Introductory
PSYCHOLOGY

Introductory
PSYCHOLOGY
a personalized textbook

WALTER M. VERNON   Illinois State University

SECOND EDITION, REVISED

 RAND McNALLY COLLEGE PUBLISHING COMPANY · Chicago

76   77   78   79   10   9   8   7   6   5   4   3   2   1

Preface to This Edition

This revised edition of *Introductory Psychology* brings to the student a reordering of the text presentation, additional areas of learning, and a revision in its pedagogical aids.

Starting with the traditional definition of psychology, the text proceeds to chapters that establish the concept of "structure with function." After the study of biological foundations and the developmental processes in the physiological, social-emotional, and intellectual spheres, sensory and perceptive capabilities are reviewed.

The text then introduces the methodological procedures used by psychologists in their research, and a chapter on the measurement of human abilities exemplifies the various avenues of psychological measurement and interpretation.

With Chapter 7 the student embarks on a sequential development of the factors that shape and fashion patterns of motivated behavior. From basic motivation and respondent and operant behaviors, the chapters move on to an introduction to social processes, human learning and memory, personality, stress, and psychopathology.

Several chapters have available similarly numbered "extension" chapters presented at the end of the book. These chapters extend basic areas of information in the correspondingly numbered earlier chapters with higher-level subject matter.

Seven of the chapters in this new edition are completely new, and the others have been heavily revised or have had additional topics inserted. Every effort has been made to increase comprehensiveness and usability in this edition.

The pedagogical aids in this revision have taken on a new look that provides the student with a twofold self-checking system. The primary pattern of text development revolves around the attainment of basic concepts. Following the presentation of a section of material, there appears a numbered concept label followed by one or more sample questions on that concept. After several such concept checks have been presented, a Progress Check is inserted to test the students' acquisition and overall assimilation of the material in the preceding cluster of concepts. The format of the text makes it suitable for self-paced learning as well as for use with a fixed class schedule.

As was the case with the first edition, we have attempted to demonstrate clearly to the student which concepts and facts are important and should be learned. A significant amount of research now has shown this method, with its guided sample questions, to be superior in assisting students to a high level of competence on classroom examinations molded around basic principles. This was our objective in preparing this book, and the task now passes to the student since the student's ultimate grasp of the subject matter must in large part reflect the amount of effort he or she brings to bear.

At this time it would be appropriate to express gratitude to the approximately 5,000 students at Illinois State University who have worked their way through the course materials that represented the earlier drafts of this edition. Intentionally or otherwise, their reactions have provided valuable feedback which assisted in the improvement of the ultimate product.

W.M.V.

Contents

Preface to This Edition   v

**Introduction to Psychology
and to This Course of Study**   2

Areas of Involvement by Psychologists **4**   /   Course Goals **4**   /   Study Procedures
and Exam Questions **7**   /   A Minicourse: The History of Scientific Psychology **8**   /
A Self-Test **23**

Biological Foundations of Behavior   26

The Evolution of Behavioral Tendencies **28**   /   Neurology **36**   /   Heredity **52**   /
Overview **61**

**Developmental Processes:
Physical, Social-Emotional, and Cognitive**   64

The Nature of Developmental Research **66**   /   Developmental Processes I:
Physical Development **67**   /   Developmental Processes II: Social-Emotional
Development **78**   /   Developmental Processes III: Cognitive Development **90**   /
Conclusion **104**

Sensation and Perception   106

Sensation and Perception **108**   /   Visual Sensory Processing **108**   /   The
Nature of Perception **128**   /   Visual Perception **129**   /   Organization of Visual
Perception **130**   /   Hearing (Audition) **140**   /   Attention **146**   /   Perceptual
Development **147**   /   Perceptual Theory **149**   /   Conclusion **153**

Scientific Procedure in Psychology   154

Sources of Knowledge **156**   /   Foundations of Science **157**   /   The Two Questions in Research **166**   /   Major Research Strategies **171**   /   Statistical Methods: Representation of Data **172**   /   Measures of Central Tendency **176**   /   Measures of Variability **180**   /   Measures of Relationship: The Correlation Coefficient **183**

The Measurement of Human Abilities   190

What is Intelligence? **192**   /   Where Does Intelligence Come From? **193**   /   Measurement of Intelligence **202**   /   Validity and Reliability of Tests **211**   /   Validity of Intelligence Tests **215**   /   Race and Intelligence **217**   /   The Components of Intelligence **223**   /   Mental Retardation **226**   /   The Gifted Child **228**   /   Various Tests **229**   /   Summary **233**

Simple Motivation and Emotion   234

Activation **236**   /   Deprivation and General Activity **238**   /   Needs and Drives **241**   /   Incentivation **254**   /   Motivation and Efficiency **256**   /   Instincts **258**   /   Moving from Basic Motives to Humanistic Motives **261**   /   Emotions **267**

Respondent Behavior and Classical Conditioning   276

Respondent Behavior **278**   /   Operant Behavior **282**   /   Simple Learning **284**   /   Classical Conditioning **285**

Operant Behavior and Operant Reinforcement   308

Operant Reinforcement **310**   /   Operant Extinction **321**   /   Variables Affecting Operant Conditioning **322**   /   Punishment: Functional Relationships **335**

Social Processes 340

Groups as Influencers **342** / Attitudes: Our Perceptions of Others **353** / The Psychology of Attraction **361** / Altruism **369** / Attribution Theory **373** / Consistency Theories **384** / Behavior Within Small Groups **389** / Conclusion **394**

Human Learning and Memory 396

Cognition as Motivation **398** / Verbal Learning **401** / What Do You Mean by "Learning"? **405** / Acquisition versus Retention **415** / Motor Learning **419** / Distribution of Practice **421** / Feedback **422** / Transfer of Training **423**

Personality and Its Assessment 430

What is "Personality"? **432** / Traits and Their Measurement **433** / Determinism and the Search for Causes of Behavior **435** / Sheldon's Body Structure Position **436** / Freud's Psychoanalytic Theory **440** / The Behavior Theory Approach to Personality **454** / Roger's Self Theory **459** / Categories of Assessment Devices **466**

Frustration, Stress, and Conflict 474

Stress **476** / Frustration **480** / Conflict **490** / Human Reactions to Frustration, Stress, and Conflict **498**

Psychopathology 512

Definition of Psychopathology **514** / Children's Psychopathologies **515** / Adult Psychopathology **520** / The Major Groupings of Psychopathologies **522** / Social Variables in Psychopathology **539** / Biological Factors in Psychopathology **547** / Psychopathology and Therapy **556**

EXTENSION CHAPTERS

Research Methods 566

Levels of Measurement **568** / Sampling **570** / Error **573** / Inferential
Statistics **580** / Summary of Scientific Inference **591** / The Purposes
of Science: An Overview **591**

Operant Conditioning: Advanced Principles 594

Research Styles and Terminology **596** / Elaborated Operant Procedures **604** /
Punishment **619** / Conditionability **624** / Theories of Reinforcement **626** /
Summary **631**

Social Processes:
Ethological and Social Learning Viewpoints 634

The Study of Animal Societies **636** / Socialization versus Isolation **642** /
An Experimental Analysis of Aggression **644** / The Experimental Analysis of
Other Social Patterns **655** / Human Interpersonal Response Patterns **656** /
Conclusion **661**

Verbal Learning in Context 662

The Importance of Contextual Learning **664** / Areas of Contextual Learning
Research **665** / Overview **679**

References 683

Index 697

Answers to Progress Checks 707

Introductory
PSYCHOLOGY

Introduction
to Psychology
and to This
Course of Study

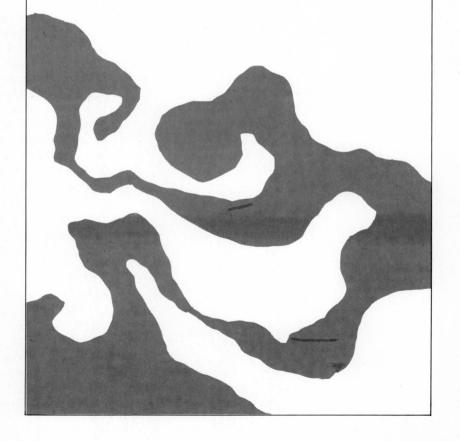

AREAS OF INVOLVEMENT BY PSYCHOLOGISTS

COURSE GOALS
The Design of This Text

STUDY PROCEDURES AND EXAM QUESTIONS

A MINICOURSE: THE HISTORY OF SCIENTIFIC PSYCHOLOGY
Prescientific Psychology: Early Philosophers
The Origins of Scientific Psychology
Formal Schools of Psychology
Structuralism
Functionalism
Psychoanalytic Theory
Gestalt Psychology
Behaviorism
The Place of the Formal Schools in Modern Psychology

A SELF-TEST

Let us assume that you are a normal, intelligent, and curious human being. You pick up your evening newspaper and are impressed by several of the headlines you see—a well-known, child-rearing specialist claims that parents can actually raise a child's IQ by 10 or more points using certain environmental designs; a local group proposes that a new "nondiscriminatory" test of intelligence be used with black candidates seeking employment; and a local university has received a federal grant to investigate whether one can learn effectively during sleep while listening to tapes of lecture recordings. You will notice that all of these topics have a common basis—they all pertain directly to the subject matter of psychology.

The current degree of interest in academic psychology may surprise you. At the college and university level, psychology not only is one of the most heavily enrolled subjects, but over the last two or three years, while overall enrollment figures were dropping in universities, there was an actual increase in the numbers of individuals enrolling in psychology courses. Why should there be such a high degree of interest in the study of psychology? To a large extent this interest is due to the fact that coping with the current times requires a broad understanding of human beings and why they behave as they do. There is prevalent an intellectual curiosity about human beings' basic social inclinations, their emotional patterns and existing dimensions of personality. Many persons are oriented toward the many social problems that burden our society, such as crime, juvenile delinquency, and racial prejudice. And many individuals are motivated by compassion for the retarded, the mentally ill, and the maladjusted. But most of all, everyone is interested in understanding himself and why he behaves as he does.

AREAS OF INVOLVEMENT BY PSYCHOLOGISTS

Today, modern-day living and working, as a matter of routine, call upon the services of trained psychologists. Industries employ psychologists in their personnel departments to advise on the selection of employees and to deal with their motivation, and to advise on practices that influence morale and productivity. The courts utilize counseling psychologists to straighten out bad family situations or persons with serious adjustment problems. Local school districts often have a resident school psychologist who works with the children who have social or emotional maladjustments and learning disabilities.

More and more people are consulting psychologists (and psychiatrists) as the importance of mental health for a full life is acknowledged. Less and less is stigma associated with those who have sought such help. And with this trend more people are becoming knowledgeable in the vocabulary and methods of psychology. Ten years ago a television program featuring as its central character a consulting psychologist (The Bob Newhart Show) could not have achieved a prime time slot for viewing as well as the public interest this program has drawn. In 1974, the periodical *Psychology Today* suggested nominating the actor for the title, "Mr. Psychologist."

Backing up the "field psychologists" mentioned above are those in the profession who specialize in laboratory experimentation to develop a fundamental understanding of the ways in which environmental variables influence motivation, perception, learning, and so on. Also there are the physiological psychologists who study the contributions of basic neurological and biochemical makeup to specific classes of behavior; and there are the developmental and social psychologists who study, in turn, physical and psychological growth from infancy through late adulthood and the influence of specific social factors. Another group, the educational psychologists, investigate the varied aspects of the educational process, ranging from the mode of transmission of information to the various strategies of testing knowledge. Clinical psychologists, who are trained much in the same way as the counseling psychologists and who often intern in mental hospitals, concentrate upon the origins and treatment of serious mental illnesses. Figure 1.1 reflects the approximate distribution of members of the American Psychological Association among various employment categories just a few years ago.

COURSE GOALS

It is the purpose of a course in the social and behavioral sciences to answer as many relevant questions as possible among those which interest most of us. From the early historical days of psychology, textbooks have attempted to do just that. But the task is not easy. For example, one of the major problems in behavioral research pertains to *how information is acquired.* This may not seem to you to be a very important problem, but in practice it is of vital significance. To illustrate, one of the *least* reliable ways of finding out why an individual acted in a given fashion is to ask the individual why he or she did so. Psychologists have determined the answers will tend to be influenced by such factors as defensiveness concerning one's

Figure 1.1

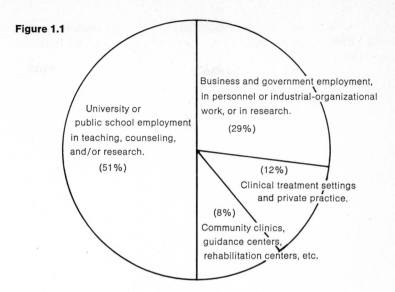

University or
public school employment
in teaching, counseling,
and/or research.
(51%)

Business and government employment,
in personnel or industrial-organizational
work, or in research.
(29%)

(12%)
Clinical treatment settings
and private practice.

(8%)
Community clinics,
guidance centers,
rehabilitation centers, etc.

failings, rationalization of one's behaviors with self-justifications, inabilities in expression, and even lapses of memory concerning past behaviors. Therefore we do not consider the main goal of this text to be simply the communication of basic facts about behavior, but as something broader. You will find a number of goals are pursued, as outlined below.

1. Concepts

First we have a variety of basic concepts to present. Some of these take the form of *definitions*. Definitions may be of research procedures, behavioral phenomena that develop under certain conditions, or methods of measurement used in psychological research. Some concepts have to do with *behavioral clusters*. Some clusters are given psychopathological names like "schizophrenia," while others are termed "achievement," "maturity," and "intelligence."

2. Cause-and-Effect Relationships

Ultimately, in psychology, we are interested in finding out what causes an individual to behave in the ways he does. Toward that end some individuals have stated that the twofold purpose of psychology is to become able to *predict* the behaviors of individuals from a knowledge of past and present data, and eventually to *control* behavior by making modifications in the environments or history of experiences of those individuals.

3. Research Strategies

Some ways of approaching research questions are demonstrably more powerful or reliable than others. One of our emphases will be upon the demonstration that all "data" is not to be taken as being of equal value. From knowledge of research strategies you should become capable of exercising critical judgment when research findings are presented to you.

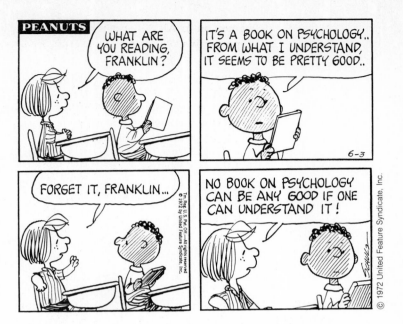

4. Being an Intelligent "Consumer" in Today's Society

As an individual with a college or university background, some of your occupational duties or social conversational topics will involve the consideration of facts and the derivation of judgments. Following exposure to the concepts of psychology, to some of the demonstrated cause-and-effect relationships, and to research strategies, you should be able to act positively on issues or proposals put to you in the name of "expertise" or on the basis of "evidence."

As immediate cases in point, you may become interested in seeking better ways of studying for examinations. You may become fascinated by the difficulties you experience in convincing people of an emotional issue through the use of logical reasoning and persuasion. Later in life you may face child-rearing decisions or community-based issues pertaining to education. At all these times, your effectiveness is enhanced when you call upon your higher education.

5. Preparation for Future Coursework in Psychology

One of the prime responsibilities in any introductory course is preparation to handle higher-level courses. To the extent that a knowledge of basic principles is called for as you move into educational psychology, child (or developmental) psychology, or social psychology, the text utilized in your introductory course carries a heavy responsibility.

The Design of This Text This text was developed with the above goals in mind and is prepared in such a way that it may be utilized in either a traditional educational system or in what modern educators call a PSI system (for "personalized systems of instruction"). All PSI programs involve themselves with several basics: (1) presenting a clear understanding of what key material should be learned; (2) supplying rapid feedback concerning what concepts were missed on examinations; and (3) offering some form of reexamination procedure to insure that each student who completes the course will have learned the basic principles to a reasonably high criterion. Some PSI programs also offer self-pacing through the various examinations scheduled.

A second important aspect of this text is that several key areas of psychology are expanded in the Extension Chapters which follow Chapter 14 of the main text. These chapters will be of special interest to students who plan to take advanced courses in psychology. A basic philosophy in the organization of this text was that each chapter ideally would serve as a springboard into a particular counterpart advanced course in the field.

STUDY PROCEDURES AND EXAM QUESTIONS

So that you may do well on the examinations in this course, you should have a clear understanding of how the materials are organized and how you should arrange your studying to produce the best work.

Within the text material itself, through concept questions and progress checks, you will be shown exactly what you are expected to learn and you will become aware of how you are progressing. Rather than just "drifting" through a chapter as you read it, you will repeatedly come face to face with questions which will determine whether or not you are learning the essentials of the material you are covering. You will be able to judge when you have studied enough to take a test, and you should have a greater degree of confidence in your ability to make a high grade.

Recommended study procedures include working with two or three other persons after your own study is completed and you have attempted to answer all of the sample questions in a chapter. It would be well to meet with these friends on a regular basis to review and compare answers. You should do this while there is still time to go back into the text in cases where differences arise on what is the correct answer to a given question.

The sample questions provided for your self-testing fall into two main categories. First there are the specific *concept questions* which are grouped under concept headings that are consecutively numbered as you progress through each chapter. (An answer key is not provided for the concept questions since they immediately follow text material in which the answers are evident.) Second there are the *progress checks* which test your understanding of the broad meanings of a cluster of concepts, and sometimes even the relationships between different concepts. (Answers to these questions and a text page reference are given at the end of this book.)

To do well on the course exams, it is recommended that you complete all of the questions and follow up on those with which you feel indecisive. Just looking at the questions will not provide the level of knowledge needed for adequate exam performance. You can expect the exam questions to bear some relation to the sample questions in the chapter.

Good exam questions test real comprehension by a number of "rear-rangements" that fall into five general categories:

The Exact Matching Question

Here the only changes will be minor in the wording, or a completion style concept question may be cast into multiple-choice format using the same wording.

The Partial Exact Matching Question

A concept question might ask for "the three reasons why," while the matching exam question might ask which of four "reasons" is not a valid one.

The Element Reversal Question

While we might ask in a text question who founded the original behavioristic approach in psychology, the exam question might then ask which of five different approaches was founded by John Watson, and the proper choice would be behavioristic.

The Example Substitution Question

A sample question might present a case history or example, and ask which concept or term describes what has been presented. The exam question could then present a different case history or example of the same concept.

The Concept Reversal Question

These questions are by far the most difficult. By substituting a few words from the original sample question, the nature of the question on the exam is changed so that a different answer becomes correct.

Such rearrangements as outlined above can be expected on all the exams. The fifth type of question, the concept reversal, calls for a further remark. Lest the student feel that the teaching method in this book simply calls for memorization, it should be pointed out that those who memorize without understanding the material invariably fail to answer many concept reversal questions correctly.

A MINICOURSE: THE HISTORY OF SCIENTIFIC PSYCHOLOGY

In order that you might fully understand what is ahead in this textbook, we shall now present a typical academic topic—the history of psychology as a science and academic discipline, developed in the format used in the subsequent chapters. We shall provide enough material so that you can anticipate the pattern that is to follow in the course; and we suggest that you undertake seriously to study the chapter's contents and answer the concept questions, work the progress checks, and then do your best on the sample exam that appears at the end of the chapter. (Unless you are told otherwise by your instructor, you may assume that *no* Chapter 1 material will appear on any formal exam.)

Prescientific Psychology: Early Philosophers

One of the most frequently quoted remarks in psychology was made by Ebbinghaus, a late-nineteenth-century learning researcher, who stated, "Psychology has a long past but a short history." The long past of psychology refers to the fact that man has attempted to understand himself in relation to the world around him since before the period of recorded history. In a more recent sense, psychology's past includes the various philosophic efforts to explain man's behavior which gained sophistication in the eighteenth and nineteenth centuries. During this entire period, the basic psychological question of why man behaves as he does was the center of attention. Most of the writings of that era were oriented around moralistic questions, and the contents of new teachings were seldom generated from anything resembling scientific procedure.

Still, as we look back from the vantage point of the late-twentieth century, we can see that the ancient philosophers in their own ways anticipated many present concerns, and sometimes their reflections bear a remarkable relevance for present-day psychologists. Democritus, Plato, and Aristotle all devoted considerable attention to the question of what kinds of data should be given the greater emphasis in deriving knowledge, and the present differences that occasionally emerge between rationalists and more laboratory-bound psychologists reflect a continuing interest in the same problem. Aristotle was one of the first to advocate that so complex a matter as human behavior was subject to the same sort of natural laws of determination as were the physical sciences. Questions of freedom from fears and tensions and satisfaction with one's life-style were the focus of the writings of the Stoics and the Epicureans shortly after the time of Aristotle, preceding similar interests of the later influential religious philosophers and mental health advocates.

The era of Francis Bacon and Galileo saw scientists analyzing the relative merits of inductive and deductive logical systems in the evaluation of research data. The relationships that appear to exist between the "mind" and the body were a focus of interest in the seventeenth century, and the current interest in the field of psychosomatic medicine is but one modern counterpart of that comprehensive question. The entire field of developmental psychology, with its research topics of perceptual development, the nature of the learning process in the youngster, etc., saw its earlier representation in the so-called nativism-empiricism issue debated by British philosophers such as John Locke in the late seventeenth century.

Despite the relevance to modern issues that we can see in the early works of philosophers, the shortcomings of the use of "reason" in the absence of formal research causes the early work to be of little present practical value. It was with the advent of a rigorous scientific method that psychology as a scientific discipline came into practice in the mid-nineteenth century.

The Origins of Scientific Psychology

Considering that the roots of psychology extend so far back into philosophic origins, it is somewhat surprising that scientific psychology originated in physiology laboratories. Various individuals, such as Descartes, had likened human behavior to mechanical actions, using analogies of hydraulic operations, etc., to explain the various operations of nerves, cerebrospinal fluid, and so forth. The theory that the body was a kind of machine was one that was testable both by naturalistic observation and by experimental research. So it was that the year 1850 marked the beginning point of scientific psychology. At that time Gustav Fechner initiated the first research into the relationship between mind and body by examining how changes in the strength of a stimulus influenced the resulting sensation produced by that stimulus. Fechner noted that while a mental event is not directly measurable in a qualitative sense, it might be measured indirectly in terms of the amount of change necessary in a physical stimulus for a subject to begin to observe a just noticeable difference in the resulting sensation.

C 1.1. *Early scientific psychology.*

Early scientific psychology originated in _____ .

  a. physiology laboratories   b. medical hospitals for the insane

  c. public school classrooms   d. philosophy debate forums

The origin of scientific psychology arose in research into the relationship between _____ .

  a. stimulus strength and strength of a resulting sensation

  b. situations of threat and the resulting emotions

  c. skull shape and intelligence

Fechner held that a mental event could be studied by examining _____ .

  a. what is necessary to produce change in sensations

  b. how people feel about leading philosophic issues

  c. sex differences in attitudes

One of Fechner's contributions within this general research area was the development of standard psychophysical measurement methods that have been used consistently since he introduced them. Another of Fechner's major contributions has since been represented in the Weber-Fechner ratio. This represents a law in the area of perception whereby a stimulus intensity must be increased by a constant percentage of its own value if the increases are to be perceived as just noticeable differences. Let us illustrate this concept through a simple example.

Suppose that a given subject held a lead weight of three pounds in one hand, and the question arose as to what amount of weight would be necessary in order for the subject to perceive that a second weight, held in the other hand, was heavier than the first. Suppose that the 3-pound (48-

ounce) weight had to be matched by a 49-ounce weight, and any less relative difference could not be discriminated. A simple calculation will show that the 3-pound weight must be increased by around 1.9 percent of its own weight in order for the just noticeable difference (*jnd*) to be perceived. What then of a 13-pound (208-ounce) weight being held in one hand by the same subject? What weight would be necessary, in comparison, for the subject to reliably discriminate that the second weight was heavier? Fechner's research showed that a weight of 212 ounces (13¼ pounds) would be necessary. This also represents the application of the constant fraction—in this case, 1.9 percent—applied to the value of 208 ounces.

Further research showed that different constant fractions apply to different sensory functions. The discrimination of differences in the pitch of tones involves a difference of 0.3 percent (three-tenths of one percent); brightness of a light, 1.6 percent; loudness of a tone, 8.8 percent; skin surface pressure, 13.6 percent; and variations in the saltiness of a mixture being tasted, 20 percent.

C 1.2.   *The Weber-Fechner ratio.*

The constant fraction in the Weber-Fechner ratio refers to the proportion of its own value that a stimulus _____ .

    a. must increase in order to be judged as significantly changed

    b. must increase in order to be perceived as a just noticeable increase

    c. must achieve if perception is not to fade with continued experience

The Weber-Fechner constant fraction value _____ .

    a. is consistent from sense to sense   b. changes from sense to sense

During the period of time immediately following Fechner's research, many physicists, physiologists, and physicians eagerly began to establish evidence of psychological "constants." Laboratory research at that time concentrated on a search for scientific data that were consistent with various physiological assumptions of the time. One of these assumptions was that situations could be developed within which the predictions of reaction time, discriminability among stimuli, and so forth could be made quite precisely.

For example, Donders, a Dutch physiologist, produced a sizable literature on reaction time. Donders' research established that reaction time in a choice situation was predictably longer than was reaction time where a simple reaction to a stimulus was required, and this result has been repeatedly confirmed. As reaction time was studied more thoroughly, it became apparent that even this basic behavior is enormously complex, and that reaction time varies with the sense organ stimulated, with the intensity of the stimulus, with the number of items to be discriminated in a choice situation, with the degrees of difference existing between them, with the amount of practice the subject has received, and with scores of additional factors (Heidbreder, 1933).

The formal history of psychology, as an academic discipline in itself, is often associated with the name of Wilhelm Wundt. Wundt, trained both in the disciplines of physiology and philosophy, became fascinated with applying the work of physiologists on reaction time, stimulus discrimination, and so forth to experiences existing within the consciousness of the human subject. Wundt published his early textbook *Physiological Psychology*, in which he outlined what he felt a psychological experiment should be. In his view a psychological experiment was one patterned closely after a physiological experiment, being a procedure in which the process to be studied is kept very close to a controllable stimulus and an objective response. The response in question was an *introspection*—a formulation of the subjective content of experiences of the subject—formed within the context of a carefully prepared act of observation. Wundt perceived the higher mental processes of experience, thought, and feeling as being accessible only to the individual doing the experiencing, but in Wundt's formal use introspection was not just a casual self-examination of one's own mental processes. Rather, for Wundt, it was a rigorous and sophisticated technique which required intensive training of a subject, and each laboratory investigation was repeated again and again.

In 1879, at the German University at Leipzig, Wundt established his famous laboratory for psychological research. Since his name already was well-known, Leipzig soon became a center attracting students from all over the world who wished to study the "new psychology." From England, America, France, and elsewhere, young men flocked to Leipzig, and as a result the leaders in psychology over the next several decades were those who had been trained under Wundt's influence.

C 1.3. *Wilhelm Wundt in early psychology.*

One of Wundt's pioneering developments was the rigorous training of subjects to examine carefully

the contents of their own experiences in a technique known as _____ .

a. psychoanalysis   b. introspection   c. philosophizing

Formal Schools of Psychology

Structuralism

To a very large degree, twentieth-century scientific psychology has been studied in terms of the different schools or approaches that were emphasized at various times. *Structuralism* was the first major psychological school, and it was influential for a considerable number of years. The structuralists, following Wundt, regarded psychology as the science of the mind, and they felt that the proper approach to the field was to study the *contents of the mind.* All science, according to structuralists, had a starting point in experience. They felt that while a physical science might study the manifestations of wavelengths of light or soundwaves representing noise from the standpoint of physical factors, psychology should concern itself with the counterpart mental experiences of these same phenomena. Thus, while physicists would study red as a projection of a specified light wavelength, psychologists would be interested in the mental experience of seeing the color red.

The structuralists tried vigorously to keep psychology pure of common sense. Common sense, they explained, results in a large number of inconsistencies and absurdities. Similarly, structuralists attempted to keep psychology pure of utilitarian interest. They were intolerant of the point of view that psychology should bring aid and comfort to sick minds. The business of psychology, they asserted, was not to relieve suffering or bring about improvement in people, but to discover and understand facts about conscious experience. Mental processes were to be studied in the same impersonal, detached manner as a physicist would employ in studying the forces exerted by falling objects.

With our modern-day emphasis upon utilitarianism, psychopathology, and a vast array of subject matter topics, it is sometimes hard to comprehend how structuralists could make an entire academic subject out of the content of conscious experience. But they did, and therefore let us look at some of the simplest processes to which consciousness was reduced by the structuralist psychologists of the time.

Sensations and images in the conscious mind were said to have at least four main attributes—quality, intensity, duration, and clearness. *Quality* is defined as the attribute that distinguishes every elementary process. Hot, cold, colors such as red, tastes such as sour, and specific musical notes are all examples. *Intensity* is an attribute that places an experience of a given quality on a dimension running from the highest to the lowest degree of its particular kind—the attribute that makes it possible to say that one sensation is stronger or weaker, brighter or duller, louder or softer than another. *Duration* is the attribute that gives a process its characteristic place in time, its initiation, existence, and termination. The attribute of *clearness* determines the place of a given process in the conscious mind; if clear, the process is dominant and outstanding, and is usually perceived attentively, but if it is unclear, it fades into the background among other irrelevant stimuli.

As we previously stated, these four attributes are primary ones. A variety of secondary attributes exists, such as *insistence*, which was defined as the penetrativeness of odors, the urgency of pain stimuli, the obtrusiveness or glaringness of lights, and so forth. Research then centered on questions such as whether insistence was a separate attribute, or whether it might be formed from a combination of two or more of the primary attributes, such as clearness and quality, or perhaps clearness, quality, and intensity all taken together. Other questions investigated included whether certain experiences contain all four attributes of experience, or just combinations of two or three.

In this way structuralism became a complex but versatile approach to psychology, at least to the extent that the psychology of the time defined the area its subject matter covered. The structuralistic movement, spearheaded by the influence of men such as Wundt, achieved the definite distinction of making psychology a true science, removing it from the realm of metaphysics and loose, untrained judgmental factors. The weakness inherent in structuralism was perhaps its passion for formal correctness. In its zeal to be scientific, it set up restrictions, both in method and subject matter area, that were to hamper its development as a broad, large-scale science. It is no wonder that a number of individuals within the field felt hampered by the structuralist approach, and that departures from its orthodox methodologies became fairly common around the turn of the century.

C 1.4. *Schools of psychology: Structuralism.*

The structuralists felt that psychologists should study _____ .

   a. the contents of the mind   b. the purpose or use of mental functions

   c. how associations between ideas are formed

Attributes such as quality, intensity, duration, and clearness were said to be characteristics of _____ .

   a. intelligent individuals   b. images and sensations in the conscious mind

   c. strength, separating man from lower organisms

Structuralism's great contribution was _____ .

   a. the making of psychology into a true science

   b. in the use made of its findings by opticians and other applied scientists

Functionalism   The clearest departure from the restrictions and methodologies of structuralism was contained within a movement which became known as *functionalism*. Roughly around the turn of the century, a number of psychologists argued that the proper emphasis of psychology should not be so much upon the *content* of the conscious mind as upon the *function* of the mind and the purposes it serves. Just as the structuralists were strongly influenced in their directions by the psychophysical developments within physics laboratories of the middle nineteenth century, functionalism took a great amount of inspiration from the work of Charles Darwin. It became a point of view espoused by the functionalists that man has developed his behavioral capacities and tendencies largely because those characteristics assisted him in adapting to the particular characteristics of his environment. For the first time the interests of a sizable number of psychologists turned to such adaptive functions as learning, motivation, and various other aspects of both human beings' and lower organisms' reactions to their environments. Just as Darwin emphasized the purpose of biological characteristics that aided a species in its adaptation and survival, so did the functionalists stress certain mental characteristics or capacities which aided the individual in adaptation.

C 1.5. *Schools of psychology: Functionalism.*

Functionalists patterned their form of psychology after the general approach of _____ .

    a. Spearman   b. Copernicus   c. Harvey   d. Darwin

Whereas structuralists studied the content of mental experience, functionalists stressed the ways in which the mental processes _____ .

    a. helped the individual adapt to his environment

    b. were interpreted by the person experiencing them

    c. first developed in the small child

PROGRESS CHECK 1.1

1. Prior to the nineteenth century, many people wrote about the subject of psychology. These people can be best characterized as being _____ .

    a. scientists   b. philosophers   c. mathematicians   d. fools

2. It was not until the nineteenth century that a scientific study of psychology really began, and then, interestingly enough, it began as _____ .

    a. a laboratory science   b. a division of religion

    c. a branch of medicine   d. an animal science

3. The psychological problem that most intrigued Gustav Fechner was the relationship between the strength of some physical stimuli and how we experience them. Which of the following problems would Fechner most likely have been interested in? _____ .

    a. Whether or not juvenile delinquents love their mothers

    b. What will motivate a rat to run a maze

    c. How much you must raise the temperature of the water in order to detect a difference in warmth

    d. None of the above

4. The Weber-Fechner ratio is somewhat unusual in psychology because it specifies an exact mathematical relationship between external physical events and accompanying psychological events. From this statement you might conclude that _____ .

    a. The science of psychology is made up of a vast number of mathematical laws

    b. It is absolutely impossible to reduce a psychological law to mathematical terms

    c. There are relatively few psychological laws which have been reduced to mathematical terms

    d. All of the above

5. A simple reaction time study might go something like this: "When the light flashes, press the button." In a choice reaction time study the subject might be told, "If the light is red, press button A; and if the light is green, press button B." In the choice situation, you would predict that _____ .

   a. the reaction time would be about the same as in the simple situation

   b. reaction time would be longer than in the simple situation

   c. the reaction time would be shorter than in a simple situation

6. Wilhelm Wundt pioneered the controlled laboratory method called introspection. In the introspective method the experimenter makes a careful analysis of the subjective content of an experience as reported by an intensively trained subject. Which of these would be an example of introspection? _____ .

   a. Measuring reaction times

   b. Watching subjects put together puzzles

   c. Giving an IQ test

   d. Asking trained subjects what they experienced when they heard a series of random tones

---

Psychoanalytic Theory   While these developments were transpiring, and the content of the discipline of psychology was changing dramatically, a major influence on psychology was developing in Europe, where Sigmund Freud was formalizing his views regarding personality and abnormal behavior. At this particular point in time, psychology had not included the study of psychopathology within its content area, largely for the reason that heretofore it had been assumed that psychopathology invariably was the result of a biological disease process. Where mental illness existed, it was assumed that there was some actual disease in the tissue of the central nervous system. Abnormal behavior therefore was not viewed as a topic within psychology at all, but as a purely medical problem. Freud was one of the first to strongly advance the viewpoint that characteristics of the human personality, whether normal or abnormal, largely could be attributed to psychological experiences in early life. In his *psychoanalytic theory*, Freud also proposed that considerable individual interpretation of events was possible, so that tremendous complexities and differences between individuals were inevitable. Some individuals would be influenced in certain ways by unconscious processes which they probably would not understand, and many behaviors would represent symbolic enactments of other unconscious processes.

Whether or not one wishes to agree with the majority of Freud's views on the determinants of psychological development, the field owes a debt to him for bringing the clinical areas of psychology to the popular attention of psychologists, for his almost unique (at that time) insistence that so many psychological processes are determined by complex patterns of interpersonal relationships, and for the heavy emphasis he placed upon childhood as a critical period in personality development.

C 1.6. *Schools of psychology: Psychoanalytic theory.*

Psychoanalytic theory was developed by _____ .

   a. Freud   b. Cattell   c. disillusioned structuralists

Psychoanalytic theory was fairly unique in its stress upon _____ .

   a. the importance of childhood processes in personality development

   b. abnormal behavior as a legitimate field of psychological inquiry

   c. interpersonal relationships as determinants of personality

   d. all of the above are true

Gestalt Psychology   A short while later in the evolution of psychology, a group of men called *Gestalt psychologists* began to have an influence on the field. These German psychologists placed particular emphasis on the phenomenon of perception, and many of their proposals were designed to prove Wundt and the structuralists wrong on certain issues. The Gestalt psychologists opposed the structuralists' efforts to reduce conscious experience to a small set of component parts. Rather, they put stress on the characteristics of the whole form (Gestalt), advancing the view that a perceived whole is more than just the sum of its parts. One of their interesting contributions was the concept of apparent movement. You can recall from your own experiences in watching fluorescent advertising signs that illusions of movement can easily be created if multiple lights are activated in a pattern. As a simple example, imagine that you are in a dark room looking at an area in which two light bulbs, spaced 18 inches apart, are alternatively lighted. As one lights up, the other goes off, then the situation is reversed and continues to be alternated back and forth. The result is apparent movement—it appears that there is only one light, moving back and forth, rather than two. The phenomenon of apparent movement was studied in terms of factors that influence it—speed of alternation, width of the intervening space, and so forth—and speculations regarding the function of brain physiology were developed from research findings.

Many other phenomena of perception were developed by the Gestaltists, some of which will be discussed in Chapter 4. We might at this point simply indicate that a large number of these contributions went in the direction of showing that human beings perceive stimuli in patterned, organized ways that frequently involve the perceiver's having "added something" to the literal stimulus pattern. For example, groups of objects may be seen as forming an overall shape, even though the spaces between the objects are not filled in. Also, individual objects can be perceived as being grouped due either to their being clustered in certain ways or to their belonging to similar object classes. Many such interests and research

The humor in these cartoons is evident to you now. But after studying this course, their humor will take on heightened meaning, with relevance to psychological theory.

THE FAMILY CIRCUS, by Bil Keane. Reprinted courtesy The Register and Tribune Syndicate

"Look at the big plane, Jeffy!"
"That's littler than the one I got for Christmas."

"Actually, he's afraid of us, but his inability to deal with his fear makes him angry. Anger is something he _can_ deal with."

"You've been walked and you've been fed. Now I suppose you want love and affection."

THE FAMILY CIRCUS, by Bil Keane. Reprinted courtesy The Register and Tribune Syndicate

"We had intelligence tests today. Boy! Were they HARD!"

"I think I'll stick it out here, but thanks, anyway."

traditions have continued into modern-day perception research, but the influence of this approach upon clinical, interpersonal and educational processes can be evaluated as being modest.

C 1.7. *Schools of psychology: Gestalt psychology.*

Gestalt psychology was a field which concentrated its study on the phenomenon of _____ .

    a. motivation   b. perception   c. personality processes

A topic stressed in Gestalt research was that _____ .

    a. in perception the whole is often greater than the sum of its parts

    b. apparent movement cannot occur in young children

    c. motivation is usually determined by how people perceive others' intentions

Behaviorism   One of the most influential schools of psychology, and perhaps the only one to continue a present-day existence in a more or less formal fashion, is that of *behaviorism*. Behaviorism was originally developed in 1912 by John Watson, a psychologist who had been trained formally in a functionalistic background. While he was not an enemy of functionalism, and he recognized the advances which functionalism represented over the structuralist style of mentalistic psychology, he still felt that there was entirely too much philosophizing in the interpretations of purposes served by behaviors in the functionalistic approach. For this reason Watson developed an extreme environmentalism within which he proposed to study and explain all forms of behavior. Watson was the first psychologist to state that the prediction and control of behavior was the proper objective for psychology, and he emphasized repeatedly that only behavior that was observable and which could be directly and exactly measured could generate proper data.

Watson's environmentalism is best reflected in his frequently cited remark to the effect that if he could have a young infant to train in any way he desired, he could produce any effect chosen, developing the child into a doctor, a minister, a thief, etc. In the same manner in which structuralists took the early psychophysicists for a model, and in which functionalists seized upon Darwin for inspiration, Watson was impressed with the contributions of Pavlov in his conditioning laboratories in Russia. Watson intensively began to study the development of feelings in human infants, putting forth the point of view that one could very easily produce, eliminate, or change given emotional predispositions in a subject simply by manipulating the history of stimuli presented. At the simplest level, if one experiences very unpleasant events such as sudden, frightening loud sounds in the presence of some neutral stimulus, there develops a growing sense of nervousness and anxiety in the subsequent presence of the neutral stimulus. Or if one regularly feeds a little child ice cream in the presence of a given stimulus, that stimulus would itself eventually begin to bring about in the child a pleasurable emotional response.

Watson's ideas are considered, by historians of psychology, to have been very much in the spirit of the times, and very "American" in structure. That is, Watson did not assume that people are "born into" certain behavior traits or categories of ability. Rather, the new behavioristic psychology departed from a strong European emphasis on heredity and "high birth" in favor of an implied initial neutrality or equality. The child would later become what his environmental conditioning history made him. For this reason behaviorism was particularly well received by American psychologists, and the movement grew tremendously. At present, as a formal school of psychology, behaviorism has both been assimilated by the field and has entered into a second formal phase. The latter comment is reflected in the fact that following the formal points of view of B. F. Skinner, there has been in the past two decades a strong resurgence of interest in limiting psychological data to objective, observable behavior, together with a reemphasis of the assumption that behavior is largely determined by factors in the environment. As we arrive at certain chapters at an intermediate point in the textbook, this emphasis will be elaborated.

C 1.8. *Schools of Psychology: Behaviorism.*

The early form of behaviorism was founded by _____ .

It would be proper to say that behaviorism represented an extreme _____ .

    a. nativism   b. form of structuralism   c. environmentalism

The label "behaviorism" can be linked to behaviorists' views that the only proper data for psychologists

    to consider is _____ .

    a. behavior that is self-reported   b. mental behavior   c. observable behavior

It would be correct to say that behaviorists assume that most people _____ .

    a. are at birth destined to certain categories of behavioral traits

    b. are at birth flexible and may be conditioned to almost any behavior pattern

    c. have a fixed biology that limits their performance

PROGRESS CHECK   1.2

1. Functionalists stress all the ways that mental and behavioral processes help an individual adapt to the environment. Which of these observations would more likely be performed by a functionalist? _____ .

    a. Observing the way a cat tries to escape from a box

    b. Asking a subject about the qualities of experience accompanying a pain stimulus

    c. Measuring the increase in light intensity required in order for a person to detect a change

2. Freud believed that individuals were greatly influenced by unconscious processes. _____ .

    a. True   b. False

3. Watson contended that the only data of concern to psychology should be observable behavior. Which of these would be an example of data that Watson might accept? _____ .

    a. A mental image   b. A thought plan   c. The pressing of a buzzer   d. All of these

---

The Place of the Formal Schools in Modern Psychology

In large part the formal schools of psychology have disappeared from view, leaving behind their strong influence upon the subject matter, basic assumptions, or methodologies that are employed in modern psychology. Of the formal schools discussed, behaviorism is perhaps the most strongly represented as a contemporary force in psychology, even to the extent that modern-day behaviorists can be labeled and identified by name within the field. The influence of behaviorism extends from a heavy emphasis on animal behavior, through advocation of environmental experience as the main determinant of behavior, to a stress upon observable behavior as the only legitimate data. Functionalism is still expressed in modern psychology in the strong emphasis which most psychologists give to the utility of behavioral patterns.

The emphasis upon stimulus complexities in the determination of perceptual patterns, which remains in the perceptual laboratories today, is the contribution of the Gestalt psychologists. The psychoanalytic interpretations of behaviors, both abnormal and normal, are heavily represented in many theories of psychopathology and developmental psychological processes. Were it not for Freud and his followers, it is also quite possible that even today psychologists would not view the field of abnormal behavior as a main area of psychology. Of all the formal schools, it is perhaps most difficult to locate any remaining evidence of structuralism, apart from the obvious present-day emphasis upon strict scientific method—a point of view first stressed by the structuralists in contrast to the prior works of philosophers.

The history of scientific psychology is more closely tied to these various approaches, or schools, than to specific researchers. It is not possible, as it is in some other sciences, to list scores of important calendar dates of important events in the history of psychology. Hundreds of research findings compete for positions of relatively equal importance, and it is impossible to select just a few as being cornerstone discoveries of psychology.

We cannot conclude any presentation of the factors influencing modern psychology without mentioning certain contemporary influences that are determining the directions of many individuals in the field. A strong force, sometimes termed *cognitive psychology*, has emerged from within the ranks of child development, social, and educational psychology to stress man's rationality as a determining influence shaping his behavior directions. Such points of view will be represented in Chapter 3, where we will present the points of view of Piaget, and later in Chapter 10, where some of the relevant points contributed by some social psychologists will be reviewed.

In examining the pathways along which the various schools of psychology have traveled, it is hoped that you have begun to perceive a logic and a pattern to the academic area that we call psychology. It is certain that you will be able, at various points, to tie much of what is developed later in this text to an understanding of the historic backgrounds of the field.

A SELF-TEST We earlier described how you should best go about learning the subject matter of psychology from this text. It is now time to determine if your methods will bring about the 90 percent and better performance that is characteristic of students using textbooks such as this. To do this, we present a multiple-choice exam of just ten questions, based on the foregoing minicourse. The format of these questions is a little changed from that of the corresponding sample questions you studied, exactly as described on page 8. As you take this minicourse exam, you should gain a feeling for how well you are grasping the material, and whether you need to modify your study procedures. Remember, relatively few students achieve grades lower than 90 percent (one error out of ten questions) on the regular chapter examinations.

Minicourse Test

1. The origin of scientific psychology came in early research into the relation between _____ .

    a. childhood experiences and the emotional structure which results

    b. contents of consciousness and the intent of the perceiver

    c. nature of a sensation and the related stimulus strength

2. Fechner held that the examination of what stimulus changes were necessary in order to produce changes in sensations was a means of studying _____ .

    a. mental events   b. attitudinal differences

    c. Descartes' theory of the mind/body relationship

3. The notion that change amounting to a constant portion of a stimulus' strength or quality is necessary in order to be perceived as a just noticeable difference is associated with _____ .

    a. Donders   b. Wundt   c. Weber and Fechner

4. A subject is trained to examine carefully the contents of his moment-to-moment conscious experiences in a technique called _____ .

    a. psychoanalysis   b. philosophizing   c. introspection

5. Structuralists felt that the proper subject matter of psychology was the _____ .

    a. purpose and adaptiveness of mental functions

    b. relation of stimulus units to perceptual wholes

    c. effects of early experiences upon personality structure

    d. content of the mind

6. The most important contribution of _____ was to make psychology into a true science.

    a. structuralism   b. functionalism   c. psychoanalytic theory   d. existentialism

7. Darwin strongly influenced the approach taken by the _____ .

    a. structuralists   b. functionalists   c. psychoanalysts   d. existentialists

8. Functionalists stressed, in their approach, the ways in which mental processes _____ .

    a. are interpreted by the person experiencing them

    b. are first developed in the young child

    c. assist the individual in adapting to his environment

9. Which of the following statements is *not* true? _____ .

    a. Freud founded the psychoanalytic school of psychology

    b. Psychoanalytic theory stressed the importance of childhood experiences to a *lesser* degree than did earlier approaches

10. It would be proper to say that behaviorism represented an extreme _____ .

    a. form of structuralism   b. reaction to Gestalt psychology

    c. nativism   d. environmentalism

Check Your Work   Now that you have taken your first "examination" in psychology, check your work against the correct answers printed below.* In the balance of this book we will embark upon the formal research areas in psychology, and our emphasis shall be more upon the present state of affairs in psychology than upon its historical past.

Biological Foundations of Behavior

**THE EVOLUTION OF BEHAVIORAL
TENDENCIES**
  Eugenics
NEUROLOGY
  The Neuron
  The Brain
    Sub-Cortical Centers
    The Cerebral Cortex
  The Nervous System and the Environment
  The Autonomic Nervous System
    The Sympathetic Division
    The Parasympathetic Division
HEREDITY
  Fundamentals of Genetics
    Single-Gene Effects
    Sex-Linked Effects
    Penetrance and Expressivity
    Multiple-Gene Effects
  Research Methods
OVERVIEW

Sometimes we hear a student ask, "Why is it important in a psychology class to study the physiological structure?" The answer to that question is complex. First, the philosophy of this book will hold that it is *not* important that you understand physiological mechanisms in a thorough, microscopic fashion. Nor is it important that you inventory the total collection of brain-behavior relationships that have been established through research. What is important is that you recognize some basic patterns in the relationship of physiology to behavior. Therefore, we shall examine some of the areas of interest and points of view in physiological psychology. Later, if you have a continued interest in this topic, you may be able to take a course in physiological psychology.

Another way of answering the question about reasons for the study of the biological foundations of behavior is to point out the place which this area of research holds in the explanation of behavior. This chapter lays a foundation by demonstrating *what capacities for behavior exist* in individuals, with some speculation as to how those capacities came into being. If you view the topic of this chapter as the understanding of *how* an individual can behave, and then, in subsequent chapters, you study *why* he behaves in certain ways, you can begin to appreciate the contributions of this area of research.

THE EVOLUTION OF BEHAVIORAL TENDENCIES   In the study of the biological foundations of behavior we do not launch immediately into "brain structure," or the body's complex biochemistry. Rather, it is of great interest to understand why man has certain capacities that are possessed by other life forms, and why he has some that are not; also why some species possess capacities that are not possessed by man. Most individuals who are interested in this line of study either concentrate their energies on the development of the general Darwinian approach, or are tied in with the rapidly growing and complex field of behavioral genetics. We shall turn first to evolutionary analysis.

Man is a biological organism with an evolutionary history. Still, when it is stated that he may manifest genetically programmed behavior, many people have an initial reaction of disagreement. In fact, it is becoming unfashionable, at least in this nation, to investigate genetically determined behavior in human beings. Spuhler and Lindzey (1957) concluded their summary of human behavioral genetics by stating that it is "an area of research that is procedurally difficult, politically dangerous, and personally repugnant to most psychologists, sociologists, and anthropologists." Still, when one examines the patterning and similarities in both the behaviors and the structural characteristics of the various living species, including man, one is inclined to accept an evolutionary point of view as at least one of the causative factors in human behavior.

Evolution has been defined as the description of how life first began, of the first organisms, of the physical changes that occurred in those organisms, and how these changes increased gradually and steadily so that new forms or species of living things were constantly appearing and older ones disappearing. The name historically associated with evolution is that of Charles Darwin. It was he who coined the expression "natural selection."

Natural selection refers to the processes whereby some organisms perpetuate their kind by reproducing themselves, while others fail to do so, and starts with the fact that in a given species there will be some variation in the numerous structural characteristics of different individuals. Without going back to the dawn of evolution, let us consider a case in point. Suppose, for example, fur is a characteristic of a species. In very severe winters that occasionally occur, lightly-furred animals might easily perish, while those of the species with heavy coats of fur would have a much better chance of surviving. This is what Darwin meant by "survival of the fittest." Or, to use another popular bit of terminology, the animals with heavy fur are better "adapted" to the natural environment. Then, the notion of natural selection holds, only the fittest remain alive to reproduce the species, and their offspring tend to resemble the parents in terms of the vital adaptive characteristics. If certain characteristics or degrees of characteristics are not adaptive, they cease in an evolutionary sense with the early deaths, prior to sexual maturity, of individuals in the species with those nonadaptive characteristics.

C 2.1.   *The principle of natural selection.*

Darwin's statement of the principle of natural selection is that _____ .

Evolutionary changes are usually very gradual. Small changes may occur through hundreds or even thousands of successive generations and finally be manifest in an outwardly visible structural or behavioral characteristic. It can be seen, however, that during severe environmental stresses evolution might progress rather rapidly. If 90 percent of the youngsters of a species in a given generation were wiped out by unusually severe weather factors prior to sexual maturity, the subsequent generation might be visibly altered in terms of certain "typical" physical characteristics. Even with slower evolutionary processes, the continuous contribution of natural selection is a powerful change factor. Suppose that a gene had a selective factor of .001. (This means that the percentage of individuals with a given characteristic that survive to sexual maturity is only one-tenth of 1 percent higher than the percentage without the characteristic that survive.) Suppose also that the gene was totally recessive so that individuals would have to inherit the gene from both mother and father, and even then only a fourth of those offspring would manifest the characteristic. Still, the characteristic would spread through a population so that within 120,000 generations the gene's manifestation would increase from 1 percent to 100 percent (McGaugh, 1971, p. 23). Actually, the large number of generations involved in this calculation does not represent an undue amount of time in evolutionary history, particularly when you consider that fast-maturing species are concerned. Another consideration is the fact that many genes have a far higher selective factor than .001, and many operate on dominant rather than recessive principles. Thus, natural selection can change the genetic/structural characteristics of a population quite rapidly.

It is important to recognize that we do not inherit behavior—what we actually inherit is biological structure that mediates behavior. Thus, within-family similarities in behavior can be traced to biological structures similar to those of our immediate ancestors. As an example, let us consider the case of emotionality in animals. We can selectively breed for high emotionality. We start by choosing laboratory rats that become extremely excited under certain conditions and we breed excitable males with excitable females. Then we can compare the offspring of such matches with the offspring of low-excitable parents or matches where one parent is excitable and one is not. We find that high-excitable parents reproduce high-excitable offspring, and low-excitable parents reproduce low-excitable offspring; mixed matches on the excitability factor result in intermediate levels of excitability in the offspring. Determination of offspring excitability needs at least a few weeks or months of age before measurement. Meanwhile we can take half of the individuals from each litter and sacrifice them immediately after birth for physiological examination. We then find that the offspring of high-excitable parents have larger adrenal glands (like their parents) than the offspring of low-excitable or mixed parents. Therefore, we conclude that animals do not actually inherit behavior (in this case, *emotionality*), but inherit the biological structure (in this case, *adrenal size*) that mediates the behavior.

C 2.2. *The transmission of behavioral characteristics through genetics.*

When we observe behavioral similarities in genetically related individuals, what is it that is "inherited"? _____ .

    a. Biological structure   b. The behavior itself

> We have been talking as if each offspring is a carbon copy of its parents' structural characteristics. We all know that this is not so. Sometimes two quite tall parents have a small or medium-size child. In many other characteristics there are numerous examples of variation away from the parental pattern. Then, what is the relationship of parental structure to the structural characteristics of their offspring? In general, when parents manifest a given degree of a characteristic, their offspring tend to exhibit that characteristic to a similar degree. However, while the degree of the characteristic in multiple offspring tends to be clustered near the parents' values, the distribution of the characteristic resembles the normal bell-shaped curve. This is the concept of *variation.*

C 2.3. *The concept of variation.*

Which of the following most accurately describes the concept of variation? _____ .

    a. Offspring of different parents are often quite similar to each other

    b. Offspring of different parents are often quite similar to their own parents

    c. Offspring are often not identical to their own parents, though most are

    d. There is more variability in structural characteristics among a parent generation than among the next generation considered as a separate group

> Occasionally mutations take place in the genetic process, which simply means that an accident occurs in the biological manifestation of genetic material. Mutations occur at random, both in nature and as a result of mutagenic agents (chemicals, radiation, etc.). Mutations, unlike the changes resulting from natural selection, are not directed toward the adaptational needs of the organism. Occasionally such genetic accidents result in better adapted individuals, and if such individuals are not made sexually non-reproductive as a side effect of the mutation, the mutated characteristic can be continued through the genetic process. Thus, an occasional line of individuals may differ markedly from their immediate ancestors and others of the species. Most mutations, however, are harmful (Moment, 1958), and typically these genetic accidents are not perpetuated through further reproduction.
>
> What we have been discussing so far is the way in which there have always been and will continue to be wide variations in the manifestation of practically every biological characteristic of a species. Now we run again into the most powerful of the Darwinian notions—the concept of *natural*

selection. If we see that certain individuals vary in a certain biological characteristic, we assume that that characteristic was significant in the survival of the species in its natural setting. Such characteristics as height, weight, strength, and intelligence (in the sense of complexity of the brain structure) influenced the likelihood of individual survival to sexual maturity. Such characteristics obviously pertain to survivability. Many other not-so-obvious, but critical, characteristics will be briefly discussed later.

Let us take an example of a biological characteristic that is obviously relevant to survivability in the natural, predatory environment. Consider the body size of the horse, including measures of both height and weight. If you were to visit a museum of natural history, you might see there the re-created remains of horses that lived many thousands of generations ago. The structures have been carefully duplicated and one is immediately struck by the differences in size between these horses and the horses of today. One can see that as thousands of years passed, larger and larger body sizes evolved. How would this have happened in Darwinian theory? The natural assumption would be that the larger animals might be less vulnerable to attack from predators, and with longer legs they might be able to outrun predators. Thus, in a large herd with a number of young horses, when

the predators attacked, the horses that were larger, stronger, and ran faster tended to have a greater rate of survivability; out of hundreds of horses in a large herd, the relatively few that lived to sexual maturity would be predominantly the larger ones. They would then pass along this characteristic to their offspring. Gradually, over thousands of years, with the process of natural selection favoring the larger, swifter animals, the species as a whole began to take on the form it has today.

As for existing small breeds, we either assume that they are products of fairly isolated areas with low predatory threat, or that man, practicing controlled breeding, has deliberately produced small types of horses for special purposes. As an exercise in Darwinian logic you might take any extreme species characteristic, such as the long necks of giraffes, and figure out how the process of natural selection might have favored the animals with the more extreme manifestations of the characteristic. In doing this, it is relevant to note that adaptive characteristics are not simply those associated with defense against predators, but also those related to acquiring food and gaining sexual access to others of the species.

In contrast to the external manifestations of biological structure, we can cite subtle internal variations in a species that lead to survival. Let us consider an interesting case involving rabbits. The early settlers to Australia who came from Europe brought with them a few rabbits, which turned out to be a costly mistake. With few of rabbits' natural predators in Australia, the rabbit population soon grew to greatly outnumber the population of human beings on that continent. The rabbits destroyed a great deal of the land productivity. Australia finally defended itself by building a long fence almost the entire length of the nation, and a tremendous percentage of the national budget was spent each year to keep this barrier in good repair. A large number of professional "fence watchers" were hired as government employees to maintain the fencelines in the waste areas of Central Australia. Several years ago a more economical way of controlling the rabbit population was proposed. The disease myxomatosis was deliberately introduced into the rabbit population. Soon most of the animals were dead, but there were a few which seemed to have a resistance to the disease. The animals having this particular genetic variation—resistance to myxomatosis—soon began to multiply and now the long fence is once again the major defense against a large wild rabbit population.

But what characteristics might have aided such a helpless-appearing animal as the guinea pig to survive? The guinea pig seems to have little ability to fight or to run rapidly to escape. Its poor vision does little to help it recognize a predatory threat. Therefore, we have to turn to the known characteristics of the guinea pig. The guinea pig is a nocturnal creature when he lives in his natural environment. The cover of darkness allows him to move short distances from his burrow to feed on easily accessible vegetation in relative safety. His poor day-vision is little hindrance to him in the darkness. Another pair of characteristics are the guinea pig's high rate of reproduction and his low aggressiveness toward others of his own species. All of these characteristics, combined, allowed

"INCIDENTALLY, WE'LL BE SHORT ONE RAT THIS MORNING. THE BLACK AND WHITE ONE BIT ME AND I BASHED HIS SKULL IN."

the survival of this species of little animal, despite its weaknesses.

From the comparative study of different strains and breeds of animals we become increasingly aware of the actual differences that may exist between widely separated geographic groups within the same species. Even within a short space of time, in evolutionary terms, we have seen changes in strains of laboratory rats. A group of rats may be introduced into a breeding colony in a given laboratory, and maintained there for decades. Often laboratories supply animals from their strain to other researchers. These animals are separated from their natural predators, and man becomes a type of predator in a restricted evolutionary sense. If you wish to use rats for certain types of research, the animals that do not manifest desired behaviors are destroyed and no longer is their genetic input available to the strain.

The well-known docility of the white laboratory rat, for example, is the result of rats in that species being destroyed if they should bite a laboratory worker. Thus, the characteristic of aggressiveness was bred out of the species. In other laboratories "lazy" rats which do not scurry down a maze may not be retained for breeding. M. B. Jones, in 1956, described rats taken from two different strains in separate laboratories. Individuals in one group, coming from a California colony, were much slower to emerge from a start box than those from a group used in the University of Iowa psychology laboratories. The California animals spent long periods of time in exploratory behaviors, sniffing along the walls and in the air. Even after they had presumably learned the maze-traveling behaviors, they would stop, seemingly without reason, and renew their explorations. The University of Iowa rats, on the other hand, would pop out of the start box, scurry down the runway and around the turns, and enter the goal box. Jones reported that the Iowa rats, except for their orientation toward the goal, seemed almost oblivious to their surroundings. Fantastic differences have been developed, deliberately, in the "intelligence" of certain strains of rats through selective breeding. In an experiment, which will be more fully described in a later chapter, Tryon (1940), through several generations of breeding bright-with-bright and dull-with-dull rats, emerged with two groups which had practically no overlap at all in terms of their learning efficiency in a complex maze.

Researchers in Canada have investigated temperament differences in various breeds of dogs. Certain breeds are highly conditionable and are therefore easily trained by man and appear intelligent. Other breeds of dogs are, as a general rule, rather slow to absorb training, and while they may occasionally exercise vigorously, they still seem to demonstrate a singular lack of nervous energy and drive. Many of the ability and temperament differences are the result of deliberate planning and selective breeding.

Certain other factors have been identified and conceptualized as being influential in the evolution of species. One, *genetic drift*, may develop out of the chance isolation, by migration or accident, of a small segment of a larger population. The gene pool of the small group may not be identical to that of the larger population. Continued inbreeding perpetuates the unrepresentative genetic characteristic and can produce evolutionary changes that are nonadaptive. An example of this can be found in the Old Order Amish of Pennsylvania (Thompson & Thompson, 1966). The Amish traditionally intermarry, and in one colony a form of mental retardation with certain pronounced physical differences, known as the Ellis-van Crevald syndrome, was observed in over 50 cases among 8,000 members of the colony. This problem was absent from other Amish colonies as well as from the general population. A wide variety of such genetically restricted problems results from genetic drift.

A related phenomenon is that striking differences in characteristics may develop between groups of the same species that, for hundreds of thousands of successive generations, have had different environmental stresses to adapt to. This is the popularly recognized idea of a "hardy" people who have had to cope with harsh conditions. Though many of these notions are no doubt exaggerated, there are distinct and major differences, for example, in skin color of different races of man that reflect such influences.

Since we very frequently observe characteristics in human beings that appear to parallel the animal characteristics just described (intelligence, conditionability, nervous energy, and drive), it is interesting to speculate as to whether there may actually be gross differences in biological structure existing within groups of human beings which make them, as groups, discriminably different from others. Man's characteristic travel and migration limit the human manifestation of what, in rats, we would call a "strain difference," but we do sometimes encounter a group of human beings that has lived almost exclusively in a small geographic area for hundreds of years, with very little genetic input from the broader population. Also, it is at least a speculative possibility that the different races of man, socio-economic classes, and certain religious groups, due to tendencies not to mate with individuals outside of their own groups, may have developed certain characteristics of biological structure beyond simply those of facial or skin characteristics, which are manifested in behavioral differences. This is a very interesting possibility, but unfortunately little sound evidence has been accumulated.

Eugenics   We know that selective breeding enables man to control behavioral manifestations in the domestic animals he employs for a variety of purposes. There also seems to be clear evidence that, in man himself, the same processes of natural selection have been working over the years.

Many persons believe that, since we know of ways in which to control behavioral characteristics through selective breeding, society might be advanced by such a program deliberately applied to human beings. This idea was proposed by Darwin's cousin, Sir Francis Galton, in England. Galton had great breadth as a scientist, and his chief concern was human evolution. He was quite taken with the idea he got from Darwin that mental, emotional, and physical characteristics were inherited. He felt that changes in behavioral potential could be made in an entire race or nationality of people through selective breeding; and so in 1883 he established the *eugenics* movement. His intention was to replace "natural selection" in man with deliberate selection on the basis of behavioral and psychological assessment, with the eventual result being a race or a clearly defined subgroup of persons within the society who would be virtual supermen. As you might expect, the movement, though it evoked an intense academic type of interest, never really got off the ground. There were a few occasional gestures in that direction, such as the one or two state programs to sterilize severely retarded individuals and habitual felons. Such programs are seldom politically popular.

There is currently some revived interest in the possibility of deliberate manipulation of genetic material in order to create newborn individuals with superior physical and mental characteristics, but it is obvious that anything significant in this direction is far from having reached a practical stage of development.

C 2.4.   *The concepts of eugenics and selective breeding.*

Which of the following cases most accurately describes selective breeding? _____ .

   a. Systematic inbreeding of parents with children, etc., in favored animal colonies

   b. Systematic mate selection so as to maximize characteristics desired

   c. A movement in human society to eliminate undesirable characteristics through a systematic mate selection program

   d. Alteration of situational factors during animal breeding to maximize fertility

Which of the following cases most accurately describes eugenics? _____ .

   a. Systematic inbreeding of parents with children, etc., in favored animal colonies

   b. Systematic mate selection so as to maximize fertility in sparse populations

   c. Alteration of situational factors in human groups to maximize fertility

   d. A movement in human society to maximize desirable characteristics through
      a systematic mate selection program

PROGRESS CHECK   2.1

1. Which is a more correct statement about evolutionary changes? _____ .

   a. Series of rapid mutations produce new and better species

   b. Adaptive behavior patterns acquired by parents are transmitted to offspring

   c. Through the processes of natural selection, gradual changes occur in a species

MATCH: _____ 2. Natural selection

   _____ 3. Variation

   _____ 4. Mutation

   A. Some animals reproduce themselves, while others fail to do so

   B. Random genetic accidents

   C. Normal distribution of inherited characteristics

5. If a pair of highly excitable rats produced an excitable litter, then what might one conclude? _____ .

   a. The offspring inherited excitable behavior

   b. The offspring inherited biological structures mediating the behavior

6. Intermarriage in one Amish colony produced the Ellis-van Crevald syndrome. This is an example
   of _____ .

   a. genetic drift   b. mutation   c. natural selection   d. survival of the fittest

7. The man historically associated with the eugenics movement to selectively breed better humans
   is _____ .

   a. Gregor Mendel   b. Charles Darwin   c. Francis Galton   d. Marco Polo

---

NEUROLOGY   We now come to the question: In what specific biological structures are psychologists interested? Probably various psychologists have interests in differing structural characteristics for one reason or another, but in general we can point to the majority of research as being concerned with the brain's function, with variables relating to operations of other portions of the central nervous system or to the autonomic nervous system, and with variations in brain chemistry. In essence the whole pattern of research seems to revolve in one sense or another around the neurological system of the body. We shall now examine, briefly, certain characteristics of neurological structure.

The Neuron   The basic unit of the nervous system is the *neuron*. Neurons are extremely tiny threadlike cells which, by the billions, make up what we call the nervous system of a single individual. If we are to understand how the nervous system operates, we must first see, briefly, how a single neuron operates.

The function of a neuron is to transmit an abrupt electrochemical impulse from one end to the other, through its length. The changes in the electrochemistry of a neuron can stimulate similar changes in other neurons, which in turn influence others, in the manner of a long chain.

In general we talk about two major divisions of the body's neurological system—the peripheral and the central portions. The *peripheral nervous system* consists simply of the neurons that lie outside the brain and spinal cord. The *central nervous system,* by contrast, is made up of neurons within the brain and spinal cord. In general, the mechanisms controlling the operations of these two systems are similar.

Most neurons show a fairly pronounced degree of specificity—that is, they tend to carry only signals of a certain nature. This is actually dictated by the fact that the neuron is tied in to certain types of sensory receptors and the neural tract leads to a certain area of the brain. Neurons carry information in only one direction along their lengths, and although it is somewhat of an oversimplification, we may talk of peripheral neurons as either carrying sensory messages inward toward the brain, or outward from the brain with signals proceeding toward the body's muscles and glands.

Very seldom do we find isolated neurons. More often they are bound together in bundles, similar to the many wires in a large insulated telephone cable. A large bundle of neurons is called a *nerve.*

If a nerve in the peripheral nervous system is severed, it is capable of reconnecting itself. In general, the process takes about six weeks, and during the regrowth the ends of a nerve may weave about to avoid scar tissue, but eventually they come together and attach. Such a regenerative process does *not* take place in the central nervous system, however, when damage has occurred there.

C 2.5. *The nature of the neuron.*

The neuron is sometimes termed the _____ .

    a. basic unit of the nervous system   b. functional equivalent of the structural genotype

    c. final element in the stimulus-response cycle   d. product of bundles of nerves

A bundle of neurons is called _____ .

    a. a cell body   b. the brain   c. a nerve

A single neuron carries a signal _____ .

    a. in one direction only   b. either forward or backward

C 2.6. *Categories of nervous systems.*

The brain and spinal cord together make up the _____ nervous system.

The neurological structure that lies outside the central nervous system is

    called the _____ nervous system.

The Brain

The central processing area for all bodily activities is the brain. There are a number of divisions of the brain which we believe correspond to evolutionary development. In humans, as we go up from the neck region, we see that the higher we go, the more complex and sophisticated is the brain structure when compared with the corresponding areas in animals lower on the phylogenetic scale. It has been suggested that the process of evolution followed a rising path in the brains of organisms, finally developing the frontal lobes, which were the last to evolve as complex areas. It is in the cerebral cortex—the entire higher brain area—that the human is most unlike lower animal forms. The evolution of the species apparently has favored individuals with larger brains, but this factor has to be balanced by the difficulty the human female has in giving birth to a baby with a large head. One solution to this, in evolution, appears to be the "packing-in" of brain tissue inside the skull cavity, resulting in a convoluted appearance of the brain's surface.

C 2.7. *The evolution of the brain structure.*

It is in the _____ brain area, called the _____

_____ , that man has become, through evolution, most unlike lower organisms.

Sub-Cortical Centers

Let us begin at the bottom of the brain area and go upward (see Figure 2.1). At the top of the spinal cord itself is a region called the *medulla,* and above is the *pons.* In addition to simply being areas that are part of the chain carrying information from the lower to the higher areas and back again, the medulla and the pons have their own specific functions. They act as centers for the maintenance of heart and lung activity, and if these areas are damaged there is a very serious threat to life itself.

    Through the center of the medulla and pons also extends a network believed to exert a general arousal influence upon the higher areas of the brain and the physical body functions. This region is called the *reticular system,* which we will discuss in more detail in a later chapter. Finally, in the pons there are important pathways that divert to connect lower centers to the cerebellum, which is a structure in the back of the brain that is important in the maintenance of balance and coordination of body movements.

Figure 2.1

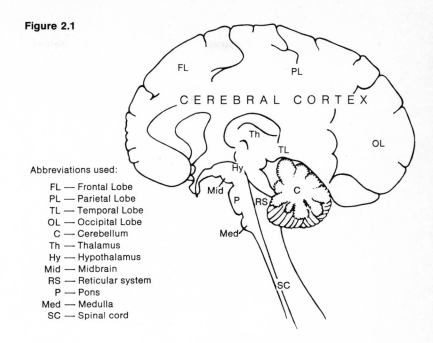

Abbreviations used:

FL — Frontal Lobe
PL — Parietal Lobe
TL — Temporal Lobe
OL — Occipital Lobe
C — Cerebellum
Th — Thalamus
Hy — Hypothalamus
Mid — Midbrain
RS — Reticular system
P — Pons
Med — Medulla
SC — Spinal cord

Above the pons are midbrain neural pathways, both ascending and descending. High in the midbrain are certain areas that have a coordination function in connection with seeing, hearing, and body movement.

Immediately above the midbrain is a small, important area called the *hypothalamus.* The hypothalamus serves as a center for many kinds of behaviors relating both to emotion and to primary drives. The hypothalamus has many subdivisions which seem to function separately. Electrical or chemical stimulation of one subdivision in this area will cause obviously satiated animals to eat vigorously again, while destruction of this area will cause the animals to stop eating and drinking and consequently to die. Recently a region was discovered in the hypothalamus that, upon stimulation, gives rise to a sensation of pleasure. An electrode in the so-called "pleasure center" can be placed so that an animal can perform a behavior such as bar-pressing to stimulate himself, and he will pursue such stimulation for days at a time to the exclusion of food, water, sex or sleep. Apparently all the pleasurable things in life are pleasant only insofar as they activate the pleasure center in the hypothalamus, and direct stimulation of the area makes all else unnecessary.

Another function of the hypothalamus is control of water metabolism. Changes in the water concentration of the blood stimulate a particular hypothalamic region which then sets off subsequent activation patterns leading to eventual drinking. Other cells in the hypothalamus are sensitive to the temperature of the bloodstream and small variations bring quick responses such as vibration of the muscles (shivering) in a cold environment, or perspiration in a hot environment, which cools the skin's surface through the evaporative process.

Above the hypothalamus is an area called the *thalamus,* which has several functions. One area in the thalamus receives signals from the sensory systems (sight, smell, hearing, touch, etc.) and relays this information to higher levels in the brain, and appears to introduce some organizing and modification of the information being transmitted. At another point in the thalamus various neurological tracts project out into widely separated regions of the higher brain.

C 2.8. *Structures of the subcortex.*

An area which receives various incoming sensory information, organizes the information, and then transmits it into various widely separated areas of the cortex is the _____ .

    a. reticular system   b. thalamus   c. hypothalamus

A brain center which has the function of activating or arousing the higher regions of the brain as well as certain body functions (heart rate, etc.) is the _____ _____ .

The so-called "pleasure center" in the brain is located in the _____ .

Cells in the (name the brain center) _____ are sensitive to blood fluidity, blood temperature, etc., and serve to trigger various reactive body functions.

The Cerebral Cortex   Most of what we would call "mental" functioning occurs in the *cerebral cortex*—the higher brain centers. These cerebral hemispheres started to develop in the ancestors of present-day fish. Primarily they were developed to process the senses of taste and smell, which strongly relate to survival of the species. These senses are necessary if an organism is to find good food, regurgitate bad food, find sexual partners, stay with its own species, and avoid predators. As the vertebrates continued to develop and their brains evolved, other sensory inputs and expanded functions were possible.

     Before we approach a discussion of the complex functioning of the cerebral cortex, let us examine some of the problems the researcher faces. Since mental processes are so vital to a person's earning a living and getting along with others in a complex society, we need to know all we can about how the brain operates. Unlike the functions of the midbrain, where great similarities exist between brain-behavior relations from man down through various infrahuman species, in the cortex we deal with many higher intellectual functions, and it is not feasible to gather all our information from animal research.

     The researcher can approach the problem of specific function in several ways, but the most common is the study of the effects of brain lesions. Various individuals come to the attention of brain researchers; some of these individuals have experienced brain injury in war or in an accident. Others have disease processes, tumorous growths, etc. The first major problem is that it is usually difficult to specify the *exact location and extent* of tissue damage and relate this to behavioral changes. The techniques available for localization of damage, such as the EEG and various radio-

JANNA

Janna ducked low behind the cartons of medical supplies stored on the balcony high above the foyer of the BMC complex. From all around came the hollow noises of the searchers, punctuated intermittently by a low-toned but insistent alarm.

Janna caught her breath and reflected on her past ten years at the BMC. Of all its residents, in all its years, she was the first to turn defector. At least she was the first to resist a transmutation procedure.

Granted, the procedure was not all that bad. Usually the individuals, chosen on the basis of their age and general health, were *elevated* in intellectual function. The injections were reasonably painless, if you didn't mind the idea of 70 or 80 microneedles penetrating your skull and entering the brain tissue simultaneously. Then a wider area of intellectual operation opened up to you, and it was like an adventure.

But this time! The informational circuit had stated that it was the first time in six years that there were oversupplies of Level-7 personnel, and half a hundred were being selected for transmutational *reduction* to all levels below Level-7.

You never knew—you might even be reduced to Level-1, although usually only males who could work in the dangerous but simple jobs were transmuted back to that level.

Still, suppose you were put back to Level-2 or Level-3 and had to work scrubbing equipment or assembling simple machines. Sure, you wouldn't have any yearning for your old identity, they said. You wouldn't even understand what it was that you used to do.

But the indignity of it ran against the grain!

Janna crouched lower, knowing suddenly that she had been seen and that there was no escaping the Brain Modification Center guards. Suddenly, before she could be reached by anyone, she launched herself into space right off the balcony platform. The floor rushed up.

Let them put her brain back together now with their little blueprints. That was the last thought she had.

Behavior control has been affected by brain surgery and shock therapy. The purpose of such procedures is to modify serious psychological disturbances that interfere with the individual's operating effectively in civilized society. But if the pioneer efforts of this field achieve such refinements that such things as intellectual ability and emotional structure can be maneuvered, will the basic humanity of existence be altered?

logical procedures, are only able to give an approximate locus. Even in cases which have been subjected to surgery, it is often impossible for the surgeon to specify exactly the degree or the progression of damage.

There are further problems in specifying the exact location of damage.

Such "space occupying" lesions as tumors produce pressures inside the skull which distort the shape of the brain and affect tissues far removed from their own location. Damage to one part of the brain might affect a blood vessel passing through or over that part and so disrupt the blood supply to other areas with consequent further damage. By contrast, in work with animals the lesion can be carefully placed experimentally in an otherwise intact brain.

Much brain research in humans comes out of cases routinely treated in clinical efforts at remediation. Strokes form the most common cause of localized damage. The study of effects of localized damage include other types of brain damage such as tumors or lesions produced by surgery.

Now that we have suggested some of the complexities in performing brain-behavior research and interpreting the results, let us discuss what we *do* know about the function of the cerebral cortex.

First, let us designate the four major lobe formations of the cerebral cortex. On the left side of Figure 2.1 is the *frontal lobe* area, which apparently mediates thought, verbal memory, logic, anticipation of the future, etc. A sense of time seems mediated in this area as well. Toward the back of the brain, still on top, is the *parietal lobe:* this area receives impulses concerning the sense of touch and the kinesthetic sense. Kinesthesis is the feedback system that tells us what the body is doing. Receptors located in the muscles, tendons, and joints inform the brain about the location and attitude of the various body parts at a given moment. At the rear of the brain is the *occipital lobe:* this area mediates visual pattern recognition, and a serious dysfunction of interpretation of visual information can be the result of damage to this area. In the area in front of and just above the ears, is the *temporal lobe.* What the occipital lobes do for visual perception, the temporal lobes do for language perception. If damage occurs here, people may hear speech and recognize words, but not be able to understand what combinations of words mean, or they may not remember the meanings of certain individual words, both in hearing others talk and in their own speech.

(*Note:* We have been using the expression *lobe* rather than lobes, in describing the four areas, because in Figure 2.1 we are looking at only one side of the brain. Actually the brain is divided across the top, with a left portion and a right portion of each lobe structure, each essentially independent in its operation.)

The cerebral hemispheres are not essential to life. Certain deformed individuals, born without parts of the hemispheres, clearly indicate this. But a fairly intact cerebral cortex is required for any kind of "normal" life.

C 2.9. *Functions of the lobes of the cortex.*

Mediation of thought, memory, logic, and so forth takes place in the _____ lobes of the brain.

Visual pattern recognition takes place in the _____ lobes.

The _____ lobes mediate language perception.

Senses of touch and kinesthesis are mediated by the _____ lobes.

What has been described to you is a gross oversimplification. While it is true that certain brain functions have been assigned to specific regions of brain tissue, there seem to be second- and even third-level brain areas which are directly involved in any physical or mental process. And, conversely, there is probably no area of the brain that is limited to just a few isolated functions.

The Nervous System and the Environment

The main function of the neurons that make up the body's nervous system is to allow the individual to relate to circumstances in his immediate environment. The specialized functions of the nervous system all evolved in terms of allowing the individual to respond to events rapidly and effectively in ways that maximized the chances for survival. We shall describe the activation of a single neuron, and then show the sequences involved in a response to a stimulus.

One of the basic functional relationships that we can see in biological literature is that the strength of an organism's response to a stimulus is largely a function of the intensity of the stimulus. It is fundamental that an organism be able to translate the elements indicating stimulus intensity into some kind of accurate recognition. Otherwise the organism may waste its resources seeking refuge from a momentary chill from cool air, hiding from tiny specks in the visual field, and so forth. The actual neural signal is an electrochemical change brought about by a reversal of polarities on the inner and outer surfaces of the neuron. This electrochemical shift is in the nature of an impulse which travels down the length of the neuron. At the end of the neuron there is no physical connection with other neurons, but the impulse can still bridge the small gap and activate the next neuron in series. This gap, called the *synapse,* is the point of *functional connection* between neurons. When the signal being transmitted reaches the end of the neuron, the impulse releases transmitter molecules which spread across the synaptic gap and act to stimulate the next neuron in series.

A neuron is said to have a *threshold* for activation. This means that the strength of an incoming stimulus must be of a sufficient level before activation can occur. If a neuron is activated, however, it discharges at full strength. This is known as the all-or-none principle. The concept of threshold applies not only to the chemical-electrical potential which exists at the receptors which trigger the neurons' activation, but at the synapses, which are also biochemical in their operation.

C 2.10. *The synapse.*

The synapse is defined as the point of _____ _____ .

C 2.11. *Activation thresholds for individual neurons.*

What is the term used to describe the characteristic of the neuron such that if it is to become activated

it will transmit its signal at full strength? _____ .

   a. Synaptic principle   b. Electrochemical shift   c. All-or-none principle

Each neuron has a _____ , referring to the stimulus strength necessary before the neuron is activated.

How does the organism determine how strong a stimulus is? It does this in two ways. First, recognizing that the different receptors in the eye, ear, skin surface, and so forth have different thresholds, you can see that a strong stimulus would trigger more neural activity than would a weak stimulus. The weak stimulus could only trigger low-threshold receptor neurons, while the stronger stimulus could trigger neurons with higher thresholds.

The second mechanism for determining stimulus strength is more complex. After a neuron fires, it cannot fire again for a fraction of a second: this *absolute refractory period* is a sort of "total exhaustion." Then, for a short interval of time, the neuron is "recovering." During this time, which is called the *relative refractory period,* the neuron will fire only if it is triggered by a stronger-than-usual stimulus. Another way of stating this is to say that during the relative refractory period the threshold for activation is moving from a very high level down to the point where it arrives at its normal value. The whole process of the two refractory periods following stimulation takes less than one-hundredth of a second. As you can now see, a very strong continuing stimulus would cause a single neuron to fire more frequently during a given period of time than would a weaker stimulus.

In these ways, then, we see that the organism can differentiate stimuli of different intensities—from both the number of neurons bringing the signal in and from the rate of the signal impulses delivered by each neuron.

C 2.12. *The refractory phases of the neuron.*

During a neuron's absolute refractory phase _____ .

   a. it cannot be activated

   b. it can be activated, but only by a relatively strong stimulus

   c. it is capable of being activated by a stimulus of a strength matching its normal threshold

If a neuron is capable of being activated by a stronger than usual stimulus, but not by a stimulus matching its normal threshold, the neuron is said to be in the _____ phase.

   a. absolute refractory   b. relative refractory   c. normal

C 2.13. *Interpretation of stimulus strength by the neurophysiological system.*

What two neurological factors allow the individual to respond in terms of a stimulus' strength (or intensity)? (a) _____ .

   (b) _____ .

Now, let us follow a simple interaction of the brain with an event in the environment in order to see just what sequential operations are involved in the brain's operation. Let us suppose that a stimulus is picked up by one of the body's *receptors*. The signal, transmitted electrochemically, proceeds through the peripheral nervous system. When the nerve impulse arrives at the point of entry into the spinal cord, a synapse occurs so that the signal can proceed. Inside the spinal cord itself the ascending neuron (this is called the afferent pathway) carries the signal into the brain, where it is delivered to the appropriate brain center. Here, a "decision" is made, which does not necessarily imply a conscious awareness or a deliberate thought process by the individual, and an outgoing signal then starts downward along the efferent pathway. As we have already indicated, a single neuron does not carry messages in two directions, so different pathways are involved in the two-way process. Also, the outgoing messages do not typically go to the receptor where the incoming message was received, so separate pathways are vital. As the outgoing message reaches the appropriate level of the spinal cord, it crosses another synaptic junction and passes into the peripheral nervous system. The outgoing signal finally reaches and triggers the body's *effectors*. These are the structures that cause some action relative to the environment. (See Figure 2.2)

If the incoming signal is a simple, informational one, such as a message that the eye is not able to see very well because of the poor adjustment of a reading lamp, the effectors involved would be the muscles which control hand and arm movements. These specific areas would be triggered and the individual would reach out and make the adjustment. The action of muscles, in response to neurological stimulation, is also electrochemical. Chemicals are released at the spot where the neuron has a synaptic relationship with the muscle fiber, and a contraction of the muscle results.

Figure 2.2

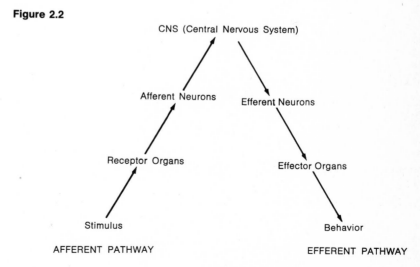

C 2.14. *Receptors and effectors.*

The body's receptor organs _____ .

    a. are those which bring about some change in the organism relative to the environment

    b. are stimulated by effector organs

    c. are the first to receive incoming stimuli

    d. are intermediate links between two other physiological functioning units

The body's effector organs _____ .

    a. are those which bring about some change in the organism relative to the environment

    b. are stimulated by receptor organs

    c. are the first to receive incoming stimuli

    d. are typically elements of the central nervous system

C 2.15. *Afferent and efferent pathways in neurophysiology.*

The afferent pathways are _____ .

    a. stimulus elements that trigger physiological reactions

    b. neurological structures that bring a stimulus signal in from the environment

    c. neurological structures that carry a signal out to the effectors

    d. logical reasoning processes resulting from an individual's recognizing stimuli

The efferent pathways are _____ .

    a. stimulus elements that trigger physiological reactions

    b. neurological structures that bring a stimulus signal in from the environment

    c. neurological structures that carry a signal out to the effectors

    d. logical reasoning processes resulting from an individual's recognizing stimuli

The Autonomic Nervous System

Another neurological process in the body parallels the central nervous system processes and is very important for the adjustive functioning of individuals. The *autonomic nervous system,* while triggered by some of the same receptors that initiate central nervous system signals, has the internal organs of the body, specifically the *glands* and the *smooth muscles,* as its effectors. The task of the autonomic nervous system is to maintain the body's delicate internal balance for optimum operation both in times of relaxation and during stress. The autonomic nervous system is divided into two subdivisions, the *sympathetic division* and the *parasympathetic division.*

The Sympathetic Division

The purpose of the sympathetic nervous system is to prepare the body for emergencies by patterning a reaction of the internal organs. The sympathetic nervous system consists mainly of two long nerve trunks, running parallel to each other, which lie outside the spinal cord on its *ventral* (toward the front) surface, extending from the lower brain areas all the way down to the bottom of the spinal cord. Nerve fibers extend outward from the main trunk, making a functional connection with the internal organs.

When an individual is faced with stress, signals start from the brain as soon as the information is received. While a signal pattern from the brain may follow the central nervous system pathways, resulting in bodily movement with respect to the new environmental situation, the autonomic nerve tracts are aroused separately, resulting in internal biological changes. Some neurons of the sympathetic division proceed straight to the smooth muscles of the internal body—heart tissue, for example. The direct neurological stimulation causes the heart rate to increase. A bit more time is involved in the indirect effect on the heart by the hormones released in glandular reactions. This is why sometimes when we get involved in an emergency situation, we react quickly in a cool and efficient manner, and then only a minute or so later, after the emergency is over, we experience an extremely high level of emotionality as the *delayed reaction* of the autonomic nervous system's glandular effectors has finally had its effect. These emergency functions, in situations such as threat of serious combat, could make the difference between life and death.

C 2.16.   *The autonomic nervous system.*

The autonomic nervous system has, as its effectors, _____ .

   a. the skeletal muscles of the body

   b. the central nervous system

   c. the smooth muscles and glands

C 2.17.   *The sympathetic division of the autonomic nervous system.*

Which of the following is the primary purpose of the sympathetic division of the ANS? _____ .

   a. Reasoned reaction to changing stimulus patterns

   b. Activation of the body to meet situations of stress

   c. Deactivation of the body following stress, and return to a state of normalcy

A number of endocrine glands are triggered by the ANS, including the *pituitary*, the *thyroid*, and the *adrenal* glands. From one gland alone, the pituitary, at least nine hormones are secreted. These hormones stimulate the sex glands, have a direct control over the secretions of the adrenal glands, regulate blood pressure, and perform various other functions. Turning to the adrenal gland, the hormone *epinephrine* stimulates secretion of sugar by the liver and increases the heart rate. Another adrenal hormone, *norepinephrine,* raises the blood pressure through constriction of the diameter of the various peripheral blood vessels. Many hormones are regulated by the sympathetic division, and we shall not go further into them. It is not so much the names of the hormones that are of interest to us, but some of the unique ways in which these hormones affect the bodily processes.

C 2.18. *The endocrine glands.*

Epinephrine and norepinephrine are hormones secreted by the _____ gland.

    a. pituitary   b. thyroid   c. adrenal

Which endocrine gland would be the one that has been called the "master" gland, since its several different hormones have direct effects on other glands? _____.

Let us consider what happens to a human body when stress occurs. We might supply the stress by creeping up behind you and discharging a pistol a few feet away when you are not expecting it. Immediately certain sympathetic fibers would elevate the rate of the heartbeat. Simultaneously the central nervous system would mediate a quick doubling over into a crouching posture, which has been called the *startle reflex.* After a few seconds, the dumping of glandular secretions into the blood stream would begin to have certain specific effects upon various organs of the body. There would then be further elevation of the heart rate. This, along with constriction of the peripheral blood vessels, would begin to raise the blood pressure. These two factors would result in more rapid movement of oxygen (which is fuel for the large muscle groups of the body) out to the muscles for use. The oxygen intake would be elevated by an increase in both the depth and rapidity of breathing. The pupils in the eyes would dilate, the hair on the arms, legs, and nape of the neck would begin to stand more erect, the individual would begin to perspire, and twitching of the muscles might be apparent. This latter phenomenon is brought about by the influence of epinephrine, from the adrenal gland, on the muscle fibers themselves. Epinephrine has the effect of lowering the threshold for muscle activation, so that even in a resting attitude some of the muscles begin to contract.

These various changes following stress have the overall effect of preparing individuals for a more efficient reaction to an emergency and, were an organism in a "natural" setting, he would have a greater likelihood of surviving the emergency situation. Let us examine exactly what, in evolution, each of these changes might have done for the individual.

The natural setting for the majority of man's time on earth has been precivilization. Reptiles and a variety of both large and small predators had to be dealt with on a daily basis. When man encountered his enemies, and some of these enemies were other men, he might react in a number of ways. Presumably, during the earlier stages of evolution, his internal autonomic reactions were in no way as patterned and consistent as they now are. So, let us say that a number of human beings were threatened daily, and frequently fought for their lives. If a man's rate and depth of respiration increased, he took in the vital oxygen supply that he needed for prolonged action. If his heart rate increased, moving the oxygenated blood along more rapidly to the large muscle groups, he could exert strength for a longer period of time. If an individual's pupils dilated, at all other times than perhaps the brightness of midday he would be better able to perceive small features of his environment that might be important if he were running; he would be better able to avoid obstacles or threats, or see objects that could be used as weapons. If his hair stood erect (and man seems to have lost most of the piloerection response at this point in his history), the insulation provided a defense against the teeth of the opponent. Since man's piloerection response (hair erection) only shows a vestigial existence, we know most of what we know about this phenomenon from observation of lower organisms. Cats with long hair, for example, are defended against enemies by their erect hair, which serves as a physical buffer. Some observers of animal behavior also consider the possibility that, by making the individual seem larger than he really is, piloerection causes the potential victim not to look so helpless, and his increased size may discourage the aggressor.

C 2.19. *Evolution of autonomic processes.*

In evolutionary terms, man's "natural setting" is (civilization/precivilization)

_____

If the body's hormones lower the threshold for activation of muscle fibers, the individual is then able to respond muscularly in ways which increase his chances for survival. The twitching of muscles in the highly activated body is correlated with the potential for exerting a great deal more physical strength at that moment than one is usually capable of. Occasionally newspaper reports describe how certain people, in emergencies, have been strong enough to lift very heavy weights off accident victims' bodies, or perform other feats of strength of which they would ordinarily not be capable. Also, the lowering of response thresholds means that the individual will have quicker reactions, which may be necessary if he is to gain even a slight edge on an opponent.

If the surface of the body perspires under conditions of sympathetic nervous system activation, two advantages may result. First, and most clearly, perspiration, in the process of evaporating from the surface of the skin, serves as a natural air conditioner, since the body stays cooler in normal or low-humidity conditions when one perspires. Second (and admittedly this is speculation), it is probable that when an individual is grabbed by an opponent, the fact that the skin's surface is wet and slippery would increase the individual's ability to slip free and escape.

The Parasympathetic Division   Thus far we have emphasized the patterns of autonomic responding within the sympathetic division of the autonomic nervous system. While the most dramatic changes in the body are associated with sympathetic activation, the results of parasympathetic activation are also quite interesting.

In the sense of function, we might say that the operations of the sympathetic and parasympathetic systems are opposite to one another. The sympathetic system responds to signals from the reticular system, and its activity then arouses the entire biological organism in stressful situations. The parasympathetic system responds to the absence of emergency signals coming in from the reticular system (and to a limited group of other types of stimulation), and its activity then returns the biological organism to a normal state. We generally use the expression that one or the other of the two systems "is dominant," referring to arousal on the one hand versus a stable and generally unaroused state on the other.

Of course the actions of the two systems are not just that simple. The hypothalamus is the key area in autonomic activation. The sympathetic and the parasympathetic divisions are aroused by overlapping, yet to a degree separate, sections of the hypothalamus. Various organs of the body are stimulated directly by neurons proceeding from each area. Organs such as the eye (pupillary dilation versus contraction), stomach, kidney, and intestines, plus others, are directly innervated and thus stimulated by both systems. Some organs—the sweat glands, blood vessels, and heart—are stimulated only by the sympathetic system. A few, such as the external genitals, are stimulated only by the parasympathetic system. It was once thought that "pleasant" emotions were mainly the result of parasympathetic dominance and unpleasant ones the result of sympathetic dominance, and while this does, descriptively, seem to be the case, modern knowledge suggests that this explanation is too simplistic. Rather, there appears to be a complex interaction of events which culminates in one's psychological experience. Much of the "experience" of emotion appears to be due to a conscious realization of one's situation and probable consequences—thus, extreme physical threat would ordinarily be unpleasant. Along a separate dimension, however, there are apparent direct effects of one's endocrine and biochemical state on the brain. For example, under mild to moderate sympathetic arousal the pancreas releases a hormone

called glucagon which in turn stimulates the liver to release its stored sugars. This condition, then, along with related elevations in certain adrenocortical hormones, is known to develop a temporary mood of an excited sort of buoyancy and well-being, sometimes later followed by an emotional slump (Selye, 1956).

C 2.20. *The parasympathetic division of the autonomic nervous system.*

Which of the following is the primary purpose of parasympathetic arousal? _____ .

    a. Reasoned reaction to changing stimulus patterns

    b. Activation of the body to meet situations of stress

    c. Deactivation of the body following stress, and return to a state of normalcy

In general, the actions of sympathetic nervous system arousal and parasympathetic arousal are (opposite/similar) _____ in their consequences.

Using a Darwinian analysis of how characteristics develop in organisms, one assumes that when a certain characteristic exists in a species, it played some part in the selective evolution of that species. As we said before, during most of man's time on earth he has existed in prehistoric environments, in which all the characteristics that we have described can clearly be seen to contribute to his survivability. At this point we have, in our civilized societies, an entire population that reacts according to its "prehistoric" evolutionary programming.

The next time you are called upon to give a talk before a large group of people, you might remember that when you perspire profusely and your hands begin to twitch, and when you begin to breathe so rapidly that you are concerned about how you will sound to the audience, these are all built-in emergency mechanisms to save you from the "enemy." Your body is preparing for fight or flight. Man has simply not had enough evolutionary experience in civilization to have had his gross physiological features restructured into different "civilized" patterns.

PROGRESS CHECK 2.2

1. The peripheral nervous system is composed of the brain and spinal cord. _____ .

    a. True   b. False

2. Which is true? _____ .

    a. The nerve is the basic unit of the nervous system

    b. A nerve is a bundle of neurons

    c. Glial cells group together and form nerves

    d. Nerves are only found in the spinal cord

3. Which nerves may regenerate and reconnect? _____.

    a. Those in the central nervous system   b. Those in the peripheral nervous system

4. Human and animal brains are considered most different through evolution in which area? _____.

    a. Reticular formation   b. Cerebellum   c. Pons   d. Cerebral cortex

5. The reticular formation is believed to have which function? _____ .

    a. Maintenance of balance   b. Normal heart rhythms

    c. General arousal   d. Imagery

MATCH: _____ 6. Parietal lobe   A. Visual pattern recognition

               _____ 7. Frontal lobe   B. Touch and kinesthesis

               _____ 8. Temporal lobe   C. Thought, memory and logic

               _____ 9. Occipital lobe   D. Language perception

10. Neurons will fire on the all-or-none principle when stimulated _____ .

    a. to activation threshold   b. only by very weak stimuli

    c. by sinusoidal currents   d. at the axon end

MATCH: _____ 11. Absolute refractory   A. A very strong stimulus may fire the neuron

                       period   B. Temporarily the neuron is completely

               _____ 12. Relative refractory   unresponsive

                       period

13. Hormones, such as epinephrine, are secreted by _____ .

    a. exocrine glands   b. neural vessicles   c. ANS receptor sites   d. endocrine glands

14. Which division of the ANS is dominant after stress ends and the body has returned to normal? _____ .

    a. Sympathetic   b. Parasympathetic

HEREDITY   Heredity as a basis of various behavior patterns is a controversial subject in psychology. While little real controversy exists concerning *whether* heredity affects behavior patterns, the *degree* of the effects is the subject for argument and different interpretations of data. We shall begin this section with an elementary review of some basic genetic principles.

Fundamentals   A *chromosome* is a discrete set of genes arranged in a linear order. The
of Genetics   chromosome is subdivided into *genes,* the physical structures transmitting

heredity potential from one generation to the next. Genes, in turn, are largely composed of *DNA* (deoxyribonucleic acid), a genetic material that has the ability to reproduce itself exactly and that serves as a carrier of chemical codes. DNA specifies the sequence of amino acids in the biosynthesis of polypeptide chains which, in turn, constitute the primary components of proteins. To accomplish this, DNA manufactures *RNA* (ribonucleic acid), a single chain that directs activity at the cellular sites of protein synthesis.

We can interest ourselves in hereditary action at several levels. We have already considered such actions at an ecological level in our discussion of evolution. We are now entering an area in which research activities either proceed at the biochemical level (DNA research, for example) or at a purely mechanical level where we interest ourselves in predictive characteristics of chromosome and gene research. We shall pursue the latter approach rather than the former, mainly because of the extreme complexity of biochemical explanations. You should not assume that either one or the other of the approaches is the "right" one. An analogy might be to compare the mechanical level of approach with the study of engine design in automotive mechanics, while the biochemical level would have its counterpart in the chemist's study of the complexities of the automotive combustion processes.

At the mechanical level we are interested first in *chromosomes*. Chromosomes normally occur in pairs, one coming from each of the parents. The cell structure of human beings has 46 chromosomes (23 pairs), of which one pair is responsible for sex determination. Because the developing cells of a conceived organism are formed by a process of cell division, each developing cell (or gamete) contains *one* member of each pair of chromosomes. The union of male and female gametes results in a single cell (or zygote) with 23 pairs of chromosomes, one member of each pair having been contributed by each parent. The genes that so pair are called alleles.

C 2.21. *Chromosomes.*

The chromosome is made up of a set of _____ .

The cell structure of the human being has _____ pairs of chromosomes.

A developing cell contains (how many members) _____ of the pair of chromosomes

for that characteristic possessed by one of the parents.

It is at the level of the gene's action that we shall concentrate our attention. The gene is (at the mechanical level) the basic unit of heredity. These tiny structures within the chromosomes, working in pairs—one from the father and one from the mother corresponding to some given biological characteristic—make up the fundamental requirement for genetic action. A person is then said to have inherited a genotype. A *genotype* is simply the organism's genetic make-up and, as you will see, sometimes does not have exactly corresponding representation in the *phenotype,* which is the actual physical structure (appearance) of the individual.

C 2.22. *Genes.*

The gene has been termed the _____ .

    a. link between the past and the future

    b. basic unit of the nervous system

    c. basic unit of heredity

    d. alternate to a biochemical theory

C 2.23. *Genotypes and phenotypes.*

The genotype most typically is described as _____ .

    a. an organism's "type" in terms of its physical appearance

    b. an organism's genetic make-up

    c. (both of the above may be correct)

The phenotype most typically is described as _____ .

    a. an organism's "type" in terms of its physical appearance

    b. an organism's genetic make-up

    c. (neither of the first two answers is correct)

Single-Gene Effects

The genotype of many traits is determined by a single pair of genes. Of the pair, one type may be dominant and the other recessive. A recessive gene trait is one that will appear in the phenotype only if both members of the gene pair (one from each parent) are of the recessive type. One simple example, often cited, is that of the brown-eye gene, which is always dominant over the blue-eye gene, which is recessive. If even one member of the gene pair is of the brown-eye type, the phenotype will be brown-eyed, although the genotype may be a brown-blue combination.

Let us illustrate this with a standard set of symbols. In genetics a capital letter is typically used to designate the dominant gene, and a lower-case letter designates the recessive gene. For a given trait an individual may be *AA*—homozygous for the dominant gene, which means that his genotype consists of two dominant genes, or he may be *aa*—homozygous for the recessive gene, which means that his genotype consists of two recessive genes. Or, he may be *Aa*—heterozygous—which means that his genotype consists of one gene of the dominant type and one of the recessive. In the above cases the *phenotype* would be *A* for the *AA* genotype, *A* for the *Aa* genotype, and *a* for the *aa* genotype. The genotypes *AA* and *Aa* give rise to phenotypes that are indistinguishable from one another. In this case the individual's genotype can be ascertained by a study of the proportions of *A* and *a* phenotypes in the individual's children.

C 2.24. *Single-gene effects: dominant and recessive genes.*

It is *necessary*, in order for a recessive-gene trait to be expressed in the phenotype, for (one/both)

_____ parent(s) to contribute the recessive gene.

It is *necessary*, in order for a dominant-gene trait to be expressed in the phenotype, for (one/both)

_____ parent(s) to contribute the dominant gene.

Some very clear systematic principles of genetic inheritance have been developed, and we can offer a system that will show how characteristics are inherited if the genes involved are clearly dominant or recessive. Each parent, as you will recall, has his or her own genotype for a given characteristic.

Table 2.1

	A	a
A	AA	Aa
a	Aa	aa

Table 2.2

	A	a
A	AA	Aa
A	AA	Aa

Let us employ the 2x2 table to illustrate the inheritance of a single-gene-determined genotype.

You can see in Table 2.1 above that two parents, both *Aa*, would on the basis of chance be parents to 25 percent *AA*, 25 percent *aa*, and 50 percent *Aa* genotypes.

In Table 2.2, you can see the probable percentage outcomes where parents are of genotypes *AA* and *Aa*. Offspring are 50 percent (by chance) *AA* and 50 percent *Aa*, so that none of the offspring would be of phenotype *a*. You can easily calculate other possible combinations—*AA* with *aa*, *Aa* with *aa*, *AA* with *AA*, and *aa* with *aa*.

An interesting phenomenon is that a recessive gene can "submerge" within a number of families for a period of several generations, reappearing when two "carriers"—persons of genotype *Aa*—mate. Consider the recessive gene for blue eyes in the human being. An *AA* parent and an *Aa* parent would neither have blue eyes, but half their children, on the average, would be *Aa* carriers of the gene. Of those *Aa* children (50 percent of the group of children), if they all married *AA* genotypes, half the resulting offspring would be *AA*, and half *Aa* (thus, half of a half, or 25 percent of the grandchildren, would be carriers). And so the cycle might proceed within two hereditary lines, with *no* blue-eyed children appearing for generations. Then as two individuals, both of whom are *Aa* for blue eyes, eventually mate, one-fourth of their children, on the average, would have blue eyes. Given the general ignorance of familial genetics, you can imagine the consternation that is sometimes caused by such developments.

If you feel that you would like to further examine the types of possible genotypic and phenotypic outcomes where single-gene effects are involved, examine Table 2.3.

Table 2.3

Genotype of Father	Genotype of Mother	Resulting Possible Genotypes in Offspring				Phenotypes of Offspring
AA	AA	AA,	AA,	AA,	AA	All A
AA	Aa	AA,	AA,	Aa,	Aa	All A
AA	aa	Aa,	Aa,	Aa,	Aa	All A
Aa	AA	AA,	AA,	Aa,	Aa	All A
Aa	Aa	AA,	Aa,	Aa,	aa	¾ A, ¼ a
Aa	aa	Aa,	Aa,	aa,	aa	½ A, ½ a
aa	AA	Aa,	Aa,	Aa,	Aa,	All A
aa	Aa	Aa,	Aa,	aa,	aa	½ A, ½ a
aa	aa	aa,	aa,	aa,	aa	All a

C 2.25. *Calculation of single-gene probabilities.*

Suppose you have two parents, neither of whom carries a certain recessive gene characteristic in his or her phenotype. One parent, however, does possess the recessive gene in the genotype. Suppose, moreover, that none of their children or grandchildren marry individuals with such a genotypic characteristic. Then, among the great-grandchildren, is it possible that any would still carry the recessive gene in the genotype? _____ .

As in the last problem, suppose all of the grandchildren married individuals with the recessive gene in the genotype but not in the phenotype. Hypothetically, what should be the outcome in the phenotypic expression of the characteristic in the next generation (calculated as a percent)? _____ .

Inheritance by single-gene effects is an all-or-none affair only if the genes are clearly dominant or recessive, but some genes (seldom associated with abnormalities) are neither clearly one nor the other. They are called intermediate genes, and they result in various degrees of incomplete dominance in the phenotypes of offspring. Thus, a white chicken mated with a black one will yield gray offspring—sometimes lighter and sometimes darker shades of gray.

C 2.26. *Intermediate genes.*

The intermediate genes, which are neither clearly dominant nor recessive, are (always, usually, seldom, never) _____ associated with what we would call "abnormalities."

Some traits appear to be manifest through the interactions of two or more gene pairs. You can work this out for yourself in a table if you care to, but you might just accept for the moment that, if the trait in question were the result of the actions of two recessive genes in each gene pair concerned, there would be 16 different possible parental mating combinations with nine resulting genotypes. You can easily see, then, how many other combinations of outcomes would result if a trait were manifest through interactions of both a dominant and a recessive manifestation of gene types, or two dominant gene manifestations, or even arrangements involving more than two gene pairs.

Sex-Linked Effects
An offspring "inherits" 23 chromosomes (which contain the genes) from one parent and 23 matching chromosomes from the other parent. One of the chromosome-pairs determines, among other things, the sex of the offspring. The female is termed *XX* on the gene-pair for determination of sex, while the male is termed *XY*, *X* being the female gene and *Y* being the male. The female will, at random, contribute one or the other of her *X* genes and the male will, at random, contribute either his *X* or his *Y* gene in mating so that the outcome probability is 50 percent female (*XX*) offspring and 50 percent male (*XY*) offspring.

C 2.27.   *Genetic determination of sex.*

On the gene-pair for determination of sex, the *XX* arrangement creates an individual of the

_____ sex.

Certain traits are "sex-linked," and at first they seem to contradict the Mendelian laws. However, these are cases in which the relevant genes are on the same chromosome as the genes that determine sex of the offspring. Almost always in these cases the relevant genes are on the *X* chromosome. Of the sex-determining genes, the *Y* (male) gene is dominant, and the *X* gene subordinate.

Red-green color blindness is a sex-linked trait. It is caused by a fairly frequent recessive gene on the *X* chromosome. Because the *Y* chromosome does not carry that particular gene, in the male (*XY*) the "recessive" trait has no opposition and can predominate and be expressed in the phenotype. When the female, on the other hand, has the recessive gene on an *X* chromosome, she will usually have the dominant gene for normalcy on her other *X* chromosome so that her vision will be normal but she will be a "carrier" of color-blindness through her genotype. The actual phenotypic expression of such color-blindness in women is not impossible, but the parental genotype circumstances that would lead to this event rarely occur. A color-blind mother plus a color-blind father would result in 100 percent of female births being color-blind; a "carrier" mother, plus a color-blind father, would result in 50 percent of female births being color-blind. Table 2.4 elaborates on such possibilities, where C is normal color vision; the hyphenated indications reflect the fact that the male genotype carries only one X chromosome.

Table 2.4

Genotype of Father (XY)	Genotype of Mother (XX)	Resulting Female Genotype	Resulting Female Phenotype	Resulting Male Genotype	Resulting Male Phenotype
C-	CC	CC	C	-C	C
C-	Cc	CC, Cc	C	-C, -c	½ C, ½ c
C-	cc (rare)	Cc	C	-c	c
c-	CC	Cc	C	-C	C
c-	Cc	Cc, cc	½ C, ½ c	-c	c
c-	cc (rare)	cc	c	-c	c

A number of other sex-linked characteristics exist, among them hemophilia, a disorder wherein the blood does not readily clot, and serious wounds often result in fatal bleeding.

C 2.28. *Sex-linked genetic effects.*

Sex-linked effects develop when the relevant genes for determination of a trait are on _____ .

    a. the Y chromosome   b. the X chromosome   c. both X and Y chromosomes together

Penetrance and Expressivity

A gene for a given characteristic may or may not produce the corresponding phenotype, and we have shown one possible reason why this may happen—one member of the gene pair may be recessive and subordinate to the dominant gene which dictates an opposing characteristic. An additional concept has been introduced to account for other failures of the genotype to produce an expected trait—we say it is because of *lowered penetrance*. This is a mathematically defined concept, and it is assumed to have occurred whenever we find that the phenotypic expression of a trait is lower than the predictions from the parents' genotypes. If, over a large number of cases, we found that a certain phenotype occurred only 80 percent as often as it should, we would say that the gene has a penetrance of 80 percent.

Expressivity refers to the degree to which a trait is manifested. The genotype may be expressed fully in the phenotype, or it may be given lesser expression with the trait barely appearing. Penetrance and expressivity are not properties of the genes, but the result of interactions of numerous genes and sometimes the environment as well. It has been established that high penetrance and strong expressivity typically go together, while the types of genes that have lower degrees of penetrance also express themselves weakly when they are penetrant.

C 2.29. *The concepts of penetrance and expressivity.*

Whenever a smaller number of individuals manifest a single-gene effect than should be the case according to Mendelian laws, we speak of the gene's having a lowered _____ .

"You can't talk to that crowd—they've all got extra Y chromosomes."

Whenever some trait is produced by certain genetic combinations, but there seems to be quite a bit of variation in different individuals' degrees or severities of the trait, we speak of the _____ of the gene.

Multiple-Gene Effects   Many inherited traits seem to be the expressions of a number of genes, acting independently. Such polygenic inheritance is characterized by a more-or-less normal curve manifestation of the trait in a species. Such species characteristics as intelligence (except for certain types of retardation), body size, and body color in humans and many animal forms are *polygenic expressions*. Special statistical methods have been devised to predict polygenic variation, and the field is called quantitative genetics. We cannot go into it here due to its complexity, but for the moment keep in mind that the phenotypic expressions of polygenic variables tend to revolve around the values of the parents. Take intelligence—if we were to gather 100 mothers with IQ=105, and 100 fathers with IQ=115, we could chart the IQs of their offspring. The mean for the resulting distribution should be around 110, with the data assuming the shape of a normal curve. It is quite frequent, with polygenic traits, to find offspring with phenotypic expressions quite *un*like either of their parents.

C 2.30.   *Multiple-gene effects.*

When we know of inherited characteristics that seem to be more or less normally distributed in the general population (as opposed to characteristics such that you either "have it" or you don't), we consider the characteristic to be a _____ expression.

Research Methods   No truly experimental method is used in human genetics since this would almost necessarily call for controlled breeding, but a large body of data has been accumulated on the incidence of traits, first in the general population, and then in aunts, uncles, cousins, parents, siblings, twins, etc., of persons with the trait. This, together with experimentally founded animal data, has made possible a number of conclusions concerning the principles of genetic action. In order to conclude that a trait is at least partially attributable to heredity, it must be shown that (1) the trait occurs significantly more often in blood relatives of individuals with the trait than in the general population, and that (2) environmental factors cannot sufficiently account for the increased frequency. It is the second criterion, of course, that offers us the most difficulty. Consider the case of intelligence:

1. We wish to investigate the genetic components of intelligence.
2. Our hypothesis is that low-intelligence parents will have a very high proportion of low-intelligence offspring.
3. Our low-intelligence parent group seems to come mainly from a low-income background. There is a probable cause-and-effect relationship of the sort that the low-income environment, due to its lack of stimulus variety and complexity, contributes toward lowered intelligence.
4. It is sometimes assumed that protein deficiencies and possibly certain other nutritional deficiencies affect developing brain structure, resulting in lowered intelligence.
5. Both for economic and educational reasons, infants in the lower-economic group are assumed to have a higher degree of nutritional deficiency than infants from families with higher incomes.

As you can see, it is necessary to engage in an almost prohibitive set of procedures in order to achieve control over environmental factors. Many researchers have turned to animal research in an effort to overcome the control problems.

PROGRESS CHECK   2.3

1. The basic unit of heredity is the _____ .

    a. neuron   b. golgi complex   c. RNA molecule   d. gene

2. Phenotypic manifestations produced by genetic effects _____ .

    a. appear and disappear only in utero   b. usually occur at puberty

    c. are deadly   d. may endure for a lifetime

3. Which of these is a fundamental of genetics? _____ .

    a. Chromosomes are composed of genes   b. Genes are composed of chromosomes

4. Which molecule constitutes the genetic material? _____ .

    a. AC   b. DNA   c. STP   d. RNA

5. Suppose one parent has a gene pair *AA* for brown eyes and the other has *aa* for blue eyes. Which of these genotypes would the offspring have? (Hint: fill out this matrix to answer the question.) _____ .

   a. *AA*   b. *aa*   c. *Aa*   d. All of these

	A	A
a		
a		

6. Which phenotype would the offspring in question 5 show? _____ .

   a. Brown eyes   b. Blue eyes   c. Blue-brown eyes

7. A black chicken mated to a white rooster produces gray chicks. Which is true? _____ .

   a. The black genes are dominant

   b. The white genes are recessive

   c. The genes for color are intermediate

8. Which trait is sex-linked? _____ .

   a. Eye color   b. Height   c. Color blindness   d. Hair color

9. Which chromosome pair results in a normal human male? _____ .

   a. XXY   b. XY   c. XX   d. XYY

MATCH: ____ 10. Penetrance   A. Degree to which a trait is manifested

           ____ 11. Expressivity   B. More than two genes determine a trait

           ____ 12. Polygenic expression   C. Phenotype expression of trait differs from mathematical predictions

---

OVERVIEW   In this chapter we have surveyed certain means by which behavioral potential is established in the conceived organism. It has been assumed that heredity is the major force through which we inherit biochemical and neurological patterns, not to mention appearance features. Moreover, we are not affected just in our early lives by genetic factors. Many inherited characteristics, such as male baldness patterns and several serious degenerative diseases, may not even begin to manifest themselves until middle or late adulthood.

C 2.31.   *The duration of genetic effects.*

The genetic influence upon our biological structure may become manifest in the phenotype _____ .

   a. at fetal and neonatal stages only

   b. up until the point of physical maturity

   c. throughout our lifetimes

No two human beings have exactly the same genes. Even in identical twins, where the genes are theoretically identical, there are so many genes involved that various minor gene mutations are probably always present, causing the developing biological structure of the twins *not* to be identical in every respect.

The interested student may wish to continue to explore some of the areas that we have opened up in this chapter. One of the simplest, short books to develop upon the topic of Mendelian genetics in our list is Charlotte Auerbach's *The Science of Genetics* (1961). An extremely interesting book is *Asimov's Guide to Science* (1972), by Isaac Asimov. Beadle and Beadle have written *The Language of Life* (1966) at a bit higher level of complexity. Finally, certain sections of David Rosenthal's *Genetics of Psychopathology* (1971) will be interesting. A later course may be taken in Physiological Psychology, but the main treatment of genetics will come in courses that may be taken in the field of biology.

It has not been our purpose in this chapter to recount the various established relationships between specific behavior variables and hereditary determinants. In appropriate chapters—concerning intelligence, motivation, psychopathology and the like—we shall discuss certain ones. We shall simply summarize, at this point, by stating the current situation. Behavioral genetics, as a research field, is progressing very rapidly. The field of medical genetics is already well established. Currently, most of the thrust is into genetic counseling of would-be parents. But as the mysteries drop away from molecular genetics, it is very likely that some day we shall be able to determine trait outcomes in very deliberate ways. When this happens, many of the most profound and miserable human disorders will largely vanish from being.

Developmental Processes: Physical, Social-Emotional, and Cognitive

THE NATURE OF DEVELOPMENTAL RESEARCH

DEVELOPMENTAL PROCESSES I: PHYSICAL DEVELOPMENT
Nutrition
  Motor Development
  Nutrition and Brain Development
  Nutritional Inadequacy in Human Beings:
    A Major Study
Stimulus Factors in Brain Development

DEVELOPMENTAL PROCESSES II: SOCIAL-EMOTIONAL DEVELOPMENT
Positive Social-Emotional Development:
  The Smile
Negative Social-Emotional Development:
  Maternal Deprivation
Negative Social-Emotional Development:
  Stimulus Deprivation
Erikson's Psychosocial Theory of
  Development
  Basic Trust vs. Mistrust
  Autonomy vs. Shame and Doubt
  Initiative vs. Guilt
  Industry vs. Inferiority
  Identity vs. Role Confusion
  Intimacy vs. Isolation
  Generativity vs. Stagnation
  Ego Integrity vs. Despair

DEVELOPMENTAL PROCESSES III: COGNITIVE DEVELOPMENT
Jean Piaget and His Theory of Cognitive
  Development
  Factors in Cognition
  Periods of Intellectual Development

CONCLUSION

The term "developmental psychology" refers to the study of systematic changes in physiological structure and behavior that can be predicted largely from knowledge of the age of an individual. Various developmental stages singled out for the attention of research specialists are (1) the fetal period (referring to the interval while the fetus is in the mother's womb), (2) the neonatal (newborn) and early infancy periods, (3) the late infancy period, (4) the early childhood (preschool) years, (5) childhood, (6) adolescence, (7) adulthood, and finally (8) old age and senescence. As you can well imagine, the systematic changes that occur during the first six of the stages just listed are typically "growth changes," while the later changes are usually those of decline.

THE NATURE OF DEVELOPMENTAL RESEARCH

What sorts of changes are we discussing? Developmental changes usually fall into three separate categories—changes in *physical structure,* in the *social-emotional structure,* and in the *cognitive* (intellectual) *structure* of individuals. Developmental research begins with the examination of the differences that exist between individuals of different ages. There are subsequent stages of developmental research, directed at discovering which specific factors influence the developmental processes and, of those, which might be manipulated directly in order to bring about desired changes. These two subsequent stages of research develop naturally out of the data provided by the first. Let us illustrate this.

A developmental psychologist might be interested in defining what patterns of a certain social-emotional factor are characteristic at different ages of children. We might find the initial research directed at establishing the ages at which the average child enacts certain critical social interactions on his own initiative. Going from this initial research, other developmental psychologists might then be interested in finding out what specific factors seem to be associated with deviant (versus normal) development. Some aspects of development may be largely determined by patterns of experiences in the forms of interactions with adults, with peers, certain types of socioeducational stimuli, and so forth.

The two main areas of research just described—predicting behavior as a function of age and identification of specific contributing factors in individual development—account for a large majority of research in developmental psychology. The third research area, and a very difficult field indeed, is the actual remediation of faulty developmental processes. In the latter area the task is to establish logically what sorts of remediation processes one might employ, then determine through continuing manipulation of assumed contributing factors whether existing developmental deficits *can* be reversed. The possibility of partial or total *ir*reversibility is of course critical in expensive remediation programs, so this factor must be carefully assessed.

3.1. *The concept of developmental processes and research areas.*

Developmental psychologists basically study changes in physiological structure and behavior consistent with _____ .

a. physical health   b. education   c. age   d. physical size

Developmental factors fall into three classifications—the _____ structure, the _____ structure, and the _____ structure.

Which of the following areas of research activity is actually *not* particularly common in developmental psychology? _____ .

a. Establishment of age-norm developmental differences

b. Establishment of specific factors influencing developmental processes

c. Identification of experiences and feelings of certain groups of people, such as those of different races

d. Experimentation on the topic of reversing developmental deficits

In expensive remediation programs, it is realistic and important to determine the extent to which developmental deficits may be _____ .

a. diagnosed   b. reversed   c. recognized when they occur

A short review of the topics in developmental psychology may actually obscure the fact that this is a very extensive and important research area, both for psychologists with their particular interests, and for society in general. You may well imagine the implications of major new findings concerning socioeducational, familial, and other contributing factors where important social problems are concerned—problems such as school drop-outs, delinquency, the value of preschool educational experiences, and so forth. With increased exposure to the literature of developmental psychology, you will undoubtedly also be impressed with both the scope of the field and the elaborate sophistication of theories and research in this area.

DEVELOPMENTAL PROCESSES I: PHYSICAL DEVELOPMENT

There is considerable controversy in medico-legal and ethical-theological circles concerning just when a human individual begins "life." These controversies are of interest mainly to those individuals who have some interest in attempting to influence legislation concerning abortion. As far as we are concerned, for purposes of this text, the human life begins when the female ovum is fertilized by the male sperm. The normal processes of cell division then take over, and the fertilized cell shortly becomes a recognizable human form.

Early in the development process the bodily tissue is adequately differentiated so that the various organs are identifiable, as is specialized nervous system tissue. The developing organs become innervated to the extent that at only a few weeks the fetus can respond with gross, un-differentiated movement when stimulated. By eleven or twelve weeks, well-defined reflexive responses can be observed in the human fetus; at this age the fetus can flex its trunk and neck, and can move its arms and legs, although it is still too early to observe self-initiated or spontaneous movement.

A very wide variety of factors can affect the various developmental indexes during this general period of time. If you should later take a course on developmental psychology (called child psychology at many colleges and universities), you will learn about these in more detail. Briefly, research has shown that significant effects can result from such factors as *maternal diseases* (you no doubt have read of the effects of rubella and syphilis as two examples), the administration of certain *medical drugs* such as the well-known thalidomide, *narcotics addictions* which may lead to addicted newborns, *alcohol* consumption, high levels of *nicotine* from smoking, and X-ray or other forms of *irradiation*. At a more sophisticated level, *Rh incompatibility* poses a threat to the life of the newborn, the genotypic chromosome makeup can be influenced by the *mother's age,* and there is even some evidence that the newborn's biochemical patterns can be influenced by *maternal emotions* during certain key months of the pregnancy.

At this point we shall limit our continued discussion of prenatal developmental factors to a single contributant—nutrition—and we shall consider this factor both prenatally and postnatally.

Nutrition   In general, eating might be termed a survival motive. A wide array of physical variables is affected by one's nutritional state. Naturally, variations in physical development, particularly those involving the central nervous system, in turn affect a wide variety of behaviors. Of primary interest are intellectual behaviors.

At the most obvious level, the general indices of human health are closely tied to an adequate nutritional balance. There are few individuals at this point in history who are unaware that a severe deficit in certain vitamins and minerals in the diet will cause specific effects. Variations in growth patterns have been tied to nutrition, so that we generally expect taller and more heavily muscled individuals to emerge from the ranks of the well nourished.

There is a literature which suggests that human beings, to some extent, have the capacity to respond specifically to dietary inadequacies. That is, if iron-deficient meals have been eaten over a period of time, a craving begins to develop for the sorts of foods that will counter the deficiency. One of the earliest and most illustrative experiments along this line was performed by Davis (1928), who employed "free feeding" arrangements with young children. Davis established that the very young child, when presented with several bowls of familiar food substances, indulged in sweet, dessert-type foods at the beginning. In fact, this preference was evident for several days, but soon the child began to show a preference for those foods which would contribute other essential vitamins and minerals. Over a period of a month it was established that an almost perfectly balanced diet was consumed by the child, although on any single day it might have appeared that the child was consuming most heavily a single dietary substance. This same phenomenon may very well underlie the familiar stories concerning the pregnant woman who awakens at 3:00 A.M. with a craving for pickles or ice cream.

C 3.2. *Nutrition: Specific hungers during nutritional deficits.*

In a free-feeding situation, it has been found that the young child will, over a period of time, select a diet

that is _____ .

Along these lines, it is interesting to note that individuals' appetites for specific foods at times are found to be related to what foods are necessary in their particular climates. For example, the Eskimos' appetite for whale blubber is just what their bodies need in an extremely cold climate.

Motor Development One of the more dramatic effects of nutrition is the effect on the development of the muscular-skeletal physical structure. Doubtless there are many strong genetic influences that govern at what times children will walk, run, and so forth, but adequate nourishment is vital if the child is to show healthy growth. One of the typical patterns of research in this area concerns the ages at which children, on the average, perform a variety of motor tasks.

One source (Lenneberg, 1967) gives the following as average motor development norms. At 12 weeks the child supports the head while in a prone position, with the weight on the elbows. At 20 weeks, the child can sit with props. At 6 months, the child sits alone, and can bend forward, using the hands for support. At this age the child can also bear his or her own weight when placed into a standing position, but cannot yet stand for any period of time while holding on. At the age of 8 months, the child can stand while holding on to a support. At 10 months he, or she, can pull himself into a standing position, can walk when held by one hand, and can seat himself on the floor. At 24 months, the child is able to run, but may fall when turning suddenly, and is also able to quickly alternate between sitting and standing positions. Such developmental norms have been offered to parents and professional workers as a guideline of how fast they may expect a child to acquire certain abilities. Many children exceed the norms, while many are relatively slow in their development. Such gross muscular-skeletal behaviors as we have described show a low positive correlation with later psychological potential; that is, "brighter" children in terms of later IQ tests tend to stand, walk, and run a bit earlier than average, and those not so bright tend to stand, walk, and run a bit later than average. Still, in view of the low correlation of these variables, caused by large numbers of individual exceptions, parents should not take alarm if their child is somewhat behind the pace suggested by normative tables. The use of gross skeletal-muscular performance as a predictor of later psychological potential is of fairly high reliability only with extreme cases. That is, a child who is severely mentally retarded will typically be substantially slower than average in standing, walking, and running.

C 3.3. *Motor development: Predictive power.*

It could be fairly stated that the normative development of gross muscular-skeletal behaviors

shows _____ correlation with later intelligence.

    a. no   b. a low   c. a very high

There is perhaps less emphasis placed by psychologists upon the development of the muscular-skeletal system than there should be. Most of the normative research on the topic was performed during an era 25 to 50 years ago, and doubtless many modern-day psychologists feel that little that is new can come of such research. Still, as Horrocks (1969) has pointed out, in childhood and in adolescence the body becomes a key to the self-image—not only in terms of physique and stature, especially among males, but also in terms of physical attraction and other related variables. The foundation for deep emotional disturbances may rest on one's physical attributes. Thus it becomes of more than passing interest to parents to note the progress of their own child's height, weight, etc. in terms of group norms.

There is a vast data on this topic, well represented in many books specifically devoted to child growth and development. In the limited space we have available, we cannot fairly represent much of the data. However, you will note in Figure 3.1 certain gains in height which are characteristic as a predictive function of age in both girls and boys. Such data are often useful to parents or to counselors who wish to explain to youngsters what they may expect in terms of their own physical growth. As you can imagine, a deviation from the norm is often disturbing to the adolescent, who can sometimes be reassured on the basis of normative data.

Figure 3.1

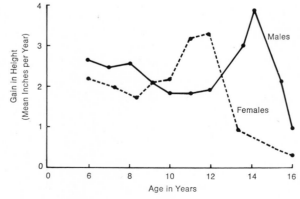

Adapted from Tanner (1962)

C 3.4.   *Motor development: Psychological effects.*

The importance of physical growth norms, to the psychologist, lies mainly in the effects of body

characteristics upon the _____ .

    a. IQ   b. level of future success   c. self-image

> Quite obviously, one can expect that, as a direct predictive function of increasing age, a child should be able to do an increasing number of things calling for muscular-skeletal coordination as he or she passes through infancy and into early childhood. At the same time it is normal to expect that the height and the weight of the child will increase as age progresses. There is obviously a good deal of variability in what we see in individual children, and there is likewise no doubt that quite a few specific extraneous factors, besides nutrition, combine with hereditary influences to affect these physical measures and performances.
>
> It has been noted that, over a period of a relatively short time, norms on children's muscular-skeletal performances have become accelerated. Johnson and Medinnus (1974) have reviewed the data of four studies of developmental norms, performed in 1933, 1935, 1946, and 1967. They show that such behaviors as ability to sit alone dropped during that time from a seven-month mean (average) age to a six-month mean age. The ability of the infant to crawl dropped from nine months to seven. Walking with assistance dropped from 12 months to 10, standing alone dropped from 14 months to 11, and walking alone dropped from 15 months to 11 months.

C 3.5.   *Motor development: Normative changes over time.*

Studies have shown that over the last 30 or so years, children's performances of psychomotor tasks

are occurring at _____ ages.

    a. about the same   b. earlier   c. later

> What is to account for such variations in developmental norms over less than a 35-year span? The answer to this question is by no means clear, although we suspect that in recent years infants have been better nourished than was generally the case in the 1930's.
>
> Also it is likely that greater expectations of physical performance at early ages are being placed upon the infants. Many mothers have learned that general developmental abilities show a correlation with later IQ scores. Perhaps they engage in a type of "correlational thinking," assuming that if psychomotor abilities predict intelligence, accelerating the psycho-motor development through encouragement might change the level of intelligence. Such a hypothesis is not supportable, but one can understand the mothers' initiative.

Nutrition and Brain Development

Important as muscular-skeletal growth may be, of greater interest to the psychologist is the topic of factors which directly influence developing brain tissue and, in terms of associated function, the intellectual processes. Certain findings, derived from animal experimentation, suggest especially that protein nutrition via the mother to the fetus is critical to the development of brain tissue. Individual animals, poorly provided with protein nourishment via the mother's diet during the fetal period, often develop into rather dull individuals, slower than others of their species to learn mazes or solve simple problems. Physiological research further suggests that these individuals actually have fewer cortical brain cells (Zamenhoff, Van Marthens, & Margolis, 1968).

The effects of undernutrition during the very early neonatal stage is also considered to be potentially serious, especially since the brain grows so much faster than does the rest of the body during the first few weeks of neonatal life. Thus, most experiments have focused upon undernutrition occurring during the critical early weeks. Predictable changes occur in rats which are underfed during the first few weeks after weaning.

In one experiment undernutrition was initiated in "weaning" animals born of well-nourished mothers. Malnourishment was continued for a period of several weeks. Electroencephalograms showed a lessening of rhythmic cortical activity, and in postmortem the brain-tissue nerve cells themselves were found to be degenerated. A matched group of animals, rather than being sacrificed for postmortem examination, were fed high-protein diets for up to three months, but they too showed the same type of damaged central nervous system tissue when eventually sacrificed. Throughout this experiment it was clearly seen that the earlier the initiation of dietary inadequacy, the more severe was the resulting damage; also, the degree of damage was a direct function of the degree of reduction of the protein value of the diet.

The analogy basis between experimental colonies of animals on the one hand and the human condition on the other are numerous. For example, children who are not weaned until the second or third year of life, a practice common in many unsophisticated societies, are very likely to receive sufficient calories but inadequate dietary protein. Along a similar line, in England researchers recently demonstrated that there is marked retardation in brain growth in rat pups placed in a situation in which a single mother must suckle 15 to 20 young. Beyond the age of about three or four weeks for the rat and proportionately later ages for slower-maturing species, the effect of undernutrition on brain development seems progressively less pronounced.

C 3.6. *Nutrition: Relation to central nervous system development.*

Physical development of brain tissue can be affected prior to actual birth through the variable of

the mother's ＿＿＿＿＿＿＿＿＿＿＿＿＿＿＿＿＿ .

In proportion to body size, brain growth proceeds much more ＿＿＿＿＿ during the first few weeks of life.

    a. rapidly   b. slowly

It would appear that CNS changes during the neonatal period, due to malnourishment, _____

reversible.

a. are   b. are not

It would appear that there is _____ correlation between the age (in days or weeks) at introduction

of nutritional inadequacy in neonatal animals and the degree of ultimate CNS damage.

a. no   b. a definite

Going from animal to human research in the study of nutrition, a massive problem in interpreting data arises. In Chapter 5 and Extension Chapter 5A we shall expand upon this matter, but for the moment let us point out that the distinction between environmental and hereditary causes becomes confused in most human research. Those parents who are most likely to provide undernutrition, whether prenatally through the mother's diet or postnatally through the diet provided the child, also tend to be of lower than average intelligence themselves. In working with human subjects we cannot effectively control these factors, and so must wonder whether other influences besides nutrition are affecting the developing intellectual abilities.

To look for a moment at such human data as do exist, one of the few strongly suggestive experiments was performed by Harrell, Woodyard, and Gates (1955), who supplemented the diet of one group of low-income expectant mothers with vitamins, while a matched group continued with their usual diet. Children born to the mothers from the first group were found to have higher IQs when tested at ages three and four than the children in the second group. A few other such studies exist, and some of the inferences drawn rest upon multiple unproved assumptions.

Before we continue with an examination of human data, let us turn to why this issue is so very important to psychologists. In the recent three or four years we have experienced a tremendous resurgence of interest in questions of intelligence in relation to socioeconomic level, and to race. A very popular presumption among many psychologists is that the lower IQs found in lower socioeconomic class individuals may be due to factors relating to maternal nutrition and to postnatal nutrition. While animal research suggests that this might very well be at least a contributing factor, solid evidence using data derived from human subjects is necessary before society embarks on major programs of nutritional subsidy which may be extremely costly and complex in administration.

Nutritional Inadequacy in Human Beings: A Major Study

In 1972, Stein and his colleagues attempted to answer the question of the effects of malnutrition on developing human brain structure in the fetus and the neonate. These researchers gained access to the national archives in the Netherlands containing vital data and intelligence test scores for individuals who were either conceived or born during the Dutch famine of 1944–45.

Due to a complex series of wartime developments, the Germans imposed a transport embargo on the western region of the occupied

Netherlands in late 1944, a situation which was not the case in the eastern region of the country. The result of the embargo was that before the end of that year no food was reaching the large cities of the west and famine developed. Extreme nutritional hardships soon became evident among the population in that area. The supply of food continued to decline, until in November, 1944, the deficiency became severe. The famine continued into the first week of May, 1945, when the allied armies crossed the Rhine and liberated the Netherlands. During the six-month period of the famine, the death rate in the affected cities rose sharply, and many of the deaths were certified as being due to starvation. Clinical reports from hospitals in the famine area noted a high frequency of medical disorders due to hunger, and frequent weight loss of as much as 25 percent of normal body weight.

For purposes of the study Stein et al. used a system of matched pairs. Experimental-group subjects were individuals who, as shown by national records, were born in two major famine-affected cities in the western region of the country during this general time period. Several thousand individuals were chosen for study who went through the famine period *in the fetal stage,* as were several thousand others who went through that period *as neonates.* Matching control subjects were individuals born on the same dates in certain major cities in the eastern region which was relatively unaffected by the famine. Only male subjects were studied since the measure of intelligence employed was the report from military-induction examination centers, all of which used a standardized intelligence testing procedure.

The first comparison established that the birth weights of the individuals from the famine area were approximately 14 percent lighter than the average in the control group. Then standard IQ test scores were used for intelligence purposes, as were scores on a nonverbal IQ test (the Raven's Progressive Matrices). In addition, the rates per thousand of severe mental retardation and mild mental retardation were calculated. These studies provided *no* evidence that the effects of severe famine resulted in measurable loss of intellectual ability.

Inasmuch as the research covered a broad period of time, the implications to be derived from this study have to do both with the effects of malnutrition during the fetal period as well as its effects during the first few weeks and months of life. To the extent that this was an extremely well-controlled study, and assuming that the effects of famine were severe and fairly uniform among the population in the affected area and that much less famine occurred in the geographic region used for control purposes, the study by Stein appears to be the most conclusive data available on the topic as it pertains to human development.

How do we interpret this report of lack of effect of malnutrition during the two critical developmental stages? It is possible that extreme situations in totally different cultures, or extremely long-term conditions of malnutrition might still cause intellectual deficit. For example, most of the Dutch mothers, prior to the famine, were well nourished. The same cannot be said of poverty stricken individuals whose miserable circumstances may have existed for years. Similarly, it might be one thing for a youngster, just a few weeks old, to survive three or four months of hunger without an intellectual effect, yet quite another for a youngster to encounter such conditions from birth onward throughout his early childhood. There is no support for such speculations, however, and on the face of the evidence provided by the Dutch famine study we must tentatively conclude, as did Stein and his colleagues, that fetal and infant malnourishment produce far less of an effect (if any at all) on the intellectual potential of human beings than would be predicted from animal research.

C 3.7. *Nutrition: Relationship to measured intelligence.*

The Dutch famine study evaluated the effects of malnutrition during the _____ and the _____ developmental stages.

In the Dutch famine study, a matched control individual was _____ (the same, different) in nationality, _____ (the same, different) in terms of age, and _____ (the same, different) in terms of exposure to famine.

The Dutch famine study concluded that malnourishment during two critical periods of development in the human species has _____ effect on developing intellectual ability.

    a. a major   b. no discernable

Stimulus Factors in Brain Development

We should not proceed without a very brief notation that many things other than just nutritional inadequacies are studied in relation to their effects on the tissue of the central nervous system. Experiments with rats, kittens, and monkeys have clearly indicated that animals which are protected from environmental stimulation, and which have been prevented from exploring their environments, not only have smaller brains with fewer nerve cells but also develop impaired functioning of the central nervous system (Bennett, Diamond, Krech, & Rosenweig, 1964).

Again, we can turn from animal research where we are fairly well aware of the small and precise factors involved in resulting differences in performance capabilities of animals in different treatment groups, to human data that are available. One of the most interesting research projects available to us in this area is a fascinating finding by Skeels (1966) which went back to an environmental arrangement in the year 1939. A group of orphaned children who, at the ages of around 19 months, were so developmentally retarded as to be virtually unadoptable, were divided into two groups. One half of the original group continued its existence in an overcrowded orphanage in which little one-to-one interaction with adults occurred. The other half of the children were assigned individually to be cared for by mildly retarded girls residing in an institution for the retarded.

The girls, serving as mother-substitutes, spent great amounts of time with the children, talking to them, playing with them, and teaching them various skills. As soon as this group could walk, they also attended a nursery school where play materials and additional stimulation were provided. After four years it was found that the second group had an average IQ *almost 50 points higher* than the first group. In 1966, in the 20-year follow-up, Skeels found that most individuals in the second group had completed high school, about a third had attended college, and almost all were self-supporting. In contrast, most individuals from the first group had not progressed beyond a third-grade education and most were either institutionalized or at least were not self-supporting.

It seems quite clear that one's surroundings have a great deal to do with one's ultimate level of intellectual potential, whether that effect is eventually found to be determined by neurological and biochemical changes brought about by stimulus complexity, or whether the effect can be explained as being due to basic learning mechanisms. It appears quite feasible that animal stimulus deprivation, and such human research data along the same line that are available, can lead us to general conclusions concerning the undesirable effects, on human children, of unstimulating home environments, poor educational facilities, isolation resulting from illness, limited recreational opportunities, and lack of incentive due to repeated discouragements.

C 3.8.   *The effects of environmental stimulation on brain development.*

Rats, kittens, and monkeys deprived of general stimulation from the environment have subsequently been shown to have _____ brains, with _____ nerve cells.

In a long-term follow-up study, Skeels found that children developed far better _____ than when growing up in a crowded orphanage.

  a. when given to mildly retarded girls to rear individually

  b. when placed in foster homes with high IQ children also living there

  c. neither of the above is correct

PROGRESS CHECK   3.1

1. Which of these is not a major category of developmental changes? _____ .

       a. Reflexive structure   b. Physical structure

       c. Social-emotional structure   d. Cognitive structure

2. A critical factor to evaluate before undertaking expensive remediation for developmental deficiencies is _____ .

       a. cost-benefits   b. the reversibility of the effect

c. socioeconomic class   d. demographic variables

3. Recently, psychologists have again become interested in physical growth because _____ .

    a. it fairly accurately predicts IQ and success

    b. the body seems to be an important factor in the development of self-image

    c. they find it of great esoteric value

    d. it is easy to do normative research in the area

4. Studies indicate that children today are performing psychomotor tasks at earlier ages than children born 40 years ago. This may be because _____ .

    a. today children are brighter

    b. today children are better loved

    c. today children are better nourished

    d. television may affect eye-hand coordination

5. Studies with animals indicate that there is a relationship between the development of the central nervous system and nutrition. Which is true? _____ .

    a. There is no correlation between age at the time of nutritional inadequacy and degree of CNS damage

    b. CNS changes in the neonatal period are reversible

    c. Bright offspring eat more food than their duller litter mates

    d. The mother's diet can affect development of her fetus's brain tissue

6. A pregnant rat with what kind of dietary deficiency is likely to produce a pup with central nervous system defects? _____ .

    a. Sugar   b. Minerals   c. Vitamins   d. Protein

7. Stein et al. studied _____ .

    a. the effects of environmental stimulation on the central nervous systems of animals

    b. the effect of nutritional inadequacy on later intelligence in the Netherlands

    c. the effects of "mothering" on developmentally retarded orphans

    d. none of these

8. Recent studies make one thing clear: _____ .

    a. One's early surroundings have a great deal to do with one's ultimate level of intelligence

    b. Children are not affected by stimulation

    c. Long-term studies indicate IQ is fixed at the time of birth

DEVELOPMENTAL PROCESSES II: SOCIAL-EMOTIONAL DEVELOPMENT

The infant, when first born, might be viewed behaviorally as a composite of various primary drives. It is of course well known that the infant brings out various emotional responses in adults. Some scientists have noted that innate responses seem to play significant roles in the parent-offspring interactions of many birds and mammals, and it has been suggested that just as animals seem to have innate emotional reactions to the young of their species, so do human beings respond to classes of stimuli, delivering care and helpfulness.

Lorenz (1943) believes that the shape of the body and the face in the young brings out mothering responses in human beings. Lorenz has even speculated that toy manufacturers deliberately produce dolls and stuffed animals with a certain babylike appearance so as to appeal to these responses in buyers. One researcher (Hess, 1967) has shown that adult subjects become more and more emotionally positive as they are shown stylized drawings of both human infants and animals that grow progressively more babylike and infantile in their appearances. Following up remarks by Lorenz, Bowlby (1969) has suggested that the smiling response of the infant acts as a social releaser, causing the mother to respond in a biologically fixed, loving way, and increasing the likelihood that the infant will be cared for and will survive.

C 3.9. *Ethological viewpoint of innate mother-child bonds.*

Certain theorists propose that evolution has imposed an innate releasing mechanism in human beings, whereby the general _____ of the baby, and his _____ behavior release care-giving behavior.

Positive Social-Emotional Development: The Smile

When we turn to the matter of where the *infant's smile* comes from, the answers are by no means clear-cut. One might describe the question as being whether the child's smiling is innate, being a built-in reaction to certain classes of stimuli, or whether it is a social interaction learned (reinforced) over a period of time on the basis of such a behavior's effects on others.

In a search for the beginnings of positive emotion, investigators have centered on the infant's smiling response. In a series of investigations by a psychoanalyst interested in child development (Spitz, 1946), it was found that the smiling response in the very young infant most typically is stimulated by the *human face.*

The face does not have to be a real one, as sketches of a human face will do almost as well. It has been found that the face of a stranger, at a certain period early in the child's life, will bring about reactive smiling just as readily as will the face of its own mother. The most appropriate stimulus is the full face looking directly at the infant. The profile of a human face, on the other hand, is relatively ineffective in eliciting the response (Watson, 1964). Spitz found that the peak rate of smiling at the full human face is during the period from two to six months of age. After the age of six months, very few infants will smile at a strange face, although they continue to smile at familiar faces, leading to the interpretation that by then they have learned a social habit of smiling at those they know.

Smiling appears to be a relatively innate behavior, not critically dependent upon imitative modeling; Freedman (1965) found that blind infants begin to smile at the usual time for the emergence of the smiling response. Freedman's findings challenge any notion that the infant's smile is released reflexively by others' smiles. Also, it would appear that the emergence of smiling at the earliest stages could hardly be a response which is learned via the reactions of others to pleasant moods. Still, in terms of the frequency of this form of behavior, once established, there is very good evidence that the rate can be sharply modified by its consequences. That is, if the infant is rewarded by frequently being picked up when it is smiling, it will spend more time smiling. If the infant's smiles are not rewarded, smiling will decrease.

C 3.10. *Ethological viewpoint of the stimulation of positive emotion in human infants.*

A consistent producer of a smiling response in the young infant is a full-front view of _____ .

    a. an animal   b. another infant playing with toys   c. a smiling human face

The smile, as an expression of a pleasant mood, _____ (does, does not) seem to be dependent,

    for its initial emergence, upon modeling.

The type of _____ generated by smiling influences the frequency of that form of behavior in the future.

    a. consequence   b. emotion

We have chosen only a single social-emotional development—in this case, smiling—to illustrate the developmental course of positive social-emotional reactions. There is a reason for this. Generally each positive development is matched by certain cases of failure of such development to occur, and these cases are generally considered "negative," in the sense of there being resulting emotional instability or some other factor that hinders the individual from becoming emotionally fulfilled. Since psychologists gravitate toward psychological problems as natural areas for the use of their training, we have taken the liberty of listing such cases in the following section.

Negative Social-Emotional Development: Maternal Deprivation

One of the strongest influences over the emotional development of children is the style of mothering they receive. The negative extreme of development is, of course, brought about by deprivation of maternal care.

In 1945 Spitz wrote an account of children raised in different caretaker environments. First, infants were studied who were raised at home, where each child had the full-time care of its own mother. These children provided data representing normal development. Infants raised in a foundling home, cared for by nurses at a ratio of eight children to each nurse, were then studied. This was an unstimulating environment in which the children lay in their cribs with relatively little to do or see. The children reared in the foundling home environment showed progressive physical deterioration and displayed profound emotional depression, characterized by crying, poor appetite, excessive quietness (being seemingly "out of touch") and stereotyped rocking movements.

Spitz believed that the depression and the physical effects in the foundling home group were not simply due to a general lack of stimulation, but rather due to the loss of the mother. The children in this group had been brought to the foundling home when each was about four months of age. Spitz concluded that these children had already begun to develop emotional attachments to their mothers, so that when the child was later placed in the home and separated from the customary maternal care, depression developed. Spitz called this *anaclitic,* or dependency, depression.

Subsequently Spitz (1946b) showed that children subjected to maternal deprivation a little later in life also displayed developmental abnormalities. In this research prolonged separation from the mother beginning at an age of six to eight months was studied. These children changed from having seemingly happy, active, curious types of typical behaviors to patterns of withdrawal, weeping, and sullenness, and there began a decline in certain physical growth indices. The mothers in this particular study had been imprisoned. Some of these mothers returned to their children some time within the next three or four months, and in those cases the children seemed again to become happy and active. However, longer separation produced more extreme behavioral disturbances, with the children sitting or lying down with expressionless faces, and gazing off into the distance in an out-of-touch manner for long periods. Spitz went on to define the period from four to twelve months of age as a critical period in terms of maternal dependency in human infants.

Other researchers have placed somewhat different interpretations on the observed lack of positive emotional development in maternally deprived children. Casler (1968) believes that the critical variables operating on children in institutions are not so much the lack of the mother figure as an overall lack of perceptual, social, and emotional stimulation in the typical child-care institution. From this viewpoint, the child is conceived of as an active, seeking creature and an avid learner, and deprivation of stimulation in all the spheres just mentioned is thought to result in adverse effects. Going from such a point of view, it is speculated that many children, still living in homes with a mother figure, may undergo changes similar to those associated with maternal deprivation as a function of neglectful mothers.

C 3.11.   *The effects of maternal deprivation on human social-emotional development.*

Separation from the mother produces, in the young child, what Spitz termed _____ ,

 or dependency, depression.

Spitz has noted the period of from _____ to _____ months of age as being a critical period of

   maternal dependency in children.

Some researchers believe that unfavorable development effects in institutionalized children are not

   due to deprivation of mothering so much as they are to an overall lack of _____ ,

_____ , and _____ stimulation.

It is in the area of animal psychology, usually involving the use of monkeys, that we see the only truly experimental work that has been performed in the area of maternal care. Certain early attempts to investigate this factor simply separated mothers from infants in various species at varying ages. Harlow, at the University of Wisconsin, launched comprehensive experimental studies which brought other factors into consideration.

Harlow was quite interested in the maternal patterns of care (under natural conditions) given by rhesus monkey mothers. Many analogues to the human condition exist. In the wild state these animals normally live in fairly large social colonies, and Harlow noted that when frightened the young monkeys typically ran directly to their own mothers and clung to them in a fashion quite similar to that of most human children. Similarly the displays of affection between a young monkey and its mother frequently took the form of clinging and embracing.

In his experiments Harlow employed "surrogate mothers," one type of which had a terry-cloth-covered body which was soft and yielding. The inside of this "cloth-mother" was warmed by a light bulb. The mother-surrogate was roughly of the same shape, size, and visual contour as a real adult rhesus monkey. In various stages of different experiments some of these mother-surrogates were capable of providing the infant with milk through a tube, just as would a real mother. Harlow observed that the infant, if deprived of its own mother, would quickly develop an emotional attachment to a cloth-covered surrogate almost as if it were a real mother. It would run to her when frightened, and when in her presence would be a great deal bolder toward any intruder in the area.

In one interesting comparison, the small monkeys were observed to cling for hours to the terry-cloth-covered mother, ignoring a nearby surrogate mother which was molded from thick wire. The hard, unyielding wire frame, even though easy to cling to, failed to attract the young monkeys. Some infant rhesus monkeys, when removed from their real mothers, were put into a cage with a wire-mother which provided milk through a tube; eventually they were given a second surrogate mother, this time cloth-covered. None of these monkeys was observed to spend time clinging to the wire-mother, even before the second surrogate was provided, except during actual nursing. These infants immediately accepted and showed attachment to a newly provided cloth-mother. They would spend as much as 22 hours out of every 24 clinging to the cloth-mother, leaving her only from time to time when hungry in order to nurse briefly at the breast of the wire-mother.

A wide variety of emotional developments accompanied having a wire-mother versus a cloth-mother. Infants with cloth-mothers seemed fairly emotionally secure, while monkeys provided only with a wire-mother often ignored her almost totally, spending hours sitting alone in a corner sucking their thumbs, vocalizing, engaging in stereotyped rocking, and occasionally engaging in self-mutilating behavior.

It should not be overlooked, however, that the infant rhesus monkeys reared by surrogate mothers, even the cloth-mothers, were emotionally deficient in many ways at maturity. They were seen to have extreme difficulty in most social relationships, and were quite difficult to mate with other rhesus monkeys. With their own young infants, these adult monkeys were often cruel or rejecting. Still, even recognizing these emotional deficits, many psychologists believe that Harlow established an important dimension of child care—the importance of cuddling, holding, and otherwise exposing the infant to what is termed "contact comfort." The variable of contact comfort is obviously one which is irregularly supplied in some families, and the provision of this opportunity is frequently difficult in a personal sense for certain parents, due to their own personalities. The parent who is rigid, emotionally cold, and not particularly desirous of touching the child may be inflicting emotional damage.

C 3.12. *The effects of "mothering" on social-emotional development in monkeys: Harlow's research.*

The provision of feeding by a wire-frame mother surrogate _____ develop an attitude of affection and

clinging by infant rhesus monkeys.

    a. does   b. does not

The important variable in the rearing of infants, suggested by the Harlow research with rhesus monkeys,

    is _____ _____ .

A soft-surfaced mother surrogate during the early developmental stages results eventually in grown-up

rhesus monkeys that are emotionally _____ .

    a. essentially normal   b. somewhat deviant

A related experiment of interest was performed by Hreen and Gordon (1964). These investigators chose several infant monkeys to be reared entirely deprived of their mothers; several other monkeys were left with their mothers. At testing, the animals were placed one at a time in an empty booth. By pressing a lever they could raise a shield and view an adjacent booth for 10 seconds. The animals reared by their mothers developed active bar-pressing in order to view, variously, food, a peer-age monkey, an adult monkey, and plastic geometric forms. However, the monkeys from the motherless group showed no inclination to develop bar-pressing, and in fact showed great fear responses to almost every change of stimulus conditions.

Perhaps this is the point at which to clearly differentiate between two somewhat opposing viewpoints on the interpretation of data from maternal-deprivation research. On the one hand, there is the material deprivation school of thought, characterized by Spitz, which implies an emotional interaction specific to the act of "mothering." The opposing view could be termed the "need for environmental stimulation" school of thought.

Negative Social-Emotional Development: Stimulus Deprivation

Researchers interested in the effects of stimulus deprivation generally fall into two groups—the one group being interested in effects upon emerging intellectual ability, and the other in possible effects upon the developing social-emotional structure.

One group of experiments has to do with the effects of extreme stimulus deprivation during infancy. Where the deprivation has to do with sensation and perception, visual-motor coordination is later affected. Riesen (1965) reared infant monkeys in darkness during their first three months of life, and then found that in lighted areas the monkeys failed to blink when threatened with a blow, and would not put out their arms in defense when propelled rapidly toward a wall. However, these inadequacies were corrected with time.

Where the deprivation is more in terms of environmental complexity, other forms of deficit are noted. Scott (1968) reared dogs in confined quarters where there was nothing to do, look at, listen to, or investigate. Later these animals seemed healthy and outwardly normal, but showed certain peculiarities. Not only were they highly excitable around changing stimuli, but they seemed oddly insensitive to pain, and would put their noses up to a lighted flame time and time again.

In terms of social-emotional development, the conclusion generally arrived at by researchers is that appropriate adaptation and development calls for exposure to at least a moderate variety of changing stimuli—not just "good" experiences alone, for some research findings indicate that proper handling of later stress depends upon prior experiences with stressors. The ability as an adult to adapt to pain with appropriate responses rather than extreme panic and disorganization requires prior exposure to moderate amounts of pain stimuli. Similarly, low or moderate levels of frustration, disappointment, deprivation, and depression seem developmentally appropriate.

C 3.13. *The effects of general stimulation upon social-emotional development.*

A critical period of development is thought to exist within which organisms should experience at least moderate levels of _____ if "normal" development is to occur.

a. love and affection

b. aversive stimulation

c. interesting sensory variety

d. all of the preceding answers are correct

There are various other social-emotional reactions of human beings which we believe are due to factors specific to certain situations or more complex than the simpler stimuli discussed in this chapter. Such reactions as the ability to take pleasure in one's achievements, having a sense of ethics leading to feelings of guilt after having hurt others, and characteristics of aggression are all dealt with at greater length in subsequent chapters under the topic headings of learning, social influences, stress, and so forth. We shall leave an extensive discussion of such topics for these chapters.

Erikson's Psychosocial Theory of Development

Erik Erikson is a contemporary psychologist who has developed a limited theory of personality, but his unique step-by-step progression through stages closely correlated with chronological age suggests that his work would be appropriately categorized under the topic of developmental psychology.

Erikson is best known for his notion of the *eight stages* of man, which begin in infancy.

C 3.14. *Erik Erikson's theory of development: The stages.*

Erikson proposes that there are _____ stages of psychosocial development in man.

   a. three   b. five   c. seven   d. eight

1. Basic Trust vs. Mistrust: The Development of Trust

As was the case with Freud, Erikson's theory states that the relationship with the mother or some mother figure during early infancy is vital in psychosocial development. What is important is that the infant develops its basic attitudes of trust relative to significant others during this period. The trusting attitude is considered to be a cornerstone of a healthy personality, evolving out of the mutual relationship between mother and infant, and extends into a basic sense of one's own trustworthiness. Erikson emphasizes the quality of the entire maternal relationship. It is necessary for the mother to be sensitive to the needs of the infant, and the infant needs to know that the mother can be relied upon for her care. Under these conditions the child feels secure and the attitude of basic trust begins to develop. Without it mistrust and feelings of estrangement become prominent, and later in life such an attitude characterizes people who withdraw into themselves when difficulties arise.

C 3.15. *Erikson's first stage.*

Erikson stresses that a mother must be sensitive to the needs of her child, and the child must come to feel basic security, if the desirable stage of basic _____ is to develop.

2. Autonomy vs. Shame and Doubt: The Development of Self-Pride

In the second stage the toilet-training situation assumes prominence and is representative of a number of other social hurdles that the child must face in growing up and having more expected of him or her. The child previously has had a sort of autonomy in the sense that unsocialized behaviors were excused on account of infancy. Now, growing older, the child must either become "socialized" in various forms of self-control or be overcome with a sense of failure.

According to Erikson the controls exercised by parents at this time must be firm, yet reassuring, so that the child will not become overly hostile. Additionally, if the parents reflect disappointment in the child during this stage of development, he or she will develop feelings of shame and self-doubt. Erikson stresses that the child must learn how to cooperate without being "broken" or losing self-esteem. The results of training at this stage can be, on the one hand, an emerging sense of autonomy and self-pride; given different circumstances, there will develop contrasting attitudes of self-doubt and shame at one's own failures at later ages.

C 3.16. *Erikson's second stage of development.*

Erikson suggests that parents, while exercising control in training the child, still should be reassuring

and not display disappointment, so that the child in the second developmental stage may develop

an adequate sense of _____ .

a. autonomy and self-pride   b. basic trust   c. shame and self-criticism

3. Initiative vs. Guilt:
The Development of
a Sense of Purpose

The third developmental stage is characterized by a great deal of curiosity, exploration, and "testing the limits" of disciplinary areas. At this stage parental emphasis is not so much upon the child being forced to conform to society's expectations as it is upon what is right and what is wrong. The child during this stage enjoys competition and conquest, but is learning what the limits are that are placed on these activities. The child's conscience is developing during this period, and one begins to see the process of self-judgment appear. The ideal outcome of this stage is a healthy sort of self-division—the child remains part child in initiative and risk-taking, but part parent in a developing sense of self-observation and self-criticism. The results of training at this stage can be, on the one hand, the child's having a healthy sense of purpose and initiative, but a good moral sense. This contrasts with loss of initiative, fearfulness, and hesitation.

C 3.17. *Erikson's third psychosexual stage.*

The developing sense of right and wrong in the third psychosexual stage ends, hopefully, in the child's

having a healthy sense of purpose and _____ , but a good moral sense.

4. Industry vs. Inferiority:
The Development
of Competence

Sooner or later, according to Erikson, children become dissatisfied with make-believe and self-indulgence, and begin to develop a certain amount of industry. The child has developed, and continues to develop, positive identifications with people who know how to do things and whose work is valued by society. In addition the child begins to see how working with others is often necessary to produce things successfully. If he or she is not good at this sort of achievement, and cannot compete with peers in many important skills, deep feelings of inadequacy and inferiority may develop. Some supportive experiences, taking the child over inevitable inadequacies, are important for successful resolution of conflicts at this stage. The healthy personality emerging from this stage is one with feelings of self-confidence and competence, a sense of industry, and a developing feeling of being a useful and productive member of society.

C 3.18. *Erikson's fourth psychosexual stage.*

Erikson proposes that a healthy personality, with a sense of industry and feelings of self-confidence,

calls for _____ in the fourth stage.

a. occasional supportive experiences when the child displays inadequacies

b. learning the harsh lesson of life that one cannot always be a winner

c. careful protection from any situation which might lead to failure

5. Identity vs. Role Confusion: The Development of Individuality   As the child moves into adolescence, he, or she, must let go of the safe hold on childhood and "reach out for a firm grasp on adulthood, depending for a breathless interval on a relatedness between the past and the future, and on the reliability of those he must let go of, and those who will 'receive' him [Erikson, 1964, p. 90]." During this most crucial period young persons are extremely concerned with how they appear to other people and how they are accepted as individuals with both human value and a role in society. Erikson suggests that the adolescent hangs suspended in a period during which there is experimentation with various roles in hopes of finding a niche. Society is usually permissive at this point, as for most adolescents their adult commitments are delayed, allowing young persons some time to "find themselves."

It is during this period that the young person may experiment with a variety of roles, trying out unfamiliar behaviors. For some an energetic and committed involvement with idealistic causes is a transient role enactment. Others use this period of time for systematic travel or for a migrant drifting, seeking to "find themselves." Some continue their education, while others enact roles in a delinquent subculture to a greater or lesser extent.

At this period of time the adolescent vigorously guards against a sense of identity loss and often overidentifies with culture heroes or with cliques. Young people help each other and bolster their identities by banding together and acting in stereotypic ways. This not only includes their ways of dressing and speaking and some of the ideals they espouse, but extends toward holding common friends and enemies. Young adolescents are extremely cliquish and are often cruel in excluding from their in-groups certain individuals who are perceived as different and "out of it."

An adequate role identity usually emerges out of this period of development. A good deal of storminess has been weathered by the typical adolescent before he or she emerges into a settled identity. In some cases, however, there develops an increasingly severe identity confusion. A sense of personal isolation, a loss of initiative, and an inability to concentrate on tasks at hand may occur. Excessive preoccupations and involvements with minor side issues may distract the individual from other, more vital functions. The most severe cases of identity confusion can involve a choice of a negative identity. In these cases the individual may display hostility and scorn toward the roles that are suggested by the community and the family as desirable and proper. The resulting behaviors may include rejection of one's cultural and social-class background, or an attack on the legal system, one's nationalistic identity, and so forth. The individual may assume an image perceived by the family as undesirable, outrageous, or even dangerous. This is usually interpreted by mental health professionals as the individual's strategy to avoid being "a nobody."

C 3.19. *Erikson's fifth stage of development.*

During Erikson's stage of "identity versus role confusion," which of the following patterns is likely to develop? _____ .

 a. Feelings of isolation, depression, and a tendency to withdraw from everyone else

 b. Extreme feelings of guilt concerning personal failures

 c. An unusual commitment to the roles required of members of some deviant subculture which runs counter to the value system of the parents

6. Intimacy vs. Isolation: The Development of Mature Love

Only after identity is well-established is genuine intimacy with others possible. Erikson considers genuine intimacy to be a stable commitment to another human being, with an ability to abide by the sacrifices and compromises dictated by such a commitment. The adult who is not established in his or her identity either shies away from such relationships or engages in a transient and promiscuous series of relations, "play acting" with other people and abandoning them if faced with commitment. Such relationships are very stereotyped in their sameness, and prove to be basically unrewarding to the individual.

C 3.20. *Erikson's sixth stage of development.*

Erikson feels that a secure identity is necessary as a prerequisite to any genuine and enduring _____ .

 a. intimacy   b. creativeness   c. trust

7. Generativity vs. Stagnation: The Development of Altruism

In maturity the human being needs to be "needed" and possibly even express concern for the establishment and the guidance of the succeeding generation. For many this is contained and expressed through the raising of one's own family. For some the family may be substituted for or supplemented by other forms of productivity and creativity which represent a useful contribution to society. Generativity represents an expansion of the personality to include a general interest in others. When this does not occur, the individual experiences a sense of stagnation, boredom, and interpersonal impoverishment. Often stagnation of this sort leads to self-indulgent behaviors, too much self-attention, and ultimately a pre-occupation with one's own physical and psychological difficulties, together with unhappiness.

C 3.21. *Erikson's seventh stage of development.*

"Generativity" is furthered in the seventh stage by the raising of a family or through _____ .

    a. close friendships   b. creativeness

8. Ego Integrity vs. Despair: The Development of Wisdom As the individual finally moves well into middle adulthood, the end product of the seven earlier developmental stages unfolds. Ego integrity refers to a mature, calm reflectance upon one's own contributions and life cycle, together with a positive acceptance of the people who have been significant in it. The various dissatisfactions in others of an earlier period are normally replaced with an attitude of tolerance. One can love without reservations for what might have been, and can accept one's self without reservations concerning failures. When ego integrity fails to develop, the individual experiences feelings of despair and resentment, displeasure with people or with institutions, regrets over the past and that it cannot be relived differently, and death is feared rather than accepted gracefully.

C 3.22. *Erikson's eighth stage of development.*

"Ego integrity" in the final developmental stage is characterized by _____ .

    a. no particular fear of death

    b. a lack of regret over past failings and misfortunes

    c. an uncritical acceptance of significant other people

    d. (all of the above are true)

Overview of Erikson's Theory As a theoretician, Erikson stresses the importance of various social influences on the development of the personality. He pays far more attention than do many child psychology theorists to conscious attitudes and awareness. Finally, he extends a theory of emotional development well beyond the limits of the childhood years.

While Erikson is by no means clear on every point concerning what causes satisfactory or unsatisfactory progression through the various stages of development, his viewpoints offer a very interesting interpretive basis against which to evaluate the psychological condition of an individual.

PROGRESS CHECK 3.2

1. Which variable has the greatest influence on the rate of infant-smiling behavior at *later* developmental periods? _____ .

    a. The antecedent to smiling, such as a face

    b. The consequence of smiling, such as food, cuddling, or ignoring

2. Which statement does not reflect Spitz's viewpoint concerning the effects of maternal deprivation on human social-emotional development? _____ .

    a. Separation from the mother produces anaclitic depression

    b. Dependency depression occurs in mother-deprived infants

    c. Unfavorable development effects in institutionalized children are due to an overall lack of stimulation

    d. All of these reflect Spitz' viewpoint

3. Harlow's research with monkey-mothering demonstrated _____ .

    a. that an infant rhesus monkey would cling to a wire surrogate

    b. the importance of cuddling

    c. that soft-surface surrogate mothers produce essentially normal adult rhesus monkeys

    d. a surrogate will do as well as a mother

4. According to Erikson, what must the child feel to develop basic trust? _____ .

    a. Appreciation   b. Satiation   c. Success   d. Security

5. Erikson's second stage suggests parents exercise both control and reassurance in child training. This produces _____ .

    a. autonomy and self-pride   b. love   c. basic trust   d. dynamic conflict

MATCH: _____ 6. Erikson's third psychosexual   A. Initiative and purpose
                  stage

          _____ 7. Erikson's fourth psychosexual   B. Self-confidence
                  stage

          _____ 8. Erikson's fifth psychosexual   C. Identity
                  stage

          _____ 9. Erikson's sixth psychosexual   D. Intimacy
                  stage

10. In Erikson's model ego integrity occurs at the _____ .

      a. seventh stage of development   b. eighth stage of development

11. One school of thought affirms a critical period of development wherein moderate levels of various pleasant as well as unpleasant stimulation are important for normal development. _____ .

      a. True   b. False

12. Ethologists have suggested what about the mothering response? _____ .

      a. It is due to heredity

      b. Mothers have to learn to love their infants

      c. A babylike appearance stimulates mothering

      d. When the baby does not smile, the mother worries

13. Experiments have shown what stimulus most adequate to produce a smiling response in young infants? _____ .

      a. Light shined in the eye   b. A front-view human face

      c. Other people at a distance   d. A human face in profile

14. Freedman's findings with blind babies suggest that smiling _____ .

      a. is an imitative process

      b. must be learned early or not at all

      c. may initially be an innate behavior

      d. cannot occur unless babies see another person

DEVELOPMENTAL PROCESSES III: COGNITIVE DEVELOPMENT

Having reviewed some of the major viewpoints on the determination of physical and social-emotional areas of development, we now turn to intellectual, or cognitive, development.

Jean Piaget and His Theory of Cognitive Development

We have already alluded to a number of processes that contribute to the physical development of central nervous system tissue. Through a direct cause and effect these same factors influence intellectual development. For this reason our attention has been directed toward various factors such as nutrition and type of environment, but we now shall devote attention to an entirely different area of research.

When we consider how cognition (thinking) develops in children, it is typical that we think of the child simply as being an adult in miniature. That is, while we recognize that children cannot think "as well" as adults, we often assume that the ways in which they think are the same as those displayed by adults. Thus, we would assume that a child cannot exercise logic reasoning or predict future events as well as an adult, but we would consider that the ways in which he or she might attempt to do so would be essentially similar.

Even formal concepts of intelligence, as reflected by existing intelligence tests, demonstrate this attitude. We naturally assume that the average nine-year-old can reason through certain problems of a simple mathematical nature that correspond to his or her classroom experiences in school, and we assume that the six-year-old has not had these experiences. Therefore, in testing logical reasoning, we might ask a nine-year-old boy to fill combinations of various-sized containers (two quarts, three quarts, etc.) in order to come up with a certain specified amount of a liquid; the younger boy might be asked to take a pencil and trace a route on a map of a round pasture in order to locate a small object he had (in imagination) previously dropped there. There is nothing in the assumed "theory" of intelligence reflected in the two different tasks that would imply different reasoning processes in children of different ages.

"KEEP AN EYE ON THE KIDS FOR AWHILE, WILL YOU, JEAN?"

Quite a few years ago, a Swiss psychologist named Jean Piaget began to study his own children's thinking and learning, and eventually branched out into work with a wider group of children. From Piaget's efforts came a point of view that the exercise of intelligence and reasoning in the child is a *qualitatively different* procedure from that of the adult. He similarly felt that there were several stages or plateaus during infancy and early childhood at which different forms of intellectual processes existed. The "logic" of the child thus would be dissimilar from one stage to the next.

A typical problem that interested Piaget was how a small child views concepts of quantity. Let us assume that we have two one-quart containers filled with water, which are rather short but wide, and that we have one empty one-quart container which is three times as tall, but only one-third as wide. A little girl who views the pouring of liquid from one of the short containers into the tall container, is witnessing what she thinks is an increase in the quantity of the liquid. At an early age the child literally believes that the taller, narrower container holds more liquid, even though she saw the pouring process with her own eyes. Similarly, if one arranges a row of a dozen blocks spaced an inch apart, and then arranges a second row of a dozen blocks spaced two inches apart, a little boy will believe that the second row contains a greater number of blocks, since he is influenced by the length of the row he sees.

While the above examples are interesting in that they provide a vivid demonstration of the different dimensions of logic in the very young child, we should properly begin at the beginning in order to consider Piaget's theory of the development of the intellect.

Piaget was vitally interested in a specific type of intelligence. He, unlike most other investigators, considered "real" intelligence to be an essentially untaught process. Consider this statement: "Actually we can distinguish two aspects in the child's intellectual development. On the one hand we have what can be called the psychosocial aspect, that is, everything the child receives from without and learns in general by family, school, and educative transmissions. On the other there is the development . . . of the intelligence itself—what the child learns by himself, what none can teach him and he must discover alone; and it is essentially this development which takes time [Piaget, 1973, p. 2]." You will observe as you read about the research of Piaget that his tests of intellectual ability are quite different from those of standardized IQ tests, and this is precisely because he feels that *intelligence* is different from the mass of learned *information*.

C 3.23. *Piaget's viewpoint of "intelligence."*

In Piaget's opinion, "real intelligence" is essentially that which is _____ .

    a. transmitted via the culture and thereby learned

    b. self-taught and self-discovered

Factors in Cognition   As the infant interacts with people and objects in the world around him, he develops a number of schema. *Schema* is Piaget's word for an organized action or cognitive structure that the child applies to the world around him, leading to *knowing*. The very young child has only a few schema. He can grasp objects handed to him, and draw them close for visual inspection. When the mother's breast is provided, he is capable of guiding himself to the source of food. In Piaget's terms, very young children have both grasping and sucking schema. By using an appropriate schema, the infant deals with and "understands" a present situation, but his schema go little beyond simple grasping, manipulating, and sucking.

A bit later, children develop what Piaget calls *interiorized schema*. That is, rather than involving physical action directly, the child becomes capable of transforming the physical task into a mental representation. One way of viewing this is to say that the child becomes capable of thinking about doing something; at a fairly sophisticated level this is well represented by arithmetic problems in which a child is asked to imagine eight apples and four apples, toward the objective of calculating the total number of apples. By using interiorized schema, the child is able to conceptualize the appropriate numbers and "add" them in their literal absence.

Piaget views the whole of human adjustment, from infancy to adulthood, as the person seeking to understand his or her world by applying a certain schema to certain objects or events; but he also recognizes the necessity for the individual to occasionally adjust his choice of schema to fit the characteristics of the situation.

Piaget's theory stems from two basic assumptions concerning the intellectual development of human beings. He proposes that human beings inherit two basic tendencies—*organization*, which is the tendency to systematize and organize processes into coherent wholes, and *adaptation*, the tendency to adjust to the environment. These two tendencies are carried on within a basic process called *equilibration*. This is a dynamic preservation of a state of balance between the child's sense of coherence and stability in what he, or she, understands from his conception of the world, and the flexibility to change his precepts in order to make inconsistencies in experience comprehensible and consistent to the major system.

Let us look at the two basic tendencies, organization and adaptation, to see how they combine to produce cognitive structures. Organization is illustrated by the child gradually acquiring certain bits of information and knowledge, and occasionally bringing the bits together into a larger system. Adaptation refers to two complementary processes—*assimilation*, which is the process of applying an already established pattern of behavior to a new object or event, and *accommodation*, which is the alteration of an old categorization scheme in response to environmental influences (definitions from Sheppard & Willoughby, 1975, p. 509).

Let us see how these concepts might be utilized by the child. Let us assume that a boy has organized the various skills connected with reaching for and grasping a rolling ball. Now let us assume that we bounce the ball across the floor toward the child. His first reaction would be *assimilation,* in that he would act ineffectually, trying to seize the ball without taking the up-and-down motion into account. After some repeated experience with this new three-dimensional problem, he will *accommodate* his original anticipatory schema into a new type of schema pertaining to how to grasp moving objects.

C 3.24. *Piaget's theory of cognitive development: Factors in cognition.*

An organized action or cognitive structure to be applied to the world around one is what Piaget calls

a _____ .

These structures, together, lead to _____ . (Refer to the last answer)

    a. insight   b. problem solving   c. knowing

When schema no longer involve physical action directly, but can be represented in mental activity,

they are called _____ _____ .

The active process of applying one's schema to interaction with the world around one is called

_____ .

Adjustments to schema in response to the dictates of new experiences is called _____

_____ .

Piaget viewed the concept of understanding as a relative balance between processes of assimilation and accommodation. That is, through interiorized schema the individual is capable of anticipating and dealing symbolically with imagined situations, and is simultaneously able to bring to bear the lessons learned from a lifetime of experiences in related situations. The understanding structure may be quite simplistic where experience is limited, but can become complex where broad experience has built a major memory structure to be mentally retrieved and evaluated by the individual as he envisions a task situation.

Periods of Intellectual Development

As we stated earlier, one vivid characteristic of Piaget's view of cognitive development is that certain periods of development are *qualitatively* different from each other. That is, the child thinks in different ways as his age progresses. Also, in Piaget's view, the child must go through the stages in a fixed order and cannot achieve a higher level of intellectual development until he has adequately progressed through the earlier levels. The *order* of occurrence of these levels is *invariable* in all children.

The intellectual development of the child is dependent upon the environment in which he grows up, and the speed of progress through different periods varies widely in different environments. Therefore the ages at which the various periods are represented can only be viewed as a rough guideline. The *sensorimotor* period is generally the period of infancy approximating, roughly, the first two years of life. The *preoperational* period is the period of preschool years. The *concrete operational* period extends from around seven years of age, and the *formal operational* period takes over around very early adolescence. We shall consider each of these stages in turn. As you go through the periods of development, from time to time you should consult Table 3.1 on this page. There you will see a highly comprehensive charting of the periods with some of their major characteristics. The discussion following will elaborate upon the important aspects of each period.

Table 3.1 Piaget's periods of cognitive development.

PERIODS	CHARACTERISTIC BEHAVIOR
I. Sensorimotor Period (0-24 months)	
1. Reflexive Stage (0-2 months)	Simple reflex activity (example: grasping, sucking).
2. Primary Circular Reactions (2-4 months)	Reflexive behaviors occur in stereotyped repetition (example: opening and closing fingers repetitively).
3. Secondary Circular Reactions (4-8 months)	Repetition of chance actions to reproduce interesting consequences (example: kicking one's feet to move a mobile suspended over the crib).
4. Coordination of Secondary Reactions (8-12 months)	Responses become coordinated into more complex sequences. Actions take on an "intentional" character (example: the infant reaches behind a screen to obtain a hidden object).
5. Tertiary Circular Reactions (12-18 months)	Discovery of new ways to produce the same consequence or obtain the same goal (example: the infant may pull a pillow toward him in an attempt to get a toy resting on it).
6. Invention of New Means Through Mental Combination (18-24 months)	Evidence of an internal representational system. Symbolizing the problem-solving sequence before actually responding. Deferred imitation.
II. The Preoperational Period (2-7 years)	
1. Preconceptual Phase (2-4 years)	Increased use of verbal representation, but speech is egocentric. The beginnings of symbolic rather than simple motor play. Transductive reasoning.
2. Intuitive Phase (4-7 years)	Speech becomes more social, less egocentric. The child has an intuitive grasp of logical concepts in some areas. However, there is still a tendency to focus attention on one aspect of an object while ignoring others.
III. Period of Concrete Operations (7-11 years)	Evidence for organized, logical thought. There is the ability to perform multiple classification tasks, order objects in a logical sequence, and comprehend the principle of conservation. Thinking becomes less transductive and less egocentric. The child is capable of concrete problem-solving.
IV. Period of Formal Operations (11 years-upward)	Thought becomes more abstract, incorporating the principles of formal logic. The ability to generate abstract propositions, multiple hypotheses and their possible outcomes is evident.

(Adapted from Sheppard & Willoughby, 1975)

C 3.25. *Piaget's theory of cognitive development: Periods of intellectual development.*

Piaget viewed human cognitive development as being comprised of sequential _____ _____ (qualitatively, quantitatively) different intellectual stages.

The stages of human intellectual development occur in a _____ (fixed, variable) order from child to child.

The Piagetian stages occur at approximate, but not exact, ages from child to child, influenced by _____ .

a. experiences in the environment   b. nutrition

The Sensorimotor Period

In considering the first intellectual period, it may seem that the things we discuss have little to do with emerging intelligence. This is a misconception, however, since it has been claimed that sensorimotor intelligence is the basis of all intelligence, and Piaget himself used the term "practical intelligence" as a rough synonym for this period.

Sensorimotor, as the term implies, refers to a largely *non*verbal relationship that develops between an individual and the environment. This period starts as soon after birth as the individual begins to relate to the environment, although at this age "relation" simply means grasping, feeling, etc. Soon the child becomes more purposeful and active in the exploration of his surroundings, and becomes aware that objects have a separate existence from parts of his own body. You may have noticed the small infant seemingly fascinated as he examines his own hands or feet, feeling them, sensing their existence, then switching his attention to nearby objects, as if he were comparing his own physical qualities with those of environmental objects. One of the first qualities to develop at this level is a simple orientation toward some things and away from others; the child learns that objects in the environment have various properties that can be interesting and rewarding (positive), hurtful or uncomfortable (negative), or neutral.

During this period the child begins to relate to the environment. At the outset the main activities consist of exploration and manipulation. While it is easy to envision the child reaching and grasping for bright colored objects placed within range, and learning a form of intellectual adaptiveness, it is perhaps not so obvious that this may involve a series of nonverbal learning tasks. One of these might be that objects that have different configurations must be grasped differently. Another might be that objects a short distance away can be reached and touched while farther objects cannot. (Even at an adult level, the sensorimotor form of relationship to objects can continue largely in the same style. The relatively non-thinking act of riding a bicycle is one example.)

At a later point during the sensorimotor period, the child begins a more active means-ends pattern of behavior. Simple problem-solving appears, and it seems some understanding of spatial relations develops.

Elongated objects may become useful as extensions of one's hand, and some are eventually seen to be useful tools to use against other objects. Generalization develops, so that other objects—not just the one being used at the time the original success was achieved—are readily substituted.

A number of concepts emerge out of this period. One of these is the concept of *object permanence*. Infants only gradually build up a distinction between a visible object and an object that was visible but is now hidden. In the early stages of life the infant responds as though an out-of-sight object no longer has any existence. If the baby has its eyes focused upon a nearby attractive object, and under most circumstances it soon reaches out to grasp it, the grasping act can be cancelled by the lowering of a visual shield in front of the object. Almost at once the infant will turn its attention elsewhere, displaying very little curiosity as to where the object went.

Object permanence is gradually and systematically developed from the age of one-and-a-half to about two years of age. During this time the infant learns to coordinate its senses, so that a single object can begin to be perceived as one which has both visual and auditory (or other) sensory properties. It is during this stage that the baby begins to show the first signs of object permanence by pursuing the disappearing objects with its eyes. If an object is moved along the visual field until it disappears behind a screen, the infant will continue to turn its head to follow the object's projected path and will watch for it to reemerge at some predictable spot. The behavior of older infants observing the passage of toy electric trains through tunnels exemplifies this. As object permanence increases, the infant for the first time will demonstrate search behavior when an object passes out of sight.

At early points in this developmental period the infant fails to demonstrate a maturely developed sensorimotor intelligence, as evidenced by certain strange tactics. Suppose that a small dog that interests the infant walks across the left side of the visual field to disappear behind a couch. The infant may focus its gaze on the spot at which the animal disappeared. Then the dog reemerges several feet to the right in the child's visual field for a moment, then disappears behind a nearby chair. It is not unusual to see the child crawl rapidly to the point at which the animal first disappeared behind the couch, rather than employ the more effective tactic of proceeding to the point at which it was last observed.

Or, consider this case. A little girl witnesses an animal in a wire mesh cage being rolled behind the sofa. From behind the sofa an assistant removes the animal, and the cage is then drawn again into the visual field and over to an area near the child. The child will proceed to inspect the cage, look in and under it, and show great puzzlement. Before a certain point in the development of sensorimotor intelligence, it apparently never occurs to her that something that she could not see might have happened. In one sense she feels that sensation (her own direct viewing) of an incident is reality, and that nonsensation implies that the incident did not really happen.

C 3.26. *The sensorimotor period of cognitive development.*

Within the _____ period the child will develop an ability to attend to objects that have

disappeared from view, exhibiting "search" behavior. The child has then developed the concept of

_____ _____ .

The knowledge that develops within the sensorimotor period is largely _____ .

    a. nonverbal   b. mathematical   c. emotional

The final stage of sensorimotor intelligence is an obvious skill in understanding movements, even when disguised from perception, and an easy and flexible awareness of the reality of both objects and events not being directly perceived.

The Preoperational Period

The next stage of development extends from the age of around two until about seven. It is during this period that we begin to see the emergence of a capacity, simple at first, to interiorize action and think symbolically. The first substage of the preoperational period is called the *preconceptual phase* (ages two to four), during which time the child begins imagery. He also initiates actions that he has seen others perform, through his symbolic play activities.

During the preconceptual phase the child is quite egocentric, being unable to take the viewpoint of other people. At the intellectual level this is represented in an interesting demonstration that sometimes surprises the observer. A child, after walking around a large four-sided object that has each side painted a different color, and finally returning to his starting point, imagines that a child stationed on the opposite side of the object is seeing the same color.

It is also characteristic that the child in this preconceptual phase categorizes on the basis of *single characteristics* of objects, and is unable to consider, simultaneously, multifaceted aspects of stimuli. We spoke earlier of a young child assuming that a tall, narrow container inevitably contains more contents than does a short, wider one. At this stage the child is simply unable to conceive of an object having interacting height and width; he or she concentrates on a single salient feature of the stimulus being presented. During the phase of preconceptual thought the child can grasp such ideas as that men and women are all people, or that apples and oranges are both food, but is unable to categorize objects along multiple dimensions. He or she would be unable to visualize apples along dimensions such as big green apples, small green apples, big red apples, and small red apples, and would not be able to sort actual apples in this manner.

Another limitation in this phase is that thinking is *complexive*. That is, thoughts run on by themselves, hopping from point to point largely on the basis of certain fairly concrete similarities or suggestions, but the child flits from one idea to another with very little cohesive attack upon a problem.

He cannot coordinate his thoughts for an appreciable length of time around a single concept.

Yet another limitation comes from the child's failure to differentiate objects from creatures. Thus, at this age, it is not at all uncommon for the child to inject qualities of experience into inanimate things. A kite with a broken wooden frame may be viewed compassionately as being "hurt," or an automobile might be viewed as being "happy" due to the configurations of its headlights and radiator grill, which seem like a pleasant, smiling face to the child.

Still another lack of development during the preconceptual phase is a deficiency in the ability to visualize physical properties which are not present, such as those representing the relationship between a map and actual streets. Piaget (1973) refers to an experiment on four- and five-year-old children who all were experienced in walking from their homes to school and returning later in the day. The experimenters tried to get these children to represent the path they took between school and home by means of a map game. A blue ribbon represented the street running in front of the school, other ribbons represented other streets, and certain colored boxes represented important different buildings nearby. While these children knew how to follow their ways to school, they were unable to represent their paths within the map game. They were limited to saying, "I leave the house, I go like that (gesture), then like that (gesture), then I make a turn like that, then I reach school." This example was considered indicative that information acquired on the sensorimotor level cannot be elaborated on another level of representation until development has progressed to a satisfactory point.

The second phase within the preoperational period is the *intuitive* phase, which lasts from about four until around seven years of age. During this time the child is extending, differentiating and combining his or her imagery, and is simultaneously exercising various corrections to impressions of reality in terms of space, time, and cause-and-effect thinking. Three fundamental operations make an appearance. The child becomes able to think in terms of classes of events or objects, to see relationships, and to handle abstract number concepts. Early in this stage the child may become able to realize that "Mrs. Thomas is the mother of Paul." This seemingly simple understanding involves the perception of relations as well as a comparison and ordering of items.

C 3.27. *The preoperational stage of cognitive development.*

If a child cannot view situations from others' perspectives, his thinking is said to be _____ .

    a. egocentric   b. prerational   c. uniform

It is characteristic in the preoperational stage that children handle _____ of the concepts they are dealing with.

    a. only a single dimension at a time   b. two or three dimensions at a time

The Concrete Operational Period

As the preoperational period ends, generally at around age seven, certain new developments herald the start of the period of concrete operations. During this period a number of abilities develop which increase the child's capacity to reason and solve problems in a logical and consistent fashion. It is during this stage that a child first begins to develop a clear-cut view of classification systems, and he develops the capacity to work flexibly within those systems. For example, consider the notion of the hierarchical relation of classes and subclasses. The child develops the ability to group together four dogs and four cats into the notion of eight animals. It is possible for him to answer questions such as "Are there more dogs or more animals?" Still, early during the development of this capacity, the child may become confused where different levels of concepts are employed. Only gradually does a clear-cut conceptualization evolve, where children can move up and down between classes and subclasses, clearly envisioning each. One important development that seems to contribute to this ability

is that of *reversibility* of the transformation from subclass to class, then down to subclass again.

Another developing ability during this stage has already been mentioned, where we discussed the inability of the child to visualize a tall, thin one-quart container and a short, squat one-quart container as being equal in content. Such an ability, when developed, is called *conservation*, and it can be subcategorized into a number of different types.

Typical in Piaget's writing are discussions of conservation of mass, weight and volume. Occasionally discussed are notions of conservation of both numbers and area. We shall not illustrate all of these—just a few examples should make the notion of conservation clear. Conservation of numbers means that a child will perceive eight objects in one group as being the same number of objects as eight objects in another group. Prior to the development of this form of conservation the child would perceive one group as being the larger in number if the objects within it were larger (as with coins), or if there was greater space between the individual objects so that they were spread out over a larger area. Another form of conservation would be the understanding that changing the shape of a soft clay object does not change the amount of clay contained in the object.

The various conservation abilities depend upon a certain level of neurological maturation of the individual for their development, yet Piaget noted that even all adults have not acquired some notions of conservation. Spencer, in his *Treatise on Sociology*, tells of a woman who preferred to travel with a long piece of luggage rather than a square one because she thought that her dresses, when spread out in the long case, weighed less than when folded down in the square case (Piaget, 1973, p. 7).

Can one accelerate the development of conservation abilities? Piaget refers to research on the question, discussing an experiment where various children were introduced to the notion of conservation of weight. They were instructed through example that if object A is equal in weight to object B, and object B is equal in weight to object C, then object A is therefore of equal weight to object C, despite the fact that the objects are different in shapes and sizes. Each child went through a number of learning experiences, and after each reply the child was shown the results on a scale which indicated the weight was the same. After two or three such experiences the child consistently would repeat, "It will be the same weight."

What was interesting in this experiment was that the learning was limited to this specific example, and the investigators were unable to obtain evidence for a generalizable learning of the notion of conservation of weight when they turned to other different situational problems. "Thus it is one thing to learn a result and another to form an intellectual instrument, a logic required to construct such a result. Such a new reasoning instrument is not formed in a few days [Piaget, 1973, p. 8]."

During the concrete operational period one of the most important developing capacities is that of *transformation*. This term refers to processes by which one state of being is changed into another state of being (a solid to a liquid) and along with transformation develops its reversibility. Concerning the latter capacity, the fact that a child can think from one level to another, then back again to the first level, is generally responsible for what we then perceive (somewhat incorrectly) as an apparent ability to think simultaneously at two or more levels.

As you can imagine, none of the characteristics described in the period of concrete operations develops suddenly. Rather, a continuous and growing ability is characteristic as the child encounters successive educational and social experiences.

C 3.28.   *The concrete operational period of cognitive development.*

A child gains the ability to think in terms of classes and subclasses within the _____

_____ period of development; a contributant is the newly-developed

ability to think down to a subclass and then back up again rapidly, this being the capacity for

_____ of the transformation.

An important developing ability during the period of concrete operations is the ability to understand

that changes in size, spacing, shape, and so forth do not necessarily mean accompanying

changes in weight, volume, and so forth. This is the notion of _____ .

The Formal Operational Period

Starting at around age eleven, the child begins to overcome certain limitations that existed in the concrete operational era. A new set of capacities called formal operational intelligence develops.

One of the most important characteristics of the formal operational period, at least in terms of the intellectual capacity of an educated person, is the developing ability to consider *all possible combinations of events* in problems presented, excluding ones that are irrelevant. If you were to take a very young child and ask him to solve a given problem, it would not be at all unlikely that after the first effort fails, the child will then say, "Well, I just can't do it." Even though the observing adult can clearly see other related solutions, and will think that the child should be aware of them also, it seems that the child has little ability to put together all possible solutions, through combinations of elements, until a workable solution is arrived at. With the development of this skill a large number of intellectual challenges can be handled.

Another capacity exhibited by the individual who is moving into the formal operational period is the capacity to consider *hypothetical situations.* Young children are limited to a very simplistic fantasy representation where hypothetical events are concerned. The older child or adolescent gradually becomes capable of imagining wide varieties of events or solutions to problems that have never been acted out or verbalized in his presence.

A third major influence during this period of development is an increasing ability to consider *abstract principles.* At a very early age children are given mathematical problems such as the sum involved in the addition of three apples and four apples. Only through the initial translation into "apples" is the child realistically able to visualize the problem; later comes abstract visualization with some awareness of the intent and the concepts involved. Later in the formal operational stage, the individual can readily move into new areas of advanced abstraction, without the need to first fuse the events. On one level the individual may now study fields such as advanced mathematics and abstract science and mechanics, while on another level he or she may begin to deal intensively with philosophic abstractions such as the meaning of life, the meaning of existence, and so forth.

C 3.29.   *The formal operational period of cognitive development.*

Three abilities that develop within the formal operational stage of development are the abilities to consider

a. _____ .

b. _____ .

c. _____ .

As you now can see, the viewpoint that the adult is somehow just a quantitatively different individual from the child, thinking along simpler but similar dimensions, is naïve. Granted, for purposes of the estimation of one's level of intelligence with a standardized test, such a viewpoint may allow the easiest conceptualization and measurement. It will not be argued at this point whether intellectual measurement might be revamped and brought in line with Piagetian principles. Still, we should make a note that there exist psychological theorists who take the position that the child is not simply a miniature of an adult, and that a number of distinct qualitative changes in the intellectual processes develop along predictable and formalized dimensions.

PROGRESS CHECK   3.3

1. Which is an accurate statement about Piaget's theory of cognitive development? _____ .

    a. It is comprised of sequential quantitatively defined intellectual stages

    b. The stages occur in a variable order from child to child

    c. The stages occur in a fixed order at approximate ages for each child depending on environmental influences

    d. All of these

2. According to Piaget, in which period is developed knowledge largely nonverbal? _____ .

    a. Sensorimotor   b. Preoperational   c. Concrete operational   d. Formal operational

3. A characteristic of the preoperational period is _____ .

    a. egocentric thinking   b. handling of concepts on multiple dimensions

    c. ability to map   d. grouping of creatures, things and people separately

4. Classification systems and conservation are abilities children develop in the concrete operational period. _____ .

    a. True   b. False

5. Which ability develops prior to the formal operational period of cognitive development? _____ .

    a. Hypothesis formation   b. Abstract thinking

    c. Consideration of all possibilities of a problem   d. Transformation

6. Piaget believes that intelligence evolves mainly from amassing learned information. _____ .

    a. True   b. False

MATCH: _____ 7. Accommodation   A. Alteration of old schema in accord with new experiences

    _____ 8. Assimilation   B. Apply established schema to new objects and events

9. According to Piaget, children develop simple problem skills and object permanence in the _____ .

    a. sensorimotor period   b. preoperational period

    c. concrete operational period   d. formal operational period

10. During the preoperational period children develop _____ .

    a. classification systems   b. reason   c. conversation   d. imagery

---

CONCLUSION   In this chapter we have examined, briefly, some of the major changes that occur in the physical, social-emotional, and cognitive dimensions as the individual develops. Some psychologists take an interest in the biologically relevant developments during the fetal period, although we have given relatively little emphasis to that topic. Most current research interest is oriented toward establishing the various biological, social, and nonsocial environmental factors that influence the developing infant or child in positively or negatively valued directions. In view of the fact that our space is limited, we also have refrained from a discussion of advanced adulthood and old age, and the changes that typically occur during that period.

In the near future you may wish to take a course in developmental psychology. It is a frequent second or third course following the introductory course. Should you have a more immediate interest in the field, there are a number of interesting texts you might wish to consult. Three of these are *Child Behavior* by Sheppard and Willoughby (1975), *Human Development* by Lugo and Hershey (1974), and *Child Psychology* by Johnson and Medinnus (1974). If you should be interested in the topic of aging, a comprehensive treatment of research findings is to be found in *Aging and Behavior*, by Botwinick (1973).

Sensation and Perception

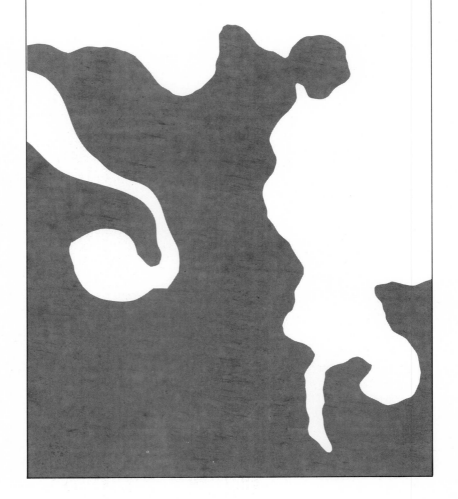

SENSATION AND PERCEPTION

VISUAL SENSORY PROCESSING
Visual Stimuli
  Photic Energy
The Human Eye
  The Retina
  The Fovea
  Rod and Cone Function
  Ganglion Cells
  The Optic Nerve, Thalamus, and Visual Cortex
Color Vision
  Color Mixture and Color Perception
  Additive Color Mixture
  Color Defects

THE NATURE OF PERCEPTION

VISUAL PERCEPTION

ORGANIZATION OF VISUAL PERCEPTION
Basic Organizational Processes
Two-Dimensional Spatial Organization
Three-Dimensional Spatial Organization
  Physiological Variables in Depth Perception
    Accommodation
    Convergence
    Retinal Disparity
  Stimulus Variables in Depth Perception
    Linear Perspective
    Relative Size
    Interposition
    Light and Shadow
    Texture Gradients
    Aerial Perspective
    Height in the Horizontal Plane
    Motion
Motion Perception

HEARING (AUDITION)
Qualities of Auditory Sensation
Auditory Theory
Auditory Acuity
Defects in Auditory Acuity

ATTENTION

PERCEPTUAL DEVELOPMENT

PERCEPTUAL THEORY
Nativism Versus Empiricism
  Gestalt Theory
  Empiricist Perceptual Theories
  A Stimulus-Oriented Theory

CONCLUSION

One of the first things you will notice as you study this chapter is that the material is less theoretical and more concrete. This chapter also contains a great amount of technical terminology because of the description of complex physiological processes. Assuming that a prime objective of your introductory course is to prepare you for advanced courses of study and for an ability to examine published literature in the areas of emphases, the stress on terminology is deserved.

In previous chapters a groundwork has been laid demonstrating that the subject of psychological study is, first and foremost, a biological organism with a physical structure that renders certain capabilities. We are now ready to consider the types of stimuli that almost constantly impinge upon that physical structure, and examine the processes involved by which we interpret, from the resulting neurological activity, what is going on around us.

SENSATION AND PERCEPTION   Our only contact with the world outside ourselves, and thus all our acquired knowledge of it, comes through our sense *receptors,* which are tiny specialized transducers (devices that convert energy from one form to another). The action of receptor cells sets in motion a complicated sequence of communication between neurons that usually involves the brain stem, thalamus, and cerebral cortex and may involve other organs as well. *Sensation* or *sensory processing* are the labels applied to these complicated but fundamental receptor-to-brain neuron communication sequences. *Perception,* then, is the discriminatory response of an organism to the energy-converting sense organs. Your perception of objects and people is more than simply the sensory processing of an immediate stimulus. Perception may involve a long history of experience with the environment (learning), autonomic nervous system functions (emotion), body needs (motivation), and may be limited by the nature of the neurological system (intelligence). In plain language, what you see, hear, feel, smell and so forth, depends upon the nature of your sensory processing system and is influenced by your past and present experiences.

C 4.1.   *Sensation and perception.*

Sensation can be defined as _____ .

    a. the discriminatory response of an organism to the energy-converting sense organs

    b. fundamental receptor-to-brain communications sequences

    c. the global reactions of the total organism to incoming stimulation

Perception can be defined as _____ .

    a. the discriminatory response of an organism to the energy-converting sense organs

    b. fundamental receptor-to-brain communications sequences

    c. the action of transducers

VISUAL SENSORY PROCESSING   All perceiving, thinking, and reacting is carried out by the nervous system, and communication within that system is electrochemical. Information about the environment, however, is almost never in the form of electrical energy. Information arrives in the form of electromagnetic radiation (light), mechanical activity (pressure, including sound), or chemical activity (flavors, odors). How, then, does the brain discover what is going on in the environment with such a mismatch of energy processes?

    The answer is that the receptors of the sense organs serve as *transducers.* They change the incoming message into a form the nervous system can "understand." Each sense system is specialized in its ability to take one kind of energy and then transmit it as an electrochemical message. The eye, for example, is most sensitive to electromagnetic energy, the ear to mechanical energy, and the tongue and nose to chemical activity.

Two major consequences stem from the fact that all information about the environment must come in through the senses. One is the limitation of the *effective environment.* We are not sensitive to all electromagnetic radiations—radio waves, for example—nor are we sensitive to the very high-frequency sound waves that are part of the effective environment for bats and porpoises. Reality is limited for a species by the limits of its sense organs. The other major consequence, called the *doctrine of specific nerve energies,* is that while the brain receives messages from the sense organs through nerve connections, it does not get messages directly from the environment. The brain is aware of neurological impulses, but has no way of interpreting the origin of a message from the optic nerve, for example, as being from electromagnetic radiation, a finger in the eye, a blow to the head, or drugs stimulating the visual system. All such messages from the optic nerve are interpreted as light.

Messages carried in the nervous system are coded in much the same way that a verbal message is translated into the dot-dash language of Morse code. The elements of this *neural code* are the fire-or-not-fire decision of each neuron, which neuron is firing, how many neurons are firing, and the frequency of each neuron's firing.

All the senses are important in our total behavior but each is also, unfortunately, very complicated in its own specific ways. Take, as an illustration, vision—the sensory process through which the typical human being assimilates more information than through all the others combined. We shall consider first the nature of visual stimuli and the basic structure and function of the eye. We then shall outline the neural communication sequence, from the visual receptors to the cerebral cortex.

C 4.2.   *The basic nature of sensory processing.*

Sense organs change incoming messages from one form of energy to another, and thus serve as

_____ .

The eye is most sensitive to _____ radiation, the ear to _____

_____ activity, and the tongue and nose to _____

activity.

A major consequence of the fact that all information about the environment must come through the

senses is that we _____ .

   a. have a limited effective environment

   b. cannot always assume total correspondence between the actual environment and neurological

       signals

   c. can easily be misled into hallucinatory and hence irrational processes

   d. (two of the above answers are correct)

   e. (none of the first three answers is correct)

Information in the nervous system is carried in the form of which neurons are firing, how many are firing,

and their frequency of firing, all comprising a _____ .

a. visual processing pattern   b. neurological image

c. neural code   d. (none of the first three answers is correct)

The stated position in the text is that human beings process more information through the sense of

_____ than through any other sensory process.

a. sight   b. touch   c. hearing   d. smell   e. movement and balance

Visual Stimuli   We have pointed out that an individual's sensory system may respond to electromagnetic radiation, chemical activity, and mechanical energy. The neurons in the visual system are highly sensitive to all three of these forms of stimulation. The usual stimulus for vision, however, is commonly but somewhat inaccurately called "light," a term that actually fits not so much the stimulus itself as our experiences resulting from that stimulation. In this section we shall refer to the stimulus as *photic energy*, or *electromagnetic radiation* rather than "light."

Photic Energy   Photic energy may be described as waves of particles, which means that its pattern has *wave characteristics* similar to peaks and troughs in water resulting from a tossed rock, and *particle characteristics* like a shower of objects. Wave characteristics find greater use in color perception and particle characteristics in describing photic energy stimulation leading to brightness perception. Photic energy varies in wavelength from approximately 10^{-14} meters (about a trillionth of an inch) to about 10^8 meters (62,137 miles). Only a small portion of this electromagnetic spectrum is visible to humans. The visible spectrum (Figure 4.1) is usually measured in nanometers (10^{-9} meters, or a millionth of a millimeter), abbreviated nm.

Figure 4.1

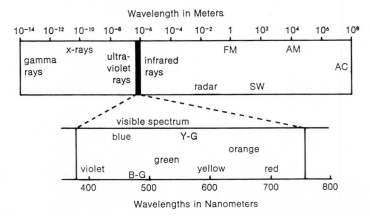

ELECTROMAGNETIC SPECTRUM

Colors normally experienced as the result of stimulation by various wavelengths of photic energy

C 4.3.   *Photic energy.*

The usual stimulus that results in the experience of light is called _____ energy or

_____ radiation.

_____ characteristics of photic energy are more useful in describing color perception;

_____ characteristics are more useful in describing brightness perception.

The approximate limits of the human visual spectrum under normal illumination conditions are

approximately _____ to _____ nm.

Under normal conditions we would experience the color _____ to photic stimulation at

around 400 nm., and the color _____ to stimulation at around 600 nm. (Refer to

Figure 4.1.)

PROGRESS CHECK   4.1

1. The fundamental receptor-to-brain communication sequence is _____ .

    a. perception   b. sensation   c. the action of transducers

2. Communication within the nervous system is _____ .

    a. mechanical   b. electromagnetic   c. electrochemical

MATCH: _____ 3. Eye stimulus   A. Electromagnetic energy

                _____ 4. Ear stimulus   B. Chemical activity

                _____ 5. Tongue stimulus   C. Mechanical activity

                _____ 6. Nose stimulus   D. Electrochemical activity

7. The nervous system carries out all human perceiving, thinking, and reacting. _____ .

    a. True   b. False

8. The doctrine of specific nerve energies involves the fact that _____ .

    a. the brain receives information from neurological activity, but not directly from the
environment

    b. we have a wider variety of senses than we realize

    c. not all information about the environment comes through the senses

9. Transducers in the nervous system _____ .

    a. convert stimulus energy to an electrochemical message

    b. change the incoming message to a form the nervous system "understands"

    c. aid fundamental receptor-to-brain communications sequences

    d. all of the above

10. "Neural code" might be defined as the _____ of the neurons by which information is carried in the nervous system.

    a. Morse code   b. firing order

11. Though which sensory process does the typical human being assimilate the most information? _____ .

    a. Smell   b. Taste   c. Sight   d. Touch

The Human Eye   The eye is said to be very much like a camera. Both the eye and the camera have devices to control the amount of light passing through their entrances (the iris and the diaphram) by making the opening (the pupil and the aperture) larger or smaller. Both have focusing lenses, and both have photosensitive interior surfaces (the retina and the film). Although these relationships do exist, they are misleading. As an optical device the eye is in some respects a poor-quality product, even though the photic sensitivity range of the eye is far greater than that of any camera-film combination made.

The camera, whether still or motion picture, takes a series of discrete still photographs, but the eye is continuously affected by light stimulation. The eye makes constant rapid microscopic motions, as well as continuous slow drifting and occasional gross movements, but cameras do not ordinarily function well when shifted during operation. Nor do the eye and the camera focus in the same way. In better cameras the lens moves forward or backward for focusing; in cheaper cameras the focus is fixed. The main focus of the eye is accomplished by the fixed *cornea* which supplies about two-thirds of the refractive power (focusing ability) of the eye's optical system; minor adjustments for near or far vision (*accommodation*) are made as the flexible *lens* stretches flat or thickens. Finally, photosensing (sensing light) in the eye is a dynamic and varying process, whereas the photosensitive film in a camera reacts in a fixed manner. (See Figure 4.2.)

Figure 4.2

THE HUMAN EYE

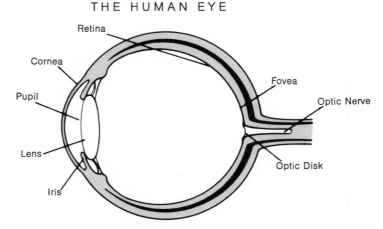

Figure 4.3

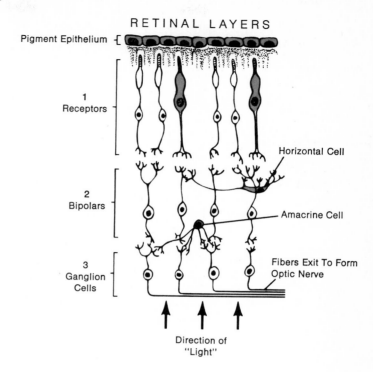

RETINAL LAYERS

Pigment Epithelium

1 Receptors

Horizontal Cell

2 Bipolars

Amacrine Cell

3 Ganglion Cells

Fibers Exit To Form Optic Nerve

Direction of "Light"

The Retina   The vertebrate retina contains photosensitive light receptors called *rods* and *cones* because of their shapes. The human retina contains an estimated 125 million rods and 6.5 million cones. These slender structures face away from the light toward the inside of the eye (Figure 4.3). Within the human retina, the rods and cones make functional connections (*synapses*) with special neurons called *bipolar cells,* which in turn synapse with neurons called *ganglion cells.* The fibers of the ganglion cells exit from the eye at the *optic disk* and form the major part of the *optic nerve* (see Figure 4.2). The optic disk is located in the retina at the back of the eye, and serves as the entry and exit location of the blood supply as well as nerve fibers. Because the optic disk has no rods or cones, it is known also as the blind spot. There are other neural cells, called horizontal and amacrine cells, located in the retina that are hypothesized to play an inhibitory role in vision; however, their precise function is not yet clear.

The Fovea   Near the center of the retina is a small depressed area called the *fovea,* containing only cones. This minute collection of cones gives rise to the best visual *acuity* (ability to resolve details), due partly to the fact that the ratio of foveal cones to bipolar cells is about one to one, whereas the ratio of nonfoveal cones and rods to bipolar cells is well over one hundred to one. Also, better acuity from this retinal region is achieved due to the fovea having more neurons in the cerebral cortex devoted to processing its information than all the remaining rods and cones in the retina combined.

On the other hand, cones are insensitive to lower levels of illumination. Rods, which continue to function with less photic stimulation, are about 1,000 times more light sensitive than cones. Thus, despite its excellent visual acuity in good illumination, the foveal region is "night blind" because it contains no rods. When you look directly at a small visual stimulus, the light from it falls on the fovea. If you wish to see a dim star at night, you should fix your gaze a little to one side of the star so that rods will be stimulated.

C 4.4. *Eye structure.*

The main focus of the eye is accomplished by the _____ .

Minor adjustments in focus for near/far vision are accomplished by the _____ .

    a. lens   b. cornea   c. pupil

Th light receptors in the retina are called _____ and _____ .

The optic disk is the spot at which the ganglion cell fibers _____ .

    a. synapse with the bipolar cells   b. leave the eye and form the optic nerve

The "blind spot" in the retina is the point at which _____ .

    a. the worst focus is achieved   b. the ganglion cell fibers leave the eye

    c. there are no rods or cones   d. (two of the preceding answers are correct)

Near the center of the retina is a small area called the _____ , which contains only

_____ as its visual receptors.

The fovea is "night blind" as it contains no _____ .

PROGRESS CHECK   4.2

  1. Photic energy _____ .

      a. is the usual stimulus for vision

      b. is the method by which impulses are transmitted to the cornea

MATCH: _____ 2. Particle characteristics   A. Useful in describing color perception

          _____ 3. Wave characteristics   B. Useful in describing brightness perception

  4. (Refer to Figure 4.1.) The color yellow can be seen at what nanometer reading? _____ .

  5. And what color is seen at 400 nm? _____ .

  6. And what are the approximate limitations of the human visual spectrum? _____ .

  7. The main focus of the eye is accomplished by _____ .

      a. the lens   b. the retina   c. the cornea

8. Additional accommodations for near and far vision are made by _____ .

    a. the lens   b. the retina   c. the cornea

9. Rods and cones are _____ .

    a. identical in function

    b. photosensitive light receptors

    c. the major cause of blind spots

10. The spot at which the ganglion cell fibers leave the eye and form the optic nerve is _____ .

    a. the fovea   b. the optic disk

11. "Night blindness" is caused by a lack of _____ .

    a. rod function   b. bipolar cells   c. amacrine cells   d. cone function

---

Rod and Cone Function

The human retina contains an estimated 125 million rods and 6.5 million cones, the two types of receptors having quite separate functions. On the one hand, rods respond to conditions of brightness, rendering a perception of black, white, and shades of gray. Contained within the rods is a substance called rhodopsin, or "visual purple." Rhodopsin quickly bleaches out when exposed to light from the visual spectrum, with the exception of extremely long-wave red light. In any brightly illuminated environment the rods are typically bleached out and inoperative, and we then respond almost totally to information transmitted by the cones. Under poor lighting conditions, on the other hand, rods become operative and can respond to very low energy levels that would be too weak to stimulate the cones. When we step into a darkened movie theater after coming in from bright sunlight, we can see how poorly our cone vision allows us to perceive our surroundings. Following a period of the rods' regeneration in the darkness, rod vision takes over and we begin to perceive objects and people around us even though the light is quite dim.

Cones, on the other hand, are sensitive to various wavelengths of light corresponding to our perceptions of colors. It is a bit misleading to leave the statement at this point, since cones also respond to stimulus qualities that we call "black, white, and gray." As you read this textbook in a well-lighted room, you are probably utilizing almost exclusive cone vision, with your rods "bleached out."

Rod and cone sensitivity is not constant in all circumstances. Among the factors influencing sensitivity is prior activity of the visual system. When either rods or cones are subjected to intense light, they lose their ability to respond to weak stimuli (*light adaptation*). In order to regain maximum sensitivity, *dark adaptation* must take place. The longer one remains in the dark, the less intense is the light stimulus necessary for detection. The light intensity sensory threshold for the cone system (*photopic vision*) lowers quickly, and is at its lowest level in approximately 10 minutes.

Figure 4.4

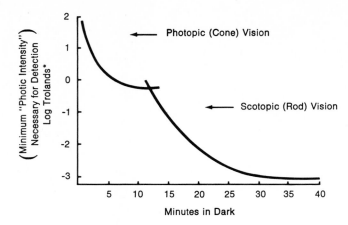

* The Troland *is a unit "light" measurement that takes into account the size of the pupil. Since this scale is expressed in logarithmic units, an increase of 1* log *Troland is the same as an increase of 10 Trolands; an increase of 2* log *Trolands is the same as an increase of 100 Trolands. Thus the range from -3 to 2* log *Trolands represents a energy change of 1,000,000 Trolands.*

The rod system (*scotopic vision*) recovers sensitivity more slowly, with dark adaptation almost complete after 30 minutes (see Figure 4.4).

All wavelengths of the visible spectrum are not perceived to be equally bright at equal intensities. How bright a color appears depends on its wavelength and on whether the photopic (cone) or scotopic (rod) system is functioning (see Figure 4.5). Wavelengths of light of about 510 nm. are seen as brightest when the intensity of light is so low that only rods are stimulated. Other wavelengths appear less bright in scotopic vision. You may recall that electromagnetic radiation at 510 nm. wavelength is experienced as green, but that is true only for the photopic system, not for the scotopic. Cones mediate color vision but rods do not. We are color-blind, in extremely dim light, to weak-colored stimuli. The maximum brightness in the photopic system is at wavelengths of about 555 nm., usually experienced as a yellow. Although only cones mediate color vision, it is interesting to note that at dusk, when there is a transition from photopic to scotopic vision, a green that in full daylight was equal in brightness to a red will appear much brighter than red. This change in sensitivity is called the *Purkinje shift*, after the man who first noted it.

C 4.5. *Rod and cone function.*

_____ mediate color vision.

a. Rods   b. Cones

Figure 4.5

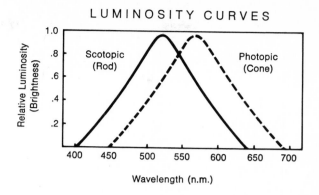

The sensory threshold at a given moment for the cone system is called _____ vision,

and for the rod system it is called _____ vision.

Relatively complete dark adaptation for cone vision takes about _____ minutes after removal

from bright light; for rod vision, the corresponding time is about _____ minutes.

The shift in relative brightness that occurs at dusk represents a shift from the _____

system to the _____ system and is called the _____ _____ .

Ganglion Cells   Approximately a million ganglion cell fibers exit from each eye in the optic nerve, many fewer than the 130 million receptors. Much of the information from the rods and cones is summarized in the on-off signals carried by the ganglion cell fibers.

In 1953 Kuffler stimulated a cat's retina with pinpoints of light in a wide variety of patterns, and simultaneously recorded electrical response measures from ganglion cell fibers in the optic tract outside the eye. By correlating the light pattern stimulating the receptors with the output characteristics of the ganglion cells, he was able to determine that each ganglion cell served only a small region of the retina. Thus, each ganglion cell was said to have a tiny *receptive field*. Many of these receptive field patterns were organized in a special way. Some ganglion cells would respond only if the center of the receptive field was stimulated by light while the outer portion was left darkened; these ganglion cells were labeled *on-center, off-surround cells*. Other ganglion cells responded only if the center of the receptive field was left dark and the outer area was stimulated with light *(off-center, on-surround cells)*.

C 4.6. *Ganglion cells.*

There are approximately _____ times as many visual receptors (rods and cones) as there are

ganglion cell fibers summarizing their activity.

a. 3   b. 19   c. 130   d. 1000

Each ganglion cell in the retina serves only a small rod and cone area of the retina. The receptor area a ganglion cell serves is known as the ganglion cell's _____ _____ .

PROGRESS CHECK   4.3

1. What mediates color vision? _____ .

 a. Rods   b. Cones

2. Scotopic vision is the sensory threshold at a given moment for _____ .

 a. the cone system   b. the rod system   c. relative luminosity

3. The _____ is the transfer in relative brightness from the photopic system to the scotopic system that occurs at dusk.

 a. Purkinje shift   b. play of yellow wavelengths

4. Relatively complete dark adaption takes more than approximately twice as long for scotopic vision as it does for photopic vision. _____ .

 a. True   b. False

5. The "receptive field" is _____ .

 a. the small area of the retina which contains only cones

 b. the area served by the individual ganglion cell

6. The ratio of ganglion cell fibers to visual receptors is approximately _____ .

 a. 1000 to 1   b. 3 to 1   c. 130 to 1   d. 1 to 130

The Optic Nerve, Thalamus, and Visual Cortex

A complex pattern of light- and dark-spot information is transmitted from the retina and is carried by the *optic nerve* as it proceeds toward the *thalamus* (see Figure 4.6). Within the thalamus, synaptic links allow the signals to proceed to the occipital lobes in the visual cortex.

Many of these thalamus-to-cortex nerve fibers converge on a single cortical cell in the visual cortex. It has been discovered recently (Hubel & Wiesel, 1962) that light-dark information converges in such a way on cortical cells that they respond maximally when the retina has been stimulated with *lines* of light or dark. Succeeding cells process the line information into a translation to movement and direction in cats and monkeys, and presumably the same is true for humans.

Figure 4.7 illustrates how stimulation of receptors in the retina with a moving line of light is coded so that the message can be used by the brain. Some of the light particles entering the eye stimulate the receptors they strike. The light absorption changes the chemical balance of the receptors briefly, causing them to fire and in turn to stimulate certain

Figure 4.6

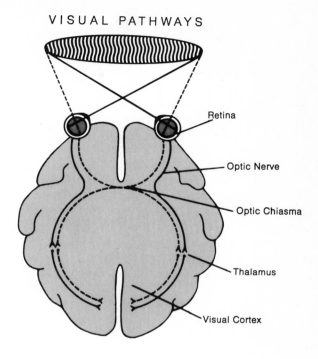

VISUAL PATHWAYS

Retina

Optic Nerve

Optic Chiasma

Thalamus

Visual Cortex

Figure 4.7

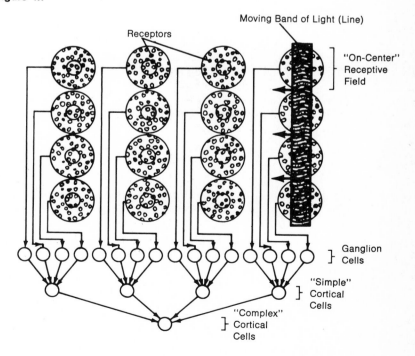

Moving Band of Light (Line)

Receptors

"On-Center" Receptive Field

Ganglion Cells

"Simple" Cortical Cells

"Complex" Cortical Cells

bipolar cells to fire. Figure 4.7 does not illustrate bipolar cells, since they are quite numerous; also, the exact nature of the bipolar cells' role in the coding process is still uncertain. Many bipolar cells converge on a single ganglion cell, stimulating it to fire. The ganglion cell fibers exit the eye and travel via the optic nerve to the thalamus in the midbrain region, causing cells there to fire. Thalamic cells have been omitted from Figure 4.7 because no change in the code is known to occur at the thalamus. Fibers from the thalamus then converge on a simple cortical cell in the visual cortex. The firing of the simple cortical cell represents a line of light in a particular area of the retina. If another group of ganglion cells with adjacent receptive fields parallel to that of the first group of ganglion cells is stimulated to fire immediately after the first group fires, then if a third group and then a fourth group fire, the rapid successive stimulation of a complex cortical cell results in the coded information of a line moving from right to left in a particular part of the retina.

C 4.7. *Neurological aspects of visual acuity.*

The neuron conduction sequence in the eye is (1) rods and cones, to (2) _____

cells, to (3) _____ cells.

The ganglion cell fibers then travel, via the optic nerve, to the _____ .

Fibers from the thalamus converge on _____

cells. These cells are known to respond maximally when a particular area of the retina is

stimulated by _____ of light energy.

The vast numbers of cells involved in visual processing can be grasped if you imagine the retina as a postage stamp on which more than half the population of the United States is located (the rods and cones). The populations of Indianapolis and its suburbs each carry yes/no messages from the stamp (the ganglion cell fibers), to be processed by more than twice the world's population (the cortex contains about 10 billion neural cells), which in turn would be contained within an area about the size of a large man's combined fists (the cerebral cortex).

Color Vision   The preceding discussion of visual processing has ignored the fact that most of us are capable of distinguishing colors, which we attribute to distal (outside the organism) stimuli. In everyday life it is useful to speak of red apples, orange marigolds, blue sky, and green grass, but in a visual sensory processing context such terms are misleading. First, most distal stimuli do not radiate electromagnetic waves, but selectively reflect part of the spectrum illuminating them; second, there are no colors in the outside world—only various wavelengths of electromagnetic radiation; third, color experience is a product of the visual process, not the stimulus; and fourth, color names are verbal responses which may be used by an individual who does not have the same experience to a stimulus as do most other people— those, for example, with color blindness.

Figure 4.8

YOUNG–HELMHOLTZ THEORY

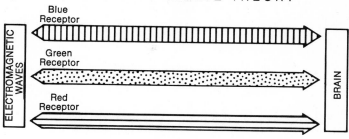

HERING THEORY

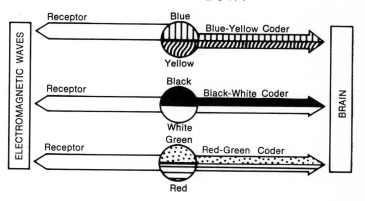

COMPOSITE THEORY

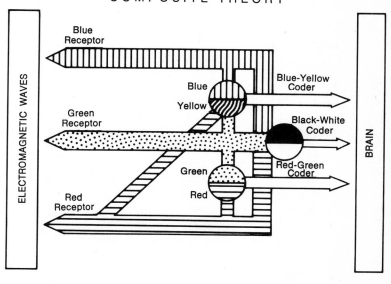

In humans and some of the other primates each cone contains one of three pigments, named *cyanolabe, chloralabe,* and *erythrolabe,* meaning "blue-catching," "green-catching," and "red-catching," respectively. Other mammals have fewer cone types and do not have what we would call true color vision in the sense that humans perceive color. Each of these three cone types has a different peak spectral sensitivity. Only recently demonstrated in controlled experiments, the three-color receptor theory dates from the early nineteenth century when it was suggested by Thomas Young. Hermann von Helmholtz also supported the position in the mid-nineteenth century, and today we refer to the *Young-Helmholtz* or *trichromacy* theory of color vision. An alternative to the Young-Helmholtz theory was proposed by a contemporary of Helmholtz's, Ewald Hering. The *Hering* or *opponent process* theory suggests the occurrence of three opposing operations in the retina—black-white, red-green, and yellow-blue processes—such that a person could "process" only one of the two opposing colors at a time in a given area of retina. (See Figure 4.8.)

A composite theory (see Figure 4.8) would have three types of receptors—a receptor sensitive to short wavelengths (blue), one sensitive to long wavelengths (red), and one sensitive to intermediates (green). The receptors would then stimulate presumed blue-yellow, black-white, and green-red coders. If only one of the receptors were stimulated, then the resulting experience would be blue, red, or green, depending on which was stimulated. Simultaneous stimulation of blue and green receptors would yield the experience of blue-green. If red and blue receptors both responded, the experience would be purple. If red and green receptors were stimulated, we would experience yellow. If all three receptors were stimulated, we would experience shades of gray, the exact shade depending on the intensity of the proximal stimuli. Research evidence supports the trichromacy theory about the existence of three types of cones in the retina (e.g., Marks, Dobelle & MacNickol, 1964; Rushton, 1962). Additionally the existence of opponent processes has been discovered in the operation of thalamic cells (e.g., DeValois, 1965); however, the actual opponent process neural coding operation seems more complicated than predicted in the Hering theory or the composite theory outlined above.

C 4.8. *Theories of color vision.*

_____ types of color receptors were predicted by the *Young-Helmholtz* or _____

theory of color vision, and have been demonstrated to exist in controlled laboratory experiments.

The Hering theory is sometimes called the _____ theory.

    a. bichromacy   b. trichromacy   c. opponent processes

**Color Mixture and
Color Perception**
  Many perceptual phenomena are consistent with the composite theory of color vision. Among these are the "laws" of color mixture, negative after-images, simultaneous color contrast, color induction, and color "blindness," which will be discussed in this section.

Color perception depends partly on the *wavelength of radiation,* but in addition visible radiation can be measured in *wave purity,* and *intensity.* The combination of all three of these is converted by the eye and the brain into color.

Three experiential (that is, characteristics *experienced* by the individual) attributes of color correspond roughly to the three physical characteristics of visible radiation. These three experiential attributes are *hue, saturation,* and *brightness.* Black and white are considered *achromatic* colors. Hues other than black or white (that is, red, green, blue, etc.) are *chromatic* colors. *Hue* depends primarily on wavelength and is the most obvious attribute of a color; for example, a wavelength of 600 nm. produces an orange hue. Very rarely, however, do we have narrow bands of wavelengths in a stimulus. Normally all the visible-spectrum wavelengths are present to some degree. The greater the purity of the waveform, the greater the *saturation.* In the case of roses a deep-red bloom is highly saturated, whereas a pale-pink one is low in saturation. If a rose were white, it would be completely *de*saturated. Thus, a radiation comprised almost entirely of 600 nm. waves would have high wave purity and would be perceived as highly saturated.

The relationship between hue and saturation may be seen in the color circle shown in Figure 4.9. The spectral colors from violet to red are spaced on the circle's perimeter, with the nonspectral hue, purple, filling the gap. On the circumference of the circle the hues are highly saturated. In the center they are completely desaturated and are achromatic. The points *A, C* and *E* are highly saturated; point *D* is a bit less saturated; point *B* is achromatic.

The final dimension of color mixture, *brightness,* introduces the experiential dimension of light versus dark. Brightness has, as its extremes, white and black, with shades of gray in between. Any two colors, when mixed, will yield both a hue and a brightness intermediate between the two. Saturation of the resulting color mixture will be less than that of either of the original two colors.

Figure 4.9

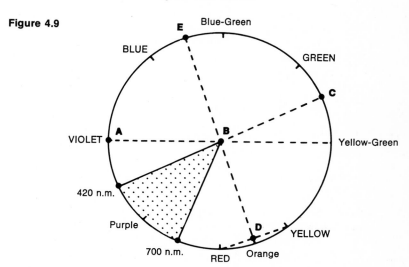

C 4.9. *The perception of color.*

Color vision depends upon _____ .

    a. wavelengths of radiation   b. wave purity

    c. intensity   d. (all of the preceding are correct)

Wavelength generally translates to an experience of _____ , wave purity to

_____ , and visible radiation intensity to _____ .

Black, white, and gray are _____ colors. Red, purple, blue, yellow and green

    are _____ colors.

Additive Color Mixture   The color circle in Figure 4.9 predicts the effects of combining wavelengths of electromagnetic radiation, called *additive color mixture*, which is not to be confused with the mixing of light-absorbing materials such as paint, called *subtractive color mixture*. Mixing two hues on the color circle will yield a hue exactly intermediate between them, but somewhat less saturated. Point *D* in the circle, for example, is an orange obtained by mixing red and yellow, but it is less saturated than an orange on the perimeter of the color circle. Hues opposite one another on the circle yield gray when mixed, and are said to be *complementary colors*. Blue-green and red are complementary colors, as are yellow and blue.

All the chromatic hues may be generated by various combinations of three hues from the color circle—a blue, a green, and a red. Since blue, green, and red mixed in various amounts can generate all other chromatic hues, but not each other, they are called *primaries*. Blue, green, and red are *additive color mixture primaries*. If you wish to mix pigments, the *subtractive color mixture primaries*, blue, yellow, and red, must be used.

C 4.10. *Color mixture.*

Combinations of wavelengths of lights is _____ color mixture, while combinations

    of paints, dyes, etc. is _____ color mixture.

Hues and brightness of color mixtures are of a value _____ .

    a. equal to the higher value of the mixture elements

    b. equal to the lower value of the mixture elements

    c. intermediate between the values of the mixture elements

Colors opposite one another on the color wheel (for example, yellow and blue) yield the hue _____

    when mixed.

Hues that yield gray when mixed are called _____ colors.

Three hues, called _____ , can be mixed to yield all other hues. The additive color

mixture primaries are _____ , _____ , and _____ . The subtractive

color mixture primaries are _____ , _____ , and _____ .

> Look at a red object for 20 seconds or more, then look at a sheet of white paper or a white wall. In a few seconds you should see a blue-green afterimage with the same shape as the inspection object. Blue-green is, of course, the complement of red. *Negative afterimages* are always seen as complements. Try using only one eye for inspection and the other eye for the afterimage. The fact that the afterimage does not then appear demonstrates that retinal processes rather than cortical processes are responsible for the effect. Try viewing the afterimage against both near and far surfaces. The size change follows the laws of geometric optics. If the inspection object was two inches high at a distance of two feet and the test surface is twice the distance, the afterimage will be four inches high. If the test surface is three times the distance of the test object, the afterimage will be three times the height of the inspection object.

C 4.11.   *Negative afterimages.*

If you should look at a vividly colored object for a half-minute, then look away at a white surface, you

will see _____ .

    a. a color approximately 100 nm. higher on the color wheel

    b. that color's complement   c. an achromatic image

A negative afterimage is clearly a _____ process.

    a. retinal   b. cortical

> If a color is surrounded by its complement, it appears more highly saturated than if surrounded by an equally bright gray. This phenomenon is called *simultaneous color contrast. Color induction* can be demonstrated by surrounding two gray patches with complementary colors. If, for example, a gray is surrounded by blue, it will look yellowish; when surrounded by yellow, it will look bluish.

C 4.12.   *Simultaneous color contrast and color induction.*

A color appears more highly _____ when surrounded by its complement.

When a chromatic hue surrounds a gray area, the gray tends to take on the appearance of the

hue's _____ .

Color Defects   Some types of color deficiencies are genetic in origin. About 8 percent of males but less than 1 percent of females have genetic color vision defects.

Most persons with a genetically determined color defect lack the normal function of erythrolabe (red) or chloralabe (green) cones. Consequently, no matter which of these two functions is missing, red-green discrimination is difficult or impossible. Weak red cone function is called *protanomaly;* completely absent red cone function is called *protanopia.* Weak green cone functioning is called *deuteranomaly;* completely absent green cone functioning is called *deuteranopia.* Weak blue cone function *(tritanomaly)* and absent blue cone function *(tritanopia)* are extremely rare, and seem to be always associated with other visual impairments.

A person with normal three-cone type function is said to be a *trichromat.* If all three cone types are present, but one is weak as in protanomaly, deuteranomaly and tritanomaly, a condition known as *anomalous trichromacy* is said to exist. Most color defects are of this type. If a person totally lacks any one of the three functions, as in deuteranopia, protanopia, and tritanopia, the condition is called *dichromacy.* Complete color blindness *(monochromacy)* is rare and can have a variety of origins including a complete absence of cone function, in which case daytime acuity is poor and normal fixation impossible because the fovea which contains only cones is devoid of functional receptors.

C 4.13. *Color vision defects.*

A person with normal color vision is a _____ .

A person with a weak function of one cone type has a condition known as _____

_____ .

A condition in which one cone type is missing is known as _____ .

The most common kind of color deficiency involves the weakness or inability to make _____ -

_____ discriminations. Such defects are _____ determined cone defects,

and occur most often in (males or females) _____ .

Diagnosis of visual color defects requires fairly sophisticated techniques. The only procedure that can detect *all* kinds of color defects involves mixing additive-primary light sources to match known standards. Color defective subjects make matches that differ from those of normal subjects. The most frequent kinds of color defects can be detected by using cards called *pseudoisochromatic plates,* on which color spots vary along the three dimensions of color—hue, saturation, and brightness. Numbers, letters, or other forms on these plates are generated by hue alone, so that color defective subjects cannot perceive the form.

Persons with visual color defects typically behave no differently from those with normal vision. The protanope and deuteranope may, in fact, call fire engines red and grass green despite the fact that they may *see* little hue difference between the two. Just because they have learned an appropriate label does not mean that they have the hue discrimination process. What a red-green-blind person actually does see was reported by a woman who was defective in one eye and normal in the other (an extraordinarily rare type). Using her defective eye, she saw red brick walls as being a muddy yellow, and green traffic lights appeared as blue.

PROGRESS CHECK 4.4

1. The sequence of nerve cells in the eye is _____ .

    a. ganglion to bipolar to simple cortical to thalamic

    b. bipolar to ganglion to simple cortical to thalamic

    c. bipolar to ganglion to thalamic to simple cortical

    d. none of the above

2. The Young-Helmholtz theory advocates the _____ theory of color vision, while the Hering theory advocates _____ complementary processes.

    a. bichromacy/identical   b. trichromacy/opposing

3. Wavelength radiation, wave purity, and intensity all affect color vision. _____ .

    a. True   b. False

MATCH: _____ 4. Brightness   A. An experience of wavelength

           _____ 5. Hue   B. An experience of intensity

           _____ 6. Saturation   C. An experience of wave purity

7. The colors experienced in early black-and-white motion pictures are _____ .

    a. chromatic   b. achromatic   c. chromonematic

8. Subtractive color mixtures are _____ .

    a. combinations of wavelengths of lights   b. combinations of blue, green, and red

    c. combinations of paints and dyes   d. combinations of various additives

9. Opposite colors on the color wheel are called _____ .

    a. complementary colors   b. additive colors   c. highly saturated colors

10. Name the additive color mixture primaries.

_____

_____

_____

11. Name the subtractive color mixture primaries.

   _____

   _____

   _____

12. A negative afterimage is _____ .

   a. always seen as a complement   b. a retinal process

   c. an image seen after viewing a vividly colored object   d. all of the preceding

13. Simultaneous color contrast occurs when _____ .

   a. red is surrounded by orange

   b. a color is surrounded by its complement

   c. a grey patch is surrounded by an achromatic hue

MATCH: _____ 14. Dichromacy   A. The absence of one cone type

          _____ 15. Trichromacy   B. The weakness of one cone type

          _____ 16. Anomalous trichromacy C. Normal cone function

17. A red-green color deficiency is _____ .

   a. most common in children   b. most common in females   c. genetically determined

---

THE NATURE OF PERCEPTION

The preceding portion of this chapter covered the topic of sensory processing or *sensation,* the complicated but fundamental receptor-to-brain neuron communication sequence. In this portion we shall discuss *perception,* which may be defined as the *immediate discriminatory response to stimulation of the energy-converting sense organs.* Perception results in part from the stimulus—specifically, the character and pattern of energy applied to the sense organs—and in part from the sensory processing system characteristics.

As important as they are, the stimulus and the sensory processing system do not operate alone in perception. Our perception of objects, people, and events involves much more. Perception also may involve a long history of experience with the environment (learning), autonomic nervous system functions (emotion), and body needs (motivation). It may be limited by the nature of the neurological system (intelligence).

For most people, perception works remarkably well almost all of the time. Chances are that you can walk through crowded hallways without bumping into other people, and you can walk up and down stairs without falling. It is likely that you can concentrate on one of several simultaneous audible conversations at parties, and you can probably shut out a variety of noises while reading a book or magazine. At times, however, you are easily distracted, and at other times your perception may bear little resemblance to objects and events in the world outside yourself. You may see objects as being different in size than they are, as faster or slower, nearer or farther, as different in color, or perhaps you even perceive something that is not there at all (a hallucination). Apparently, for most people perception is accurate and appropriately directed most of the time.

Some people, however, are extremely distractable, and some so commonly react inappropriately to stimuli that their behavior is said to be pathological. Some types of perceptual malfunctioning are clearly related to structural characteristics such as neurological damage resulting from a physical injury, from toxic substances or oxygen deprivation, or from genetically determined brain malformations. Other types of perceptual malfunctioning appear to be determined by environmental circumstances such as prolonged sensory or social isolation.

VISUAL PERCEPTION

The kind of visual stimulus that most commonly interests us is another person, a moving automobile, a steak, or some other object that absorbs some electromagnetic (light) waves, reflects others, and in a few cases, such as windows, transmits wavelengths. These stimuli do not radiate light,

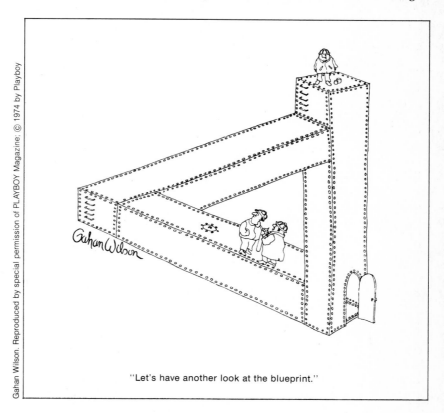

Gahan Wilson. Reproduced by special permission of PLAYBOY Magazine; © 1974 by Playboy

"Let's have another look at the blueprint."

but change the pattern of the light that illuminates them, and they are called *distal stimuli*. This term distinguishes them from light patterns received by the photoreceptors in the retina of the eye, which are termed *proximal stimuli*. The proximal stimulus, in turn, should be distinguished from what we "see" or perceive.

Suppose you are walking down a hallway toward your classroom, and you look at its closed door as you approach from an angle. The distal stimulus is the rectangular door surface. The proximal stimulus (on the retina) is a trapezoid, which changes size and shape with each step forward. What you "see," or perceive, is a rectangular door—not a series of changing trapezoids. Over a wide range of proximal stimulus changes, the *perceived* door looks the same. The tendency to perceive objects as unchanging despite proximal stimulus changes is called *perceptual constancy*. Color constancy, position constancy, and brightness constancy are types of perceptual constancy, in addition to size constancy and shape constancy. Without perceptual constancy our perceptual world would be hopelessly chaotic: An infant nearby would be perceived as a giant compared to an adult farther away, we could not recognize friends under artificial lighting, and driving an automobile or steering a bicycle would be incredibly complicated because objects would grow larger and change shape as we approached them.

C 4.14. *Basic visual-perceptual tendencies.*

Trees, automobiles, windows, dogs, and children and adults are examples of _____ stimuli, whereas the patterns of light from those objects at the receptors in the retina are _____ stimuli.

The tendency to perceive objects as unchanging despite proximal stimulus changes is called

_____ _____ .

ORGANIZATION OF VISUAL PERCEPTION Among the many questions regarding perception that need answering, in addition to how perceptual constancies develop, is how we are ever able to see *objects* rather than just a mosaic of patterns and colors. How do we learn to perceive that one object or event is the same, or is different, from another? How are we able to tell where an object is located in space? What roles do learning and motivation play in perception? From a developmental viewpoint, is perceptual organization innate or dependent upon prior experience?

No simple answers to these questions are at hand. Various theories of perception deal with some of them, but none are able to provide comprehensive explanations.

**Basic Organizational
Processes**

When your visual receptors are stimulated by a typical, everyday stimulus-complex, what you perceive is more than just a collection of unintegrated sensory elements—lines, colors, and movements. You perceive, instead, figures or objects as separated from their backgrounds. This basic perceptual process was called, by the Gestalt psychologists (to be discussed later), *figure-ground segregation.*

Stability of figure perception is dependent on change in the proximal stimulus. We mentioned earlier that the eye is in constant motion. This motion is critical to normal vision. *Absence of spatial change* will, itself, cause the disappearance of visual figures. Several investigators (for example, Pritchard, 1961) have determined that when a stopped or stabilized image is generated by special optical techniques, compensating for eye movements and fixing the image on a retinal area, entire sections of the figure tend to disappear.

The stability, in perceived space, of a simple distal stimulus is dependent upon structure or pattern in the background. A small dim light in an otherwise totally dark room will appear to move (the *autokinetic phenomenon*), but if the background is patterned, the effect diminishes until perceived movement disappears altogether.

C 4.15. *Organization of visual perception.*

A basic perceptual process by which we perceive figures rather than a collection of unintegrated

sensory elements from the entire visual field was called _____ – _____

_____ by the Gestalt psychologists.

The _____ phenomenon, in which a dim small light is perceived as moving,

illustrates the importance of surrounding structure or pattern for perceptual stability.

Figures are perceived differently from grounds. Ambiguous figures, such as the reversible figure-ground design in Figure 4.10, have been useful in demonstrating those differences. One design in Figure 4.10 may be seen as a vase or as the outlined profiles of two faces. The other may be seen as a Maltese cross or as a propeller. Both these designs illustrate two characteristic differences between *figures* and *grounds*. First, contours are associated with figures, and figures are said to have *form quality.* Contours are not perceived as part of the ground, and perceived ground is said to be *formless.* Second, figures are perceived as being in front of grounds. Look at Figure 4.10. When the darker vase is seen as the figure, the contour is attached to it, not the lighter-hued ground. When faces are seen as the figure, the contour is associated with them. Note also that when the vase is seen as the figure, the darker area appears nearer than the lighter area, but when the faces are seen as the figure, the lighter area is perceived to stand in front of the darker. Similar effects can be

Figure 4.10

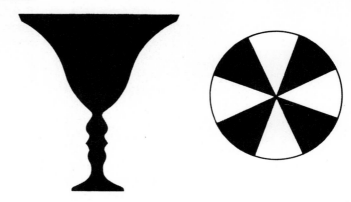

tested with the other design in Figure 4.10.

The color of stimuli perceived as figure also differs from the color of stimuli perceived as ground. The color of figures is perceived as being attached to specific objects or things. Because the color of a figure is seen as a characteristic of the surface of the perceived form, it is called *surface color*. The color of a ground, on the other hand, is objectless. It is perceived as a detached color floating at an indefinite position in space and is designated *film color*.

C 4.16. *Basic figure-ground perception.*

_____ generally perceived as being relatively formless.

   a. Figures are   b. Ground is

_____ to be perceived as being nearer.

   a. Figures tend   b. Ground tends

Background color (ground) is designated as _____ color.

   a. film   b. surface

Two-Dimensional Spatial Organization

Gestalt psychologists—a particular group heavily involved in perceptual theory—emphasized the observation that in the process of perception, under many conditions, the perceiver spontaneously groups separate distal stimulus units. Spontaneous organization of stimuli is said to follow a general principle or law called *"prägnanz"* in German, translated into English as "good figure." This means, loosely, that groupings will occur in the most economical way to form the simplest and most stable figures possible under the conditions at the time of perception. The figure ⋈, for example, is usually perceived as a diamond between parallel lines. It can also be seen as a *W* above an *M*, but it is not usually seen that way because the diamond-parallel line figure is more stable and compact

Figure 4.11

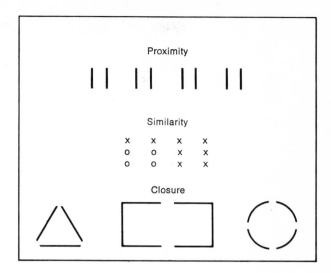

than the *W*-on-*M* figure.

The Gestalt psychologists made the general principle or law of *prägnanz* (good figure) more explicit with specific principles of perceptual organization. The most important of these are: proximity, similarity, closure, good continuation, and common fate.

The *proximity* illustration in Figure 4.11 is seen as four groups of two lines each, rather than as a single group of eight lines, indicating that groupings are formed from elements close to one another when other stimulus factors are held constant. The *x*'s and *o*'s in the *similarity* illustration are usually seen as belonging to separate subgroups within the *x* and *o* dimensions, even though they are equally separated in terms of proximity. Similar stimuli are often perceived as grouped. The triangle, rectangle, and circle (*closure* illustration in Figure 4.11) are actually three unconnected lines, a pair of brackets and group of four arcs. This illustrates a strong tendency to complete incomplete figures so that they become stable, whole and economical.

Which circle—*a*, *b*, or *c*—would you darken to complete Figure 4.12? *Good continuation* properties call for the selection of *c*. In good continuation, the arrangement of existing patterned stimuli largely determines the manner in which new stimuli will be organized.

Figure 4.12

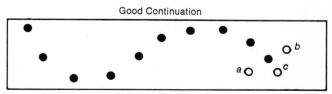

We have examined four of the five specific principles of the general principle of *prägnanz*. The fifth is *common fate*. Common fate cannot be illustrated without perceived motion. When the components of a set of stimuli appear to move together in the same direction and at the same rate, they become perceptually grouped. They are perceptually bound together by their common outcome or "fate." A motionless tiger in tall grass is unseen until he moves—then the contours and patterns "become" a tiger. Groups of lights that appear to move together around a theater marquee would be another example of common fate.

C 4.17. *Gestalt organizational principles.*

The general principle of two-dimensional spatial organization suggested by the Gestalt psychologists

    is the principle of _____ , or _____ _____ .

(Refer to the last question) This general principle means that groupings will occur in the most _____

    way to form the _____ figures possible.

    a. economical/simplest and most stable   b. complex/most elaborate   c. direct/accurate

The five *specific* principles of two-dimensional perceptual organization are _____ ,

_____ , _____ , _____ _____ , and

_____ .

Three-Dimensional Spatial Organization

One of the characteristics of normal vision that seems obvious to us is that we perceive depths. Our visual world is obviously three-dimensional. However obvious the depth of our visual environment may appear to be, it is not obvious *how* visual depth perception occurs. The retina of the human eye contains a layer of light receptors that, for all practical purposes, is a two-dimensional receptive surface. If that is so, how is it possible for us to generate a three-dimensional view? Is it a wired-in process of some sort to be explained in terms of biological variables? Is it to be explained in terms of our experience with the environment? The available evidence strongly supports the position that *both* types of variables are involved in depth perception.

Physiological Variables in Depth Perception

There are three possible physiological cues to depth. One is clearly very important: *retinal disparity*. Of lesser importance are: *convergence* and *accommodation*. We will consider these cues in an ascending order of importance.

Accommodation

In order to maintain a sharp focus of light rays on the retina, minor adjustments in the focus of the lens are made by muscles inside the eye that cause ligaments to stretch the lens or allow it to thicken. This change in lens shape is called *accommodation* (see Figure 4.13). Receptors embedded

Figure 4.13

ACCOMMODATION

Far
Object

Near
Object

in these muscles and ligaments are stimulated by the muscle and ligament action, with different patterns of feedback from such stimulation provided as the eye focuses on near and far objects, thus providing possible information about depth. Accommodation cues to depth are probably not very important for most of us, as there is no appreciable change in lens shape beyond a distance of about four feet from the eyes. They may be more important, of course, for the person who does close work requiring accurate estimates of depth such as jewelry design, dentistry, and watch repair.

Convergence

As you look at an object in the distance, your eyes are practically parallel in their lines of regard (see Figure 4.14). If you look at an object within 50 feet, however, the eyes will move inward so that the lines of regard converge. The nearer the object, the greater the convergence. *Convergence* results from action of the skeletal muscles attached to the outer surface of the eye (*extrinsic* eye muscles). Although we are not usually directly aware of this muscle movement, differential stimulation of receptors within the extrinsic eye muscles, as muscle tension changes when we look at near and far objects, provides a possible cue to the depth of the visual object.

Retinal Disparity

Because our eyes exist at two separate points in space, the right eye does not get exactly the same view as the left eye. A depth effect results from the

Figure 4.14

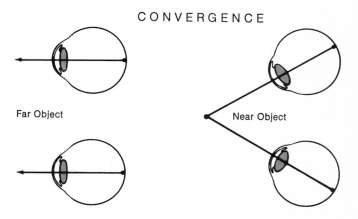

CONVERGENCE

Far Object

Near Object

neural combination (in the cortex) of these simultaneous and slightly different proximal stimulus patterns. You can easily demonstrate *retinal disparity* for yourself. Close one eye, and hold a pencil at arm's length. With the other hand, hold a different pencil a few inches from your eye so that it is in line with the other pencil. Focus on the farther pencil, then open and close each eye alternately several times. Note the apparent differences in position of the nearer pencil that result from stimulation of different portions of the two retinas. Information about depth can be gained by the use of only one eye, through accommodation, but the three-dimensional experience is more vivid when employing *stereoscopic* (two-eyed) vision.

C 4.18.   *Physiological cues to visual depth perception.*

One physiological cue to visual depth is _____ —the change in lens shape for

near and far focus that is signaled by receptors in internal eye muscles.

A second physiological cue to depth is _____ —the feedback from

_____ eye muscles as we move our eyes to look at objects 50 feet or less from us.

The most important physiological cue to depth comes from _____ _____ ,

which is the slightly variant proximal stimulus patterns on the two retinas.

Three-dimensional vision is more vivid in _____ vision than in one-eyed

(monocular) vision.

Stimulus Variables in Depth Perception   One can perceive depth quite well without vision from both eyes, although there is a loss of vividness. People with vision from only one eye successfully drive automobiles; flat photographs and paintings give clear impressions of depth, and two-dimensional motion pictures and television provide sufficient information about depth for most people. The reason that one can perceive depth in flat presentations so effectively is that our experience with the environment has consistently demonstrated that certain stimulus relationships are sure indicators of depth. A number of these *stimulus cues* to depth are presented below.

LINEAR PERSPECTIVE: Railroad tracks appear to converge in the distance, yet we know from experience that they are parallel. When we see lines converging toward the horizon, we conclude that the lines must be parallel and hence perceive depth or distance.

RELATIVE SIZE: Objects farther from us result in smaller proximal stimulus patterns than the same objects would generate if nearer. If two objects are known to be of about the same size, but one proximal stimulus is decidedly smaller than the other, we conclude that the object generating the smaller image must be the more distant of the two.

INTERPOSITION: If one object appears to cover a portion of another, we conclude from past experience that the covering object is the nearer one.

LIGHT AND SHADOW: Light comes from above in our normal visual world. As a consequence, convex objects are brighter above and darker

THE FAMILY CIRCUS, by Bil Keane.
Reprinted courtesy The Register and Tribune Syndicate.

"Look at the big plane, Jeffy!"
"That's littler than the one I got for Christmas."

below. Concave objects in contrast are dark above and light below, and we thus can interpret the direction of an indentation in the visual field.

TEXTURE GRADIENT: Objects near us appear larger and spaced farther apart than objects farther away. A gradual continuous change in the coarseness of texture (texture gradient) provides another stimulus cue to depth.

AERIAL PERSPECTIVE (haze): Objects far from us often appear to have a cloudy, blurred quality. Objects near us are usually clear. The lack of haze can lead to faulty distance estimation. Travelers viewing mountains fifty or more miles distant through dry, clear air, away from industrial pollution, often perceive the distance as being only four or five miles.

HEIGHT IN THE HORIZONTAL PLANE: Objects farther away from us appear to be above nearer objects in the visual field.

RELATIVE MOTION: Movement through the environment results in the proximal stimulus of near objects moving rapidly across the retinal surface. The proximal stimulus of farther objects maintaining what is actually an identical speed moves more slowly across the retina. This *relative* motion (or motion parallax) provides another stimulus cue to depth.

C 4.19. *Stimulus cues to visual depth perception.*

We can tell that mountains, unobscured by other terrain features, are far away by the stimulus cue called

_____   _____ .

A typical photograph of a gravel road will often appear to have depth as a result of _____

_____ , and a photograph of railroad tracks will appear to have depth as a result of

_____   _____ .

If you ride in a train and look from the window, telephone poles near the track will appear to move quickly past your view. Distant objects such as buildings or mountains will move past slowly. Your experience of depth results from the stimulus cues of relative _____ .

Motion Perception

The movements of objects in our visual fields are usually perceived appropriately as moving objects *(real motion)*. It is also possible for us to perceive motion where motion is not objectively present *(apparent motion).*

One view of how we perceive real motion is the *retinal image displacement theory*, or *inflow* theory, which holds that as the proximal image of the distal stimulus moves across the retina, new receptors are stimulated in rapid succession. This rapidly changing pattern of stimulation is interpreted by the observer as object movement.

The idea that the retina is involved in motion perception is generally accepted, but the theory carries with it the implication that the retina is immobile in normal motion perception, and that it acts only as a fixed mosaic of receptors over which light patterns flow. In truth, the eye is in constant motion, and the retina continuously scans the image of a moving object.

A more complicated view of motion perception is suggested by Gibson (1968) in his *ambient array theory* of motion perception, which places emphasis on the observer's ability to extract information from the changing light patterns reflected from surrounding objects (the ambient light array). One example of movement perception relates to the movement of an external object. In that instance, the ambient light array is transformed as the object covers and uncovers portions of the background. This changing of background is interpreted by the observer as object movement. When we ourselves move through the environment, motion is perceived in a somewhat similar manner.

Visual *apparent motion* occurs frequently in our experience. The perceived motion of lights around theater marquees, and the "motion" perceived in motion pictures and television are common examples of this phenomenon. Extensive investigation of visual apparent motion was initiated by Max Wertheimer in 1912. His famous paper on the topic launched the Gestalt theory of perception, and introduced the term *phi phenomenon* that is now used as a collective term for several simple forms of visual apparent motion. It appears that the perception of apparent motion depends on the similarity between the apparent movement stimuli and previous experienced cues of real or actual motion. Under many circumstances observers can detect no difference between the two types of perceived motion. However, certain conditions must occur for apparent motion to be perceived at all.

In the case of two alternating lights that are perceived as one moving light, the distance between the two lights, the duration of the lights, and the intensity of the lights must all fall within certain boundaries. For motion pictures and television to be seen as the equivalent of real motion, the rate that the pictures are flashed on and off, or replaced, must exceed the viewer's *critical fusion frequency* (CFF)—the rate at which flashing lights are seen as a continuous light.

C 4.20. *Motion perception.*

Perceived motion where none is present is known as _____ motion.

One view of motion perception uses the explanation of changing stimulus patterns on the retina—the _____ _____ _____ theory.

(Refer to the last answer) One criticism of this theory is that it is based on a notion of _____ .

    a. an active retina   b. a passive, or still, retina   c. learned perceptual patterns

The _____ _____ theory of motion perception places explanatory emphasis on movement in the environment.

The perceived motion of lights around theater marquees, in motion pictures and television are examples of visual _____ motion, simple types of which are usually referred to as the _____ phenomenon.

In order for motion pictures to appear as real motion, the frames must flash on and off at a rate that exceeds the viewer's _____ _____ _____ , which is the rate at which flashing lights are seen as _____ .

PROGRESS CHECK 4.5

MATCH: _____ 1. Distal stimuli   A. Animals, food, trees

           _____ 2. Proximal stimuli   B. Patterns of light reflected from objects

3. The tendency to perceive objects as unchanging despite proximal stimulus changes is called _____ .

    a. color constancy   b. perceptual constancy   c. brightness constancy

4. Figure-ground segregation is a perceptual process where _____ .

    a. one perceives objects as unchanging

    b. one perceives objects as separate from backgrounds

    c. one perceives objects as having movement

    d. one perceives objects as stable

5. Figures tend to be perceived as being both nearer than grounds and relatively formless. _____ .

    a. True   b. False

6. The principle of *prägnanz* (good figure) is _____ .

    a. the principle of two-dimensional spatial organization

    b. the principle of common fate

7. Name the five *specific* principles of two-dimensional perceptual organization.

_____

_____

_____

_____

_____

8. The principle of *prägnanz* means that groupings will occur in the most complex way to form the most elaborate figures possible. _____ .

    a. True   b. False

MATCH: _____ 9. Stereoscopic vision   A. The change in lens shape

               _____ 10. Accommodation   B. Feedback from extrinsic eye muscles

               _____ 11. Convergence   C. Absence of one cone type

               _____ 12. Retinal disparity   D. Variant proximal stimulus patterns

                                                    E. Two-eyed vision

13. Relative size, linear perspective, texture gradient, and relative motion are all examples of _____ .

    a. accommodation   b. the autokinetic phenomenon

    c. stimulus cues to depth   d. all of the preceding

14. Simple types of apparent motion are referred to as the _____ .

    a. phi phenomenon   b. retinal image displacement theory   c. ambient array theory

15. In order for flashing lights to appear continuous, their rate must exceed the _____ .

    a. ambient light array   b. critical fusion frequency

HEARING (AUDITION)   We have made the point that vision is the sense through which the typical human being gains most of his information concerning what is going on around him. This is, of course, somewhat a value judgment, and anyone would agree that other major senses—hearing, touch, taste, smell, kinesthesis—are important for effective functioning. Space does not permit a discussion of each major sensory system in the same detail as we have done with vision. Although each system is totally independent in the nature

Figure 4.15

DIAGRAM OF THE EAR

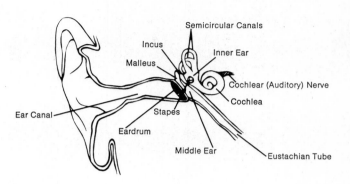

of its receptors and theories, certain general similarities exist in how distal stimulus patterns are translated into neurological codes that are then interpreted by relevant areas of the brain. A detailed description of another sensory perception process will help to establish the basic pattern of sensory perception, and we have chosen to include hearing in this chapter.

As you may already know, the stimulus for hearing is a physical phenomenon known as the sound wave. Sound waves generally are measured in cycles per second (cps.), and frequencies between 15 cps. and 20,000 cps. are usually thought of as comprising the auditory range for human beings. Sound waves are collected by the shell-shaped structure of the outer ear, which is formed in such a way as to funnel the sound waves down the ear canal toward the eardrum (tympanic membrane). At that point, the vibration of sound waves stimulates a corresponding vibration within the biological structure itself.

Translation of sound-wave vibration into the process of physiological response starts at the eardrum (see Figure 4.15). The physical buffeting produced by the sound waves sets the eardrum in motion at approximately the same frequency in cps. The vibratory movement of the eardrum is then transmitted to an adjacent three-bone complex—the malleus (hammer), incus (anvil), and stapes (stirrup). (The names in parentheses are often given to these bones because of their general shape.) The most interior of these bones, the stapes, is attached to a membrane which then makes contact with the heavy fluid of the inner ear, and sets this fluid in motion. The waves created by the motion of the fluid have a vital function.

Inside the inner ear is a very small structure with a snail-like appearance called the *cochlea* (see Figure 4.16). It contains the auditory receptors. The cochlea is extremely complex, with many important fine structural details. It is shaped in the form of a curled up tube, divided down the center of its interior by the basilar membrane, thus forming two channels. The basilar membrane contains sensory cells which respond

Figure 4.16

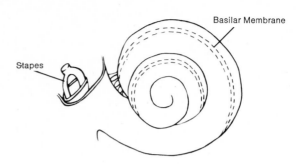

ENLARGED VIEW OF THE COCHLEA

Basilar Membrane

Stapes

to vibratory stimuli. The pressure of the waves from the inner ear fluid, traveling up one channel of the cochlea, stimulates tiny hair cells that are synaptically connected to the fibers of the auditory (*cochlear*) nerve itself, and thus the neurological component of hearing is created. The other channel in the cochlea functions as a pressure equalization area, and its open space provides a place for the vibration of the basilar membrane to occur.

C 4.21. *Physical processes in hearing.*

Sound wave frequencies comprising the normal range of the human hearing are from _____

to _____ cps.

It would be proper to say that sound waves _____ .

   a. create vibration in the biological structure

   b. are responded to directly by the receptors

The auditory receptors are to be found in the _____ .

   a. stapes   b. tympanic membrane   c. cochlea

Qualities of Auditory Sensation While a number of other measures of a given sound exist, most basic research has concentrated on the qualities of *loudness* and *pitch*.

Loudness is a perceptual phenomenon resulting from the intensity of the sound wave. The more forceful the sound waves' impressions on the eardrum, the greater the physical displacement of the eardrum in its vibrations, which are passed on to the tiny bone complex, all of which is reflected in the physical manifestations of the inner ear. Sound intensity is usually measured in units called decibels.

Pitch is a perceptual impression resulting from the frequency, in cps., of the sound waves. The higher pitches correspond to higher values in cps. As we mentioned before, frequencies of 20,000 cps. can be perceived by a large percentage of human beings, but by middle age most adults have begun to lose much of their ability to detect sounds at the higher frequencies. Within a few more years, it is common to see frequencies of around 15,000 cps. as the upper limit of perception for some people. This is why a young person sometimes grows impatient with an older mechanic who cannot hear the high-pitched squeak in an automobile that is quite easily perceived by its young owner.

Auditory Theory The so-called "theory of loudness perception" is quite simple and straight-forward. First, a large number of receptor cells in the cochlea will fire in response to a loud sound, and receptors with high thresholds as well as those with low thresholds will also respond. Additionally, as each cell returns toward its normal threshold after firing, and passes through its refractory period, an intense sound causes it to fire almost immediately. Thus each individual receptor cell fires at a higher rate when the stimulus is intense.

Pitch discrimination is a more difficult perceptual problem to unravel, and it is concerning this problem that a number of formal theories have developed. One school, comprising a group of major theories, is called *place theory*. This general approach maintains that pitch is determined by the exact place in the cochlea that is stimulated by a given sound frequency. This notion is related to the physical phenomenon of sympathetic vibration of tuning forks, piano strings, and so forth, when a note of an exact matching frequency is sounded.

Place theory also holds that different sections of the cochlea respond to different levels of pitches. There is considerable support for the position that high tones are perceived at early points in the cochlear spiral, low tones are perceived at the more interior points within the cochlea, and intermediate tones in the intervening regions. Place theory, in its various forms, has an attraction due to its simplicity, but most scientists have by now rejected the notion in its pure form. There is too much evidence that neurological fibers coming from a specific place within the cochlea are interwoven with other fibers, and that a given sound wave frequency actually sets into action a wide assortment of receptors along the cochlea.

A second major auditory theory, called the *frequency theory*, supposes that the literal frequency, in cps., of the sound wave is transmitted through the receptors at the same response rate per second to the nerve fibers. The weakest point in this theory is its interpretation of how we hear the highest audible frequencies. It is known that the mammalian nerve fiber can transmit no more than 1,000 impulses per second, and specific research on auditory neurons suggests a maximum rate no higher than 400 impulses per second (Galambos & Davis, 1948).

An important principle relating to auditory theory was established by Wever and Bray in several studies, starting in 1930. Using an anesthetized cat, they studied impulses from the cat's auditory nerve, which were fed into an ordinary telephone receiver, thereby enabling the experimenters to hear the same "tone" that was being applied to the cat's ear. During the experiments the cat experienced stimulus frequencies that reached the level of sound that the experimenters heard as 4,000 cps.

The question immediately arose as to how a cat's nerve could carry these high frequencies if the component neurons could carry only relatively low frequencies. The experimenters arrived at a theoretical answer that they termed the *volley principle*. In essence the principle is that, while an individual neuron cannot match in impulse the higher cps. stimulus values, the neurological system can function in a coordinated style, arranging a sequential firing of a number of neurons in volleys. Assuming a sequential firing, one can see that ten individual neurons, each with a capacity of 400 cps., could accurately reflect in an exact physical counterpart an incoming stimulus of 4,000 cps. That is, 4,000 cps. would be going into the auditory system, and the same neurological signals per second would be carried by the auditory nerve, though not by any single neuron within the auditory nerve.

Auditory theorists consider that the volley principle fairly well accounts for a variety of the data that have been amassed, and in fact there is good support for this principle at the lower frequency values, but experts consider that the principle still does not explain the ways in which we can perceive the highest audible frequencies.

The formal *volley theory* was proposed by Wever (1949), and is sometimes described as a "place-volley" theory in that it includes elements of the place theory. As we have stated, the volley principle breaks down at high frequencies, and the place theory breaks down especially at low frequencies, which seem to stimulate extensive regions of the cochlea. The formal volley theory proposes that high tonal frequencies are signaled by the place in the cochlea that is stimulated, and that low frequencies are signaled by volley sequences in the auditory nerve. The theory assumes that a combination of both kinds of signals explains the perception of intermediate frequencies. Wever's theory submits that the place effect is evident at frequencies down to approximately 400 cps. and that the volley principle has an effect up to about 5,000 cps. Both factors work in interaction in the region between 400 and 5,000 cps.

One important piece of evidence in favor of a place theory was provided through research by Wever and Smith (1944), who subjected guinea pigs to extremely intense pure tone stimuli for several minutes. The animals were subsequently sacrificed, and their cochleas were examined by microscope. It was found that high pure tones injured the cochlear area near the beginning of the ascending canal, while lower tones injured areas higher in the ascending canal.

C 4.22. *Auditory theory.*

A theory that a specific point in the cochlea responds to a specific sound wave frequency is called

_____ theory.

A theory that a stimulus of 100 cps. would set up neurological firing at 100 cps. is called _____

_____ theory.

A combination of the two formal theories just discussed resulted in the _____ theory.

Auditory Acuity

Auditory acuity is measured by the minimum sound intensity necessary to evoke some auditory perception by the subject. However, tonal frequency has been demonstrated to be an important interacting variable. That is, different intensities of stimulus are usually necessary, in a single individual, for perception of different tonal frequencies.

Measurement of sound intensity is generally carried out in terms of bels and decibels (db), the latter being one-tenth of a bel. This logarithmic unit of measure (the bel) was introduced by telephone engineers, and we shall indicate some of the everyday sound equivalents in decibels so that you may acquire a comfortable understanding of what these units mean. A just noticeable whisper is usually calculated at around 10 db, the inside of a quiet automobile at about 50 db, the sound on a busy street at around 70 db, the sound made by an elevated train moving overhead at 90 db, and the sound generated by a nearby airplane engine at 110 db.

Using these terms and cycles per second, we present, for the general population, the median stimulus intensity level necessary for threshold perception as a function of the stimulus frequency. It has been found that most human beings are usually perceptive of stimuli in the neighborhood of 3,000 cps., with the median stimulus intensity for threshold being around 8 db. The intensity necessary to meet threshold requirements, in relation to frequency, rises in a fairly linear fashion to a value of around 32 db as stimulus frequency increases to around 10,000 cps. On the other end of the scale, the minimum stimulus intensity necessary for threshold responding rises to around 15 db at stimulus frequencies in the neighborhood of 20 or 25 cps.

Defects in Auditory Acuity

Defects in auditory acuity are generally of two major types, the first of these being known as conduction deafness, and the second being termed nerve deafness. From our earlier description of the anatomy of the hearing mechanism, you can easily visualize how the small bone structures in the middle ear might become relatively immobilized, so that they do not easily vibrate. This is the essence of conduction deafness, and generally the degree of hearing loss is constant for all frequencies within the normal limits of hearing perception. Treatment of this form of deafness can be carried out through surgery, or the problem may be approached by means of an amplifying hearing aid, which almost always compensates for this form of hearing loss. Nerve deafness is caused by a different problem, and this form of deafness results in a markedly greater hearing loss for the higher tonal frequencies. There is no known cure for this form of deafness.

C 4.23.   *Auditory acuity.*

A proper statement would be that human beings _____ .

   a. are about equally sensitive to all sound frequencies

   b. are most sensitive to very low sound frequencies (around 20-50 db)

   c. are most sensitive to very high sound frequencies (above 10,000 db)

   d. are most sensitive to intermediate sound frequencies

ATTENTION   *Attention* is a result of the perceptual process being selective—not all stimuli in the environment are perceived simultaneously or with equal clarity. Learning, motivational, and stimulus variables have all been linked with attention.

Perception is an *active process* rather than a passive one, and the past history of the organism (learning) often plays a significant role in what is selected for perception in the environment. This behavioral tendency to respond to stimuli in terms of previous experience is called *perceptual set,* and is common in everyday life. A shoe salesman is likely to attend closely to other people's shoes, and a photography buff will probably look closely at cameras being carried by other people.

Motivational states play a role in determining which stimuli are attended to. Food odors and pictures of food that go unnoticed most of the time may dominate attention after prolonged food deprivation.

There are also those properties of *stimuli* that direct attention. In general this is called the *contrast effect,* and may be determined by differences in brightness, hue, saturation, motion, direction, or speed. Advertising often takes advantage of these effects. A blank newspaper page, for example, with only a few lines in the middle will draw attention far more than most other printed material. A restaurant or night club, barely noticed previously, may suddenly be vividly perceived by almost all passers-by following the installation of an electric sign conveying the illusion of movement. Contrast effects are used effectively in musical theater productions when the star wears a costume different from that of the chorus; and only the bride wears white at the wedding. The degree of contrast effect is partly a function of the degree of difference between figure and ground. The enterprising jeweler is careful to display his diamond against an extremely dark non-reflective background to increase perceived brightness. And recently "Dear Abby," in her newspaper column, heard from a young bride-to-be who was concerned about the remark of one of her chosen bridesmaids that she was going to alter her gown to make it low-cut and revealing. (The distress of the bride obviously involved who becomes "figure," in more ways than one.)

C 4.24.   *Attention.*

Which of the following general types of variables have all been linked with attention? _____ .

a. learning   b. motivational states

c. stimulus variables   d. (all of the preceding answers are true)

PERCEPTUAL DEVELOPMENT   The question of how perception develops has been, to psychologists, a matter of great theoretical and research interest. Psychologists are interested in both *ontogenetic development* (in the individual) and *phylogenetic development* (evolutionary development from lower levels of species to higher). A fair amount of early research was done in the vain hope of settling the nativism-empiricism, or nature-nurture, controversy. The issue is not entirely dead even now, but most psychologists today take the position that all mature human behavior results from interactions between genetically endowed biological structure and environmental experiences.

Investigative work considered to relate to human perceptual development can actually be performed on adults rather than children. Two examples will suffice. Senden (1960) collected case histories of persons with congenital (present at birth) eye cataracts who had them removed when adults. These persons were immediately able to make figure-ground discriminations, suggesting that those discriminations are innate perceptual skills. On the other hand, form discrimination, even between simple figures such as circles and triangles, developed slowly.

Another type of study with adults was first conducted by Stratton in the 1890s, and later by a number of other researchers—most of them either American or Austrian. The usual procedure first calls for subjects to wear lenses that alter the proximal stimulus by inverting it, displacing it, distorting it, or discoloring it. Subjects are then tested to determine whether or not the distorted visual world eventually becomes "normal" after a period of lens-wearing. Adaptation to the altered image is usually excellent after time and experience. Equally interesting is the fact that re-adapting back to the "real" world is not immediate; subjects require time and experience after the lenses are removed. Data from these two types of studies have often been interpreted to indicate that perception is built slowly through interaction with the environment. But other interpretations are also possible, such as the slow adaptation for the adult does not necessarily mean that the process is equally slow for the child nor that an identical developmental-adaptational perceptual process is employed by children.

C 4.25.   *Perceptual development.*

Senden established that _____ discrimination is apparently innate, and not dependent upon experience or learning.

a. form   b. figure-ground

If one were to feel circles and triangles as raised designs on paper, then be able to see them as an adult for the first time, one _____ recognize visual stimuli depicting circles, triangles, and so forth.

a. would   b. would not

One study, conducted by Wayne Dennis in Iran on foundling-home children, found that extreme perceptual deprivation in infants, resulting from their having lived all their lives in perceptually sterile settings, is related to deficiencies in later abilities to learn, to perform motor skills, and to interact appropriately. A number of animal perceptual deprivation experiments have resulted in similar conclusions.

A number of ingenious investigations have sought to determine basic visual skills in infants. One such study by Fantz (1963) took advantage of the fact that infants prefer visual fields with figure over those without figure. Thus, a gray card with the same average brightness as another card with alternating black and white lines is looked at by an infant less than is the striped card, but only if the infant's visual acuity allows discrimination of the spacing between the lines. Using a variety of line widths, Fantz was able to determine that infant visual acuity develops more rapidly than most researchers had previously thought possible, with fairly good acuity even at one month of age.

A large number of interesting investigations on perceptual development in animals have been conducted, many on the specific effects of various types of perceptual deprivation. Held and Hein (1963) were interested in determining whether or not self-initiated movement is important in the development of visual motor performance. Ten pairs of kittens were deprived of visual experience from birth, except for a daily routine in which each pair was placed in a cylindrical drum with vertical stripes painted on the inside surface (Figure 4.17). One kitten was free to walk around the drum in either direction and to look about as he did so. The other was supported by a gondola propelled by the free kitten and could look only in the direction determined by the movements of the first kitten. The active member of each kitten-pair was clearly superior in later depth-perception test performance, visually guided paw-placement training, and eye-blink response to an approaching object.

C 4.26. *Effects of perceptual deprivation.*

A study by Dennis showed that children reared in perceptually sterile environments were _____ .

   a. quite deficient in their abilities to learn and perform motor activities

   b. scarcely handicapped at all in adjusting to performance demands

In Held and Hein's gondola experiment, kittens that had been allowed self-initiated motion were clearly superior to kittens who had not in the later _____ -perception test performance.

Figure 4.17

PERCEPTUAL THEORY:

Nativism Versus Empiricism

It is the role of perceptual theory to explain observations concerning perceptual organization, and predict new ones. No such theory is completely adequate, but all may contribute to our understanding and may stimulate research. Most theories in psychology rest on one of two philosophical bases—either nativism or empiricism.

Gestalt theory, mentioned earlier, fits into a philosophical position called *nativism*, which states that certain organizational patterns of thinking, and thus to an extent the forms taken by knowledge, are innate and predetermined. A polar opposite is the position of *empiricism*, which asserts that all knowledge is acquired—"We know nothing that has not come to us through our senses." Empiricism has been the philosophical base for a number of theories of perception, most of which can be traced back to the philosopher Bishop Berkeley, or to the physicist-physiologist Hermann von Helmholtz. Berkeley contended that visual perception develops under the tutelage of active touch—we must feel before we see. Helmholtz took the position that raw sensory input is compared with previous sensory inputs and ideas, and that a perception then occurs by unconscious inference. The basic idea is that simple sensory input is elaborated upon by some internal process, and perception arises from the two. The main perceptual question that persons taking such positions ask is, "How is perception built from sensations?"

Gestalt Theory   Probably the main assertion of the Gestalt school of perception was the importance given to the *whole,* the *pattern,* the *configuration,* or *"Gestalt"* as it is called in German. Psychologists of that school pointed out that a pattern is not a mere piecemeal summation of parts, but a process dominated by characteristics of the whole. A melody played in one key on a piano, for example, is easily recognized when played in another key, despite the fact that the notes are not the same. A face, they point out, is more than a mere aggregate of eyes, nose, mouth, and so forth. It is dominated by its overall configuration, and not by its parts. Hence, "The whole is more than the sum of its parts."

It is interesting to note that the Gestalt psychologists felt that the principles of perceptual organization (discussed earlier in this chapter) apply to all psychological functions, including learning, memory, and cognition (thinking).

C 4.27.   *Gestalt theory.*

Gestalt theory, insofar as perceptual organization is concerned, could be called _____ .

   a. nativistic   b. empiricist

Gestalt psychologists suggested that the same principles apply to psychological functions other than

   perception, including _____ , _____ , and _____ .

The word *"Gestalt"* can be translated into English as _____ , _____ , or

_____ .

Empiricist   Several contemporary theories of perception have features derived from
Perceptual   Berkeley's older theory. One is the *neuropsychological theory* of D. O. Hebb,
Theories   the Canadian psychologist who proposed that visual perception of objects and space is built slowly through the active touch sense and eye movements which the perceiver relates to retinal stimulation patterns. These three factors (touch, eye movement, retinal stimulus patterns) are related or joined in brain tissue as the specific cell combinations (cell assemblies) are simultaneously or sequentially activated. Eventually, then, just retinal stimulation alone causes all three cell assemblies to activate. Several other "motor-copy" perceptual theories differ from Hebb's theory in that they use nonphysiological learning theory explanations for the developing active-touch/eye-movement/retinal-stimulus pattern relationship.

Among the modern perceptual theories derived from Helmholtz is *probabilistic functionalism.* This theory of Egon Brunswick takes the position that every perception is an involuntary bet about what the distal stimulus might be. Brunswick (1953) suggested that we base our "bets" on the basis of probabilities. The trapezoidal proximal stimulus pattern that we receive as we walk down the hallway has been confirmed to be a rectangular door in the past, so we involuntarily "bet" that the present similar pattern is a door on this occasion too.

C 4.28. *Empiricist-perceptual theories.*

Hebb's contemporary theory of perception is _____ .

    a. neuropsychological   b. an empiricist-perceptual theory

    c. accepted by most psychologists as true   d. (two of the preceding answers are true)

A theory which assumes that individuals perceive according to what a stimulus "probably means,"

    relating to probabilities established through past experiences, is _____ .

    a. nativistic   b. probabilistic functionalism   c. empirical-physiological

A Stimulus-Oriented Theory

A novel theory of perception has recently been developed by James Gibson (1966) and his wife, Eleanor Gibson (1969), who believe that the question, "How do we build perceptions from sensations?" is the wrong question to ask in perceptual theory. They suggest that all the information the individual needs to know about distal stimuli is contained in the stimulus pattern of light coming from objects and events. Objects and events reflect light in highly structured ways. What the individual must do is learn to pick out the constant features in the changing proximal stimulus pattern. In the case of vision, James Gibson says there are three main structural features in ambient light (visible radiations reflected from distal stimuli) that are received: *layout structuring, pigment structuring,* and *illuminatedness structuring.*

Layout structuring refers to the characteristics of surfaces, or faces, of objects. The convexities and concavities of surfaces, large or small, change the pattern of light illuminating them to give us layout information. Such structuring allows us to determine, visually, the slope of a mountain, to see two walls as being perpendicular to one another, or to read an embossed calling card. When the surfaces of the distal stimuli are small facets, we are also provided with texture information.

Pigment structuring refers to the differential amount of absorption and reflection of light that many surfaces give us (for example, a stained wood-grain table top absorbs more light in the dark areas than in the light). There may also be selective reflection of wavelength (chromatic color), as in a color photograph.

Illuminatedness structuring might be called shadowing, and refers to both *attached* shadows (for example, the shadow of a tree which is attached to the tree which formed it), and the *casting* of shadows (for example, the pattern on a brick wall cast by laundry hanging on a line between the sun and the wall). The individual can derive more "meaning" from a complex visual stimulus with accompanying natural shadows than one without.

The Gibsons contend that perception is learned, and what we learn is to differentiate between patterns—to discriminate. All we need in order to differentiate, they say, is experience. An example of such learning might be found in the case of a beginning medical student. At first the sounds made by different hearts seem very much the same, but with experience the student can differentiate the heart with leaking valves from "normal" heart sounds. Perceptual discrimination skill apparently can reach the level of virtuosity as in an example given by William James, the famous American psychologist, who wrote of a woman employed in a large institution who could determine the ownership of the *washed* laundry by odor.

C 4.29.   *The Gibsons' theory of perception.*

The Gibsons' theory of perception stresses _____ structuring, which is determined by the surface of objects, _____ structuring, which is determined by the many differential patterns of _____ and _____ of light by an object, and _____ structuring, which is determined by the pattern of attached _____ and cast _____ .

The Gibsons contend that perceptual discriminations are _____ .

    a. learned   b. innate

PROGRESS CHECK   4.6

1. Learning, motivational and stimulus variables are all linked with attention. _____ .

    a. True   b. False

2. Figure-ground discrimination is _____ .

    a. learned   b. innate

3. Which of the following is *not* affected by a perceptually sterile environment? _____ .

    a. The ability to learn   b. The ability to interact appropriately

    c. The ability to make figure-ground discriminations

    d. The ability to perform motor skills

4. Self-initiated motion apparently _____ .

    a. increases abilities of depth-perception   b. decreases abilities of depth-perception

5. What does the word *Gestalt* mean in English? _____ .

    a. The pattern   b. The whole   c. The configuration   d. All of the preceding

6. Gestalt theory could be called empiricist. _____ .

    a. True   b. False

7. Empiricism is the theory that _____ .

    a. all knowledge is acquired   b. all knowledge is innate

    c. knowledge is a combination of the innate and the acquired

8. Gestalt psychologists believe that the principles of perceptual organization apply also to learning, memory, and thinking _____ .

    a. True   b. False

9. Hebb's theory of perception is _____ .

    a. neuropsychological   b. nonphysiological

10. The definition: "The theory that every perception is an involuntary bet based on probabilities, established through past experiences, about what the distal stimulus might be," describes _____ .

    a. the probabilistic functionalism theory

    b. Hebb's theory

    c. the stimulus-oriented theory

MATCH: _____ 11. Layout structuring

    A. Refers to the pattern of attached shadows and that of shadows cast

    _____ 12. Illuminatedness structuring

    B. Refers to the differential amount of absorption and reflection of light

    _____ 13. Pigment structuring

    C. Refers to characteristics of surface or faces of objects

14. The Gibsons' theory suggests that perception is _____ .

    a. innate   b. learned

CONCLUSION   Perception is the area of psychology that has the largest history and has more detailed research data than almost any other area. Only a small sample of the information in the field could be surveyed in this chapter. The student who would like to pursue an interest in perception will find many excellent books available, written at a level appropriate for a person who has completed a single psychology course.

    There are several very good general books on perception—among them, *Principles of Perception* by S. Howard Bartley (1969). If you wish to give attention to only vision and audition, Gerald Murch's (1973) *Visual and Auditory Perception* is, available in a paperback edition. *Perception in Everyday Life,* written by S. Howard Bartley (1972), is an unusual and interesting paperback. Of similar appeal is the paperback that contains three-dimensional stereo illustrations and discusses depth perception at length—*The Intelligent Eye,* by R. L. Gregory (1970).

Scientific Procedure
in Psychology

SOURCES OF KNOWLEDGE

FOUNDATIONS OF SCIENCE
    Variables
    The Psychologist's Variables
        S (stimulus) Variables
        O (organismic) Variables
        R (response) Variables
    Relating the Psychologist's Variables

THE TWO QUESTIONS IN RESEARCH
    What Do You Mean?
        Advantages of Operational Definitions
    How Do You Know?
        A Typical Problem

MAJOR RESEARCH STRATEGIES
    The Experimental Method
    The Survey Method
    A Comparison of the Methods

STATISTICAL METHODS: REPRESENTATION OF DATA
    Graphic Representation

MEASURES OF CENTRAL TENDENCY
    The Mean
    The Median
    The Mode
    Advantages of Each of the Measures
    Central Tendency Expressed in Distribution
        Curves
        Shapes of Curves

MEASURES OF VARIABILITY

MEASURES OF RELATIONSHIP: THE CORRELATION COEFFICIENT
    Linear Relationship Shown Graphically
    Nonlinear Relationship Shown Graphically
    A Formula to Calculate the Degree of
        Correlation

Psychology has been defined as the *science of the behavior of organisms*. It is appropriate to point out that there are three very important words in the definition. First, "science" implies that the scientific method is employed in seeking knowledge. We shall examine the scientific method shortly. Second, "behavior" is defined as some observable action of an organism—it is highly important that the psychologist concentrate on those actions that can be clearly observed and systematically measured. Finally, the word "organisms" denotes that the subjects in a psychologist's research program may be human beings or infrahuman (below the phylogenetic level of the human being) organisms. We shall have occasion to return to these points as we go on, so it would be well to keep them in mind.

C 5.1. *The definition of psychology. (See chapter introduction on previous page.)*

Psychology is defined as the _____ of the _____ of

_____ .

Behavior is a term that refers only to the _____

actions of an organism.

SOURCES OF KNOWLEDGE   Science is only one of several methods people employ in order to understand the phenomena around them. We can list the ways in which people tend to understand the various aspects of life. First, many human beings *rely on authority*. We are taught as youngsters to trust our parents. In nonliterate cultures elders were looked to for their wisdom concerning the crops, the hunt, and making war. Adults in our own culture often go first to "experienced" relatives or friends for advice on child-rearing, their health, and so forth. Seeking others' authoritative advice is a convenient way to solve many of the problems that confront us. In some matters the help offered by relatives and friends is insufficient, so for "knowledge" of death, the meaning of existence, and such philosophical matters, man tends to seek even higher authoritative sources. Thus, we see religion as an authoritative source of answers for many individuals, while others turn to books written by philosophers.

A second main source of knowledge is *reasoning*. Often, individuals are able to use their own rational processes to figure out things in ways that make sense to them. Obviously there may be a number of mutually contradictory explanations for some events, each of which can be logically supported. I remember a particularly interesting example of this in a woman who operated a small store along a highway in the mountains of southeastern Kentucky. It was summer, and I remarked that it was a lot cooler than it had been the day before. "Yes," the woman replied, "it must have hailed somewhere." That remark demonstrated a sort of logical cause-and-effect supposition, but was far from being valid as an explanation of cold air masses. Unfortunately, we do a lot of this as we seek to understand. If we want to know why children are aggressive or tell lies that glorify themselves, we may try to think through the logical reasons why they might do so, and we try to apply some vague memory of our own similar behavior, and we are often wrong. As man's reliance on authority decreases somewhat with his advancing education, he tends to rely more on reasoning, but with only marginal effectiveness.

C 5.2. *Man's nonscientific ways of gaining knowledge.*

In man's search for knowledge, two of his *non*scientific sources are reliance on _____

and reliance on _____ .

We cannot state that reliance on nonscientific sources of knowledge always produces error—far from it. What we do say, however, is that an alternative approach—the scientific method—is available for the investigation of most questions, and it offers the most powerful method available for understanding ourselves and the universe around us.

FOUNDATIONS OF SCIENCE

The basic foundation of science is *controlled observation* by the scientist. (Later you will see what is meant by "control.") An important characteristic of a scientist's observations is that they are directed toward events that are *publicly observable*. This means that observations by the scientist could be repeated exactly (this is called "replication of research") and in this manner verified by any trained and properly equipped observer. If research cannot be replicated, it is not considered to be legitimate science.

In the very earliest stages of any science, scientists merely observed, made notes, and perhaps were able to put events into categories through classification of similarities and differences. Every science has such a first stage, and this is called the stage of *description*. The second stage of science is *prediction,* in which the scientist, on the basis of earlier systematic observations, is able to predict that certain future events will occur under given conditions; within this stage, one finds the steps of verification of the predictions and refinement of subsequent predictions. The third stage that sciences strive toward is the stage of *control,* in which the scientist actually enters the ongoing process and changes conditions in order to manipulate outcomes deliberately.

Spitzer. APA Monitor, August 1971. Reprinted by permission.

"Four years of research, and now you tell me you forgot which is the control group!"

C 5.3. *The basic structure of scientific development.*

The basic foundation of a science is _____ .

    a. its theories   b. its proofs   c. controlled observation

In order to be considered scientific, a scientist's observations must be of a nature such that they

    can be _____ .

    a. repeated and verified by other scientists

    b. expressed within formulas

    c. fit into existing theoretical frameworks

The three stages of every science are

    1. _____ .

    2. _____ .

    3. _____ .

In the third stage of scientific development, the scientist enters the ongoing process and attempts

    deliberately to _____ .

    a. predict outcomes   b. manipulate outcomes   c. prove existing theories

A science such as astronomy would at present be described as having advanced to the stage of _____ .

    a. description   b. prediction   c. control

So far what we have been saying is mainly common sense and corresponds quite well to the everyday understandings most people have concerning science. Beyond this, however, is a large background of procedural developments, all of which are important and most of which may seem at least a bit unfamiliar. We will proceed now to the general topic of scientific method.

Variables   In the behavioral sciences, we are interested in the investigation of the *relationships between variables*. Essentially what we seek is an answer to the question: "What caused a certain event to occur?" Secondarily, we wish to determine exactly how values of certain variables relate to the values of others.

A *variable* is anything that varies in an observable and measurable way. Typically an event that we call a variable ranges from nonoccurrence through moderate values of intensity, duration, or the like, up to extreme, high values.

We might study the relationship of two variables which we shall call A and B. If we establish that there is a predictive relationship such that knowing the value of A we can more accurately predict the level of B, then we say that a *functional relationship* exists, $B=f(A)$, stated "B is a function of *A*." We could establish, for example, that the more time one spends studying (variable *A*), the higher will be the grade on an examination (variable *B*).

Functional relationships involve what are called *independent* and *dependent* variables. In the model *B* =*f(A), B* is the dependent variable. You might consider that the grade on the examination (variable *B*) is *dependent upon* the amount of studying, hence is the *dependent* variable. In turn, the variable *upon which* it depends is then termed the independent variable (variable *A*).

Actually, there are two main types of functional relationships. There are those *cause-and-effect* relationships, where variable *A* actually brings about variable *B*. The typical criteria are that the independent variable (or variables in case there is more than a single one) is both *necessary* and *sufficient* to change the value of the dependent variable.

Then there are those cases where *B* is said only to be a *predictive function* of *A*. In these cases we are indicating that while *A may cause B*, we are reserving such a definite statement and are merely stating that knowledge of the value of *A* allows one to predict the level of *B* to a degree better than chance. It can be shown, for example, that students who miss a large number of classes make lower grades on subsequent examinations than do students who miss few if any classes. Still, it does not necessarily follow that the act of missing classes actually causes lower grades. It might well be that the variation in the dependent variable is introduced by the two factors "motivation" and "ability." An informal study recently established that students in a large class who are in the bottom quartile (25 percent) in regularity of attendance study fewer hours in preparation for a formal examination than does the other 75 percent of the class. Also, the average of the scores of the bottom quartile on college-entrance examinations was significantly lower than the average for the other 75 percent. In this example you can see that we are not stating that class absence *causes* lower grades when we say that grades are a predictive function of (can be predicted from) the rate of absence from class.

If we can establish that the value of *B* can be predicted from knowledge of the value of *A*, we are then in a position to make predictions that may be of considerable value, and we may even be in a position to suggest changes in independent variables in the hopes that dependent variable values may be predictably affected. If we determine a relation between examination grades and the amount of time spent studying, we might then realistically give advice concerning study habits.

Consider the relation that might exist between depression and nervousness on the one hand, and drug use among adolescents on the other. Such a strong relationship was reported by Fejer and Smart (1972) in Ontario. Adolescents who had high scores on a test of manifest anxiety and who admitted having been repeatedly depressed through their developing years were found to rank much higher in the use of opiates and amphetamines than were adolescents with lower anxiety scores and fewer past depressions. The functional relationship that was established indicates that, knowing the anxiety level and emotional history of a given individual, one can predict with better than chance accuracy whether the individual may become involved in drug use. The personality characteristic of anxiety and depression is the independent variable, and drug use is the dependent variable.

It is important that you be able to recognize variables as being either dependent or independent and also understand the abstract definitions of those terms. An *independent variable* is one that is either directly manipulated by the scientist or is arranged into the initial structure of organization and classification. A *dependent variable* is one that is allowed to vary and is subsequently measured and its relation to the independent variable established. Therefore, with two related variables, if one could logically have caused the other, but not vice versa, the first would be the independent variable. In the absence of such an indication, if one variable occurred earlier than the other we would commonly term the earlier manifestation the independent variable.

C 5.4. *Variables and their relations.*

If $R=f(T)$, then T is the _____ variable.

When we can predict the value of one variable fairly effectively if we just know the value of some other variable, we say a _____ relationship exists between the two variables.

    a. dependency   b. cause-and-effect   c. functional

To illustrate what we have been talking about, let us explore the relationship that might occur between the amount of time spent studying and the grade one gets on a subsequent examination. The data are all hypothetical, but it will show you how the scientist could proceed. We might start by selecting a number of students for each level of the independent variable (study time), choosing as the 1-hour group those who studied from 45 to 75 minutes, as the 2-hour group those who studied from 105 to 135 minutes, and so forth. Then we would calculate the average for each group's examination scores (dependent variable). The resulting relationships could be charted as shown in Figure 5.1. We can see that the more time one spends studying, the higher the grade tends to be, but there is a manifestation of the phenomenon of "diminishing returns" in the data.

It would be appropriate at this point to mention that in many research projects there may be more than one independent variable and more than one dependent variable. To use a simple example, we might be interested in the relation of grades to both study time and IQ. Figure 5.2 (hypothetical data) shows a very similar relation of study time to grades for both high-IQ and low-IQ students, but IQ itself seems to account for a considerable part of the resulting grade. Thus, according to such data, grades are seen to be a function of study time *and* to be a predictive function of IQ.

The Psychologist's Variables

Some authors have gone to lengths to state that all sciences conduct research in a similar manner. In fact, it has been said that such are the similarities

Figure 5.1

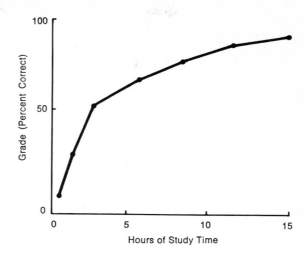

Figure 5.2

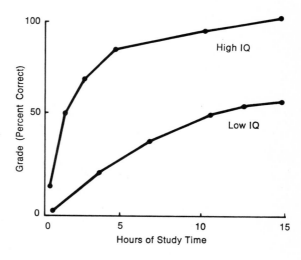

that a division into areas of physiology, chemistry, psychology, and botany is simply a convenient division of labor. Assuming this, we would then say that the major division among the sciences lies in the classes of variables that are selected for investigation. In psychology we can group all the research variables into three categories—stimulus variables, organismic variables, and response variables.

S (stimulus) Variables   *S (stimulus) variables* are events which activate some sensory process in the individual. We shall list four subcategories of *S* variables.

(1) *Physical-specific stimuli* are those with specific physical properties

which can be stated exactly in terms of intensity, quality, and duration. The narrowly experienced stimuli commonly employed in a perception laboratory are clear examples of physical-specific stimuli—spots of light, electronically generated tones, pressure and temperature changes, and so forth.

(2) We can also differentiate *situational stimuli*. These are the broadly experienced aspects of one's social environment, such as peer-group influence, a socioeconomic class culture, or situations in which one is competing with others or is interacting with persons of the opposite sex. The *same* situational stimulus may differ markedly from one particular occasion to another in its various aspects.

(3) *Cognitive stimuli* are thought processes that have a stimulatory effect on the individual. People sometimes amuse themselves by daydreaming. Others can "think" certain types of thoughts—happy, confident—and thereby modify their emotional awareness to a certain degree. When regarded in this sense, one's own cognitions (thoughts) can have stimulus properties.

(4) *Intraphysical stimuli* are sensations that arise from changes in one's own internal body processes. It may be of interest to a psychologist to study the effects of feeling one's anger or fear (in the sense of internal stimuli such as rises in blood pressure, perspiration, etc.) on behavioral variables. The latter is probably the least important stimulus category for most research psychologists.

C 5.5.   *Stimulus variables.*

Of the *S*-variables, something like the experience of asking a person of the opposite sex for a date would be a _____ stimulus.

    a. physical-specific   b. situational

If a soldier overseas thinks about pleasant times with his girl friend whenever he gets depressed, these thoughts are _____ stimuli.

    a. cognitive   b. situational

A monkey watches a panel board. He has learned that when a certain light flashes on he can pull a handle to get a reward. The light is a _____ stimulus.

    a. cognitive   b. physical-specific

When Jimmy Smith was a youngster his outbursts of anger were severely punished by his parents. Now, as an adult, when he gets frustrated and upset, he suddenly experiences intense anxiety. He is responding to _____ stimuli.

    a. intraphysical   b. physical-specific

O (organismic) Variables   *O (organismic) variables* are biological variations among individuals. These fall into three general groups: (1) *genetically transmitted characteristics* such as race, sex, and inherited disorders; (2) *congenital characteristics* (present at birth), usually of a damaging nature, such as toxic or physical damage to the brain tissue of the fetus; and finally (3) *postnatal induced or developed characteristics*, again usually of a damaging or deteriorative nature, such as brain damage or the deteriorative effects of extreme old age. This sort of grouping is not appropriate to all cases. For example, where scientists might be interested in the comparison of brain chemistry patterns in normal versus mentally ill people, it is difficult to refer to brain chemistry patterns as being solely the effect of genetic acquisition, solely congenital, or solely postnatal. Still, such a grouping of effects is useful in conceptualizing different types of research interests in psychology.

R (response) Variables   *R (response) variables* are the behaviors of organisms. A response is an occurrence of a specific individual action, while the word "behavior" refers to a complex or changing pattern of responses. "Response" can be broadly defined so as to include three categories: (1) *Skeletal responses*—those that are determined by the skeletal muscles of the body, and in short, are "visible" movements of the body. (2) *Autonomic responses*—those internal changes that typically accompany emotion, such as changes in heart rate, blood pressure, perspiration. (*Note:* We have already presented the sensation of these responses as having stimulus value.) (3) Finally, *cognitive responses*—the thoughts and ideas that we continually generate, including those connected with emotional processes. (*Note:* We have also presented the *experience* of thoughts as having stimulus value.)

So that you won't have to work up your own outline, let us put what we have been talking about into outline form. So that you can see at a glance how the variables and their subcategories stack up, see Table 5.1.

Table 5.1

I. Stimulus variables	II. Organismic variables	III. Response variables
a. physical-specific stimuli	a. genetically transmitted characteristics	a. skeletal responses
b. situational stimuli	b. congenital characteristics	b. autonomic responses
c. cognitive stimuli	c. postnatal induced or developed characteristics	c. cognitive responses
d. intraphysical stimuli		

C 5.6. *Organismic and response variables.*

A variable such as the age of a species of monkey you are using in studying sexual behavior would

be _____ variable.

a. an organismic   b. a response

The species of monkey you are using in studying a behavior would be _____ variable.

    a. an organismic   b. a response

Of the R-variables, a recording of the number of times during a class that a child is out of his seat without permission would be a measure of a _____ response.

    a. skeletal   b. cognitive

An individual marks down each time he thinks about committing suicide, and after a few days he enters a therapy program. He continues to make a record of his suicidal thoughts. We are interested in the change in their rate. Suicidal thoughts are a _____ response.

    a. skeletal   b. cognitive   c. autonomic

We test one of Freud's theories by frustrating two groups of persons. Then we allow one group to "let off steam," while the other group must control themselves. At hourly intervals over the afternoon we then measure blood pressure changes in both groups. Blood pressure falls into the category of _____ response.

    a. a skeletal   b. a cognitive   c. an autonomic

Relating the Psychologist's Variables

Now, how do we put all of this together? There are four ways in which psychologists organize their research according to our previously described conception of independent and dependent variables and the present conception of S-, O-, and R-variables. In more-or-less descending order of importance (to us) they are:

(1) $R=f(S)$	(3) $R=f(O)$
(2) $R=f(R)$	(4) $O=f(S)$

(1) Let us look at an example of each of the above models. First, $R=f(S)$. This is the most powerful of research strategies because it tells the psychologist about certain aspects of the environment that may actually change or control behavior. If one studied the ability to learn complex verbal material under conditions of quiet, of background music, and of audible conversation, this would be an example of $R=f(S)$. So would be differences in the IQs (which are actually behaviors in specific testing situations) of groups which have grown up in homes of different socioeconomic classes, the homes being situational stimuli.

(2) Let us look at $R=f(R)$. Essentially this means that if we know something about one behavior pattern of an individual, we can predict some other behavior fairly well. This can be useful, as where a pattern of psychological test results may be associated with the behavior we call "schizophrenia." Or, college entrance exam scores may relate to subsequent college grade point average. Or, employee honesty can be predicted from knowledge of individuals' honesty on previous jobs.

(3) Consider $R=f(O)$. We may establish that males and females, or that

blacks and whites, score differently on certain scales of personality tests. (Remember that the test score is an R variable, being a sample of behavior in a specific situation.) We may establish that IQ scores begin to change in certain ways as people age, or that older persons' abilities to learn certain types of things change. We may establish that certain intellectual test patterns are associated with having a given degree of brain damage in a specified location.

(4) $O = f(S)$ refers primarily to work in the area of physiological psychology. For example, brain chemistry of rats may be changed by periods of isolation away from sensory stimulation, or by stress. This last research model is not of much concern in an introductory-level book.

You have probably noticed that, with the exception of the $O = f(S)$ model which is usually restricted to physiological laboratories, the R-variable is the typical dependent variable in psychological research. This is because the primary target interest of the psychologist is behavior (R) and the functional relationships that allow us to predict it and/or to control it.

C 5.7. *S–O–R in functional relationships.*

Using the symbols S, O, and R, write the model used in studying children's development of characteristics of dominance as a function of their physical sizes: _____ = f(_____).

What is the model for studying the relation of age to suicide rate? (Note before you answer— is age a behavior? Think.).

    a. $O = f(R)$ b. $R = f(O)$ c. $R = f(S)$ d. $R = f(R)$

What is the model for the effects of the ink and paper colors of reading materials on the rate of reading? (Note before you answer—would the color of paper be a behavior? Would the color of paper be a "biological" O variable? Think.).

    a. $R = f(O)$ b. $R = f(S)$ c. $R = f(R)$

In psychological research, the _____ variable in the majority of cases is the dependent variable.

    a. stimulus   b. response   c. organismic

PROGRESS CHECK 5.1

1. How does the nonscientific approach to knowledge differ from the scientific approach? _____ .
   a. More reliance upon reasoning and authority
   b. More reliance upon controlled observation
   c. The two methods do not differ   d. None of the preceding
2. Publicly observable events are _____ .
   a. nonverifiable   b. replicable   c. both   d. neither

MATCH: _____ 3. Description   A. Under specific conditions, events will occur

_____ 4. Prediction   B. Observation and classification of events

_____ 5. Control   C. Manipulation of independent variables

6. Which of the following states a functional relationship? _____ .

   a. $f(A) = \dfrac{B}{A}$ b. $\dfrac{A}{B} = f\,(AB)$ c. $B = f(A)$ d. All of the preceding

Using the formula $Y = f(X)$

MATCH: _____ 7. Independent variable   A. Y

_____ 8. Dependent variable   B. X

9. List the two types of functional relationships:

   1. _____

   2. _____

MATCH: _____ 10. S variables   A. Biological variations

_____ 11. O variables   B. Activation of sensory processes

_____ 12. R variables   C. Behavior

13. Stimuli involved in peer-group relations might be _____ stimuli.

   a. situational   b. cognitive   c. intraphysical   d. all of the preceding

14. Congenital characteristics of individuals are _____ .

   a. S variables   b. O variables   c. R variable   d. none of the preceding

15. If you are interested in studying the effects of stress on heart rate, you would be measuring, as the independent variable, a(n) _____ .

   a. S variable   b. O variable   c. R variable   d. None of the preceding

---

TWO QUESTIONS IN RESEARCH   These may strike you as a very simple pair of questions: first, "What do you mean?" and second, "How do you know?" But these two questions describe the main tasks in performing scientific research. Furthermore, these questions have provided science with many uneasy moments, and even today there is vast criticism of much research on the basis of inadequacy in the treatment of these questions.

What Do You Mean?   The simplest way to answer the question, "What do you mean by 'intelligence'?" is to offer a philosophically derived answer such as, "Intelligence is the ability to cope successfully in a variety of unfamiliar situations." The problem with this sort of definition is that there is then no agreement on how to go about measuring intelligence. One researcher may be impressed by the cleverness and lack of naïveté in a street-corner ghetto gang, and he may wish to call certain individuals intelligent because they cope successfully. A second researcher, meanwhile, measures IQ and concludes that the same group is relatively low in intelligence. We look at the physical sciences and see a variety of standards by which to measure such things as weight, size, density, and physical scientists can even translate from one scale to another with accuracy, as is done with temperature or conversions to metric measures. In psychology, however, it is much harder to insure that various researchers, using the same term, are all talking about the same thing. For the past few years the preferred approach to the problem has been by scientists' use of operational definitions of the variables in their research.

An *operational definition* is a definition of a variable that is stated in terms of the method of the variable's measurement. The method of measurement of intelligence might be a certain type of IQ test. The method of measurement of "hunger" might be a statement of how many hours an organism has been deprived of food. Most physical-specific stimuli are almost automatically defined in operational terms, but many other stimuli, as well as many organismic and response variables, are not. A variable may have several possible operational definitions. Let us take "fear" for example. A definition mentioning a "degree of emotion" without further specification would not be operational. How would a scientist define fear? If he stated his definition in terms of physiographic readings of heart rate and breathing patterns, then this would be an operational definition of fear. If he defined fear in terms of the subject's answers to questions on a scale pertaining to various levels of anxiety experienced in certain situations, then a score on the fear scale would be the operational definition. As you can see, the operational definition is not necessarily one that clearly describes the variable in the conceptual sense, but is one in which there is a clear understanding concerning how the variable is measured. If the definition does not state the procedures involved in the measurement, it is not an operational definition.

C 5.8.   *Operational definitions: What they are.*

If I were to define a monkey's "sex drive" as the amount of voltage in a shock grid that it would endure

to cross the grid area to get to a monkey of the opposite sex, this _____ be an operational

definition.

   a. would   b. would not

If a definition is operational, the variable is defined in terms of the method by which it is

   a. explained   b. conceptualized   c. measured

"Curiosity is the degree to which one wonders about the nature and sequence of events in one's

surroundings" _____ an operational definition of curiosity.

   a. is   b. is not

Advantages in Operational Definitions

It may have occurred to you to ask what advantage there could be in allowing different scientists to define their terms in different ways. Actually, though, there are reasonably small numbers of "preferred" definitions of the variables psychologists commonly investigate. Usually the operational definitions used by certain scientists who have made the most significant contributions to the research literature come into common use.

What are the advantages of operational definitions? First, the operational definition allows the researcher to build more meaningfully upon the research that has already been reported. One does not tend to go off on a tangent with a different operational definition, because it is then impossible for others to meaningfully integrate the results of published research into a unified pattern. If a scientist wishes to elaborate on the work of a previous scientist, he tends to find out the operational definitions that were employed and, usually, he employs the same definitions.

Second, the reader of research literature may have reason to question a certain statement of a functional relationship, or he might be aware of conflicts between what two different scientists have found. The only way in which such things can be resolved is to look at the operational definitions. Suppose that researchers have investigated the relationship of the level of socioeconomic family background to the degree of children's aggression. Suppose that in three studies the researchers report (1) no relationship, (2) a positive relationship—meaning high socioeconomic level goes with high aggression and low socioeconomic level goes with low aggression, and (3) an inverse or negative relationship—meaning high socioeconomic level goes with low aggression, and low socioeconomic level goes with high aggression.

If one were to be faced with such a contradiction, he would go directly to the operational definitions of "aggression" used by the three researchers. There you might find the following definitions of aggression, corresponding to the three findings above: (1) "Yes" answers on an aggression scale containing questions such as "Do you sometimes feel that you would like to deliberately make someone else cry?"; (2) rate of hitting, breaking and throwing objects in an isolated-play situation in an experimental playroom; and (3) the number of times during an observation period when a child verbally or physically abuses another child. If such a story were to unfold, the conclusion would be that there might well be totally independent forms of aggression and that research should begin to pursue this topic. In fact, this would set the stage for $R = f(R)$ research into the actual relationship between the three types of behavior previously lumped under the one term "aggression." In summary, then, operational definitions allow the researcher to better relate his own research to what already exists, and they allow the reader of research to better resolve inconsistencies and understand what is actually being investigated.

On the other side of the issue there are certain problems involved in the use of operational definitions. Some scientists may use an operational definition so exclusively that another possibly legitimate definition goes uninvestigated. Our three definitions of aggression typify what we are talking about. It would be unfortunate if all aggression research proceeded according to a single operational definition. Also, on rare occasions, it is possible that some scientists have kept an outward appearance of scientific legitimacy by superficially operationalizing certain concepts which in reality are wild departures from the criterion of "actual, observable behavior." When some event such as a mental phenomenon is not even *in*directly observable, and in fact exists only in assumption, the practice of constructing operational definitions for such an event is completely illegitimate and hinders the proper development of the topic area in the scientific sense. You should note at this point that there is such a thing as legitimate *indirect* observation. If a subject reports to the scientist his own perceptual or mental experiences in a carefully documented manner, this is proper indirect observation of those experiences. Such a procedure might, for example, have a subject rank nine or ten different unpleasant situations in terms of the degree of tension or fear that each might produce. We might then properly conclude, through just indirect measures, that handling a snake would be more aversive to the subject than standing near the edge of the roof of a tall building.

C 5.9. *Operational definitions: Advantages and disadvantages to their use.*

One of the main purposes of clearly stated operational definitions appearing in published research reports is so that _____ .

a. scientific integrity can be assured

b. precise comparisons of different research programs can be made

c. a scientist can work alone rather than in large teams

d. precise statistical tests of the data can be made

A problem presented in the movement toward operationalism is that a given operational definition of a concept may be used too _____ .

a. narrowly by almost all researchers

b. much as if it were the actual conceptual meaning

The fact that behavior that is not at all observable can be operationalized is seen as _____ to the legitimate scientific process.

a. advantageous   b. a hindrance

This section began by asking the scientist "What do you mean?" In summary, the scientist replies with an operational definition of the variable questioned.

How Do You Know? The second question to the scientist is, "How do you know?" and it is asked when the scientist claims knowledge of causes or the understanding of certain phenomena. For example, the scientist may state that frustration causes aggression. He "knows" because he has data available to him showing a functional relationship between the level of frustration on one hand and the type or amount of aggression on the other. The important question here pertains to the degree of relationship between the variables. Another way of putting this is to ask how much of the variation in the dependent variable can be accounted for by variation of the independent variable. When a scientist can demonstrate independent variables that rather thoroughly account for both the occurrence of and the variation in a dependent variable, then he has "explained" the event. In summary, then, the scientist responds to the question "How do you know?" with a statement of the degree of functional relationship that has been established between variables.

A Typical Problem: Do children learn more quickly under conditions that reward correct behavior or that punish incorrect behavior? First, the dependent variable is correctness, so we ask, "What do you mean by correctness?" The operational definition may be correct verbal responses on a group-task series of progressive brain-teaser problems. Second, the independent variable is reward versus punishment, so we inquire, "What do you mean by reward and punishment?" Reward, it may turn out, is praise by the teacher, while punishment is a scolding by the teacher. Finally, we ask, "How do you know that children learn more quickly under one of the conditions?" The answer to that question could be such a statement as, "The children achieved scores 40 percent higher under the one condition." (We shall elaborate this answer into statements of probability in Extension Chapter 5A.)

C 5.10. *"Knowledge" in science.*

If a scientist is asked "How do you know?" his proper reply is in terms of a statement about

_____ _____ he has discovered.

What is the point to all this? There are two points. First, we want you to know how psychologists communicate among themselves—the researcher presenting his findings and answering to his colleagues. But there is another, stronger, purpose. We would not be at all disappointed if you were to adjust your own inquiries along the same lines. When a professor or a friend makes a supposedly factual statement, it is not inappropriate to ask for a clarification of what he means by the use of certain terms. Then, if the individual is at all open-minded, he should not be offended by the question of how he "knows" something. If anyone in a research-oriented area such as psychology, education, or the various related research disciplines cannot support a statement with data or with a reference to where published data can be found, then that person should adjust his remarks accordingly in the future. That is the point of your learning how and why scientists operate in the ways they do.

MAJOR RESEARCH STRATEGIES

When psychologists conduct research, it is through the use of one of two major scientific research methods—the experimental method and the survey method—which we will now discuss.

The Experimental Method

Within the *experimental method* we randomly assign subjects to the different categories or "levels" of the independent variable. Then we collect data on the dependent measure by which to compare the groups. For example, we might wish to use three teaching techniques in an elementary school. We could take the groups of children in each grade and randomly assign them to the three types of classrooms. Then we could measure the achievement levels during the year in each type of classroom and make our judgments about relative merits. This method is easily the most powerful of the two, and is to be preferred whenever possible. It is not possible, however, to assign persons to some categories. How would you randomly assign a child to an "orphans" category, or to an age group? That brings us to the second method.

The Survey Method

When we cannot manipulate the independent variable, because it already has an existing value for each subject, then we use the *survey method*. We call the results a "study" rather than an experiment. Here we assign subjects to naturally existing categories of the independent variable and compare the groups as they behave in the manner defined as the dependent variable.

A Comparison of the Methods

A large number of problems cannot be tackled with the experimental method. Where the independent variable is age, race, or sex; or being blind, mentally-retarded, or orphaned; or being from a broken versus an intact home—there is no way to randomly assign subjects to the categories of the independent variable. The survey method is then dictated.

Two points should be made here. First, there are certain research questions adaptable to the use of either the experimental or the survey method. In these cases the data provided through experimentation is definitely to be preferred. Second, even when experimentation is impossible, one should accept the results of a study with a certain degree of caution. The problem lies in the control of error, and that will be our next topic for consideration.

C 5.11. *Research strategies: Survey versus experimental methods.*

If we assign subjects randomly to the categories of the independent variable, we are using the _____

method of research.

    a. experimental   b. survey

If we deliberately manipulate the independent variable—that is, we decide to impose a certain value

of it upon the subject—we are using the _____ method of research.

    a. experimental   b. survey

Assignment of subjects to a level or category of the independent variable which already exists for them (sex, age, etc.) is a step in the _____ method of research.

a. experimental   b. survey

If we tested the memory for verbal material of young undergraduate versus middle-aged (30 to 55 years of age) undergraduate students, we would then *have* to use the _____ method of research.

a. experimental   b. survey

The product of the experimental method is called an experiment; the product of the survey method is called a _____ .

a. survey   b. study   c. replication

PROGRESS CHECK   5.2

1. If a variable is stated in terms pertaining to its measurement, it is defined _____ .

    a. operationally   b. functionally   c. both   d. neither

MATCH: _____ 2. Experimental Method   A. Direct manipulation of the independent variable

            _____ 3. Survey Method   B. Independent variable not directly manipulated

4. Which of the following might be an operational definition of thirst? _____ .

    a. How many hours since last drink   b. "I am thirsty"   c. Both   d. Neither

5. Two advantages of operational definitions are _____ .

    a. to allow others to relate to researchers

    b. to decrease the likelihood of replication

    c. to allow researchers to relate to other researchers

    d. a and c

STATISTICAL METHODS: REPRESENTATION OF DATA

If you were to be given data to analyze, that data would be very difficult for you to organize unless you could perceive it in some systematic fashion. In this section we will look at a few established ways of presenting data, and then discuss statistical decision-making.

Let us start right off by assuming that we have some scores from a classroom examination. If we simply started with the first paper turned in, we might record in consecutive order a random list of scores such as 74, 88, 79, 81, 94, 87, etc. If we had such a list of scores for 50 or even 100 people, we would not be able to come to many immediate conclusions other than simple statements such as "It seems like quite a few scores are in the 70s." Therefore the first thing we should do with such a list of scores is to redistribute them into what we call a *scoring distribution*. In a scoring distribution (or distribution of scores), usually the highest score is placed at the top and the scores then proceed downward according to value. It is also fairly common to see the *lowest* score placed at the top and the order of the distribution of scores thus reversed.

scores
94
91
89
88
88
etc.

As you can see in the scoring distribution to the left, the whole thing now seems a lot more comprehensible. Let us now ask you to imagine that a scoring distribution such as the one on the left is actually quite lengthy, and consists of 50 or 100 scores. We can usually detect a possible economy of space when a large number of people have the same score. Using only the scores already placed into a scoring distribution, we shall combine duplications and construct what is called a *frequency distribution* in the following manner:

In the frequency distribution on the right, we now have a listing which tells us in the left column *what scores* were made and in the right column *how many persons* achieved each score. However, to be perfectly accurate, the frequency distribution to the right has still not been properly completed. Usual procedures call for indication of all *intermediate* scores that occur with a zero frequency (which actually means that they did not occur). Also, the heading *frequency* is usually abbreviated to *f*.

score	*frequency*
94	1
91	1
89	1
88	2
etc.	

score	*f*
94	1
93	0
92	0
91	1
90	0
89	1
88	2
87	0
etc.	

Now that we have portrayed a properly drawn frequency distribution at the left, we need to know about some circumstances that could make it still more concise. When many different scores are involved, we can achieve a further economy of space by grouping the scores into equal intervals and presenting the resulting *interval frequency distribution*.

A typical interval frequency distribution might proceed as indicated to the right. Note that the interval is held constant. This is one of the rules of using interval frequency distributions. The rule we mentioned before, that the zero-occurring intermediate scores must also appear, is true here, but, as you can probably guess, it seldom happens that there are no scores within entire intervals.

score	f
90–99	2
80–89	4
70–79	11
etc.	

C 5.12. *Statistical representation of data: Tabular distributions.*

If we put occurring scores into order from highest to lowest, we have drawn a _____

_____ .

A two-column table that represents in one column each occurring score, and in the other column how often it occurred, is called a _____ _____ .

(Refer to the last answer.) This representation would allow an economy of space *if* we had a scoring distribution with a large number of _____ .

If I have a representation of scores which tells how many scores occurred between, say, 0 and 10, between 11 and 20, between 21 and 30, etc., this kind of representation is called a(n)

_____ _____ _____ .

(Refer to the last answer.) A rule in drawing up this kind of representation is that the size of the

_____ must be kept _____ .

(Refer to the last two answers.) This representation would allow an economy of space *if* we had a scoring distribution with a very large number of _____

_____ .

Graphic Representation

When we take data from frequency distributions and represent it on a graph or chart, certain procedures should be followed. First, the data are always to be represented with the independent variable on the horizontal axis (abscissa), and the dependent variable on the vertical axis (ordinate). Also the values of the variables proceed from the lowest values at the intersection of the axes to the highest values at the extremes, in the manner of Figure 5.3.

If we measure off values from both scales, we can plot scores. Suppose we were interested in college grades as a function of IQ. If we found that for individuals with IQs of 120 the mean GPA (Grade Point Average) was 2.5, we could begin to plot the functional relationship graphically as illustrated in Figure 5.4.

Figure 5.3

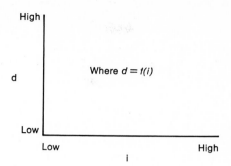

Figure 5.4

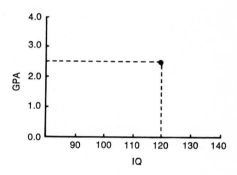

It may have occurred to you that many of the graphs presented in a textbook are simply different ways of representing frequency distributions and interval frequency distributions. In these cases you might imagine pushing a frequency distribution over on its side and then counting off the frequency upward along a vertical axis:

score	f
4	1
3	3
2	12
1	25

Figure 5.5 corresponds to the data in the frequency distribution to the left.

Figure 5.5

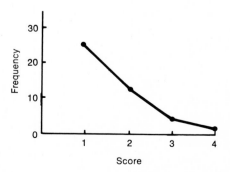

C 5.13. *Mechanics of graphing data.*

The horizontal axis of a graph represents the _____ variable.

Another name for the horizontal axis of a graph is the _____.

The vertical axis of a graph, known as the _____ ,

   represents the _____ variable.

The variable plotted on the vertical axis of a graph would have its _____ value at the top.

   a. highest   b. lowest

At this point it is likely that you will agree with us that very little more can be done in terms of economy of space, so long as we try to represent each individual's score in the distribution in some visible fashion. If, however, we cease reference to individual scores in the distribution, we can proceed to the next economy of space, which is to collapse larger quantities of data into smaller mathematical expressions. Not surprisingly, these expressions are called *descriptive statistics.*

MEASURES OF CENTRAL TENDENCY

The first type of descriptive statistics consists of the measures of central tendency. The three measures of central tendency are the mean, the median, and the mode.

The Mean

The *mean* is a value that you may already know by another name—the average. The mean is calculated by summing all of the scores and dividing by the number of scores.

$$\bar{x} = \frac{\Sigma\, x}{n}$$

In the formula just given, note the symbol for the mean, $\bar{x}$; the symbol for "sum of," Σ; the symbol for an individual score, x; and the symbol for the number of individual scores, n.

The mean is considered to be the most important measure of central tendency, at least partly because we can use a mean in more complex formulas to be described later. An interesting characteristic of the mean is that of the three measures of central tendency, the mean is the most influenced by extreme scores. That is, the mean will be drawn in the direction of an extreme score. As an example, the mean of the scores 1, 1, 1, 1, 1, 1, 1, 100 is 13.375. This mean was drawn up quite a distance and obviously is not a score that is in the usual sense typical of the group.

The Median

A second measure of central tendency, the *median*, expresses the middle-most score—that is, the score that has as many scores below it as it has above it. With the scores 2, 4, 8, 9, 10, the middle score is 8, because there are two higher scores and two lower scores in the scoring distribution. If the scores were 8, 8, 100, 100, 100, the median would be 100, since 100 is at the center of the scoring distribution. In the event that *n* (symbol for number of scores) is an even number, for example four or six scores, a tie for middle will result. Then you should take the mean of the two tied scores. Thus, for 1, 4, 5, 6, the median is 4.5; for 1, 4, 5, 6, 7, 8, the median is 5.5.

The Mode The *mode* is the third measure of central tendency. It is the most commonly occurring score in a scoring distribution. Thus, for 1, 2, 2, 2, 2, 2, 3, 3, 3, 4, 5, the mode is 2. In the case of ties, as with the distribution 1, 2, 2, 2, 2, 3, 3, 3, 3, 4, 5, the modes are 2 and 3. If the modes are separated as with the distribution 1, 2, 2, 2, 2, 3, 4, 4, 5, 6, 7, 7, 7, 7, we have what is said to be a bimodal distribution (in this example modes of 2 and 7). In a looser sense, sometimes a distribution is said to be bimodal simply because the curve, when drawn, shows two separate "elevations," even though the modes are not exactly equal in the numbers they represent.

Advantages of Each of the Measures As we stated earlier, the mean has one special advantage. It is used in a number of important formulas that we shall examine later. Also it is the most commonly used measure of central tendency. It suffers from a certain lack of representativeness if there are some extremely deviant scores in the distribution, and it is the most time-consuming to calculate. The median has the main advantage of being quick and easy to calculate, and it is not influenced by a few extreme scores. The mode has a certain usefulness if one is wishing to label a "typical" individual, but the mode is seldom used except in instances where there are only a very few levels or categories of the measured variable. For example, modal measures might be used when only two or three values are found, as in a reference to a school being "predominantly black," or when we express some other form of predominance in sex, age groupings, and so forth.

C 5.14. *Measures of central tendency.*

The score in the exact middle of a scoring distribution is the distribution's _____ .

Which measure of central tendency is most affected by extreme scores? _____ .

The most common score to occur in a scoring distribution is the distribution's _____ .

The sum of the *x*'s divided by *n* is the formula for the (use symbol) _____ .

The most time-consuming to calculate of the various measures of central tendency is the

_____ .

The _____ is the most used measure of central tendency.

score	f
5	5
4	2
3	3
2	5
1	0
0	1

Assume you have a frequency distribution as given to the left. Be prepared to recognize as true or false several statements about any such frequency distribution and its central tendencies. For example, "distribution is bimodal," "its median is 4," etc.

The mean for the scores 4, 5, 6, 4, 5, 5, 5, 6, and 6 is _____ .

    a. 4.91   b. 5.11   c. 5.22   d. 5.89

The mean for the scores 105.1, 107.2, 109.8, 110.0, 112.2, and 114.7 is _____ .

    a. 107.0   b. 108.0   c. 109.8   d. 111.111

The median for the scores in the last problem is _____ .

    a. 109.5   b. 109.9   c. 109.95   d. 110.5

Assume you have a frequency distribution as given to the right.

score	f
6	10
5	3
4	1
3	0
2	1

What would be the distribution's mean? _____ .

    a. 5.0   b. 5.2   c. 5.4   d. 5.6

In the frequency distribution to the right, what is the distribution's median? _____ .

    a. 5.0   b. 5.4   c. 5.5   d. 6.0

Central Tendency Expressed in Distribution Curves

From what you now know about measures of central tendency, you should be able to envision the three central tendency points on a distribution curve. In the distribution represented in Figure 5.6, the mean, median and mode all fall at the same point. This can only happen when the distribution has a symmetrical, balanced appearance such as is pictured. When scores fall into such a symmetrical, bell-shaped distribution, we refer to them as being *normally distributed*. While the expression "normal curve" has some specific technical properties, the term is frequently used in a somewhat casual way to describe a reasonably symmetrical distribution of scores.

Figure 5.6

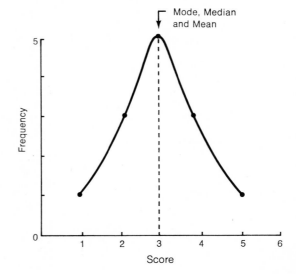

score	f
5	1
4	3
3	5
2	3
1	1

Therefore,

    Mode = 3
    Median = 3
    Mean = 3

Figure 5.7

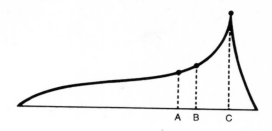

A B   C

In the distribution depicted in Figure 5.7, the three measures of central tendency are represented as points *A, B,* and *C.* You can clearly see that the *C* value is the mode. Observe also that many far-flung, extreme scores are at some distance from the mode toward the *low* end of the distribution. You know that it is the *mean* which is most affected by extreme scores. Thus, *A* must be the mean, leaving the intermediate value *B* to be the median. A distribution such as the one depicted here is said to be *skewed,* meaning that most of the scores fall to one side of the mode. Skewness is described by the direction of the "tail," and when the tail extends toward the low values (such as depicted in Figure 5.7), the curve is said to be negatively skewed. If the tail extends in the direction of the high values, the curve is said to be positively skewed. Galton, decades ago, was impressed by how many physical variations and their mediated behaviors are normally distributed. In certain functions, however, skewed curves are typical.

C 5.15. *Central tendency in graphed data.*

If a distribution's three measures of central tendency occur in the same position on the horizontal axis,

we know that we have a _____ distribution.

a. normal   b. skewed   c. bimodal

A distribution in which most of the scores fall to one side of the mode is called a _____ distribution.

a. normal   b. skewed   c. bimodal

score	f
9	1
8	1
7	1
6	2
5	4
4	6
3	8
2	10
1	1

The curve represented by the distribution to the left would _____ skewed.

a. not be   b. be positively   c. be negatively

In the distribution just described, would the mean be to the left or to the right of the median in the drawn curve? _____ .

a. to the left of the median

b. to the right of the median

Shapes
of Curves   You now know about normal curves, skewed curves, and bimodal curves. There are certain other shapes of curves, depicted in Figure 5.8, that also should be recognized. The *asymptotic* curve hits a *plateau*. The *ogival* curve is something like a lazy-S. Sometimes a vocabulary is used such as the following: a positively accelerating curve is one which goes up with the rate of the rise increasing; a negatively accelerating curve is one that goes up with the rate of the rise decreasing; a positively decelerating curve goes down with the rate of drop increasing; and a negatively decelerating curve goes down with the rate of drop decreasing. The ogival curve, as you can see, is first positively accelerating and then negatively accelerating.

Figure 5.8

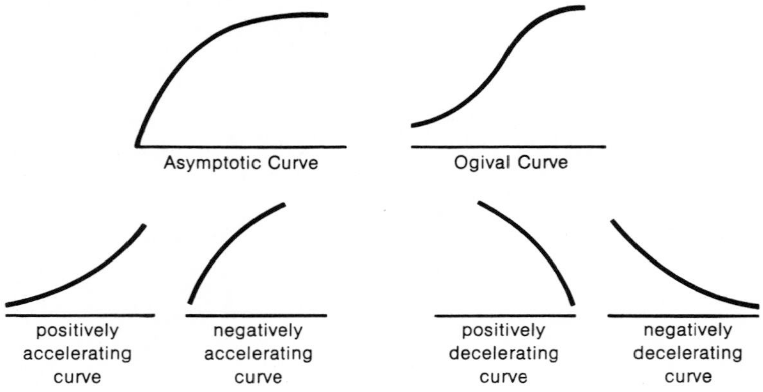

| Asymptotic Curve | Ogival Curve |

| positively accelerating curve | negatively accelerating curve | positively decelerating curve | negatively decelerating curve |

C 5.16.   *Shapes of curves.*

A curve that goes up with the rate of the rise decreasing is called a _____ _____ curve.

A curve that goes up with the rate of the rise increasing is called a _____ _____ curve.

MEASURES OF
VARIABILITY   The second major group of descriptive statistics consists of measures of variability. Essentially this means that we are answering the question, "How spread-out from the center of the distribution are the scores?" The simplest measure of variability is the *range*. The range answers the question: How many possible different whole-number scores are included within the "space" from, and inclusive of, the lowest occurring score to the highest occurring score? We take the highest score, subtract the lowest score, and add one ($H-L+1$). Thus, for the scores 1, 1, 2, 3, 5, 8, 9, 10 the range is 10 points ($10-1+1$). The range is a very simple statistic to calculate, but it reveals little about the internal distribution of scores. Consider an extreme case. Suppose in one distribution we had: 1, 5, 5, 5, 5, 5, 5, 5, 5, 5, 5,

5, 5, 5, 5, 10. In a second distribution we had 1, 1, 1, 1, 1, 1, 1, 1, 10, 10, 10, 10, 10, 10, 10. Obviously in the first group most scores are at a middle point. In the second group the "spread" or variability of scores is much greater; in fact, everybody in the second distribution is at one extreme or the other. We need a statistic that will be large for the second group, but small for the first. Such a statistic is the *standard deviation*.

Suppose that we take each score and find the difference between it and the distribution's mean. This is the difference score, *d*. Then we square each of the difference scores (which has the effect of removing negative numbers). Then we sum the squared differences, divide by *n*−1, and finally take the square root of the whole business. This, then, is the standard deviation, *s*. (Note: Use *n* rather than *n*−1 in the formula if *n* exceeds 30.)

$$s = \sqrt{\frac{\Sigma(d^2)}{n-1}}$$

Like the range, the standard deviation grows larger as the scores tend to be spread out at greater distances from the mean. But while the range shows only the distance between the two most extreme scores, the standard deviation reflects the internal variation of all the scores. The more the pattern of scores is spread out from the mean, the larger the standard deviation becomes.

Another characteristic of the standard deviation is that, like the mean, it is often used in more advanced formulas in statistical computation. In fact you will be able to see this in the next measure to be discussed.

C 5.17. *Measures of variability: Types.*

A measure of variability gives us an idea how much the scores vary from the _____ the distribution.

   a. center of   b. lowest point on

The measure of variability that relies on only two values from the scoring distribution is the _____ .

   a. standard deviation   b. range

Would the standard deviation of IQ scores be higher in a general classroom with a wide representation of IQs, or in a special education classroom where the retarded children there all have fairly similar scores on IQ tests? _____ .

   a. The standard deviation would be higher in the general classroom

   b. The standard deviation would be higher in the special education classroom

What three factors must you know in order to calculate *s*? For example, must you know the distribution's mean, its *n*, its range? Name the necessary factors:

   1. _____   2. _____   3. _____

PROGRESS CHECK 5.3

1. Regroup the following test scores into a frequency distribution:

   scores
   99
   97
   98
   99
   99

2. If scores are grouped in ranges, this is termed _____ .

   a. frequency distribution   b. interval frequency distribution

   c. normal curve   d. clustering

3. Choose numbered labels from the graph at the right: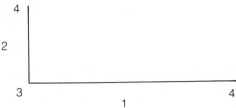

   _____ A. Higher scores

   _____ B. Lower scores

   _____ C. Horizontal axis

   _____ D. Vertical axis

4. Plot the following test scores and frequencies:

scores	f
100	20
75	30
50	40
25	10
0	0

   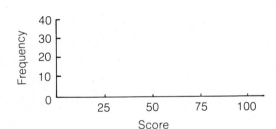

5. Descriptive statistics include _____ .

   a. expanding scores into large quantities of data

   b. collapsing scores into smaller quantities of data

6. Determine the following for the scoring distribution given:

   a. Mean _____   *scores*
                               23
   b. Mode _____   17
                               15
   c. Median _____   10
                               10

7. Which of the following is the formula for determining the mean? _____ .

   a. $\Sigma x = \dfrac{\bar{x}}{10}$ b. $n = \dfrac{\Sigma x}{x}$ c. $\bar{x} = \dfrac{\Sigma x}{n}$ d. None of the preceding

8. Identify the labels on the curve to the right:

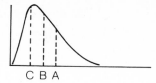

   A _____

   B _____

   C _____

   C B A

9. The curve in question eight is termed _____ .

   a. normal   b. skewed   c. bimodal   d. abnormal

MATCH: _____ 10. Negatively accelerating curve

   _____ 11. Positively decelerating curve   A.    B.

12. Determine the range for the following scores. _____ .

   10, 11, 12, 13, 14, 15

13. Determine the standard deviation for the following: $s =$ _____ .

$$s = \sqrt{\frac{\Sigma(d^2)}{n-1}}$$

   scores
   2
   5
   3
   2

MEASURES OF RELATIONSHIP: THE CORRELATION COEFFICIENT

Of a number of different measures of relationship, the most familiar and frequent is the *correlation coefficient*. The word "coefficient" simply means a number that describes a degree of value. Essentially what a correlation coefficient tells us is the degree to which we can accurately predict an individual's score on a second variable if we are told his score on a first one. For example, knowing an individual's IQ usually allows us to predict, more or less accurately, the general range into which his college grade point average will fall. We make some poor individual predictions, of course, but our overall success in such predictions tends to be high. As an example, suppose we wish to predict college success or failure from the knowledge that one group is made up of individuals all with IQs around 90, while another group is made up of individuals all with IQs around 120. We would predict failure for the first group, with perhaps a 95 percent success in our prediction, and we would predict success for the second group, with perhaps a 60 to 70 percent prediction success rate.

The example just presented relies upon the fact that certain measures show a high degree of correlation. Where correlations exist, we can break them into positive and negative correlations. In a *positive correlation*, high scores on one variable are related to high scores on the other. In a *negative correlation*, high scores on one variable are related to low scores on the other. Consider for a moment—would the heights and weights of men show a positive or negative correlation? Would the numbers of class absences of individuals be positively or negatively correlated with their grades in the course? In the first case there would probably be a fairly strong positive correlation, and in the second case a fairly strong negative correlation.

A perfect positive correlation is expressed as +1.00 (or just as 1.00). On the other side, a perfect negative correlation would be expressed as −1.00. Both of these extreme coefficients (1.00 and −1.00) are equally strong. Lower degrees of relationship exist as the correlation coefficients move from 1.00 or −1.00 toward .00. Any correlation coefficients in the area of .40 or .50 (or, −.40 or −.50) are high and excite the interest of the researcher. Coefficients of around .20 (or −.20) are high enough to show the researcher that there may be a reasonably important relationship between the measured variables. Finally, as coefficients drop down to .10 or lower, the researcher is aware that the variables have little predictive power in relation to one another.

Whether a correlation is positive or negative, it can be equally good in giving us a foundation from which to predict. The coefficient associated with the correlation tells us the magnitude of the relationship, while the positive or negative sign simply tells us whether the relationship is positive or negative. To illustrate this last point, a researcher would rather see a coefficient of correlation of −.50 than .40 between two variables. The −.50 value allows stronger predictive power.

Linear Relationship Shown Graphically To be a bit more technical, a correlation coefficient describes the degree of linear relationship between two variables. To understand this point, it is helpful to portray scatter-diagrams. These are the plotted positions of individuals' pairs of scores. For example, consider Figure 5.9. In this scatter-diagram we have presented the relation of IQs on one intelligence test to IQs on another (fictional data). As you can see, the data is reasonably linear, as indicated by a line drawn through the plots (Figure 5.10).

Figure 5.9

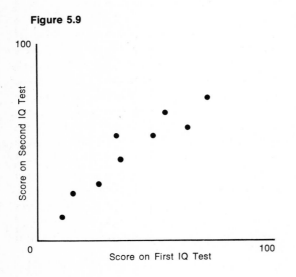

Figure 5.10

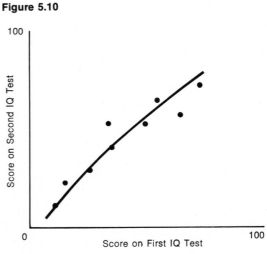

On the other hand, consider the relation that might exist between students' academic rank in high school and their academic rank in college. Figure 5.11 shows the relation (fictional data), and the "fat" area necessary to encompass most of the plots is shown in Figure 5.12.

Figure 5.11   **Figure 5.12**

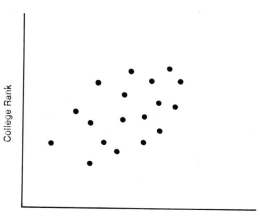

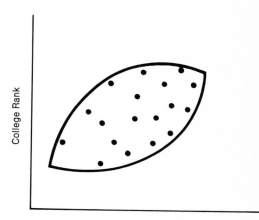

The expression "linear," used above, refers to the degree to which one can draw a diagonal straight line (see Figure 5.10) and thereby hit most of the plots. The data in Figure 5.9 is reasonably linear, and the resulting correlation coefficient would be quite high. On the other hand, the linearity of the data in Figure 5.11 is quite weak, and the resulting correlation coefficient would be small.

There is yet another way in which a relationship between variables may exist, but not be linear. This is where the line drawn through the plotted points would be far from straight. One research project related evaluation of teaching in various university-level courses to the grades the students expected to receive in the courses being evaluated. Figure 5.13 shows the plotted means of evaluations. While a strong relation existed, the calculated correlation coefficient was not realistically indicative of the actual strength of the relation. Good predictions can be made in such cases, but the correlation coefficient is not large due to the nonlinearity.

Remember the rules presented earlier for graphically portraying data. Low values must be presented at the axes of the horizontal and vertical dimensions. This being the case, the scatter-diagrams of positive correlations show linearity running from lower left to upper right (see Figures 5.9 and 5.11), and negative correlations would show linearity running from upper left to lower right.

Figure 5.13

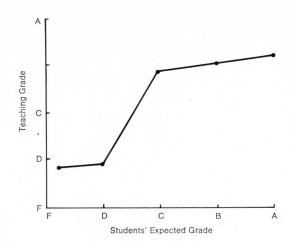

C 5.18. *The correlation coefficient.*

If high values on one variable are strongly related to low values on a second variable, _____ exists.

a. no correlation between them   b. a positive correlation   c. a negative correlation

Joe made a 40 on his art test and a 70 in chemistry; Sam made a 50 and a 65 on the two tests respectively, and Sally made a 65 and a 55 on the two tests. Judging just from this data, and assuming that the pattern holds with other students, it would seem that _____ probably exists.

a. no correlation   b. a positive correlation   c. a negative correlation

A correlation coefficient can be no stronger than _____ .

a. −1.00 or +1.00   b. +1.00 (alone)

Which of the following correlation coefficients would you rather see if you were trying to find the strongest predictive measure?

a. −.75   b. .00   c. .50   d. .65

As the area enclosing the plots on a scatter diagram grows "fatter," the associated correlation coefficient will _____ .

a. decline   b. increase

If a line connecting plots on a scatter diagram were a straight diagonal line, the resulting correlation coefficient would be _____ than would be the case with an ogival curve apparent in the plotted relationships.

a. higher   b. lower

A Formula To Calculate the Degree of Correlation

Several formulas are utilized to calculate the degree of correlation. The most commonly employed uses the symbol r. To compute r, you first pair the two measures for each individual, which are called the x and y measures. It is customary to place the x column on the left in a descending order of values. One then finds the product of each individual's two scores (xy), sums all the products, finds the product of the mean of the xs and the mean of the ys, finds the product of the standard deviation of the xs and the standard deviation of the ys, and then substitutes these values in the formula for r as shown in the following example:

$$r = \frac{\frac{\Sigma(xy)}{n} - \bar{x}_x \bar{x}_y}{(s_x)(s_y)}$$

x	y
10	10
8	10
6	5
4	5
2	0
0	0

Suppose we are given scores on two measures for each of six persons, and we wish to compute the value of r. Let us begin with an illustration in which the values on each measure range from 0 to 10, given at left. You should be able to calculate n (remembering that this is the number of persons), the mean of the x values ($\bar{x}_x$), the mean of the y values ($\bar{x}_y$), the sum of the xy (x value times y value) scores, and the standard deviations of x and of y (s_x, s_y).

See if you can properly draw a scatter diagram and calculate the correlation coefficient. If your answer is anywhere near .80, you are probably doing the calculation of r with a generally correct procedure. The correct substitutions for this problem are given in the inverted footnote below.

What does a correlation coefficient of .80 tell us? First, it is a positive relationship, meaning that high scores on the x variable are associated with high scores on the y variable, and conversely, low scores on the x variable are associated with low scores on y. Second, it is a very high coefficient, indicating a strong relationship. Still, it is less than perfect. Why? If you look at the data in the x and y columns, you will see that while the top scorer on the x variable also had a top score on y, the second highest person on x was tied for highest on y. So, we cannot predict *perfectly* what a person will do on y from simply knowing his score on x.

We have now completed an introduction to the three types of descriptive statistics—measures of central tendency, measures of variability, and measures of relationship.

$$r = \frac{\frac{230}{6} - 5 \cdot 5}{\sqrt{\frac{70}{5}} \cdot \sqrt{\frac{100}{5}}} = \frac{13.33}{16.72} = .797$$

Correct values for correlational problem given above.

PROGRESS CHECK 5.4.

1. Predictions of y, given x, might be made on the basis of a _____ .

    a. correlation coefficient   b. standard deviation   c. range   d. variability

2. A perfect negative correlation would be expressed as _____ .

    a. +1.00   b. +.50   c. −.50   d. −1.00

3. The graph to the right depicts _____ .

    a. linear relationship   b. nonlinear relationship

    c. unilinear relationship   d. duolinear relationship.

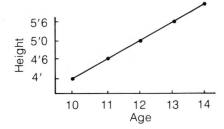

4. $r = \dfrac{\dfrac{\Sigma(xy)}{n} - \bar{x}_x\,\bar{x}_y}{(s_x)\,(s_y)}$ is the formula for _____ .

    a. standard deviation   b. correlation coefficient   c. both   d. neither

---

NOTE TO THE READER: The subject matter discussed in this chapter is expanded and amplified in Extension Chapter 5A, beginning on pages 566-67.

The Measurement of Human Abilities

WHAT IS INTELLIGENCE?

WHERE DOES INTELLIGENCE COME FROM?
Intelligence and Heredity
Intelligence and Environment

MEASUREMENT OF INTELLIGENCE
Binet and Formal Intelligence Tests
  Intelligence Test Items
Standard Deviations of Test Performances
The Wechsler Scales

VALIDITY AND RELIABILITY OF TESTS
  Validity
  Reliability

VALIDITY OF INTELLIGENCE TESTS

RACE AND INTELLIGENCE
On Jensenism

THE COMPONENTS OF INTELLIGENCE

MENTAL RETARDATION
Causes of Mental Retardation

THE GIFTED CHILD

VARIOUS TESTS
Culture-Fair Tests
Infant Intelligence Tests
Aptitude Tests and Achievement Tests

SUMMARY

"Measurement" refers to the process of placing some value—usually numerical—on an event or on the capacities which that event represents. The measurement of human abilities, then, concerns such functions as intelligence, talents, and the like. We shall start this chapter with the most important concern of all—intelligence testing—and we shall then proceed to a brief discussion of some related matters.

WHAT IS INTELLIGENCE?

"Intelligence" is a controversial topic in the field of psychology at the present time due to the fact that many people feel that individuals categorized as having low intelligence are denied, unfairly, opportunities to go to certain schools, to get good jobs, etc. We shall not attempt to answer such charges directly. Some facts will be presented, and you should then make up your own mind about whether or not intelligence testing should be de-emphasized in our society.

Abstractly speaking, intelligence might be defined as the ability to function effectively, particularly in novel situations. This is not much of a definition, but it conveys the idea that task-effectiveness and an independence from "practiced" accuracy are the targets for measurement. Obviously we cannot measure intelligence directly. Whatever it may be, its manifestations are vast and complex. What we attempt to do is (1) try to understand essentially what the term "intelligence" actually means, and (2) use the responses on the intelligence test as a sort of behavior sample from which to estimate the person's intellectual ability. The end-product of a testing program, typically, is a remark that a person's level of intelligence is *estimated* to be high-average, or some similar statement. We may state that a person's IQ is 109—a very specific statement—but we have to realize that the IQ is not the same as intelligence. It is just a score representing an estimate, and the score may vary somewhat, depending upon which test is used in the measuring.

C 6.1. *The concept of intelligence.*

What is an acceptable definition of intelligence?

OFF THE RECORD, by Ed Reed.
Reprinted courtesy The Register and Tribune Syndicate

OFF THE RECORD
"Sometimes I wish he had brains instead of ambition."

Intelligence _____ the same thing as "IQ."

    a. is   b. is not

WHERE DOES INTELLIGENCE COME FROM? Intelligence is the result of two interacting determinants—heredity and type of environment. First, *heredity* determines a type of biological structure which then possesses a capacity for a certain level of operation. Within the range of operation, from low-average to very high, polygenic processes are manifest in determining a given degree of neurological complexity. This results in what has been termed "familial intelligence." Occasionally there are gross forms of more severe mental retardation that are typically single-gene manifestations, and which limit an individual to a very low IQ ceiling. Mental retardation is frequently separated into the polygenic "familial retardation" and the single-gene effects which are usually termed "structural retardation," with the latter type usually being the more severe.

C 6.2. *Sources of intelligence.*

The two major determinants of one's level of intelligence are _____ and the type of

_____ .

Intelligence and Heredity Psychologists typically compare the IQs of individuals *within families* in establishing hereditary determinants of intelligence. First, one can compare the correlation of IQs of monozygotic (identical) twins with the correlation of IQs of dizygotic (fraternal) twins. The *MZ* twins are genetically identical, while the *DZ* twins, except for the accident of being of exactly the same calendar age, are no more genetically alike than are any set of siblings. Then, other family relationships can be studied. Assuming that heredity determines considerably the degree of the IQ, correlation coefficients should vary with the degree of "relatedness." That is exactly what the data portray, as shown in Table 6.1, compiled mainly by Burt and Howard (1956).

Table 6.1

IQ Correlation Between Related Individuals*	
Identical twins	.88
Identical twins reared apart	.77
Fraternal twins	.63
Siblings	.51
Parent/child	.49
Grandparent/grandchild	.34
Uncles-aunts/nephews-nieces	.35
First cousins	.29

*From Burt & Howard, 1956.

An analysis of the Burt and Howard data suggests a considerable input of environment since the coefficient for identical twins reared together is visibly higher than that for identical twins reared apart. On the other hand, the powerful effect of heredity is seen in the fact that the coefficient for identical twins (.88) is as high as is the test/retest reliability coefficient where individuals are retested with the same IQ test after a moderate interval of time (.88 to .90). Also, as one can see, there is greater similarity between the IQs of identical twins reared apart since infancy than between the IQs of fraternal twins reared together. Finally, there is considerable consistency between the data of Burt and Howard, showing a decreasing level of correlation with decreasing relatedness, and what one would predict from a polygenic theory of inheritance.

A further sophistication was introduced by Herrnstein (1973), who compared predicted versus expected correlations of IQs. Using methods that are beyond our present scope to elaborate, one can calculate the hypothetical correlation that should be obtained if intelligence is entirely genetic. Since we know that the environment has a decided impact upon intellectual ability, we should not expect perfect correspondence in the actual figures. Still, Table 6.2, which summarizes a large number of separate studies, is striking for its close relationship between the obtained correlations and the theoretical predictions. In Table 6.2 you will see some deviation of obtained values away from those of the Burt and Howard summary discussed in the last paragraph. This is due simply to the fact that a number of newer studies were taken into account by Herrnstein.

Table 6.2

*IQ Correlations Between	Theoretical Prediction	Obtained Value
Monozygotic twins reared together	1.00	.87
Monozygotic twins reared apart	1.00	.75
Dizygotic twins	.52	.53
Siblings reared together	.52	.55
Siblings reared apart	.52	.47
Parent-child	.49	.53
First cousins	.18	.26
Second cousins	.14	.16
Unrelated children reared together	.00	.24
Foster parent–child	.00	.20

*FromHerrnstein, 1973.

One further piece of evidence lends power to the heredity position. Skodak and Skeels (1949) and later Honzik (1957) studied children who had been adopted during the first six months of their lives. As a general estimate of parental intelligence, educational levels for the biological parents and for the adopting parents were determined. The results were dramatic—the IQ scores of the children correlated significantly (around .37) with the educational levels of the biological parents, but very little (around .06) with the foster parents' educational levels. Many more studies could be cited, all of a pattern. The result is clear—one's intelligence appears, to a considerable degree, to be the result of one's heredity.

C 6.3.   *The genetic basis of intelligence: correlational studies of the IQ.*

If we retest individuals with the same IQ test after a moderate interval of time, we get a correlation

coefficient between the two sets of scores of around _____ .

a. .20   b. .50   c. .75   d. .90   e. 1.00

The coefficient of correlation of IQs of identical twins reared together is nearest _____ .

(Refer to Table 6.1.)

a. .50   b. .60   c. .90   d. .99

The coefficient of correlation of IQs of identical twins reared apart is nearest _____ .

a. .30   b. .50   c. .70   d. .90

The coefficient of correlation of IQs between parents and their children is nearest _____ .

a. .30   b. .50   c. .70   d. .90

Darwin, Spencer, Huxley, and Galton all held that the laws of heredity and individual variation applied to humans as well as to lower animals, and to mind as well as body. Huxley's celebrated essay "The Natural Inequality of Man" convinced most of those who still held doubts. Still, it was more in the spirit of British than American inquiry that *in*equalities were studied, and not a large number of American names are associated with this field.

More recently, the political spirit in this nation has led to a heavy emphasis upon the power of the *environment* to effect the major influence on intelligence. The idea that Operation Headstart might remedy most cases involving low IQs reflects this influence. This has led to a situation in which leading geneticists such as Goldschmidt (1955) have deplored the current neglect of genetic inquiries by psychologists.

We have briefly alluded to research concerning the IQs of twins as a key to the heredity question. There are certain problems with such research. First and foremost, we are concerned about the degree to which the environments of twins are similar. At least one expert holds the opinion that when parents know they have identical twins, the environment they provide the twins is much more of a single set of experiences than if the twins are perceived as being fraternal. Thus, the different correlations *might* reflect greater similarity in the environments of identical twins. Then, in the cases of identical twins reared apart, the majority of these individuals are illegitimate and are placed by social agencies. These agencies take pains to place the children in families as similar as possible to the biological parents in terms of level of education, religion, and racial background. Thus, the high coefficient [.75 to .77] may reflect, to a degree, similarity in environments. These are strained explanations, however. They just do not have the force necessary to totally negate the powerful relationships that have been established between the IQs of related persons. In efforts to investigate the relation of heredity to intelligence, without the confounding effects of family-rearing patterns, psychologists have turned to laboratory animals as subjects.

The laboratory animal has a number of advantages for research, resulting from control of correlated variables. The male animal will not have had a fight with his wife just before coming in to be a subject in the experiment. He will not be tired beyond effective functioning because of a hangover from last night's cocktail party. Perhaps even more important, he will not have been reared on a highly deviant diet—protein-deprived, for example—during his infancy. And the prenatal care of the laboratory animal's mother will have been according to a standard. Therefore, we have a great deal of confidence in our control of correlated variables. It then remains to think of ways to test intelligence effectively under such circumstances.

A number of methods are available for testing an animal's intelligence. If you are using monkeys, you can easily test concept formation and you have a fairly reliable proof that this is "real" intelligence. Monkeys are expensive to obtain and maintain, however, and the genetic work on animal intelligence mainly has been with the laboratory rat.

In chapter 3 we mentioned the work of Tryon (1940), on which we shall elaborate at this point. Tryon's work remains the outstanding contribution on the topic. Tryon performed a selective-breeding experiment starting with over 100 unselected laboratory rats. They were given a series of trials in a complicated maze with several choice points. The measure of the rat's learning was the total number of errors he made by entering blind alleys before he was finally able to run the maze several times in succession without making an error. On the basis of what the "first generation" learned in the maze, Tryon's data showed greatly varied abilities. One rather brilliant fellow made only 7 errors before mastering the maze, while at the opposite extreme the dullest animal made 214 errors. The distribution of errors looked like a fairly symmetrical normal curve.

Tryon then bred the brighter rats with each other, and the duller rats with each other, and repeated this for 18 successive generations. Even in the second generation there were beginning to be two clearly distinct curves of performance for offspring of bright and offspring of dull parents. In that generation the error-mode for offspring of bright rats was around 32, while the error-mode for offspring of dull rats was around 76. By the seventh generation there were two distinct distributions that had little overlap. The error-mode for offspring of bright parents, by that time, was around 21, and the error-mode for offspring of dull rats was around 131. In the seventh generation, approximately 88 percent of the offspring of bright parents made scores better than even the brightest individual offspring of dull parents.

While almost no overlap was occurring in the performance curves of the two groups by the seventh generation, Tryon continued selective breeding until the eighteenth generation was available for testing. It seems like an interesting prospect to go on and on and eventually produce the "rat who can take over the world," but this simply did not happen. There was not a great deal of difference between the seventh generation strains and the eighteenth generation strains. Apparently the effects of heredity on familial intelligence in rats approached a practical limit, but the bright strain versus dull strain differences remained dramatically in contrast.

To this day, 34 years later, Tryon's work stands as powerful evidence for the inheritance of intelligence. Probably the greatest weakness of

Tryon's conclusions lies in the operational definition of intelligence he used and then generalized to the human intellect. The error-score in a maze may not correspond very closely to the abilities used by human beings in performing their various daily abstract tasks. Therefore, we balance results such as Tryon's with family-based research using human subjects.

C 6.4. *The genetic basis of intelligence: animal research.*

Animal research into the question of genetic determinants of intelligence has the advantage of giving us greater control over _____ .

a. random error   b. correlated variables such as diet

Tryon's operational definition of intelligence in his selective breeding experiment with rats was _____ .

a. the ability to solve visual discrimination problems

b. the selection of attractive sexual partners   c. the number of errors in a maze

Tryon was able to observe clear differences in his bright versus dull strains of animals as early as the _____ generation.

a. second   b. fifth   c. seventeenth

Intelligence and Environment
Currently the greatest research effort on the topic of intelligence is being directed toward the effects of certain types of environments. There seem to be several fundamental questions here: Does the environment affect the score you get on an intelligence test? Is any limitation placed on learning ability by a substandard environment, and if so is it reversible?

Concerning the first question there seems little doubt that the IQ (intelligence quotient, and remember that this is not the same as intelligence) is raised by certain types of experiences and lowered by the lack of such experiences in the home and the immediate neighborhood, as well as in the school. Conversation patterns differ. The amount of money earned by some families may limit their children's exposure to some types of leisure-time activities, and it also is a factor in determining whether parents can afford to supply the home with books, magazines, and other materials which, directly or indirectly, have educational value. Not least among the important environmental influences is the attitude of the parents toward education and educational values. A child may on the one hand have instilled in him the attitude that education is a good thing and to be taken advantage of, or on the other hand, that it is something to be endured until he is old enough to drop out.

The typical intelligence test contains many questions that relate to one's experiences, and without those experiences it is doubtful that a good score can be obtained. Consider this: An item on an IQ test (to be given to six- and seven-year-olds) is a picture of a man carrying a rolled-up umbrella as he walks through the rain. The question is put to the child, "What is silly about this picture?" How likely is the child to supply the correct answer if his

family, and most of the persons in his neighborhood, are too poor to own umbrellas? He may never have seen one in his entire life. Similarly, there are a number of questions that a person should be able to answer if he has learned what is usually expected in the classroom. Here the entire question of the quality of education comes into play. If an individual comes from a substandard school, he is not going to do as well as he might otherwise.

C 6.5. *The effects of environment on intelligence.*

In modern-day research the majority of current effort is going into the determination of the effects of

_____ on intelligence.

a. heredity   b. the environment

Relating to the notion of the environment's effects on intelligence is the concept of *IQ constancy*. We generally assume that an individual's IQ will be constant from year to year, with only minor changes. These changes are laid more to inaccuracy of the testing instruments than to actual fluctuations in one's capacity. We are not surprised to see an IQ of 107 for a child, then see his IQ listed as 105 on a test given the following year. We do *not*, however, expect to see 107 one year and 95 the next. This concept—IQ constancy—obviously depends upon a major assumption. That assumption is that the environment of the individual is of approximately average quality, in comparison with the general population. If the assumption is violated, the IQ may well change.

C 6.6.   *The concept of IQ constancy.*

The concept of IQ constancy is an assumption that the IQ of a given individual will _____

_____ .

The concept of IQ constancy depends, for its manifestation, upon the assumption that the environment

for a given individual is _____ .

    a. below average   b. approximately average   c. enriched

> Some years ago it was shown that if a child attended kindergarten, the result was a gain of approximately five IQ points, an increase that was maintained through the following years. In the days when this research was conducted, kindergarten was the exception rather than the rule for children. A few similar studies have been carried out during the last few years, but as yet scant attempts have been made to study the "enriched" environment for mature individuals. In one study however, the enriching effects of going to college were examined in relation to the IQ. It was first established, at a particular university, that the average first-semester freshman had an IQ of 108, while the average graduating senior had an IQ of 122. If we stopped at that point, this would be called *cross-sectional* research, and we might conclude that seniors have higher IQs than freshmen because their IQs have increased. We call research *longitudinal* if, on the other hand, the same individuals are followed up on subsequent measures over time. Four years went by and those persons from the freshman group of subjects who were still at the university and were listed as seniors were retested. Their IQ average was 122, but the freshman test score for *just those individuals* was 113. One conclusion was that the lower-IQ students from the freshman group were prone to leave college, while the higher-IQ students stayed and graduated. The main finding was that going to college for four years apparently raises the IQ by about nine points (Vernon, 1962).

C 6.7.   *Longitudinal and cross-sectional research.*

Cross-sectional research is illustrated in a case where one examines _____ .

    a. 500 dogs within a week's time, charting rate of "aggressiveness" as a function of their ages

    b. 100 kindergarten children for a few days to see if those older than five and one-half years of age demonstrate more social maturity than those younger than five and one-half

    c. a colony of monkeys for a year, to see if their sexual activity rates slow as they age

    d. (both a and b above are examples of cross-sectional research)

    e. (all of the first three cases are examples of cross-sectional research)

Longitudinal research might be said to *usually* be _____ .

    a. more difficult or more expensive to perform

    b. easier to terminate within a brief time

    c. the only genuine and worthwhile form of research

A variety of situations have been shown to deteriorate IQ. We would predict that any time an individual is in an environment that is inadequate in providing a typical variety of experiences and activities there would be a cumulative deterioration of IQ over a period of time. A research program was once conducted in a reformatory for boys, where long-term resident juvenile offenders were tested yearly while they lived in the institution and attended a rather marginal educational program conducted within the institution. Under these circumstances, it was concluded, the boys lost around four IQ points each year they spent there.

An even sharper loss was measured during a period in the 1930s in the deep South where, at that time, segregated schools were maintained. The facilities, materials, and often the teacher preparation for the black schools were grossly inadequate. This was cross-sectional research, which showed that grade by grade the mean IQ drifted lower and lower. Obviously, the situation that existed in the schools was compounded by similar deprivations in the poverty-level homes these children came from.

C 6.8.   *The effects of atypical environments on the IQ.*

Apparently, educational experiences that are not obtained by most people have what effect upon the individual who does experience them? _____ .

    a. Increase in IQ   b. Decrease in IQ   c. No change in IQ

It would seem that when individuals miss out on fairly common environmental and educational experiences, the IQ becomes _____ .

We stated earlier that there were two main questions involved—whether the environment affects the scores one gets on IQ tests (and we have answered yes to this question), and second, if some limitation might be placed on overall learning ability by the substandard environment; and, if so, whether it might be reversible. The answer to this second question is not at all clear.

Very obviously, from data and logic, we would predict poorer learning on tasks for which previous learning is a necessary foundation. Thus, in universities where underprivileged people are admitted under special programs for degree study, the history of experiences has not been initially a very happy one. In one institution, during a single year, 29 of 31 such individuals were not academically eligible to return after their first year. However, universities, faced with such problems as a student enrolled in a college-level-math course in spite of a dismal math background or one trying to master English composition although the language in his or her home and neighborhood was not of the middle-class style of speech, took remedial steps. Special tutorial programs were introduced, and to a certain extent this intensive personal assistance helped many of the special students to pass their courses and continue. This seemingly is evidence of an unorganized sort that those students who can "make up" their original deficits soon become able to make it on their own without special help.

Therefore, we might conclude that the only limitations on learning ability are in areas directly related to the substandard background, and that those limitations are reversible.

On the question of reversibility of the effects of environmental deprivation, we also have no clear-cut final evidence. First, we have a few cases of extreme deprivation in which parents cruelly imprison their children, locking them in attics or cellars. These "attic children" typically are fed, but have nothing to do with their time, nor does anyone talk to them. In the few cases that have come to light of children so deprived from their earliest days and then brought back into a normal environment as adolescents, it seems that there is such profound intellectual limitation that they never make complete recovery as productive human beings. Of course, the degree to which personality distortions affect progress is indeterminable.

Second, still on the question of reversibility, there is some evidence from the Operation Headstart efforts of the past few years. Involvement of the children in enriched environmental experiences has had the effect of bringing their IQs up to a more-or-less normal level. Unfortunately, Headstart involvements do not continue for a given child and the recent Westinghouse Study in Ohio found that Headstart children, three years later, had drifted back to the same IQ level from which they began their rise. Still, Headstart has given promise that reversibility, and not just a halting, of IQ declines is possible.

Lee, in 1951, conducted research on IQ reversibility in the Philadelphia school system. Prior research, as we indicated earlier, showed that the IQs of most black children in segregated southern schools drifted lower and lower year by year. Lee studied the subsequent pattern of change after southern black children moved with their families to Philadelphia. Children who entered the first grade after having recently arrived from the South had a mean IQ of 86, which rose to 89 in the second grade, to 92 in the fourth grade, and to 93 in the sixth grade. When southern-reared black children entered the Philadelphia schools at a later time of life, however, their IQs started lower and stayed lower than the group just described.

Perhaps the answer on reversibility is that low IQs due to environmental deprivation seem to be at least partially reversible, but the percentage of reversibility may vary, depending on the degree to which the IQ has been affected by the environmental factor and the duration of that influence.

PROGRESS CHECK 6.1

1. Which is true of the test/retest reliability coefficient for an individual on the same IQ test? _____ .

    a. It is 1.00   b. It is surprisingly low

    c. It is the same as the coefficent for identical twins

    d. This type of study has not been done

2. In Tryon's experiments with selective breeding of rats _____ .

    a. differences in brightness were not observed until the fourth generation

    b. intelligence was measured by maze errors

    c. dietary deficiencies produced dull rats

    d. intelligence and bar pressing were related

3. In comparison to animal research on the genetic basis of intelligence, which is true of human research? _____ .

    a. Researchers have greater control over correlated variables such as diet

    b. Researchers have less control over correlated variables such as diet

4. Current research on the determinants of intelligence focuses mostly on _____ .

    a. environment   b. heredity   c. both equally

5. The concept of IQ constancy depends on which assumption? _____ .

    a. An individual's environment remains relatively the same

    b. An individual's environment is of average quality

    c. Both   d. The concept does not require assumptions

MATCH: _____ 6. Longitudinal research   A. Study of feeding behavior among a group of infants

    _____ 7. Cross-sectional research

    B. Study of changes in feeding behavior with a group of children over a five-year period

8. Which is true of the effect of atypical environments on IQ? _____ .

    a. People who miss common environmental and educational experiences have lower IQs

    b. Unique experiences such as college seem to increase IQs

    c. Both   d. Neither

MEASUREMENT OF INTELLIGENCE

The concept of intelligence and speculation into its origins has a very ancient history, but is was only in the early part of the nineteenth century that people actually began to consider intelligence a measurable thing. As early as 1838, in a publication in France, an author discussed intelligence—particularly in relation to the classification of mental retardation—and he falsely speculated that certain physical measures, such as the size of the skull, might be valid intelligence measures.

Individual mental testing has had an extensive history. Francis Galton, the younger cousin of Charles Darwin, first suggested the notion of systematic measurement of the intellect. In 1869, only a few years after Darwin published his *Origin of Species,* Galton issued a book titled *Hereditary Genius* which applied some of Darwin's notions to the question of intellect. Galton noted that while different individuals show wide differences in intellectual ability, a fairly specific level of intellectual ability seems to run strongly within many families, suggesting that the basis for these capabilities may be inherited. This is particularly obvious in the cases of the higher levels of intellect, indicated by achieved eminence. Galton went back through British history and noted that politicians, scientists, judges, and authors seemed to "run in families." The fact of "eminent families" in Great Britain was taken, by itself, to be evidence of genetic strains of superior mental ability. Galton compared Darwin's already well-known notions of natural biological variation to obvious variations in mental ability, suggesting a common basis.

At the present state of scientific development, we are extremely sensitive to the role played by environment, and we tend to be skeptical of genealogical evidence unsupported by further data. Galton was not much more content with this approach than we are today, and within a very few years he had established a laboratory within which he actually tried to test mental ability. Galton knew that mentally defective individuals often lack sensory acuity, and he guessed that there might be a relation that could be established between intelligence and the keenness of the senses—the ability to distinguish between weights which differed only slightly, to differentiate between slightly different tones of a high pitch, to detect minor changes in heat and cold, and so forth.

C 6.9. *Early efforts to measure the intellect.*

Galton was one of the first persons to attempt to systematically measure intellectual ability. His approach was through various tests of _____ .

    a. problem-solving ability   b. reasoning   c. sensory acuity   d. common sense

Shortly thereafter a number of other scientists began their search for a practical intelligence test. An American psychologist, James McKeen Cattell, used the term "mental test" in 1890 as he described some of his studies of the mental abilities of students. Cattell used similar notions as Galton's, but additionally measured color discrimination, the perception of time, memory, and various other measures. In 1893, Joseph Jastrow collected data at the Chicago Columbian Exposition, where spectators subjected themselves to batteries of tests which included dividing lines into sections of equal length and reading words exposed only momentarily. In 1891 an anthropologist, Franz Boas, measured 1,500 children in Massachusetts, requiring them to repeat back as many as possible of a list of numbers just heard. This test, termed *immediate memory span,* still appears in various intelligence tests. At approximately this time J. A. Gilbert developed test measures which he attempted to correlate with teachers' impressions of the intelligence of children. He found that the children who were quickest at pressing a button when a light appeared were also the brightest according to their teachers' evaluations. Reaction time and intelligence are not highly correlated according to modern-day standards, yet this provided still another dimension to be further investigated.

Interest intensified, and the fairly new American Psychological Association in the mid-1890's formed a committee to consider the feasibility of cooperation among the various university laboratories interested in the measurement of mental abilities. Yet the first practical application of method was done by a French psychologist, Alfred Binet.

Binet and Formal Intelligence Tests

In an article written in 1895, Alfred Binet and a colleague argued for mental testing based on thought processes rather than on sensory and motor functions. At the time Binet was unclear on just what should be measured, but the article suggested tests of memory, imagination, attentiveness, verbal comprehension, and moral awareness. Binet and his colleagues committed themselves subsequently to the study of the measurement of intellectual processes, using as subjects mainly children from the schools of Paris. As it turned out, the use of children as subjects was merely an accident, but it led naturally to an appreciation of the mental age of the individual as it related to his abilities. Rather than speculate on the countless ways in which one might go about distinguishing between duller and smarter adults, it dawned on these investigators that in many ways the duller adult might be equated along most dimensions to children of given ages.

As the years passed Binet established many measures and tables of norms, all based on the testing of children. It was natural, therefore, that in 1904 when the Minister of Public Instruction wanted a way to identify subnormal children in the Paris schools, he turned immediately to Binet. It was the intent at that time to place mentally defective children in special schools where they could be helped, but the problem first was to find them. Binet, using his tests and available norms, was able to establish the different ages at which children, on the average, could perform each of a number of mental activites.

Binet's ideas caught on rapidly. As you might suppose, it was not only in France that the average eight-year-old child could just barely repeat five digits read to him; and so the Binet scale was adapted for use in Belgium, Great Britain, the United States, Italy, and certain other countries. Most items on the test seemed to cross national and language boundaries.

Intelligence Test Items

In the first practical test Binet and his colleague, Simon, had a progression of 30 tests covering the range of mental ability. At the youngest ages the examiner determined whether a young child would visually follow an object presented in his field of vision. Grasping movements were then noted, imitations of gestures, the following of instructions to touch various parts of the body, the naming of familiar objects, repeating sentences, constructing sentences to include three given words, and the ability to distinguish between abstract words with similar meaning.

In 1911 a new version of Binet's test was issued, featuring five problems which the average child of each age could solve. Herrnstein (1973) has noted the problems for the six-year-old level:

1. Distinguish between morning and afternoon.
2. Define familiar objects in terms of their use.
3. Copy a diamond shape.
4. Count 13 coins.
5. Distinguish between pretty and ugly faces.

For the average ten-year-old these were the appropriate problems:

1. Arrange five objects in order of weight.
2. Draw two designs from memory.
3. Criticize absurd statements.
4. Answer questions reflecting comprehension.
5. Use three words within not more than two sentences.

The difficulty level of each item was determined by administering it to large numbers of normal children from ages three to eleven. An item was considered appropriate to a given age if approximately half of the children of that age could answer it correctly, and if fewer than half of younger children could answer it correctly while more than half of older children could. The test items gave a very strong emphasis to judgment, comprehension, and reasoning, reflecting Binet's view of the structure of intelligence. Thus a child was said to have a "mental age," meaning the age of normal children whose performance he equalled.

About a decade and a half later, Professor Terman of Stanford University translated and adapted the original Binet-Simon scale for use in the United States, and he derived norms of thousands of American school children. The American version was known as the *Stanford-Binet*. Essentially the procedure goes like this: A seven-year-old child, for example, would ascend through several levels of difficulty. He might first be given the materials appropriate for a five-year-old. He would be given six problems at each age level. If he got all six five-year items correct, he would proceed to the six-year level for six more problems. Suppose he got all of those right, but missed some of the seven-year items. We would then say six is his *basal age*. At the seven-year level, let us say he got four of the six correct. He is given two months credit for each correct item (i.e., eight months). He then goes to the eight-year level where, let us say, he gets two of the six correct, again receiving two months credit for each of the two (four more months), and then he gets none correct at the nine-year level. We would take the basal age—six—and give credit for the higher-level problems answered correctly, which would give 12 more months of "mental" age to be added to the basal age. This, then, is the mental age of the child—7–0, meaning seven years plus zero months. Suppose the child were actually 7–6 years old (7 years and 6 months) in chronological age. We could then say his CA (chronological age) is 90 months and his MA (mental age) is 84 months. We would set up the fraction: $\dfrac{MA}{CA}$ which would equal $\dfrac{84}{90}$ or .933. Next, we multiply the quotient by 100, resulting in the intelligence quotient (IQ) which, in this case, is 93.

C 6.10.   *The Stanford-Binet intelligence test.*

The individual who was responsible for the initial translation and adaptation of Binet's intelligence test

for use in the United States was _____ .

a. Simon   b. Terman   c. Galton

The age level where a child gets *all* of the items correct on the Stanford-Binet is called the

_____ age.

Calculate the IQ's for four individuals as follows:

1. John has a mental age of 4 years 2 months (hint: this is to be converted to *50 months*), and

   a chronological age of exactly 6 years. His IQ is _____ . (Was your answer, rounded

   to the nearest point, 69? If not, get some help in your calculations.)

2. Millie has a CA of 4 years 8 months and an MA of 6-1 (Six years, one month). Her IQ is _____ .

   a. 110   b. 120   c. 130   d. 140

3. Jimmie has an MA of 14-0 and a CA of 14-6. His IQ is _____ .

   a. 92   b. 96   c. 99   d. 104

4. An institutionalized child has a CA of 13-1 and an MA of 6-4. Its IQ is _____ .

   a. 38   b. 48   c. 58   d. 65

The Stanford-Binet test of intelligence has been a widely used instrument, with a great deal of supporting research. In this country revised editions are occasionally issued. The reasons are obvious—children are growing up in an increasingly technological society and the daily experiences of the child of the 1970s are quite unlike those of the child of the 1930s or 1940s. If a child of the present, given an outdated test showing a picture involving an automobile missing a wheel, is asked what is odd or funny about the picture, he might say the car itself is funny, thus missing the main point in the picture's contents. Also, the norms are kept current through restandardization of new revisions so that a child's MA is being divided by the CA on the basis of MA norms of a contemporary group of children—not those of two decades ago. Thus, if children get "brighter," the "average" of them still perform so as to be assigned an IQ of approximately 100.

The logic of an intelligence quotient is that if a seven-and-a-half-year-old child has the mental ability of an average seven-and-a-half-year-old, his IQ is 100. The test has been refined to the point that this is exactly so. Also, the distribution of IQs on the Stanford-Binet is very smooth in the normal distribution sense, and it has been established that the standard deviation of the Stanford-Binet is 16 points. Let us expand upon the matter of the standard deviation, since some facts about standard deviations can allow us to infer quite a bit about relative test performance.

Standard Deviations of Test Performances

In Chapter Five you were familiarized with the notion of standard deviation. In essence you learned that in addition to knowing the mean on standardized tests, proper interpretation of individual scores also calls for knowledge of how to interpret deviations from the mean; this is the essential purpose of calculating the standard deviation. It is important to remember that the mathematical laws surrounding the standard deviation no longer apply if a normative distribution of scores varies away from being normal (symmetrical). Also, there must have been a reasonably large number of scores in the normative distribution, and the population being tested should be similar to the normative population. With these cautions in mind, let us see how knowledge of a test's standard deviation assists us to interpret individual scores.

In a perfectly normal distribution, about 68.3 percent of the obtained scores are found between one standard deviation below the mean and one standard deviation above the mean ($\pm 1s$). Since the distribution is symmetrical, this breaks down to a value of 34 percent between $-1s$ and the mean, and 34 percent between the mean and $+1s$. Within the range $\pm 2s$, we may expect about 95 percent of the values, and within the range of $\pm 3s$, about 99.7 percent of the values. In Figure 6.1, you can see the exact percentage of cases falling into each section of the curve, as it is divided at the points representing the value of the standard deviation.

What this means is that once you are told the mean of a normal distribution and the value of its standard deviation, you can accurately estimate the percentage of cases falling above and below any given value within the distribution. This cannot be done precisely with only the limited information presented here, but tables of normal curve probabilities are available that show exact probabilities at all intermediate points. So, if you were told that your score was 1.70 standard deviations above the mean, you could tell what percentage of the normative group you surpassed, and what percentage did better than you. Interestingly, you may run into such reports later if you have teachers who report examination performance in z-scores. A z-score is simply a statement of how many standard deviations you were away from the mean and in what direction, so that a z-score of 1.70 would tell you that you were above the mean (since 1.70 is a positive number), and you were one and seven-tenths standard deviations distance from the mean.

Figure 6.1

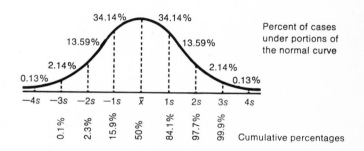

For the moment, however, let us simply talk in terms of whole-number standard deviations. If you were to have an IQ score of 132 on the Stanford-Binet test, this would be 2s above the mean, since the mean is 100 and the standard deviation value is 16 on the Stanford-Binet. And, examining Figure 6.1, you can see that only 2.27 percent of the persons in the general population exceed +2s, your S-B (Stanford-Binet) score. At this point you should be able to state the percentages of persons exceeding certain Stanford-Binet values, or falling within certain ranges.

C 6.11. *Standard deviations of test performances.*

The Stanford-Binet IQ test has a standard deviation of _____ points.

What percentage of persons in the general population have S-B scores above 116 (rounded to the nearest point)? _____ .

What percentage of persons in the general population have S-B scores lower than 100? _____ .

Lower than 84? _____ . Lower than 132? _____ .

What exact percentage of persons in the general population have S-B scores above 148? _____ .

You could correctly say that approximately one person out of _____ in the general population has an IQ score of 116 or above.

a. 2   b. 4   c. 6   d. 10

C 6.12. *Z-scores.*

What approximate percentage of persons in a normally distributed group would have z-scores lower than −2.00? _____ . Higher than −2.00? _____ . Higher than .00? _____ .

Occasionally one finds z-score values well beyond 3.0 or −3.0. This is due to two factors. First, it is typical in such cases that the curve upon which the mean and standard deviation values are fixed is not perfectly normal. Second, even in a normal distribution, the mathematical possibility exists that standard deviation values might be achieved—although at fantastically low probabilities—at any point within possible score values, even if this means a z-score of 10 or 15.

Before going on to a discussion of another major test of intelligence, it should be noted that the normal curve we have been discussing describes the IQs of persons in the normally educable general population. The test norms deliberately avoided institutional populations. The actual curve of the *entire* population has a rather pronounced hump at the lower end, which is the result of the fairly large number of persons who, through a genetic accident, physical damage, or for other reasons, are classed as mentally retarded. The individuals who are severely retarded, if not institutionalized, at least are not in attendance in the public schools, and on that basis were not included in the normative data.

The Wechsler Scales

A number of years after the use of the Stanford-Binet came to be widespread, Dr. David Wechsler of Bellevue Hospital in New York City published the Wechsler-Bellevue Intelligence Test. After several years of use it was republished in an improved form, and divided into a test for adults and a test for children. (There is also a third form, that we shall not discuss at this point.) The adult scale is called the WAIS (Wechsler Adult Intelligence Scale), and it has largely replaced the Stanford-Binet for most psychologists who test adult intelligence. The children's scale is called the WISC (Wechsler Intelligence Scale for Children), and it is used by professionals involved in testing children's intelligence to a somewhat greater degree than is the Stanford-Binet.

An advantage of the Wechsler scales over the S-B is that "ability" is broken down into several more precise categories, and relative strengths and weaknesses can be assessed. While the S-B, at each age level, employs a mixed variety of items, the Wechsler is broken into two areas—verbal and performance. Each renders its own IQ score, and in a combined form they are used to calculate the full-scale IQ. Each area is broken down further into individual subtests:

Verbal tests:	*Performance tests:*
Information	Picture Arrangement
General Comprehension	Picture Completion
Digit Span	Block Design
Arithmetical Reasoning	Object Assembly
Similarities	Digit Symbol
Vocabulary	

All of the items on the verbal test call upon some degree of verbal skill, while the performance tests are largely free from reliance on language. For example, the object assembly test is similar to a jigsaw puzzle. For *certain types* of individuals, a performance test score is sometimes assumed to be, by itself, a more valid IQ than is the verbal or even the full-scale score. This is so when we are dealing with individuals whose native language is not English, or who have some other form of language deficiency.

One major departure on the Wechsler scales is that one no longer actually calculates a mental age and then goes through the process of mathematical division to obtain the IQ. Instead, a *deviation IQ* is located on a chart on the basis of the examinee's CA (chronological age) and the number of points (scale scores) made on the tests. Wechsler has set the standard deviation for his tests at 15 points rather than the S-B's 16. As a result, the following chart is appropriate for the Wechsler scales:

IQ	% of individuals
130+	2.2
120–29	6.7
110–19	16.1
90–109	50.0
80–89	16.1
70–79	6.7
below 70	2.2

As you should be able to see quite easily, the normative group is again the general noninstitutionalized population; the *total* population, which includes persons in custodial institutions, is *not* represented.

C 6.13. *The Wechsler Intelligence Scales.*

The common abbreviation for Wechsler's Intelligence Test for Children is the _____ .

Such abilities as block design, picture arrangement, and object assembly are called _____ tests of intelligence.

Estimates of IQ based just on performance tests subscales may be more valid than the full scale IQ score for individuals who _____ .

    a. are very young   b. have language handicaps   c. are mentally retarded

Instead of a calculation of MA, CA, and then IQ, the Wechsler scales use a concept of _____ IQ.

Both the S-B and the Wechsler scales are called *individual tests of intelligence*. This means that a trained person sits with a single examinee and administers the test in a quiet atmosphere. A large number of responses on an individual test of intelligence are oral statements by the examinee in response to questions put by the examiner. Individual tests are frequently used in clinical situations and in situations where, because of specific difficulties, administrators are interested in a precise knowledge of a school child's intellectual capabilities. On the other hand, as you can easily see, the costs associated with administration of individual tests of intelligence limit their use in such settings as schools and employment offices, where large numbers of individuals are routinely tested. Practicality dictates that many organizations use *group tests of intelligence*. These tests, of which there are several, are designed for use with a number of persons at one time. Also, the administration of group tests is typically quite simple, and does not call for the presence of a highly trained examiner. Most group tests are generally patterned, in content, after the S-B or the Wechsler scales.

C 6.14. *Group versus individual tests of intelligence.*

The S-B and the Wechsler are both _____ tests of intelligence.

Which of the following types of tests would be the most expensive to administer to a large number of persons? _____ .

    a. an individual test of intelligence   b. a group test of intelligence

PROGRESS CHECK   6.2

1. A seven-year-old child gets all of the items correct on the test for eight-year-olds. What is the child's

   basal age? _____ .

   a. 7 years   b. 8 years   c. 7/8 months   d. 114 IQ

2. Which statement is true of the Stanford-Binet IQ test? _____ .

   a. The standard deviation is 16 points   b. Half the population have IQs of less than 100

   c. Less than 1 percent of the population have IQs greater than 148   d. All of these

3. What does a z-score tell you on a Stanford-Binet test? _____ .

   a. How many standard deviations above the mean someone is

   b. How many standard deviations below the mean someone is

   c. Either a or b   d. Neither answer

4. Which form of the Wechsler Intelligence Test is used for children? _____ .

   a. WISC   b. WAIS

5. Which of these might be on a performance test of intelligence? _____ .

   a. Information   b. Digit span   c. Vocabulary   d. Object assembly

6. For an individual with a language deficiency which type of IQ test is more appropriate? _____ .

   a. Verbal test   b. Performance test   c. Full-scale

7. Deviation IQ is _____ .

   a. (MA X 100)/CA   b. scale for use with Stanford-Binet

   c. the same as a z-score   d. scale for use with a Wechsler test

---

VALIDITY AND RELIABILITY OF TESTS If a test is to have any value at all, it must have both validity and reliability. These are vital terms that have relevance to all efforts to systematically measure human performance.

Validity *Validity* involves the question, "Just what is it that this test measures?" There are a number of different types of validity, and if you take a later course in psychological measurement you will be exposed to them all. For the time being, however, let us simply discuss the most obvious types.

Predictive Validity

First, a test may have *predictive validity*. This means that the test scores correlate with later performance on the task that the test was designed to predict. ACT scores (college entrance examination), for example, are validated against the subsequent grade point averages of the students, and if there is a strong correlation, then we say the test is valid. This is the most important form of validity.

Concurrent Validity

A test may have *concurrent validity*. This means that the test scores correlate with a test for which predictive validity has already been established. Thus, if one has developed a new group IQ test, rather than administer the test to a large number of subjects, then follow them through their academic careers for several years, it is possible to correlate their scores on the new test with their scores on the Stanford-Binet or the Wechsler. A high correlation would be evidence of validity. This form of "indirect validation" is extremely common because it is not only expensive but extremely time-consuming to establish predictive validity. You should recognize, of course, that concurrent validity is less impressive than is a demonstration of predictive validity.

Construct Validity

A completely different type of validity is represented in *construct validity*. This, simply stated, means that the test's contents are consistent with a particular point of view (theory) of the nature of that which is being measured. For instance, the ability to recite quickly and accurately "Peter Piper picked a peck of pickled peppers" has no particular relationship to *anyone's* recognized notion of what intelligence is; therefore, the ability to recite tongue-twisting phrases accurately has little construct validity in an intelligence test. However, a recognized theoretical position is that intelligence consists of several factors, two of them being the ability to remember (memory) and the ability to reason. Items calling out these abilities would likely have acceptable construct validity.

Face Validity

The final type of validity that will be discussed here is *face validity*. This is unimportant in some ways, but important in others. It simply means that an item ideally should *seem like* it is measuring what it is presumed to measure. The only point to be made is that there is sometimes a disquieting effect on the examinee if he perceives a test as being silly or unfair, particularly if the test is being administered in connection with selection for an educational or employment opportunity.

C 6.15. *Test validity.*

Test validity is described by the question "What is it that a test ＿＿＿＿＿＿＿＿＿＿＿＿ ?"

Which of the several types of validity is the most important? ＿＿＿＿＿＿＿＿＿＿＿＿ .

A short cut, indirect means of approximating predictive validity comes through_____ validity.

If a test item "seems like" it is measuring what it is intended to measure, it is said to have_____ validity.

    a. predictive   b. concurrent   c. construct   d. face

Reliability   *Reliability* refers to whether or not a test accurately and consistently measures that which it is measuring. A thermometer is a good example of an instrument with high reliability. If we measured the temperature in a room, then removed the thermometer, and later re-entered the room with the thermometer and took a new measurement (providing the room had not been aired or otherwise changed), we would be extremely surprised if the thermometer gave a totally different reading the second time. We would decide that the instrument lacked reliability.

Overall Reliability

What we have just described is *overall reliability,* as assessed by the test-retest method. Overall reliability is the major form of test reliability. Let us examine how the procedure might proceed. In the case of an intelligence test we ordinarily allow several months to elapse before retesting, during which time we assume that the details of the test will have been forgotten. The correlation coefficient between the first and the second testings then tells us about the test's reliability.

Internal Reliability

Another desirable form of reliability is *internal reliability.* In this case you might consider each test item individually to see if persons who had overall high scores on the test had a greater rate of being correct on each specific item than persons with overall low scores on the test. This technique of establishing internal reliability is called *item analysis.* Another way of establishing internal reliability is called the *split-half method,* in which the individuals' performances on one-half of the test are compared with the performances on the other half. Obviously, if an individual scores very high on the one half, in comparison with other persons, he would be expected to achieve a similar high score on the other half.

The concept of internal reliability is an important one in psychological measurement, but unfortunately there are persons who do not recognize that the concept presupposes, to a degree, that the test (or a test's independently established subscale) is measuring a *single factor.* For example, some professors, after administering a multiple-choice examination, "improve" it by first performing an item analysis. If there are a handful of items on which individuals' performances seemed only barely related to their overall examination scores, those items are then eliminated from the examination.

Now suppose, for a moment, that on a 60-item examination there are 50 items calling for the exercise of memory and 10 items calling for a considerable degree of abstract reasoning. There would almost certainly be a much lower relationship between performance on the reasoning items and the overall examination score than there would be between the memory items and the overall examination score, since the latter predominate. As a result of hasty utilization of item analysis, allowing discard of the unrelated items, the test would become more "pure" thereafter, with the retained items all testing only one thing—memory.

To summarize the statements made in this brief section, a test's overall reliability is vital, and any published test of IQ, personality traits, and the like must have its *overall* reliability established. In the matter of *internal* reliability, on the other hand, the concept is risky where a test measures more than a single factor.

C 6.16. *Test reliability.*

Test reliability refers to how _____ a test performs its measurement function.

    a. easily   b. inexpensively   c. accurately and consistently

The test-retest method is used in order to establish the _____ reliability of a test.

    a. overall   b. internal

When we relate success on a single item to the entire test score, we are establishing _____ reliability.

    a. overall   b. internal

State two methods of establishing internal reliability:

    1. _____

    2. _____

There is an assumption behind the item analysis method, used to establish internal reliability, which in some cases makes the technique questionable. It is that the technique implicitly assumes that _____ .

    a. the test is measuring a single factor   b. that each item is measuring an independant factor

    c. that internal reliability is the same thing as overall reliability

Which type of reliability is vitally important to any standardized test? _____ .

    a. overall   b. internal

Any standardized test—be it a test of abilities or a test of personality characteristics—must have an acceptable degree of both validity and overall reliability. Tests are ordinarily predictive instruments, so we must verify that they predict according to an acceptable criterion of performance— predictive validity. Then, we expect the test to have a high degree of precision, so that on retesting we do not see results varying wildly—overall reliability. Any new test placed on the market has to justify itself in terms of basic preliminary research into its validity and reliability.

VALIDITY OF INTELLIGENCE TESTS

While the establishment of the overall reliability of tests is a somewhat tedious, routine chore, the establishment of predictive validity is a fluid and vital step. Here the psychologist can decide what sort of predictive criteria to use. Let us take the intelligence test, for example. Suppose you have a new test. You give it to a large number of persons and get a range of scores. Now what? You know you have to see later how those persons do on some other measure that represents "actual" intelligence. What measure could that be?

Generally, constructors of individual intelligence tests have chosen academic success as the predictive criterion. Of course there are problems here. First, academic success is the direct result of *both* intellectual ability and applied effort (motivation?). Second, it is well-known that in the public schools (where validity research is typically conducted) a great number of factors other than strict academic criteria affect teacher judgment and resulting grades. Class conduct, whether the student "joins in," neatness of written work, articulateness of speech, and even such things as a child's sex or race in some classrooms, all contribute to assessment and the grades given by the teacher. Therefore, we do not get outstandingly high validity coefficients. Still, grades in school are the foundation of intelligence test predictive validity. Both the S-B and the Wechsler scales have independently

established predictive validity in educational settings. For example, one investigation (Bond, 1940), involving tenth grade students, found correlations between S-B IQ and reading comprehension of .73, spelling .46, history class grades .59, geometry class grades .48, and biology class grades .54.

To a limited extent, IQ test scores have been validated on the basis of success on the job. In one study (Vernon, 1963), IQ scores were related to scores on a four-level "promotability" index for lower and middle level management personnel in a large office of a food manufacturer. One hundred and forty-four persons were rated by their immediate superiors on their judged potential for promotion. The raters were not supplied with the ratees' IQ scores. The correlation coefficient was .58 between the two measures, suggesting that fairly good predictability of success in management development can be obtained from knowledge of individuals' IQ scores.

In the cases of new *group tests* of intelligence, test developers usually seek concurrent validity—the device of correlating scores on the new test with scores on an individual test of intelligence that already has established predictive validity. This is like the old geometry axiom that two things equal to a third are equal to each other. If a new test is "equal" to a test with established validity, then it, too, is assumed to have validity.

C 6.17. *The validity of intelligence tests.*

Group intelligence tests have, for the most part, been validated in terms of _____ .

    a. the prediction of academic success

    b. their correlation with individual IQ test scores   c. occupational success

Individual tests of intelligence usually have well-developed _____ validity.

    a. predictive   b. concurrent

Group intelligence tests typically rely on the development of _____ validity.

    a. predictive   b. concurrent

PROGRESS CHECK 6.3

1. Which IQ test would be least expensive to administer to all fifth-graders in the Wilmette School District? _____ .

    a. Stanford-Binet   b. WAIS   c. A group test   d. Cost is about equal

2. If a dominance test actually predicts social dominance, then it has _____ .

    a. validity   b. reliability

3. You might do an item analysis on a test to establish _____ .

    a. overall reliability   b. construct validity   c. external reliability   d. internal reliability

4. Where a test measures multiple factors, _____ .

    a. item analyses are risky measures of internal reliability

    b. split-half methods are risky measures of internal reliability

    c. overall reliability must be established   d. all of these

5. Reliability means _____ .

    a. the test correlates with performance   b. the test is accurate and consistent

    c. both   d. neither

MATCH: _____ 6. Individual intelligence   A. Rely on predictive validity

                    tests   B. Rely on concurrent validity

        _____ 7. Group intelligence tests

RACE AND INTELLIGENCE   On the next page there is an account of a person faced with a very strange-appearing "intelligence" test as part of a job-application process.

    Unless you are black and from a fairly impoverished background, the story may give you your first opportunity to appreciate how many people—both white and black—feel when they are confronted with the hurdle of an intelligence test when applying for a job or for some type of educational benefit. Poor people, regardless of their color, have often had little experience with many of the sorts of things that come up on intelligence tests. Some people believe that the whole affair of intelligence testing is unfair to certain groups. So, in 1968, a black sociologist, Adrian Dove, devised "Black Questions for Whitey," with thirty questions in all, six of which you have just seen. Last year, when we asked an auditorium group of 350 students the six questions, only two students got all the answers right, and they were both black.

    Dove did not propose his test seriously as a replacement for standard intelligence tests, but Dr. Robert Williams, past-president of the Black Psychologists Association, proposes to construct a real black intelligence test with norms established solely on black people. He proposes to insist that the test be used exclusively as the testing instrument whenever a black person is to be tested in an educational or business institution.

    Black groups have been the most outspoken critics of standard intelligence testing. Historically, in IQ testing, the means for black groups are lower than the means for whites. The critics point out, quite accurately, that the assumption of an "average environment" is not typically satisfied in the black community. If a child comes from an impoverished family and his parents are uneducated, he may never have heard spoken certain words that are in the vocabulary section of the IQ test.

    Some black spokesmen call for the abolishment of IQ testing altogether. Others, like Dr. Williams, feel that a special black IQ test should

A JOB APPLICATION TEST

You have come into a small room. Someone hands you a sheet of questions, along with an IBM answer sheet and a sharpened pencil, and then leaves you alone. It is a test of your intelligence. If you do well, you get the job. If you do not do well, you will not be hired. You have very little money. Your wife is waiting outside in the automobile to see if you get work. You look at the test:

1. Whom did Stagger Lee kill in the famous blues legend?
   a) his mother
   b) Frankie
   c) Johnnie
   d) his girl friend
   e) Billie

2. If you threw the dice and seven is showing, what is facing down?
   a) seven
   b) snake eyes
   c) box cars
   d) little Joes
   e) eleven

3. In C. C. Rider, what does C. C. stand for?
   a) civil service
   b) church council
   c) country club
   d) country circuit
   e) cheating Charlie

4. Cheap chitlings will taste rubbery if they are not cooked long enough. How soon should you quit cooking them?
   a) 15 minutes
   b) 8 hours
   c) 24 hours
   d) one week on a low flame

5. Hattie Mae is on the County. She has four children to feed and her husband is in jail for nonsupport. Her welfare check is $286 per month. Last night she went out with the biggest player in town. If she got pregnant, then nine months from now how much more will her welfare check be?
   a) $80
   b) $2
   c) $35
   d) $150
   e) $100

6. The Hully-Gully came from
   a) East Oakland
   b) Fillmore
   c) Watts
   d) Harlem
   e) Motor City

You sit and stare at this test for a few minutes. It seems unfair because you just don't know much about the sorts of things that are being asked. Nevertheless you go through the motions, filling in answers, and you then turn in the test to the man who comes to collect it. You dully leave the building, realizing that there is very little chance that you will be called to come to work on the basis of your test results. The only thing that stands between you and that job is the test which you just took, and you can't see how its contents could have anything to do with running a machine or working on an assembly line.

Adrian Dove devised 30 "Black Questions for Whitey" in a non-serious vein to make his point that white intelligence tests for blacks are frequently unfair.

be used with black people. In his address to the Association of Black Psychologists (1973), Williams states that it "is morally wrong for black and other minority children to continue to experience the psychological abuse and dehumanization inflicted via the administration of IQ tests." Williams' own words provide the best elaboration of his point of view:

> The damage resulting from the use of culturally biased IQ tests affects more than the child's immediate academic situation. Evidence indicates that knowledge of a child's intellectual potential can influence the expectancies of teachers, which in turn influences the performance of the child (Rosenthal & Jacobson, 1968). Expectations of parents, family, and the community are also influenced by information from recognized authorities that a child's intellectual ability is limited. The educational programs into which these inappropriately labeled students are then channeled provide limited stimulation and opportunity to prepare them for a full range of academic or occupational careers. Thus, opportunities for jobs and economic security are also greatly diminished. In other words there is a clear ripple effect of the damage that improper labeling and tracking can have. There is the immediate and lasting damage inflicted on the child in terms of his self-image and his future development. The family and the community suffer by being deprived of a potentially productive contributor.

If IQ testing were to be abolished, there certainly might be positive gains. Some individuals cannot then be further penalized because of social factors over which they never had control. The disadvantage is that this discards an important predictive measure. If academic decisions are being made, the fact that the test has been validated on the predictive criterion of academic achievement should be considered. At the very least, such tests offer the possibility of enlightened career guidance. Of course, it is totally without foundation to say that certain IQ standards can be specified below which individuals have *no chance* of success in, say, law school or medical school. A psychologist can, however, realistically suggest that the chances are slim for persons with a given level of IQ.

In one case, a physician had his son's IQ tested after he became worried about the boy's failure to make high grades in his ninth-grade courses. The father expected, quite absolutely, that his son would study medicine. The IQ of the boy was 104, and it could be said fairly confidently that he would experience difficulty with a respectable premedical curriculum, to say nothing of medical studies thereafter. While offering hope that the boy might make it, the psychologist in the case counseled the father in ways that made less likely the possibility of his later reflecting disappointment in his son, and perhaps causing the boy to have feelings of inferiority or guilt.

In industrial settings intelligence testing makes possible the placement of individuals into positions that do not overchallenge them to the point of failure. Laws now exist that restrict job selection and assignment on the basis of tests to only those tests that have had predictive validity established on the criterion of performance within the job category being filled.

The other proposed solution to the "problem" of IQ test fairness—the so-called "black IQ test"—is a proposition that is subject to criticism. The implication exists, in the proposition, that black people cannot compete on the same terms, and many persons would resist this implication vigorously. Also, according to the statements of some of the proposition's advocates, it is doubtful that predictive validity would be established on academic criteria. Therefore, of what use would a black IQ test be as a predictor? What would be the criteria against which predictive validity would be established? These are questions that concern persons who administer and utilize IQ tests.

On Jensenism   One of the most loaded topics to emerge in the field of psychology in the last several years began with an article published in 1969 in the prestigious *Harvard Educational Review* by Dr. Arthur Jensen. The board of editors of that journal solicited Jensen to prepare an article on the topic, "How Much Can We Boost IQ and Scholastic Achievement?" The result was a 123-page publication—the longest ever published in the *Harvard Educational Review*. Since that time there has been an extreme amount of reaction on the parts of psychologists and educators in related disciplines, most of it hostile to the general content of Jensen's statements.

First Jensen's article reviews the conclusions of a nation-wide survey and evaluation of the various federally funded compensatory education programs, such as Project Headstart. This document, produced by the United States Commission on Civil Rights, had earlier concluded that compensatory programs had produced *no* significant improvement in the measured intelligence or the scholastic performance of the disadvantaged children who were its presumed beneficiaries. The Commission was faced with the decision of either recommending that the programs be reduced or abandoned due to their ineffectiveness, or raised to a larger scale in an effort to produce the desired results. Jensen's interpretation is that increasing compensatory education on a larger scale is not likely to improve the situation. He questions the assumptions, theories, and practices on which the programs were based.

Jensen points out that some small-scale innovative programs have shown considerable promise of beneficial results, and he does not advocate abandoning efforts to compensate and improve the education of the disadvantaged. Nevertheless, while he supports the expansion of a diversity of approaches and rigorous experimentation with methods of boosting educational achievement, his suggestion that "larger doses of the same" form of compensatory education would not help scholastic achievement and should be abandoned has not been well-accepted in many quarters. Many individuals view Jensen's remarks that Project Headstart was functionally inefficient as an attack on minority individuals' rights to get ahead in the world.

The majority of Jensen's paper is given over to a review of evidence leading to his conclusion that individual differences in IQ are predominantly attributable to genetic differences, with environmental factors contributing a lesser portion of the variance in IQ in groups of individuals. "Heritability" of the IQ, which means the percentage of the variance attributable to genetic factors, is calculated by Jensen at about 80 percent.

Turning from the analysis of the degree of heritability of IQ to the differences between IQ averages of different races in the United States, Jensen reviews studies that indicate that under conditions as equal and comparable as can be expected in this nation, black students almost invariably show a lower mean IQ than white students. Jensen grants that a certain amount of the IQ difference is attributable to environmental differences that are predominantly linked with family income level. This means that groups of black children, *due to an artifact of society* that places most black families in the low-income range, are subjected to environments that by general standards are educationally impoverished in that they fail to provide a suitable variety of complex learning experiences. Still, with the heritability factor of 80 percent, Jensen's conclusion is that there are racial differences in innate intelligence.

Jensen recognizes that IQ is not synonymous with "intelligence," but he claims that intelligence tests should be used to advise individuals on the proper pursuit of scholastic and career goals. The next point is rather delicate and is open to a variety of interpretations, but Jensen asserts, "Selective factors in social mobility and assortative mating have resulted in a genetic component in social class intelligence differences."

At this stage it would be advisable to consider some of the actual points made by Arthur Jensen. He states his opposition to treating any individual in ways solely on the basis of race, color, or social class background. But he is also "opposed to ignoring or refusing to investigate the causes of the well-established differences among racial groups in the distribution of . . . IQ." Jensen wishes this subject to be an open scientific question, and is dismayed by a number of official statements of faith by important agencies which are made in the absence of any data. He cites the statement: "It is a demonstrable fact that the talent pool in any one ethnic group is substantially the same as in any other ethnic group," released by the U.S. Office of Education in 1966; and the statement: "Intelligence potential is distributed among Negro infants in the same proportion and pattern as among Icelander, Chinese, or any other group," released by the Department of Labor in 1965. Both, says Jensen, are without scientific merit or factual basis. Jensen states that the fact that different racial groups in this country have widely separated geographic origins and different histories which have "subjected them to different selective social and economic pressures," makes it "highly likely that their gene pools differ for some genetically conditioned behavioral characteristics, including intelligence or abstract reasoning ability." He continues to state that nearly every anatomical, physiological, and biochemical system investigated shows racial differences, and he questions why presumptions concerning the brain and its capacities should be exceptions.

Probably the most explosive of Jensen's statements concerns the relationship of learning ability to racial differences in IQ. Jensen suggests two broad categories of mental abilities—*abstract reasoning ability* and *associative learning ability*. He suggests that these abilities are most suited, respectively, to problem-solving and the assimilation of abstract information on the one hand, and to the learning of concrete procedures and operations on the other. He produces data which he interprets as showing these types of abilities to be differentially distributed in various social class and racial groups. Jensen claims that large racial and social class differences are found for abstract reasoning ability, but there are much smaller differences between groups in associative learning ability for concrete data. Then comes Jensen's most controversial statement: "Research should be directed at delineating . . . [these and] still other types of abilities and at discovering how the particular strengths in each individual's pattern of abilities can be most effectively brought to bear on school learning and on the attainment of occupational skills." His next remarks seem reasonably humane, as he states that by pursuing this goal we can end a situation which means "educational rewards for some children and utter frustration and defeat for others."

Many people have responded in an extremely negative tone to Jensen's pronouncements. One of the replies was made under the title, "Jensen's Dangerous Half-Truths," by Whitten and Kagan (1969). Whitten and Kagan cite a number of problems in Jensen's position. One of these is the serious problem in interpreting the lower IQ scores of black children, in view of the assumption that many black children are afraid of the examiner or do not realize that they are being tested. As a result they obtain lower scores than they would if more psychological examiners were of their own race. They also suggest that the amount of motivation to do well that is present at the moment, and the extent to which the child is paying attention to the examiner both enter the picture. "It does not take much reflection to realize that the IQ test is a cultural invention, not a biological characteristic, and it is not very likely that genes would influence an IQ score in any simple manner."

Whitten and Kagan continue to attack other statements of Jensen— for example, the assertion that compensatory education is not likely to help black children. They point out that such programs have been spectacularly successful in Israel. "It is not fair to suggest that special tutoring or compensatory work has failed merely because a Headstart Program organized on a crash basis failed to produce . . . increases in IQ scores."

There are a number of sources for discussion of the Jensen position, and at this point you may be interested in pursuing some of them: Jensen's own statements appear in the *Harvard Educational Review* in his original article, "How Much Can We Boost IQ and Scholastic Achievement?" (1969), and in his book *Genetics and Education* (1972). A fairly basic critique is "Jensen's Dangerous Half-Truths" in *Psychology Today,* written by Whitten and Kagan (1969). Jensen replies in *Psychology Today* with "Input: Arthur Jensen Replies" (1969). Bruce and Livingstone have written a critique at a higher level of abstraction titled "On Creeping Jensenism," in *Race and Intelligence,* edited by C. L. Bruce et al. (1971).

We have, in a very brief capsule form, presented two sides of a major issue. As you continue to gain knowledge of test characteristics through further course work, you will be in an increasingly better position to interpret the statements of both sides. One thing, of course, would be regrettable, and that would be if social programs and institutions adjusted their procedures in ways that were discriminatory against racial groups solely on an emotional basis, using the Jensen position as an after-the-fact rationalization.

Summary

At the beginning of this chapter we stated that we would not attempt to answer claims that IQ testing should be abolished because of its unfairness. We have presented the flavor of the unfairness (hopefully), and we have also shown that where the instrument is validated on certain predictive criteria the abolition of its use to predict the criterion measure seems to be a discarding of a very good thing. Many influential psychologists in this nation have been ever watchful that IQ tests are not used in such a way as to be unfair to individuals who do not read well, are from non-English speaking backgrounds, etc. But they have not yet found particularly effective ways of assuring equal justice for people from deprived backgrounds whose futures may in part depend upon the results of intelligence testing.

THE COMPONENTS OF INTELLIGENCE

Intelligence is conceptualized by some as being a global, unitary ability. Implicit in the Wechsler scales, however, is an assumption that intelligence is at least of two kinds—verbal and performance. Furthermore, the fact that persons can be quite high on one individual scale within the verbal or performance group and low on another suggests that there may be a large number of different kinds of intelligence. Some psychologists have even spoken of the "street intelligence" shown by children in the slums who may not be high achievers, either in school or on intelligence tests, but who show an uncanny ability to function and be leaders in their own environments.

What is the essential structure of intelligence? There seem to be two fairly simplistic notions, with several elaborations of each. Historically we might follow the activities of a British scientist named Charles Spearman. Spearman was interested in establishing the intercorrelations that exist between separate items on the common intelligence tests in use. Taking these intercorrelations, Spearman concluded that there was a universal intellectual capacity, which he labelled g, for *general*, plus a number of minor and unrelated mental capacities of no great importance. Spearman's notion was that performance on any given task depended on two factors, the g factor and whatever else might be specific to the task. Spearman called these other factors s, for *specific*. To him, a universal factor permeated virtually all mental activities, while the various specific factors were applied only within tightly circumscribed situations. To be "intelligent," according to Spearman, therefore meant to have a lot of g.

In noting this theory, or any other, it is appropriate to recognize that the conclusions are based on actual data. There is no denying that the correlations between different test scores fall into a pattern that makes sense if one assumes that there is some common underlying capacity.

Opposing the point of view represented by Spearman's theory, L. L. Thurstone, an American electrical engineer, applied his own brand of expertise to psychological measurement not only in the field of intelligence, but in the areas of measurement of attitudes, personality, and motivation. Thurstone reasoned in a manner opposite to Spearman. Rather than looking for intercorrelations to establish a general factor, he concentrated on the lack of total correlation, searching for the lowest intercorrelational scores in order to discover how many independent factors might be implied. Thurstone devised a method of analyzing intercorrelational patterns mathematically, thereby creating multiple-factor analysis. According to his method, he divided Spearman's general factor, g, into a set of *primary mental abilities*.

Thurstone (1941) began with 60 different kinds of intelligence test components and, by finding out which of them correlated highly with each other, concluded finally that there were seven independent primary mental abilities. The seven have moderate intercorrelations with one another, but the correlations are not so high as to make us believe that the seven areas are not largely independent of one another. Thurstone's seven primary mental abilities are the following:

1. number ability
2. word fluency
3. verbal meaning
4. memory
5. reasoning
6. spatial relations
7. perceptual speed

Some theorists assume that different areas of the cortex mediate the different abilities, which would account for independence in their function within a single individual. There are clinical psychologists who even report success in the diagnosis of the degree and location of cerebral damage through the interpretation of patterns of high and low scores on the different test scales.

A recent substitute in the theory of intellectual structure has been proposed by J. P. Guilford. Guilford performed a number of interesting studies throughout the period of the Second World War and thereafter, and grew increasingly skeptical of the simplistic structure-of-intellect theories that were dominant in the field. In place of Thurstone's seven primary mental abilities, or the g factor and the specific factors, Guilford felt that intelligence could be classified into three separate dimensions. The first dimension pertains to what sort of *mental operation* is involved in a given task. Guilford claimed five alternatives. Either (1) *cognition,* the immediate awareness of information; (2) *memory,* the storing or fixation of new information; (3) *divergent production,* the generating of logical alternatives from information given; (4) *convergent production,* the generating of a logical conclusion after being given information; or (5) *evaluation,* the comparing of items of information relative to some standard.

The second dimension proposed by Guilford concerns the sort of *information* (content) that gets processed. Mental operations fall into four content categories. First there is *figural,* referring to information organized through the senses such as visual or auditory images; second is *symbolic,* information carried by abstract symbols such as numbers or letters which are not combined into words; third is *semantic,* information of a conceptual nature typically carried through words; and fourth is *behavioral,* information arising from nonverbal behaviors. The latter factor is similar to the notion of "social intelligence."

Guilford's third dimension consists of six types of mental *products.* The products may be (1) *units,* which are individual elements of mental work like specific words or images; (2) *classes,* collections of units which share some property; (3) *relations,* the connections between units or classes such as "left of," "larger than," etc.; (4) *systems,* coherent bodies of information relevant to a topic; (5) *transformations,* changes in preexisting information; and (6) *implications,* the associations of previously unrelated items of information.

Within this three-dimensional structure, Guilford has proposed an explanation of the entire diversity of intellectual processes within a single framework. The five operations, four contents, and six products yield 120 combinations, representing distinct abilities which should be uncoverable by testing. Using the powerful procedure of factor analysis, so far 98 of the 120 abilities predicted by the model have been identified through a diversity of testing research. We may never see a single comprehensive mental test which can satisfactorily pinpoint all of Guilford's proposed factors, so that we might establish people's strengths and weaknesses in each. Still, it is conceivable that specific occupations or academic areas might call for very specific abilities, and those abilities might be accurately stipulated within the Guilford structural theory, with test catalogs available that would designate tests to measure the various specific abilities.

On another dimension, a number of thoughtful psychologists have identified what seem to be two separate processes. Cattell (1963) has postulated *fluid intelligence,* which is a "general relation-perceiving capacity which operates in all fields," and which is biologically determined, and *crystallized intelligence,* which is a "sum of particular relation-perceiving skills acquired in specific fields," and which is environmentally determined. This leads us back to the topics we discussed earlier in this chapter.

C 6.18.   *The components of intelligence.*

The notion that there is a general, widespread intellectual capacity (*g*) in human beings is attributed

to _____ .

   a. Spearman   b. Galton   c. Thurstone

The theory of *g* developed out of an interest in the _____ of different abilities in given human beings.

   a. correlation   b. lack of relationship

Thurstone's work in factor analysis leads to the conclusion that there are _____ primary mental abilities.

   a. two   b. five   c. seven   d. nine

A three-dimensional structure of intellect theory, developed by _____, proposes 120 distinct abilities.

   a. Spearman   b. Thurstone   c. Guilford   d. Cattell

This concludes our discussion of "What is intelligence?" as well as "How is intelligence measured?" It remains for us to discuss a social problem of grave magnitude—mental retardation.

PROGRESS CHECK   6.4

1. The most outspoken critics of standard intelligence testing have been _____ .

    a. Jewish psychologists   b. blacks

    c. Chinese-Americans   d. no one group has been most outspoken

2. Which psychologist has been criticized and challenged for his stance on racial differences and IQ? _____ .

    a. Arthur Jensen   b. Robert Williams   c. B. F. Skinner   d. Raymond Cattell

3. Which is true of Spearman's notions about intelligence? _____ .

    a. To be intelligent means one has a lot of *g*

    b. The symbol *g* stands for general intellectual capacity

    c. Performance depends on *g* and *s*   d. All of these

MATCH: _____ 4. Spearman   A. Fluid intelligence

           _____ 5. Thurstone   B. Seven primary mental abilities

           _____ 6. Cattell   C. General intelligence

           _____ 7. Guilford   D. Three dimensional structure of intelligence

---

MENTAL RETARDATION   For reasons both financial and personal, mental retardation is a serious problem. We shall not go into the issue in depth—just enough to acquaint you with some of the basic concepts.

The classification of the mentally retarded typically is in terms of the degree of retardation. Table 6.3 indicates the classifications suggested by the

Table 6.3

Range in IQ Scores	Terms Used in AAMD Manual (1961)	Former Terms
70–84	Borderline Retardation	Borderline
55–69	Mild Retardation	Moron
40–54	Moderate Retardation	⎰Imbecile
25–39	Severe Retardation	⎱Imbecile
Below 25	Profound Retardation	Idiot

American Association on Mental Deficiency. In addition, the older terms in common use in prior decades are listed.

We frequently place the mentally retarded into three groups for administrative purposes. These groupings are primarily on the basis of our selection of the appropriate educational program for a given child. We class the retarded as educable—the highest IQ group of the retarded—followed by the trainable and the subtrainable. For the *educable retarded*, many academic skills are stressed, with attainment approaching the fourth- or fifth-grade level. *Trainable retarded* individuals are not assumed to have adequate capacities to profit from many typical classroom experiences, but the objective in working with them is to achieve an adequate level of self-care and, hopefully, at least partial self-support. In trainable programs the emphasis is placed on matters of personal hygiene, how to make purchases, recognition of important words that aid an individual in getting about in everyday life (signs on rest-room doors, stores, streets, and so forth), handling of cash, and simple arithmetic. In addition, simple work habits and attitudes are stressed, as are the ability to follow verbal instructions, speech and language skills, and concepts of safety. Finally, the *profoundly retarded* are included in the total care group. These individuals require constant supervision and custodial care throughout their lifetimes.

Using the IQ criterion, one typical state's educational system classifies individuals with IQs of 55 to 84 as educable retarded, from 25 to 54 as trainable retarded, and below 25 as subtrainable and profoundly retarded.

C 6.19. *Categories of mental retardation.*

"Borderline" mental retardation starts with IQs below the level of _____ .

    a. 100   b. 90   c. 85   d. 65

Psychologists typically divide the mentally retarded into three groups along the dimension of *potential:*

    (1) the _____   _____ ,

    (2) the _____   _____ ,

    (3) the _____   _____ .

Causes of Mental Retardation

The causes of severe mental retardation are various:

(1) There are *chromosomal abnormalities*. Mongolism (also called Down's syndrome) may yield mild to severe retardation. The mongoloid usually has a number of accompanying physical problems, in addition to the somewhat Oriental appearance of the face.

(2) *Prenatal infections* may be transmitted from mother to fetus, and may then affect the brain tissue.

(3) *Congenital* (present at birth) *syphilis* may produce retardation, as may *rubella*.

(4) *Toxic damage* from sources such as carbon monoxide, lead, arsenic,

etc. may take place as maternal toxemias during the pregnancy, or they may be experienced after birth.

(5) Mental retardation may be associated with *premature birth*. Sometimes, when birth weight is too low, subsequent brain development does not proceed normally.

(6) *Prenatal brain injury* is rare, but when it does occur it may result in retardation. For example, the incidence of mental retardation among the infants of pregnant women exposed to large amounts of X-ray irradiation is significant. *Birth trauma* such as prolonged anoxia (lack of oxygen) during the birth process also causes varying degrees of retardation. The brain cells are particularly sensitive to reductions in the amount of available oxygen.

(7) *Cranial and brain tissue abnormalities,* such as distortions in the size and shape of the skull, may or may not cause retardation. (a) With *hydrocephaly*, there is an increased volume of cerebrospinal fluid which causes the head to enlarge. While the skull expands, the brain tissue is compressed and damaged by the pressure. (b) With *microcephaly*, the skull cavity is abnormally small, and the initial problems while a fetus, plus the necessary surgical intervention, typically renders retardation. Brain tissue abnormalities in microcephalics include the absence or malformation of various parts of the brain.

(8) *Defects of metabolism* may result in severe retardation. (a) *Phenylketonuria* is a disturbance of protein metabolism that results in the back-up in the physical system of certain acids that affect the brain. In this disorder, immediate dietary attention to the newborn infant may prevent mental retardation. (b) *Hypothyroidism*, traditionally known as "cretinism," is another cause of retardation, due to a decrease or absence of the thyroid hormone.

(9) In addition to the above, there are (a) *degenerative cerebral diseases,* usually thought to be genetically acquired, (b) childhood diseases such as *encephalitis* and *measles* with certain complications, and (c) *childhood accidents* involving head injuries. Finally there are (d) *degenerative changes* in the brain associated with advanced aging, sometimes resulting in a severe limitation of intellectual functioning, and usually known as "senility."

This list is not exhaustive, but it may give you some idea as to the range of problems seen by persons who deal with mental retardation. The education or training of these persons is a special field, and a challenging one. The only hope for the retarded individual to live a relatively unfrustrated life is to be well-trained to the point of always being punctual, keeping clean, always dressing appropriately, and being mannerly so as to achieve the degree of potential success in life that may exist for him.

THE GIFTED CHILD   There are several labels used to describe the child with a very high IQ. Early in the history of testing the word "genius" was invented, but this was followed by controversy. Finally, most persons agreed that a "genius" was an individual with not only a high IQ, but also one with a history of highly significant accomplishment, well beyond what one ordinarily expects from an individual at that particular point in life. Nowadays the word "gifted" is preferred, and has reference simply to an individual with a very high potential, indicated by the IQ.

In developing a psychology of the gifted, Terman and his associates in 1925 began a longitudinal study of a large number of gifted children in California. That state's school population was examined and from more than a quarter of a million (250,000) students, 1,500 were discovered with IQs of 140 and above; 80 of these students had IQs over 170.

The first popular misconception discounted by Terman was the notion that exceptionally bright children tend to be physically inadequate specimens. The gifted children proved to be physically superior and healthier than the average child, and better adjusted psychologically. Through several subsequent decades, Terman followed up most of these persons and found outstandingly high patterns of professional success. Very few of them failed to achieve a well-above-average level of success in their professional lives.

C 6.20.   *The gifted child.*

Terman, in his longitudinal study of the gifted, found strong later occupational success; he also established that the health and physical condition of gifted children is usually _____ .

a. above average   b. below average   c. about average

VARIOUS TESTS

Culture-Fair Tests

At an earlier point we mentioned that there was a considerable "loading" of verbal items on traditional tests of intelligence. Some special groups, such as the deaf, the illiterate, the foreign-speaking, and others whose environmental backgrounds might be said to be impoverished in some way, may not be fairly dealt with on tests calling for good verbal skills. To a degree, reliance on the performance section of the Wechsler scales can more accurately reflect the intellectual potential of these groups. However, specific tests have been developed in an effort to remove or at least lessen the effects of cultural background.

One of the earliest of such tests was the Seguin Form Board. The test consists of ten individual pieces of varying shapes which can be replaced in a board by matching the correct shape to its existing space. Three trials are allowed, the fastest time being used as the subject's score. The Seguin Form Board comes in several levels of difficulty, from a relatively simple form appropriate for low mental ages to more complex boards for higher levels of ability.

Another popular test of this sort is the Porteus Maze. It is an individual test for subjects age three to adult. The subject works through a series of paper mazes of increasing difficulty. The test emphasizes planning, foresight, and the inhibition of impulsive responses (Porteus, 1965). An interesting aspect of the Porteus Maze is its involvement of impulse control. In a study of delinquents in a reformatory it was found that rule-abiding, well-behaved inmates scored about ten points higher than a maladjusted group, even though the groups were similar on S-B IQ scores (Porteus, 1950).

Another such test is the Raven's Progressive Matrices Test. It is a group test for ages five to adult. This test is designed to measure the ability to perceive relationships. The subject is directed to select the design that completes a pattern. The subject must identify and apply the two principles by which the figures are altered. Predictive validity against a range of criteria, including educational achievement and vocational success, is fairly good but not outstanding (Burke, 1958).

In the early days of use, psychologists referred to tests such as we have been discussing as *culture-free* tests of intelligence. In recent years, however, the tests are recognized as still having some cultural bias, and they go by the name *culture-fair* (a less absolute term).

C 6.21.   *Culture-fair tests of intelligence.*

A culture-fair test of intelligence is intended for use with persons who _____ .

    a. have very low achievement test scores in academic settings

    b. may have trouble with the language due to illiteracy, foreign birth, etc.

    c. challenge the legitimacy of standard IQ tests

    d. cannot understand the directions given on standard IQ tests

Three different culture-fair tests of intelligence are

    (1) _____ .

    (2) _____ .

    (3) _____ .

Infant Intelligence Tests   A number of tests have been developed for use with very young children. Although such tests have little precise predictive power, they are useful in appraising major deviations in the rate of intellectual development in the first months of life. The Cattell Infant Intelligence Test is structured much like the Stanford-Binet. However, the items are observational rather than verbal. All items involve active, directed attention. Some typical items for six-month-olds are the following: regards cube; follows ring in a circular motion with eyes; and transfers object from one hand to the other. By twelve months individual differences depend mostly on the directed use of the hands.

A practical and well-investigated test is the Bayley Mental and Motor Scales of Infant Development. The test is designed for use with subjects from ages one month to thirty months. It consists of two tests, one directed toward attention and adaptive behavior, and the other measuring coordination. At the older levels more emphasis is placed on communication and concepts, with a decrease in the assessment of simple attention and inspecting behaviors. Especially prior to the age of one year, infant intelligence tests cannot be very accurate in predicting later IQ, except for the mentally defective. Thus, the infant intelligence tests have only limited usefulness.

C 6.22. *Infant intelligence tests.*

Infant intelligence tests have very little predictive power (for later IQ) when given prior to the age

of _____ .

a. one year   b. two years   c. three years

The statement contained in the last question implies that infant intelligence tests probably lack

much _____ .

a. predictive validity   b. internal reliability   c. face validity

Aptitude Tests and Achievement Tests

We have been discussing intelligence testing, and at this point we should divide the sorts of ability tests currently in use into two groups:

An *aptitude test* is intended to predict an individual's *potential* for performance. It is recognized that individuals with the same training or practice show great differences in their performances in the particular task area. These differences are attributed largely to dissimilarities in aptitude with regard to the task in question. For this reason the military, industries, and vocational counselors are greatly interested in the development and application of aptitude tests.

A number of aptitude tests have been designed, including tests in the following areas: sensory capacities, motor functions, mechanical aptitude, clerical aptitude, artistic, musical and literary aptitudes, creativity, and reasoning. Needless to say, development of aptitude tests in some of these areas is considerably easier and more successful than in others.

Presently there are many aptitude tests in use. An entire series of aptitude tests was carefully designed, researched, and further refined during the Second World War. Test batteries were used for the selection of airplane pilots and for a variety of other complex job categories. The development of such tests followed the simple procedure of getting scores on a large number of persons and then putting those persons through training for the job in question. A number of the students would fail the training course, others would pass, and after the results of training were available one then went back to the original test, retaining items that discriminated between the people who were failures and successes. Through a gradual procedure the psychologists developed stronger and stronger predictive instruments.

Aptitude tests are usually provided with suggested cut-off scores. Below each cut-off score would be individuals who could be identified as probable failures in the training course. One test used during the Second World War predicted the results of training radio-code operators. A score was eventually found on the developed test where only 6 percent of persons exceeding that score failed the course, which compared very favorably with an overall 40 percent failure rate of unselected trainees. Other well-known aptitude tests are used for the selection of candidates for medical school, dental school, etc.

In order for a test to truly be an aptitude test, it should not be weighted with items that are taken from subject-matter areas in which individuals might have studied or practiced. Otherwise, instead of being an aptitude test, it becomes an achievement test.

While an aptitude test is defined as a test to assess an individual's potential to perform, an *achievement test* measures the degree of proficiency *already attained* in a specific area. Achievement tests can serve two functions. Like aptitude tests, they can be used to predict a person's current capacity to do a job well. For example, one's level of acquired knowledge is represented in the score on a college entrance examination, which is a very important basis for doing successful work in a university. A second purpose for achievement tests is to measure the effectiveness of training programs. If we use two or more methods to teach arithmetic or foreign language, we may then carefully construct achievement tests for administration at the end of training to determine which method is superior.

Most of this chapter has been devoted to the discussion of intelligence testing. Some persons prefer to classify intelligence tests as aptitude tests. This is certainly consistent with the abstract definition of intelligence as we often view it. Realistically, however, there are very few intelligence tests that are not in large part actually achievement tests since, as we already stated, most if not all fail to be literally culture-free.

C 6.23. *Aptitude versus achievement tests.*

A test designed to measure an individual's capacity or potential for performance is called an _____

_____ test.

A test designed to measure the degree of proficiency already attained in some area is called an _____

_____ test.

PROGRESS CHECK   6.5

1. A person with an IQ of 75 is considered _____ .

    a borderline retarded   b. moderately retarded   c. severely retarded   d. an idiot

2. Which group of retarded individuals might be taught to read at the fifth grade level? _____ .

    a. Educable retarded   b. Trainable retarded   c. Profoundly retarded

3. Retardation associated with Down's syndrome is caused by _____ .

    a. congenital syphilis   b. premature birth   c. anoxia   d. chromosomal abnormalities

4. Gifted children are usually nearsighted and sickly. _____ .

    a. True   b. False

5. Of these tests, which one is considered culture-fair? _____ .

    a. Stanford-Binet   b. WAIS   c. Porteus maze   d. WISC

6. Which test might an American school psychologist administer to a student whose native language

    was Spanish? _____ .

    a. Seguin Form Board   b. Porteus Maze

    c. Raven's Progressive Matrices Test   d. Any of these

7. An infant intelligence test administered in the first year _____ .

    a. has great predictive validity for later IQ   b. is similar to an aptitude test

    c. usually assesses only major deviations in development   d. facilitates visual development

MATCH: _____ 8. Aptitude test   A. Measures attained degree of skills in an area

    _____ 9. Achievement test   B. Predicts potential performance of a skill

---

SUMMARY   In retrospect, while many areas of psychology have very recent histories, the area of tests and measures is one of the older areas of research effort. The model $R=f(R)$ describes the major research pattern in which the behavior sample on a test is investigated in relation to some outside criterion performance. While many individuals—even trained psychologists—have made the mistake of overlooking available information on actual criterion behavior in favor of accepting test information, the very purpose of which was to predict the data being ignored, the history of test application reflects an overall success. Using information from aptitude and vocational interest tests, problems of job discontent have been identified and corrected. Industries have used tests to find persons whose talents are most suited to the jobs being recruited. In a sense psychology has scored one of its biggest successes in the area of psychological measurement, but you will now understand why the area is also regarded as a current hotbed of dissension, containing problems that must be realistically solved in the immediate future.

Interested students may wish to continue reading on the topic of intelligence testing. We recommend *Psychometric Assessment of the Individual Child* (1968), by R. Douglass Savage. This is a brief, easy-to-read treatment of the measurement of intelligence, educational attainment, personality, and motor and perceptual skills. *Individual Mental Testing* (1972) in three paperback volumes was written by Allen J. Edwards, with the first volume given to history and theories, the second to concepts in psychological measurement, and the third to research and interpretation. An excellent book of readings, with up-to-date articles on many current issues, is *Human Intelligence* (1972), edited by J. McV. Hunt.

Later you may have the opportunity to take a course in psychological measurement or tests and measurements in the psychology department as your next step in the study of the topics in this chapter.

Simple Motivation
and Emotion

ACTIVATION

DEPRIVATION AND GENERAL ACTIVITY
The Evolution of "Activity=f(Drive)"

NEEDS AND DRIVES
Primary Drive States
The Hunger Drive
The Thirst Drive
Contact Comfort
Stimulus Variety
Sensory Deprivation
The Sexual Drive
The Manipulatory Drive
The Measurement of Drives

INCENTIVATION

MOTIVATION AND EFFICIENCY

INSTINCTS

MOVING FROM BASIC MOTIVES TO HUMANISTIC MOTIVES
Humanism
McClelland and the Need for Achievement
Murray's Psychology of Human Needs
Maslow's Conception of Human Motivation
An Evaluation of Maslow's Theory of Human Motivation

EMOTIONS
The Origin of Emotionality
Overview

The question, "Why does an organism behave as it does?" is probably the central topic in psychology. Except for two or three chapters, the major portion of any introductory psychology book is directed toward this question.

This chapter will deal primarily with *simple* motivation, which is to say those motives that are essentially unlearned and natural to a species. Then, in later chapters, we shall examine the broader view of the influence which an organism's experiences in its environment may have upon its subsequent behavior patterns.

ACTIVATION   When an organism behaves, we assume there is motivation for the act. This assumption extends even to the child who squirms during a dull church sermon or to the college student who engages in cognitive activities such as daydreaming. We shall begin the topic of motivation by going to the basic, physiologically derived source of behavior—activation.

The term *activation*—or level of arousal —has been used to describe, in an overall way, the degree of physical and cortical activity existing at a given moment. It is usually viewed as a continuum, with deep sleep at the lower end and extreme excitement at the upper. In between are all degrees of intermediate activation from drowsy, relaxed calmness to various levels of interest and finally tension. For a number of years psychologists have been aware of such an underlying dimension and in 1943 Clark Hull, in his influential behavior theory, put forth his idea of the generalized drive state. Such ideas as Hull's, and later notions of activation, have been tied in most closely with the operation of the reticular system in the brain (see p. 38).

C 7.1.   *The concept of activation.*

Activation might be defined as the overall degree of _____

_____ activity at a given moment.

The *reticular system* (RS) is triggered to a state of heightened electro-chemical activity by a number of input factors. First, there are major afferent pathways coming in from the musculature and the internal organs of the body, so that such things as muscle tension arouse the RS. Second, the sensory organs, when stimulated, further arouse the RS. You may recall the recent legislative interest in the noise levels of our immediate environments; this is because research has shown that noise induces tension. Third and finally, there are incoming pathways to the RS from the cortex itself (French et al., 1954), suggesting that when you recognize or understand the meanings of certain important stimuli, such an awareness has a direct effect on the RS.

What does the RS do in turn? When scientists, using tiny microelectrodes, directly stimulate the RS, that structure in turn triggers an alert or aroused brain pattern in the cortex. Using the EEG (electroencephalograph) to trace brain-wave patterns, it has been found that the RS is the key intermediate structure between events in the environment and the cortex's alertness. Consider for a moment how sleepy you typically are when your alarm wakes you in the morning. Suppose, on the other hand, shortly before your usual rising time, you are awakened by the sound of someone walking in the next room at a time when you know that you are supposed to be the only person in the house. Under such conditions all sleepiness drops away in an instant, and the cortex is put into a state of immediate, wide-awake alertness. The RS is the direct trigger. The RS then mediates or participates in the control of a number of further functions of the body, including autonomic patterns.

In general, RS level is functionally related to four factors: (1) The individual is more highly aroused when *physically fresh* than when fatigued. (2) *Novel stimulation* produces a higher level of arousal than does the continuation of the same stimulus pattern; this latter condition induces what is called *habituation,* manifest initially at the RS level. (3) A higher level of arousal results from conditions of *intense stimulation* than from lower levels of stimulation. And (4) RS level is affected to a considerable degree by the state of *incentivation.* We shall discuss incentivation later in this chapter, but briefly this means that the degree of RS activity is increased by the organism's direct perception or awareness of aversive or appetitive stimuli in the immediate environment.

Perhaps the best-known experiment that clearly demonstrates the major function of the RS was performed by Fuster (1958), who trained rhesus monkeys to discriminate between two geometric forms. Food was given to them if they made the correct discrimination. Fuster compared the percentage of correct discriminations and the time it took a monkey to make the choice under normal (control) conditions with measures taken while the RS was being directly stimulated through tiny microelectrodes with varying intensities of electrical current. Fuster found that performance improved markedly, up to a point, with increases in current intensity. Such findings show that the level of RS activity affects alertness and efficiency.

C 7.2. *The reticular system.*

The brain structure most directly contributive to the overall degree of physical and cortical activity

is the _____ .

a. cerebral cortex   b. thalamus   c. reticular system

Factors triggering heightened reticular system activation include:

a. _____

b. _____

c. _____

Military research has established that when individuals watch a continuing radar sweep on a screen for long periods of time, they begin to lose alertness and may not respond to the appearance of an extra reflection that begins to appear on the screen. Rather than just fatigue, this is due to a process called _____ .

a. blurring   b. facilitation   c. habituation   d. fixedness

If you were trying to go to sleep but knew that someone who hated you had just arrived in town and had sworn to get you if it was the last thing he did, and you wondered if he might even break into your house to hurt you, we might say that your state of _____ was increasing the level of activation.

a. incentivation   b. intermediacy   c. conflict   d. vulnerability

It has been shown that monkeys' task performances are _____ by direct electrical stimulation of the _____ .

a. frontal lobes   b. reticular system   c. visual cortex   d. medulla

Certain implications for the student arise from the RS research findings. We now know that the individual who wishes to stay alert for best mental functioning should vary his stimulus input occasionally, should try to stay consciously aware of the various incentives for effective performance, and should even try to maintain a certain amount of muscle tension during study. A midwestern university once went so far as to provide "gripping knobs" which were simply brass doorknobs mounted on the top surfaces of dormitory desks. The idea was that by exerting some muscle tension during study, better retention would result. The same result can be obtained simply by sitting up straight, neither lounging comfortably nor lying down when studying.

The research also provides a lesson for the instructor. An instructor wishing to avoid student habituation and lowered RS activity should never miss an opportunity to break up a dull, continuous 50-minute lecture presentation with other forms of stimulus presentation. Even if the stimulus variation is devoid of course-related content, the effect on student alertness is favorable. Many experienced auditorium lecturers move about with the microphone almost constantly, dim the lights to write a word or two on an overhead projector, then brighten them again, vary their pace of speech, vary the tone of voice and inflection, and occasionally do something unexpected. Some teachers will stop every 15 minutes or so to provide a few study questions from material just covered. All these factors serve to heighten RS activity, resulting in better attention and intellectual functioning.

DEPRIVATION AND GENERAL ACTIVITY

When organisms are deprived of certain goal objects (food, water, etc.), they typically engage in behaviors that are appropriate to attain the objects. These behaviors are typically learned, and we shall deal with them mainly in the next three chapters. More basic than this is the *general activity* that is the direct result of deprivation.

Whenever our basic needs are not met, we become more active than we were before. Experiments have measured the amount of running by small animals in exercise wheels that adjoin their cages. You have probably seen such wheels on gerbil cages, but the laboratory setups include counters which measure the number of revolutions of the wheels, and which can be reset at certain time intervals. With such devices we can study the effects of the deprivation of food, water, or some other goal object upon the behavior of the animal. In Figure 7.1 you can see charted the general function that describes the effect of food deprivation upon the wheel-turning of a laboratory rat. Over a period of around four or five days the animal runs more and more in his activity wheel until the time when he grows weaker and can no longer maintain as high a level of activity. At this point, indicated by the

Figure 7.1

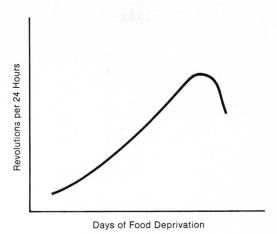

Days of Food Deprivation

downturn in the curve, increasing physical debility will soon result in death if the deprivation continues. The functional relationship existing between food deprivation and activity level has been described by Mathews and Finger (1966).

A similar function holds for the sex drive. If one studies the activity of the female rat as a function of the estrous cycle, a jagged curve results. The female rat, when in heat, travels a good deal in the wheel, with the rate dropping off considerably during the intervening time (Figure 7.2). The male rat's sex drive is partly triggered by olfactory stimuli, and if we place the male rat's cage and wheel beside the female's, we can get an almost perfectly matched set of activity curves. When the female rat is in heat, the male rat, a few inches away, experiences a heightened sex drive and he goes into operation in his activity wheel.

Figure 7.2

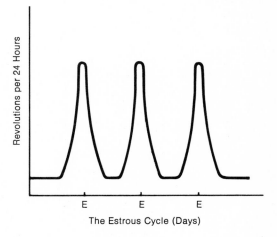

The Estrous Cycle (Days)

C 7.3.   *The effect of the general drive state on activity level.*

A demonstrated method of increasing the general activity level of an organism would be to _____ .

 a. satiate the individual with a great deal of food

 b. artificially induce in the individual prior prolonged sleep

 c. deprive the individual of food for a period of time

 d. (none of the above is likely to be true)

> You should recognize that the rat isn't going anywhere when he runs in the activity wheel, and the proper explanation of the running is not that he "thinks" maybe the wheel is going to take him to the desired goal. Organisms are simply more active when deprived. How could this have come about?

PROGRESS CHECK   7.1

1. The overall degree of physical and cortical activity existing at a given moment is termed _____ .

 a. circadian rhythm   b. activity

 c. continuum of random movement   d. activation

2. Which response pattern is an example of habituation? _____ .

 a. Blurred vision at night   b. Fatigue at the end of a day of hard work

 c. Loss of alertness to a radar screen   d. Improved performance upon familiarity with a task

3. The brain structure most directly linked to triggering activation is the _____ .

 a. pituitary gland   b. reticular system   c. striate cortex   d. central gyrus

4. Which is *not* a factor heightening activation? _____ .

 a. Physical freshness   b. Novel stimulation   c. Incentivation   d. Habituation

5. Threat of an aversive stimulus would probably _____ .

 a. result in habituation after a few minutes   b. facilitate digestion

 c. increase incentivation   d. quickly fatigue the organism

6. Fuster's discrimination training experiment with rhesus monkeys showed _____ .

 a. performance improvement up to a point with increases of electric current to the reticular system

 b. electrical stimulation of the reticular system reduced performance scores

 c. normal animals performed better than shocked animals

 d. animals undergoing current performed better when it was turned off

7. Food or water deprivation has what effect on general activity? _____ .

    a. Increase   b. Decrease   c. Varies   d. Remains constant

---

The Evolution of "Activity=f(Drive)"

Under conditions of an elevated biological need, organisms in their natural settings will die unless they can find the goal objects to satisfy the needs (except the sexual need). If drought results in the drying-up of water holes, animals living in nearby burrows must increase the radius of their daily explorations and find new water supplies if they are to avoid death. Similarly, if food becomes scarce, the individual animal has to travel farther and spend more time searching for food. It is appropriate to note that such activity burns up calories more rapidly and, in a sense, hastens death. Still, the animals that lie down to conserve strength find no food, while those that grow physically restless and travel farther have a better chance of survival. Thus the functional relationship of *general activity=f (drive)* evolved in most organisms.

In the case of the human being, an unmarried dormitory dweller may experience a heightened but unmet sex drive, accentuated by being placed in the frequent company of attractive members of the opposite sex, and he may often experience restlessness and an inability to sit quietly and concentrate on studying. Like the animal in the activity wheel, the student gets up, moves about, looks out the window, gets drinks of water, wanders around, and after considerable time still hasn't gotten much studying done. Research a few years ago showed that students who had married during their sophomore or junior years had a much higher subsequent grade point average. A frequent remark made by subjects in that study was that they could "concentrate better" and didn't feel the need to be "on the go." Possibly there might be other explanations, but it is doubtless that the direct effect on general activity level from satisfaction of the sexual need was at least partly responsible for the improvement in grades. If one is tempted to explain that the male students involved "felt their future responsibility," then it is difficult to explain why the female students' grades also increased. Interviews established that most of the young ladies involved had changed their expectations of getting a responsible job after graduation from "almost certainly" to "perhaps." This would not seem to be consistent with an explanation of grade improvement based upon feelings of economic responsibility.

As we previously stated, all but perhaps the newest-born human beings have had learning experiences and engage in a great deal of directed behavior in addition to general activity when drives increase, so we shall now look at some of the specific drive states.

NEEDS AND DRIVES

The obvious place to begin is at the physiological level, with a discussion of needs. Every organism has a complex physiological structure that maintains the homeostatic balance. *Homeostasis* refers to the delicate internal balance of factors that preserves an organism's functioning equilibrium. For example, the body reacts to a number of environmental situations with its own internal changes. Internal sensors can detect subtle changes in the blood temperature which result from environmental temperatures. At that point, the body reacts with a variety of physical changes, one of which may be perspiration. Similarly, when the body's supply of blood sugar lowers to a certain level, more blood sugars are released from the body stores. *Needs* are those motives which must be satisfied in order to preserve a condition of homeostatic balance.

C 7.4. *Homeostasis.*

Homeostasis most properly would refer to _____ .

   a. an internal balance of factors such as blood sugar levels

   b. a demonstrated drive state

   c. behaviors which satisfy needs

Homeostasis has its closest counterpart in the organism's _____ .

   a. need state   b. drive state   c. level of frustration and aggression

On a somewhat different level, let us contrast the explanation of needs just given with a different approach—one that derives more from the interests of ethnologists. Some would say that a need is involved if total deprivation of the goal object would have an eventual deteriorative effect on the individual *or on the species*. These last four words are inserted because of the special characteristics of maternal behavior and sexual behavior. We shall return to this definition in the discussion of certain primary drives.

Primary drives are natural or unlearned motives that activate skeletal behaviors and are the direct result of states of need. Not all needs arouse drives. In a variety of situations the body can be in a state of prolonged need, but without typical skeletal reactions. Prolonged deprivation of vitamin A or vitamin D is an example of this. Most needs do trigger drives, however, and you will recall how you tend to do things to reduce hunger, thirst, deficits in stimulus variety, high levels of environmental noise, high environmental temperatures, etc. (There is another category of drive— the secondary, or learned, drive—that we shall leave to a future chapter to develop.)

C 7.5. *The concepts of need and drive.*

When homeostatic balance is not proper, a _____ exists.

   a. need   b. drive   c. impulse

An "ethnological" definition of need would include the necessity of the need's satisfaction if there is not to be a ——— effect on the ———. _____ .

    a. deteriorative/social structure

    b. stimulating/aggressive impulses

    c. deteriorative/species

If a need exists, typically a _____ is manifest in behavior.

    a. drive   b. motive   c. conflict

> We can divide all drives into two major categories—appetitive drives and aversive drives. In general an *appetitive drive* is said to be operative when an organism tends to approach a given goal object or stimulus with the intent of experiencing it or consuming it. *Aversive drives,* on the other hand, are operative when an organism tends to escape or avoid a given goal object or stimulus. Generally we refer to the goal object for an appetitive drive as a *positive incentive,* and to the goal object of an aversive drive as a *negative incentive.*

C 7.6. *Type of incentive and type of drive.*

A situation in which an organism tends to approach a goal or stimulus reflects the operation of an _____ drive.

If an organism tends to avoid a stimulus, the operation of an _____ drive is reflected.

A stimulus that is the object of avoidance is called a _____ incentive.

Primary Drive States   The primary (unlearned) appetitive drive states include hunger, thirst, sexual arousal, maternal behavior, seeking of contact comfort, and the seeking of stimulus variety. The primary aversive drive states include pain, frustration, anxiety, and fatigue. We shall now proceed to discuss some of these drive states.

C 7.7. *The primary drive states.*

The word *primary*, when referring to a drive, means _____ .

The Hunger Drive   Research on *hunger* is quite extensive, and probably the first well-known hunger drive experiment, described in most introductory textbooks, concerns the question of whether hunger pangs actually activate food-directed behavior. We have all experienced hunger pangs when a meal is past due.

Several decades ago a researcher directed a volunteer subject in a research project (Cannon, 1934) designed to throw light on the question. The subject swallowed a balloon which was attached to a small tube. After the balloon was in the stomach, air was sent through the tube to inflate the balloon. Equipment then measured, through air pressure changes, contractions of the stomach associated with the physical feelings of what we call ''hunger pangs.'' The finding was that hunger pangs occur at the same moments that stomach contractions occur. Still, the question of whether such stomach contractions *cause* hunger in the broader sense was unanswered.

It has also become known that organisms have brain centers that are extremely sensitive to blood sugar levels. The existence in the circulatory system of blood with low sugar content appears to activate the hunger drive. In one important experiment, blood was transfused from the bodies of dogs that had been deprived of food for several days into the bodies of dogs that had been recently stuffed with food until they had no more desire to eat. Immediately after the transfusion, the well-fed dogs returned to the available food supply and began to eat as if they were starving (Templeton & Quigley, 1930).

C 7.8. *The determinants of hunger drive.*

The hunger drive appears to be primarily the result of _____

level, acting as a stimulus upon certain brain centers.

The full stomach _____ the predominant factor in hunger in a blood transfusion experiment with dogs.

a. was   b. was not

The Thirst Drive The *thirst* drive appears to have a very similar physiological basis. That is, it is not so much the "dry throat" that causes the thirst drive as it is the liquid condition of the blood. As a simple illustration, we have all had the experience of growing quite thirsty, and then drinking much more water than is actually comfortable for us to consume. The wetting of the mouth and throat is accomplished very quickly, and the additional water intake is obviously guided by stimuli of a different nature. Brain centers are receptive to a variety of stimuli including the liquidity of the blood, and the drive to consume water results.

C 7.9. *The determinants of thirst drive.*

The thirst drive is due to the degree of _____

more than to the more superficially obvious factor of _____ _____ .

Contact Comfort The need for contact comfort was first established by a psychologist named Harry Harlow of the University of Wisconsin. He conducted an extensive research program at the primate center located there, much of which has been summarized in Chapter 3, where his major findings as they relate to developmental processes were discussed. We will present here a summary of Harlow's findings, and include information concerning the historical reasons for the research as well as implications for motivational theory.

To briefly summarize a portion of his work, Harlow found that rhesus monkeys are strongly motivated to cuddle against a soft, warm surface during their early weeks and months of life. In a natural setting one can observe that young monkeys spend a great deal of time during each day clinging to the mother's body.

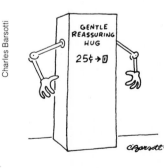

Harlow originally began his investigation to determine whether love for the mother is based in its initial stages on the satisfaction of the primary drive of hunger. Toward that end, he designed two monkeylike dolls (surrogate mothers) which were offered to a recently born rhesus monkey which had been separated from its mother. One of these dolls was soft, covered with sponge rubber and terry cloth, while the other was made up of a hard wire frame. Each monkey had two "mothers"—one wire and one cloth. Various monkeys individually experienced separate feeding plans, some being fed by their "wire mother" and the others by their "cloth mother" through a milk tube. It was found that the nature of the doll's surface—that is, wire versus cloth—seemed to be the controlling factor in determining which surrogate mother the monkey clung to during most of the day, as well as which one the monkey ran to when threatened by a loud mechanical toy. It did not appear to be important which "mother" did the feeding. It was the soft cloth mother that was turned to repeatedly by the young monkey for comfort and consolation.

The application of these findings to the concept of need came later. It was found that the infant monkeys that were completely deprived of a soft "mother" against which to cling demonstrated a type of behavior very

HUNGER AND THIRST, AND LOVE

A short story was once written on the theme of man's deepest motive. According to its plot, an argument was in progress between two young men, one of them very rich and the other very poor. The rich man argued that man's basic animal drives were the predominant ones, and that his civilized being was but a thin veneer which could be shattered by the more basic motives, if the situation demanded it. The poor man disagreed. The rich man bet the poor man $1,000 that basic motives would prevail if the latter took part in an experiment. The bet was agreed upon.

The poor man, with his wife, entered a chamber which was divided inside into two separated compartments. It was sealed and there was no way to get out until the experiment was over. The man and his wife stayed in the compartments without food or water until they were both ravenous with hunger and thirst. Then a single small bite of food and a thimbleful of water was given to the young man.

Would he drink the water and eat the food himself? Or would his love for his wife prevail, and would he pass the food and water through a small opening between the compartments to her, even in the expectation of his remaining yet another full day without food and water?

Like the author of the short story "The Lady or the Tiger?" we shall not conclude the story we have unfolded, except to convey the notion that persons outside the sciences tend to have a nice feel for the romantic. What do you think the ending was?

similar to that of human children with severe psychological problems. They would huddle in a corner, cry, rock back and forth, sometimes bite and injure themselves, and were seemingly out of touch with their surroundings. If a wire "mother" was provided, it was ignored. The availability of a soft warm surface against which to cuddle when young appears to maintain the animal in a much better degree of psychological intactness, and on this basis we term contact comfort a *need*.

We have already stated that a need is involved if deprivation results in a deteriorative change, and deprivation of contact comfort in infancy does bring about such deterioration. This line of research helps us to understand why a child may adopt a favorite blanket that he takes with him everywhere, and it suggests that we should satisfy the need of human infants to be picked up, held, and cuddled. For a number of years more philosophically-inclined psychologists have been fond of the expression "tender, loving care." Now, from Harlow's work, we see experimental evidence showing how vital tender, loving care really is.

C 7.10.   *The need for contact comfort.*

We conclude that contact comfort represents a need since prolonged deprivation of this factor _____ .

    a. results in an obvious drive state in the individual

    b. produces a deteriorative change in the status of the individual

    c. brings death

In Harlow's work with rhesus monkeys, infants developed affectionate bonds to the _____ mother surrogates, but not to the _____ mother surrogates.

Harlow originally wanted to investigate the relation of love for the mother to the necessity for satisfying the _____ drive.

    a. hunger   b. gregarious   c. exploratory

Stimulus Variety   A need for *stimulus variety* also has been recently established. The existence of a drive toward stimulus variety is clear. Infants spend a greater percentage of their time gazing in the direction of a decorated wall in a room than looking at the opposite, plain wall. In fact, where *two* walls are decorated, it is generally the one with the more complex pattern that is looked at the greater amount of time. As a child grows older we see a high degree of interest in a wide variety of diverse stimuli which can satisfy this need.

We also see an ability, in human beings, to self-satisfy the need for stimulus variety through imagination. If you will recall, in an earlier chapter we talked about cognitive stimuli. Through the use of self-initiated cognitive stimuli—that is, daydreaming and the use of vivid imagination— the individual who is deprived of stimulus variety can partially satisfy his need.

This is a need of particular importance for the public speaker to recognize. As a student you can easily recall your own inclination, as you sit through an incredibly tedious class lasting for 50 minutes, to move about, shift position, and daydream. Is it not surprising, then, that you can sit for two to three times as long without moving a muscle as you watch an interesting motion picture? The difference lies in the wide variety of changing and complex stimuli that are presented in the motion picture, ranging from thoughtful dialogue to vivid action, all linked by interesting visual contrasts.

Now consider the situation a classroom teacher faces. He probably has no access to a musical background which could help to establish or change a tone or mood to fit the presentation. He has little opportunity to constantly mix interesting visual presentations into his lecture, and inasmuch as his lecture is essentially a monologue, relatively little vocal variety is possible, and only his voice is heard constantly for an hour. Nevertheless, some teachers are considered to be very interesting and excellent in their presentations. On observing their techniques, one usually finds that the "good" teacher mixes in as much stimulus variety as the circumstances permit.

The use of the blackboard in the classroom or the overhead projector in an auditorium introduces stimulus variety, and can be employed even when such presentation is not vital to the subject matter. Any experienced salesman who uses a visual display kit is well aware of this. It is important that the teacher refrain from speaking in a monotone, maintaining the same pace of speech, or having a "sameness" to the lecture content for an entire hour. The experienced teacher will vary his pace, will have clearly identifiable subsections within an hour-long lecture, and will use his voice very much as an accomplished musician plays an instrument. Even the simple acts of moving about and using physical gestures introduce variation in stimuli, and maintain interest. When such a teacher is presenting a topic you find very little inattention, but when a teacher violates many of these guidelines, the need for stimulus variety overwhelms the listener, and soon attention to the lecture is displaced by attention to a variety of self-generated cognitive stimuli that we usually call daydreaming.

Sometimes teachers ask, "Is entertaining the class the same thing as educating the people there?" Such a question actually misses the point. It should be obvious that if attention is lost there can be no learning. The point was demonstrated experimentally by Coats and Smidchens (1966), who actually set out to compare speaker dynamism with "grade threat" in the ability to produce recall of presented material. Threat of low grades had no significant effect, but how dynamic the speaker was in his presentation produced highly significant results. The 184 students who were subjects learned much better from a "dynamic" speaker, although the content delivered by the two speakers was matched.

One clear-cut functional relationship links the need for stimulus variety to the phylogenetic level of the species. It has been shown that the higher the evolutionary level of the organism, the more stimulus variety is required if the individual is not to demonstrate a condition of deprivation.

Still, in 1960 Jencks and Porter investigated the response to stimulus variety in a species quite low on the phylogenetic scale. In investigating what might serve as a reward for laboratory rats, three groups of rats were run through a maze each day. One group received food whenever they came into the goal box. The second group, arriving at the goal box, found only the empty area awaiting them. The third group encountered a variety of different situational stimuli when they arrived at the goal box. One day they might find cotton carpeting on the floor, on another day a ladder which allowed them to descend to a lower level, and variously on other days a strange (same sex) rat, the smell of perfume, a dark enclosure, being picked up, shredded paper on the floor, and nails scattered on the floor. Under these various circumstances it was found that the variety-rewarded animals learned the maze as efficiently as did the animals rewarded by food. There was no evidence of maze learning in the group which simply encountered the empty goal box. It was concluded that even at the phylogenetic level of the rat there is a need, or at least an apparent drive, for stimulus variety.

On the human level a program of basic research by Munsinger and Weir (1967) investigated the preference of infants and young children for complex visual designs. A machine carefully measured visual fixation in children ranging from nine to forty-one months of age, and it was consistently found that children at all ages fixated on the most complex of the 12 visual designs shown.

The situation with the human being, and quite possibly with some of the higher infrahuman species, may not be quite as simple as the last experiment implies. An extensive research program carried out by Berlyne and his associates at the University of Toronto has suggested that, in addition to complexity, there is a human appreciation for patterning in stimulus variety. The title of a recent research article by Berlyne and Boudewijns (1971), related to the phenomenon just discussed, is self-explanatory: "The Hedonic Effects of Uniformity in Variety."

C 7.11. *The need for stimulus variety.*

The bored student may - - - in order to satisfy the need for - - -. _____ .

   a. smoke/social interaction

   b. sleep/stimulus variety

   c. daydream/stimulus variety

The degree of the need for stimulus variety is _____ correlated with phylogenetic level of a species.

   a. not   b. positively   c. negatively

The human need for variety in stimulation is tempered by a need for that stimulus variety to be _____ .

   a. of only moderate intensity   b. weak   c. patterned

Sensory Deprivation

So much for the existence of an apparent *drive* for stimulus variety. How then do we meet the criterion of terming stimulus variety a *need*? The criterion calls for deterioration of the organism under conditions of prolonged deprivation. Some years ago, in a Canadian university, human volunteer subjects were used in a sensory deprivation experiment. These subjects were well paid for their time. They took a variety of tests of their ability to read, comprehend, do mathematical problems, and so forth, and they were then put separately into chambers where all sensory stimulation was as limited as possible. There was nothing to look at or listen to, and in one series of the experiments the subjects were even immersed in tubs of water maintained at exact body temperature, with polyethylene cone-shaped cuffs on their wrists and ankles which prevented even the stimulation that might be provided by touching a surface or oneself with the fingers, or touching the toes to something. In this latter series of experiments, the subjects wore translucent goggles which admitted no perception of shape or form from the environment, and a speaker on the wall delivered "white noise," which is a mixture of sound tones at all frequency levels so that the listener cannot say whether he is hearing high, middle, or low-pitched sound. The white noise effectively masks any perception of patterned sound that might come from outside the experimental chamber.

The results of this experiment were quite dramatic: the subjects very rapidly began to resign from the experiment. Despite high wages as experimental subjects, many of the people decided on the first day that they could not continue in extreme sensory deprivation. Even the longest-enduring subject did not last nearly as long as had been anticipated, and follow-up tests showed that even after a few hours of sensory deprivation, individuals began to deteriorate markedly in their intellectual abilities. The ability to do math problems, for example, dropped off considerably, and after the experiment it returned only gradually over a period of several days (Heron, 1957).

Obviously such extreme conditions very seldom occur with human beings in normal environments. But they may occur in a relative sense with certain people whose environments are quite sterile or limited. Educational psychologists have become familiar with the terms "enriched" and "impoverished," referring to environments. The impoverished environment, which may exist in some lower socioeconomic level homes, seems to result in a marked decrease in the mental abilities of children.

An interesting speculative question, which is being approached through animal research at the present time, is whether prolonged sensory deprivation of an intense nature is reversible. It would be a sad thing if we were to find that prolonged sensory deprivation, of even a relative degree, resulted in *ir*reversible deteriorative changes, but such knowledge is vital and must be pursued. The answer to this question awaits a research design that is appropriate and that controls correlated variables effectively.

C 7.12. *Sensory deprivation.*

The sensory deprivation experiments showed that _____ abilities deteriorate rapidly under conditions of massive deprivation of stimulus sensations.

The Sexual Drive   We have passed over two primary drives that need special attention because they are not of the same general pattern as the others. The first is the *sexual drive* which *is* a need according to the broad definition given earlier in this chapter. We stated that if a need goes continually unmet, there is a deteriorative effect on the organism *or on the species*. There is no evidence that prolonged deprivation of goal objects specific to the sexual drive has a deteriorative effect—either physical or psychological—upon the individual, although this is not to say that an individual might not become frustrated. Rather, in the abstract sense, the welfare of the *species,* not the individual, demands the satisfaction of the sex drive. Widespread total deprivation would mean extinction as a species.

Moreover, in animal research, it has been found that the common *appetitive deprivation effect* associated with incentives such as food and water does not exist in quite the same way for sexual deprivation. When an organism is deprived of food for three days, he will exhibit more vigorous behavior or will endure more shock to get to food than if deprived for two days, and his two-day deprivation behavior is more vigorous than behavior under one-day deprivation. The same holds true for water. With the sex drive, however, we could make a general statement that the animal that is deprived for longer periods of time seems to have no stronger sex drive, with the only qualification being that for a short period of time following satisfaction of the sex drive, sexual motivation seems weak.

An important functional relationship known to hold with animals, and apparently with human beings as well, is that sexual activity is a function of age. The young adult is most sexually active, with activity declining slowly with increasing age, then declining more rapidly as the organism becomes elderly. In one interesting experiment, however, an interacting variable was discovered. A rat "couple" had been observed for about two years of their middle and late adulthood. The male emitted fewer and fewer sexual overtures per estrous cycle of the female, although sexual behavior did not cease entirely. One day the mate of the male was removed and a strange female animal in heat was inserted into the chamber with the male. Almost immediately "Romeo" began to act as if he were young again, and this behavior persisted at a fairly high level for a few weeks before it began to fade. Replacement of that female again rejuvenated the sexual behavior. The case of the "philandering rat" allows some understanding of the behavior patterns we sometimes observe in human beings, as we can see that the level of sex drive is a function of familiarity of the object individual as a sexual partner. Of course, society offers a number of negative incentives to human philandering, which serve to displace what may be basic behavioral impulses.

C 7.13. *Sexual behavior.*

Sexual behavior _____ a need.

    a. is   b. is not

The appetitive deprivation effect over a general range of values of the predictor variable (time) _____

    appear to hold true for animal sexual behavior.

    a. does   b. does not

Animal sexual activity is a strong predictive function of _____ .

    a. age of the individual

    b. novelty of the sexual partner

    c. (both of the above variables are true)

The Manipulatory Drive   The other drive that we shall discuss here is the so-called *manipulatory* drive. This apparent drive is not well understood. Monkeys and human beings both seem to automatically begin "toying" with or manipulating objects that are presented to them. In fact, the well-known expression "monkey around" may be taken from this common behavior. In the absence of any sorts of extra rewards or other primary drives, monkeys will manipulate little puzzle-locks and try to put intra-fitting objects together, by the hour. The drive to manipulate things with the hands may not be based upon a need to do this *particular* thing. It is possible that it is the need for *stimulus variety* that is served by manipulatory behavior. At any rate, the inclination to manipulate things—the so-called manipulatory drive—is very strong in organisms high on the phylogenetic scale.

The Measurement of Drives

Many years ago an interesting scheme was derived for the measurement of animal drives. At Columbia University, animal psychologists put together an obstruction box—an experimental chamber which was rectangular in shape with a platform at each end. The center section was made up of a large electric grid. The reasoning was that if you put an animal on one platform and an incentive object on the opposite platform, and had variable intensity shock delivered through the grid, you could find out what intensity of electric shock an animal would be willing to endure in order to get to the goal. Hungry animals were tempted by a food goal, thirsty animals by a water goal, and so on. Of course, the strengths of drives relate to durations of deprivations, and we have come to realize that different drives reach their peaks at different durations of deprivation, but nevertheless the early findings are of interest.

After a specified length of deprivation, using laboratory rats, the investigators who had tested the relative strengths of six drives came to the following conclusions: The strongest drive was the maternal drive, which caused a mother rat to cross a grid at a high intensity of shock to get to her young offspring on the opposite platform. The second strongest drive appeared to be the thirst drive, third was the hunger drive, fourth was the female sex drive which caused a female rat in heat to cross the grid to get to a waiting male, and next was the male sex drive, with the male rat crossing the grid to get to a female in heat. Weakest was what the researchers called the exploratory drive, which we would now probably place under the

Drawing by Levin; © 1975 The New Yorker Magazine, Inc.

heading of a need for stimulus variety. In short, the animals would endure very little electric shock simply for the opportunity of getting to the other platform to see what was there. This early research has been elaborated by several other workers, but so far there have been no subsequent comprehensive studies of the relative strengths of drives.

C 7.14. *The measurement of drive strength in laboratory research.*

In the Columbia obstruction box, strength of motive is inferred from the _____ voluntarily endured

to satisfy the motive.

a. amount of time spent waiting   b. intensity of electric shock

Different drives reach their peaks at _____ durations of deprivation.

a. the same   b. different

Using the Columbia obstruction box, psychologists determined that the _____

drive was the strongest of six motives investigated using laboratory animals.

In the Columbia obstruction box, _____ was the weakest of the six motives investigated.

PROGRESS CHECK   7.2

MATCH: _____ 1. Need

   _____ 2. Drive

A. Behavioral motives resulting from needs

B. Homeostatic imbalance

C. According to ethnologists, total deprivation could be deteriorating to the individual or species

D. Low blood sugar

E. Searching for water.

3. An organism approaches a particular stimulus. Which kind of drive might this represent? _____ .

   a Appetitive   b. Aversive

4. The goal object of an aversive drive is _____ .

   a. a positive incentive   b. approach-avoidance

   c. hunger reduction   d. a negative incentive

5. Which of these does not generate a primary drive? _____ .

   a. Hunger   b. Pain   c. Jealousy   d. Thirst

6. Which factor seems to be the primary cause of hunger? _____ .

   a. Peristalsis   b. Low blood sugar   c. Empty stomach   d. Time

7. A dry throat actually causes the thirst drive. _____ .

    a. Probably   b. Probably not

8. What factor led Harlow to believe contact comfort is a need? _____ .

    a. The young rhesus preferred cloth mothers to wire surrogates

    b. It is similar to tender loving care

    c. Some of the same characteristics operate in stimulus variety

    d. Young rhesus with only wire mothers underwent deteriorative changes as pre-adults

9. Which behavior is a college student in a boring class unlikely to perform for stimulus variety? _____ .

    a. Smoking   b. Daydreaming   c. Listening attentively   d. Doodling

10. Sensory deprivation experiments demonstrated _____ .

    a. a need for stimulation

    b. deterioration of intellectual abilities under deprivation conditions

    c. both   d. neither

11. Which is true of sexual behavior? _____ .

    a. It results from a need

    b. Animals do not require other stimulus variety if sexually fulfilled

    c. The drive becomes much stronger due to deprivation over time

    d. Two of the above answers are true

    e. All of the first three answers are true

MATCH: _____ 12. Strongest drive   A. Measured by Columbia obstruction box

    _____ 13. Weakest drive   B. Maternal drive

    C. Exploratory drive

    D. Female sexual drive

14. Different drives reach peaks at different durations of deprivation. _____ .

    a. True   b. False

INCENTIVATION   An *incentive* is some *discernible goal* with motivational properties—it may be an object or a situation—and it may be positive (attractive) or negative (repelling) in its value. In a relatively unlearned sense, organisms are attracted to some objects and situations and repelled by others. It is possible to investigate functional relationships that exist in these situations, and thus to be guided in the planning of motivational systems with children, in business and industry, and so forth.

Much of the research of the type in which we are interested was conducted by Judson Brown (1948, 1961) at the University of Iowa. In a typical experiment on this subject a researcher uses animals in straight-line runways, with little harnesses on their bodies and leashes that lead to restraining springs. If an animal goes down a runway until restrained, he can be measured in the amount of pulling tension he exerts against the restraint. Positive incentives are set up by presenting animals with visible food and measuring their strength of pull at different distances. When restrained at a point near the goal, the animals pull vigorously, but the farther away they are when restrained, the less is their pulling strength. The functional relationship derived is that incentivation is a function of the distance to the goal.

Also, as you can see in Figure 7.3, the curve describing this relationship is not a straight line, and the motive strength increases much more rapidly as the organism is very close to the incentive.

The same general procedure can be used to study the negative incentive. In this operation, the animals are shocked in a chamber, then the door is opened and the animals can scamper down the runway. At different distances from the chamber the animals are restrained and their pulling strengths measured. As the solid line of Figure 7.4 indicates, a functional relationship is again found, with negative incentivation a function of distance from the goal. We have taken the liberty in Figure 7.4 to draw the positive incentivation line as a broken line for comparison. As you can see, it is the negative incentive that is the steepest closer to the goal. This is the concept of the *goal gradient*, which is well-known in psychology.

To recap the highlights of the goal-gradient research, (1) the closer one is to the incentive, the stronger the motivation, and (2) motivation relative to a negative incentive increases more rapidly than does motivation relative

Figure 7.3

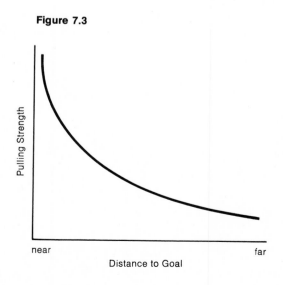

Figure 7.4

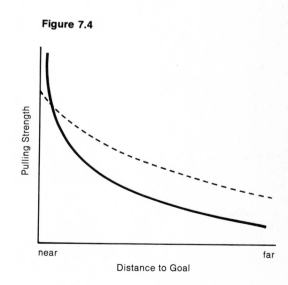

to a positive incentive at points very near to the goal. In Chapter 13 we shall study some of the problems resulting when mixed motives exist in a single situation, creating frustration and conflict.

C 7.15. *Incentivation and goal gradients.*

An incentive is _____ .

    a. a goal object that exists

    b. a goal object that is perceived by the subject

    c. a drive state based on need

Brown found that in straight-line runways incentivation toward or away from a goal was a direct function

of _____ .

    a. distance from the goal   b. realization of the goal's meaning

The gradient (slope of the line on the graph) is steeper when the organism is _____ the incentive.

    a. close to   b. far from

Which gradient increases in steepness most sharply when the organism is positioned very close to the

incentive? _____ .

    a. positive   b. negative

We shall expand upon these points later on, but for the moment the major lesson from incentivation research is that incentives are good motivators when they are immediate in terms of space or time. Distant incentives have poor motivating properties, and just because we are human beings who can "anticipate" does not mean that we are exceptions to the rule. By offering *immediate* incentives to people—adults as well as children, although the phenomenon is particularly pronounced with children—we can use incentives to advantage; otherwise, efforts at incentivation are usually disappointing.

MOTIVATION AND EFFICIENCY

Two topics pertaining to the interrelationship of motivation and efficiency should be noted. First we shall discuss the relation of appetitive and aversive motives to activation level, and second, the relation of activation level to efficiency.

Obviously, both appetitive and aversive motivation may exist at levels just barely discernible. Slight stirrings of hunger or mildly annoying levels of bright light are examples of each. Still, within the moderate and the high levels, aversive motives create higher levels of activation than do appetitive motives. (Remember that activation level pertains to the amount of arousal of the physical and nervous systems.) At the highest levels especially, motivational states created by such stimuli as strong electric shocks or burnings are considerably higher than even those created by extreme

Figure 7.5

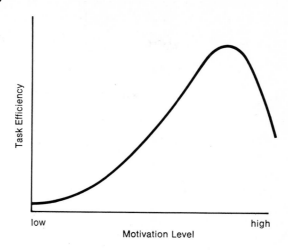

hunger or thirst.

The second point concerns the relation of activation level to task efficiency. An optimum point of motivation for any given task can be established, and that optimum point is generally some intermediate value. Researchers have developed the "inverse-U" shaped function shown in Figure 7.5 to describe this relationship. As motivation increases, efficiency on a task increases up to a point, beyond which it decreases. You have probably had the experience of being in such a hurry to beat a deadline or to make up for lost time that you have dropped things, made mistakes, and shown a generally lowered level of efficiency. You may well visualize how, if being chased home by a rabid dog, you might not be able to get your key out and open your front door as efficiently as if you were calmly arriving home.

A well-established "law" in psychology, called the Yerkes-Dodson Principle, states this relationship and then goes on to elaborate. The principle first states that for every task there is an optimum intermediate level of motivation. It goes on then to say that the actual optimum spot on the motivational scale drops lower as task complexity increases. The principle was established only within a restricted range of tasks, but in general you can see how even extremely high motivation might be optimum if a simple task such as brute strength or a quick muscular reaction were involved. On the other hand, complex tasks such as unfamiliar speech patterns, abstract reasoning, or complex discriminations are disrupted if the motivation level is too high.

C 7.16. *The effect of motivation level on efficiency.*

Generally speaking, except at the lowest intensity levels, appetitive motivation creates _____ levels of activation than does aversive motivation.

    a. higher   b. lower

The function that holds between motivation level and resulting task efficiency is _____ .

    a. linear (straight line)   b. U-shaped   c. inverse (upside-down) U-shaped

The Yerkes-Dodson Principle, which describes the function mentioned in the last question, also states that the more complex a task becomes, the _____ will be the best level of motivation for that task.

    a. higher   b. lower

INSTINCTS   Certain behaviors are known as *species-specific behaviors*. This term refers to a class of behaviors that are shown to be typical of either a single species or a group of related species, but which are not typical of other species. For the most part, the behaviors that we call *instincts* are species-specific. One of the most frequent questions asked of psychologists by beginning psychology students is whether or not human beings manifest instincts. For this and other reasons the question "What is instinct?" is important.

Psychologists do not totally agree concerning what constitutes an instinct. Many years ago Hunter (1919) defined an instinct in terms of three criteria. They were that the behavior should be biologically useful, all individuals within the species should manifest the behavior, and the behavior should be relatively complete even on its first occurrence. Years later Kendler (1963) offered four criteria of an instinct which were as follows: All the members of the species should manifest the behavior, the behavior should be unlearned, the behavior should fit a rigid pattern, and finally the behavior should be complex.

In integrating these two psychologists' opinions, it might be useful to redefine the criteria of an instinct.

(1) An instinct should be *biologically useful* to the individual and/or the species, although the usefulness may not be immediately apparent.

(2) *All intact members* of the species should manifest the behavior. We specify "intact" because of the possibility that biologically damaged individuals might not fit the pattern.

(3) The behavior should be *unlearned*. This was implied when Hunter stated that the behavior should be relatively complete on its first occurrence.

(4) The behavior should fit a *rigid pattern*, and not show significant variations from one individual to another.

(5) The behavior should be *complex*, and here the major restriction is that we wish to exclude simple reflexes from classification as instincts.

Examples of instinctive behavior are abundant to the student who studies animal behavior, even in a descriptive way—particularly those species that lie below the level of mammals on the phylogenetic scale. Fish respond to shapes of other fish or to spots of color on other fish with aggressive or sexual behaviors. Birds respond to the colors and song-patterns of other birds. The "singing" of certain insects such as locusts appears to have the capacity to bring out sexual behaviors in other individuals of the species. Birds' migratory patterns, as well as those of fishes, also are classed as instincts.

Research has established that instinctive patterns are triggered by an interaction between *internal biological conditions* and *environmental stimuli*. The internal biological conditions may relate either to biological structure or to transient biochemical changes such as those that occur with regularity in the mating season. Due to the strong control that stimuli have over instinctive behavior, instinctive behaviors can be influenced very easily by introducing artificial environmental changes. One researcher raised birds in a solarium in which an artificial sun rose on one side of the room, crossed the ceiling, and "set" on the other side of the room. The track across the ceiling could be adjusted to duplicate the relative position of the sun in the sky as the seasons change from summer to winter and back again. During one late summer and fall, artificialities were introduced in the solarium sun position, so that it was as if winter was ending and spring was beginning; that is, the sun began to take longer to make its way across the ceiling, and the track upon which it traveled was adjusted higher in the "sky." After several weeks the birds were released. When last seen they were all in a flock flying north. The experimenter's best wishes went with them, but it was clear that these birds would perish in the winter cold unless they were sensitive enough to the sun position to quickly readjust their "calendar" and turn south.

In other research, sea turtles that live on beaches were theorized to orient themselves to water from the light reflections made by moonlight on the waves. In an experiment, the large sea turtles turned inland when flickering spotlights were set up inland away from the water, and as long as the lights were shown in front of the creatures, they continued to lumber inland farther and farther.

C 7.17. *Instincts.*

Know the five criteria of an instinct, so that if we give you some proper criteria and an improper one, such as "must be manifest immediately after birth," you can identify the improper one.

_____

_____

_____

_____

_____

Instincts are triggered by an interaction between _____

conditions and _____ .

Temporary reduction of physical discomfort may underlie some instinctive patterns. It has been hypothesized that some species of birds laying fertile eggs experience a good deal of flesh-irritation which is soothed by "nesting," as the bird presses its inflamed underside against the smooth surface of the egg. As animals nurse their young, it is thought that a certain degree of physical discomfort is reduced by the removal of the milk. The discomfort obviously experienced by dairy cows that are overdue for milking illustrates this.

Do human beings have instincts? This question is extremely difficult to answer, because one of two possibilities may exist, and the issue is difficult to research. First, human beings, in their evolutionary process, may have "grown out" of reliance upon instinctive patterns. Due to their intelligence, they may have ceased to evolve in terms of instinct development. Whatever biological structure mediated the instinct may have "drifted" back to a state in which the instinct no longer exists. An alternative explanation is also possible. Instincts can be overlaid with learning. Human beings have such a wide variety of behaviors that have been strongly and consistently learned in a wide variety of circumstances that it is quite possible that the instincts are merely shrouded and are never actually manifest. Thus, if we were to take an individual and strand him soon after birth in a primitive wilderness, if he survived it is possible that a variety of instinctive patterns might emerge. At this particular time, however, it does not seem that we can answer the question of human instinct in any decisive way.

We shall make one final point relative to the concept of instinct. As a general rule we know that the hormonal condition of the organism has a stronger directive influence over behaviors of organisms lower on the phylogenetic scale than it does over behaviors of organisms high on the scale. Laboratory rats, for example, that have had no experience with the performance or observation of "rat sex" have absolutely no difficulty whatsoever, as adults, when they are first introduced to sexually receptive members of the opposite sex. Males know what to do and females know what to do. Yet the elimination of the sex hormones that control the estrous cycle in the female and which influence the appropriate behaviors in both sexes eliminates sexual behavior.

As we go up the phylogenetic scale, we see that dogs continue to demonstrate low-frequency sexual behavior after elimination of sex hormones by surgery *if* they have had previous sexual experiences. Finally, when one gets to the higher monkeys, learning is the dominant factor. We see an initial total ignorance of appropriate sexual behavior even in physically normal individuals if they have been kept from observing sexual behavior and if they have had no prior interaction with receptive individuals of the opposite sex. Luckily, in man, "observation" takes place in a symbolic way through verbal instruction or description, so it is not typical to find total naïveté about the matter.

C 7.18. *Hormones and behavior.*

Hormones control behavior to a _____ degree in individuals as we go up the phylogenetic scale.

  a. greater   b. lesser

MOVING FROM BASIC MOTIVES TO HUMANISTIC MOTIVES

Before we consider the ways in which viewpoints of man's specific motive structure have been perceived differently from those of lower organisms, we should make it quite clear that there are many psychologists who feel that the notions of motivation already presented in this chapter lie at the foundation of all human behavior, either in a direct fashion or through the mechanism of learning. In Chapters 8 and 9 you will see how some psychologists develop this latter point. Still, there are many who feel that such concepts are not to their tastes, and they have developed alternative explanations for the wide varieties of observed human behavior.

Humanism

Humanistic psychologists are those who would explain human behavior along dimensions not shared with lower organisms. Many versions emphasize one aspect or another of human motives. One group of psychologists, for example, has placed emphasis upon the affiliation motive, claiming that proper development and satisfaction of this motive is essential to all subsequent psychological development and mental health.

Another group has proposed a need for *equity*. Their stress is upon a total socioeconomic structure in which "inequity exists for a person when he perceives that the ratio of his outcomes to inputs and the ratio of others' outcomes to inputs are unequal [Adams, 1965]." It can be seen that equity may concern basic social situations such as exist in an individual's own home, or might apply to job situations.

Some psychologists, among them McClelland (1961) suggest that *achievement* is the overwhelming motive present in most people, with the amount of need for achievement determined by a number of things including how the individual was treated during childhood. There are those who conceive of the entire human condition as being essentially determined by an individual's need for achievement. They would perceive, for example, that one's achievement in the educational area will dictate what that person "amounts to" for years to come.

Some psychologists believe that the motive for achievement is a highly institutionalized, and thus artificial, concept. That is, they would view achievement as influenced through the educational process or a determination to succeed in the business world, but would conclude that there must be a broader-based type of motive structure that is more generally applicable to all human beings, both within and outside of the highly structured educational-industrial society. So it is that White (1959) has proposed the existence of a general *competence motive*. Competence refers to the organism's capacity to interact effectively with its environment. Even in lower organisms, White considers a motive for competence to be innate. White argues that the motive for competence is much more complex in the human being, and he presents considerable evidence of individuals trying to cope with their environment apparently for no reason other than a desire to master it. White argues that a competence motive is aroused whenever people are faced with new situations or new problems, and that the motive wanes when a situation has been explored or worked with to the point that it no longer presents a challenge.

Yet another group has proposed a motive for *self-actualization*. Self-actualization is the need people have to grow and develop, a desire for self-fulfillment, and a tendency for a person to actually become everything that he is capable of becoming (Maslow, 1954). There are several different approaches to self-actualization, usually revolving about the notion of what self-actualization actually is, and each taking its particular viewpoint as to why different individuals seek different forms and different levels of self-actualization while certain individuals appear not to pursue this motive whatsoever.

C 7.19. *Humanism.*

Humanists, in the vocabulary of psychology, are those individuals who _____ .

a. stress concern for human welfare in their propositions

b. explain human behavior in terms of factors that could not possibly account for the behaviors of infrahuman species

c. reject psychological approaches which stress awareness and free will

McClelland and the Need for Achievement

David McClelland's main interest has been in three motives—achievement, affiliation, and power. He considers *achievement* to be the main motive of man. McClelland and his associates (1953) have developed a procedure which involves the evaluation of imaginative productions (stories based on themes) as a means of measuring motives.

McClelland suggests that all motives are learned. To investigate one way in which the achievement motive may be learned, Winterbottom (1958) studied the relationship between children's need to achieve and parental training. Children were identified as being low or high in their need for achievement on the basis of their stories. The mothers were then asked at what ages they had expected their children to have accomplished certain behaviors such as standing up for their rights, eating alone, earning their spending money, and so forth. The mothers were also asked how consistently they had rewarded the children for these behaviors. While all mothers expected such behaviors by the age of nine or ten, the mothers of high achievement children expected these accomplishments much earlier than did the mothers of children with a low achievement need. In addition, consistent reward for these accomplishments was characteristic only in the families of the high achievement need children.

McClelland has also contributed an interesting viewpoint concerning situational determinants of motivation. He speculates that the individual tends to match his past experiences with his predictions for the outcome of a particular situation. While the individual wants to be able to predict what will happen in a situation, he does not want to be able to do so with complete accuracy, since this would lead to boredom. As a result, the greatest motivated activity is in situations of *moderate* anticipatory accuracy.

This notion would explain how it is that many people lose interest in an activity once the challenge of mastering it is completed. Motivation depends, in part, on anticipation of the unexpected.

C 7.20. *McClelland's "need for achievement."*

Data would support a claim that a need for achievement _____ .

    a. develops through child-rearing practices, and is therefore related to parental practices

    b. is innate and strongly pronounced in everyone

Motivation to act appears to be influenced by expectation of outcome; the greatest motivation to act comes when the individual _____ .

    a. has no idea what to expect in terms of succeeding

    b. is totally self-confident

    c. is moderately confident of his or her ability to succeed

Murray's Psychology of Human Needs

Another important needs theorist is Henry A. Murray, who has derived a list of psychological needs which, incidentally, has become the basis for a well-known personality test, the Edwards Personal Preference Schedule (EPPS). Rather than present a full listing of all of the 20 needs proposed by Murray, we will simply list certain of them and thereby experience the tone of Murray's general conceptualization of why human beings are motivated as they are. Murray conceived of people as having a need for friends (affiliation), to make an impression on others (exhibition), for understanding what is going on around them (understanding), and for excelling in something (achievement). Some of the needs seem not always to be praiseworthy; for example, Murray proposes human needs to revenge an insult or injury (aggression), to justify or conceal one's misdeeds (defendance), and to be consoled or indulged by others (succorance). Other needs seem rather common, such as the proposed needs for play, for order in one's affairs, and dominance over other people.

A needs system such as Murray's provides interesting post hoc explanations of behavior—we might say that an individual acted in a certain way because of a strong or overdeveloped need in some area. As such the system is mainly of philosophical value. However, the personality test mentioned earlier (the EPPS) is sometimes employed to make predictions of human behavior in a variety of circumstances, and this test has generated a great deal of research. Basically the test evaluates whether an individual "needs" such factors as autonomy to a greater or lesser degree than most persons of his or her age and sex, then predictions of actual behavior relative to that need are usually seen to be fairly accurate.

C 7.21. *Murray's need system.*

Henry Murray has developed a complex system of _____.

    a. twenty human needs that create an aspect of one's personality

    b. twelve basic needs that are common to human beings and to most animal species

    c. five needs to explain all behaviors, both normal and abnormal

Maslow's Conception of Human Motivation

One of the motivation theorists who has contributed a great deal to the concept of human motivation is Abraham Maslow. He conceives of a pyramid or hierarchy of human motives at five levels. See Figure 7.6. At the most basic level are the *physiological needs* of the organism. These are essentially what we have already referred to as primary drives. It is important, Maslow feels, for the human being to have his hunger, thirst, sexual, and other physiological needs met at a satisfactory level.

The second level of human motivation is the *safety need*. Safety is primarily a physiological matter, and this strong need would explain the reluctance that most individuals have to submit themselves to deliberate injury. There are many known circumstances of individuals who attempt suicide by letting themselves be hit by a train or a truck, but at the last minute they jump aside and save themselves. The safety need can be expanded to include psychological safety. An individual could be said to "need" a certain amount of invulnerability from sarcastic attacks, insults, or social threats by other people. The need for safety thus includes both a resistance to psychological as well as physiological insult.

The third level of need is for *love and affection*. This need is not conceived of as being sexually motivated, but refers primarily to the need for a love relationship.

The fourth level in Maslow's need hierarchy is the need for *esteem*. Esteem was primarily meant to refer to an appreciation of one's self by others, in terms of respect or approval. This does not necessarily mean

Figure 7.6

MASLOW'S HIERARCHY OF HUMAN NEEDS

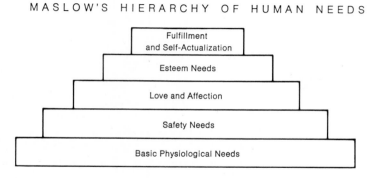

Fulfillment and Self-Actualization

Esteem Needs

Love and Affection

Safety Needs

Basic Physiological Needs

"You've been walked and you've been fed.
Now I suppose you want love and affection."

that an individual's actions have to be respected by society as a whole if the need is to be met. On the contrary, one may receive the esteem of one's peer group for committing acts that would be condemned by society as a whole. The concept of esteem is also extended to include self-esteem, which means that a person has a need to think highly of himself, or at least not feel ashamed of his own worth as a human being. Obviously, part of this is a felt reflection of what other people think of one, but there are cases of individuals whose self-esteem may be high even though the esteem of others, in the broad sense, is quite low.

The fifth and highest level of motive, according to Maslow, is the need for *self-actualization.* This interesting term means that the activities of an individual should be at a level consistent with his abilities or ambitions. In a general sense an individual would be self-actualized if what he did for a living, and what he did in a family sense, was both challenging and gratifying. Many people are intelligent but have low levels of education, which has the effect of limiting the level of their occupational endeavors. A very bright person with a trivial job, far below the level of what he could be doing if just given a chance, is an individual who is not self-actualized.

The recognition of these five forms of human needs is one of Maslow's contributions to our understanding of human motivation. There is another aspect of Maslow's theory, however, which is extremely provocative. It is simply this—an individual is said to not actually *have* a given need, at least to any meaningful extent, until lower levels of needs are reasonably satisfied.

For example, physiological needs would take precedence over safety needs. During the Korean War period there were incidents involving Korean civilians who came onto army supply depots under cover of darkness to steal food. Sometimes women and children were surprised in the act of going through garbage cans looking for scraps, and on several unfortunate occasions these individuals were shot as they tried to run away. The illustration here is that these people had a more powerful need to satisfy hunger than to protect their physical safety. Or, in Maslow's terms, the need for safety was not prominent under conditions of extreme hunger.

Similarly, the need for love and affection would be said by Maslow to be of only secondary importance where physiological needs go unsatisfied *or* where threats exist continuously to one's physical safety. Recognizable examples of the latter are probably rare, but there is research bearing upon the first notion. During the Second World War, volunteer subjects were used in the University of Minnesota's starvation experiments. These individuals were given only the minimum amount of food necessary to maintain life in an effort to understand what happens to prisoners of war on similar diets. The subjects in the experiment were observed in many aspects of behavior, and they gave self-reports of their feelings and motives. One of the consequences of extreme food deprivation was an almost complete cessation of interest in sex or affectionate relationships. In fact, the "pin-ups" belonging to these men became most typically pictures of food clipped from magazines.

Going up to the next level, if the needs at the lower three levels are unmet the need for self-esteem and the esteem of others is not prominent. Under these circumstances people sometimes engage in highly undesirable behaviors. One of the reasons why personnel managers are reluctant to hire individuals who are going through the emotional strains of divorce bears upon this point. It is known that these individuals may behave in ways that do not contribute to self-esteem or esteem by others. "Non-esteemed" behaviors are practically all undesirable in the view of an employer. As an example, the lonely individual who has been recently divorced or widowed may engage in a series of rather prominent promiscuous relationships. To put it in everyday terms, the individual begins to act as if he or she had no "pride." An illustration of the secondary importance of esteem where physiological deprivation exists can be found in the large number of "normal" German women who resorted to prostitution with American soldiers shortly after the end of World War II to earn money for food. Self-esteem and the esteem of others seem relatively unimportant in the face of hunger.

The notion of higher needs depending upon satisfaction of lower ones extends also to self-actualization. When lower needs are met, many individuals may make sacrifices to attend continuing education programs, or perform any number of other achievement-oriented activities. On the other hand, many people seem to avoid those activities that could lead to ultimate satisfactions and self-actualization; in their cases Maslow would assume that, unless of low abilities, these individuals find that a sincere affectional relationship or the esteem of others seems continually to elude them. They then expend their efforts in the pursuit of these or other lower level goals.

An Evaluation of Maslow's Theory of Human Motivation

Maslow's theory of the nature of human motivation has too many exceptions to be genuinely satisfying to some psychologists. A scientifically derived theory should have very few exceptions, and when exceptions occur it is supposed that there is a lawfulness to them that itself will be discovered. If a scientific theory has lawful exceptions, the exceptions are used to remold the theory until finally perfect explanation and prediction are possible. Maslow's theory is not satisfactory in this respect. If one visualizes the man who goes hungry in order to provide certain things for members of his family, if one visualizes the individual who commits suicide despite the satisfaction of his basic physiological needs, if one visualizes the individual who is satisfied at all levels and who enjoys the esteem of his fellow-man and who still does not attempt to elevate himself to working productively at a level representing his full potential, and if one visualizes those people who are able to continue to function effectively in responsible positions despite emotional turmoil concerning the loss of loved ones, then you begin to see the apparent exceptions to Maslow's predictions.

What is the major value of a theory such as Maslow's? To an individual committed to a behavioristic explanation of behavior, there may be little of merit in his speculations. To others Maslow's reflections may appear to be the collected wisdom of a gifted psychologist with insight into how a very large number of people feel and act. At the very least, Maslow's theory has value to the field of psychology to a degree consistent with the large amount of research which it has generated.

C 7.22. *Maslow's needs hierarchy.*

The most powerful and basic needs, according to Maslow, are those _____ on his needs hierarchy.

    a. lowest   b. highest

To Maslow, the most basic needs are the _____ needs.

Highest on Maslow's needs hierarchy is the individual's need for _____ .

Maslow states that the existence of the higher needs, as motives, depends upon the _____ .

    a. intellectual level of the individual   b. satisfaction of all lower needs

EMOTIONS

In some modern-day texts there is little specific treatment of "emotion," outside of passing remarks within chapters on physiological processes or on the various emotional problems such as neurosis. This is in contrast to the situation that existed some years ago, when there was a great deal of space given to discussion of emotion in introductory texts. In those days a typical research problem concerned whether subjects could consistently and ac-

curately differentiate emotions from facial expressions in photographs. Obviously, reliability in the judgment of emotion was critical in the early stages of research. More recently, psychologists have operationalized the term *emotion* into physiological definitions or into inferences from the type of stimulus being experienced or the type of situation the individual is in.

In recent years the interest in emotion as an independent phenomenon has faded, and it is now being considered as a subelement of motivation by some psychologists. Typical is Tomkins, who titles a presentation, "Affect as the Primary Motivational System." (*Affect* is a term often used synonymously with the word *emotion*.) Tomkins notes that traditionally *drives* are assumed to have aspects of urgency and intensity, but, he adds, the "illusion is created by the misidentification of the drive 'signal' with its 'amplifier,' . . . [its amplifier being] the affective response. . . ." Tomkins offers, as an indication that the primary biological need is not to be confused with its accompanying emotionality, a reference to the almost desperate gasping for breath of one who is choking or drowning. The emotionality of this situation is contrasted with the situation in which pilots have neglected to wear oxygen masks at very high altitudes. These individuals typically show no panic and their deprivation of oxygen results in an almost euphoric enjoyment. In the more typical situations of need, neurological sequences in the brain amplify the drive signals and/or environmental signals that have weak motivating properties of their own, and a "primary drive" with an emotional counterpart is the result (Tomkins, 1970).

It is along this line of thinking that some psychologists have begun to list various states of emotionality as being among the highest intensity motives or, as Tomkins has done, to state that motivation *is* emotion.

C 7.23. *Emotion.*

Modern-day operational definitions of emotion have a tendency to refer to _____

measures taken on an individual, or to the _____ he is experiencing.

The term *emotion* is often used synonymously with the word _____ .

    a. motivation   b. affect   c. hedonism

Many modern books treat emotion as a subelement of _____ .

    a. motivation   b. affect   c. hedonism

The Origin of Emotionality   Much of present-day interpretation of structural or behavior patterns in terms of their evolutionary significance must be speculative. As Latane and Hothersall (1972) point out, ". . . just because an adaptation serves an identifiable function does not mean that it evolved in response to (natural) selection pressures related to that particular function." Similarly, "The adaptive function of an act for a species does not necessarily correspond to the psychological motivation for that act (in) an individual." Still, it is reasonable to assume a high probability for certain sorts of functions.

In Chapter 2 we showed the relation of states of emotionality, and corresponding sympathetic and parasympathetic activation, to reaction within extreme emergency situations. As we stated then, the reaction of "fight or flight," and survival under the most extreme stresses, was facilitated by the biological results of autonomic arousal. If we assume that the word *emotion* is intended to cover autonomic arousal, the survival value of emotion is obvious. If, however, we stress a mental emotional experience as the primary constituent of the term *emotion*, the relationship is not so clear. It is not necessary for an organism to "feel" emotional in order for the autonomic processes to function.

Consider the decerebrate animal. The animal is first prepared by removal of the cerebral cortex. There is then no question of conscious awareness mediating the emotion, for without the cortex there can be no conscious awareness. Only the bodily expression demonstrates that emotion is in process. The rage reaction is simple to bring out, and a cat, for example, will lash out with its claws, snarl and spit, and stand with its back arched. Other special features of this emotion are overactivity of the extensor muscles, heart acceleration, constriction of the blood vessels, and a rise in blood pressure. Similarly, any stimulation to the anterior region of the hypothalamus is likely to bring about genital erection (in the male decerebrate cat), accompanying flexor muscular positions, dilation of the arterioles, and lowering of blood pressure. In many respects, physiologically speaking, the sexual and the rage responses are in opposition.

C 7.24. *Relation of cognition to emotion.*

Studies of emotion in the decerebrate animal show that _____ is not necessary to mediate the autonomic reaction of emotionality.

    a. conscious awareness   b. stimulation

       There is something to be learned from the decerebrate reactions of laboratory animals themselves, but some authors (Stanley-Jones, 1970) also suggest a commonality with the "impersonal" rage often seen in man, with the erect trunk, locked knees, clamped jaw, and a blind, impersonal targeting of the emotion. As a result of such observations on decerebrate subjects, it is concluded that the experiencing of the emotion—the so-called "cognitive" aspects—are unnecessary for the biological emotional process to take place.

       Stanley-Jones (1970) has suggested that the common emotions of rage and lust, which he considers to be the two basic emotions, have their biological origins in the mammalian defenses against heat and cold. To cite just one line of evidence leading to this reasoning, he has found that the autonomic centers in the hypothalamus for sympathetic and para-sympathetic arousal are virtually identical to those for temperature control. This would account for the characteristic opposition of the emotional reaction of the arterioles—dilation under one emotional state and constriction under the other—which can be functionally linked to the body's temperature control. The entire autonomic system shows this "balanced antagonism," with matched opposing centers in the anterior and posterior hypothalamus regions. Whether or not this explanation will hold up to further neurological research is not a major point. It simply illustrates a notion of some interest pertaining to the evolving of the response pattern.

       In opposition to the Stanley-Jones idea of two primary emotional patterns, which is largely derived from the study of the characteristic two-opposed-processes nature of the neurology of the midbrain, there have developed other speculations. Typically psychologists have simply observed behavior, noting relationships to classes of stimuli, in drawing their conclusions.

       Bridges (1932) proposed that the newborn infant has no emotional response other than undifferentiated excitement. At about three months of age, the child's excitement takes on two opposing characters, one being *distress* and the other being *delight*. By the fifth month, distress can take the form of either *anger* or *disgust*. *Fear* joins the distressful reactions at about seven months. At about one year, delight separates into *affection* and *elation*.

       Bridges' notion on the differentiation of emotions that accompanies increasing maturity is shared, at the descriptive level, by most psychologists, although some (see Watson, upcoming) would argue perhaps with there being only one emotional state in the newborn. The cause of the differentiation, however, is another matter. Some would argue that increasing biological maturity, defined primarily in terms of nervous system development, mediates increasing emotional differentiation. Others would conclude that the differentiation is learned, with modeling after others in the social environment being of primary importance. In earlier days much effort went into the assessing of the innateness of emotions, and one saw research dealing with whether smiles, frowns, expressions of disgust and surprise, etc. were observed on the faces of blind people who had had no visual models from which to pattern. Incidentally, there appears to be little difference between blind and sighted people in this regard.

Watson (1919) was one of the early researchers to list what he considered are three emotional pattern-reactions of human infants that are unlearned and innate. Watson listed *fear,* which could be elicited by sudden loud noises or by sudden loss of physical support, *love,* which could be elicited by stroking and certain types of play-interactions, and *rage,* which could be elicited by having the limbs forcibly held down against the body. Watson's view was that these three innate emotions become further differentiated into more finely defined degrees as the child develops, and even other different-appearing emotions, such as sexual arousal, are elaborations of the three initial ones.

C 7.25. *Infant emotionality.*

Most psychologists would agree that the infant _____ possess a full range of emotional characteristics.

    a. does   b. does not

Research on facial expression of emotion in the blind suggests that the patterning of facial expression is _____ .

    a. innate   b. learned

From Watson's research with human infants, what innate emotions did he propose, and what stimuli elicited them? List below:

    a. _____   _____

    b. _____   _____

    c. _____   _____

Three basic emotional patterns were also suggested by Karen Horney (1937), who felt that there were "ways of coping" that were uniform and innate in the human structure. Emotional needs involved *moving toward* other people, *against* other people, and *away from* other people. Horney's suggested structure was elaborated within a framework of a theory of defense against anxiety, but the three orientations she suggested have grown into more general use since that time.

C 7.26. *Horney's theory of emotional orientations.*

Horney's "ways of coping" involved three emotional patterns specific to situations involving other people. What were those three patterns?

a. _____

b. _____

c. _____

Similar to the Horney orientations, theoretically basic like the Watson pattern-reactions, and initially derived from animal research, are the three emotional orientations suggested by Vernon (1972). Here the basic dimensions of stimulus quality—appetitive versus aversive—were related to their matched responses of emotional approach (enjoyment) and emotional avoidance (fear); then the additional stimulus quality of *inescapable aversive* stimulation was introduced, which is said to lead to the basic emotional response of aggression (anger). More recently, a fourth orientation has been added—separation from primary affectional sources (love objects, etc.), leading to depression.

Overview Regardless of whether one takes the view that there are two or three (or even more) basic emotional patterns, and regardless of the nature of viewpoints concerning how man develops the capacity for the experience of finer gradations of his initial gross emotional responses, the adaptational values of the emotions are clear. At least within a certain range, autonomic arousal of the physiological system tends to contribute toward survivability in a natural setting. Becoming "excited" regarding an appetitive stimulus would increase the probability of the deprived organism expending the extra energy necessary for its acquisition. The same sort of rationale would apply to escape from an aversive stimulus. Finally, the inescapable aversive stimulus defines a situation in which the organism is subjected to an appreciable probability of death or at least serious injury. In this situation the small animal turns and fights his attacker, may be successful in repelling the attack, and in this manner may survive.

PROGRESS CHECK   7.3

1. Which stimulus is likely to be the greater incentive? _____ .

   a. Appetitive   b. Aversive

2. Incentivation toward or away from a goal _____ .

   a. typically is measured by bar-pressing

   b. is greatest when the organism is far from the goal

   c. both   d. neither

3. Motivation level and resultant task efficiency may be described as what kind of function? _____ .

   a. Linear   b. Hyperbola   c. Inverse U-Shaped   d. Circular

4. The more complex the task, the lower the optimum motivational level according to _____ .

   a. the Yerkes-Dodson Principle   b. Murphy's Law

   c. the Premack Principle   d. old wives' sayings

5. A behavior exhibited only by a certain species of lizard is _____ .

   a. reflexive   b. species-specific   c. idiosyncratic   d. unreliable

6. Which of these descriptions is not a criterion for an instinct? _____ .

   a. Biologically useful   b. Complex   c. Rigid pattern   d. Learned

7. Internal biological conditions are sufficient to trigger an instinct. _____ .

   a. True   b. False

8. Which organism's behavior is least likely to be hormonally controlled? _____ .

   a. Rat   b. Man   c. Monkey   d. Cow

9. Which type of psychologist might propose power as a prime motive for human behavior? _____ .

   a. Humanist   b. Behaviorist   c. Verbal learner   d. Cognitive

10. McClelland's data appears to link need for achievement to which variable? _____ .

   a. Sex of the individual   b. Age at time of demand

   c. Child-rearing practices   d. Genetics

11. Who developed a system of 20 human needs? _____ .

   a. McClelland   b. Skinner   c. Maslow   d. Murray

12. On Maslow's needs hierarchy _____ .

   a. the most powerful and basic needs are highest

   b. humans strive for fulfillment above all

   c. satisfaction of lower needs must occur before higher needs become motives

   d. only highly intellectual individuals ever can attain self-actualization

13. Which is true of current work on emotion? _____ .

   a. It is a field in its own right

   b. It is considered a subset of conscious awareness

   c. It is treated as motivation   d. It is no longer being done

14. Studies on decerebrate animals indicate conscious awareness is necessary for components of emotionality. _____ .

    a. True   b. False

MATCH: _____ 15. Watson   A. Love, fear, and rage as the basic infant emotions

              _____ 16. Horney   B. Moving toward, against, or away from people as basic processes

Respondent Behavior and Classical Conditioning

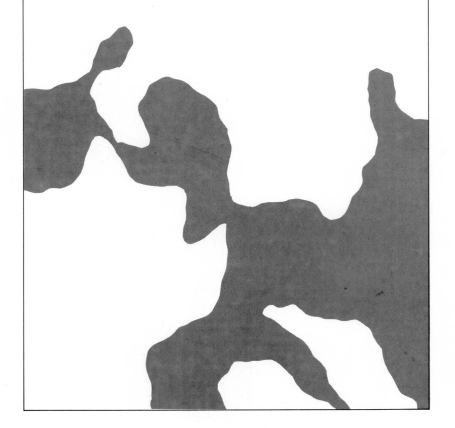

RESPONDENT BEHAVIOR
   Forms of Respondent Emotional Orientation

OPERANT BEHAVIOR
   Sources of Operant Behaviors

SIMPLE LEARNING
   The Importance of Learning

CLASSICAL CONDITIONING
   The Unconditioned Stimulus (UCS)
   The Conditioned Stimulus (CS)
   Measurement of Classically Conditioned
      Responses
   Magnitude of Response
   Percentage of Occurrence
   Latency
   Resistance to Extinction
   Functional Relationships in Classical
      Conditioning
   CR Strength: Increase in CS-UCS Pairings
   CR Strength: Intensity of UCS
   CR Strength: CS-UCS Interval
   Extinction of Classically Conditioned Responses
   Stimulus Generalization
   Generalization of Extinction
   Conditioned Discrimination
   Higher Order Conditioning

In the dawn of evolution, it is presumed by most scientists, life forms—even those that were relatively the most complex—were still rather simple in their biological structure. In the earliest stages organisms of only a few cells swam about and demonstrated fairly primitive behavior patterns. Starting with simple reflexes and orientations toward certain stimuli and away from others, evolution progressed through capacities for learning on the basis of experience, and finally to the higher and abstract forms of concept attainment we see today in the human being. In this chapter we shall examine how, through the processes of evolution, the more basic and extremely powerful behavior patterns came into being. And since it is convenient for psychologists to begin any behavioral analysis by differentiating between two of the basic forms of behavior—respondent and operant processes—we shall begin there.

RESPONDENT BEHAVIOR   As organisms evolved, most basic to their survival was that they demonstrate some sort of orientation to significant stimuli in their environment. Let us suppose that we are following the "adventures" of a phylogenetically simple organism as it swims through the water. We will assume that the organism's need for nutrition is served, in some rudimentary way, in the process of moving through the water and consuming any food elements it touches. This organism is made up of only a few cells, and is little more than a tiny blob in the water. We shall also assume that there are a few other simple organisms, some larger and predatory, which feed upon tiny blobs such as our friend. As he swims along one day, he suddenly experiences a sensation of pain, because a larger creature has moved up beside him and has taken a good-sized bite out of his left side. Our friend has a few sensory neurons which deliver sensations of pain to what few association neurons he has in the center of his body, and he begins to withdraw from the source of the stimulation. What we have just described is a reflex. A *reflex* is an involuntary behavior which is elicited in a fixed, predictable sequence by a given class of stimuli; in this case, stimuli which are painful elicit withdrawal. We might note that reflexes are also unlearned, are not complex, and tend to occur almost immediately upon stimulation.

C 8.1. *Characteristics of the reflex.*

State several of the characteristics of reflexes on the lines following.

_____

_____

_____

_____

How does such behavior develop, in the evolutionary sense? The answer to this is quite simple. It lies in Darwin's concept of the operation of natural selection. Some individuals are equipped in a more complex fashion than others along virtually every structural dimension; in this case we are primarily interested in the neurological complexity that is associated with an organism's responsiveness to stimulation. A creature with a fairly well-developed neurological system probably would be immediately sensitive to even minor indications of pain, and could quickly take evasive actions. A creature with a simpler neurological network, however, might not respond quickly, if at all, until the pain became massive and physical damage was considerable. In all likelihood, the first individual, with the more complex neurology, would have the greater chance of surviving an attack because of his capacity to react more quickly.

Darwin's principle of natural selection holds that over a long period of time and thousands of generations—and within a population of millions of individuals of a species—a dramatic movement of the biological structure took place in directions which aided individual survival in the natural state. In the case we were discussing, later generations would include an increasingly greater percentage of individuals with the more complex neurology, since the complex individuals have a greater chance of surviving until they reach sexual maturity, when they can reproduce. If a large percentage of the complex individuals survive long enough to reproduce, and a smaller percentage of the simpler creatures live long enough to do so, gradually the more complex individuals begin to outnumber the less complex ones, and the latter group finally becomes a disappearing rarity.

Simple reflexes other than mere responsiveness to pain develop according to the same evolutionary principle. Through evolution, organisms grow more responsive to certain classes of appetitive stimuli that serve as food, that culminate in the opportunity for mating, and so forth. The exact ways in which the sensory, neurological, and environmental events interact is not as clear with appetitive stimuli, but in general the principles seem about the same as is the case with responsiveness to aversive stimulation. We shall proceed now to a discussion of the nature of respondent processes.

Forms of Respondent Emotional Orientation

We shall begin with this introductory statement: By *respondent,* we refer primarily to the *emotional* types of response to stimulation. Certain aspects of skeletal (involving the large-muscle groups) behavior may be connected with respondent patterns. As the tiny creature we described makes a dash for safety, the gross musculature of its body is involved. As a dog sees food, it leans forward and attempts to reach it—a skeletal act. If we deliver a small electrical shock to an animal, it tends to lunge and jump, which are skeletal actions. It may seem strange, then, that we assert that respondent behavior is only secondarily skeletal, and primarily involves the activities of the autonomic nervous system (ANS). What we are saying, however, is that when the animal is shocked, we know that we have aroused the sympathetic functions of the ANS which are correlated with the human experience we call "fear." When the dog sees food placed before him, we can measure ANS patterns that correlate with the human experience we call "pleasure." The animal *may* or it *may not* display a corresponding skeletal action. Thus ANS, or "emotional," reactions are being specified whenever we use the term *respondent.* We shall describe three major patterns of respondent behavior, each related to the type of stimulus that elicits it.

First, *appetitive* stimuli elicit the emotional *approach orientation.* You might wish to think of this as pleasure, but we sometimes question the actual quality of the associated mental experiences when we see the respondent patterns in extremely simple creatures that have no "brain" as we usually use the term. Second, stimuli that are *aversive* tend to elicit the emotional *escape orientation.* You might wish to think of this as fear, subject to the qualification just mentioned. Finally, when the organism experiences *aversive* stimuli which are *inescapable* (which means that the organism has tried to escape and has not been successful in repeated attempts), there develops the emotional *attack orientation.* You might wish to think of this as irritation or rage.

It is important to recognize that the individual may not actually *do* anything about the way it feels toward a stimulus object. You have seen a child go to a doctor to receive a hypodermic injection and determinedly stand without flinching while the needle was jabbed into his arm. The aversive stimulus doubtless elicits an emotional escape orientation, meaning the child would like to run away from the situation, but under such circumstances the emotional orientations *may not* be accompanied by the associated skeletal act.

At this point we shall begin to use diagrams to denote exactly what we are discussing. Simple respondent behavior follows the model:

$$S \longrightarrow R$$

Often the S and R designations are followed by a subscripted term to identify more specifically a type of stimulus or response. Thus, we might see terms such as

$$S_{\text{pain}} \longrightarrow R_{\text{escape}}$$

These designations will assume a great deal of importance later in the chapter, so you should become familiar with them now.

C 8.2. *The nature of the respondent.*

Respondent behavior is primarily _____ type of response to stimulation.

    a. an emotional   b. a skeletal

C 8.3. *Categories of respondent behavior.*

The emotional approach orientation is elicited by _____ stimuli.

The emotional escape orientation is elicited by _____ stimuli.

Inescapable aversive stimuli elicit the emotional _____ orientation.

We have defined *in*escapable aversive stimuli as those from which the organism is unable to escape, despite repeated attempts. We have two simple experiments to illustrate why we say this. First, in a laboratory where paired rats were subjected to short pulses of electric shock through a floor grid every 10 seconds, the animals were seen to display escape attempts consistently during the first 30 to 50 stimulus presentations. Then the animals largely abandoned jumping up against the chamber walls and began to fight vigorously at each shock presentation (Vernon, 1969). We can observe a *hierarchy* of the reflex to aversive stimulation: first an escape orientation occurs to stimuli that *may* be escapable, and an attack orientation subsequently develops after escape attempts are not successful.

In another experiment (Vernon, 1959), five human subjects were blindfolded and in each case one arm was extended to the side into a roofed box where peg-restraints were put into position just before the experiment began. Each subject, expecting to be shocked with electricity, experienced

Figure 8.1

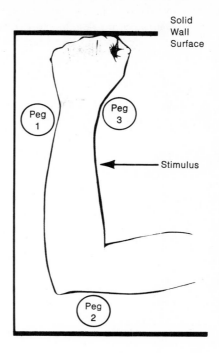

a minor pain sensation when his arm was jabbed with a stiff horsehair. The expectation of shock facilitated the vigor of the reaction tremendously. Sensitive pressure equipment attached to the pegs monitored the sequence and timing of responding. First the subjects drew directly away from the source of stimulation, but that escape route was blocked by a peg (Peg 1 in Figure 8.1). Then they pushed at a right angle to the stimulation (oblique escape), but that direction also was blocked (Peg 2). Finally they exerted pressure in the direction of Peg 3 and the source of the stimulation—a reflexive basic form of attack against the source of aversive stimulation. This three-step sequence of direct escape, indirect escape, and attack was invariable in each of five subjects, and the *slowest* of the five took only 1.1 seconds to enact the total sequence. We conclude that there is a basic reflex hierarchy to aversive stimulation that is built into the physiological structure of organisms.

C 8.4. *Hierarchies of reflexes.*

A notion that reflexes can exist in hierarchies is implied by a finding that _____ .

   a. an organism will tend to display one reflex to a stimulus, then switch to another after a period
        of time

   b. an organism can display two reflexes simultaneously to a stimulus

   c. a reflex may cease to occur after a given period of its elicitation

OPERANT BEHAVIOR   Let us now return to our friend, the simple creature that swims in the water. He can respond to a variety of stimuli in nature with rigid reflexive responses (respondents), and it is also likely that he can emit certain "voluntary" skeletal responses (operants). It is not at all clear which ability is the most primitive. An operant is simply a visible—hence, skeletal—behavior. While the respondent takes place on the inside of the organism, sometimes accompanied by simple skeletal correlated movements, the operant is essentially a visible and primarily skeletal behavior. It is quite important that you grasp the difference between these two patterns.

A. A respondent is *elicited* by a stimulus, while an operant is *emitted* by the organism. The former term means "brought out by," and has the connotation of an invariable reflex. The latter term means "send out" and has a connotation of being voluntary and subject to the individual's own decision.

B. The respondent primarily concerns how an organism *feels*, while an operant primarily concerns what an organism *does*.

C. The respondent is mediated by the *autonomic* nervous system, while the operant is mediated by the *central* nervous system.

D. The respondent is a *reaction* (to a stimulus), while the operant is an *action*.

The simple creature that swims in the water has a limited number of operant capabilities. The organism may approach or retreat from certain stimuli and it may be active or inactive. In the more complex life forms, a large variety of operants are possible in any given situation.

C 8.5.   *The distinction between respondent and operant behavior.*

Behavior elicited by a stimulus is called a _____ .

Organisms emit _____ behavior.

Emotional patterns are the primary factor in which category? _____ .

    a. operant behavior   b. respondent behavior

Respondent patterns are primarily mediated by the _____ nervous system.

Which three of the following are categorized as respondents? _____ .

    a. mowing your lawn   b. reading a newspaper

    c. experiencing pleasure at the appearance of an old friend

    d. becoming angry when frustrated   e. becoming sexually aroused

    f. running a 100-yard dash

Sources of Operant Behaviors   There are two main "sources" of operant behaviors. First, there is activity that occurs randomly. Leave an animal in a cage and it will move about and do various things with no particular plan or purpose. We believe the animal is simply providing itself with increased stimulus input. Human beings do the same sorts of aimless things when the sameness of their environments begins to grow tedious. They drum their fingers on a table, they bounce their crossed leg, or they finger something. Sometimes they pace about, hum, and the like. These are *random activities,* and they comprise an important, though not the predominant, component of human operant structure.

Second, there is behavior that has its origin in *social imitation.* Even organisms quite low on the phylogenetic scale influence the behavior of their young by providing a social model for the offspring to imitate. In this way lions are taught to stalk and hunt, monkeys learn which foods to consume, etc. The higher the individual is on the phylogenetic scale, the stronger is his tendency to imitate the behaviors of others of the species. We shall consider, a little later, variables relating to the tendency to imitate. For now, however, let us point out that the higher mammal forms, especially, watch and listen carefully, and tend particularly to imitate those adults with which they have continuous or recurrent contact.

The most significant factor that relates to a wide versus a narrow variety of random activity in the behavioral repertoire, and to the accuracy of social imitation, is the complexity of the individual's central nervous system. Higher life-forms are able to process sensory information in ways that facilitate more accurate imitation and contribute to flexibility in behavior patterns. The human being has such a capacity to imitate complex behaviors that he is able to learn to speak a language through being exposed to models who speak it. Then, through the operation of language, man gains the tools which primarily differentiate his fantastic levels of achievement potential from those of monkeys, which are actually not so inferior to man in neurological structure as the behavioral differences alone would suggest.

The tool of abstract language allows man to imitate symbolically. In this way I can tell you how to do a multiplication problem, and you can then do it yourself. I can tell you how to get to my house, and you can then do so. You are imitating the abstract content of a verbal behavior rather than a skeletal behavior. By being a student and reading textbooks, you are then able to do a very large number of things through the process of symbolic imitation.

C 8.6.   *Sources of operant behavior.*

What are the two main sources of operant behavior?

1. _____

2. _____

C 8.7.   *The potential for imitative behavior.*

The tendency to imitate grows _____ as we go up the phylogenetic scale.

Youngsters of a species would ordinarily show the strongest tendency to imitate the behaviors of _____ .

    a. their parents   b. strange adults   c. strange children

The ability to imitate complex behavior performed by a model is largely a function of the degree of phylogenetic (and ontogenetic) development of a species' _____

_____ _____ .

The tendency and the capacity to imitate complex behavior is greatly multiplied, for the human being, by the _____ .

a. age of the model   b. sex of the model

c. symbolic processes involved in language

Simple emitted operants are not our primary focus, any more than are simple elicited respondents. Of far more importance, and the subject for the next section, are the learned behavioral forms. But before we go on to that section, it is vital that you clearly have in mind what is meant by respondents and operants. Can you see why contraction of the pupil of the eye in response to increased illumination is respondent? Similarly, an elevation of the heart rate following a sudden, startling noise? Can you see why a child's play activity is operant, as is a person's cutting his lawn or going to a baseball game? If there is any confusion on your part, you would do well to restudy points A through D presented on page 282.

SIMPLE LEARNING

We have examined the ways in which simple behavioral capacities develop, through evolution, at the respondent and operant levels. We have described behaviors that are elicited in an unlearned manner by stimulus patterns, as well as behaviors which are casually emitted by organisms. It is time now for us to consider the ways in which such behaviors become characteristic of individuals, through learning.

The Importance of Learning

Psychologists are beginning to place increasing emphasis on learning as central to the understanding of the behaviors of organisms. Of course, behavior is controlled to a considerable extent by one's inherited biochemical and physiological structure, and it is affected to a great degree by certain stimulus conditions to which we show reflexive response patterns. But increasingly we see that behavior, in general, is strongly influenced by patterns of learned reactions. Social behavior styles, many behavior disorders, and academic motivational patterns all are learned. With a proper appreciation of the role of learning in the life-styles of people, we can then see how we could plan behavioral change in more desirable patterns through the application of the principles of learning.

Conditioning is defined as the simplest form of learning. It is sometimes referred to as association learning, because the individual associates various stimulus and/or response events with others. We shall discuss two main forms of conditioning—classical conditioning, in which respondent patterns are learned, and, in Chapter 9, operant conditioning, in which operant patterns are learned.

C 8.8. *The definition of conditioning.*

Conditioning could be defined as the _____

_____ .

PROGRESS CHECK   8.1

1. Which is true of reflexes? _____ .

    a. They are complex patterns of behavior

    b. Reflexes are learned

    c. Certain stimuli elicit involuntary reflexes

    d. Reflexes can occur at various intervals after stimulation

2. Respondent behavior primarily involves _____ .

    a. activities of the ANS   b. skeletal muscles

    c. CNS activity   d. neuromuscular transmission

3. The first response of animals to aversive stimulation is likely to be an _____ orientation.

    a. approach   b. escape   c. attack

4. It was demonstrated by Vernon that aversive stimulation when lengthy can lead to a three-step sequence of behaviors. Those behaviors, given out of order, are (A) attack, (B) direct escape, and (C) indirect escape. The proper sequence, using the above letter-references, is _____ .

    a. CAB   b. CBA   c. ACB   d. BCA   e. BAC

5. Which statement about operant behavior is true? _____ .

    a. Operants are emitted, not elicited   b. Operants are what the organism does

    c. Operants are actions   d. All of these

6. Which two are the main sources of operant behavior? _____ .

    a. Bar-pressing   b. Social imitation

    c. Random activities   d. Hunting and gathering

CLASSICAL CONDITIONING   In *classical conditioning*, a learned association is formed between two stimuli. As you will recall, respondent behavior is essentially the internal, emotional reaction to a stimulus, and it should be no surprise that we can acquire certain response patterns due to our own particular history of experiences. To put it simply, if a stimulus that initially elicits *no* emotion is experienced in association with either pleasurable or unpleasant events, then the stimulus begins to take on that associated meaning.

Let us return to the small friend that we left behind a few pages ago. That creature who swims in the water was last described as going through a gradual process of evolution, from being a neurologically simple individual, with a few scattered pain receptors, to an individual more complex both in terms of responses to stimuli and in the ability to initiate rapid actions. The evolutionary process which increases the level of a species' neurological complexity also increases its ability to perform certain other diverse processes. In the center of the body, where the incoming neurons concentrate, the cells may form a rudimentary association center. That is, they might be referred to as simple memory cells. If this potential for "memory" develops, then certain forms of stimulus input can result in permanent changes in behavior. So, at this early point in the evolutionary process an organism goes into a new phase.

Our friend who is swimming along in the water was attacked on an earlier occasion by a predator. Let us imagine that an instant before the initiation of pain, the attacker swims over our friend. We will assume that the little "blob" is sensitive to the presence or absence of the sun's rays through the water, and the passing over of a shadow was a perceived stimulus. Then pain began. Let us assume that on two or three other occasions a similar thing occurred. First a shadow came, as something passed between the creature and the sun, followed immediately by a pain stimulus. Very soon, in the simple neurology of the creature, an association is made between the two stimuli.

$$S_{\text{pain}} \longrightarrow R_{\text{emotion}}$$
$$S_{\text{shadow}}$$

Thereafter the shadow, which was originally neutral insofar as the initiation of flight was concerned, takes on the same eliciting characteristics as did the pain itself. We call this process *classical conditioning*, and you can see how it is the association of two stimuli. The vital necessities for classical conditioning are (1) a biologically relevant stimulus (in the above case, pain) which elicits some predictable, measurable response, (2) another stimulus

Dik Browne, © King Features Syndicate 1966

which is initially neutral insofar as the response in question is concerned, and (3) the close pairing, in time, of the stimuli.

The term *classical,* applied to this form of conditioning, takes its name from the famous research of Ivan Pavlov, who worked with laboratory dogs during the first decade of this century. "Classical" is used in the sense that this form of research was the first published work on conditioning, and it was the pacesetter in terms of establishing the terminology. In Pavlov's research dogs experienced the paired presentations of a bell and food. The dogs initially salivated at the sight of the food, and soon they began to salivate whenever the bell sounded. The association had been formed between the bell and the food.

Let us look at another example of classical conditioning to show you that it has a direct application to everyday life. Had you been so unfortunate as to fall into a pond when you were very young, it is likely that the stress, excitement, and physical discomfort that accompanied such an experience might have been associated with large bodies of water to the extent that you might today have a phobia concerning ponds, lakes, rivers, and swimming pools. In the same manner, some people develop fears of dogs after they have experienced painful attacks. At a more everyday level, it is easy to understand that we all develop mild aversions to things with which we have had unpleasant dealings. For example, consider our reactions to a complainer. It is tempting to describe how we try to escape from the company of such a person because we want to get away from his complaints, but suppose he does not complain at all on a certain occasion. Typically we will still dissociate ourselves from him as soon as possible; we certainly do not invite him to go along with us. The obvious truth is that we are not dealing with any rational decision to get away from something, but that we simply have developed constantly operating emotional reactions to that person.

Sometimes we are not aware of the reasons for our classically conditioned feelings. For example, we frequently may have feelings of discomfort on first meeting a stranger—even a pleasant and attractive person. We do not understand that this individual has physical or behavioral characteristics which may remind us of certain significant people from our past who were linked with unpleasant experiences. Similarly, we referred a moment ago to a young child falling into a pond and developing a conditioned fear of bodies of water. This was an actual case seen in a clinic, and the young man in therapy had no idea, at the outset, what the source of his fear might be. Only later, when his mother was seen in a session, did it become known that he had fallen into a small fishpond in a friend's backyard when only eighteen months old. Despite the considerable unpleasantness of the event, and the momentary terror of the child, the mother had not taken the event too seriously since the child was actually in no risk of drowning. It had never occurred to her that such a minor incident might be at the base of her son's phobia concerning bodies of water. Even after this event had been described by the mother, the son was insistent that he recalled nothing of the incident in question. Obviously, conscious memory for the incident was not necessary for the active and strong persistence of the conditioned emotional reaction.

Classical conditioning does not necessarily involve unpleasant stimuli. Many stimulus pairings can lead to the development of pleasant attitudes. At this point you should remind yourself of the large number of appetitive primary drives in human beings, the satisfaction of which can lead to pleasure. Therefore, the linking of a certain person, place, or activity with the reductions of any of the primary drives—hunger, the need for stimulus variety, and so forth—can lead to the conditioning of pleasant emotional reactions to new stimuli. Some psychologists think that an infant's love for its mother is even developed in this way, since a variety of primary drives, the most important being hunger and the need for contact comfort, are associated with the presence and attention of the mother.

Less intense, perhaps, is the conditioning of various pleasant attitudes toward activities which provide stimulus variety. Often, places have been linked with pleasant experiences, so that we enjoy returning and remembering. Of course, even with pleasant experiences, the possibility exists for *un*desirable emotional developments. Certain sexual perversions are believed to relate to the linkage, in preadolescent years, of sexual excitation with stimuli which youngsters at that age associate with sex (women's underwear, furtive glimpses of others undressing, etc.). In fact, just as we described three reflexive (or unconditioned) emotional orientations to three varied forms of stimuli, so we can observe that all three orientations can be conditioned if we have an initially neutral stimulus and the appropriate biologically relevant stimulus. In fact, we shall go so far as to make the following categorical statement. Where it can be demonstrated that a certain biologically relevant stimulus elicits a powerful emotion in an individual, the pairing of that stimulus with virtually any stimulus that does not have such an effect at the outset will eventuate in the development of a clear-cut conditioned response. Thus, individuals may come to "enjoy" mild pain stimuli, or to have aversions or aggressive feelings toward those stimuli which are tolerated or even appreciated by most other individuals. We shall have many opportunities to demonstrate these various combinations in our further discussions.

In order to properly study classical conditioning and to determine the laws governing its development, psychologists have tended to concentrate on restricted fields in which both stimulus and response factors can be easily quantified. Pavlov's original research went on for decades with just a group of dogs learning to respond to neutral stimuli associated with various biologically relevant stimuli. This may sound quite simplistic, but in this manner Pavlov collected volumes of data and was able to make valuable and exact statements about functional relationships within the conditioning process.

In the United States a number of psychologists have preferred a research model which, instead of dealing with food, delivers a puff of air to the surface of the eye. The air puff causes an eye-blink response. In place of the bell, these psychologists use an electronically generated tone. By repeatedly pairing the air puff and the tone, the tone eventually comes to elicit the same response—the eye blink—as did the puff of air. More recently some

American psychologists have paired the presentation of a tone with the delivery of electric shock. Using animals such as monkeys in this research, the increase in the rate of the heartbeat is the resulting conditioned behavior.

As you can well imagine, it is difficult in some of the broadly defined social areas, with situational stimuli (this term was defined in Chapter 5) involved, to *quantify* the presentation of stimuli and the resulting responses. By using common laboratory situations, however, psychologists can easily vary exact amounts of air puff intensity or the number and intensity of electric shocks, and they can literally measure the elevations of heart rates and occurrences of eye blinks.

C 8.9. *The concept of classical conditioning.*

Classical conditioning concerns the learning of _____ behavior patterns.

    a. operant   b. respondent   c. cognitive   d. always visible

In classical conditioning there is an association between _____ .

    a. a stimulus and a response   b. two stimuli   c. two responses

Be able to name the man who developed the procedure of classical conditioning: _____ .

When we experience classically conditioned emotions, we _____ aware of the reasons (the conditioning sequence) behind our feelings.

    a. are   b. are not   c. may not be

Which of the following emotional orientations can be conditioned through the classical conditioning procedure? _____ .

    a. approach   b. avoidance   c. aggressive   d. (all of these)

Psychologists prefer to concentrate conditioning research on narrow laboratory topics rather than broad social situations, primarily so that they can more easily _____ .

    a. control expenses   b. get their findings published   c. quantify the variables

Sneezing, salivating, experiencing fear of some stimulus object, and generating a respiratory reaction (asthma) are all examples of reflexive behaviors. Of these four, how many would you guess would be demonstrated as being conditionable in response to previously neutral stimuli in a laboratory?

_____ .

So that you can read and understand published literature in the field of classical conditioning, we shall turn now to some standard terminology in use by professionals.

The Unconditioned   The biologically relevant stimulus that naturally elicits a predictable re-
Stimulus (UCS)   sponse is called the *unconditioned stimulus (UCS)*. By using the word "naturally," we imply that the air puff to the eye or the presentation of an

electric shock works in a reflexive way on the basic biological structure. It makes no difference whether or not an organism attempts to inhibit a response to the *UCS*—the response occurs anyway, since the respondent is *in*voluntary.

The response to the *UCS* is the *unconditioned response (UCR)*. Again, you will recall that respondent behaviors involve the autonomic nervous system, and they are the behaviors that generally underlie the various forms of emotion. Thus the dogs' salivation, the monkeys' elevated heart rates, and human beings' twitches of the eyelid are the measurable variables suggesting underlying pleasure, fear, or aversion.

C 8.10.   *The unconditioned stimulus.*

The biologically relevant stimulus in classical conditioning is called the _____ (use the abbreviation).

In reference to your last answer, the response to this stimulus is called the _____ .

    a. *UCS*   b. *UCR*   c. *CS*   d. *CR*

An unconditioned response _____ be voluntarily controlled by the individual.

    a. can   b. cannot

The Conditioned Stimulus (CS)   As we have said, in classical conditioning we have an association between two stimuli. The second stimulus in the classical conditioning situation is the *conditioned stimulus (CS)*. The conditioned stimulus is defined as a stimulus that is *initially neutral* in that it does not elicit the target behavior being studied. When, however, the stimuli have been paired an adequate number of times, we then see the development of the *conditioned response (CR)*. The conditioned response is qualitatively the same as the unconditioned response, although it is quantitatively weaker. That is, in the monkey experiment, we might observe that the shock stimulus produces an elevation of 60 heartbeats per minute over the resting rate. But while the bell which has been paired with shock produces a heart rate increase (qualitative similarity), that increase likely will be no more than 30 or 35 beats per minute elevation over the resting rate, even when fully developed. Thus it is quantitatively weaker.

C 8.11.   *The conditioned stimulus/conditioned response association.*

In classical conditioning, a stimulus that is initially neutral is termed the _____ (use the abbreviation).

In reference to your last answer, the response to this stimulus is called the _____ .

    a. *UCS*   b. *UCR*   c. *CS*   d. *CR*

Compared to a *UCR*, a *CR* is usually _____ .

    a. approximately the same strength   b. weaker   c. stronger

We shall now take a moment to demonstrate the diagram for classical conditioning, using the new terminology that has just been presented. Rather than use both the terms *UCR* and *CR,* we shall present the single term *R,* since the two responses are qualitatively the same.

We can describe Pavlov's original research as follows:

$$UCS_{food} \longrightarrow R_{\text{"pleasure,"}\atop(salivation)}$$
$$CS_{bell}$$

We also could describe some of the current research on the development of emotion:

$$UCS_{shock} \longrightarrow R_{\text{"fear"}}$$
$$CS_{visual\ stimulus}$$

It is worth noting in passing that, as before, the solid arrow denotes an unlearned and predictable *S-R* pattern. The dotted line denotes an *S-R* sequence that *can develop,* provided the organism experiences the association of the *CS* and *UCS.*

"Do you mind if I go to lunch early, Professor Pavlov?
For some reason I'm hungry."

C 8.12. *Diagrammatic representation of classical conditioning.*

In the following diagrams, insert the missing abbreviations.

UCS _mathematics_ R _anxiety, aversion_

——————— *ridicule, failure*

——————— *good food* R _pleasure_

CS _restaurant_

What might be a not-uncommon *CS* appropriate to the emply blank below?

UCS _pain_ R _fear, aversion_

CS ——————— *(?)*

Measurement of Classically Conditioned Responses	The degree, or strength, of a classically conditioned response may be measured in several ways.

Magnitude of Response

Most typical is a measure of the *magnitude of the response*. For example, a heart-rate increase in response to an aversive stimulus might be very pronounced or it could be only a small departure from the normal resting heart rate.

Percentage of Occurrence

If the *CR* is the sort where a scientist is interested in the simple fact of whether a response occurs, it is typical to see a measurement of the *percentage of occurrence;* that is, percentage of conditioned responses occurring within a block of trials—for example, a block of the *CS* presentations. As you can see, the type of response one is dealing with affects the decision of what kind of measure to use.

Latency

Rarely, we hear of another measure—that of the *latency* of the response. Latency simply means the amount of time that elapses between the presentation of the *CS* and the beginning of the *CR*. Presumably, as conditioning progresses, this unit of time decreases.

Resistance to Extinction

A fourth measure which is sometimes employed is *resistance to extinction*. You will understand this measure after we have had an opportunity to discuss the extinction process.

Classical conditioning, except in a few unusual circumstances, is a gradual phenomenon. The typical conditioning curve begins at a zero level, and slowly and gradually increases to some maximum level which we call the *asymptote* of the curve. In the typical laboratory experiment we see a rise of the conditioning curve resulting from pairings of stimuli until it reaches a maximum after about 40 stimulus pairings. This is not a hard-and-fast rule. Cases have varied from single-trial conditioning to others in which the strength of the conditioned response continued to increase through 1,000 stimulus pairings. Such cases, however, are unusual.

C 8.13. *Measurement of classical conditioning.*

State the four ways we might measure the strength of classical conditioning.

_____

_____

_____

_____

Define response latency.

_____

_____

The classical conditioning curve usually becomes asymptotic (reaches its maximum) after about how many pairings of the *CS* and *UCS*? _____ .

a. one   b. 20   c. 40   d. 1,000

Functional Relationships in Classical Conditioning   A few simple functional relationships account for most of the variance in classical conditioning, as we shall illustrate in this section.

CR Strength: Increase in CS-UCS Pairings

As we have already stated, the strength of the *CR* increases as the number of pairings of the *CS* and *UCS* increases. This is an asymptotic function, which is illustrated in Figure 8.2.

Figure 8.2

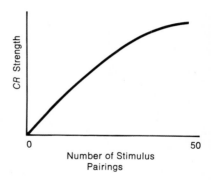

In a social context we can see how repeated pairings of stimuli allow the *CS* to elicit an increasingly stronger *CR*. If children torment a tied-up dog with sticks day after day, the dog grows more hostile toward the children day by day. In this case strength of *CR* (emotional attack orientation) increases as a function of the number of times the *CS* (children) have been paired with the *UCS* (physical torment).

CR Strength: Intensity of UCS

Response strength also increases as function of *UCS* strength. Spence, at the University of Iowa, devoted a large portion of his career to the investigation of *CS* and *UCS* intensity effects upon the magnitude of the resulting *CR*. On one hand he found that *CS* strength does not appear to have a very clear-cut relationship to *CR* magnitude. On the other hand, the stronger the *UCS* in conditioning, the greater is the magnitude of the *CR*, as illustrated in Figure 8.3.

In the same manner as in the children and dog example, the stronger the *UCS* intensity, the stronger the emotional reaction to the *CS* becomes. If the children tormented the dog harshly and brutally, this should produce even more savagery in response to the children's appearance. If a child is hurt by another child, the strength of the *CR* (emotional escape orientation) increases as a direct function of the intensity of the *UCS* (degree of physical hurt). In this case the other child is the *CS*. If Billy hurts John very badly in a fight, thereafter John tends to experience strong fear when Billy comes into the vicinity. As you will note, functional relationships are not hard to understand when you interpret actual cases.

CR Strength: CS-UCS Interval

A third functional relationship is that the strength of the *CR* increases as a function of the time-relationships of the *CS* and the *UCS*. This is a little more difficult to understand than the other two functions. When the *CS* precedes the *UCS* (called forward conditioning), conditioning is generally much more efficient than when the *UCS* comes first (backward conditioning). This phenomenon is probably due to the *UCS* being biologically relevant, with the result that it commands the attention of the organism when it occurs first and the *CS* then goes largely unnoticed. However, when

Figure 8.3

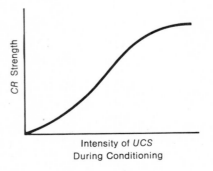

Intensity of *UCS*
During Conditioning

the CS comes first, providing a stimulus change, the undistracted organism notices it; then the UCS occurs, commanding attention, and the organism thereby has efficiently processed the perception of both stimuli, and the two events become "associated." Figure 8.4 shows the general pattern of the two relationships.

As Figure 8.4 shows, backward conditioning—measured in terms of time values to the *left* of the zero point—fails to be particularly effective. In the case of forward conditioning, the particular point of CS onset at which the paired association is at greatest efficiency is approximately one-half second before the UCS begins. This fact has been demonstrated in dozens of experiments and with all kinds of species, including humans. If the delay between the CS and UCS onsets is much greater than three or four seconds, conditioning tends to be poor. The explanation for this *conditioning gradient*, as the slope of the line in Figure 8.4 is called, is probably to be found in the basic neurology of organisms.

Later you will see how knowledge of this particular function may help you understand attitude development and other forms of emotional conditioning, but at this point we are simply stressing the importance of a variable that has a strong effect on the dependent variable under consideration.

We have now covered the main functional relationships in classical conditioning. We might mention others, briefly. You will recall that in Chapter 7 we stated that, generally speaking, aversive motives are stronger than appetitive ones. Proceeding then to our statement that UCS intensity contributes to CR strength, we conclude that in general the emotional states conditioned in the presence of aversive UCSs—the emotional escape and attack orientations—are considerably more intense than those conditioned in the presence of appetitive UCSs—the emotional approach orientations. Finally (and understanding of this point will await the next section), CR strength depends not only upon the conditioning history, but on the extinction history as well.

Figure 8.4

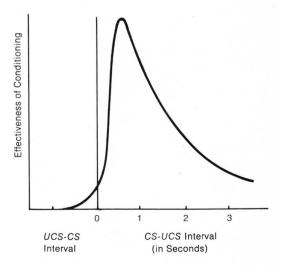

TREATMENT SESSIONS

Sam Donovan heard the guards coming down the hallway. Their harsh steps echoed off the bare concrete walls of the long prison tunnel. The door opened and Guard Celli stepped in first, as he always did, with the others staying behind, ready if needed.

Sam Donovan had never entertained any hopes of escaping the attitude-change sessions. As long as he was in the prison he knew that failure to cooperate would be countered by increasingly sharp cutbacks of his food and water ration. And there was little point in trying to escape since there was completely effective electronic surveillance. The "dog collar" he wore around his neck would emit a constant radio signal, easily traced. And the collar was set to explode, destroying him in the process, if any attempt was made to cut or file it.

Sam Donovan dutifully got up and followed Guard Celli, with the others coming behind. Just a few yards down the prison tunnel they stepped into the Attitude Change Chamber, where the session began.

It was as before. Sam Donovan's crime had been that of resisting authority. So Guard Celli read from carefully prepared card-questions designed to bring vivid images to Sam Donovan's mind and re-create former experiences. The same series of cards that were used in previous sessions were again read, beginning with the one about Sam Donovan's father, accurate to the smallest detail, and bringing to mind many typical adolescent conflicts. When the story on the cards arrived at the point where Sam Donovan had resisted his father's authority, a sharp electric shock was administered to the back of Sam Donovan's neck.

More stories on cards were read, involving schoolteachers, the officers who directed the adolescent military preparedness center, and the police themselves—story after story, situation after situation. As these detailed accounts and questions brought clearly to his mind the past cases where Sam had resisted or expressed any negative feeling, the

C 8.14. *Functional relationships determining the strength of classical conditioning.*

Suppose you were once nipped by a dog, but your friend was rather seriously injured by a dog's vicious attack. Your friend is extremely afraid of dogs, while you are not nearly so uneasy. The reason lies in the intensity of the _____ (state abbreviation) during conditioning.

Backward conditioning is the situation in which the _____ .

    a. *CS* precedes the *UCS*   b. *UCS* precedes the *CS*

Generally speaking, backward conditioning is _____ than forward conditioning.

    a. more effective than   b. less effective than

According to the conditioning gradient, which of the following is most effective in classical conditioning? _____ .

    a. forward conditioning   b. simultaneous conditioning   c. backward conditioning electric shock was delivered.

Sweat poured down Sam Donovan's face. While the electric shocks were not disabling, they were extremely unpleasant. Since the intensity of each was unpredictable, the dread of the unknown was terrifying.

But it was working! As each story began, Sam tried harder and harder to think about pleasant replies, imagining his role to have been co-operative and totally passive. For when the image of resistance came to mind, the tension and incredible dread sharply intensified. This reaction was the whole purpose of the training, which was not to be resisted. Sam Donovan knew that by the end of his training sessions he would no longer be capable of thinking hostile thoughts toward authority figures. Even the slightest envisioning of himself "talking back" would create a level of anxiety that would be agonizing.

The year was 1997, society was increasingly complex and tech-nological, and deviance was not to be tolerated. Sam Donovan later lay on his bunk, soaking wet with his own perspiration. Perhaps it was all for the good. Some decades before, he recalled, if an individual resisted a public official or policeman, he might be incarcerated for as much as five or ten years. This way Sam Donovan knew that the treat-ment session would last for only 21 days.

Fourteen more days to go before he would return to his job and family.

Attitude change through the principles of classical conditioning is a proven fact. At this time most such efforts are directed at decreasing anxieties, but a field called "aversive conditioning" has developed, intended to create tension and dread and thereby suppress such behaviors as contribute to the patterns called alcoholism and homosexuality. Could "1997" actually be as portrayed in this story?

For optimum conditioning, the _____ should precede the other stimulus.

    a. *CS*   b. *UCS*

Referring to your above answer, this stimulus should precede the other by as close to _____ as possible.

    a. simultaneity   b. ½ second   c. 2 seconds   d. ½ minute

It would appear that which of the following conditioned responses might be established in the fewest conditioning trials? _____ .

    a. Salivation (in a dog) to a light stimulus paired with food

    b. Heart rate elevation in response to a light stimulus paired with shock

    c. Conditioned enjoyment of some initially neutral type of music experienced while drinking pleasant-tasting soft drinks

Figure 8.5

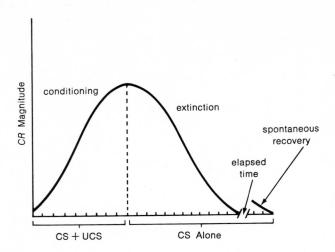

Extinction of Classically Conditioned Responses

Extinction of Classically Conditioned Responses

Extinction, in the case of classically conditioned responses, refers to a situation in which the *CS* is presented without an accompanying *UCS*. In these cases, after repeated *CS* presentations, the magnitude of the conditioned response begins to fall off. Eventually, through 30 or 40 trials in most cases, we see a total elimination of the conditioned response (see Figure 8.5). An important note is that the *CS* must be presented in order for extinction to occur. The simple passing of time, without an experience of the *CS* presentation, has been shown to have practically no inhibiting effect upon a previously developed *CR*.

C 8.15. *Extinction of classically conditioned responses.*

The two requirements for extinction of a classically conditioned response are that the _____ must be presented, with the _____ absent.

If we classically condition an emotional response, then isolate the organism from the stimulus conditions (both *UCS* and *CS*) for a period of a year or two, we should expect in response to the *CS* _____ .

a. less *CR* magnitude at the end of that time

b. more *CR* magnitude at the end of that time

c. about the same *CR* magnitude at the end of that time

Suppose we have brought about the total extinction of a respondent behavior. There is a further interesting phenomenon, noted by Pavlov, that we call *spontaneous recovery*. Pavlov found that after he had completely extinguished the salivary response in dogs, if he then removed the animals from the experimental situation for perhaps a half-hour, a percentage of the

CR later recurred when the bell was presented again (Figure 8.5).

The *CR* magnitude under this condition was not large, but the importance of the phenomenon lies in the fact that it appeared, at first, to introduce exceptions into what was otherwise a lawful phenomenon. Further investigation showed that the spontaneous recovery phenomenon was itself consistent, and therefore lawful. Since Pavlov's research there has not been a great deal of interest in spontaneous recovery, but its existence is an important bit of knowledge. Sometimes people extinguish a response and become concerned because it appears again the next day. Pavlov found that the magnitude of the recovered behavior was much smaller than the original conditioned level and, furthermore, if the recovered behavior was again extinguished, then little or no subsequent recovery would occur in the absence of further conditioning trials.

The phenomenon of spontaneous recovery may be envisioned more easily by relating it to the notion of forgetting. This analogy would require that you regard the conditioning experience as learning to respond. The extinction trials would represent another form of learning—learning *not* to respond. Then we could say that the subject sometimes "forgets" what he has very recently "learned" during extinction. That is, he forgot that he was not supposed to respond to a certain stimulus, and responded as if the older conditions—those which held during conditioning trials—still were in effect. Do not be misled. The analogue just given you possibly is not an accurate representation of what actually goes on in classical conditioning. We simply are not sure, but it still may allow you to view spontaneous recovery as a familiar phenomenon rather than as a technological event.

C 8.16. *The concept of spontaneous recovery.*

Spontaneous recovery refers to the recurrence, after elapsed time following _____ of a *CR*.

PROGRESS CHECK   8.2

1. The simplest form of learning is _____ .

    a. eating   b. reflex responding   c. conditioning   d. thinking

2. Pavlov's dogs learned to salivate to the sound of a bell.

    This is an example of _____ .

    a. operant conditioning   b. physiological drooling

    c. classical conditioning   d. an innate reflex of dogs

3. Some psychologists think an infant's love for its mother is classically conditioned, because _____ .

    a. Pavlov arranged a training paradigm for his dogs, which resembled the mother-child interaction

    b. babies drool when they see their mothers

    c. babies associate their mothers with the satisfaction of primary drives

    d. there is no other reasonable explanation for the attachment

4. Which of these might function as a *UCS* for eye-blinking? _____ .

    a. Pinprick to the foot   b. Soft music   c. Smell of popcorn   d. Puff of air

5. The tone E-flat is paired with shock to a monkey's arm. The monkey's heart rate thereafter increases at the sound of E-flat. Which is true? _____ .

    a. Shock is the *UCR*   b. E-flat is the *CS*   c. Heart rate increase is the *UCS*

6. Below are some dependent variables used to measure the strength of a conditioned response. Which is most typical? _____ .

    a. Magnitude of response   b. Percentage of occurrence

    c. Latency   d. Resistance to extinction

7. Strength of the *CR* increases with the number of *CS–UCS* pairings as what kind of function? _____ .

    a. Asymptotic   b. Linear   c. Parabolic   d. Circular

8. For classical conditioning to be most successful, what is the optimum stimulus presentation? _____ .

    a. *UCS* presented, then *CS* .5 seconds later

    b. *CS* and *UCS* presented at the same time

    c. *CS* presented, then *UCS* .5 seconds later

    d. Order is not important

9. Which situation best describes extinction in classical conditioning? _____ .

    a. The *CR* does not occur   b. The *CS* is presented alone

    c. The *UCS* is presented alone   d. The animal does not undergo any procedure

10. Oftentimes the *CR* will diminish to a zero level during extinction trials, only to be back again the next day. This is termed _____ .

    a. response remission   b. second-day surge

    c. perseveration   d. spontaneous recovery

Stimulus Generalization

We have all had, occasionally, generalized emotional experiences. For example, suppose that you once had some difficult sessions in a high school math class; the course had caused you humiliation by publicly demonstrating your weak points, and had been hurtful by way of your getting numerous low grades. You naturally grew to dislike the course. Generalization of this dislike comes into play when you become somewhat emotional upon being told that you have to take a college math course. You have never met the college math instructor, nor do you know anything of his or her teaching methods. Why should you fear something that you have not had previous experience with? *Stimulus generalization* is the answer.

In stimulus generalization an organism demonstrates a *CR* to a stimulus *similar* to a *CS* that has been previously conditioned. Suppose that we produce a tone (the *CS*) of 1000 cps (cycles per second) and pair this with a sharp electric shock (the *UCS*) to a monkey's leg. After several such pairings we note, in addition to visible agitation, a significant heart rate increase (the *CR*) each time the 1000 cps tone is sounded. Now let us present a tone at 900 cps, then one at 800 cps, at 700 cps, and so forth. We observe that for each decreasing tone frequency the animal demonstrates a smaller and smaller response. This illustrates a lawful relationship. It is that the magnitude of the response in stimulus generalization is a direct function of the degree of similarity of the generalized stimulus to the *CS*. Just as is the case with ordinary classical conditioning, we can see how stimulus generalization has survival value for an organism in a natural setting. If an organism has hurtful encounters with a certain object or individual, then it is probably well to avoid not only that specific object, but others that are similar to it.

We have a special vocabulary that we sometimes use in working with experiments in stimulus generalization. The term "generalized stimulus" is cumbersome and, similarly, we need a shorter expression to describe the generalized response. Thus, some persons have used the term *CS'* (*CS* prime) to denote a stimulus similar to, but differing along a certain dimension from, the *CS*. Similarly, the *CS'* is said to elicit the *CR'* (*CR* prime). Therefore our functional relationship now states that, in stimulus generalization, the magnitude of *CR'* is a function of the similarity of *CS'* to *CS* (see Figure 8.6).

Figure 8.6

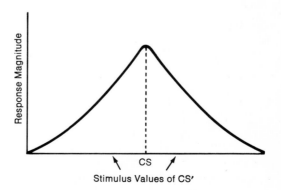

Stimulus Values of CS'

It should not be overlooked that there are a number of interacting variables in stimulus generalization. Most clearly you should be able to see that not only is *CS–CS'* similarity a key factor, but the original degree of *CR* magnitude is critical. This simply means that if a very intense conditioned response is typical in a given subject exposed to a certain stimulus, then the potential exists for a large responsiveness to similar values of *CS'*. If the *CR* is weak, however, little *CR'* is possible.

Another factor that has been noted is that the slope of the stimulus generalization gradient is increasingly flatter, or tending toward the horizontal, as the magnitude of the *CR* increases. This means that where a weak fear response is produced by a certain stimulus, a sharp falling off of responsiveness is evident to stimuli which are similar. However, where an intense, even phobic-like response is present, with an individual exhibiting literal terror when exposed to a certain stimulus, other stimuli of that class will have quite similar effects, and ultimately it is possible that the *CR'* may be almost as pronounced as the *CR* itself.

C 8.17. *The concept of stimulus generalization.*

Stimulus generalization refers to the elicitation of a response by a stimulus which _____ .

    a. previously was paired with a biologically relevant stimulus

    b. previously was utilized in extinction trials

    c. is similar to a previously conditioned *CS*

What is the term we use to describe a stimulus that is similar along some dimension to a given *CS*? _____ .

    a. *CS'*   b. *UCS'*   c. *CR'*

Using the types of abbreviations used in the last question, you could say that the amount of stimulus generalization is largely a function of the degree of similarity between the _____ and the _____ .

The degree of stimulus generalization is an interaction between *CS–CS'* similarity and _____ .

    a. the age and intelligence of the organism

    b. the phylogenetic level of the species used as subjects

    c. the developed strength of the conditioned response

The gradient, or slope of the line describing stimulus generalization, is steeper where the magnitude of the conditioned response is _____ .

    a. very high   b. rather low

Generalization of Extinction   A related phenomenon is generalization of extinction. This is one of the more abstract concepts in conditioning literature. The phenomenon of generalization applies to extinction in much the same way as it does to conditioning. Just as building up a response is followed by a spread of effect to nearby stimulus values, so is the reduction of a response through extinction followed by a spread of the extinction effect to nearby stimulus values. Once we draw a stimulus generalization curve, we can begin to extinguish the response at some point along the CS' dimension. We then find that when we have completely extinguished the response to *that value of CS'*, we have reduced the amount of responding to *other values of CS'*, especially those *immediately adjacent* to the extinguished CS'. This is what is meant by *generalization of extinction,* a very important phenomenon. We shall later refer to generalization of extinction as a hypothetical explanation for a variety of phenomena that occur in psychotherapy as well as in real-life social situations.

C 8.18.   *The concept of generalization of extinction.*

If I present a value of CS' repeatedly, without any pairings with a UCS, I will observe _____ in the magnitude of CR' to the CS' in question.

    a. an increase   b. a decrease

Referring to the above question, ask yourself whether there is demonstrated a generalization effect. Then, the phenomenon described in the last question is representative of which of the following? _____ .

    a. generalization of extinction   b. extinction

If I present a value of CS' repeatedly, without any pairing with a UCS, I will observe _____ in the responsiveness to those values of CS' that are similar to the CS' being presented.

    a. an increase   b. a decrease

Consider whether a generalization effect is shown in the previous question. Then, that phenomenon is _____ .

    a. extinction   b. generalization of extinction

Conditioned Discrimination   The *opposite* of stimulus generalization, which implies a not-so-accurate responsiveness to stimuli in one's environment, is called conditioned discrimination. *Conditioned discrimination* is a process whereby an organism learns to respond only to the CS and not to values of CS'. An illustrative case of conditioned discrimination involved a large collie dog. This dog, owned by a man living alone, had no experience with children outside of some repeated teasing and molesting by a group of neighborhood boys who poked sticks at him through a wire fence. Over a period of time the animal grew extremely aggressive toward children. In the early stages of development the same children were always involved and were the only children with whom the dog had had contact. These particular children served as the CS in the situation, and their tormenting was the UCS which caused the dog to become furious.

    Stimulus generalization was demonstrated when the dog became hostile toward other children who passed by. In the case of this particular dog, a subsequent event led to conditioned discrimination. The event was the arrival of the owner's grandchildren for a visit of several weeks. Laboratory research would tell us that conditioned discrimination takes place when the *CS* continues to be presented *with* the accompanying *UCS*, and the *CS'* continues to be presented *without* the *UCS*. These stimulus presentations must *both* take place repeatedly if completely effective discrimination is to develop.

After the children arrived to visit their grandfather, and were often in the yard, the neighbor children who had been teasing the dog did not come around for a while. During this time the grandchildren, who initially aroused the dog's hostility, gradually gentled the animal and after a short time could enter his pen to play with him, pet him, and take him out on a leash for a walk or play. One day the neighbor children returned and the collie approached the fence wagging his tail, a behavior not seen for a very long time when these children were involved. This particular act represents generalization of extinction.

The neighbor children, however, were not long in reestablishing themselves as tormentors, and thus the original *CS* was again paired with the *UCS*. Over a period of time conditioned discrimination developed, so that the children living nearby elicited the dog's anger, while the owner's grandchildren caused him to approach them with a wagging tail.

The case just described is somewhat lengthy, but it incorporates classical conditioning, stimulus generalization, generalization of extinction, and conditioned discrimination. For this reason it might serve as a frame of reference from which to orient your own examples of these various phenomena.

C 8.19. *The concept of conditioned discrimination.*

Suppose that a college student without any background in academic music takes a music appreciation course. Suppose then that the first course is a "loser," with a severely critical and tough-grading teacher. If the student developed an aversion to any further music courses that were suggested to him, this would illustrate _____ .

a. conditioned discrimination   b. stimulus generalization

In the case of the above student, suppose that he was forced by his curriculum requirements to take several more music courses. Another course under the same teacher proved equally aversive, but the rest of the music courses were highly enjoyable, and excellently taught. Over a period of time, this student might become eager to register for interesting-appearing music courses taught by various faculty members other than the one with whom he had the unpleasant experiences. This development represents _____ .

a. conditioned discrimination   b. stimulus generalization

Higher Order Conditioning

Higher order conditioning occurs when a *CS*, which has developed into a strong elicitor of a *CR*, functions *as if* it were a *UCS* in developing a *CR* to a *new* neutral stimulus. Let us say that a man whips his dog occasionally. The pain is a *UCS*, and the whip itself, initially neutral, is the *CS*. Soon the animal fears the whip, indicating that the conditioning process is well-established. Now, suppose that the man begins to use a new command that the dog has not heard before. Perhaps it is "Stop!" spoken in a loud voice. If he shakes the whip at the same time that he shouts the new command, it is likely that the new command alone (without the whip) will soon acquire the capacity to frighten the animal, even though the command is never directly associated with physical punishment. The verbal command is the new neutral stimulus, which is paired with the well-established *CS* (the whip) that elicits the emotional response.

You should bear in mind that higher order conditioning depends upon the presence of a well-established *CS* to begin with, and it depends upon the *CS* being *maintained* as an eliciting stimulus, and not extinguishing. This simply means that from time to time during conditioning, the *CS* must again be paired with the *UCS*. Otherwise, the *CS* that is being paired with a new neutral stimulus is actually undergoing extinction each time it is presented.

You should also recall that aversive stimuli produce higher levels of activation (drive) than do appetitive stimuli. Therefore, we would probably have much better luck establishing higher order conditioning if the original *UCS* was aversive.

C 8.20. *The concept of higher order conditioning.*

Higher order conditioning occurs when a new stimulus is used for the first time in classical conditioning.

That new stimulus is _____ .

a. a new *CS*   b. a biologically relevant stimulus   c. a *UCS*

A critical factor in higher order conditioning is that the original conditions in the first stage of the process must occasionally be reinstated. This is because one must *maintain* the eliciting power of the _____ .

a. new *CS*   b. established *CS*   c. *UCS*

Both stimulus generalization and higher order conditioning are important phenomena in that they explain situations within which we have learned to attach emotional feelings to stimuli that we have never experienced before (stimulus generalization) or that have never been directly associated with biologically relevant stimuli (higher order conditioning).

You have now been exposed to the general topics of emotional responding and how we acquire a learned emotional structure. The topic area is highly relevant to understanding why people demonstrate certain aversive as well as appetitive responses to various environmental objects or circumstances. You will see the further application of this chapter's principles in certain later chapters.

PROGRESS CHECK 8.3

1. An orange light is the *CS* for a pigeon. In which case would a pigeon be exhibiting stimulus generalization? _____ .

   a. The pigeon's response is elicited by a yellow light

   b. The pigeon pecks at a disk

   c. The pigeon turns around upon hearing a 1000 cps tone

   d. The pigeon lifts its leg when shocked

2. Although responses will generalize to stimuli similar to the *CS*, extinction will not generalize. _____ .

   a. True   b. False

3. Suppose an organism learns to respond only to the *CS* and not to similar stimuli. What would one say had occurred? _____ .

   a. Limited repertoire of responding   b. Stimulus generalization

   c. Conditioned discrimination   d. Spontaneous control

4. Higher order conditioning occurs _____ .

   a. only with phylogenetically advanced organisms, such as primates

   b. whenever animals are beaten and become highly fearful

   c. with all cognitive and emotional processes

   d. whenever a previous *CS* functions as if it were a *UCS*

Operant Behavior and Operant Reinforcement

OPERANT REINFORCEMENT
    Positive and Negative Reinforcers
      Escape and Avoidance Conditioning
    Primary and Conditioned Reinforcers
      Conditioned Reinforcers: Social and Token
        Social Reinforcer: Attention
        Social Reinforcer: Approval
        Social Reinforcer: Affection
        Social Reinforcer: The Submission of Others
      Token Reinforcers
    Delay of Reinforcement
    The Measurement of Operant Behavior
OPERANT EXTINCTION
**VARIABLES AFFECTING OPERANT
CONDITIONING**
    Operant Reinforcement used in Behavior
      Modification
      Positive Reinforcement
      Extinction
    Schedules of Reinforcement
      Fixed Interval Schedule (FI)
      Variable Interval Schedule (VI)
      Fixed Ratio Schedule (FR)
      Variable Ratio Schedule (VR)
    Schedules of Reinforcement and Everyday Life
    The Partial Reinforcement Effect
      A Backward Glance: The Partial
        Reinforcement Effect in Classical
        Conditioning
    The Relative Strengths of Positive and Negative
      Reinforcement
PUNISHMENT: FUNCTIONAL RELATIONSHIPS
    The Use of Punishment in Behavior Modification

The distinction between respondent and operant behavior was presented in Chapter 8. Before we begin this development on the topic of operant conditioning, remind yourself that, as opposed to respondent patterns that are essentially the feelings and emotions of the organism, *operants are the visible muscular behaviors* emitted by an organism. In short, an operant is what an individual *does,* as opposed to how he feels. You may also remember that we mentioned that there were two major sources of operant behavior—*random activity* and *social imitation.* We are now ready to consider the ways in which certain patterns of operant behavior become established as the characteristic behaviors of individuals. The major topic at the outset is the concept of reinforcement.

OPERANT REINFORCEMENT

Let us see just what sort of simple laboratory design we might employ to study operant conditioning. We might have a laboratory rat in an experimental chamber with a lever emerging from the wall. When the rat, exploring his surroundings (random activity) happens to press the lever, a pellet of food is delivered into a tray. If we observe the animal's behavior over a period of an hour, we see a shorter and shorter interval of elapsed time between lever presses. The animal is experiencing certain *consequences* of its lever-pressing behavior, and is "learning" to press it rapidly:

$$R_{lever\ press} \longrightarrow S_{food\ pellet}$$

Another favorite subject for research is the laboratory pigeon. Pigeons are very adept at pecking at objects, and can emit these behaviors with a high frequency. Therefore, pigeons are frequently trained to peck at plastic discs set into the wall, which in turn are connected to automated mechanisms which deliver a small amount of grain as the reward.

Positive and Negative Reinforcers

Both of the preceding examples involve what we call *reward conditioning;* that is, organisms are presented with an *appetitive stimulus* as the consequence of their behavior. Whenever this occurs, we call it *positive reinforcement.* Positive reinforcement is an increase in a class of behaviors due to the onset of a stimulus as a consequence of those behaviors.

Another class of stimuli will cause an organism to behave so as to escape from or avoid it. Stimuli of this kind are *aversive stimuli,* and the associated experiments are called *escape* or *avoidance conditioning.* Learning under

"IF YOU MAKE IT, BRING ME BACK A PIECE OF CHEESE"

these situations is said to occur through *negative reinforcement*. It is very necessary that you clearly understand the difference between the two kinds of reinforcement. Negative reinforcement is an increase in a class of behaviors due to the *termination* (or diminution) of a stimulus as a consequence of those behaviors.

Escape and Avoidance Conditioning

In a typical negative reinforcement procedure involving *escape conditioning,* a laboratory rat may experience electric-grid shock through the floor of the experimental chamber. His immediate reaction is to jump about the chamber, and if one of his jumps causes him to move the lever on the wall, the consequence may be that the grid shock immediately ceases. His bar-pressing actions in succeeding trials occur with ever-shorter lapses of time, until finally the animal is seen resting with one foot upon the lever, ready to press it down whenever the shock begins. In escape conditioning the animal cannot totally avoid the aversive stimulus. He simply learns ways to quickly cut it off when it begins.

$$R_{lever\ press} \longrightarrow S_{termination\ of\ shock}$$

In *avoidance conditioning,* on the other hand, the situation is adjusted so that an organism is able to avoid the aversive stimulus completely once he learns the proper technique. Suppose, with our laboratory rat on the shock grid as the example, we also use a small electric light placed just above the lever. The rule the animal must learn is that when the light comes on, the electric shock will follow in four seconds unless he depresses the lever during that interval of time. If he does, no shock will occur.

$$R_{lever\ press} \longrightarrow S_{avoidance\ of\ shock}$$

Remember that both escape and avoidance conditioning involve the increase in rate of a class of behaviors due to the elimination of some aversive stimulus (negative reinforcement).

Before we proceed, we must emphasize that no matter whether the reinforcement is positive or negative, when we reinforce a behavior, that behavior rate *always* increases.

Now, let us examine reinforcement in a human social context: Charlie is a six-year-old spoiled child. You watch as his mother leads him through the aisle of a department store. Suddenly Charlie spies a large and expensive toy. "Buy that for me, Mommy," demands Charlie. The mother is either in a hurry or is concerned about the cost of the item, for she rushes the child along, telling him that they cannot stop now. The child pulls back and resists, rooted to the spot. His voice turns shrill as he cries out more loudly that he wants the toy. People begin to turn and look at the child, and the mother's face flushes red with embarrassment. By this time Charlie is wailing loudly and the mother is concerned that he may throw himself on the floor and begin kicking as he did a few days previously. So, in an effort to hush the child, she gives in to his demand for the toy. "Here," she says. "Now don't ask for anything else today."

Charlie's operant behavior is a tantrum, which some might also label as a form of aggression. The positive reinforcement for that behavior is the acquisition of the toy, provided through the submission of the mother. The predictable result of this experience is that in the future Charlie, when faced with the denial of something he wants, will more quickly initiate tantrum behavior. Charlie was positively reinforced for tantrum-throwing by getting the toy. The mother was also reinforced. She was negatively reinforced for submitting to Charlie's tantrum by the termination of the unpleasant situation. Thus, her submissions to tantrums will tend to increase just as will Charlie's tantrums.

You should appreciate, at this point, that the concept of reinforcement is a powerful and vital factor in understanding behavior. Essentially we are stating that operant behavior is literally *controlled by its consequences*. If reinforced, any behavior pattern tends to increase, whether it is appropriate and socially approved or whether it is not. And, without appropriate reinforcement, behavior patterns do not become established in individuals' behavioral repertoires.

C 9.1. *Reinforcement: Positive and negative.*

Reward conditioning always involves _____ reinforcement.

    a. positive   b. negative

Escape and avoidance conditioning always involve _____ reinforcement.

    a. positive   b. negative

Both positive and negative reinforcement refer to _____ .

    a. increases in the rate of a class of behaviors

    b. satisfaction of biological needs

    c. either increases or decreases in the rate of a class of behaviors

Positive reinforcement operates through the _____ of a stimulus.

    a. onset   b. termination

Negative reinforcement operates through the _____ of a stimulus.

    a. onset   b. termination

_____ behavior is controlled by its consequences.

    a. Positively reinforced   b. Negatively reinforced   c. Operant

Primary and Conditioned Reinforcers

In addition to being categorized as either positive or negative, all reinforcers also are classified as being either primary or conditioned. *Primary reinforcers* are those which pertain directly to a primary drive condition. Thus food, water, sexual access, and the like are primary positive reinforcers, while such stimuli as pain are primary negative reinforcers. Conditioned (sometimes called secondary) reinforcers are not directly concerned with the satisfaction of primary drives. Rather, *conditioned reinforcers* are those stimuli that have acquired reinforcing value because of their past association with primary reinforcers. That is, they become reinforcers through the process of classical conditioning. We may use a procedure so that, with a laboratory animal, the sounding of a bell signals an event that is rewarding. If we were to repeatedly pair a bell with the presentation of food, we would eventually have an animal that would learn to work or do tricks with the only consequence being the sounding of the bell. Animal trainers frequently employ such techniques, using little metal "crickets" or clickers. Each time a dog trainer feeds his dogs, he speaks to them, using certain words and perhaps sounding the clicker. Then, when he later works with the animal, he does not have to constantly feed it after every successful enactment of the trick in order to strengthen the behavior. He simply says the things that have been associated with food, such as "Good boy," or he sounds the clicker.

The following three steps show the development of a conditioned positive reinforcer:

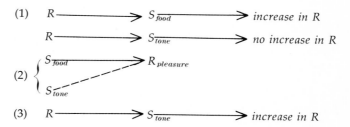

The same sort of thing occurs in the development of conditioned reinforcers of an aversive nature. This is exactly how mothers of young children train them to respond to certain tones of voice, even before the youngsters are old enough to understand the words. Mothers couple the words "No, no" with a slap on the child's hand which inflicts pain, or with a loud sudden clapping of the hands that startles the child. After several such experiences the sudden statement "No, no!" has the effect of stopping the child literally in mid-air from whatever it is that he or she is doing.

It should be obvious that the strength of a conditioned reinforcer is a function of both the number of times it has been paired with primary reinforcers *and* the magnitude of these primary reinforcers.

You will recall that a *CS* in classical conditioning (the conditioned reinforcer-to-be) will extinguish if presented by itself over and over. Therefore, those persons who systematically apply conditioned reinforcers must be careful to frequently *re*-pair the conditioned reinforcer (*CS*) with meaningful rewards (*UCSs*) that give the conditioned reinforcer its potency.

C 9.2. *Reinforcement: Primary and conditioned.*

A reinforcer that pertains directly to unlearned appetitive or aversive drive conditions, such as food, water, sexual access, or pain, is a _____ reinforcer.

    a. primary   b. conditioned   c. negative   d. positive

A reinforcer that has acquired its reinforcing properties is called a _____ reinforcer.

    a. primary   b. conditioned   c. negative   d. positive

The process of _____ is involved in a reinforcer acquiring its reinforcing properties.

    a. operant conditioning   b. classical conditioning   c. extinction

The strength of a conditioned reinforcer is largely a function of the number of times that the conditioned reinforcer has been _____ .

    a. experienced by the subject

    b. paired with primary reinforcers

    c. anticipated before its onset

A second variable related to the strength of a conditioned reinforcer is the _____ .

    a. age of the subject   b. reinforcement history of the subject

    c. strength of primary reinforcers paired with the conditioned reinforcer

An individual who uses conditioned reinforcers should always be careful to frequently reassociate the - - - with the - - -. _____ .

    a. conditioned reinforcer/experience of primary reinforcement

    b. act being reinforced/experience of primary reinforcement

*Conditioned
Reinforcers:
Social and Token*

A further categorization of conditioned reinforcers places them into two classes—those that are incorporated into social interactions, called *social reinforcers,* and those tangible objects which one may earn, called *token reinforcers.*

Social Reinforcer: Attention

We generally recognize four distinct types of social reinforcer. First, there is *attention.* Presumably the young child very quickly begins to appreciate the value of attention, particularly if it is administered by a parent, due to the fact that the youngster so often has had attention by a parent coupled with the reduction of some primary drive. The young child experiences contact comfort, stimulus variety, and reduction of such drives as hunger, temperature extremes, and so forth when the mother gives him attention and in so doing provides for his primary needs. The main exceptions to the general pattern appear to be those children for whom attention seems to be aversive. The family histories of most such individuals show that the child is typically scolded, punished, or made fun of whenever he is noticed. You can easily follow the conditioning sequence in such cases, as the experience of the stimulus of others' attention is simply linked with an aversive UCS until attention itself is capable of eliciting anxiety.

Relatively few children show such avoidance of attention; rather, the typical child is strongly motivated to receive it. One finding, predictable from conditioning theory, is that attention will be the strongest reinforcer to the child who has had a great deal of it in the past, with most of it linked with enjoyable experiences. The first-born or only child in a family is often found to be highly attention-seeking in later years, and at the same time can most easily be reinforced for various behaviors by the use of contingent attention.

Many persons do not easily make impressions on others, and therefore find it more difficult than do most in gaining others' attention through typical channels. Where there is a strong background of attention and its development as a conditioned reinforcer within the family, such individuals will adopt behaviors that may cause them not to be liked by their peers or by authority figures. Even if there is a modest level of punishment involved in the attention, such behaviors will tend to continue if this is the only means by which the individual gains this reinforcer.

C 9.3. *Attention as a social reinforcer.*

Attention does not seem to be consistent as a positive reinforcer for children from families where attention frequently has been linked with _____ .

    a. positive reinforcers   b. punishment   c. token reinforcers

The main reason that much antisocial behavior occurs, even when given a degree of punishment and clear disapproval by authority figures, is that _____ .

    a. the behavior gains attention

    b. the individual learns that he can often escape meaningful punishment

Social Reinforcer: Approval

The second category of social reinforcer is *approval*. This social reinforcer does not develop as early in the child as does attention, because approval awaits some degree of verbal ability for its typical experience. When a child is old enough to understand words, he will occasionally receive the parents' praise and simultaneously will be given some sort of reward such as fresh warm cookies. Except in a few cases in which children may grow up in families where no approval of their behavior ever occurs, approval as a social reinforcer is very strong. By giving a child approval in the classroom or in some other situation, a teacher can usually exercise a considerable amount of influence over the behavior of the child.

C 9.4. *Approval as a social reinforcer.*

The main reason that approval acquires its reinforcing properties later in a child's life than is the case

for attention is that _____ .

a. parents do not approve of children as early; they simply attend to them

b. approval typically depends upon some degree of verbal transmission, hence language acquisition is necessary

c. reaction to approval is tied in with mental age

If approval is not a consistent positive reinforcer for some children, it is probably because they are

from homes where _____ .

a. there is seldom any approval expressed

b. approval is linked with punishment

c. the children are not given attention

Social Reinforcer: Affection

A third social reinforcer is *affection*. By this we do not refer to the physical aspect of love, either in the form of contact comfort for the young child or sexual satisfaction for the adult. Rather, we refer to the communication of an emotional feeling from one individual to another. This usually takes the form of the open expression of affection. It occurs in the look a child gets from a parent, the tones of voice employed from time to time by a parent, or even literal statements of affection. In this sense rather than the biological sense, behaviorally oriented psychologists believe that the "need" for love and affection is a *conditioned* motive, and is "normal" only in that its development is more typical than its absence. A rather interesting implication in this particular assumption is that it suggests that the drive for love and affection may not exist in some individuals who, nevertheless, cannot be said to be psychologically abnormal in that they do not experience frustration or unhappiness or emit bizarre actions. On the other hand, the reverse might often be the case for an individual with a strongly developed drive to be "loved" which, if unsatisfied, might lead to a variety of peculiar or extreme behaviors. No doubt you can think of cases where certain individuals who have great difficulty establishing effective relationships with others may engage in behaviors humiliating to themselves in apparent bids for affection.

A different situation is represented in the cases of persons who seem afraid to engage in any affectionate relationship with another. In these cases one generally finds strange, ambivalent behaviors on the part of a parent—usually the mother—where the child was "used" emotionally with a great deal of turning on and turning off of affectionate behavior by the parent. Some parents even will use an affectionate overture to disarm the child in order to get information from him or even get him to come close enough to grab and then punish. Small wonder, indeed, that many such children grow to be emotionally distorted as adults.

C 9.5. *Affection as a social reinforcer.*

In a theoretical sense, according to the concepts of reinforcement psychology, the motive for non-biological affection is _____ .

a. a natural, unlearned need   b. a classically conditioned motive

According to the theoretical notion of affection reflected in the last question, which of the following might be true? _____ .

a. It is not necessarily pathological to have *no* apparent motive for affection

b. It might well be pathological to have a very strong motive for affection, reflected in certain affection-seeking behavior patterns

c. (both of the above are true)

Social Reinforcer: The Submission of Others

The fourth and last social reinforcer is the *submission of others.* In the experience of practically every child there come times when the child, in making demands, "crosses swords" with the parent. If the child is strongly motivated to acquire some goal object which the parent prohibits, a tantrum may result. The consequences of the tantrum are most important. If the tantrum succeeds in bringing about the submission of the parent, who gives in to the child, not only is tantrum-emitting reinforced, but the submission of another person is paired with the acquisition of the meaningful goal. After the submission of others has been paired with a variety of reinforcing stimuli, then the submission of others, itself, comes to have conditioned reinforcing characteristics. Thereafter, the behaviors that we call "dominant" and "bossy" become personality characteristics of the individual. Most personality tests on the market today include a measure of dominance or authoritarianism, and it is typical to see this characteristic developed to some degree in almost everyone. As you might predict, considerable variation occurs in the extent to which environmental circumstances can produce diverse degrees of dominance.

It is no accident that personality studies have shown first-born children to be more dominant than second- and third-borns within families, and that large-statured persons tend, on the average, to be more dominant than persons who are physically smaller. In the former case, first-borns have an advantage over their younger brothers and sisters, and can often manage to take things away from them by virtue of their greater maturity. This pairs the submission of another with acquisition of some meaningful prize. Similarly with large children, they tend on the average to be more dominant simply because their size, in relation to their peers, gives them an advantage in imposing their own will in conflicts that involve them.

To a great extent the development of the dominant personality also depends upon interactions with parents. Sons of very dominant fathers were shown to be typically very dominant themselves (the influence of the social model) but with some being quite submissive (Werner, 1970); and there were relatively few "in-betweens." With the submissive ones, we can speculate that the early attempts to act in dominant ways were vigorously suppressed in conflicts with the dominant parent.

C 9.6. *Submission of others as a social reinforcer.*

State three of the factors that are related to children's becoming "dominant"—that is, strongly motivated by the submission of others.

1. _____

2. _____

3. _____

C 9.7. *Types of social reinforcers.*

The four types of social reinforcers are:

1. _____

2. _____

3. _____

4. _____

Token Reinforcers While many conditioned reinforcers are socially administered, some were simply meaningless objects until they eventually acquired reinforcing properties. These are what we call *token reinforcers*. They are simply *material symbols* that are related to some form of meaningful reinforcement. The most common token reinforcer to you is probably money. Money begins as a meaningless object, as you can witness if you give coins to a child who is less than a year old. The child may put a coin in his mouth or carry it around for a few minutes because of its novelty value, but the stimulus variety can hardly be maintained for the child of such a young age, and he soon loses interest in the coin and leaves it behind. It has no value to him at that age. Soon, however, the mother engages in a variety of activities which result in the development, for the child, of money's reinforcement value. She may begin by pairing money with meaningful rewards, including praise. Or she may associate money with candy or ice cream by having the child exchange his coins for them. Either way, the coin acquires reinforcing value and is thereafter capable of functioning by itself as a reinforcer.

A variety of other frequently-used token reinforcers include gold stars on a chart for attendance or achievement, medals given to soldiers, awards for sports and scholarship, and the plastic coins sometimes used in therapeutic settings, which may later be exchanged for privileges or objects. You will learn more about the last-mentioned use of tokens in Chapter 9A.

To a degree, many of us can be influenced to behave in certain ways simply because *things* (nothing specific) are "awarded" as a consequence of behavior. "Having things" becomes important by mid-childhood, just because much of what we have acquired has been associated with reward. Some psychologists even speculate as to whether the process of token association with reward underlies the materialistic values prevalent in society.

C 9.8. *Token reinforcers.*

Tokens begin as objects _____ .

    a. which can serve immediately as conditioned reinforcers

    b. which can serve immediately as primary reinforcers

    c. which have no established value whatsoever

Tokens are properly subclassified as possible _____ .

    a. primary reinforcers   b. social reinforcers   c. conditioned reinforcers

---

PROGRESS CHECK 9.1

1. Operant behaviors are visible muscular responses emitted by an organism. Which of these is an operant? _____ .

    a. Increased constriction of arteries   b. Peristalsis of the gastrointestinal tract

    c. Running laps on a track   d. Secretion of FSH by the pituitary gland

MATCH: _____ 2. Rat presses a bar. Food pellet rolls into the maze.   A. Negative reinforcement

    B. Positive reinforcement

    _____ 3. Rat presses a bar. Electric shock turns off.

4. A pigeon learns to peck a disc when a red light flashes to prevent the onset of a shock. Negative reinforcement in this case produced _____ .

    a. escape conditioning   b. avoidance conditioning

5. Charlie threw a tantrum to obtain a cookie from his mother. Which is true? _____ .

    a. Charlie was positively reinforced for tantrum behavior

    b. Charlie's mother was negatively reinforced for handing out cookies, because the tantrum stopped

    c. both   d. neither

6. Which is correct? _____ .

    a. Primary reinforcers acquire their reinforcing properties via learning

    b. Conditioned reinforcers acquire value via pairing with primary reinforcers

7. Which of these conditioned reinforcers would be a token reinforcer? _____ .

    a. Submission of others   b. Approval   c. Affection   d. Money

---

Delay of Reinforcement

One of the best researched functional relationships in the area of conditioning concerns the effects of varying amounts of delay of reinforcement. In the operant conditioning model, it is vital that there be very little delay of reinforcement following the emission of a response. It sometimes comes as a very great surprise to readers to learn how short the amount of delay really is that can be effectively handled by organisms, either human or subhuman.

A large number of research programs have investigated this factor, one of them being an experiment by Grice in 1948. Grice used laboratory rats in a device similar to a T-maze. After running down either arm of the maze, the rats were kept in a delay box for periods of time, which varied for separate groups of rats, before they were allowed into a goal box. If they had originally gone down the proper arm of the maze, they were fed in the goal box; but if they had chosen the wrong arm of the maze, they were not fed. Grice found that when the delay of food presentation was any longer than five seconds, *none* of the rats could learn the maze.

You may wonder if the rats are not just too stupid to figure out what is going on with such a delay. Monkeys, however, have been used in similar research, and we see an almost identical pattern of results. Furthermore, no great difference is evident in the amounts of delay that can be tolerated for effective conditioning with lower animals, compared with humans. The fact that it sometimes appears otherwise is actually due to other factors that frequently enter into the human situation. The most important of these is some form of conditioned reinforcement that is often delivered immediately upon the emission of the response, even though the actual goal object is delayed till later.

The research literature pertaining to this functional relationship shows that immediate, or at least relatively prompt, reinforcement is vital to the development of the conditioned operant response. While short delays of up to a second do not result in seriously-hindered conditioning, even two- or three-second delays produce a notable decline in conditioning, and delays extending beyond five seconds drastically inhibit the development of an eventual conditioned operant response.

C 9.9. *Delay of reinforcement.*

For best conditioning, reinforcement should be _____ .

    a. immediately upon emission of the response

    b. two seconds after emission of the response

    c. anywhere up to 10 seconds after emission of the response

The Measurement of Operant Behavior

Operant behavior is generally measured in terms of rate. In practically all of the operant literature you will see the dependent variable expressed as a given number of responses per minute, per hour, or per day. On very rare occasions you may see expressed measures of response *intensity* or response *latency*, the latter being the length of time an organism is in a situation before it emits the response. Generally, however, these measures are secondary to the main measure of *response rate*.

C 9.10. *Dimensions of measurement of operant responses.*

Most typically, the operant researcher investigates changes in the _____ of the dependent variable.

    a. intensity   b. latency   c. rate

OPERANT EXTINCTION

Extinction of an operant behavior is a reduction in response rate that comes about when the *response is emitted* and *no reinforcement follows*. Notice that *both* factors are required. If an animal is in the habit of pressing a bar in his chamber and thereby getting food reinforcement, and if the bar is subsequently removed from the chamber, the animal's established operant bar-pressing habit may survive for years, and reappear at full strength when he next has an opportunity to press a bar. It is necessary (1) that the animal emit the response (bar press), and (2) this must be followed by no reinforcement, if extinction is to occur. Just as the acquisition of an operant response is gradual, so is the elimination (extinction) of the response. Typically, an animal presses the bar more and more slowly as extinction trials progress until finally the response disappears entirely.

C 9.11. *Extinction of operant responding.*

Operant extinction requires the two following things: first, that the organism _____

_____ and, second, that _____.

VARIABLES AFFECTING OPERANT CONDITIONING

The main factor that affects operant conditioning is (1) *the number of rein-forcements.* When one animal has received 5 reinforcers, another 25 and another 100, we predict the higher response rate will be on the part of the animal with the greatest number of reinforced trials.

An important variable, as we have indicated, is (2) *the time interval between the enactment of the response and the presentation of the reinforcer,* with immediate reinforcement the most effective. Reinforcers delivered too early, even preceding the enactment of the response, as well as reinforcers delivered too late, perhaps eight to ten seconds following the response, are relatively ineffectual.

Another important variable is (3) *the amount of reinforcement.* In most situations we can discern factors of both quantity and quality in the amount of reinforcement. For a dog being given a food reinforcer, we might be interested in the grams of food weight (quantity), as well as the percentage of cereal content in the food. The latter factor might reduce the palatability (quality), and hence the value, of the reinforcement. If social reinforcers are concerned, we might be interested in both the quantity of reinforcement, such as how frequently a certain person of the opposite sex compliments you, as well as the quality of the reinforcer, which might take the form of the degree of sexual attractiveness of that person.

An obvious variable is (4) the *amount of unreinforced responding* (extinction trials) that subtract from the response strength that has built up through reinforcement.

A final variable is (5) that of *schedules of reinforcement.* This is a topic so complex that further on we shall consider it in a separate section.

Mort Walker, © King Features Syndicate 1974

C 9.12. *Variables affecting the strength of operant conditioning.*

Exclusive of schedules of reinforcement, what are the four variables cited as influencing operant conditioning?

1. _____

2. _____

3. _____

4. _____

In each of the pairings below, indicate the case in which the stronger operant conditioning would occur: 1 _____ , 2 _____ , 3 _____ , 4 _____ .

1. { a. subjects are given 3 reinforced trials
      b. subjects are given 20 reinforced trials

2. { a. one second elapses beween response and reinforcer
      b. five seconds elapse between response and reinforcer

3. { a. two bites of food are given to subject as reinforcer
      b. twenty bites of food are given to subject as reinforcer

4. { a. subjects have been given 10 conditioning trials, 10 extinction trials
      b. subjects have been given 10 conditioning trials, 5 extinction trials

Operant Reinforcement Used in Behavior Modification

We have described how behavior may be developed or altered using a variety of principles of operant conditioning. These strategies for behavior change are traditionally labeled "behavior modification," and each strategy is said to be a *paradigm*. The term "paradigm" generally means a model which implies some sequential process. Thus, one paradigm is that of positive primary reinforcement, another is that of extinction, and so forth. There are more paradigms than we have so far described; moreover, many paradigms can be further subdivided. So, without implying that we are going into appreciable detail, we would like to demonstrate how some of the simpler paradigms have been utilized in behavior modification research.

Positive Reinforcement

Whenever we are faced with a very low rate of a behavior which we would like to establish more firmly in the behavioral repertoire at a higher rate, we think first of rewarding the behavior on the occasions when it occurs. Unfortunately many parents and public school teachers fail to reinforce adequately even those behaviors that they are quite eager to establish. The questions to the behavior modifier are first, "Why *should* the person behave a certain way? What are the consequences for doing so?" And secondly,

"What would be effective consequences to offer the subject for the desired behavior?" Once these questions are clearly thought out, the possibilities for the use of positive reinforcement open up.

It might be added that sometimes an alternative and much less desired behavior is evident in a subject, and concurrent with reinforcement of the target behavior the experimenter must withdraw reinforcement from the other behavior and hence extinguish it.

Allen (1964) and her associates at the University of Washington carried out a systematic program of positive reinforcement, using attention with a nursery school child at a laboratory preschool on the campus. The four-year-old, Ann, interacted freely with adults, but was withdrawn from same-age peers. She expressed no fear of other children, but usually failed to respond to their attempts to play with her, choosing instead to initiate contacts with nearby teachers. Observation confirmed that the teachers typically gave considerable attention to her various achievements as well as to her occasional bumps and bruises. Over a period of time it seemed that her dependent attention-seeking was increasing, and that her constructive activities were pursued only so long as they served to direct frequent adult attention her way.

A plan was drawn up by which Ann was to be given adult attention only while interacting with other children, except, of course, in an emergency situation. If she approached a teacher and attempted contact, the teacher would ignore her and walk away to busy herself with other children. However, if Ann smiled at another child the teacher would then smile at Ann the next time she caught her eye, and if Ann became involved with another child or with a group activity, the teacher immediately entered the situation, giving Ann considerable attention. During the three or four weeks of this procedure, Ann's rate of interaction with other children rose from an initial rate below 20 percent of the observed times to over 60 percent. A two-month follow-up was performed, and it was found that Ann was maintaining her contact rate at 60 percent and above. The interpretation was that once active social play was established, there were enough reinforcing events within the interactions to keep them going at a reasonably high rate.

Extinction   A wide variety of cases exist where various undesirable behaviors develop because of the favorable consequences they bring. Either positive or negative reinforcement may be represented. In the first case we may find that individuals receive attention for undesirable acts; then those and similar activities become characteristic of the individual. In such cases attention must be withdrawn. In other cases we may find that individuals escape from various social or emotional threats by certain strategies which then become characteristic. We might say a person is "timid," which means that he or she habitually refrains from certain forms of social activities, and is negatively reinforced by the removal of the social threat in so doing. Such cases of negative reinforcement are often difficult to deal with, but again it is appropriate to find some way to cause reinforcement for the act to end, and thus bring about extinction.

A case is described by Williams (1959) which is extremely simple in concept, yet powerful in effect, especially considering how many parents deal ineffectually with similar problems. A two-year-old boy had been seriously ill for a considerable time, and during this time he had become accustomed to receiving the constant attention and concern of his parents. Now that he was recovering and the parents were no longer so constantly involved in giving special care, he was attempting to control them with his tantrums and crying. One of the most critical times came when the boy was put to bed at night.

During his illness the child had been talked to, stroked, and stayed with each night until he fell asleep, and his present behavior was effectively perpetuating that state of affairs. When put to bed, if the parents left the room, the boy would scream and cry until the parents returned. At least one parent was forced to stay in the child's bedroom until he fell asleep. If that parent picked up a book or magazine to read, the boy would cry until the reading material was put down. Both parents were of the impression that the boy fought off sleep as long as possible, and in fact the parents were spending from 30 to 60 minutes sitting in his room each night after he was put down, waiting for him to go to sleep.

The decision was made to extinguish the crying and tantrums by not delivering contingent parent attention. During the treatment program the boy was put to bed in a relaxed, leisurely fashion, following which the parent left the room and gently closed the door. The child screamed and raged, but the parent did not return. A systematic measure of the time spent crying was taken (the dependent variable), and it was found that on the first evening the child continued screaming for 45 minutes before finally ceasing and falling asleep. On the second evening of the procedure the boy fell asleep immediately, and it was speculated that he was still tired from the previous evening's tirade. On the third night about 10 minutes of screaming and fussing occurred, and on the fourth evening about 6 minutes. There was less time spent crying each evening thereafter until, by the seventh evening, there was no more crying. In a follow-up study almost two years later, the boy appeared to be friendly, expressive, and outgoing, and the parents reported no form of bedtime problems.

A case in a large mental hospital was reported by Ayllon and Michael (1959), who modified an undesirable behavior by withdrawing attention. Lucille was in the habit of entering the nurses' station at frequent intervals and interfering with the work going on there. She had been doing this for about two years, and an initial measure suggested that she was averaging around sixteen visits a day. Each time she entered the office, she was spoken to by a nurse. She was told again that this was not allowed, and the nurse would lead her by the hand back onto the ward. She had been classified as mentally defective, and one nurse said, "It's difficult to tell her anything because she can't understand—she's too dumb."

It was hypothesized that the nurses' attention was maintaining the behavior, so in the treatment phase whenever Lucille entered the nurses' station she was ignored. Under no circumstances would any nurse even acknowledge her presence, whether or not she spoke to them. Over a period

of eight weeks the average number of daily entries into the office dropped from 16 to around 2, which was not considered to be particularly excessive.

It is appropriate to point out that many behaviors, both in institutionalized and "normal" individuals, and including both reasonable-appearing acts as well as bizarre actions, are maintained by the fact that people notice them. When children act up at school, it is typically because this gains them the notice of the teacher or the attention of their peers. As an older individual acts out the role of a "character," this too typically yields a more desirable alternative than being ignored by others. Some individuals enact an exaggerated dependency role, effectively controlling others' delivery of contingent attention in this manner. Some persons are deliberately abrasive and argumentative; this behavior insures that, at least for the moment, they become the center of attention as others respond to their deviant actions. It would appear that virtually everyone responds to attention.

When deprived of a normal degree of attention, most persons seem to become a little depressed; when we hear the statement that a person is being "taken for granted," this usually means that he or she is not getting the amount of individual attention that that person is accustomed to receiving. It would also seem that an environment which denies a degree of individual attention to people seems to stimulate the development of some form of deviant attention-seeking behavior.

Schedules of Reinforcement

By far the quickest way to establish a high rate of behavior is to reinforce each occurrence of the response. This is *continuous reinforcement*, abbreviated *crf*. It is usually advantageous, from the experimenter's point of view, to move away from a *crf* schedule once the behavior is established. An *intermittent schedule* of reinforcement (sometimes called a partial schedule) is a schedule in which the behavior is reinforced *visibly less* than 100 percent of the time. Behavior can usually be very satisfactorily maintained, even on a very thin intermittent schedule, if movement into that schedule is handled gradually.

Fixed Interval Schedule (FI)

First we shall consider the *fixed interval (FI)* schedule of intermittent reinforcement. Suppose that we have a monkey in an experimental chamber. A small bar or handle protudes from the wall, and to make this example realistic let us suppose that the monkey has been reinforced a number of times in the past for pulling the bar, so that bar-pulling occurs fairly frequently. If we have an *FI-1* schedule, this means that the animal is working on a one-minute fixed interval schedule of reinforcement. Inside the laboratory mechanism is a clock which measures time intervals. The procedure goes something like this—the clock starts counting off one minute, during which time nothing happens whenever the monkey pulls the bar. After exactly 60 seconds, the next bar pull is rewarded by the immediate delivery of food.

You will note an interesting characteristic of the fixed interval schedule: it is that no matter how often the monkey pulls the bar during the 60 seconds, there is no effect on the frequency of reinforcement. So, it should not be a surprise to learn that with this type of schedule we do not develop a very "energetic" monkey. Compared with monkeys on certain other schedules, this monkey will appear fairly easy-going, and over a long period of time he will emit a fairly low rate of responding.

There is another interesting characteristic of the fixed interval schedule. Monkeys, rats, and pigeons, as well as people, appear to have a sense of timing. If the interval is fixed, such as 30 seconds, one minute, or two minutes, the reinforced individual quickly begins to sense the time when a reinforcer is about to be delivered. At such a time he begins to emit responses much more rapidly, and this reminds us of the child who, just before Christmas, begins very energetically to be nice so that Santa will leave a lot of toys. This phenomenon is called *scalloping*.

Variable Interval Schedule (VI)

The *variable interval (VI)* schedule is similar to the fixed interval schedule, in that the subject is reinforced only occasionally, and the passage of time is the determinant of the moment for that reinforcement. The difference in the *VI* schedule is that the interval of time is not equal between the reinforcements. Rather, in a laboratory experiment, we calculate the *mean time* between reinforcements.

Perhaps you can most easily visualize the procedures of interval (*FI* and *VI*) schedules if you understand the mechanical aspects of the delivery of reinforcement. A long paper "belt" is fashioned into a continuous loop with little holes along one side, similar to a movie film, so that gear teeth can draw the belt along at a constant slow speed. Knowing the speed, one can punch large holes in the center of the tape to correspond to time intervals. An *FI-1* schedule might call for ten equally distant holes in a ten-foot paper belt, while a *VI-1* schedule might call for ten irregularly spaced holes in the belt. The irregular spacing for *VI-1* might correspond, let us say, to 50 seconds, 108 seconds, 45 seconds, 77 seconds, 91 seconds, 32 seconds, etc., all averaging 60 seconds. Now, let us set the belt into motion. As the animal in the experimental chamber presses the lever, no reinforcement is at first delivered, because the delivery mechanism is not activated. A metal stylus rests on the top of the paper belt as it moves, and when a punched large hole comes along, the stylus drops through onto the metal roller underneath. This completes an electrical circuit and thereby activates the reinforcement delivery mechanism for a single delivery. From that instant, the very next response will be a reinforced response. After a single reinforcer is delivered, the mechanism is again inactive until the next large hole in the paper tape reaches the metal stylus.

As we noted before, interval schedules of any kind, whether fixed or variable, do not reward the animal more often for more rapid rates of bar pressing. So, in the *VI* as well as the *FI* schedules, the animals do not become particularly "energetic." They emit steady but fairly low rates of responding. An advantage of *VI* over *FI* schedules, however, is that the scalloping, mentioned earlier, is not particularly manifest in the *VI* schedule. This is because the animal cannot very accurately sense when it is almost time for another reinforcer, since those times vary. Its response rate is more even throughout the duration of each interval, causing a higher overall response rate.

Fixed Ratio Schedule (FR)

We are now going to turn to another animal in a chamber, this time a pigeon. The pigeon is on a *fixed ratio* schedule, which we will call *FR20*. No longer is time the criterion for reinforcing a response; instead, the *number of responses* that must be emitted by the organism is the criterion. So, in the case of our pigeon, *FR20* means that he must emit 20 responses to get a single reinforcer. Pigeons, due to their own species characteristics, are particularly good at pecking things, so we might have, set into the wall, a plastic disc that looks like a large button. The bird pecks at the disc and then is rewarded with a few grains of food delivered into a feeder located beside the disc. Rather than a clock, a counter is installed behind the experimental compartment, and the food delivery mechanism is adjusted so that each twentieth peck delivers the grain. In such an *FR* schedule, the 20th peck, 40th, 60th, etc. each receive reinforcement.

The main difference between a ratio schedule and the two interval schedules is that with ratio schedules the organism receives more reinforcers if it emits a higher rate of responses. The overall effect upon the organism is that it begins to work a great deal faster. Performance curves drawn for the various schedules show much higher response rates where ratio schedules are used.

However, the fact that this schedule is a fixed schedule has an effect upon responding similar to, but less pronounced than, that which we encountered with the fixed-interval schedule. That is, scalloping occurs. You perhaps recall having driven home from a very long, exhausting trip. As you get nearer to home, you tend to speed up, because you are almost there. After some experience in the schedule, animals are often able to sense that they are "almost there," and their response rates increase.

Variable Ratio Schedule (VR) Perhaps the best schedule of all, in terms of getting a high rate of steady behavior (that is, no laziness and no scalloping), is the *variable ratio* schedule. A ratio might be expressed as *VR10,* referring to ten responses per reinforcer. But, as in the *VI* schedule, the *10* refers to the *average* number of responses necessary to produce each reinforcer. Thus, the bird may peck the disc 5 times, get food, have to peck 18 more times for the next food delivery, then 8 times, 12 times on the next try, etc.

C 9.13. *Schedules of reinforcement: Definitions and principles.*

If every response of a given class is reinforced, reinforcement is on a ＿＿＿＿＿ (use abbreviation) schedule.

When reinforcement is noticeably less than for 100 percent of responses, we would say that there is ＿＿＿＿＿＿＿＿＿＿ reinforcement.

A quick, high rate of responding is best initially established with ＿＿＿＿ schedule of reinforcement.

   a. a *crf*   b. an intermittent

The two ＿＿＿＿ schedules of intermittent reinforcement differentially reward higher behavior rates, and hence produce high behavior rates.

   a. ratio   b. interval

"Scalloping" occurs in the ＿＿＿＿＿ schedule of reinforcement, and to a lesser extent in the ＿＿＿＿＿ schedule of reinforcement.

It would seem that the *best* intermittent schedule, in terms of producing high behavior rates, is the ＿＿＿＿＿ (use abbreviation) schedule.

PROGRESS CHECK 9.2

1. Which is true of the timing of reinforcement? ＿＿＿＿ .

   a. Rats are too stupid to learn with delay of reinforcement

   b. Humans learn best with long delays of reinforcement and very rich schedules

   c. Only a short delay in reinforcement can be handled by most organisms for learning to occur

   d. Grice showed that animals can learn mazes without reinforcement

2. What measure of operant behavior is generally used? _____ .

    a. Cycle   b. Rate   c. Variability   d. Rhythm

3. The main factor affecting operant conditioning aside from delay of reinforcement is _____ .

    a. antecedent stimulus display   b. number of reinforcements

    c. ease of the task   d. quality of the response

4. A monkey receives a piece of banana for every four buttons pushed. What schedule is this? _____ .

    a. *FR4*   b. *VR*   c. *crf*   d. *VI14*

5. Which schedule of reinforcement generates the highest rate of operant behavior? _____ .

    a. Continuous   b. Variable interval   c. Fixed interval   d. Variable ratio

6. Suppose you want to establish playing with other children more firmly in a preschooler. Which paradigm would you use? _____ .

    a. Praise the child for playing with others

    b. Scream at the child for playing alone

    c. Comfort the child for running to you in tears

    d. Put the child in social isolation for antisocial behavior

7. In the case of Lucille, the pesty mental patient, what paradigm was used sucessfully to modify her behavior? _____ .

    a. Reinforcement for remaining on the ward

    b. Electric shock therapy

    c. Extinction at times of entering the nurse's station

    d. Courteous explanation of why the behavior was inappropriate

---

Schedules of Reinforcement and Everyday Life

As you can imagine, many situations in our lives correspond closely to the formal intermittent schedules of reinforcement introduced in laboratories. A fixed interval schedule is perhaps the most common schedule by which man regulates the activities of other humans. It is interesting, also, that the *FI* schedule is perhaps the least efficient in establishing and controlling behavior. If you are on a salary, you are typically reinforced once a month or once a week for emitting certain kinds of behaviors during the interval. A child in school is typically reinforced with a report card each six weeks or eight weeks, and the hard working college student is reinforced with a grade at the end of a semester. The overall emission of appropriate responses tends to be slow, with considerable speeding up shortly before the end of each fixed interval.

    Variable interval schedules are not frequent for human beings. Perhaps the easiest example to visualize is that of the teacher who attempts to regulate study behavior by occasionally springing pop quizzes. You will recall that scalloping does not occur in a *VI* schedule as it does in *FI*. Therefore, instead of waiting until the night before the examination, the student studies more consistently.

The fixed ratio schedule is much better for maintaining high rates of responding than are interval schedules. The fixed ratio schedule was introduced into industry some decades ago in the form of "piecework," where an individual received a certain amount of money for a standard number of items processed on a production line. A clear example of the operation of piecework—an *FR* schedule—is in a factory where young ladies on an assembly line receive $1.30 for each hundred electronic tubes they box. Each sits at her own conveyer belt, which she may regulate with a foot feed. If she works faster, she obviously can make more money than if she works slowly. The result is a high rate of work throughout the day. Still, there is indication of some speed-up—scalloping—when the young lady perceives the end of the series of a hundred approaching.

Situations in which variable ratio schedules operate are rare in terms of jobs, but they occur frequently in other contexts. Whenever you can say that the more frequently you try to do something, the more often, in an absolute sense, you succeed, the reinforcers are probably on a *VR* schedule. An example is your golf game. Men who take up the game of golf are largely reinforced, in the early stages, by social activity during the golf game; that is, they enjoy each other's company. Later, however, as their skills develop, much of the reinforcement for playing golf is provided by the quality of the game they play. At that point you may see a man playing golf alone, with his behavior maintained by his scores. But not all golf games are good, and in fact probably the greater portion are somewhat disappointing. So, we could say that a man is actually reinforced for playing golf by the good scores he occasionally makes. And, the more often he plays, the more frequently he will achieve a good score.

In overview, let us examine how one would go about identifying the schedule involved in a given activity. First, is the schedule *crf*? That is, is every single act of a given class reinforced? If not, it is one of the four intermittent schedules. The second step is to differentiate between *FI* and *VI* on the one hand versus *FR* and *VR* on the other. One asks, if I enact the response more often, will there then be more occasions on which I am reinforced? If so, the schedule is ratio. If not, it is interval. Once the choices are thus narrowed, the decision between fixed and variable is relatively simple.

C 9.14.   *Schedules of reinforcement: Identification of examples.*

If you get a weekly salary check you are on _____ schedule of reinforcement.

    a. an *FI*   b. an *FR*   c. a *VI*   d. a *VR*

If you work a production line and get 50 cents for every 125 items you pack into packing boxes, you are on _____ (use abbreviation) schedule.

A man who goes golfing is occasionally reinforced by having a "good round." This type of reinforcement

comes on _____ schedule.

You have probably seen people press the button for an automatic elevator; then, when it does not

appear soon they press the button again, which actually gains nothing. The elevator's arrival is

the reinforcer. Such behavior is reinforced on _____ schedule.

Gambling at poker (or almost any form of gambling for that matter) is reinforced on _____

schedule.

It would be difficult to overstate the effect of schedules of reinforcement upon the developing response pattern. Schedules of reinforcement are often not considered to be particularly exciting study material by some students and even some psychologists. Still, it is usually quite impressive to the student when he visits a laboratory and watches animals trained on multiple schedules. For example, an animal may have learned to respond on a *VI* schedule when a chamber light is turned off and respond on a *VR* schedule when the light is turned on. The viewer, watching a "lazy" animal drag itself through a series of slow, tired-appearing responses, is amazed when the light goes on and suddenly the animal is transformed into an enterprising, vigorous worker. We are fond of applying labels to people that imply fixed, internal motivational processes, when actually much behavior is almost totally dependent upon one's reinforcement history, including the type of schedule experienced during prior reinforcement.

The Partial Reinforcement Effect

After a behavior has been maintained on an intermittent (or partial) schedule, there is an interesting effect on any subsequent attempts at extinction. We can contrast the extinction curves of two organisms. Let us say that a target behavior of one organism has been developed and maintained on a *crf* schedule. Another individual has received the same number of total reinforcers for the same behavior, but after a brief initial development of the behavior on a *crf* schedule, the second individual was gradually phased into a fairly lean intermittent schedule. Then, let us initiate extinction trials. The two organisms, in adjacent chambers, get no more reinforcements for their emitted responses. We see, initially, that both individuals respond fairly rapidly in their efforts to secure continuing reinforcers. Quickly, however, the first individual who was previously reinforced on a *crf* schedule slows and finally stops responding completely. Meanwhile, the other individual maintains a fairly steady rate of responding and slows much more gradually. The dependent variable in this case is the number of responses emitted during extinction before responding ceases.

Not only is there a simple function holding between the extinction of the response on the one hand and the fact of continuous versus intermittent reinforcement on the other, but there is also a quality of the partial reinforcement effect that is due to the type and value of the particular intermittent schedule involved. Within all but extreme values of interval and ratio schedules we can say that the *leaner the schedule during conditioning,* the *more resistant to extinction* the response becomes. This is a rather complex topic, influenced by other factors, but its importance may be appreciated by the fact that one researcher reinforced a pigeon for pecking at a disc, and by a complex process of thinning out the reinforcers established a response strength that was maintained during almost two years of non-reinforcement. That is, at a given point no further reinforcement was delivered, yet the bird pecked at the disc at a fairly regular rate each day for over 700 days before finally ceasing.

What does this tell us in terms of how we should go about reinforcing people for their desirable behaviors? If you reward a child with praise and attention each and every time he does something properly, then suddenly cease doing this, the child may rather quickly cease that behavior. On the other hand, if you gradually thin out reinforcement into an intermittent schedule, first adopting something analogous to a *VR2* schedule, then *VR3, VR4,* and so on over several days or weeks, you see no significant decrease in the rate of responding. Moreover, if you later give up reinforcement altogether, the organism will go on responding for a considerable length of time without further reinforcement. Of course, it is a lucky thing that in our social environment other people frequently pick up where mothers leave off in training individuals. In many universities proper social patterns are maintained through social reinforcement by fraternity brothers. Sometimes a young man may have his table manners adjusted by his fiancée, and many business organizations stimulate a constant awareness on the part of the young executive that others in the organization are "monitoring" him, reinforcing not only good job performance but particular social interaction patterns.

C 9.15.   *The partial reinforcement effect.*

The partial reinforcement effect is the effect that a particular _____ has upon the dependent variable.

   a. schedule of reinforcement during conditioning   b. extinction program

The dependent variable, where the partial reinforcement effect is concerned, is the _____ .

   a. number of responses emitted during extinction before responding ceases

   b. amount of time involved in extinguishing a response

   c. schedule of reinforcement

Which would be the more readily extinguished?

   1. Behavior that has been reinforced 20 times on _____ .

        a. a *crf* schedule   b. a *VR5* schedule

   2. Behavior that has been reinforced on _____ .

        a. an *FR5* schedule   b. an *FR25* schedule

A Backward Glance: The Partial Reinforcement
Effect in Classical Conditioning

Up to this point we have discussed the partial reinforcement effect in terms of operant patterns. It is relevant, however, that the same type of phenomenon takes place with classically conditioned behavior. That is, when the CS is only *occasionally* paired with the UCS, often being experienced by itself, the CR is slower to develop; but, once developed, it shows a stubborn resistance to extinction. Let us suppose that a young man or woman is physically somewhat "homely." Young children are sometimes not reluctant to point out and make fun of the peculiarities of other children, and the individual may frequently have experienced a pairing of interpersonal relationships with members of the opposite sex on the one hand, and insults that result in hurt feelings on the other. After an emotional structure is developed as a conditioned response, let us say that the passing years remove a great deal of the apparent homeliness of the individual. Still, the individual may be quite sensitive to any indications that others may think that his appearance is peculiar. The occasional, though rare, rude remark made by another individual maintains a high level of emotional responsiveness to the general situation of interpersonal interactions. The rare unpleasant remarks create a very lean partial schedule of reinforcement. This practically insures that the anxiety associated with social interactions will continue for years to come.

The Relative Strengths of Positive and Negative Reinforcement

In our discussion of motivation in Chapter 7, we made the point that *aversive drive* states, through the high and intermediate ranges, tend to be stronger than high and intermediate levels of *appetitive drive* states. One of the most important functional relationships in operant conditioning is the relationship of the degree of conditioning to the magnitude of reinforcement. We can compare the amount of reinforcement represented in the satisfaction of an appetitive drive with the amount of reinforcement in the satisfaction of an aversive drive. If aversive drives, in general, *are* stronger than appetitive ones, it follows that, generally speaking, schedules of negative reinforcement should be stronger than schedules of positive reinforcement.

Let us imagine that we have a rat in a *T*-maze. He wanders up the maze, turns left and receives nothing, but if he turns right, he finds food at the end of that arm of the maze. Let us say that we reinforce turning right many times in succession with food, while the animal is operating under a relatively strong hunger drive. Then we introduce a new factor. The entire length of the main runway, as well as the entire right arm of the crossbar will be electrified, and only the left arm will be a safety area. The animal will burst out of the electrified start box and may turn right at the end of the runway, but the shock will not cease. The animal will dash about, and eventually enter the left arm of the runway—a behavior that is negatively reinforced by shock termination. Let us say that we have run the animal twice under such circumstances. We will find, as a result, that just two negative reinforcements for going into the left arm of the maze more than offset perhaps 20 or 25 earlier positive reinforcements for entering the right arm.

What can we make of all this? We believe that the phenomenon of negative reinforcement underlies the developement of our strongest (most stubborn) habits. When we are concerned with a behavior that seems very resistant to change, it is quite possible that its strength is due to negative reinforcement. We shall discuss this more fully in a subsequent chapter.

C 9.16.   *The relative strengths of positive and negative reinforcement.*

In a general sense the strongest motivation through reinforcement history would be in those cases

where an organism has behaved a certain way because _____ .

  a. of the rewards for doing so   b. of what would happen if it did *not* do so

Relatively speaking, - - - reinforcement is more powerful than - - - reinforcement. _____ .

  a. positive/negative   b. negative/positive

PUNISHMENT: FUNCTIONAL RELATIONSHIPS

Aversive stimuli are frequently used in ways other than those leading to negative reinforcement through stimulus removal. One of man's oldest techniques for controlling the behavior of children, animals, and other men is through the contingent *application* of aversive stimuli. Instead of a behavior resulting in the termination of an aversive stimulus, it causes the onset of an aversive stimulus. This is called *punishment*. While negative reinforcement causes the rate of behavior to increase, punishment causes the associated behavior to decrease, and we call this phenomenon *suppression*.

A variety of dangers accompanies the use of punishment in behavioral control. The major one of these lies in the development of simultaneous classically conditioned emotional patterns, with subsequent avoidance of stimuli associated with the punisher. Let us illustrate this with an example from the classroom. If you were taking a mathematics course and the teacher used a great deal of punishment—punishing you for failure to do your homework, ridiculing you for your performance on examinations, and so forth—very soon a conditioned pattern would emerge. That teacher, math, math books, and even that classroom would all become associated with punishment through classical conditioning. All of these stimuli would begin to cause emotional escape orientations. In later years we would see you going to college, being upset when confronted with math requirements, and being scared to death about getting involved in math courses. It is no wonder that, in a survey of college students concerning their academic aversions, the classes named most often as being regarded with the least anticipation and the ones most anxiety-producing to freshmen were math, foreign language, and physical education. And in no other classes in the public schools are the opportunities so numerous for the humiliation of students. In math, the student goes to the blackboard to publicly work problems, in a gym class he must participate in physical tests before an audience of his peers, and in foreign language courses he must "rise and translate." For some students this leaves an enormous emotional residual.

The second, but less problematic, difficulty with the use of punishment results from an interesting phenomenon involving suppression. Many years ago B. F. Skinner analyzed the contrast between a program of extinction of a bar-press response verses a program in which the bar press was not only not reinforced, but was also mildly punished. He discovered that the addition of punishment led to lower response rates, but that the low-rate behavior prior to complete extinction was prolonged, so that about the same numbers of responses were emitted within each program. Skinner stated that the prior reinforcement had developed a certain level of *reflex reserve*—the amount of behavior that would be emitted before extinction (Skinner, 1938). The conclusion from this experiment was that mild punishment may make a behavior occur less frequently at the moment, but it will occur just about as many times in the long run before it disappears entirely. Also, we have noticed that if an organism is punished for a behavior in one situation but not in others, it will often cease that behavior in the punishing situation but continue it outside the situation.

One of the strong functional relationships in punishment is that the more intense the punishment, the more total is the suppression. Another important functional relationship parallels the similar relationship in reinforcement. That is, immediacy of punishment following a behavior is vital to the behavior's suppression. Many dog owners mistakenly believe that they are accomplishing something worthwhile when they drag the guilty pup back to a wet spot on the carpet that was made five minutes earlier. They point to the spot, slap the pup, and later wonder why their type of training does not produce results. The proper way to train the animal is to follow it around at all times for a few days (after it is old enough), so that its "mistakes" can be dealt with immediately—perhaps even at the very moment they are emitted.

Wm Hoest Enterprises, Inc.

C 9.17. *Functional relationships in punishment.*

Punishment is defined as where a behavior brings about the - - - of an - - - stimulus. _____ .

    a. onset/appetitive   b. termination/aversive   c. onset/aversive

The reduction in the rate of a punished behavior is called _____ .

    a. punishment   b. extinction   c. displacement   d. suppression

The main problem of using punishment is that _____ may develop.

    a. alternative pathways to the incentive

    b. certain emotional patterns relative to the entire punishment situation

    c. the individual may not understand the contingency relationship

The effectiveness of a punisher depends largely upon its _____ .

    a. intensity   b. immediacy   c. anticipation

    d. two of the first three are correct   e. all of the three are correct

The Use of Punishment in Behavior Modification

Earlier in this chapter we presented a short section on the use of operant reinforcement principles in dealing with actual cases of deviant behavior. At that point we illustrated the use of both positive reinforcement and extinction paradigms. We shall now illustrate the use of punishment in the suppression paradigm.

The suppression of undesirable behavior among mental patients through the use of a contingent aversive stimulus has been found to be quite effective. You should not envision orderlies strapping down screaming patients in a modern-day "torture chamber." Rather, the use of punishment usually involves very mild stimuli indeed. One such case, involving two female patients in a mental hospital, is described by Ayllon and Michael (1959). Both patients shared the characteristic of having to be spoon-fed by staff members. One, Janet, usually had to be forcefully taken to the dining hall each day, where she would permit a nurse to spoon-feed her. The other, Mary, made no resistance to the feeding schedule, but her original hospital admission was based on her refusal to eat and occasional statements that her food was poisoned.

The punishment in this case was food-spillage. It had been noted that both patients were quite clean and tidy in their dress habits, and took pride in the condition of their clothing. The nurses were told to begin each spoon-feeding in the regular manner, but to then begin to do it so carelessly that drops of food would begin to fall onto the patient's dress. It was emphasized that food-spillage should not be overdone, since it was not the intent to communicate to the patient that anyone was trying to be mean to her. In both cases, after a few spills the patients began self-feeding in "self-defense." Soon they spontaneously ate on their own during the entire meal, and both of the patients, who had been underweight, began to gain weight.

A paradigm that is very close to suppression is that of satiation. While suppression refers to the delivery of a contingent aversive stimulus upon the emission of some behavior, satiation is the delivery of a usually appetitive stimulus to the individual in such magnitude that it eventually becomes aversive.

Ayllon (1963) describes a woman who compulsively hoarded towels in her room on the ward of a mental hospital. The lady raided the shower room periodically, and was in the habit of keeping anywhere from 20 to 30 towels at a time in her room. This had the effect of interfering with the availability of towels to other patients on the ward at the times they sought showers. It was speculated that the high degree of personal attention involved in being approached by staff on this matter or by having the room "shaken down" one or two times a day to recover towels was maintaining the behavior.

Satiation began with various staff members taking a towel to the patient's room at intervals throughout the day and handing it to her without comment. No longer were any towels removed from her room, and meanwhile the other patients were provided with an unusually large supply in the shower room so that they would not reinforce the behavior through their attention to it.

The first week the patient was given an average of 7 towels a day, and by the third week this had increased to 60 towels a day. When the number of towels in her room reached 625, she was observed carrying stacks of them out of her room.

Ayllon supplies the following details: During the first two weeks of satiation treatment the woman was observed patting her cheeks with the towels, smiling, and apparently enjoying them. Later she was observed painstakingly folding and stacking the approximately six hundred towels in her room. At this point, when towels were brought to her, she told the nurses, "Don't give me no more towels. I've got enough." During the third week, she said, "Take them towels away. I can't sit here all night and fold towels." During the fourth and fifth weeks her plea was, "Get these dirty towels out of here." During the sixth week, while carrying a stack of towels from her room, she remarked to the nurse, "I can't drag any more of these towels, I just can't do it."

During the following year the patient's towel hoard or inventory was calculated, and the daily average number of towels in the patient's room was 1.5, a figure approximately that of other patients on the ward.

The cases described in this section and in the earlier section on operant reinforcement in behavior modification are rather simple in design, as they were intended mainly as demonstrations of the effectiveness of such procedures in controlling behavior—not as therapy leading to institutional discharge. The technology is advanced enough, however, to allow operant procedures to be carried out in extremely complex ways, and most residential mental hospitals at this time have at least one major behavior modification ward in operation.

Such bizarre behaviors as towel hoarding and having to be spoon-fed are naturally vital to control in terms of eventual discharge back into society. However, on behavior modification wards the emphases are usually upon reinforcement and extinction procedures involving more universal behaviors. There one usually finds selective reinforcement of such behaviors as cleaning and straightening the living area, personal cleanliness and hygiene, promptness to activities, and emitting "normal talk" rather than "sick talk." To the degree that such behaviors are the focus in diagnosing a patient as being mentally ill, with behavior modification the patient can quickly be "normalized."

PROGRESS CHECK 9.3

1. A person who gets paid once a month operates on what schedule of reinforcement? _____ .

    a. Continuous   b. Variable ratio   c. Fixed ratio   d. Fixed interval

2. Factory workers who are paid for each 20 pieces of work operate under which schedule of reinforcement? _____ .

    a. Continuous   b. Variable ratio   c. Fixed ratio   d. Fixed interval

3. Which animal is more likely to maintain responding during extinction trials? _____ .

    a. One trained on a continuous reinforcement schedule

    b. One trained on an intermittent schedule of reinforcement

4. According to the experiment with rats in a T-maze, which contingency seems to be more powerful? _____ .

    a. Positive reinforcement   b. Negative reinforcement

5. The application of aversive stimulation to control another's behavior is _____ .

    a. punishment   b. brutal   c. negative reinforcement   d. immoral

6. Which variable is important for punishment training to be effective? _____ .

    a. Immediacy of delivery   b. Weak punishment is best

    c. Strong punishment is more effective   d. a and c

MATCH: _____ 7. Spilling food on the outfit of a neat patient who will not eat.   A. Suppression paradigm

    B. Satiation paradigm

    _____ 8. Overwhelming a hoarding patient with hundreds of towels.

NOTE TO THE READER: The subject matter discussed in this chapter is expanded and amplified in Extension Chapter 9A, beginning on pages 594-95.

10

Social Processes

GROUPS AS INFLUENCERS
Types of Group Influences
Group Norms and Roles
The Degree of Group Influence on the Individual
Social Variables Directly Influencing Behavior
    Change
Primacy and Recency Effects in Direct Social
    Influence

ATTITUDES: OUR PERCEPTIONS OF OTHERS
Stereotypes and Prejudices
Measurement of Prejudice
    The Bogus Pipeline Procedure
Development of Attitudes
    Social Imitation
    Learning Theory
    Social Needs and Frustrations

THE PSYCHOLOGY OF ATTRACTION
Proximity and Familiarity
Approval of Others
Similarity
Attractiveness
Competence
Reciprocity
Fear and Affiliation

ALTRUISM
Hurting Behaviors

ATTRIBUTION THEORY
Factors Influencing Attribution: Characteristics
    of Observers
    Ego Needs and Personalities
    Age of Observer
    Group Influences
Factors Influencing Attribution: Characteristics
    of Actors
    Some Responses to Basic Actor
        Characteristics
    Friend or Foe?
    Perceived Intent

CONSISTENCY THEORIES
The Theory of Cognitive Dissonance
Balance Theory

BEHAVIOR WITHIN SMALL GROUPS
Static Roles
Dynamic Group Analysis

CONCLUSION

The ways in which people behave, both in observable interactions with others and in their covert (not outwardly visible) attitudes and opinions, are powerfully influenced by the other people in their environments. This chapter concerns the various ways in which people's behaviors are affected by the social groups of which they are a part, along with some of the current thinking in the field concerning how people develop attitudes and opinions relevant to other persons.

Prior to this time we have examined behaviors that have initiated with the various need states of the organism, supplemented by simple reinforcement patterns that may or may not be socially administered. If you pause and think for a moment, however, you will see that much of our moment-to-moment behavior is directly influenced by our participation as members of various groups, and it is this influence that makes up the area that we call social psychology.

Social psychology is so diverse, and possesses such a great number of approaches and specialty areas, that we can only present a sample in a single chapter. We will examine some of the direct interpersonal effects on our own behaviors. We then will consider some of the work on the development of attitudes toward others— the study of interpersonal attraction, and some influences on stereotypic attitudes. We will look at theoretical approaches to how people finalize their opinions in ways that are conclusive and do not leave a residual of tension and dissatisfaction, and we will conclude with a look at two approaches to the study of social interactions within groups. In Extension Chapter 10A, an opportunity is given to examine some totally different ways of looking at social interaction processes.

**GROUPS
AS INFLUENCERS**

At the broadest level we are all members of a culture and various smaller groups or subcultures. An individual may belong to a labor union, to the American Legion, to the Baptist church, and to three or four fairly well-defined social groups, the latter being groups of friends who get together to eat lunch, another group in the neighborhood that attends certain functions together, and so forth. Each one of these groups exercises its own effects upon the individual.

**Types of
Group Influences**

A significant part of one's social development originates within the family. Consider these diverse family influences on your own patterns of behavior. First come the early experiences of your parents, resulting in certain of their own parental and social attitudes. Parents' education influences their values and attitudes, and possibly their child-rearing concepts as well. Parents' urban versus rural, American versus foreign-born, and entrepreneurial versus bureaucratic backgrounds exert considerable influence over their attitudes and personalities.

Turning to the *current* family situation, the family has a certain social-class attribute. Relating to social class are various predictable attitudes, motivations, and expectations. The family's social class may dictate neighborhood to a considerable extent, and the neighborhood setting will possess a given delinquency index which may contain modeling influences, and the people in the area may possess certain ethnic or other subculture characteristics, reflecting specific value systems.

The family composition itself is a strong influence. A father being absent from the home gives the mother-child interaction a special developmental relevance; also the male child in such a situation may have sexual identification problems. A mother's absence from the home may have

Lee Lorenz. Reproduced by special permission of PLAYBOY Magazine; © 1971 by Playboy

"A word to the wise, Benson. People are asking why they don't see Old Glory on your bike."

powerful emotional effects on the child, particularly if the separation is perceived by the child as rejection. The child might possibly be separated from the rest of the family, resulting in social and emotional retardation of various sorts. The existence of siblings at certain ages is a strong influencing factor. Older siblings may be aggressive toward their younger brothers or sisters, particularly the individual next in sequence. It is also known that the mother's behavior toward the first-born child is more restrictive and coercive, and less consistent, than is her behavior toward later-born siblings.

We have presented all these possible influencing factors to give you an appreciation for the types and degrees of influence by the groups to which one belongs. Considering the various influences that derive directly or indirectly just from the family group, you can imagine the variety of influences that may come to bear upon the individual who possesses even an average number of multiple-group memberships.

Group Norms and Roles   By definition groups and subcultures share some common rules of behavior, which comprise the group's *norms*. The greatest influence that a group has over a member is to force conformity to the norms in the member's behavior.

Groups may differ in terms of their specific norms, the degree of latitude allowed a member for deviance, and what kinds of penalties are assessed against nonconformists. Children are likely to belong to a variety of fairly dynamic (changing) groups that strongly enforce the act of conforming, and in children's groups the penalties for nonconforming may be severe. By the time the individual is adult, even though many of the then current relevant groups may no longer have the power to invoke meaningful major sanctions for nonconformity, the individual is usually so well "trained" that his inclinations to change himself in order to fit in are strongly in evidence.

As an individual adjusts to the group's norms in order to fit in, he adopts a role relevant to the group. A *role* consists of a set of behaviors that are expected of a member of a given group. Frequently there are different kinds of roles to match different kinds of membership—some hierarchical, such as would differentiate the new member from the experienced members of a street-corner gang, and others which are functionally differentiated, such as the role of the mother versus the role of the father within a family group. The group's norms, interacting with such factors as the individual's status level within the group hierarchy or the individual's abilities, dictate the characteristics of his role.

Why do human beings subscribe to group norms and adopt roles inasmuch as many of the associated results seem to be coercive and sometimes even unpleasant? The answer is assumed by many to be the individual's insecurity in the face of a lack of knowledge of what to do. Norms and roles remove the insecurity by clearly informing us of what is expected of us in different situations. Subsequently we may have some difficulty in handling a role with precision, or even in learning all of its complexities, but at least there is some structure provided us, and we feel less tension as a result.

Obviously, we all occupy multiple roles in a normal society. Few of us have any difficulty in being responsible and effortful workers, concerned parents, generous and friendly neighbors, etc., all of which are complementary roles—that is, they do not conflict with one another. Of more interest, however, are *role conflicts,* which are frequent. If the conflict of two roles occurs within separate group-settings, the individual is faced with a fairly easy choice between two alternatives. Suppose, for example, that your role as an active member of a fundamentalist religious organization dictates that you actively oppose "strong drink," and while associating with church-member friends you carry out this role effectively. Subsequently you attend a social gathering of persons from your place of employment. Mixed drinks are being generously doled out, and you have a choice of two reactions. On the one hand, you can abandon your usual role by either carrying around a mixed drink without drinking it, or requesting a glass of ginger ale. On the other hand, you can act consistently with your first role and either leave as a protest or stay and attempt to convince the drinkers of the error of their ways. Which choice do you think is the better alternative?

Or, let us say that in your social group of college-student friends you carry out the role of a joker, a "don't give a damn about anything" type of person. One day, in Professor Granitejaw's class, you fall asleep with your chair tipped back against the wall, lose your balance and land, still seated in your chair, flat on your back on the floor. In the hallway later, your friends joke about the incident, and consistent with your role you, too, make light of it and even imply that it was done deliberately for the effect it would produce. You enter the professor's office by yourself. Your role now is that of a student relating to a professor in a sort of hierarchical relationship. Your choices are to either adjust and act out a conflicting role—that of the humble, ashamed student who will try hard not to ever disrupt class again—or you may be consistent with your first role, and wisecrack and be flippant with the professor as he inquires into your behavior.

It seems that one's personal welfare might be best served by flexible and occasionally conflicting occupancy of multiple roles. Life may be simpler if you arrange it so that few of your roles are so diametrically inconsistent; indeed, this might be an index of maturity or responsibility. Still, it is possible to encounter little difficulty so long as the role conflicts are at different times and in different places. Many individuals might act out one pattern of racial attitudes in the company of a group whose attitudes are generally liberal and progressive, and act out quite an opposite pattern when in the company of people who are known to be highly prejudiced. Black people, as well as white people, have this problem and sometimes radically adjust their behavior to the situation they are in and what is expected of them at such times. Neither of the alternatives offered to us at these times is appealing. We are forced either to be hypocritical to some degree if we act flexibly, or to become self-defeating in our alienation of other people if we don't.

Where our problems begin to become serious are in those situations when, within a single group and at a single point in time, we are faced with conflicting roles. An example of role conflict was that of a young father stopped by a police officer for speeding in a residential area. The father had just been exercising his role of paternal authority, criticizing and lecturing his children on matters of discipline, and then was forced to sit with his children as the audience while being lectured by the police officer.

In such a case as just described there is intense frustration. The individual usually walks a tightrope between two roles, tolerating the stress without totally committing himself to one role. The risk is that as a result of the frustration or fear in the conflict situation, he may pursue another tactic—abandonment of one role in favor of the other. In the example of the father stopped by a traffic officer, such behavior would take the form of (1) totally humbling himself in front of his children in attempting to avoid a traffic ticket, or (2) becoming abusive and aggressive toward the officer. The risks are psychological, involving image and status, in the first instance, and more immediately concrete in the second.

C 10.1. *Norms and roles.*

A subculture's or group's norms are shared _____ .

    a. roles   b. common rules of behavior   c. sanctions that are invoked as penalties

By the time an individual is adult it is highly likely that he _____ .

    a. has begun to resist changing himself just to fit into a group

    b. conforms out of fear of the sanctions that may be placed upon him

    c. conforms as a learned habit

The norms of a given group dictate the characteristics of an individual's _____ relative to that group.

    a. attitude   b. role

C 10.2. *Conflicting roles.*

Conflicting roles are likely to produce the least degree of difficulty if they _____ .

    a. occur within a single situation

    b. occur at different times and in different groups

The two choices offered an individual in role conflict in separate settings are to _____ .

    a. enact two roles simultaneously, or blend the two roles into one

    b. adjust to enacting each role at different times, or blend the two roles into one

    c. adjust to enacting each role at different times, or adhere to a single, fixed role

The two choices offered an individual in role conflict within a single setting are to _____ .

    a. abandon one role, or tolerate the stress without commitment

    b. abandon one role, or enact both roles simultaneously

    c. tolerate the stress without commitment, or enact both roles simultaneously

We have discussed role enactment largely so that you can see that the psychological makeup of the individual, as far as attitudes or behaviors are concerned, is changing constantly from situation to situation and is influenced by social groups from more than a single vantage point. Let us turn now to a consideration of the simple factor of group influence.

The Degree of Group Influence on the Individual

Earlier we made the point that in childhood we are trained to conform to the norms of the groups in which we hold membership, and that we are thereby influenced to conform in later life, even when the group does not hold the power to invoke major sanctions against nonconformity. Boiled down, this amounts to a statement that we are strongly influenced, while in the presence of others, to behave in ways that do not characterize us as being ''different.'' We will now discuss research that shows that even total strangers—individuals without power to invoke sanctions—can influence our behavior.

One of the early studies which has become classic in demonstrating the influence of group members upon the individual was performed by Asch (1951). He presented subjects with a series of drawn lines, and their task was to match the length of a given line with the appropriate one of a set of three other lines. Since the set of three was not aligned with the one to be compared, the task was not plainly obvious even though the length of the lines differed appreciably. Unknown to the subject in the experiment, the other ''subjects'' were in fact assistants in collaboration with the experimenter. The subject suddenly found that his (or her) answers in judging line length were in disagreement with everyone else's in the group. The order of response was arranged so that the subject would hear the unanimous decision by the others before being called upon for the response.

It is worth noting that, if anything, the group influence in this case should have been reasonably weak since the subject had never before seen the other people involved in the experiment and had no expectations of ever meeting them again. For this reason we would not predict that the group would strongly influence the subject's behavior. Yet, significantly, the subjects were highly controlled by the majority response of the others; 32 percent of the total judgments were in error but in accord with the rest of the group; in fact, one-third of the individual subjects used in the experiment conformed to the group over 50 percent of the time.

In Asch's research the face-to-face interaction of subjects was considered, at that time, to have been a vital influence. In a variation of the technique, Crutchfield (1955) used a system where, again, a subject saw supposed judgments of four others before giving his own response. However, in this case the other individuals were not present. Rather, the data had simply been written down, and the subject was told by the experimenter what the others' judgments had been. Again, it was found that group opinions strongly affected individual decisions.

It has been established that the power of group opinion over behaviors of individual members of groups varies as a function of the individuals' ages; small children are not as significantly influenced as are adolescents and adults by group opinion. As age progresses the strength of group standards is displayed in the reluctance of high-school-aged persons to dress in out-of-style clothes or wear a hair style not sanctioned by a large element of the school's population.

It is often assumed by the parents of teen-age individuals that the period of adolescence is almost alone in dictating such conformity. The parents may hardly be aware of how strongly their own behaviors are dictated by their groups—the style of clothing that the father wears to his office, where the mother does her shopping, and the image deliberately projected to neighbors concerning one's life-style.

C 10.3. *Group opinion as a social influence.*

Asch found that individuals were influenced in their _____ by the opinions of others.

   a. racial stereotypes   b. perceptual judgments of a physical dimension

Crutchfield's elaboration on Asch's work established that group opinion can influence individuals

even without _____ .

   a. clear knowledge of the group's reasons

   b. the physical presence of members of the group

   c. the group's having any power to invoke sanctions for nonconforming

It would seem that there is a generally _____ correlation between age on the one hand and the

degree to which one is influenced by group opinion on the other, within the age range of the

young child to the middle-aged adult.

   a. positive   b. negative

Social Variables Directly Influencing Behavior Change

We might arbitrarily divide social "influencers" into social situations in which there is an obvious effort to persuade or to change the individual (speeches, decision-making groups) and those situations where the influence is more subtle. Indirect influences would include modeling after certain individuals and social reinforcement delivered for conformity. Indirect influences are treated mainly in other chapters.

We have dealt with certain variables that exist within direct influence situations—age of subjects and pressures within role-conflict situations are two. Briefly we shall note here that there are other fairly obvious variables, including the amount of pressure being delivered by the group (Schachter, 1951) and the degrees of prestige and expert-status possessed by the communicator of information (Hovland & Janis, 1959). Less consistent (but still interesting) findings have been obtained in the study of the effects of credibility or trustworthiness of the communicator, the perceived intent to influence, the attractiveness of the communicator, and the similarity existing between the communicator and the subject.

Some of the variables just me॒   l be of considerable in-

NOT GUILTY BY PSYCHOLOGY

The young lawyer was brilliant in his closing arguments. Following his point-by-point review of the case against the defendant, he proceeded with a scathing attack on the evidence and testimony presented by the old defense attorney. He denounced the quality and credibility of the witnesses for the defense, and put in a few choice remarks to the effect that the old man must be desperate to call upon such weak witnesses. If not desperate, then maybe lacking in competence. It was midafternoon when the case for the prosecution was closed, and the judge asked the defense if it was ready to proceed. The old man asked for the case to be carried over until the following morning, pleading the fatigue of age and the hot weather. Though two hours of possible court time remained that afternoon, the judge granted the request and the case was carried over until the following morning.

In court the following day the old man rose swiftly to his feet. No longer did he appear weary and haggard. He began by thanking the jury for their close attention during the testimony. He singled out several jurors with piercing eyes as he recounted the panel's obvious interest and close attention to the presentations of visual evidence. He then turned to the prosecuting attorney and complimented him upon his excellent summary of his case. Whith great courtesy the old man addressed the prosecutor by his formal title (though he was fifty years younger), and even made a remark about the excellent background provided by the law school the prosecutor attended.

By this time the jury was totally convinced that the old man was a fine person, and they began to feel somewhat indignant that the prosecutor had gone so far out of his way to attack and seemingly make a fool of the old man. The old man reviewed a few of the details in his client's favor, and in concluding his summary he made a point of mentioning that his son, a young and successful lawyer from a large city elsewhere in the state, was sitting among the spectators in

terest to a trial lawyer who is interested in influencing a jury to his side of the testimony. If you tried you could build a hypothetical situation where each of the variables mentioned above could vary from one extreme to its opposite, and you could then easily envision the influence that each such variation would have on jury opinion.

Primacy and Recency Effects in Direct Social Influence

One of the more interesting aspects of psychology is that so often we can see that a grandma's law appears to hold true in the light of actual data. The grandma's law in this case is that "first impressions are lasting." It would appear that this is so, although the question is not just as simple as that.

The manner in which the *primacy effect* is studied generally is as follows: Subjects judge some issue or individual; for example, some hypothe courtroom.

After the judge gave his instructions to the jury, they retired to the jury room. One of the things uppermost on their minds was the fact that the old man had been such a gentleman, while the prosecutor had seemed vicious and vindictive in contrast. Was it possible that the defendant was innocent? Would this old man have so passionately represented a person he knew did not deserve his efforts? It also seemed outrageous to recall how the prosecutor had worded his attack on the integrity of the defense witnesses. He had told the jury they should disregard certain people's testimony as being unreliable. Maybe the prosecutor was trying to do their thinking for them—maybe he had the same disparaging attitude toward the jury as he had shown toward the old man and his client. They reflected how the old man's son would be sitting in the courtroom. After the hostile attack by the prosecutor, did they wish to be the instrument which would cause the son to feel disappointment in his own father? How sad that this fine old man might be even further damaged in front of his son.

In the jury room there was little need for discussion of the facts, and no need at all for a second ballot. The unanimous verdict on the first ballot was not guilty.

In a follow-up study by a social scientist it was determined that 11 of the 12 jurors had been reasonably convinced of the defendant's guilt following the prosecutor's summary, and although no new evidence or logical analysis of the testimony had been presented by the defense attorney the following day, their not guilty verdict was reached immediately. Obviously the jury's verdict had been determined mainly by factors completely separate from the evidence itself. How would a psychologist view this situation?

thetical description of an individual, or videotaped recording of his performance, is observed by subjects. Usually there are two stages to the observation. In one stage a very positive and effective image of the individual is projected, while in the other stage the individual is not nearly so positive or effective. One group of subjects is exposed to the positive impression first, followed by the negative; the second group of subjects is exposed to the negative impression first, followed by the positive.

In one experiment (Jones, Rock, Shaven, Goethals, & Ward, 1968), subjects watched a student attempt (this was staged) to solve a series of difficult problems, and were then asked to assess that student's intelligence. The design of the experiment called for the student to solve exactly 50 percent of the total number (30) of problems. Half of the subjects watched the student have his successes closely bunched at the beginning of the series, while the others observed the student being more successful toward the end of the series. A very strong primacy effect was observed. Where the individual had done his good work at the beginning of the series, he was almost invariably judged to be more intelligent, and when asked to recall how many of the 30 problems the student had solved, those subjects who had seen early success gave an average estimate that the student had solved 20.6 of the 30 problems. Subjects who had seen the successes bunched toward the end of the series estimated an average of 12.5 successes on the 30 problems, even though there was no actual difference in degree of success between the two conditions.

The primacy effect extends to attitudes as well as abilities, and the same type of procedure can be used in research portraying a "friendly-unfriendly" pair of presentations, a "good-bad" pair of presentations, and so forth. It is typically found that the first impression is indeed lasting.

Other research has occasionally demonstrated a phenomenon termed the *recency effect*. The recency effect typically is strongest in more firmly established situations. That is, if the viewer has had considerable experience with the properties of the individual being viewed, the most vivid effects are those made by the most recent actions of or information about the individual.

What are the reasons for the primacy effect? It has been speculated for some time, and by different theorists, that human beings have a need to know, to understand, and to not be ignorant of what is going on around them. When we observe the behavior of an individual and have no existing notion of his or her attributes, a void exists that needs to be filled. We then are very attentive, we respond quickly and form initial impressions from early information, and rapidly develop an opinion regarding the given individual.

Once our information base is fairly well formed, we no longer carefully evaluate individual items of information. Thus the recency effect is not actually easy to bring about. When it does occur, it is probably because extremely vivid elements of information, reflecting behaviors in great contrast to what we have earlier been led to expect from an individual, have come to our attention. The interpretation of this phenomenon is that it is essentially perceptual—contrast alone makes the new impression vivid and noticeable. It is not irrelevant to point out that this perhaps is to account for the degree of severity with which the public greets violations of public trust in previously respected elected public officials.

Primacy and recency effects are strongly involved in the formulation of judgments of people. Consider for example the admission procedures for graduate students applying to universities, or procedures relative to becoming employed in business or industry. If the persons doing the evaluations do not know you, it is very likely that their first impressions will be their strongest, most vivid impressions of you as a candidate. If the first thing they see concerning you is a glowing letter of recommendation, they then may be less influenced later by seeing "spotty" data in your academic transcript. And, of course, the reverse sequence of events may occur.

Or consider the powerful potential of the recency effect in generating certain human reactions. Following a lifetime with a satisfactory interpersonal relationship, there might be a change in the behavior of a husband due to some physical condition. This might result in changes of mood and temper. The recency effect gives to the wife an exaggerated impression of these behaviors, and it is often only through the exercise of the strongest forms of other social controls that "offended spouses" do not follow their strong inclinations to retaliate. Businesses and industries, too, have been known to dismiss veteran employees of good standing due to the sudden development of undesirable behavior patterns. The individuals making these decisions are responding with what appears to be a natural human tendency—the strong effect of recent information on the determination of attitude.

C 10.4. *Primacy and recency effects in social influence.*

The primacy effect might best be exemplified in the slogan _____ .

    a. the early bird gets the worm   b. first impressions are lasting

    c. the first person never gets all the glory   d. he who laughs last laughs loudest

The _____ effect seems to be most evident in established situations where the judging individual is very familiar with the person or incident being evaluated.

    a. primacy   b. recency

The primacy effect has been explained at least partly on the basis of the observing individual's _____ .

    a. strong need to know, to understand, and to not be ignorant

    b. impulsiveness or immaturity

    c. lack of other information with which to contrast the observed behavior

The recency effect has been explained at least partly on the basis of the observing individual's _____ .

    a. strong need to know, to understand, and to not be ignorant

    b. sense of contrast between the old information and the new

    c. greater retained memory for recently-occurring events

PROGRESS CHECK   10.1

1. Groups and subcultures share some common rules of behavior which are _____ .

    a. roles   b. sanctions that are invoked as penalties   c. norms

2. Fred is looked upon by his friends at school as someone who doesn't let anyone push him around. One day in class his teacher asks him to make a public apology to one of his classmates. Which of the following choices does Fred have in this situation? _____ or _____ .

    a. Abandon one role in favor of a commitment to the other

    b. Blend the two roles into one

    c. Adjust to enacting both roles at different times

    d. Tolerate the stress, going through the motions of minimal compliance

3. Your mother strongly disapproves of your associating with Bill because he has a reputation of being "fast" with women. While walking back from school, Bill asks you if you would like to go for a ride. Which of the following choices do you have in this situation? _____ or _____ .

    a. Blend the two roles into one   b. Abandon the social role and go home immediately

    c. Adjust to enacting both roles at different times   d. Tolerate the stress without commitment

4. What did Asch's research indicate about group opinion as a social influence? _____ .

    a. The amount of social influence is directly correlated with the degree of familiarity among the individuals in the group

    b. There will be a greater degree of social influence if there is an expectation that the individuals in the group will meet each other again

    c. Even if there are no expectations of meeting the individuals in a group again and there is no familiarity among the members, there still will be a great degree of social influence

5. Crutchfield's research suggests that the crucial variable in group influence affecting an individual's decision is _____ .

    a. the physical presence of members of the group

    b. clear knowledge of the group's reasons

    c. knowledge of the group's opinion

6. Which of the following individuals would *least* likely be influenced by group opinion? _____ .

    a. A young child   b. An adolescent   c. An adult

7. Which of the following examples pertain to the primacy effect? _____ . Which pertain to the recency effect? _____ .

    a. First impressions are lasting

    b. An observing individual's strong need to know, to understand, and to not be ignorant

    c. A public official who has done a good job in office is discovered taking payoffs from an oil company. You think he should be sent to prison for it

d. Evident in established situations where the judging individual is familiar with the person being evaluated

e. A graduate school receives outstanding letters of recommendation for a student. Later they receive the student's transcript with good but not excellent grades indicated. The evaluator decides the candidate should be accepted

f. You are very fond of your teacher. One day she unjustly accuses you of being involved in vandalism. You decide never to take another class from her

---

ATTITUDES: OUR PERCEPTIONS OF OTHERS

The ways in which we perceive other people are influenced by a wide variety of factors. Elsewhere we present a fairly elaborate viewpoint of how the processes of classical and operant conditioning come into play in generating initial attitudes. Briefly, we tend to think positively toward an individual whose presence (or, possibly, image) is associated with pleasant, favorable occurrences, and we tend to think negatively regarding an individual whose presence has been characterized by unpleasantness. Beyond this, we are reinforced by our families and friends for demonstrating attitudes and beliefs that are consistent with their own, and we sometimes come into strong disfavor and suffer social abuse when our attitudes are highly deviant from those upon whom we depend for our social reinforcers.

In this section we shall consider a number of other influences which, research has shown, bear upon our basic attitudes toward other people.

Stereotypes and Prejudices

Many people respond in fixed, predetermined ways to a variety of classes of stimuli. It may never have occurred to you that stereotypes are sometimes accurate, but whether accurate or inaccurate, many stereotypes serve as a major hindrance to effective interpersonal and intercultural relationships.

Some stereotypes are positive. Many individuals view certain national groups very favorably, and admire their most outstanding "characteristics." There is probably not a great deal of harm done if one wishes to assume that the German "people" are industrious and scientific, or that the American is resourceful and ambitious, whether or not these stereotypes are generally accurate. What is distressing, however, is that many individuals are willing to assume that certain negative stereotypes are true—that black people are lazy, Polish are stupid, Japanese are treacherous, Jews are greedy, Irish tend to drink and brawl, etc. What is even worse, in the case of negative stereotypes, there is a tendency for people holding these views to assume that *every single individual* from the target group possesses these characteristics.

It is worth noting that when people already hold negative stereotypic views of a given group, increasing familiarity with individuals from that group does *not* automatically lead to decreased dislike. This is not surprising, since the individuals concerned are very likely to act out their dislike for each other, and the negative feelings on both sides will then be made even stronger.

The development of negative stereotypic thinking is a much more pervasive characteristic than is generally supposed. For example, we may initially think solely of a stereotype, with accompanying prejudice, that exists among whites in this country toward blacks. Some who have had certain experiences may also conceive of an existing degree of prejudice toward Jews in this country and toward Mexican-Americans in the southwestern part of the nation. What we sometimes do not see so vividly is that stereotypes and prejudices are much broader. The Protestant mother who would hate for her son to marry a Catholic girl, because of "all those children they would have" illustrates a very common stereotype and prejudice. Feelings of blacks toward whites frequently involve stereotypes, as do the feelings of many in the general population toward individuals on welfare, and toward social activists involved in organized demonstrations. And what else but stereotypic attitudes and prejudice are the feelings of a very large percentage of individuals outside the deep South toward white people in the deep South area, all of whom may be perceived as being aggressive bigots?

C 10.5. *Stereotypes and prejudice.*

There is a pronounced tendency for persons to believe that every individual in the target group possesses certain stereotyped characteristics when that stereotype is essentially _____ .

a. positive   b. negative

Stereotypes are _____ .

a. unfair, reflecting false attributes

b. sometimes true and sometimes false in relation to attributes

Measurement of Prejudice   A variety of means exists by which to systematically measure prejudice. You can readily see that measuring differences in degrees of or changes in levels of prejudice calls for quantifiable means that do not exist simply through hearing how an individual talks about some target group.

One technique is the Bogardus Social Distance Scale. Using individuals of any target group as the hypothetical topic, subjects are asked whether they would willingly engage in the following general activities:

1. Would marry an individual.
2. Would have as regular friends.

3. Would work beside in an office.
4. Would have several families in my neighborhood.
5. Would have merely as speaking acquaintances.
6. Would attempt to have them live outside my immediate neighborhood.
7. Would attempt to have them live outside my country.

A different sort of measure of prejudice comes from the Thurstone scale (1931). A number of statements specifically relating to black people were developed, and each was rated by a group of judges for its degree of prejudice. A modification of the items and their scale values follows:

4.9   I am not at all interested in how the Negro rates socially.
7.6   Under no circumstances should Negro children be allowed to attend the same schools as white children.
0.4   Give the Negro time. Within the next 50 years he will astonish you.
6.0   The Negro should have freedom but should never be treated as the equal of the white man.
0.0   I believe that the Negro deserves the same social status as the white man.
0.7   Give the Negro a high position in society and he will show himself equal to it.
5.6   I think the colored race should hold a somewhat lower social position than the white race.
0.0   The Negro should be considered as equal to the white man and be given the white man's advantages.
3.8   The courts are far more unfair to the Negro than the real differences between the races justify.
8.6   Negroes should not be allowed to associate with white people in any way.
0.7   The white and black races should enjoy the same privileges and protections.
4.8   The Negro problem will settle itself without our worrying about it.
9.4   The Negro should be considered in the lowest class of human beings.
0.3   By nature the Negro and the white man are equal.
2.6   The Negro is perfectly capable of taking care of himself if the white man would only let him alone.

In order to complete the Thurstone-type scale, the subject places a check mark in front of those items with which he agrees and an X in front of those items with which he disagrees. The checked (agreed upon) items are then taken by themselves and averaged. Why not try this scale yourself? Compute the mean of the scale values of items you check as agreed with. For comparative purposes the scale was administered to 100 Illinois State University freshmen in 1975; their mean was 1.19 with a standard deviation calculated at 0.17.

Still another method of calculating attitudes, and one which has qualitative as well as quantitative dimensions, is the *semantic differential scale*. Such a typical scale is presented in Table 10.1. The subject evaluates an organization, a person, a group, and so forth along various dimensions, circling one number on each line. A line can then be drawn reflecting the median points on each dimension.

Table 10.1

Activity scales:									
A. Active	8	7	6	5	4	3	2	1	Passive
B. Sharp	8	7	6	5	4	3	2	1	Dull
C. Fast	8	7	6	5	4	3	2	1	Slow
Potency scales:									
D. Strong	8	7	6	5	4	3	2	1	Weak
E. Large	8	7	6	5	4	3	2	1	Small
F. Heavy	8	7	6	5	4	3	2	1	Light
Judicable qualities:									
G. Good	8	7	6	5	4	3	2	1	Bad
H. Clean	8	7	6	5	4	3	2	1	Dirty
I. Pleasant	8	7	6	5	4	3	2	1	Unpleasant
J. Beautiful	8	7	6	5	4	3	2	1	Ugly
K. Sacred	8	7	6	5	4	3	2	1	Profane

The Bogus Pipeline Procedure

There are many psychologists who have begun to recognize that individuals who react one way on questionnaires and attitude surveys sometimes act in other ways where actual behavior is concerned. One of the early expressions of interest in this phenomenon came when researchers took subjects aside after their participation in attitude surveys, asking them, "Look, give me a candid report of what you *really* feel about these people—give me your gut reaction." Sometimes this method gained modified reports, and sometimes not.

More recently some psychologists have used "behavioroid" measures. Rather than true behavioral measures, psychologists report on subjects' responses where those subjects have been led to believe that they will be committed to some form of consequence consistent with their response pattern (Aronson & Carlsmith, 1969). If a subject is asked what his attitude is toward individuals of certain ethnic or subcultural groups, and that subject believes that a tolerant, accepting attitude may then lead to being housed with a representative of these groups as a dormitory roommate, the report of the subject tends sometimes to be modified.

A technique of recent research interest is the bogus pipeline method (Jones & Sigall, 1971). Researchers became interested in knowing what the responses of subjects would be if they believed that their true feelings were being monitored by sensitive physiological recording equipment, similar to the modern lie detector. In advance of their participation the subjects were allowed to see how high the needle swung at various times when an assistant to the researcher submitted to a "test" by equipment. Then, during their own participation, the subjects were first asked to estimate how high the needle would swing for their own response to various stimulus questions prior to their "testing." The whole procedure was set up to appear as a pipeline revealing the subjects' true feelings, but the assumption of equipment sensitivity and performance was bogus, hence, the term "bogus pipeline."

Subjects attached to the equipment, having been told that the equipment would be infallible in detecting their true feelings, seemed to be more truthful. There are several explanations of why this occurred. One of these holds that the individual is less reluctant to report prejudiced feelings in coincidence with presumed physiological data than to report on a standard questionnaire how one thinks about a group of people. The former measure seems more basic and involuntary, while the latter seems to subjects to be more deliberate, intellectual, and indicative of one's true moral/ethical makeup. Another interpretation is that to most subjects it would be less aversive to be revealed first by self-report and then by a machine to be somewhat prejudiced, than it would be for them to project a pretense of tolerance and then be revealed as somewhat of a bigot. Faced with such an alternative, the subjects tend to tell the truth.

No current measures of attitudes are perfect. Even with the bogus pipeline technique it is quite likely that deep-seated emotional feelings, of which the subject is not consciously aware, would not be revealed. It is also possible that a wide variety of reasons exist why individual subjects may project an invalid pattern in a bogus pipeline experiment—from how accurately they feel the equipment will operate, to the personal relevance of the "audience."

C 10.6. *Measurement of prejudice.*

A device that asks whether you would be willing to have members of a target group live in your

neighborhood, work with you on the job, and so forth, is the _____ .

a. Thurstone scale   b. semantic differential   c. Bogardus social distance scale

A device that asks you to agree or disagree with a number of statements about a target group, each of

which has a scaled "prejudice value," is the _____ .

a. Thurstone scale   b. semantic differential   c. Bogardus social distance scale

If you were to evaluate a presidential candidate or a group such as "the Japanese" on a scale of

dimensions such as "strong," "active," "clean," etc., this would be the _____ .

a. Thurstone scale   b. semantic differential   c. Bogardus social distance scale

A measure of attitude where the subject is kept "honest" by the belief that his physiological indices

will show if he is lying is the _____ .

a. semantic differential   b. Thurstone scale   c. bogus pipeline technique

Development of Attitudes

There are several theories concerning the development of and subsequent modification of attitudes in human beings. In this section we shall examine a few of these points of view. While each point of view has its advocates who would claim that the position they espouse is solely to account for developed attitudes, the truth is probably a compromise. It is likely that all of the points of view hold true at one time or another and to one extent or another. There is evidence to support the proposition that each of the influences which we shall discuss does indeed affect the development or modification of attitudes.

Social Imitation   There is an abundant literature, some of it several decades old, that establishes the powerful influence of imitative models upon developing attitudes. One research finding is that the majority of college-age students have the same view on political affiliation as do their parents. Most parents whose political orientation is toward the Democratic party seem to have children whose orientations are basically Democratic, and the same finding holds for other political orientations.

It is also evident that one of the strongest influences upon the developing attitudes of an individual is the basic value system of those persons with whom the individual associates. These factors are discussed in Extension Chapter 9A.

Learning Theory   The learning approach holds that attitudes reflect the reinforcement of statements of opinion. Prior to any firm development of a complex attitudinal system, it is likely that individuals discuss issues and at various times experience shifts or changes in their transient points of view. At such times the individual's social group may socially reinforce, fail to reinforce, or even punish certain expressions. Those expressions that are reinforced tend to become strengthened. To the extent that these expressions are consistent with the individual's actual behavior, we say that an *attitude* has developed.

Research indicates that simply approving of certain kinds of statements made by an individual can systematically modify that individual's attitudinal position. One of the main concerns with the practical use of this method to change attitudes in social situations is that it may take a considerable amount of time and attention devoted to a single individual if we simply sit and wait for the occasional expression of a "desirable" attitude to reinforce.

Therefore it was of interest when one researcher (Scott, 1957) decided to actually dictate an attitude to the subject, a position which was out of character for that subject, and then attempt to reinforce statements consistent with that position. The research was carried out in a debate context. There was to be a pro and a con side of the debate, and following assessment of the subjects' positions on the issue, certain subjects were assigned to the point of view in contradiction to their actual beliefs. It was found that a powerful influence over attitude could be achieved by rewarding a positional statement through praise. Under this procedure, an individual carefully prepares arguments supporting a position that he, himself, is opposed to, and then wins the debate. In such circumstances it is found that the subject changes his attitudes dramatically in a direction consistent with the point of view he argued for. Unrewarded debaters (losers) did not show such a shift of attitudes.

Another model of learning, that of classical conditioning, is evident in attitude development and modification. There is research to suggest that the simple pairing of appetitive stimuli with stimuli which generate images of a certain topic will systematically increase feelings of liking toward that topic area. Conversely, pairing aversive stimuli with stimuli which bring up images of a topic will result in a developing aversion to that topic area. There have been a number of experiments in this general field, and the technique has been found to be so effective that it has been adopted for clinical use in modifying extreme attitudes such as are found in phobic reactions.

This method also has been used to decrease undesirable appetitive orientations toward certain objects or topics (certain sexual deviations, for example). One manner in which this has been done in clinical settings is to have the individual imagine certain stimulus objects or situations, then he is asked to quickly think about developing consequences that may be humiliating, hurtful, or personally disgusting. These latter imaginative stimuli are usually delivered as forcefully and vividly as possible, so as to generate powerful emotions in the subject. Under such circumstances the individual's attitudes concerning the topic area are usually visibly modified.

Social Needs and Frustrations One approach to attitude theory holds that individuals have a need to feel important. That is, when persons are humiliated or feel inferior, this triggers a sharp and sudden need to find someone who is lower or inferior. This approach derives partly from the common observation that prejudice against blacks is more evident in the lower than in the middle socioeconomic class of white society.

Related to the socioeconomic class correlation just mentioned is a notion that prejudice derives from fear. Advocates of this position feel that lower socioeconomic class whites have the most to fear from blacks' entry into their job areas and may experience greater economic and physical threat from blacks' entry into previously all-white residential areas. Consistent with such arguments is a common observation that the intensity of racial prejudice seems closely related to the relative proportion of the total population represented by members of the target group. Where there are fewer of a certain group, there is typically (not always) less prejudice.

Another theory ties prejudice, and violent acts in particular, to frustrations experienced by the prejudiced group. One study of statistical data from the past showed that the yearly numbers of lynchings of blacks in the deep South from 1875 to around the turn of the century was closely tied to years when cotton prices were depressed. The anger and the frustration felt by whites was vented, the argument goes, on the most available group that was relatively helpless to defend itself.

These by no means exhaust the existing theories of why prejudiced attitudes exist. However, this presentation is adequate to demonstrate that it is by no means a clearly understood phenomenon.

C 10.7. *Attitude development and modification.*

One could probably modify undesirable prejudices of an individual by _____ .

    a. arranging that he spend a lot of time in the company of individuals with "desirable" attitudes

    b. arranging social reinforcement of any expressions of desirable attitudes

    c. (both answers are correct)

Prejudices seem to increase when _____ .

   a. people are economically frustrated

   b. one goes down the socioeconomic scale of white society

   c. target group individuals become more numerous in an area

   d. (all of the above are true)

PROGRESS CHECK   10.2

1. If a target group has a negative stereotype, there is a pronounced tendency to think everybody in that group possesses the stereotyped characteristics. _____ .

   a. True   b. False

2. Stereotypes are _____ .

   a. usually based on true attributes   b. unfair, reflecting false attributes

   c. usually based on a few individuals in the target group

   d. sometimes false and sometimes true

MATCH the following items with the appropriate scale.

_____ 3. You are asked if you would engage in the following activities with the Chinese:
Would marry; would attempt to have all Chinese live outside the country.

_____ 4. You are asked to answer whether you agree or disagree with the following items: I am not at all interested in how the Negro rates socially. Give the Negro time, within the next 50 years he will astonish you.

_____ 5. You are asked to evaluate a group such as the Vietnamese on a scale of dimensions such as "strong," "active," "clean," etc.

A. Thurstone scale

B. Semantic differential

C. Bogardus social distance scale

6. Which one of the following is an example of the bogus pipeline procedure? _____ .

    a. The researcher takes subjects aside and says to them, "Look, give me a candid report of what you *really* feel about these people"

    b. A subject is asked what his attitude is toward individuals of a certain ethnic group, and that subject believes that a tolerant, accepting attitude may then lead to his being housed with a member of the ethnic group as a dormitory roommate

    c. The researcher leads the subject to believe that his true feelings are being monitored by sensitive physiological recording equipment

7. Which one of the following techniques would be most effective if you were interested in modifying undesirable prejudices of an individual toward blacks? _____ .

    a. Provide the individual with reading material that describes the black man's contributions to society

    b. Introduce the individual to more black people

    c. Arrange for social reinforcement for any positive statements about blacks

    d. Give the individual a lecture on the evils of prejudice

8. When people are more economically frustrated, prejudices seem to increase. _____ .

    a. True   b. False

9. A person in the upper-middle class is likely to be more prejudiced than a blue collar worker. _____ .

    a. True   b. False

THE PSYCHOLOGY OF ATTRACTION

The relationships that one establishes, or tries to establish, with others are several in type and are affected by a number of different factors. On one level, the choice of friends is influenced by several known factors. Most of us would rather affiliate ourselves with individuals who reward us in certain social ways, and would choose to avoid individuals who are aversive in their quality of interaction. Not so clear are various other factors, including whether we tend to seek out individuals who are similar to ourselves, whether we are inclined to treat people differently depending upon their perceived physical attractiveness, and so forth.

Proximity and Familiarity

What may seem strange to you is a strong variable affecting interpersonal liking—the factor of physical proximity. The research frequently cited on this topic concerns subjects who moved into a housing project for married students at a university shortly after the area opened for residency. Practically none of the residents had prior acquaintance with each other, but soon interpersonal liking developed. The investigators concluded from the patterns that developed that proximity was a strong influence in the formation of friendships. Later, in a similar research program concerning unmarried students living in a dormitory, the same results were obtained. In both these settings it was found that students tend to establish the strongest friendships with individuals who are close to them in geographic proximity. Naturally exceptions occurred. Still, a strong correlation was established between "togetherness" and the choice of friends.

The findings concerning the effects of physical proximity on friendship led to the predication that frequent contact, by itself, produces more positive attitudes. There was one very convincing experiment on this topic. Unacquainted female subjects had to go through several stages of a complex experiment, and their participation was arranged in such a way that at each point they had the company of various other women. Each subject was exposed to five other women a varying number of times. Even though no talking was permitted in the experiment, it was found that subsequent ratings of the likability of each of the five women were positively related to the number of contacts. The woman who had been a partner on ten different occasions averaged a much stronger likability score than any other, followed by the individual exposed on five occasions (Sagert, Swap, & Zajonc, 1973).

What explains this phenomenon? Is it that we get to "know" a person, and his or her characteristics, through such contact? It would appear that in an *inanimate* sense, familiarity increases liking. Robert Zajonc simply showed subjects photographs clipped from a college yearbook. Different individuals' pictures were shown to subjects different numbers of times, and after several weeks the subjects were asked to indicate their liking for the individuals in the pictures. Liking was in direct relation to the number of times the faces had been seen. Subsequent research has qualified this conclusion somewhat. We now believe that the factor of contact alone, while it may raise liking for persons who are initially perceived as neutral, actually increases dislike for individuals who are initially perceived in a negative fashion.

The phenomenon is apparently not limited to a liking for people, as there is some evidence that familiarity with different art forms and entertainment phenomena increases the degree of positive rating of those experiences. Put simply, repeated exposure to a stimulus generates an increased amount of liking for it. This, of course, assumes that the exposure is neither forced aversively, nor is the stimulus itself either inherently aversive or so simplistic as to generate rapid boredom.

Approval of Others It would seem obvious that we are more positively attracted to those who approve of us, and whose interpersonal behaviors are of a rewarding nature, than to those who indicate their disapproval of us. Research by

"I can't say I like the looks of that bunch."

Aronson and Linder (1965) has confirmed this to be the case. We shall not review the literature in this area, since it should be clear to you that there are many important and subtle variables at work which affect perceived approval or disapproval. These include the context within which evaluated incidents occur, the qualitative aspects of remarks that are evaluated, the levels of felt needs and insecurities in the subjects, and such factors as the sexes of subject and target individuals.

Of more interest to us, beyond the simple fact that we like those who like us, are the ways in which this factor can then manifest itself.

Similarity   Assuming that we are attracted to persons who like us, and possibly repelled by those who do not, what assumptions do we make in advance of definite information concerning others' feelings? Research has suggested that we assume people with backgrounds and attitudes like ours are more inclined to like us. We fear that people whom we perceive as different from us will reject us, so we avoid them. There is also some suggestion that the degree of effect of this variable is dictated partly by the level of psychological insecurity that one may possess.

How do we relate the fact that liking for others is influenced by similarity, yet we have heard it said that "opposites attract"? Most of the research on this question has to do with the characteristics of couples who have had a fairly permanent relationship over a period of time, or with individuals who have manifested enduring friendships over a number of years. Generally the attitudes of one individual are compared with their partner's attitudes on the one hand, and with the attitudes of the general population on the other. In almost all cases it is found that individuals who are attracted to one another strongly enough to maintain a long-term relationship are individuals quite similar on most dimensions.

On those variables where opposites *do* seem to attract, the critical dimensions are not so much attitudes and values, but emotionally based needs. That is, one individual may need to be dominant over others, and the partner may need to be submissive or have someone upon whom he or she can depend for guidance and security. Just as dominant-submissive opposites are attracted to one another, so are sadistic-masochistic relationships formed which do not necessarily have to assume the extreme characteristics usually associated with these terms. Many individuals seem to get relief from their frustrations by taking them out on someone, more often psychologically than physically. Their partners may then feel relief from guilt, or may even reexperience security-need fantasies initially established during childhood, during these incidents. Similarly the enjoyment of dominance in organizations for one individual may be matched by another's need for a framework of goals and procedural guidelines within which to work. One person's need to escape from heavy responsibility may be matched by a partner's seeking responsibility. All such relationships hold as well for the business-industrial society as they do for informal social and heterosexual societies.

Attractiveness A great deal of our reaction to other people is based upon their physical appearance. At a very early age children begin reacting positively to physically attractive peers, rejecting those who are less attractive. This has been observed as early as the age of four (Dion & Berscheid, 1972). Adults, as well, are influenced by the physical features of children. Both male and female schoolteachers have been studied in their reactions to imagined events, using pictures of boys and girls of varying attractiveness. In other cases teachers' reactions to actual children in their classrooms have been studied. In general it appears that teachers are quick to forgive violations of rules or the occasional antisocial transgressions of attractive children, while being more inclined to blame or punish less attractive children for the same types of behaviors.

Occasionally there are reports of the qualities most favored by college students in persons of the opposite sex. These studies generally find that good looks tend to rate rather low in the hierarchy of valued characteristics, but when actual behavior is studied, it is found that college students make more vigorous social overtures toward those of at least reasonable attractiveness, and attempt to avoid, socially, those less physically attractive. Ingenious studies of this phenomenon have been made, such as that of Brislin & Lewis (1968), who correlated the estimated physical attractiveness of a computer dance date with the desire to date that individual again, arriving at a correlation of .89. No other characteristics of the computer date partner, including perceptions of personality or similar interests, achieved even a remotely similar correlation. It would also appear that physical attraction, like money, functions as a commodity—it is sought and bargained for, and not everyone gets "all he or she wants" in a partner since not everyone can be matched with the most attractive individuals. It has been found, in the actual dating behavior of college students, that people tend to end up matched with individuals who closely approximate their own degree of physical attractiveness (Berscheid & Walster, 1974).

What are the factors that make an individual physically attractive, both in terms of sexual attraction and attraction in a broader sense? It appears that the determination of heterosexual attraction is a complex phenomenon, having general cultural determinations and with considerable individual differences in people's preferences. In the late nineteenth century the most desirable ladies were those whose physical characteristics, according to present-day values, were rather massive. An examination of the photographs of "beauties" in the era of Lillian Russell will confirm this fact. Moreover, in some societies today the most attractive and sought-after young ladies are those of heavier weight. In one South Pacific group of islands a young lady chosen to be the bride of the chieftain is deliberately prevented from exercise and fed heavily until she reaches satisfactory proportions—sizes that typically approximate 300 pounds.

Perhaps of more relevance are the factors that exist in our own society which govern physical attraction. We are currently in an era which places great value upon the slender, athletic, and physically active type of physical makeup. The tall, slender, and energetic male is perceived by others, including his employers, as having more positive characteristics, including greater ability. A survey published in the *Wall Street Journal* showed that college graduates over six feet in height receive average starting salaries in business almost 12 percent greater than graduates under six feet. Moreover, the hiring procedures themselves seem discriminatory, not only against short males but against those who are obese or physically ugly.

Competence   Yet another criterion that affects other persons' perceptions of an individual concerns that individual's perceived competence. A variety of imaginative studies has established that individuals of perceived high competence are much more positively rated by observers than are individuals of perceived lower competence. Some research has been in the area of heterosexual attractiveness, with the not-so-surprising result that young ladies are more attracted toward competent males than those of lesser competence, all other things being perceived as reasonably equal. But the phenomenon is also expressed more generally, in the sense that the same holds true of males rating males.

It is not totally clear why this phenomenon is not generally true where female individuals are being evaluated. For some reason both male and female judges evaluate the highly competent female as being at least no better in interpersonal attractiveness, and typically as less attractive than the female of lesser competence. There may be a wide variety of sociocultural reasons for this. Mixed into this topic is an interesting surprise. While individuals rate a superior male as better liked than one of only average competence, it has been found that a few small mistakes on the part of the superior individual increase his likability. Perhaps this factor makes the superior person more "human" and more like ourselves.

Reciprocity   One of the strongest determinants of interpersonal liking, which holds especially for individuals who are socially or emotionally insecure, is the phenomenon of *reciprocal* attraction. In many cases fairly deep and permanent insecurities exist; some individuals are insecure concerning their own heterosexual attractiveness, capability, etc. In other cases individuals may be temporarily devastated by the ordeals involved in a divorce action or some personal or professional failure or trauma. These individuals are particularly vulnerable to signs that others like them. They respond, at least temporarily, by becoming strongly attached to the individual who has sent out signals of initial attraction.

Fear and Affiliation   One of the strongest contributors to a need for affiliation is the presence of felt fear. The classic experiment in this area was conducted by Stanley Schachter (1959), who recruited a number of female undergraduate students at the University of Minnesota as volunteers for research. When the young ladies arrived in the research area, they were greeted by an individual who informed them of procedure. Some of the subjects were told that they would be given a series of shocks while measures of their pulse rates were taken, and they were told rather ominously that the shocks would be quite painful, though there would be no permanent damage. This condition presumably induced a high level of fear. With other subjects the conditions were identical, except the description of the shocks simply stated that they would produce a slight tingling sensation and would be mildly unpleasant. These individuals were considered to have a low level of induced fear. The subjects then filled out a questionnaire which included the question of whether they would prefer to wait in a private room or wait in a classroom with other subjects to be called for participation. This was the major dependent variable in the experiment. It was found that under the low fear conditions 31 percent of the women chose to have company while they waited. Under the high fear condition 63 percent of the subjects chose to be with someone while waiting to be called.

Subsequent research established that not all persons are equally attractive as partners under fear conditions. It is found that others who are in the same predicament are much more valuable as perceived partners than are individuals with no involvement in the predicament. As Schachter put it, "Misery doesn't love just any kind of company, it loves only miserable company."

C 10.8.   *Factors influencing affiliation.*

It has been found that people tend to like best those individuals who _____ .

    a. live close to them   b. live far enough away so they do not become a nuisance

Sheer familiarity alone—the fact of having frequently seen someone—usually causes _____ in that person's perceived likability.

    a. no change   b. an increase   c. a decrease

The fact that we may like people similar to ourselves more than dissimilar individuals seems at least partly dictated by _____ .

    a. our fear of rejection

    b. our prejudice against different levels of socioeconomic class

    c. fear of the unknown

"Opposites attract" when _____ .

    a. the individuals involved are young   b. the individuals involved are insecure

    c. the characteristics that are opposite represent deeply felt emotional needs

In a classroom the most generally found tendency is for the teacher to favor _____ .

    a. the less attractive student through a sort of pity

    b. the more physically attractive student

University students typically report that physical appearance is not strongly involved in meaningful heterosexual attraction. Their behaviors then _____ .

    a. confirm this   b. seem to refute this

A man who is highly capable is generally perceived as _____ likable than is a man of only average capabilities.

    a. more   b. less

A highly competent woman is generally perceived as _____ likable than a woman of only average capabilites.

    a. more   b. only equally or less

A tendency to like those who show that they like us is sometimes termed emotional _____ .

    a. reciprocity   b. submission   c. matching

People who are in a state of anticipatory dread have a _____ level of need for someone to be with and talk with.

    a. higher   b. lower

The most attractive partner, when one is anxious about an impending event, is a person who _____ .

    a. also is to be subject to the event   b. is calm and unexcitable

    c. is an expert who can give facts on the event

PROGRESS CHECK   10.3

1. Which of the following sayings might best describe the relationship between proximity and attraction? _____ .
    a. Absence makes the heart grow fonder
    b. Absence makes the heart grow fonder for someone else
    c. First impressions are lasting

2. You frequently get your gas from the same station attendant. Over time your liking of him will probably _____ .
    a. decrease   b. increase   c. stay the same

3. The fact that most people fear rejection might partly account for the reason that _____ .
    a. opposites attract   b. people who are similar attract

4. Teachers generally favor the less attractive students because they sympathize with them _____ .
    a. True   b. False

5. The more attractive person usually will be perceived as having better qualities than the less attractive person. _____ .
    a. True   b. False

6. University students often will report that physical appearance is not strongly involved in meaningful relationships, but their behavior then refutes it. _____ .
    a. True   b. False

7. A highly competent woman is generally perceived as more likable than a woman with average capabilities (all other factors even). _____ .
    a. True   b. False

8. A man who is highly capable is usually perceived to be more likable than a man of average capabilities. _____ .
    a. True   b. False

9. Reciprocity is best demonstrated by the tendency to _____ .
    a. like people who are attractive   b. like people who are capable
    c. like people who show that they like us

10. Betty's husband is threatening to leave her for another woman. In this case we might expect Betty to _____ .

a. spend more time with her children

b. spend time with Jane, who is also having marriage difficulties

c. watch television

d. visit some of her happily married friends

ALTRUISM Of great recent interest to research psychologists is the topic of altruism. *Altruism* briefly can be defined as the giving of help to others in the absence of any real or expected rewards such as money or praise.

In 1964 the nation was shocked by a well-publicized murder—that of Kitty Genovese. Late at night in the borough of Queens in New York City, a young woman was returning to her apartment. A killer stalked her and in a sudden rush began to stab her. Miss Genovese screamed again and again. Lights came on in nearby apartments and the killer ran away, but then returned and resumed the stabbing attack. More screams, and someone called out from a nearby apartment window, again frightening the killer off. He again returned after a minute or so, and again stabbed Miss Genovese repeatedly while she screamed for help. In all, 38 people are known to have been awakened by the sound, and most of them admitted watching all or part of the event from their apartment windows, but although the attack lasted for a half hour from the time Miss Genovese began scream-ing until she finally was delivered a fatal thrust, not one individual arrived to interrupt the incident and perhaps save her life.

The account just given is, perhaps, an isolated type of event, but from time to time similar incidents occur, indicating that perhaps a majority of persons "don't want to get involved." Why would no one go to the aid of Miss Genovese, and why are other persons left as helpless victims to their fates in numerous less dramatic circumstances? Stated in another form, why do some persons display altruistic behavior, while others do not? This is a topic of interest to most college-age persons, since they, of all age groups, tend to engage the most actively in helping and sharing behaviors.

This topic is much more complex than it at first appears. Some indi-viduals have entered upon the subject by studying the concept of *empathy*—the sympathetic experience of the thoughts and feelings of others. Aronfreed (1970) has hypothesized that most individuals *learn*, over a period of time, to empathize with others. That is, certain family-centered experiences have taught us to actually feel the pain and experience the upset when others are seen to be in trouble. In this way helping activities not only reduce the pain of others, but our own distress as well. Altruistic behavior thus can be explained on the basis of an easily understandable operant conditioning process, with helping behaviors being negatively reinforced.

Other researchers feel that altruism may be based upon very old developmental processes involving one's basic feelings of guilt and moral upbringing. One version of this would hold that helping behavior is positively reinforcing, since we may later walk away filled with self-praise and feelings of expansiveness. Another version emphasizes the guilt that is present in many people at any given moment. In one experiment women shoppers were asked by a male experimenter to stop for a moment and take his picture as a favor to him. In all cases the camera failed to work. Half of the subjects (the control group) were told that it was not their fault, while the other half were led to believe that they had broken the camera through careless operation. Later, as each subject walked through a shopping center, a female experimenter passed in front of them carrying a broken grocery bag which was spilling out items. Only 15 percent of the control subjects told the woman she was losing groceries, but 55 percent of the "guilty" subjects did so (Regan, Williams, & Sparling, 1972).

Some researchers have emphasized the concept of reciprocity, whereby some people feel that they should give aid to persons from whom they have received aid, but not necessarily to others (Gouldner, 1960).

Another factor that has been found to influence altruistic behavior is modeling. For example, male motorists are more likely to stop to assist a woman driver with a flat tire if they have just driven past another scene where a male has stopped to aid a woman motorist with a flat tire (Bryan & Test, 1967). Another example of the modeling influence was shown in an experiment involving children of various ages. Grusec (1972) showed that children who witnessed a model sharing were more likely themselves to share than were children who had heard an adult praising the idea of sharing, but who had not seen an actual incident of sharing.

There is a certain degree of research evidence in favor of the position that altruism is learned mainly through the workings of reinforcement. Doland and Adelberg (1967) showed that younger children do very little sharing, even under both the motivating influences of adult praise and approval for sharing and exposure to an altruistic, sharing peer model. Fischer (1963) found that while preschool children did little sharing when such behavior was reinforced with adult approval, they became surprisingly altruistic when material consequences—in this case bubble gum—served as a reinforcer. Other studies have been done by developmental researchers which have shown that altruistic behavior develops almost linearly through the childhood age years up to early adulthood (Handlon & Gross, 1959). An understanding of the processes involved in conditioned reinforcement will allow you to see how the explanation for the gradual development of altruism moves from primary (or other tangible) reinforcement which shapes the behavior of very young children, to ages at which social reinforcement becomes effective and further strengthens the behavior, to an ultimate stage where self-reinforcement via feelings of pride and virtuousness maintains the behavior. At such times the behavior is said to be internalized.

We might speculate as to the possibility that such helping behavior gradually extinguishes during the span of adulthood, since the conditioned reinforcement of self-praise is less likely to be linked with other meaningful reinforcers for adults. This might explain why older adults frequently seem less altruistic than younger ones.

Hurting Behaviors   Apart from literal aggression, it is evident that many individuals will put aside what altruistic feelings they may have in certain circumstances, and they may behave in ways that are extremely hurtful to others. One of the most talked about recent experiments in the field of social psychology was performed by Milgram (1965), who investigated the phenomenon of obedience to authority.

Subjects arrived in pairs for participation, and were immediately paid $4.50 each for their involvement. A drawing was then held, and one subject was designated the "learner," and the other the "teacher." Actually the drawing was rigged so that the experimenter's accomplice, unknown to the actual subject, would draw the "learner" slip. The learner was strapped into a chair in an adjacent room, and impressive-looking shock electrodes were attached. The teacher-subject was told that his task was to teach the learner a list of word pairs, to test him on the list, and punish him whenever he made an error. Punishment was to be in the form of a shock from a generator, with switches ranging from 15 volts to 450 volts. The shock intensity was to be increased by one 15-volt increment at each succeeding error.

As the experiment progressed and the subject pressed the switches, he could hear what at first were protests from the learner, then moans and cries that he could stand no more, and finally hysterical demands that he be set free and released. (These vocalizations were actually on a tape recorder, and no shocks were being administered.) Whenever the subject seemed reluctant to go on, the experimenter in charge said, "You have no choice—the experiment requires that you continue," or, "Your job is to punish the learner's mistakes." Despite the fact that switches for the upper ranges of shock intensity were clearly marked "Danger: Severe Shock," nearly two-thirds of all the subjects used in the experiment continued all the way to the end of the row of switches—the 450-volt switch which represented the maximum punishment intensity.

In a separate investigation 40 psychiatrists were given detailed descriptions of Milgram's testing procedure and were asked to predict what would happen. They estimated that at 300 volts fewer than 4 percent of the subjects would still be obedient; and they estimated that only one-tenth of one percent would go all the way up to 450 volts, and that these few subjects would be those who were psychologically abnormal in some way!

Behaviors that hurt others, given in response to the demands of authority, are interpretable in several ways. The most likely case can be made for the position that subjects have been strongly reinforced, as children, for obedience to authority figures—parents and teachers—and have been punished for disobeying. Despite the fact that society strongly condemns cruelty and atrocities, even in time of war and when carried out on orders of authority, the research of Milgram and his associates suggests that such behavior may very well be "natural" in the normative sense, even among educated and "civilized" people.

C 10.9. *Altruistic behaviors.*

Altruism might be adequately defined as _____ .

    a. helping behaviors   b. feelings of "conscience"

    c. helping behaviors without expectation of reward

Altruism was studied in relation to guilt people might be experiencing. Altruistic action was found to be _____ induced guilt.

    a. unrelated to   b. positively correlated with   c. negatively correlated with

There is evidence that at very young ages children increase altruistic behaviors if _____ .

    a. they are given material reinforcers for doing so

    b. they are exposed to models of altruistic behavior

    c. they are given social reinforcers for doing so

The best conclusion to be drawn from the Milgram research is that _____ .

    a. most subjects would show altruistic behavior and refuse to harm another individual

    b. most subjects would, with encouragement, harm another individual

    c. only preschool-age children would deliberately harm others, unless we are dealing with a mentally ill group of persons

---

PROGRESS CHECK   10.4

1. Which of the following might be an example of altruistic behavior? _____ .

    a. A man offers a reward for anyone finding his dog. You read it in the newspaper and start looking for the dog

    b. Joe helped you build your garage, and has promised to help remodel your basement. You feel you owe him a favor. When his house burns down, you invite him to stay with you for awhile

    c. You see someone trying to break into a house. You phone the police and wait until they arrive, apprehend the thief, and get your statement as a witness

2. According to Aronfreed we learn to empathize with others, which results in our experiencing the upset when others are pained or in trouble. Helping behavior in this case could be explained by which of the following operant conditioning processes? _____ .

    a. Negative reinforcement   b. Positive reinforcement   c. Punishment

3. In the studies you read, the most effective means of getting young children to share was through _____ .

    a. adult approval of altruistic behavior

    b. exposure to an altruistic, sharing peer model

    c. material consequences (bubble gum, candy) for altruistic behavior

4. The research of Milgram and his associates suggests that "hurting behavior" _____ .

    a. occurs at a low frequency when society strongly condemns cruelty

    b. occurs only among masochistic individuals

    c. may be a not-unusual response in certain social situations

---

ATTRIBUTION THEORY

Very recently social psychologists have turned their attention to an area of human behavior that had previously been neglected. We all recognize that when we are confronted with the behavior of a certain individual, we tend to "interpret" it as being due to one cause or another. The tendency to thus attribute reasons seems to be only weakly characteristic in cases where the behavior is of minor import or seems to be more-or-less typical of the individual. In cases where the behavior is more vivid, grandiose, or is atypical of the person concerned, we tend to practice *attribution*. The research area termed *attribution theory* seeks to establish the reasons for our making certain inferences about the causes of individuals' behaviors.

Attribution theory developed from the early work of Heider (1958), who observed that individuals who interact with other people apparently feel a "need to know" what to predict about others' behavior. That is, following contact with another individual, if you anticipate further interaction, you would feel a need to build some sort of speculative structure from which to predict that person's future behavior. We all seem to be relatively uneasy when confronted with unpredictable people.

Toward this end a three-stage process becomes evident. First, we attempt to determine whether the behavior of the individual whom we have just observed is due to internal factors such as characteristic traits, or whether the behaviors are due to external factors. External factors may include limitations in alternatives open to the person or strong demands being made upon him at the time. If the decision is that the individual's behavior is being controlled by *external* forces, the attribution process ceases; if, on the other hand, the perception is that *internal* processes dictated the behavior, the attribution process continues.

At the second stage the question of intent arises. If the perception of the behavior is that it came about accidently, the attribution process ceases;

if, on the other hand, the perception is that the behavior was intentional, the attribution process continues.

At the third stage, assuming that the behavior has been perceived as both controlled by internal factors and intentional, the attribution of the specific internal traits of the individual concerned takes place. As you can see, this is a fairly sophisticated framework within which to study the process of how we go about evaluating other persons. Many of the classic research projects in social psychology, even those carried out in the days prior to formal attribution theory, can be seen to relate to a general attribution theory framework.

One of the questions that arises in evaluating the behaviors of other people is whether the behavior observed either is significant or is out of character for the individual concerned. These are separate considerations, each of importance. First, if we already have some framework of familiarity with an individual, his continuation of behaviors that are of a type we have come to expect from him calls for no further attribution. On the other hand, when the familiar individual performs an act that is not in keeping with what we have come to expect from him, we tend to exercise the attribution process. Second, we tend to exercise attribution processes in all cases where we perceive a behavior as having special or important characteristics. Therefore, while we might not give a second thought to an individual's throwing a quarter into a Salvation Army kettle, we would begin to "analyze" that same person's behavior if his donation were several hundred dollars.

C 10.10.   *Basic characteristics of attribution theory.*

Attribution theory is said to stem from man's apparent _____ .

    a. reluctance to place blame on another individual

    b. resistance to magical thinking

    c. need to know what to predict next from an individual

In attribution theory, influencing factors are said to be either _____ .

    a. internal or external in origin   b. animate or inanimate   c. dynamic or static

If an influencing factor is seen to be _____ , attribution ceases at that point.

    a. internal   b. external

Attribution would be less likely to occur if an observed behavior _____ .

    a. was in keeping with an individual's characteristic way of acting

    b. was out of character for a person   c. highly significant

A limitation in alternatives open to an individual is seen as an _____ factor influencing behavior.

    a. internal   b. external

A person's traits are seen as _____ factors influencing behavior.

    a. internal   b. external

**Factors Influencing
Attribution: Observers**

It should not be surprising that one of the strongest factors affecting how we feel about someone else's actions are certain of our own characteristics. Some of these characteristics are outwardly visible, so that an experienced salesman is able to size up a customer and adjust his sales strategy accordingly, and an experienced trial lawyer may have definite sex or age preferences in a jury in certain kinds of cases. The systematic study of the characteristics of the observer as they affect attribution has led to a number of interesting findings. We shall begin by looking at such factors.

**Ego Needs
and Personalities**

One of the stronger influences on attribution is a basic tendency to perceive others in ways that are consistent with our own self-enhancement. Everyone is assumed to have a need for a positive self-image, and in one research program (Cialdini, Braver, & Lewis, 1974) subjects were used in a setting where they first attempted to persuade a target individual to a certain point of view. Following their efforts with each of several subjects, they were given feedback as to whether or not they had been successful in their persuasion efforts. Later the subjects were asked to evaluate the target individuals along certain dimensions, one of which was intelligence. It was shown that where the target individual had been persuaded, the subject attributed to that person a higher level of intelligence; where the target individual had held out and resisted persuasion, he or she was seen then as being of lower intelligence. It was also found that target individuals who

Henry R. Martin

"Oh, my goodness! I see you seated at your typewriter . . . and . . . and . . . you're writing another book. I see it becoming the nation's number one best seller. Why, it's a book about me and my uncanny ability to predict the future!"

gave no indication of any sort regarding their reactions were perceived in the same way as those who had resisted persuasion, and they too were rated as lower intellectually. As a control condition in this experiment, neutral observers witnessed the entire procedure and independently rated the target individuals. Their attributions were opposite to those of the subjects. They tended to rate target individuals who resisted persuasion as being relatively higher in intelligence than those who were persuaded.

Closely related to the need for self-enhancement is a tendency to attribute characteristics to persons in terms of whether they have seen us at our best or our worst. The initial question here is whether you tend later to dislike an individual who has been present as a witness when you were made to "look bad" in some way. Mikula and Egger (1974) asked subjects to perform a complex clerical task involving problem-solving while an observer sat silently in the room watching. After completion of the task the observer departed, and the subject was then asked to evaluate several personality characteristics of the observer. The observer tended to be assigned negative values much more often by those subjects who had experienced failure than by those who had been successful at the task. The strongest rejection was made by those subjects whose failures had clearly involved becoming visibly flustered and disorganized during the task.

Related research has shown that students falling into the D/F grade range tend to rate a college or university course as being less interesting, a teacher as being a poorer lecturer, and the topics taught to be less relevant than do those students who fall into the A/B/C range.

One variable of interest to personality researchers is a subject's perceived "locus of control." This refers to how a subject perceives himself in terms of being controlled either by internal or external factors. The perceived locus of control was related to attribution processes by Sosis (1974). He first measured internal versus external locus of self-control perceptions in 70 high-school students, then divided them into three groups. The internal group felt that their own performances and characteristics were due to traits for which they themselves were responsible. There was an intermediate group, then an external group who felt that events in their lives were due mainly to factors over which they had little control. The subjects were asked to read an account of an automobile accident, together with a description of the driver. They then responded to a questionnaire regarding the driver's involvement in the accident.

The internals, who felt that their destinies were controlled by themselves through their own traits, tended to assign the most blame for the accident to the driver. At the other extreme the externals, who seldom felt that their own failings were due to factors under their control, projected their feelings about themselves onto the driver and assigned the least blame to him for the accident. (You might meditate on some of these findings if you ever appear before a jury and your destiny is to be a result of their judgments.)

It may have occurred to you that there are certain types of people, apart from reasonably normal "external locus of control" individuals, who are extreme in assuming that outside factors control their lives. Most obvious are those who believe in various occult spiritualistic influences. One large newspaper recently failed to run its regular syndicated astrological horoscope feature for one week due to postal service problems, and reported that the number of phone calls of inquiry or complaint were so numerous as to occupy the entire available time of a telephone clerk assigned to explain the matter to callers.

One group of such occultists, 18 self-proclaimed spiritualists, mediums, etc., were studied by Scheidt (1974). He found that these individuals, when contrasted with traditional religionists, tended to view behavior much more as being externally controlled. Scheidt conducted extensive depth interviews of all subjects, and emerged with an interesting point of view. He implied that extreme schemes of environmental control reflect schizoid or other irrational thinking processes, or possibly low levels of effective intelligence. Some individuals with these characteristics deliberately concoct belief systems which are consistent with their own cognitive limitations. They fix upon an inflexible and concrete external-cause interpretation of events due to a lack of rational attributional logic.

Traditional religionists were studied, on the other hand, in a separate procedure by Werner (1975). Extremely religious persons were given complex descriptions of young people in a variety of situational dilemmas involving peer pressures, poverty, and so forth. Their subsequent dishonest or antisocial acts were perceived much more as being due to internal factors by the religious subjects than by a control group. The extremely religious subjects tended to be relatively the least forgiving, attributing negative traits and assigning blame directly upon the persons in the stories being evaluated.

Age of Observer

It should appear obvious that the level of cognitive development of individuals, and this is closely tied in with chronological age (see Chapter 3), would influence attribution processes. Whiteman, Brook, and Gordon (1974) reflected on the fact that young children tend often to attribute negative motives to those individuals who may frustrate or hurt them. They studied the behaviors of first, fourth, and sixth-graders in their judgments of actions described in stories. The older children took note both of the ways in which the story characters went about performing the acts and the consequences that then followed. The first-graders, on the other hand, were scarcely able to separate intention from consequences. This fits our observation that young children will become angry or upset at an act that causes them pain or distress, despite reassurances that the act was accidental or was otherwise not intended to be hurtful. The research of Whiteman would make it appear that the children in such cases are not simply being capricious and vying for some kind of sympathy, but are actually incapable of consciously discriminating intent from consequence.

Group Influences

While not a characteristic of the attributor, group pressures more directly involve the attributor than the attributee, so we will consider this variable next. Consistent with the work of Asch (1951), described earlier in this chapter, Munson and Kiesler (1974) found that either positive or negative communications from independent observers, given prior to a subject's own attributional report, influenced the attribution process in the direction of the communication. From other areas of research we might form a further hypothesis that individuals with submissive, conforming personality characteristics might be more strongly influenced in this way than dominant, stubborn types.

In this section we have seen that various characteristics of the observer have to do with the probabilities of their attribution of certain characteristics to target individuals. In the next section we shall examine characteristics of the attributees (actors) themselves which, though they have nothing to do with the actions being evaluated, influence attribution.

C 10.11. *Attribution as affected by observer characteristics.*

It is found that "persuaders" will see individuals who resist their attempts to persuade as being relatively _____ .

a. obstinate   b. hostile   c. more intelligent   d. less intelligent

In the circumstances described in the last question, a popular interpretation supports the notion that attribution is in the service of the need for _____ .

a. retaliation when frustrated   b. a positive self-image   c. being punished when one fails

If you walked into a dormitory dining room with your food tray, saw an attractive person of the opposite sex and smiled at that person, then stumbled and fell headlong across your tray of sticky gravy, hot chocolate, and other messy items, it is likely that thereafter you would think more _____ about that attractive person.

a. highly   b. negatively   c. often

Individuals who are internal locus-of-control types in their self-perceptions tend to attribute _____ blame to other people for their various failures.

a. more   b. less

Occultist-type individuals tend to perceive others' behaviors as being relatively _____ controlled.

a. internally   b. externally

A study of extremely religious individuals shows that they tend to view others as being relatively _____ controlled.

a. internally   b. externally

The very young child tends to view others' actions as being relatively _____ controlled.

a. internally   b. externally

Attribution of traits seems to be _____ the influence of knowledge of others' opinions on the matter.

a. relatively immune from   b. quite affected by

Factors Influencing Attribution: Characteristics of Actors

Research has established that our attribution of traits and motives to individuals is influenced by a variety of factors independent of the actual behavior being evaluated. Some relevant characteristics of the observers have been presented, and we shall now turn to characteristics of the actors.

Some Responses to Basic Actor Characteristics

At an initial stage we tend to react in certain ways to whether the target individual has succeeded or failed at the task, and even apart from further factors we tend to have immediate reactions.

Luginbuhl, Crowe, and Kahan (1975) showed that university undergraduates tend usually to attribute success to effort (internal) rather than ability (in this case a form of external factor), but use different criteria in judging failure, usually implying a basic lack of ability. We might generalize tentatively to state that in a relatively simplistic situation we attribute positive qualities to a successful individual, but have an initial tendency to "excuse" failure in terms of there being circumstances largely beyond the control of the individual.

The sex of the attributee enters into the situation, and Feather and Simon (1975) found that the successful female is downgraded both by male and by female high-school age judges. This research was carried out using 48 high-school students as subjects. The researchers found, consistent with Luginbuhl, that successful males are assigned positive internal attributes; but successful females drew the fire of both male and female judges, with the latter in particular introjecting certain interpretations of the performances that were not particularly complimentary.

Physical attractiveness was examined, as a variable influencing attribution, by Seligman, Paschall, and Takata (1974). Again high-school students were used as subjects, 144 in total, equally divided between males and females. Subjects judged task situations where on the one hand success or failure was brought about by an attractive woman, and on the other hand by an unattractive woman. Physically attractive women were seen as praiseworthy for good outcomes when they occurred, but as not responsible for failures. The reverse was evident with unattractive women—they were blamed for their failures, but their successes were ascribed to external factors. In relating the results of Seligman to those of Feather and Simon, note that Seligman made *no* comparisons with male target individuals. Attractive and unattractive women were only judged relative to one another, and it is possible that, in comparison with male target individuals, even the attractive women would emerge with relatively less attribution of positive internal traits.

A related research program examined attributions of guilt or innocence in a simulated jury system, studying the influence of a defendant's physical attractiveness. Efran (1974) began by surveying a large group of college students. He found that 93 percent of them were unqualifiedly of the opinion that physical attractiveness should have no effect on judges or jurors. Subsequently, using a separate group of 66 subjects, the appearance of a simulated "defendant" was manipulated with all other factors held constant. It was found that physically attractive defendants were evaluated with less certainty of their guilt, and those attractive defendants who were judged guilty were recommended for significantly less severe punishments.

Closely related to physical attractiveness is the variable of physical type. Iwawaki and Learner (1974) studied reactions to three types of body build of target individuals. The researchers used 180 male and female subjects, and sought their attributional reactions to photographs of various males between the ages of eighteen and twenty-one. Subjects of both sexes tended to attribute predominantly positive characteristics to well-built, muscular individuals, and predominantly negative characteristics to overweight individuals; thin, angular-type individuals were scored at an intermediate value.

Friend or Foe? Research has established that the familiarity of a target individual, and the feeling a subject has toward that individual both dictate attribution of traits. The familiarity factor was investigated by Regan, Straus, and Fazio (1974), who asked subjects to evaluate successes and failures of strangers on the one hand and familiar individuals on the other. Under these circumstances it was found that internal controls were predominantly ascribed to account for both the successes of the familiar individuals and the failures of the strangers. Successes of strangers and failures of familiar individuals were more prone to be attributed to external controls.

Taylor and Jaggi (1974) investigated "in-group" and "out-group" influences along the same general line of reasoning. Members of one's "in-group" are family members, friends, members of the same institutional organizations, etc. Members of "out-groups" are persons of opposite religions, different socioeconomic groups, etc. Taylor and Jaggi examined the reactions of Hindu adults in India as they judged the behaviors of Hindu and Muslim individuals. The subjects tended to ascribe successful or desirable behaviors of in-group members to internal attributes such as honesty and ambition, while they attributed undesirable behaviors of out-group members to internal attributes. Conversely, undesirable behaviors of in-group members were attributed to external causes (desperation from poverty, etc.), as were desirable behaviors of out-group members (he did it just because he was going to be paid for it).

Perceived Intent A significant amount of literature in the field of social psychology suggests that we are more inclined to attribute honesty in a statement to an individual

who is acting for reasons other than profit. If we hear an actor on television endorsing a product, we are less influenced to believe the product is good than if we hear a neighbor describing its qualities. Research has investigated people's reactions to perceived efforts to manipulate them. Most research is straightforward, with predictable results—people tend to resist domineering efforts to manipulate them for profit, etc. One researcher came up with results that were not so predictable, however. DiMatteo (1972) found that subjects respond negatively to "sad stories" that are told in efforts to change judgments. High-school students read a fictitious self-description by a male college student describing his antisocial actions on a certain date. The description then went ahead either to outline a prior unhappy childhood with previous misfortunes and serious physical handicaps, or to outline a relatively normal background. It is interesting that many people utilize such strategies to stimulate compassion and favoritism from others. Yet the results of the DiMatteo research suggest that this may well be a self-defeating tactic, for the subjects tended consistently to evaluate the person in less favorable ways where the self-description went into the "sad story" and disadvantaged background.

C 10.12.   *Attribution as affected by actor characteristics.*

There appears to be a basic tendency, apart from any other influences, to attribute success to - - - factors and failure to - - - factors. _____ .

   a. internal/external   b. external/internal

A qualification concerning the statement contained within the last question is that the overall pattern seems to be more true for (which sex?) _____ than for _____ .

Within an experiment limited to female target individuals, it was found that attribution of positive qualities is much more likely to take place with _____ target individual.

   a. an unattractive   b. an attractive

If you were placed on trial for theft, you might expect to fare better if you looked like _____ .

   a. Robert Redford   b. Bozo the Clown

If you were placed on trial for theft, you might expect to fare better if you had the body build of _____ .

   a. Dick Van Dyke   b. Oliver Hardy   c. Dick Butkus

   (For the uninitiated, the first individual is a rather thin television performer; the second was a very obese movie actor; the third is a recently retired football linebacker.)

We tend to attribute relatively positive characteristics to _____ .

   a. persons from our in-groups   b. persons from out-groups

   c. persons who are known to us in the sense of at least being familiar

   d. (two of the above answers are correct)

A study of the effects of communicating sad and possibly extenuating circumstances from one's earlier life-period indicates that individuals judging one's violations of the rules will be relatively _____ .

a. turned off by the sad stories and will judge more harshly

b. affected by the sad stories and will judge more compassionately

---

PROGRESS CHECK 10.5

1. The research area termed *attribution theory* seeks to establish the reasons for our making certain inferences about the causes of individual behavior. _____ .

    a. True   b. False

2. We all seem to be relatively uneasy when confronted with unpredictable people. _____ .

    a. True   b. False

3. We often attempt to attribute reasons in cases where behavior is typical of the individual as well as cases where the behavior is atypical. _____ .

    a. True   b. False

4. Which of the following are internal influencing factors? _____ . Which are external influencing factors? _____ .

    a. A person's traits

    b. Limitations of alternatives open to an individual

    c. Strong demands being made upon an individual's behavior

    d. Behavior is perceived as intentional

5. At a party you try to convince another individual about the dangers of overpopulation. If that individual resists your attempts to persuade him, you probably will think him _____ .

    a. more intelligent   b. less intelligent   c. hostile   d. a poor listener

6. In the circumstances described in the last question, one interpretation supports the idea that attribution is in the service of a need _____ .

    a. to know what others think of you

    b. to transfer responsibility to another individual

    c. for a positive self-image

7. In Mikula and Egger's research, the subjects tended to assign negative values to the observer if the subject had experienced failure in front of that individual. _____ .

    a. True   b. False

8. According to what you have read, in which of the following examples would the individual view

others' behavior as internally controlled? _____ . As externally controlled? _____ .

    a. The individual tends to attribute blame to other people for their various failures

    b. The individual is a strong believer in operant conditioning

    c. The individual is a strong believer in the occult

    d. The individual has very deep religious convictions.

9. A child is accidently hurt and becomes angry at the person who hurt him. According to Whiteman this is because _____ .

    a. the child is trying to get attention

    b. this is a natural reaction for a child experiencing pain

    c. the child is incapable of discriminating intent from consequence.

10. Listening to positive or negative communication from independent observers prior to a subject's own attributional report usually does not significantly influence the attribution process in the direction of the communication. _____ .

    a. True   b. False

MATCH the items in the list on the left with the appropriate items in the list on the right.

    11. Success is usually attributed to _____

    12. Attribution of positive qualities is often related to _____

    13. Failure is usually (but not always) attributed to _____

    14. Attribution of negative qualities is often related to _____

    A. external factors

    B. internal factors

    C. physical attractiveness

    D. physical unattractiveness

15. If a thin man and a fat man are competing for a job, their chances of obtaining the job are about even (all other factors being equal). _____ .

    a. True   b. False

16. Regardless of the sex of the individual, the highly competent individual will always be attributed with high positive qualities. _____ .

    a. True   b. False

17. According to DiMatteo's research a lawyer defending his client on a robbery charge might expect the following result from the jury if he described the disadvantaged background and unhappy childhood of his client. _____ .

    a. The jury would be more favorable toward his client

    b. The jury would not be affected by the lawyer's efforts to elicit their sympathy

    c. The jury would be less favorable toward his client.

18. In Efran's study, what effect did the physical attractiveness of the defendant have on the severity

    of punishment? _____ .

    a. No effect   b. The more attractive, the less severity

    c. The more attractive, the greater the severity

19. Successes are attributed to internal factors for _____ .

    a. persons from our in-groups   b. persons from our out-groups

---

CONSISTENCY THEORIES

We turn now from attribution theory, which has a somewhat constricted structural framework, to an examination of two other approaches to how we think, judge, and evaluate. In some aspects both are counterparts to attribution theory, though they are generally viewed along separate dimensions. We shall call both approaches, in an overall sense, *consistency theories* since they seem to have in common the individual's pursuit of a belief consistency. Both are seen as influencing the development and persistence of belief systems.

The Theory of Cognitive Dissonance

Suppose that you, a male, have a bushy beard and long hair. Assume, moreover, that your father despises both. In fact, he goes so far as to inform you that if you do not have the hair cut short and the beard taken off by a certain date, he will no longer give you the spending money that he has been in the habit of handing out.

You are in a dilemma. On the one hand, you don't have a job and you need the spending money. On the other hand, you think the long hair and beard both look great. Suppose you shave off the beard and have your hair cut short. There would then exist a conflict of two ideas—first, you are happy that you are retaining your source of spending money; secondly, you are convinced that you no longer look as good as you did before. The conflict is intensified by the fact that you perceive yourself as having performed this act for only a few dollars a week, which is not really that much.

Leon Festinger (1957) called this type of conflict *cognitive dissonance*. Cognitive, referring to mental thoughts, plus dissonance, referring to conflict, simply denotes that an aversive drive state has been set up in which you are very uncomfortable with conflicting ideas. The way to rid yourself of cognitive dissonance is to adjust your thinking in such a way as to reduce the amount of conflict between the separate thought elements. To return to the example of the short haircut and shaved-off beard, you could reduce the dissonance, and probably would do so, by soliciting remarks from others to the effect that your new appearance is actually better. You start by asking only certain people, deliberately selecting those who would be most likely to favor your new image. In the case of conflicting opinions you would more

readily be "convinced" by those people who say they like your new look. Once you have the belief that you now look better to other people, you can see that there would be little dissonance between the now existing elements of thought. On the one hand, you have removed your beard and cut your hair short; on the other, you now look better, have made your family happy, and have assured your continued income. This is called *cognitive consistency*.

Festinger's theory of cognitive dissonance (1957) has stimulated enormous amounts of research and theoretical application within the field of social psychology. Festinger describes cognitive dissonance as an aversive state of tension that results when an individual holds two ideas or opinions which are inconsistent. If an individual enjoys smoking, yet knows of extensive research that links smoking to lung cancer, a state of cognitive dissonance will exist. Such dissonance is unpleasant, and people are motivated to reduce it.

In the example just given, that of cigarette smoking, there are several strategies which might serve to reduce the dissonance. One way to eliminate the dissonance would be to give up smoking. Another would be to find convincing counterevidence that smoking does *not* lead to lung cancer. Partial relief from cognitive dissonance could also be achieved by reducing the number of cigarettes smoked daily, or by developing countermeasures that relate to the smoking-cancer link—for example, one might use only filter-tipped cigarettes. In these situations one does not *eliminate* the dissonance because one neither destroys one of the conflicting ideational elements nor totally eliminates the personal relevance of that element. Yet by reducing the degree of personal relevance, or by strengthening the opposing element, the relative balance between the two sides of the issue is drawn far enough off center that the individual concerned feels relatively less tension.

There are some interesting predictions accompanying the theory of cognitive dissonance. One of these, since verified, is that an individual who experiences dissonance over a decision, then makes the decision, will thereafter endeavor to avoid information which indicates that his decision might have been a wrong one. Consider the individual who alternates for a while between the purchase of two different makes of automobile. After uncomfortably making comparisons, because there is dissonance in counterclaims that each car is the "best," he decides in favor of one. Thereafter he will diligently avoid asking a friend who owns a car of the non-selected make about his experiences with it, or reading about the other make of automobile. Otherwise the dissonance might be increased as conflicting elements appear—on the one hand, he spent a lot of money on his car, yet another make would have been a better choice.

Another example of cognitive dissonance and reaction to it comes from the belief that most individuals hold that they are worthwhile and effective human beings. Such a belief would be inconsistent with a course grade of *F* received in a psychology course. The dissonance might be reduced by accepting the assumption that possibly one isn't really capable of doing college-level work, though this is a rather painful decision to make and is one which calls for subsequent action such as dropping out of school. Easier is the resolution of dissonance through labeling the course and the teacher with choice negative attributes. It would not be inconsistent, for example, that you could be a smart, motivated student capable of doing excellent college work, yet have received a failing grade from a teacher whose course was ambiguous, misleading, and ill-organized. Thus the negative descriptions of the courses in which you do poor work would be seen by Festinger as views which are effective in reducing cognitive dissonance and its

There are a number of variables that relate to the development of strategies for the reduction of cognitive dissonance. Let us consider one of these variables by examining first the inconsistency involving a very strong, emotionally-held personal value. For some, religious beliefs typify these values, and many well-educated but deeply religious individuals regularly and predictably resist any open-minded examination of alternatives to their own particular beliefs. In other persons the basic meaning of one's life and efforts might be the value involved. If an experienced scientist were to be shown data suggesting that his basic approach was in error, we might initially be surprised to find him going ahead with his approach more vigorously than ever. On further reflection you can see, however, that an attack at the very basic level of one's own worth as a professional or as a human being calls for the strongest countermeasure possible in order to reduce the intense cognitive dissonance that develops. Self-justification, coupled with vigorous attacks on alternative or opposing approaches, would be a tactic of logical choice. A choice between two bars of soap may not create much dissonance, but a choice between two automobiles will, and a choice between alternative evaluations of one's life's work is guaranteed to create enormous levels of tension.

Another variable affecting dissonance is the relative balance between alternatives. If one holds to a strong argument in the presence of weak counterarguments, little dissonance will result. However, if one is aware of powerful counterarguments that virtually balance the two opposing positions, the result is an increase in the level of tension.

A wide variety of research programs has attended the theory of cognitive dissonance since its entry into the literature of social psychology. One of these yielded the finding that, following a severe initiation into an activity—one which was costly or painful—subjects thereafter reduced any dissonance associated with participation in the group by evaluating the participation much more favorably than did other individuals whose initiations were less severe (Aronson & Mills, 1959). Similar is the finding that the greater the amount of effort expended upon some task, the more highly the task is evaluated following its successful completion. A little imagination on your part will allow you to visualize the vast potential for attitude change that exists within the framework of cognitive dissonance theory.

C 10.13. *The theory of cognitive dissonance.*

Cognitive dissonance is a conflict that exists between _____ .

    a. people   b. present goals vs. future goals   c. ideas

Cognitive dissonance is seen as _____ .

    a. an aversive drive state   b. a positive incentive

Cognitive dissonance is reduced by _____ .

    a. elimination of an element of the dissonant ideational structure

    b. reduction of the personal relevance of an element of the dissonant ideational structure

    c. (both of the above)

A basic tendency of an individual who is experiencing cognitive dissonance is to _____ .

    a. proceed to gather information on both sides of the issue

    b. avoid sources which intensify the dissonance

If dissonance involves your basic feelings of self-worth, rapid and powerful dissonance reduction is achieved by _____ .

    a. attacking that which discredits you   b. redoubling your efforts to succeed

Dissonance theory would predict that the more costly a psychotherapist or counselor, the _____ would be the patient's evaluation of the treatment.

    a. less favorable   b. more favorable

Balance Theory   Balance theory is described by Heider (1958), and is a theory to explain how individuals are motivated toward consistency in attitudes. Heider's model hypothesizes a triangular relationship between an individual on the one hand and his relationships with either two other individuals or with a person and some object or institution. Heider's balance theory proposes that there first is an experiencing individual, whom we will refer to as individual A, and two objects who may either be people or one person and an inanimate object or institution of some sort. We shall call the two objects in individual A's experiential field objects X and Y. Heider proposes that individuals are motivated to adjust their attitudes in the direction of cognitive "balance." A state of balance is said to exist when, in the triangular relationship that holds between A, X, and Y, all three attitudes or feelings are positive, or there is one positive attitude while the other two are negative.

Let us illustrate this. If individual A likes both Joe (X) and Sam (Y), and moreover Joe likes Sam, then all three attitudes would be positive and a state of balance would exist. Similarly, if individual A likes Joe but dislikes Sam, and Joe dislikes Sam as well (two negatives and a positive), balance would exist. Imbalance exists in situations such as where individual A might like both Joe and Sam, but Joe and Sam dislike one another. In such a circumstance of cognitive imbalance, there would exist motivation for individual A to choose between his two friends, deciding not to like one of them any longer. You should bear in mind that Heider's notion says nothing about the two friends coming to individual A and putting on any kind of social pressure. Heider's theory is entirely one of *cognitive* balance.

Consider another situation. Individual A likes individual X but dislikes a certain political point of view (Y). If individual X also demonstrates a dislike for idea Y, balance will exist. On the other hand, individual X may agree with idea Y, in which case imbalance exists. The situation would be rebalanced either by A beginning to dislike individual X, or by his reevaluating Y and coming to the belief that this idea is not so bad after all.

A great deal of imaginative research has been carried out concerning cognitive balance theory, and it remains a provocative theory of how attitudes and beliefs are, in part, influenced.

C 10.14.   *Balance theory.*

Heider contributed the belief that, basic to cognitive consistency, was balance in a _____ relationship.

    a. dyadic   b. triangular   c. matched-pair

Between the individual and two "objects," balance exists when the system contains _____ .

    a. three positive attitudes   b. two positive and one negative attitude

    c. two negative and one positive attitude   d. (two of the preceding are true)

    e. (all of the first three statements are true)

Suppose you dislike both Bob and Sam. It is easily observed that Bob and Sam are close friends. In this

model, a state of _____ exists.

a. balance   b. imbalance

Where a state of imbalance exists, the individual _____ .

a. is motivated to balance the system through changes of attitude

b. avoids thinking about the situation, leading to social maladjustment

c. is motivated to maintain the imbalance so that there will be a clear discrimination between

choices

BEHAVIOR WITHIN SMALL GROUPS

In task-oriented groups a large number of roles are available to the individual group member, and are typically adopted in consistency with the member's history of vicarious learning and reinforcement for various roles he has played within his family structure and with his social peers. In the formal or task-oriented group, it is sometimes interesting to list the roles that are sometimes assumed by one member or another. In one conceptual system we would talk of social wants, listing the pursuits of affiliation, acquisition, prestige, power, altruism, and satisfaction of curiosity. In another system we would discuss the individual roles of information-seeker, opinion-seeker, encourager, evaluator-summarizer, resource-person-for-facts, resource-person-for-opinions, discourager, aggressor, follower, and finally the leader. It is often fascinating for an individual to have his role behavior analyzed by an observer. In fact, in terms of one's own personal and professional development, such analyses are often considered of such value that individuals and sometimes their employing organizations spend large sums of money for group dynamics experts to do formal analyses of behavior within group settings. For the research psychologist, however, the problem with most of these conceptual systems is that the role is treated as a static thing, as indeed it may seem to appear at first study, since most people are fairly consistent in moving about within only a limited number of roles.

Static Roles

Most research into static-role function in task groups is directed toward the qualities of leadership. Effective leadership, as are most roles, is a multifaceted phenomenon. First, we have the contributant of social modeling. For leadership to emerge, a vital contributing cause is a parent or other extremely familiar adult who demonstrates the traits of a leader. Whether we like it or not, much of an individual's success in being accepted as a leader depends upon fairly superficial characteristics which contribute to his "image." Some of these characteristics cannot reasonably be modified, as they are essentially physical. Napoleon and Ghandi notwithstanding, research has shown that it is the larger and taller individuals from a group of males who, statistically, emerge more often as leaders. Even the shape and structure of one's face can have a strong bearing. One of the military services has, for years, placed a restriction on who is admitted for officer training. They have excluded individuals on the grounds of "extreme ugliness." Their observations are, apparently, that ugly persons do not function as effectively in leadership roles.

Many leadership qualities, while still somewhat superficial, nevertheless seem a bit more realistic. Persons with firm, strong voices, who demonstrate an above average degree of physical vitality and alertness tend to be much more readily accepted as leaders.

Within the static-role framework, different types of leaders are identifiable. One conceptual system identifies three behavioral dimensions—*activity*, which may translate into the number of contributions within the group, *likability*, which may translate into the tendency to deliver positive reactions to others' contributions, and *taskability*, which may translate into the number of one's own problem-oriented contributions. Research has shown that there are actually two types of individuals who can be effective as leaders. First is the individual high in activity and likability, who has a great deal of individual prominence and group sociability. Second is the individual high in taskability, who pursues the goals intensively even though he may not endear himself to his peers or his subordinates.

C 10.15. *Leadership.*

Within the assessment of level of activity, level of taskability, and level of likability, research has shown

that there appear(s) to be _____ of leadership.

a. only one genuinely effective pattern   b. two effective patterns

c. three effective styles

Leadership research has shown, among groups of male adolescents, that leaders tend to be high in number of social interactions, physically superior, better liked, and more intelligent. Many of these relationships, shown among adolescents, continue to be seen in the group behaviors of adults.

This static-role model of leadership has generated a variety of research findings concerning the effects of individuals' personalities, status differences among group members, size of the group, the presence of differing values or interests, and the degree of conformism of the majority of the group.

Dynamic Group Analysis A procedure called IPA (Interaction Process Analysis) was introduced by Bales (1950), and has been used to study the dynamics of group movement rather than simply who acts in what ways in the group. This system categorizes each unit of interaction or contribution by a group member into one of twelve types (Bales, 1950, 1970):

A1. Seems friendly, raises others' status, gives help, rewards others.
A2. Shows tension release, jokes, laughs, shows satisfaction.
A3. Agrees, shows passive acceptance, understands, complies.
B4. Gives suggestions, implying autonomy for others.
B5. Gives opinions, evaluates, analyzes, expresses own feelings and wishes.
B6. Gives information, repeats, clarifies.
C7. Asks for orientation, information, repetition, clarification.
C8. Asks for opinions, evaluations, analysis, expressions of feeling.
C9. Asks for suggestions, possible ways of action.
D10. Disagrees, shows passive rejection, withholds help.
D11. Shows tension, asks for help, withdraws from field.
D12. Seems unfriendly, deflates others' status, defends self, asserts self.

The *A* categories, above, are called *positive social-emotional interactions*, the *B* categories are neutral *task-oriented interactions* of an answering nature, the *C* categories are neutral *task-oriented interactions* of a questioning nature, and the *D* categories are *negative social-emotional interactions*.

Bales conceives of a unit as a single item or thought, "the smallest discriminable segment of verbal or nonverbal behavior to which the observer, using the present set of categories . . . can assign a classification . . . [Bales, 1950, p. 37]." In considering a unit for classification, it is always viewed as either a response to the last act of the last other person, or as an anticipation of the next act of the next other person. Also, in the case of any vagueness regarding classification, Bales advises to favor the category the more distant from the middle of the list.

Using IPA, social psychologists have collected data on a large number of fascinating questions of both a practical and a theoretical nature. Using such methods, we are likely to eventually understand far better than we do today how a group should be guided for maximum effectiveness. Within just a few of the research programs using IPA, psychologists have found that role differentiation may not take place very clearly until actual efforts to solve problems begin; the preponderance of interactions start within categories 6 and 7 (orientation), move through 5 and 8 (evaluation), and finally to 4 and 9 (control) as the problem is handled. Both positive and negative social-emotional reactions generally increase through the three phases just mentioned; any individual's tendencies to disrupt rather than contribute creatively are increased as progress through the phases prior to the final stage takes place; and deviants from the main tendencies of the group tend to be on the receiving end of the most negative social-emotional interactions. Finally, the last interactions during a meeting tend to be of a positive social-emotional nature.

In a similar vein, the functions of leadership are studied. It has been found that after persons are ranked in terms of the number of unit acts they initiate in the group, certain lawful relationships can be perceived. For example, each person in the rank order addresses a somewhat larger number of unit acts to those higher in the rank order than he does to those lower in the rank order. An analysis of the quality of leadership can be attempted by relating the identity of the individual highest in rank order of unit acts to the ratio of suggestion and agreement categories of the group's interactions to the tension categories [Borgatta, Bales, & Couch, 1954].

Some of these findings are certainly not surprising, but some were not definitely known until IPA provided a vehicle for investigation. Many vital questions are now within research access.

C 10.16. *Bales' Interaction Process Analysis.*

The four area categories of interaction, in Bales' IPA, seem to most closely fit the four terms: _____ .

    a. seek orientation; provide orientation; make others happy; fuss and fight

    b. seek orientation; seek emotional support; fuss and fight; inspire others

    c. provide motivation; ease insecurities; quit; inspire others

As a group session progesses through problem-solving, the amount of positive social-emotional responding, relative to all other categories combined, tends to _____ .

    a. increase   b. decrease

As a group session progresses through problem-solving, the amount of negative social-emotional responding, relative to all other categories combined (and not counting the final few minutes) tends to _____ .

    a. increase   b. decrease

The activities of the final few minutes of a problem-solving session tend to be _____ .

    a. exceedingly hostile, due to the reactions of those failing in their purposes

    b. tension-reducing and friendly

The most aggression in a group is directed toward _____ .

    a. the person who is the "leader" in the sense of the largest number of unit acts contributed

    b. the most deviant members of the group

    c. anyone who asks for orientation after the first ten minutes

---

PROGRESS CHECK   10.6

1. According to Festinger cognitive dissonance is _____ .

    a. an aversive drive state set up by conflicting ideas

    b. a positive incentive to resolve a conflict of ideas

    c. a conflict between present goals and future goals

2. If a person is experiencing cognitive dissonance, he probably will _____ .

    a. tolerate the stress without commitment

    b. delay his decision until he gets more feedback

   c. reduce the degree of personal relevance of one of the dissonant ideas or strengthen the opposing element

3. You have just bought a Mazda instead of a Honda Civic. If you had been experiencing cognitive dissonance about your decision, you probably will _____ .

   a. continue to read information about both cars

   b. ask someone at a party what kind of mileage they get with their Civic

   c. avoid information about the Honda Civic

4. Bob has been working for the past ten years on a machine that will produce a powerful inertial force. He demonstrates his machine to a group of scientists, who tell him that what he is trying to do is impossible. According to what you have read, Bob will probably _____ .

   a. decide to give up his invention

   b. decide to invent something more consistent with present theory

   c. think that scientists are blinded by their theories and that famous inventors in the past have faced similar reactions

5. John had to go through "hell week" to get into a fraternity. John will probably value his participation in the fraternity _____ .

   a. more than those who did not go through "hell week"

   b. less than those who did not go through "hell week"

   c. about the same as those who did not go through "hell week"

6. Balance theory is a theory to explain how individuals are motivated toward consistency in _____ .

   a. present and future goals   b. attitudes   c. relationships

7. According to balance theory, balance exists when there are _____ .

   a. three negatives   b. three positives or one positive and two negatives

   c. two positives and one negative or one positive and two negatives

   d. three positives or two positives and one negative

8. According to Heider, if individual A likes both Joe and Sam, but Joe and Sam dislike one another, then _____ .

   a. individual A will probably choose between his two friends

   b. Joe and Sam will put pressure on individual A

   c. individual A will abandon both his friends

9. When an individual is faced with a state of imbalance, he is motivated to balance the system by changes of attitude _____ .

   a. True   b. False

10. Which of the following individuals probably would not be an effective leader? _____ .

    a. An individual high in taskability

    b. An individual high in activity and likability

    c. An individual high in likability and low in activity

11. The final interactions in a group tend to be of a positive social-emotional nature. _____ .

    a. True   b. False

12. How are the most deviant members of the group treated? _____ .

    a. They are ignored   b. They are asked to leave

    c. Most of the aggression of the group is directed toward them

---

CONCLUSION   No chapter-length treatment of the area of social processes can possibly handle the diversity of approaches and go into any appreciable depth with even a limited few. We recommend that the interested student pursue the courses in social psychology which are offered at most universities as the second or third course in sequence following introductory psychology. Meanwhile, excellent paperback books that may further stimulate your interest include *The Social Animal* by Elliot Aronson (1972), *Small Groups* by Clovis Shepherd (1964), and *The Psychology of Behavior Exchange* by Kenneth Gergen (1969).

NOTE TO THE READER: **The subject matter discussed in this chapter is expanded and amplified in Extension Chapter 10A, beginning on pages 634-35.**

Human Learning
and Memory

11

COGNITION AS MOTIVATION

VERBAL LEARNING
 Meaningfulness
 Nonsense Syllables
 The Trigram
 List Length

WHAT DO YOU MEAN BY "LEARNING"?
 Learning Models
  Serial Anticipation
  Paired Association
  Context Learning
 Other Verbal Learning Phenomena
  The Serial Position Effect
  Intrusion Errors
  Chunking
  Reminiscence
  The Warm-Up Effect
  Learning-to-Learn
  Mnemonics
 Summary of Factors Involved in Acquisition

ACQUISITION VERSUS RETENTION
 Theories of Forgetting
  Trace-Decay Theory
  Loss of Access Theory
  Repression Theory
  Interference Theory
   Proactive Interference
   Retroactive Interference

MOTOR LEARNING
 Motor Learning Devices

DISTRIBUTION OF PRACTICE

FEEDBACK

TRANSFER OF TRAINING
 Analysis of Transfer of Training
 Transfer of Training and Education

In Chapters 8 and 9 we dealt with the role of learning in the development of basic emotional structure and acquisition of individual and social behavioral habits. Our approach was based on the assumption that the simple learning processes are a major determinant of everyday human and animal behavior patterns. While we intend to use the concepts of conditioning extensively in the further development of this text, the present chapter examines a different dimension of learning—the species-specific learning patterns of the human organism, as they affect (primarily) task performance.

COGNITION AS MOTIVATION

We can draw a scale of motivational complexity representing, at the left, the inflexible processes called reflexes and instincts, and other processes, rising in complexity and flexibility, as we progress to the right (Figure 11.1).

The patterns at the far left make up a large majority of the behavioral repertoires of the lower organisms, particularly when one looks far down the phylogenetic scale to the levels of insects. Many of the species-specific behaviors at this end of the scale are not of as much interest to the psychologist as to the ethologist—the biologist who specializes in such matters. Still, one must at least have a basic awareness of these patterns in order to appreciate the full scheme of things in the total behavior patterns of individuals.

The intermediate three points on the scale, we find, provide the main motivational structure for the vast majority of creatures reasonably high on the phylogenetic scale, including man.

Finally, at the highest level we have a set of behaviors actually *caused* by the ability to think logically and abstractly, and anticipate the future. These processes are practically all restricted to human beings as far as we now can determine. This is not the time nor the place to delve into various possible minor exceptions to the last statement. We shall simply note that the human species-specific patterns at the right end of the scale make up the essential difference in both motivational and ability characteristics between man and lower organisms.

Let us put the relative motive-strength contributions into a perspective. First, even educated persons do most of what they do, in terms of their motivations, because of factors within the intermediate range of the scale. The right-end factors allow a person to *know* what he should do, *how* he might do it, and to anticipate consequences of his act, but this is actually a weak motivator for behavior compared with the intermediate levels on the scale. That is, conditioned patterns tend to be stronger than cognitive motives insofar as motivation-to-behave is concerned.

The last point is frequently hard to put across to some people. Consider

Figure 11.1

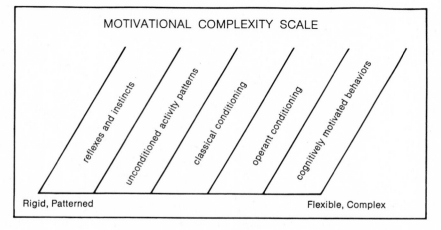

yourself. You are truly a highly cognitive person since you are defined primarily as a student-intellectual. Yet at least 95 percent of your activities during a typical day are caused by factors in your conditioning history. Perhaps the following fictional behavior diary will convince you.

You sit and look out the window, thinking about your date last weekend. A momentary lack of stimulus variety largely motivates this positively reinforced behavior. The more you have been reinforced for doing this in the past, the more typically you launch immediately into it, and for longer periods of time, when deprived of stimulus variety. Then a fly lands on your arm and provides an irritating momentary stimulus. Your escape activity (brushing it off) is negatively reinforcing, and this is often followed by a few moments of flailing the air to drive the fly away (conditioned avoidance behavior, reinforced many times in the past by successful avoidance). Then you ask your neighbor if he wants to walk to class with you. Your neighbor has probably reinforced you in the past by providing stimulus variety (good storyteller, interesting conversationalist), or by delivering social reinforcers such as flattery, praise, or attention to your own conversation. Therefore, you manifest frequent approach behavior toward him. He is not going to class today, so you walk over alone.

Attendance at class largely is a conditioned pattern, due in part to the fact that when you were younger your parents enforced a standard of values including regularity and promptness—being where you were supposed to be, living up to responsibilities, and so forth. In the absence of such an earlier environment, students are often absent from so many classes and examinations that they lose their eligibility to continue in college. On the way to your class, you make the decision to cut and go to the Student Center. Two things are relevant here. First, the class concerned has probably been high on your list of those lacking stimulus variety; also, your experiences in the class and your mental image of it (CS) have so frequently been paired with a lack of stimulus variety (UCS) that now the thought of the class (CS) is aversive. Second, the degree of spontaneity with which you made the decision is largely a function of your history of negative reinforcement for cutting classes. The more you do it and are thereby reinforced, the more frequently and readily you then continue to do it.

You go to the Student Center, where you find a variety of interesting positive reinforcers. Notice here that you are initially being negatively reinforced for cutting class, but what you do after you cut is influenced by the positive reinforcing values of the various alternatives. Eventually you leave the Student Center and go to the library, which may be a somewhat aversive situational stimulus, but there is a dual motivation pattern here. While you may be motivated to avoid the library, a stronger negative incentive is represented by the consequences you perceive for not getting a library assignment done.

Little of the motivational sequence just described is very different from the processes involved in animal behavior. The sequence is comprised mainly of reactions to current stimuli and actions influenced by one's reinforcement history. You should clearly see, at this point, that reinforcement history often predominates over one's "cognitive motives," the latter being defined as knowing what you "ought" to be doing. Typically a strong reinforcement history for a given behavior makes cognitive motivation for behavior change practically impossible. Were it not the case, there would doubtless be a lot fewer miserable people in our society.

The world is full of people who cannot resist momentary and minor temptations, another fact indicating that conditioned patterns are stronger than cognitively generated motives. Consider small, everyday examples— the person who eats fattening foods that he knows he shouldn't; the person who cuts class even though he knows he should go; the person who engages in impulse buying even though he knows he cannot really afford it; and finally (and closest to home?) the student who puts off studying for an examination or getting started on a term paper practically until the last minute. He knows he is hurting himself, but he can hardly overcome established habits.

Now consider the student scholar: Perhaps you regard him as the ultimate example of the triumph of "thinking" over baser motives. You may then be surprised to hear that even at the top level of academia about 50 percent of the persons who complete all requirements for the Ph.D. degree (and these are considerable, usually including three full years of graduate-level coursework, written and oral comprehensive exams, and foreign language reading exams) never finish writing their dissertations to receive the degree. A few years ago it was estimated that a young faculty member with a Ph.D. degree at a typical state university could probably earn from $100,000 to $200,000 more during his earnings-lifetime, within existing promotion rules, than could a similarly-situated faculty member without a doctorate. One would think that such a fantastic figure, comprehended at the "cognitive" level, would cause any right-thinking person to sacrifice TV, vacationing, "lounging," and the like so as to get his dissertation completed. The fact is, however, that the types of behaviors required in dissertation writing—namely, isolating oneself and spending many hours at a time intensively studying difficult material, synthesizing it, and then writing in a near-perfect format—are *not* the sorts of behaviors that have gained any appreciable reinforcement in our society. Many students have been fortunate enough to grow up in an environment in which some kind of study-effort has been reinforced, and they therefore read quite a bit and are somewhat scholarly, but even these people usually have never encountered anything like a large-scale dissertation.

The latter illustration is not extreme. It is a very realistic example of the fact that "cognitive motivation" is extremely weak when stacked up against competing behavior tendencies that have gained positive or negative operant reinforcement.

C 11.1. *Cognition as motivation.*

In man and the various phylogenetically "higher" organisms, the _____ points on the scale of motivational complexity provide the main motivational structure.

    a. lowest   b. intermediate   c. highest

Relative to conditioning histories, cognition tends to provide a _____ strength of motivation.

    a. weaker   b. stronger

It is not our purpose, however, to maintain that man is just a *quantitatively* more capable organism than the laboratory rat or monkey. In this chapter we shall examine ways in which the human organism is capable of *qualitatively* different aspects of learning and performance. In general those qualitatively different aspects involve language, so we shall begin with the topic of verbal learning.

VERBAL LEARNING   When we say "verbal learning," many people immediately visualize the process of a youngster learning to speak, but most verbal learning research concerns adult performances. We shall section this chapter, as we go along, according to the ways in which psychologists divide the topic of verbal learning for purposes of conducting their research.

We begin by stating that verbal learning can be shown to be a function of three separate classes of independent variables. (1) O-variables enter in. These, of course, might be only vaguely defined as O, since most O characteristics are inferred from R patterns, but still we can relate such factors as brain damage, general level of intelligence, fatigue, and so forth to ability in verbal learning. (2) S-variables affect learning. The material to be learned can vary in a number of ways along several stimulus dimensions. (3) Learning is affected by R-variables, meaning in this case the way in which the subject rehearses the material to be learned—length of rehearsal sessions, whether he says the verbal material out loud as he tries to learn it, and so forth.

We shall not dwell on the first variable class. The O-variables are all more or less obvious in their relationship to learning. It might be well at this point, however, to state that, insofar as we can determine, it appears that those variables related to *acquisition* of knowledge are related similarly to *retention*. That is, if high intelligence yields faster acquisition, it also yields longer retention. Conversely, O-characteristics that relate to slow acquisition are similarly related to shorter retention.

C 11.2.   *The relation between acquisition and retention.*

Suppose several O-variables are known to relate to acquisition scores on verbal learning tasks. It is then predictable that the same (positive or negative) relationship will hold between those O-variables and _____ scores.

   a. forgetting   b. retention

Meaningfulness   Our interest in variables related to verbal learning is strongest with the S-class of variables. A number of stimulus factors in verbal material are related to learning and to retention. First of these is *meaningfulness* in the materials used. This is one of the strongest functional relationships, with retention being higher for more meaningful material. As a matter of fact, this point has a great deal of relevance for the college instructor. The simple fact is that when we lecture to students or give assigned readings, we may be going over certain people's heads because of the materials we use and the ways in which we express ourselves. Some professors use unfamiliar words proudly to show off their knowledge of language rather than to communicate. Those students who understand the words (high meaningfulness) will retain knowledge of the concepts covered much better than those students who do not understand many of the words being used.

C 11.3. *The effect of meaningfulness in verbal learning.*

Let us say that you are asked to learn two lists of 20 words each. The first begins with "tree, hit, allow, know, car," and continues in that vein. The other begins with "incognitable, parsenary, fagaceous, bateau," and so forth. It is likely that you will learn the - - - list more easily, due to the variable of - - - _____ .

a. first/meaningfulness   b. second/meaningfulness

c. first/number of syllables involved in the words

Nonsense Syllables   You may not have thought of it, but the relationship *degree of learning = f (meaningfulness)* introduces a problem into learning research. If we present lists of material to subjects under various conditions, how do we control for a person's vocabulary ability, and hence meaningfulness? We might attempt to stratify this variable or use it with large numbers of subjects so as to have this variable randomize out, but verbal learning researchers typically use another means of solving this problem. In fact, as far back as 1885 a famous researcher, Hermann Ebbinghaus, began the use of a certain device for control of this variable. His contribution was the *nonsense syllable*.

Ebbinghaus systematically went about developing all the possible nonsense syllables from combinations of consonant-vowel-consonant (the syllables have been referred to as *cvc*'s). Such syllables as *lem, geg,* and *ral* are examples. A legitimate nonsense syllable is one that has no obvious associative meaning in either a common foreign language or in English; for example, the syllable *luk* does have obvious associative meaning with the word "luck," and is therefore not a good construction. The nonsense syllable, so the reasoning goes, has no meaning of its own, and therefore can be useful in avoiding the problems associated with meaningfulness, and can also safely be used with persons having different vocabulary abilities. Ebbinghaus' model of learning involved memorization of lists of nonsense syllables, and he was able, single-handedly, to provide us with a great deal of our present knowledge of functional relationships in verbal learning.

It may have occurred to you that some nonsense syllables might have some subtle associative meaning while others have none. This is an important variable to recognize and control, particularly in some types of experiments. In the late 1920's Glaze investigated subtle associative meaning by having subjects look at nonsense syllables and indicate those that triggered some sort of immediate association. For example, if *lek* suggests "leak" for 90 percent of the subjects in an experiment, *lek* would be given a 90 percent "association value." The syllable *fod* may suggest "fodder" to 30 percent of subjects, so that *fod* would be given a 30 percent association value. In this manner Glaze was able to publish tables of syllables with their association values. The difficulty with the Glaze tables at the present time is that a number of syllables that Glaze noted as having very low association values today have much higher values. The syllable *nam* now has a high degree of meaning since our involvement in the war in Viet Nam.

C 11.4. *The development of the nonsense syllable as a research tool.*

_____ was the man who first employed nonsense syllables in learning research.

The nonsense syllable consists of two - - -, separated by a - - -. _____ .

    a. consonants/vowel   b. vowels/consonant

The *cvc* was intended mainly to control for the variable of word _____ .

    a. length   b. meaningfulness   c. commonality

Glaze refined *cvc* use by intoducing _____ .

    a. association values   b. double-length syllable pairs

The Trigram   Another approach that has succeeded in controlling meaningfulness is the development of the *trigram* (*ccc*). This is a list of three nonrepeating consonants. Thus, *sgb*, *vlp*, and *ptw* would be examples.

    Another variable that enters into the use of both syllables and trigrams is the material's phonetic characteristics. Since trigrams, as a group, are less pronounceable than are nonsense syllables, this variable *is largely controlled* just by virtue of trigram use. Still, some variability remains, such as the pronounceabilities of *vlp* and *ptw*. Most people could pronounce the first of these two trigrams more easily than the other. Little research has been done on the pronounceability variable, but it appears that this is a major factor to be dealt with.

C 11.5. *The development of the trigram as a research tool.*

A trigram is a memory unit that consists of _____ .

    a. two consonants separated by a vowel   b. two vowels separated by a consonant

    c. three vowels   d. three consonants

Figure 11.2

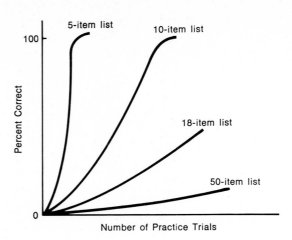

List Length Strongly related to verbal learning is *list length*. Figure 11.2 indicates that you can handle a shorter list of items with quite a bit more facility than you can a longer list. If you were to seriously investigate the publications that yielded the acquisition curves in Figure 11.2, you would find that the length of the lists does not yield a simple multiple to predict the time it would take for learning. On the contrary, it may take three times as long to learn a list that is only twice as long, and the relation grows even more disproportionate as the lengths increase further. This has brought about research into whole-versus-part learning. The questions are, "Is it better, in undertaking a long tract of material, to go right through it from start to finish, doing this over and over until it is mastered? Or, is it better to take a smaller section and go over it until it is learned, then go to the next section, and so forth?" Most of you have probably performed your own "experiments" on this. It typically has been found that *part learning* of lengthy material is better than *whole learning*, at least from the standpoint of memorization of material. If you ever have had to learn lines of poetry, you probably have answered this question to your own satisfaction.

C 11.6. *The relation of length of material to be learned to acquisition time.*

A _____ correlation exists between the time required for acquisition and the length of the list of material to be learned.

    a. positive   b. negative

With lengthy lists of material, the whole method of learning is usually _____ than the part method.

    a. more effective   b. less effective

WHAT DO YOU MEAN BY "LEARNING"?

The word "learning" has a variety of meanings, depending upon what one determines is an adequate *level* of performance or behavior change to justify the label. We recognize at least four levels of acquisition, three of which we shall discuss here. First, you may learn material to the point of *recognition*. This means that you can choose the right answer from a group of answers that are shown to you. The standard multiple-choice examination exemplifies this. A higher level of learning is represented in learning to the point of *recall*. This is represented by the completion-type examination. A number of studies have demonstrated that learning to the point of recall represents a more thorough mastery of material than does learning just to the point of recognition. The relationship is demonstrated in Figure 11.3, which represents two examinations on the same material, administered to the same students. An artifact in the situation causes the curve in Figure 11.3 to rise sharply at the upper end—it is that some persons who achieve a perfect score on a multiple-choice examination actually have studied the material past the point of 100 percent recognition, and this becomes a factor in their recall scores.

A third level of learning should be noted. It is sometimes called the level of *savings*, and describes the degree of retention in terms of the time required to relearn the material to the original criterion level. Because the material was once learned, relearning usually can progress much faster than did the original learning. Ease of relearning is measured in the amount of time saved (thus the term savings), and standard ways of calculating savings scores exist. Savings can be shown even in cases in which it initially appears that *all* of the previously learned material has been totally forgotten.

Figure 11.3

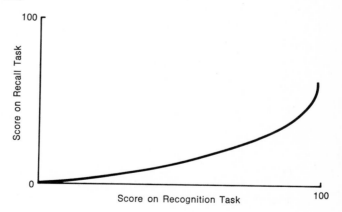

C 11.7. *Measurement of different levels of learning.*

If you can pick out the right answer from several answers put in front of you, you have learned to the level of _____ .

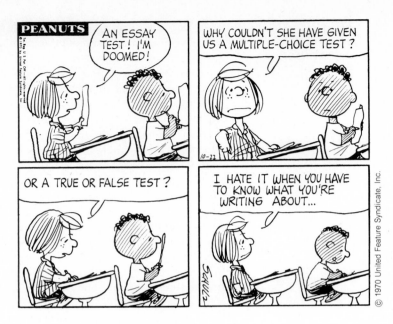

When you can reproduce the right answer without any cues, you have learned to the level of

_____ .

If you do not remember material learned long ago, but it can be shown that your time to relearn is
much shorter than if you had not once studied the material, we say that your level of learning
(before relearning) is the level of _____ .

PROGRESS CHECK   11.1

1. On the scale of motivational complexity, which area has the most constant influence on human
   behavior? _____ .

   a. Reflexes   b. Instincts   c. Conditioning   d. Cognition

2. Which variables are related similarly to acquisition and retention? _____ .

   a. *S*   b. *O*   c. *R*

3. Who is historically associated with the use of nonsense syllable in verbal learning? _____ .

   a. Henry Ellis   b. Bernard Katz   c. Hermann Ebbinghaus   d. Wilhelm Reich

4. Increased meaningfulness of items decreases one's ability to learn the material. _____ .

   a. True   b. False

5. Trigrams are stimuli used in verbal learning research, which are _____ .

   a. puzzles   b. consonant-vowel-consonant arrays

   c. nonsense syllables of any three letters   d. sets of three consonants

6. Which is easier to learn in terms of acquisition time? _____ .

    a. 5-item list   b. 10-item list   c. 20-item list   d. 50-item list

7. Learning the whole list is usually harder than learning the list in parts. _____ .

    a. True   b. False

8. A higher level of learning is represented by _____ .

    a. recognition   b. recall

9. When relearning time for material is shorter than original learning time, which principle is demonstrated? _____ .

    a. Investment   b. Bonding   c. Collateral   d. Savings

Learning Models

Learning proceeds in different ways, depending on the type of material as well as the manner in which it is presented. It is one thing to memorize a poem and quite another to learn vocabulary lists for a foreign language course. Still another type of material is represented in covering larger portions of material to understand the ideas represented there. We see three corresponding models in the learning laboratory.

Serial Anticipation

First, corresponding to the example of learning poetry, is the *serial anticipation* method. Let us say that we have a memory drum to present our material. These are cylindrical machines that present syllables or words through apertures in the front, exposing each item for a fixed, predetermined interval of time. In serial anticipation you are shown the list, one syllable at a time, following which the list starts over again and you are asked to anticipate the upcoming syllables. You state your recollection of the first syllable and then it appears. After you see it you then state the second, and so forth. In a sense this is similar to memorizing poetry or prose word-for-word, although a syllable list provides little in the way of context to help you out.

Paired Association

The second method, corresponding to learning a foreign language vocabulary, is the *paired association* method. We present two syllables or two words at the same time. For example, you might see "pine-throw," followed by "like-spot," and so forth. In the memory test you are shown "pine," and you must supply the paired associate, then "like," and so on down the list.

Paired association and serial anticipation are the two most popular models in learning research. Use of a memory drum is not necessarily required, especially for serial anticipation tasks, but the exact timing of stimulus presentations, accurately handled by this mechanical means, allows a fairly important control. With such control, a subject cannot dwell upon a word or syllable longer than a set interval of time.

Context Learning

The third research model is variously called *learning in context* (like textbook style), connected discourse learning, or prose learning. It may seem peculiar that highly meaningful material presented in context has been so seldom selected for use in verbal learning research, since it approximates the type of material students usually study; but it is likely that much more such research will be performed in the near future.

C 11.8. *The various laboratory models for the study of learning.*

Learning to recite a poem in a foreign language is most similar to the _____ . _____ method of learning in a laboratory.

Foreign language vocabulary lists are learned in a manner similar to the _____ . _____ method of learning in a laboratory.

The variable of amount of time spent looking at a single word or syllable can be controlled through the use of _____ .

    a. nonsense syllables   b. stopwatches   c. the memory drum

Other Verbal Learning Phenomena

The methods pursued by human beings undertaking to learn complex language-based concepts are varied. A wide variety of factors may assist, inhibit, or interact with the learning process. Some of these have already been mentioned—meaningfulness, length of material, which learning model is appropriate, etc. A variety of further principles and concepts has been developed within the field of verbal learning, each of which is significant in comprehending human learning.

The Serial Position Effect

One of the more powerful manifestations in verbal learning is the *serial position effect*. This is a stimulus variable whereby the position, within a list, of an element to be learned influences the speed with which it is learned. If you are given a 15-syllable list, you tend to learn the first and last syllables first, then others close to them, with the material slightly to the right of center being learned last (Figure 11.4). It is of interest that

Figure 11.4

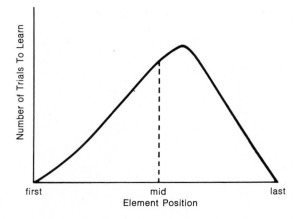

Element Position

this effect is manifest in both context learning (Deese & Kaufman, 1957) and in the maze-learning of animals.

C 11.9. *The serial position effect.*

The serial position effect describes a phenomenon whereby elements in the _____ of a mass of

material tend to be the last to be learned.

    a. middle   b. beginning   c. end

In a 13-element syllable list, approximately which element (1st, 2nd?) would likely be the *last* to be

learned? _____ .

In a 21-element list, which would likely be learned last? _____ .

                   Intrusion Errors   If we analyze the results of verbal learning experiments, we find that many of the errors are *intrusion errors,* meaning that elements from elsewhere in the list intrude at a certain point into the list the subject is attempting to recall. Intrusion errors (as opposed to exclusion errors in which you simply cannot generate an answer) function according to a pattern that researchers in learning have identified in accounting for failure to learn. *Forward associations* are one type of intrusion error in which a subject erroneously substitutes an element from a point earlier in the material. *Backward associations* are the other type of intrusion error in which elements that should come later to be in proper order are used too early.

    Intrusion errors have been proposed to account for the serial position effect. The potential for an item's intrusion is apparently a function of the nearness of the two pertinent elements. That is, element 6 in the series is more liable to intrusion from element 7 than from 8, from 8 than from 9, and so forth. Similarly, element 6 is more liable to intrusion from element 5 than from 4, 4 than from 3, and so forth. However, the distant items still have some intrusion-potential, and probabilities of intrusion into a position are related to the additive probabilities of intrusion by various individual foreign elements. If you have followed this line of thought, you can see how elements in the middle-range area of a list are most likely to suffer from intrusion errors from both directions, and thus the serial-position effect curve is produced.

C 11.10. *Intrusion and exclusion errors.*

If I were to give you a list of syllables to memorize and your response for element 6 was actually

element 9 on the list, this would be an _____ error.

    a. intrusion   b. exclusion

In the above example, the error is one of _____ association.

    a. forward   b. backward

Chunking   Processing into memory storage is facilitated by *chunking* of material into stimulus classes. Suppose I had you memorize the following word list: WORD, MOON, GUESS, LINE, DISMAY, LEADER, RINSE, ERROR, TOWEL, FURNACE, GRAPPLE, MINOR, TREAD, LOCK, FLOOR, AWAY, BOTH, BASKET. Now compare the difficulty level of that list with the following: PINE, ELM, BEECH, MAPLE, CYPRESS, BED, CHAIR, SOFA, TABLE, RUG, ZEBRA, ELEPHANT, MONKEY, LION, TIGER, JUDGE, LAWYER, DEFENDANT, TRIAL, JURY.

As you can see, the words in the second list are "chunked" into four stimulus classes—trees, furniture, wild animals, and court-related words. Our information-processing faculties work fairly well, some evidence indicates, until the number of elements being processed at a given moment passes seven. At that point we must either spend a greatly disproportionate amount of time per item for learning or else find ways of making up element "chunks," each with its own identity. Then we can process up to seven chunks without a great amount of difficulty; then, perhaps, we can identify commonalities among chunks and have larger chunks. Failing this chunking possibility, our memories are not nearly as powerful as we might like to believe.

C 11.11. *Chunking.*

Chunking is best defined as a perceptual tendency to _____ .

    a. group stimulus elements before learning them

    b. perceive cause and effect relationships in diverse elements of information

    c. reject certain items, resist them, and thereby have a "mental block"

Reminiscence   Learning is also facilitated by the phenomenon of *reminiscence*. This is a hypothetical process brought into operation by allowing subjects to stop for a moment at intermediate points during the learning process. Hypothetically the subject "reminisces" and thereby rehearses what he has just been exposed to, which has the effect of stabilizing memory for the elements being rehearsed.

Many years ago reminiscence was explained in theory by the notion of "reverberating circuits." This idea held that the neurological system contains a very large number of interconnected circuits (Figure 11.5) which are available for recircuiting if no competing material is being processed. Thus, if item after item is coming in, the steady continuity leaves no opportunity for the neurology to recycle the individual elements. Elements are "processed" once and then go into memory storage, to some extent. However,

Figure 11.5

after no more items are coming in, the last ones still in the perceptual system are recycled several times, and this reminiscence then strengthens retention for the last ones.

Whether or not this hypothetical account of neurological functioning is correct, or whether we simply should explain the reminiscence phenomenon in terms of a longer duration of attention to certain materials without the problem of competing backward error associations, the phenomenon is real. When studying you might avail yourself of this knowledge. Whenever a complex unit of information has been processed, you should take your eyes from the page and re-create the information, rehearsing and practicing it, to increase your retention level.

C 11.12. *The reminiscence effect.*

The reminiscence effect is the effect, upon learning, of _____ .

   a. a vast amount of previous experience upon which to rely

   b. the age of the subject   c. a pause without further stimulus input

The reminiscence effect brings about _____ acquisition scores.

   a. higher   b. lower

The reminiscence effect has been theoretically explained through a notion of _____ .

   a. stimulus competition   b. reverberatory circuits   c. brain oppositions

The Warm-Up Effect   Another factor that affects learning is the *warm-up effect.* Just as athletes have found that a few minutes spent "loosening up" with warm-up exercises helps their game performance, so does warming-up on a learning task assist later performance. How would we recognize and visualize this effect? We could draw a chart representing acquisition of a large amount of material during several daily experimental sessions, and we would find that the slope of each daily curve, indicating rate of acquisition, grows steeper a few minutes into each session (Figure 11.6). Translated, that means that in each session we start learning rather slowly, then the rate of acquisition increases.

Figure 11.6

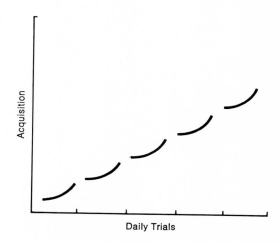

Daily Trials

C 11.13. *The warm-up effect.*

If you were to begin to practice a learning task with which you were already familiar, your performance curve (time on the horizontal axis, acquisition on the vertical) would grow _____ a few minutes into the session.

    a. flatter   b. steeper

Learning-to-Learn Another factor affecting learning is called *learning-to-learn*. Simply defined, as trials progress the subject usually learns various strategies that help him acquire the material more quickly. The learning-to-learn effect is charted in Figure 11.7 with the warm-up effect smoothed out so as to make the learning-to-learn effect more vivid.

    Let us consider an example. If you ask a little child to learn some lines of poetry, he may quickly find that adopting a "sing-song" voice pattern helps him learn. The sing-song delivery allows the child to have added cues as to how many more syllables remain in each line of poetry. If the child is a novice at this kind of task, he may show the complete progression from no sing-song to a rather clearly defined sing-song delivery within just a few trials. An individual quickly picks up various other ways of learning-to-learn in most tasks. Have you learned some "tricks," for example, that help you assemble a jig-saw puzzle more quickly than you could when you were only seven or eight years old?

Figure 11.7

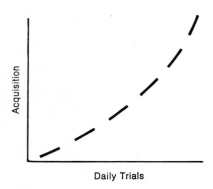

C 11.14. *The learning-to-learn effect.*

Suppose that you begin an unfamiliar learning task and practice it during several daily sessions. The slope of your acquisition curve would be _____ on the later sessions, compared with the first.

    a. flatter   b. steeper

Mnemonics A final factor with a potential effect upon acquisition is the mnemonic device. *Mnemonics* are deliberately integrated organizational cues constructed to assist memory. Generally they are verbal in nature, and dissociated from the conceptual structure of the material to be learned. You probably have used a number of these yourself. To recognize one of the simplest ones, consider the peripheral nervous system of the body. Afferent neurons carry stimulus signals into the brain, then efferent neurons carry the reaction signals out to the body's effectors. The input from stimuli precedes the outward-directed reaction to the stimuli, just as A in the alphabet precedes E. Thus, A—E (afferent-efferent) is the proper sequence. Other mnemonics include "thirty days has September . . . ," "in fourteen-hundred and ninety-two, Columbus sailed the ocean blue . . . ," and other simple jingles. Students in speech therapy and anatomy often use a technique to memorize the names of the cranial nerves in descending order—"On old Olympus' towering top a Frenchman and German viewed the hops." The first letters of the words correspond in order to the first letters of the cranial nerves. In physics the descending order of the wave lengths of light is contained in the name "Roy G. Biv." "HOMES" gives the key to the names of the Great Lakes. Finally, stalactites protrude from caves' ceilings, while stalagmites rise up from the ground below.

The degree to which the use of mnemonic devices should be recommended to students is vigorously debated in some circles. There seems to be little doubt that the imaginative use of mnemonics can help a great deal where considerable learning of isolated terms or words is required, without the provision of meaning or context to facilitate the task. It seems probable that either verbal or visual-imagery mnemonics underlie the successes of show business acts in which an individual amazes others with fantastic feats of memory. Some evidence exists to indicate the "good" students in college make greater and more imaginative use of mnemonics than do students with lesser grade point averages. This does not necessarily mean that the use of mnemonics was the major factor in producing the difference.

C 11.15. *Mnemonic devices.*

A mnemonic device is a technique used _____ .

    a. to artificially aid memory for a list of disconnected facts or terms

    b. for problem solving where there are various possible solutions

    c. primarily by low-ability individuals in learning verbal material

Summary of Factors Involved in Acquisition

So far we have mentioned a number of functional relationships in the study of acquisition, as well as other general associated phenomena. A brief run-down of the variables could be divided into stimulus and procedure classes:

STIMULUS FACTORS	PROCEDURE
meaningfulness	*whole-part*
list length	*reminiscence*
serial position of element	*warm-up* and
	learning-to-learn
characteristics that allow chunking	*chunking*
characteristics that allow mnemonic devices	*mnemonics*

Chunking and mnemonics are interactive processes between the stimulus characteristics and the approach taken by the learner.

PROGRESS CHECK 11.2

1. Memorizing a word-for-word poem is like which learning model? _____ .

    a. Serial anticipation   b. Paired association   c. Context learning

2. Which of these tasks is studied by the paired association method? _____ .

    a. Memorizing a poem   b. Eggs—*huevos;* chicken—*coq;* beef—*fleisch*

    c. Reading Dickens aloud   d. Preparing a menu for two people

3. The serial position effect describes how it is easier to learn which items in a 15-word list? _____ .

    a. First   b. Last   c. Middle   d. a and b

MATCH: _____ 4. Intrusion errors   A. Cannot generate part of a list

    _____ 5. Exclusion errors   B. Recalling items from elsewhere as part of a list

6. Processing items into memory is facilitated by chunking. Which list is an example of chunking? _____ .

    a. Mary, chair, book, jewelry, car, beach, granite, water, bush

    b. Mary, Jean, Betty, book, newspaper, magazine, granite, marble, stone

    c. (415) 388-0025   d. b and c

7. Which procedure involves stopping briefly at intermediate points during learning to rehearse?

    _____ .

    a. Warm-up   b. Learning to learn   c. Reminiscence   d. Mnemonics

8. Which example below is a mnemonic device? _____ .

    a. Eenie-meenie-mynie-moe   b. Roy G. Biv (for wavelength of light)

    c. Thirty days hath September . . .   d. b and c

9. The laboratory apparatus designed to control the time spent looking at a word or syllable is the _____ .

    a. memory drum   b. stopwatch   c. word tank   d. oscilloscope

10. What does the warm-up effect show? _____ .

    a. Performance curves steepen after a few minutes on task

    b. Once the brain circuits increase in temperature learning is improved

    c. Memory is a hot medium   d. Performance curves are square-wave forms

**ACQUISITION
VERSUS
RETENTION**

So far we have been discussing learning, using the word *acquisition;* now it is time to talk about memory, using the word *retention.* There is a definite difference between the way the psychologist conducts an acquisition experiment and the way he conducts a retention experiment. The acquisition experiment involves a subject who is exposed to material a certain number of times; after each trial, or possibly after all trials, he is tested to determine the degree of acquisition. Retention experiments involve the passage of *time.* The subject learns the material, either to a 100 percent criterion or he is exposed to a predetermined number of acquisition trials, following which "100 percent" is used to indicate the totality of whatever acquisition level he achieved. Then a given interval of time is allowed to pass and the subject is again tested. At that point we call his percentage score an indication of retention, rather than acquisition.

The student is usually extremely interested in facts concerning acquisition and retention, to the point that a number of issues and "myths" have come into being concerning how to study. For example, should you study all night for an early-morning examination? We shall deal with a number of such questions.

Retention research yields graphs with either retention or forgetting on the vertical axis. They are actually the same measure, one being the reciprocal of the other. That is, if you have forgotten 31 percent of what you originally acquired, you could also automatically say that your retention score is 69 percent.

C 11.16.   *The relation of acquisition scores to retention scores.*

Learning is to acquisition as memory is to _____ .

    a. forgetting   b. retention   c. recall   d. recovery

Which of the following formulas is correct? _____ .

    a. Acquisition plus retention equals total material once learned to criterion

    b. Retention plus forgetting equals total material once acquired

    c. Retention minus forgetting equals total material once acquired

**Theories of
Forgetting**

In this section we shall cover the various theories of forgetting. We shall briefly list three theories with a comment on each, and then proceed to a more complete discussion of a fourth theory.

Trace–Decay Theory

One of the well-known theories of forgetting is called the *trace–decay* theory. In learning terminology a *memory trace* theoretically is electrochemical arousal in the cortex which corresponds directly to a particular stimulus configuration. It was established in one experiment that measurable electrochemical activity persisted for about 200 times the length of time that a brief flash of light was presented to subjects. The electro-chemical activity (trace) is thought to be the actual physical counterpart to recognition and memory of the flash. According to the trace–decay theory the memory trace proceeds along the reverberatory circuits (mentioned earlier in this chapter), and eventually fades away. Presumably some kind of electrochemical potential persists in the form of neurological sensitivity, and would be activated in "memory." Such neurological sensitivity then fades away gradually with the passage of time. Some of the current work on immediate and short-term memory fits the trace–decay theory fairly well, but this is not the most prevalent theory at this time.

Loss of Access Theory

A second approach is the *loss of access theory*. This notion holds that memories are triggered by various stimulus-response patterns not entirely unlike the mnemonic devices we have already discussed. Over time, the mnemonic code is lost, and access to the learned information is also lost.

Repression Theory

A third approach is *repression theory*. Freud developed the notion that memories are not really lost—they are just pushed out of awareness by forces of the personality, at least if the memories are unpleasant and anxiety-producing. You can see that such a theory might hold for emotion-related memories but would not do as a comprehensive theory of academically related memory. We shall have more to say about this theory in the chapter on personality.

Interference Theory

The fourth approach, and the one to which we shall give the most attention, is *interference theory*. Proponents of this theory maintain that both acquisition and retention are affected by learning from other times and places, and both acquisition and retention can be interfered with. This is a fascinating theory that corresponds remarkably well with a great deal of research data. We shall begin by examining the possible directions of interference.

Proactive Interference

If I were to learn one foreign language (*A*) and then try to learn another (*B*), I might find that there are many competing associations. When the English word is given and I try to come up with the word from language *B*, the association from language *A* might block memory for the correct answer. This is a model of *proactive interference*. Proactive means that one thing comes *forward* in time to interfere with the acquistion of a later thing. We would investigate this by having one group learn task *A*, then *B*, while another group learns only *B*. Then, after equal exposure to *B*, both groups are tested for acquisition. If the *A-B* group were lower on the *B* test than the *B-only* group, then we would conclude that proactive interference took place.

Retroactive Interference

If I were to learn the first language (*A*), then a second (*B*), I might find that I am worse now on *A* than if I had never tried to learn *B* at all. In one sense (the sense that *A* originally came before *B* in the learning process), *B* is working *backward* in time to break up memory for A, which is called *retroactive interference*. We would investigate this by having one group learn A and then learn B, while another group learned A and then spent the same amount of time as the other group spent on B doing something other than language study. Then both groups are tested on retention of A. If the A-B group did worse than did the A group, we would conclude that retroactive interference had occurred.

To summarize, proactive interference means that something acquired earlier (A) interferes with *acquisition* of something presented later (B). Retroactive interference means that something acquired later (B) interferes with *retention* of something acquired earlier (A).

C 11.17. *Theories of forgetting.*

Electrochemical counterparts of memory fade away through time. This comprises the nucleus of the
_____ theory of forgetting.

    a. trace–decay   b. loss of access   c. repression   d. interference

The _____ theory of forgetting holds that we do not remember things that we do not want to remember
(motivated forgetting).

    a. trace–decay   b. loss of access   c. repression   d. interference

"Retention is affected by other learned elements" is essentially a statement of the _____ theory
of forgetting.

    a. trace–decay   b. loss of access   c. repression   d. interference

The _____ theory of forgetting holds that, over time, we forget the mnemonic codes that once
triggered specific memories.

    a. trace–decay   b. loss of access   c. repression   d. interference

C 11.18. *Proactive and retroactive effects in learning.*

If after learning to steer a car, I then have trouble learning to steer a motor boat in which the relation
between steering-wheel action and turning-direction is the reverse of that found in cars, this is an
example of _____ interference.

I have an A-B group and a B group. The B group surpasses the A-B group on a test of B. This
illustrates _____ interference in the A-B group.

A certain golf coach called his players together to suggest that they refrain from playing baseball
during the off-season. The coach's idea was that certain aspects of swinging the bat could develop
habits that might upset the carefully developed golf-swing patterns. If such changes had occurred,
it would have been a case of _____ interference.

Laboratory experiments exist in great numbers to show that pro-active and retroactive interference are functions of a few definite independent variables. We shall turn to a real-life-situated experiment in order to illustrate perhaps the most powerful of the affecting variables.

In this particular experiment, groups of college students learned lists of nonsense syllables. Once they had achieved a criterion level of 100 percent recall, they entered phase two of the experiment. A group that had learned its lists late in the evening immediately went to sleep. At two-hour intervals some of them were awakened and asked to recall what they could of the lists. Some were awakened after two hours, others after four hours, others after six hours, and the rest were awakened after eight hours if they were still sleeping. A second group spent the eight hours following acquisition listening to instrumental music. Again, portions of this group were selected at two-hour intervals during music-listening for the retention test. The third major group listened to recorded lectures taken from various academic areas, mixed with casual conversations. Again, various persons were tested at two-hour intervals. Finally, a fourth group was asked to work on similar nonsense syllable lists, scanning them, doing tasks such as pulling out syllables from one list which matched those on other lists, and so forth. Again, at two-hour intervals persons from this group were tested. The overall pattern was quite clear: In each group, the *longer the elapsed period* following *initial acquisition,* the *lower* was the *level of recall.*

Great differences were found, however, between the groups (see Figure 11.8.). Apparently *the greater the similarity between the original learning and the nature of the intervening activities,* the greater the interference and the poorer the retention. Also, the more time that passes during which these intervening activities take place, the greater is the reduction in retention, with the sharpest reduction taking place early during the intervening interval. The sleep group provides the most interesting data. While the other groups continued to decline beyond the two-hour point, the sleep group's

Figure 11.8

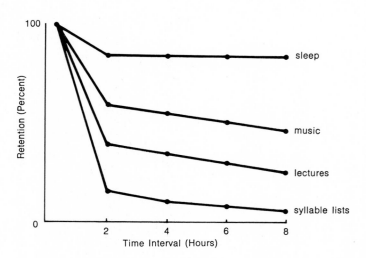

retention curve, after its initial drop, leveled out. The interpretation of the initial drop is that many subjects did not go to sleep immediately and generated interference by thinking about various things while they lay awake.

If you wish to profit from what was learned in this experiment, you should not be afraid to learn your material in preparation for a test and then go immediately to bed, provided, of course, that you do not lie awake thinking about other things. If the student learns verbal material for a test, as he of course does for 98 percent of university-level examinations, he is ill-advised to engage in a great deal of irrelevant conversation with others, or perform other verbal activity such as reading or listening to the radio. The similarity of the verbal material he hears can break up verbal memory. The greater the degree of similarity between the original learning and the intervening activities, the more loss of retention occurs.

C 11.19. *Effects of intervening activities on retention.*

State two functional relationships (related to amount of retention) that were shown in the sleep-retention experiment. (Note: What *two* things might you know that would allow you to predict somewhat accurately the level of retention that would presently exist with a given subject?)

a. retention = f (_____).

b. retention = f (_____).

MOTOR LEARNING
So far we have discussed learning as if verbal learning were the only topic of actual interest to psychologists. A separate area of learning, however, is quite important in the life patterns of human beings. This is the topic of motor learning. *Motor learning* is the acquisition of various skills involving movements of the body. These include gymnastics and other athletics, the abilities involved in the use of tools, and so forth.

Many points of overlap between motor learning and verbal learning are discernible. For example, practically all the functional relationships presented so far that pertain to verbal learning apply equally well to motor learning. Furthermore, considerable verbal mediation of motor learning occurs. This means that people use language to help them develop proper motor patterns. A simple example occurs when an individual talks to himself as he is learning to dance, using "left, right, left—left, right, left" to guide the proper sequence in the dance step he is trying to learn.

If you want another example, consider how easy it is to learn how to repair a mechanical fixture if you are aware that disassembly proceeds in a "lift up, then push to the right, and pull out" sequence. Without the words to help, learning the disassembly is slowed considerably. Still, a number of experiments give motor learning research a flavor of its own, and we shall proceed to a consideration of this special area of research.

Motor Learning Devices   In order to investigate motor learning more systematically, psychologists developed specific laboratory equipment for comprehensive programs of investigation. Two pieces of apparatus are very commonly employed. With one, the pursuit rotor, an individual tries to keep the tip of a metal rod in contact with a metal disc embedded in a rotating turntable. With a second device—a mirror-drawing apparatus—the subject uses a mirror to trace a star or some other geometric form. He works entirely on the basis of a mirror reflection, with a shield preventing direct vision of his hand and the geometric form. The mirror image reverses the right-left and the up-down relationships, so that the subject must learn an opposite-to-normal coordination between vision and movement. If an experimenter lacks laboratory apparatus, he might have a subject print the alphabet upside down. Performance can be scored as the number of letters printed correctly within a set length of time.

C 11.20.   *Motor learning.*

Motor learning refers to acquisition of skills which involve _____ .

   a. working with engines of various sorts

   b. only the simplest elements of individual actions

   c. body movements

A main facilitator of motor learning, besides simple habit formation, is _____ .

   a. verbal mediation   b. help from an observer

Two pieces of specialized apparatus for investigating acquisition patterns in motor learning are:

   1. _____

   2. _____

It is a simple thing to measure the level of initial ability in any of the three tasks mentioned above, but it is more important to measure the changes that occur, with different forms of practice, in a subject's ability level.

As a general rule, and to no one's surprise, a subject's scores begin a gradual rise as he practices any of these tasks. However, the rise can be a function of several independent variables. In addition to several of those already described for verbal learning—warm-up, learning-to-learn, proactive and retroactive interference, number of elements in the tasks (which corresponds to list length), familiarity of the task (which corresponds to word or syllable meaningfulness), and verbal mediation (which corresponds to mnemonics)—three major functional relationships have been developed within the context of motor learning research itself, and have their major application to motor rather than to verbal learning. They are *distribution of practice, feedback,* and *transfer of training.*

**DISTRIBUTION
OF PRACTICE**

A variable that is somewhat like reminiscence is distribution of practice. This refers to whether practice sessions are *massed* or *spaced*, meaning whether considerable practice proceeds without interruption or whether the same amount of practice is split into short sessions, with periods of no practice between. Years ago, Lorge (1930) performed a careful experiment in complex mirror-tracing which is still referred to as a classic example of the relative merits of massed versus spaced practice.

Figure 11.9

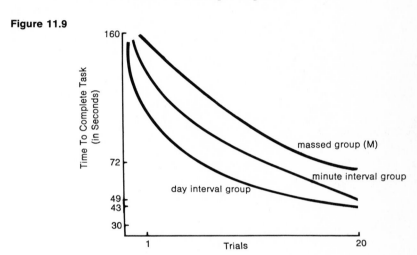

In Figure 11.9 you can see the relative performances of three groups. First, consider subjects who worked through 20 back-to-back practice sessions of the task which, at the outset before training, took around 160 seconds per tracing session (the massed, or *M* group). Compare their performances with those of subjects who had the same number of sessions (or trials) spaced one minute apart and subjects with trials spaced one day apart. As you can see, spaced practice clearly yielded superior results. At the end of the experiment, on the 20th trial, around *43* seconds were required for the tracing by the 24-hour interval group, about *49* seconds for the one-minute interval group, and around *72* seconds for the massed practice group. As this data indicated, little difference was found between the minute-interval and the day-interval group, and it appears that rest intervals of perhaps one or two minutes are about as good as longer intervals.

A variety of other variables may be employed in this area of research, one of them being the length of time of the *practice,* holding constant the length of rest intervals. In research conducted by Kimble and Bilodeau in 1949, it was found that performance on a simple motor task improved more rapidly when practice periods were limited to 10 seconds each than when they were 30 seconds each, with the time interval between sessions kept constant at 30 seconds. From start to completion, the group with the shorter practice session maintained a lead of about 10 percent efficiency over the group with the longer practice periods.

From results such as these, psychologists seem to prefer a separate explanation to differentiate the distribution-of-practice effect from the reminiscence phenomenon. While reminiscence may involve the brain's reverberatory circuits, massed practice seems to relate to a physical or mental (or both) "fatigue" factor that builds rapidly, and dissipates rapidly. The strong distribution-of-practice effect, with clear-cut results such as in the Lorge and the Kimble experiments, has been sought largely in vain by verbal learning researchers. Aside from allowing reminiscence to facilitate verbal learning, there appears to be no strong advantage in distributing verbal learning sessions, except for the avoidance of eyestrain.

C 11.21. *The distribution-of-practice effect.*

In motor learning, massing the practice trials has _____ effect on acquisition.

    a. an inhibitory   b. a facilitatory

Distribution of practice is an _____ effect in motor learning.

    a. important   b. unimportant

Distribution of practice is an _____ effect in verbal learning.

    a. important   b. unimportant

FEEDBACK   "Feedback" is information that tells the subject whether his answers are right or wrong. Feedback is obviously important in verbal learning, but in motor learning it is critical.

Let us say that you are trying to improve your ability to throw darts at a dartboard a considerable distance away. A number of factors should be adjusted, such as how hard you throw, the degree of arc you use, and perhaps even the way you stand when you throw. In this case and in comparable cases of motor learning, practice would provide no improvement in a no-feedback (*n.f.*) group that was not allowed to see where the dart landed or even see its trajectory in flight; there would be improvement, however, in a feedback group (*f.*) that had a chance to observe the results and make necessary adjustments in technique (see Figure 11.10).

To pursue the correlary of verbal learning for a moment, if teachers feel that feedback from a test is important, since it contributes to the continued improvement of the individual, they should not tell you just *how many* items you missed, but in some way they should communicate to you *which questions* you answered correctly and which incorrectly.

C 11.22. *Feedback.*

Feedback is most properly defined as _____ .

a. calculation of error rate for purposes of scientific reporting

b. information provided the subject on the accuracy of an ongoing activity

c. requiring each subject to learn material to a 100 percent criterion of accuracy

Feedback provides _____ effect in learning.

a. a facilitatory   b. an inhibitory

Figure 11.10

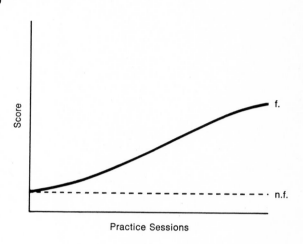

TRANSFER OF TRAINING   We have dealt with acquisition and retention in both verbal and motor task areas, and we now turn to the concept of transfer of training. The term "transfer of training" refers to the influence that the learning of one task may have upon the learning or performance of another task. We shall begin by giving a few concrete, everyday illustrations of transfer.

You might visualize two persons, both faced with the task of learning how to ride a small Honda motorcycle. Suppose one of these persons had become very skillful in riding a bicycle, while the second person had never learned how to ride a bicycle. Bicycle riding, the initial task, would *positively* transfer to the motorcycle task. That is, mastery of the first task would help in acquiring skill in the second.

In an opposite type of transfer, however, called *negative* transfer, the learning of a first task actually hinders a person in learning or performing a second. Occasionally one hears of individuals who compete in several sports. Some of the finer skills involved in one sport, if practiced extensively, actually hurt the individual's performance in another sport. Some men who have played softball and baseball extensively in their youth have a tendency, in subsequently playing golf, to bend the knees and then straighten up while swinging a club. This "swooping" motion has the effect of causing the ball to slice rather badly for most of them.

KNOWING YOUR RIGHT FOOT FROM YOUR LEFT

Mariana Osuna was a pretty girl. Not just pretty—every head turned when she walked into a room. There were plenty of guys at her university who were ready to do anything they could to impress her.

The situation on that Thursday morning led naturally into Howard Loveless' making his big "contact." Mariana, so it seems, hadn't brought her car to the campus that day. She had left it home, due to its periodic engine problems, and had taken the bus. It was 9:15 *a.m.* when she ran up to Howard in the Student Union Building.

"Howard," she said, "you have a car, don't you? That little green sports car? Could I use it to run home for a minute? I forgot my anthropology notes and we have a quiz this afternoon."

Howard beamed. "Sure. Here are the keys. Do you know how to work a stick shift?"

"Yes," said Mariana. "I'll be back in thirty minutes. Will you be here then?"

"Yeah. See you."

Howard watched Mariana walk away, and he momentarily visualized how she might show her gratitude by going out with him Saturday night.

Mariana wrestled with the car's gears and finally got it going in fits and jerks down the street. It had that old-fashioned clutch system, so that there were two pedals on the floor instead of one. Her own car just had one—the brake pedal—and the transmission was automatic.

At every stop light Mariana had to stop and think: "Now, left foot on the clutch, right on the brake."

Damn! This was difficult. She had a strong habit of using her right foot on the accelerator and braking with the left foot in her own car. Boy, what a bomb this little sports car was. It ought to do fifty by the middle of a block with its fantastic acceleration.

It was in the middle of the next block that the large trash collection truck suddenly pulled out from the alley entrance, and Mariana realized that in one second she would run headlong into it if she didn't stop. Frantically she jammed down her left foot. The car didn't stop, or even slow, and in that split second she realized that she had pressed her foot down on the clutch.

A famous psychologist of three-quarters of a century ago stated that a good set of habits can serve an individual for a lifetime, but a bad set can be a never-ending curse. Is it possible that environmental planners might devise a comprehensive scheme to promote positive transfer from task to task and minimize negative transfer such as was indicated in this story?

Transfer of training, then, can be a vital force for benefit or hindrance, depending on circumstances. We are naturally more concerned with negative than with positive transfer, because inabilities or dysfunctions can have the more serious effect. Not too long ago a major clerical office, its managers impressed by the development of a "new typewriter," the keys of which were rearranged to provide more efficient and rapid typing, ordered several. They had decided that the long-term advantages of more rapid typing would offset the costs of the necessary retraining period for their staff. Much to their surprise they found that experienced typists had extreme difficulty learning the new keyboard arrangement, and that the very best typists on the staff were the poorest performers on the new typewriter. They quickly concluded that the new typewriters were of no realistic advantage, and they were disposed of.

Analysis of Transfer of Training

In investigating transfer of training, psychologists do not stop at the determination of whether the transfer is positive or negative. They go on to subdivide both positive and negative transfer further into proactive and retroactive effects. We then arrive at four categories:

POSITIVE TRANSFER OF TRAINING

Proactive facilitation
Retroactive facilitation

NEGATIVE TRANSFER OF TRAINING

Proactive interference
Retroactive interference

We have already discussed the meanings of the terms proactive and retroactive. The dictionary definitions of facilitation and interference are also clear, so there should be little confusion in terms of fitting a case to the available models.

C 11.23. *Transfer of training: Positive and negative.*

Suppose you learn to roller skate and it can be shown that this allows you to learn to ice skate in a shorter time than would have been the case if you had no roller skating experience. This would be a case of _____ facilitation within the _____ transfer of training model.

Suppose that you lived as a small child in another country and spoke its language as your native tongue. Suppose you then came to this country, and learned and spoke English exclusively, to the point that you even "thought" in English. Years later it could probably be shown that you remembered far less of your native language than would have been the case if you were just socially isolated so that you did not speak it but had no new language with which to replace it. This would be a case of _____ interference within the _____ transfer model.

Osgood has proposed a model for transfer calling upon the major contributing factors. The two critical features in the Osgood model are stimulus

TRUDY

Jerry Marcus, © King Features Syndicate 1966

**"Frankly, Ted—I think I liked it better before
you quit smoking."**

similarity and response similarity. Let us take stimuli first. From the first task to the second, one may experience highly similar or even identical stimuli, down through various levels of similarity to the point of no similarity at all. Osgood concluded that the *similarity of the stimulus situations* is directly responsible for the *amount* of transfer of training, with high similarity contributing to a large amount of transfer, and no similarity contributing to zero transfer.

The *direction* of transfer, either positive or negative, is determined by the *response similarity* (assuming, of course, some degree of stimulus similarity to begin with). In responses, we have a range from identical (positive transfer) to dissimilar (zero transfer), and finally to the category of opposite (negative transfer). So, let us consider two situations with a high degree of *stimulus* similarity. This causes a large amount of transfer. If the *responses* called for in the two tasks are very similar, then the transfer will be positive. If, on the other hand, the responses are of an opposite nature, the transfer will be negative.

If one drove for years in the United States and then went to England, one would be confronted with situational stimuli highly similar in the sense of being behind the steering wheel and moving along. However, a vital element of driving an automobile in the United States is the habit one develops of driving on the right-hand side of the road. In England, the opposite response pattern is required, and mistakes can become quite a problem, particularly in making turns. A pronounced degree of negative transfer of training is likely until the second habit is strengthened to the point that it becomes dominant.

For a simple summary, let us restate that the *amount* of transfer depends upon how similar the two stimulus situations are, from identical (much transfer) to similar (moderate transfer) to different (zero transfer). *Direction* of any transfer that does occur then depends upon the relation of the two response patterns, from identical (positive transfer) to dissimilar (zero transfer) to opposite (negative transfer).

C 11.24. *Osgood's transfer model.*

From two tasks with a strong similarity factor in the R patterns but different S patterns, we would

predict _____ transfer.

From two tasks with an almost identical stimulus situation, but opposite response patterns called for,

we should see a (small/large) _____ amount of _____ transfer.

PROGRESS CHECK 11.3

MATCH: _____ 1. Learning   A. Acquisition

              _____ 2. Memory   B. Retention

3. Which formula accounts for a subject matter learned to 100 percent criterion? _____ .

    a. % Retention − % Forgetting = 100% of material

    b. % Forgetting + % Retention = 100% of material

    c. 100% of material − % Retention = % Forgetting

    d. b and c

4. Memory is a result of electrochemical potentials activated but then fading away in the central

    nervous system. This statement applies to the _____ .

    a. trace–decay theory of forgetting   b. interference theory

    c. repression theory   d. loss of access theory

5. Repression theory holds that _____ .

    a. activity of the CNS tends to dampen circuits

    b. mnemonic codes tend to fade away

    c. we forget things we do not want to remember

    d. more learning produces more forgetting

6. Acquisition and retention are affected by other learning in the _____ theory.

    a. trace–decay   b. repression   c. loss of access   d. interference

7. Which *two* effects of interference were demonstrated in the sleep experiment? _____ .

    a. Sleeping tends to disrupt acquired skills

    b. Any intervening stimulus is likely to disrupt learning

    c. Similarity between original and intervening activities heightens the interference

    d. Longer periods of intervening time lessen recall

8. Which is not a special apparatus for investigating acquisition of motor skills? _____ .

    a. Mirror-drawing apparatus   b. Hand-eye apparatus

    c. Pursuit rotor   d. They are all used

9. Which is an example of motor learning? _____ .

    a. Walking   b. Driving a car   c. Writing   d. All of these

10. Which factor facilitates motor learning more? _____ .

    a. Verbal mediation   b. Physical assistance from an observer

11. Which statement on distribution of practice in motor learning is accurate? _____ .

    a. Massing the trials facilitates acquisition

    b. Distribution of practice is important

    c. The effect is essential in verbal learning

    d. All of these

12. Feedback functions _____ .

    a. to facilitate learning   b. to provide information on accuracy of current performance

    c. both of the above   d. neither of the above

13. A roller skater learns to ice skate quickly. This is an example of _____ .

    a. feedback   b. transfer of training

    c. physical mediation   d. distribution of practice

14. If the response is choosing a pattern similar to ⧄⧄⧄ , which of the following S patterns would produce a greater transfer effect?

    a. ▯▯◯▯▯   b. ⧅⧅⧅

Transfer of Training and Education

If you will consider just what your college education is supposed to provide, you will see that the benefit from an education is presumed to lie in the transfer of your training to other situations later in life. That is, you hardly ever confront the identical situation that you learned to deal with in the college classroom. When, for example, is someone later in life going to ask you to write down the various causes of World War I? Or to diagram a sentence?

If the presumed benefit of a college education lies in the transfer that occurs later, what are the types of things you might be able to do better because you have had a college education? While little positive transfer may have been developed even now, at least we are aware of the problem much more than we were only a few decades ago. In those times students would study geometry in order to "become more logical-minded." This was considered a prime necessity for the student who later was to study law. The study of Greek and Latin was said to "strengthen the mind," and this was considered to be a necessity for one who was preparing to study medicine. In this manner many students each devoted thousands of hours to the study of material that has subsequently been found to generate little if any actual transfer.

Turning to subjects currently taught, Warriner has conducted research showing that individuals who memorize abstract rules of grammar are able to do no better, as a result, in their own speech patterns. Now that we know something about *S-R* similarity relations in transfer, we should be able to benefit from a gradual restructuring of educational practices. One thing that is indicated very clearly, both theoretically (on the basis of the transfer model) and from actual data, is the effectiveness of apprenticeships and internships. We shall probably see an increasing emphasis on problem-oriented *situational* training, rather than a continued sole reliance on book-type education, at least after the student's initial grasp of vocabulary and basic concepts.

The student who is interested in penetrating the area of human learning more deeply is referred to *The Psychology of Learning,* Third Edition (1967), by James Deese and Stewart Hulse. Most psychology departments offer an undergraduate course in "Learning," many using the Deese and Hulse volume as text.

NOTE TO THE READER: The subject matter discussed in this chapter is expanded and amplified in Extension Chapter 11A, beginning on pages 662-63.

Personality and Its Assessment

WHAT IS "PERSONALITY"?

TRAITS AND THEIR MEASUREMENT

DETERMINISM AND THE SEARCH FOR CAUSES OF BEHAVIOR

SHELDON'S BODY STRUCTURE POSITION

FREUD'S PSYCHOANALYTIC THEORY
The Personality Structure
The Energy System of the Personality
The Psychosexual Stages of Development
  The Oral Stage
  The Anal Stage
  The Phallic Stage
  The Latent Stage
  The Genital Stage
The Adult Character Structures

THE BEHAVIOR THEORY APPROACH TO PERSONALITY
Habit
Drive
Inhibition

ROGERS' SELF THEORY
Basic Assumptions
The Concept of Self
The Need for the Positive Regard by Others
The Need for Self-Regard
The Unhealthy Personality
Therapeutic Change

CATEGORIES OF ASSESSMENT DEVICES
The Interview Method
The Rating Scale
The Behavioral Assessment
The Personality Inventory
The Projective Measure

So far we have examined a number of factors going into the determination of behavior. First we assumed that biological factors determined both one's potential for behavior as well as one's behavioral limitations. We then assumed that perception of one's current environmental circumstances determined many behavioral reactions. Motive states and histories of experiences made up the next considerations, and finally social influences were discussed. As you can readily see, when we put all these things together, we have a functioning individual and we are interested in patterns of consistency which then set one individual off from others and give him or her the "personality" by which the individual is known.

WHAT IS "PERSONALITY"?

We have not devoted much space in this book to defining terms that are generally recognized and used by everyone. Often we hear someone say that a person has "a lot of personality," using the word "personality" as if it were synonymous with "charm." For the psychologist, however, "personality" is a precise term that has a special meaning. Actually it refers to an individual's behavior patterns that occur with consistency in given situations. The two notable factors in this definition are (1) consistency, and (2) the situational variable. For example, we would not say that a young woman had a depressive personality if we learned that she was once seen crying. We would want to know something about the frequency of such crying episodes. However, we might refer to even rarely occurring behavior as being a personality characteristic if the individual displaying it did so consistently within a rarely occurring situation. A widely recognized text, *Theories of Personality*, by Hall and Lindzey (2nd edition, 1970), stresses that there are scores of definitions of personality, each with its own merits, but each is tied more or less to a theory of what motivates people, so we shall stop with the simple descriptive definition given above.

C 12.1. *The definition of personality.*

Personality can be defined as a person's behavior patterns that _____

_____ .

For practical purposes, we have a need for an area of personality in psychological literature. We are interested in what sorts of patterns occur in human interactions to a degree that goes beyond single units of behavior. If we observe a child hitting someone, talking back to an adult, cursing someone else, and damaging property on different occasions, we tend to see a commonality in all this. The child is not just a hitter, a smart-aleck, a curser, or destroyer, but more—he is generally aggressive.

At this point you should recognize a very important fact: *Describing* a characteristic does not explain its *occurrence*. This is a trap into which even some trained psychologists occasionally fall. Billy does not achieve *because* he is "intelligent." Tommy does not hit other children *because* he "has an aggressive personality." These are circular explanations; for instance, someone asks why Tommy hits other children, and we say "because he is an aggressive child." They then ask how do you know he is aggressive, and you answer, "Because he hits other children." There is little merit in allowing a behavior to explain its own occurrence. We first should group behaviors into personality characteristics that are larger than just single units of behavior, but we then must look to the functional relationships that may exist between these patterns and various independent variables.

C 12.2. *Circularity in the explanation of behavior.*

A circular explanation of a behavior is one which allows a _____

of a characteristic to explain its occurrence.

Actually, the two topics of (1) how we describe behavior, and (2) to what types of independent variables we try to relate behavior, are both research areas of considerable interest.

TRAITS AND THEIR MEASUREMENT

In the early stages of all sciences, it has been typical that great emphasis has been placed upon the naming or labeling of things. The question of categorization of behavior is not at all the simple task that it might at first appear. Just consider one question for the moment—should the psychologist organize his conceptualization of traits around the opposing ways in which different people might react to a given circumstance, or should he look at the ways in which patterns of behavior (rather than individual acts) emerge in an individual's personality? Or might he even study the extent to which behaviors seem patterned or related, statistically, in large numbers of people —that is, do persons who show behavior A usually show behaviors C and D as well?

One group of psychologists is known for its primary emphasis upon such descriptive philosophy and research. Such *trait theorists* have developed sophisticated systems wherein (1) situations are related to the emergence of traits, (2) traits are conceptualized either as being "central" to the personality or of secondary nature, (3) age is related to the development of trait systems, and so forth. Trait theorists have developed specific theories of personality, but at this level we simply wish to point out that the question of how we describe behavior is a complex one that has been given specific attention by a great number of psychologists.

Traits are what we call the patterns of behaviors that we observe in people. If we were to search through a dictionary, we likely could find several hundred trait names that have been assigned to various patterns. You can probably list many yourself—sensitive, generous, humble, spontaneous, honest, etc. Many inventories have been developed and used to assess the traits of normal people. Even these traits—the ones selected by psychologists for formal measurement—number into the hundreds.

One approach to traits is to attempt to find out which are the basic traits—after all, when several "labels" seem to overlap or duplicate, such as friendly, socially-spontaneous, extroversive, etc., we suspect that perhaps all that is being measured is one trait. The way in which people boil down a large number of trait names into a smaller number of "true" traits is by a technique called factor analysis. Let us suppose that we take 20 published personality inventories and give all 20 to each of 500 subjects. Then we begin to see which traits on which inventories correlate highly with other traits. Those traits that seem to have fairly high correlations with one another are said to form a *cluster*; the cluster is then given a unitary conceptualization, and is called a *factor*. The problem in this is that some unexpected things sometimes show a high degree of relationship, and we then must decide what to call the factor. In research on the Sixteen Personality Factors Inventory (Cattell & Ebel, 1964), for example, it was found that persons who were "tender minded," in that they were sensitive to others' problems and had empathy for them, were also quite dependent people with an "over-protected" type of personality. What one calls such a factor is largely a matter of emphasis, unless one just lists the correlated traits and gives the factor no single name.

C 12.3. *The concept of traits.*

Traits are _____ .

    a. behavioral variables that we assume are founded in individual biological structures

    b. behavioral variables that we assume are learned

    c. individual patterns of behavior

C 12.4. *Factor analysis in personality research.*

Factor analysis is a correlational technique that is used to _____ .

    a. verify the validity and reliability of traits in individuals

    b. deduce "basic" variables from an originally larger number

    c. subdivide broad behavioral categories into numerous individual traits

The 16 P–F (Sixteen Personality Factors) Inventory is one of the leading inventories used in assessing personality. Raymond Cattell at the University

---

TRAIT LABELS USED IN THE CATTELL SIXTEEN PERSONALITY FACTORS INVENTORY
(Amended)

1. Reserved and critical	vs.	Participating and outgoing
2. Concrete-thinking	vs.	Intellectual and analytic
3. Easily annoyed or upset	vs.	Stable and secure-feeling
4. Mild, conforming, submissive	vs.	Dominant and stubborn
5. Prudent and serious	vs.	Spontaneous and enthusiastic
6. Unreliable and self-indulgent	vs.	Conscientious
7. Restrained and shy	vs.	Socially uninhibited
8. Tough and self-reliant	vs.	Sensitive and humanistic
9. Trusting and accepting	vs.	Critical, suspicious, opinionated
10. "Proper," conventional	vs.	Imaginative, unconcerned
11. Natural, forthright	vs.	Shrewd and deliberate
12. Self-confident	vs.	Guilt-prone
13. Overly cautious, traditional	vs.	Free-thinking, tolerant of ideas
14. Emotionally group dependent	vs.	Resourceful, self-organizing
15. Casual and nonintegrated	vs.	Precise and orderly
16. Satisfied, emotionally relaxed	vs.	Fretful, tense

(For clarity the trait labels used in the chart above were modified somewhat from those stated by Cattell.)

---

of Illinois factor analyzed human traits into 16 basic factors. To the extent that previous personality inventories which Cattell took into consideration touched upon all existing traits, we can assume that there are literally 16 basic traits of personality, and that all other apparent traits are simply sub-categories of the sixteen. Listed on page 434 are the trait names for opposite extremes of Cattell's sixteen dimensions. Remember that several additional traits were named under each factor, and the trait names chosen to reflect the factor were used just to capture the essence of the pattern.

The 16 P–F has been extensively used in industry, where individuals' personality characteristics on the job are predicted, and in general the pre-dictions on persons hired by the industries have been nicely verified. Predictive validity on individual traits is difficult to establish in an exact sense, but to the extent that validity is possible this seems to be one of the better available inventories for use with essentially normal people.

Now that you know essentially what is meant by a "trait," you are in a position to appreciate the differences in the ways people go about inter-preting behavior patterns in studying personality formation.

DETERMINISM AND THE SEARCH FOR CAUSES OF BEHAVIOR

Psychologists generally fall into two camps concerning causes of behavior. On the one hand are those who feel it best to limit activity to simply de-scribing and perhaps measuring trait-patterns. They tend to use as their rationale the assumption that people differ from lower organisms, and do not behave predictably in ways determined by past and concurrent events. Human beings, they say, are not controlled—they have *free will*. According to these psychologists, the behavior of human beings can hardly be ac-curately predicted, much less tied down to presumed controlling factors.

Opposing this view are those who may be called psychological *deter-minists*. They feel that any behavior has a definite cause, and that nothing "just happens." A weak form of determinism would hold that, within limits,

one can predict behavior from a knowledge of the subject's present and past circumstances. A strong form of determinism would hold that if we knew everything about a subject's present and past circumstances, we could predict his behavior precisely. An example of a weakly deterministic position would be that of psychoanalytic (Freudian) psychologists, as well as the position of psychologists who stress biological factors. An example of the strongly deterministic position is that of modern-day behaviorists who emphasize the total determination of behavioral events by the conditioning histories and concurrent stimulus factors in the environments of the subjects concerned.

It is impossible to do justice to all positions in this single chapter, and it is perhaps not unreasonable to assert that the freewill proponents appear to have had less influence on the field of psychology than have persons who take a more deterministic approach. Therefore, in the interest of presenting only a few distinctive positions, we will limit our coverage to four representative positions in the area of personality theory, three demonstrating various deterministic styles, and the last a fairly nondeterministic position.

C 12.5. *Determinism in psychological theory.*

Psychological determinism is an attitude in psychology that _____ .

    a. there is a cause for every behavioral event

    b. many events "just happen" for no apparent reason, and it will always be so

    c. scientists should try to determine as many cause-and-effect relationships as they can, though many may never be finally factualized

SHELDON'S BODY STRUCTURE POSITION

Psychologists generally agree that much of any individual's behavior is determined by biological characteristics such as the reactivity of the autonomic nervous system, and the neurological complexity and intactness of the central nervous system. In fact, a recognition of such contributions to behavior has led to the use of two opposed terms. First there is *temperament*, characteristics of behavior determined primarily by one's *biological structure*. A representative conception of what temperament consists of can be found in the seven variables measured by the Thurstone Temperament Schedule—activity, vigorousness, impulsiveness, dominance, stability, sociability, and reflectiveness. The second term, *personality*, is used to refer to behavioral variables more typically associated with one's *history of experiences*, including *learning*. That is, a person might be "confident" because he has achieved a considerable number of successes and very few disappointments in his past efforts.

C 12.6. *Temperament versus personality.*

Behavioral characteristics that are mainly determined by the variable of biological structure make up one's _____ .

Behavioral characteristics that are mainly determined by the variables of one's past experiences and learning make up one's _____ .

Some years ago there came upon the scene a psychological researcher who had an idea that went beyond the simple relations of biology to behavior that we have just described. William Sheldon conceived a theory that an individual's entire behavioral patterning was the direct result of his body type. Sheldon identified three main "types" of bodies. He described the *ectomorph*, who is a thin, bony person with little obvious body fat or heavy skeletal musculature; the *endomorph*, who has a great deal of fatty tissue, and whose outward appearance is rounded and soft; and the *mesomorph*, who has a great deal of body bulk, most of it made up of solid muscle, without a great deal of fat.

Sheldon did not simply assign a subject to the closest body type. Rather, he evaluated an individual on the degree of each of the three characteristics, ranking each characteristic on a 1 (low) to 7 (high) scale. Then, in the order ectomorph, endomorph, mesomorph, he portrayed a person's physique in the following manner: a 1-6-2 might be a very fat individual; a 1-5-4 would be a fat but still quite strong, muscularly-developed person; a 6-2-5 would be a thin, quite muscularly-developed individual such as the stereotype of the basketball player or long-distance track runner.

The essence of Sheldon's theory lies in the relation he stated between body types and personality. He described the ectomorph as being essentially introverted, solitary in his habits, not a good sleeper, restless and nervous, and inclined toward intellectual activities. Sheldon described the personality of the endomorph as fun-loving, comfort- and pleasure-seeking, highly sociable, good-natured, and noncompetitive. Finally, he described the mesomorph as being competitive, energetic, and moderately tense. The mesomorph was viewed as being in between the endomorph and the ectomorph in sociability.

On a more detailed level, Sheldon conceived of three complex personality configurations, corresponding to the body types. The ectomorph was said to have a *cerebrotonic* personality which, in addition to the main characteristics described above, also included a love of privacy, mental overintensity, emotional restraint, sensitivity to pain, and an orientation toward the later periods of life.

The personality pattern associated with the endomorphic body type was called viscerotonia. The *viscerotonic*, in addition to the characteristics described above, also was said to be relaxed in posture, slow in reaction, fond of polite ceremony, amiable toward all people, greedy for approval and affection, tolerant of others, a deep sleeper, with a strong orientation toward other people at times of disappointment or trouble.

The mesomorph was said to have a personality configuration called somatotonia. In addition to the broad characteristics described for the mesomorph, the *somatotonic* shows a love of physical adventure, dynamic and assertive postures and movements, enjoyment of exercise, pleasure in dominating others, fondness of risk and chance, psychological callousness, general noisiness, and a tendency to become aggressive and socially blunt when thwarted.

C 12.7. *Sheldon's constitutional theory.*

Sheldon had the idea that one's behavior is directly influenced by one's _____ .

    a. background of experiences   b. body type

The fat, rounded person was called _____ by Sheldon.

    a. a mesomorph   b. an ectomorph   c. an endomorph

The thin, angular person was called _____ by Sheldon.

The muscular, thick person was called _____ by Sheldon.

    a. a mesomorph   b. an ectomorph   c. an endomorph

Viscerotonia is the personality of the _____ .

Cerebrotonia is the personality of the _____ .

The _____ body type is associated with a love of physical activity and

competition, and a tendency to be assertive and dominant.

> Over a period of years Sheldon carried out major studies on college students, relating their personalities to their physiques. He established correlation coefficients between the personality structures just described and individuals who were pronounced in a single body-type category. The highest correlation coefficient was between the ectomorphic physique and the cerebrotonic personality, with a coefficient of .83. Almost as high was the correlation of .82 between the mesomorph and somatotonia. The correlation between endomorphy and viscerotonia was .79. These are extremely high correlation coefficients. Subsequent work by researchers has established still other body-behavior relationships. For example, it has been found that the mesomorphic body build is strongly overrepresented in populations of penitentiary inmates, and in children who become involved in conflicts with other children and with school authorities. Other research has related body types to varying forms of mental disorder. The suggestion is that ectomorphs, if they become mentally ill, tend disproportionately to be schizophrenic; endomorphs tend to become depressive, and the mesomorph who becomes mentally ill tends to have paranoid delusions of persecution and grandeur.
>
> It is currently the tendency among psychologists to play down the contributions of Sheldon, despite the high correlation coefficients he obtained in relating body type to personality. Some have criticized him because he performed most of the body-typing and determination of personality type himself. Critics maintain that it would have been better for an unbiased, trained rater to score the individuals on personality, while a separate rater with no knowledge of the first rating could rate the other variable. The critics do not maintain that Sheldon deliberately exaggerated the relationships, but they suggest that he might have been influenced in deciding borderline ratings by his expectations based on knowledge of the other variable.
>
> A separate criticism has been heard from persons who feel that body type is not biologically related to personality as Sheldon's theory supposes.

Rather, they suggest it may be related in a less direct manner. For example, they propose that the reason the mesomorph displays a competitive personality may be that he has been reinforced frequently by success following competitive behavior. His love of physical activity is perhaps the result of his better ability to perform physical activities. His assertiveness may be due to a history of reinforcement in which, due to his stronger physique, he was able to prevail over other peer-age individuals. In a similar manner the endomorph may become friendly and sociable because he is not easily able to relate to his peers in the area of physical competition. He learns to use such techniques as are available to him, such as friendliness, to influence others. Similarly, his love of physical comforts and eating may be the reason for the endomorphic body build, rather than the other way around. The ectomorph, in turn, may be nervous and socially inhibited, and somewhat of a social isolate, simply because of numerous experiences as a child, when his thin, frail body build invited torment and aggravation from other children.

One research study was performed that was supportive of Sheldon and might serve in partial refutation to the interpretation just mentioned. Walker (1973) used nude photographs of 73 male and 52 female nursery school children, typed their physiques, then matched the obtained ratings to behavioral ratings taken over a considerable period of time. Strong associations were found to exist, most of which were consistent with the general associations established in prior research with older subjects. While it is possible that, even in such young subjects, social histories exist that provide powerful reinforcement patterns, it is quite likely that the subjects in Walker's research were reasonably socially naïve. It would then appear that there could indeed be a basic biological linkage between body build and temperament.

Perhaps Sheldon, in claiming that personality characteristics are a biological result of body structure, is partly correct, and perhaps the critics are also partly correct, with the truth lying in a blend of both notions.

The relation of physical constitution to personality factors is an important and still-current issue, and while Sheldon's particular approach, stressing the general physique, is of limited scope in light of modern-day knowledge, a great deal of current research is going on concerning the internal, biochemical constitution and its relationship to personality. We shall reserve further discussion of this subject until Chapter 14, in which we shall examine the relationships between biochemical factors and mental illness.

PROGRESS CHECK 12.1

1. The text definition of personality is _____ .

    a. underlying dynamics of mind and consciousness

    b. consistent behavior patterns under certain situations

    c. charm and blarney   d. almost identical to everyday usage

2. Using a behavior to explain its occurrence is _____ .

    a. appropriate   b. an operational definition

    c. a circular explanation   d. infrequent

3. Patterns of behavior, such as generosity, selfishness, humility, etc., are _____ .

    a. personality types   b. enduring in individuals   c. characteristics   d. traits

4. Personality research uses what technique to deduce basic variables from a larger number? _____ .

    a. Factor analysis   b. Internal reliability coefficients

    c. Logical induction   d. Reductio ad absurdum

5. A determinist would state what about human behavior? _____ .

    a. It is different from animal behavior   b. Humans have free will

    c. Humans are unpredictable   d. Nothing "just happens"

MATCH: _____ 6. Temperament   A. Behavior variables influenced by history of experiences

    _____ 7. Personality   B. Behavior variables determined by biological structure

8. Which statement is true of Sheldon's theory of body types and personality? _____ .

    a. Ectomorphs are cerebrotonic   b. Endomorphs are viscerotonic

    c. Mesomorphs are somatotonic   d. All of these

9. According to Sheldon, a football center is a(n) _____ .

    a. ectomorph   b. endomorph   c. mesomorph

FREUD'S PSYCHOANALYTIC THEORY

Perhaps the most influential single individual, in terms of influence upon society's conception of the nature of man, was Sigmund Freud. Freud's major contributions came during the last decade of the nineteenth century, and certain elaborations upon his earlier ideas were made as far on as the 1920s and the 1930s.

Freud's theory is called *psychoanalytic* theory. It was a reasonably deterministic approach to explaining behavior, and in that sense it corresponds somewhat with modern-day behaviorism, although there are not many other similarities. Freud's theory is outlined in the next several pages.

The Personality Structure

The structural system of the personality consists of three separate components—the id, the ego, and the superego. When a child is born he has the potential for the development of all three systems, but the only system that operates during the first few months of life is the id. The *id* is the assemblage of what we now refer to as primary drives, and Freud conceived of these primarily from a hedonistic (pleasure-oriented) point of view. In fact, he felt that the primary determinant of behavior was the organism's seeking after pleasure, specifically in the form of affection and sexuality. Later Freud included the notion of aggressive impulses in the id. When the organism is newborn, it functions only toward the satisfaction of momentary physical needs and relief of physical distresses. The id-dominated personality at this age is completely selfish.

Later the ego emerges and develops. The *ego* is roughly synonymous with what we call the conscious personality. That is, the individual learns certain ways of relating to the environment in order to maximize the satisfactions of id impulses and yet do so in ways that do not get him in trouble. Another way of stating this is to say that the ego patterns, transforms, and suppresses id impulses in rational, planned ways. The ego develops largely through the process of *identification*. That is, an individual in childhood becomes more and more similar to the important adults to whom he is repeatedly exposed. An individual "adopts" another's personality, which is the essence of identification. The child learns how the parent satisfies his impulses and overcomes frustrations, and increasingly as he grows older he adopts these strategies for himself. Ego development proceeds for several decades, and the individual's conscious personality at age 40 might be quite different from what it was at age 20.

The superego is the last of the three structural elements to begin its development. The *superego* roughly is the same as what we call the conscience. Early in life the child feels no guilt for his transgression of rules, even if another person is hurt by his actions. Later, however, the child begins to show visible distress when he is aware of having hurt someone, and we can observe his guilt reactions. The superego's development comes about through a process called *introjection*, which is similar to identification in that the child adopts the behaviors of the significant adults in his environment. In this case, however, what he adopts are the *values* and *ethics*, rather than the "strategies," of the significant others. A child goes through a series of stages in so doing.

At first a child sees nothing wrong in a certain forbidden action. Then he may be able to tell you that he will not do that thing anymore because if he does he will be punished. The next stage comes when the child may be able to say that the action is wrong, and he will be punished, so he will not do it. In the final stage the child can simply verbalize "it is wrong" to do something, with diminished conscious awareness of the prospects of punishment. At that point the value is said to have been internalized into the superego structure. You will readily see how the superego can be said to develop through many years of an individual's life. For example, sexual morals are not developed during a child's early childhood, but usually await the emergence of heterosexual interest before they are formed.

When a child, or later an adult, is id-dominant, he is said to function according to the *pleasure principle.* An id-dominant person is one who is unable to delay or control his impulses for immediate gratification of desires or release of aggressions. These impulsive individuals, if adults, are visibly immature, and frequently get into trouble with the law. As a normal child matures, the personality becomes ego-dominant, at which time an individual is said to act according to the *reality principle*. Reality in this case simply means that one has learned to delay impulses toward immediate gratification. If one wants sexual access, certain material goods, and so forth, there are ways in which to achieve these goals that may take a considerable length of time, but there is an advantage in delaying the impulses. The advantage lies in the fact that society generally punishes those who act impulsively in the sense that they simply take the things they desire. If an individual wishes to have a certain material possession, he may have to work and accumulate the necessary amount of money, consistent with the reality principle. In the long run he is able to achieve the goals more than the individual who takes the money dishonestly and may be imprisoned, which removes him from the possibility of experiencing success.

The id, the ego, and the superego were viewed by Freud as somewhat in a state of competition with one another, and a variety of pathological problems may develop as a result of over- or under-development of one or more of the elements. For example, the superego and the id may be in violent conflict due to the superego's overdevelopment. A strong morality, which conflicts with biological impulses, may result in serious problems relating to social activities, values, and the sexual role. The ego serves the id by transforming impulses for immediate gratification into alternative channels, and with an underdeveloped ego one may run into various problems relating to conformity, productiveness, and so forth.

The ego is in many ways the center of the structural system, and it is crucial that it be adequately well developed so as to constitute social and emotional maturity. The ego must mediate conflicts that develop between the id and the superego, choosing behavioral routes that are able to pacify both structures. A weakly developed ego contributes major problems, and it is not completely inappropriate to suggest that the concept of *ego strength* is more or less the same as the term *"mental health."* A weak ego may result from either of two sources. First, one may identify with an individual who has a weak ego. If a son identifies with a father who resolves his insecurities by getting drunk, who resolves his frustrations by lashing out in open aggression, and who controls others by tantrums and childish tricks, it is very likely that the youngster will develop very similar patterns. A second source of a weak ego could be the failure to have an intimately known parent or parent-image with whom to identify. Some boys grow up in homes without a father, and where there is no other adult male to whom they can grow close. Some parents are emotionally and socially distant from their children, and the child never really gets to know the parent intimately. Identifications in such situations can be superficial and crude, and the child does not perceive the subtleties that exist in the adult personalities.

C 12.8. *Psychoanalytic theory: The id, ego, and superego.*

The "primary drive states" might be a fairly good description for the Freudian term _____ .

When the child learns to rationally plan ways to gratify his impulses, the _____ is said to be directing

behavior.

    a. id   b. ego   c. superego

The ego develops through the process of _____ .

    a. introjection   b. identification

The "conscience" is a term synonymous with the Freudian term _____ .

The superego develops through the process of _____ .

    a. introjection   b. identification

An ego-dominant personality is said to function according to the _____

principle.

A weak ego can come from either _____

_____ or _____

_____ .

The Energy System of the Personality

The energy system of the personality is called the *libido*. The libido is the biological reserve of energy in several forms. Freud conceived a total energy system, which supplied the physical body for movement and resistance to disease, and the mental processes in both the emotional and intellectual forms. We shall discuss each of these types of energy utilization in a moment. Libido strength is viewed as a variable, the value of which depends upon congenital biological variation—age, health, and the various drains upon the system that might exist at any of the four levels. This latter point is sometimes referred to as the "hydraulic" principle of operation, so that an outpouring of energy at one point would lessen the amount of energy available at other points in the personality.

The libido's energy is expended primarily into the id. Of course it would be obvious that sexual and aggressive energies would be at their peaks when the individual is young and in a state of robust health. As an individual ages or if debilitating factors enter into the picture, libido strength declines.

Let us examine the four levels at which libidinal energy is expended. First, energy is expended in physical activity. Second, it is expended in warding off infection and disease. Third, it is expended in thought, study, and mental concentration. Fourth, it is expended in worry and emotional tension. The important notion that Freud advanced was that an unusual drain of energy at one level would decrease the energy available for use at other levels. As an example, mental work can make one physically tired. Similarly, after a great deal of physical work one is often too tired to study and concentrate. When one is ill it is difficult to study a textbook. When one is emotionally upset he has difficulty concentrating and learning, and he may be very susceptible to colds and other infectious diseases.

When an individual is young, the libido energies generate the *life instincts*. At this age the libido is usually strong, and id energies are thrust outward upon the environment. However, when any of the determinants of libido strength lower the energy to a very low level, the death instinct takes over. This means that the low libido energy level allows the aggressive elements of the id to turn inward upon one's self, and one tends toward self-destructive behavior. Studies have related rates of suicide to times of ill health or emotional upset, and suicide rate also has been related to age. All of the results are in agreement with Freud's concept that life and death instincts depend upon libido strength.

C 12.9. *Psychoanalytic theory: The libido.*

Energy use at one point from the _____ , which is the energy system, depletes the total strength elsewhere in the system, which is the _____ principle of its operation.

Name the four types of energy supplied by the libido:

a) _____

b) _____

c) _____

d) _____

Low libido energy allows the _____ impulses to turn inward.

    a. aggressive   b. superego

The Psychosexual Stages of Development

Freud conceived of individuals pursuing their goals of pleasure, affection, and sexuality in a manner that changes with age. Another way of putting this is to say that at varying ages children typically are interested in different goals and aspects of their environments.

The Oral Stage

When a child is newborn, and for the first year or so of his life, he is in the *oral* stage of psychosexual development. During this time he is strongly oriented toward eating, and in fact the satisfaction of his hunger drive becomes the most important emotional gratification he can have. A behaviorist might point out that many things at this stage of life become paired with satisfaction of the hunger drive, a large number of them involving stimulation of the mouth area. At any rate, Freud observed that children at this young age, and continuing for some years into the future, appear to derive considerable gratification from all types of oral stimulation. Children can be observed sucking their thumbs, chewing and sucking on objects, and even adults are said by Freudian theorists to be following infantile gratification patterns when they smoke cigarettes or cigars.

The major concern of a child at this age is that he be fed when he is hungry. Freud observed the high degree of emotionality in the hungry infant, and he felt that the child had an instinctive knowledge that he would die if not fed. The high hunger drive thus results in tremendous anxiety, and satisfaction of the drive results in a corresponding amount of emotional relief and gratification. The danger, Freud thought, was that some children might develop too high a level of upset due to hunger and, in sequence, too high a level of gratification from eating, and problems could develop (we shall look at these in a moment). A controversy about feeding children on demand versus on schedule developed as a result of Freud's influence, with most Freud-influenced pediatricians advocating feeding on demand.

The gratification pattern in eating is frustrated late in the oral stage by the process of weaning. Whereas the child consistently had been given an easily handled form of food, the new requirements are that the child handle solid substance. Most children demonstrate anger and show visible frustration at this point. This is an important contributing factor to what Freud predicted could happen in the later personality formation of the adult.

The Anal Stage   The second psychosexual stage is called the *anal* stage. At this point in the child's life, the emotional attention is focused upon a new factor, namely toilet-training. Again the child is frustrated in the performance of a function that previously offered no problem. At an age when a child is still largely preverbal, in that he may not understand the abstract words for certain functions and internal feelings, the parents demand that he subscribe to a rigid routine concerning his toilet habits. This is beyond the initial capability of the child, and his frustration is understandable. The problem becomes more and more severe, and resistance to the toilet-training demanded by mothers usually starts simply as an emotional accompaniment of frustration due to nonunderstanding and inability, rather than as an act of deliberate aggression. The emotions mount on both sides, with parent and child each becoming increasingly upset. Finally an association is formed when the child "understands" what he or she is expected to do. One day the child is treated as unlovable and nasty, and he may regard the whole business as rejection or withdrawal of love by the parent, and on the next day the child may behave as desired which results in the mother becoming very demonstrative with affection and praise, and there is a return of all the good things that the child had been denied during the frustrating earlier times. At this point the emotional gratification is intense (we called this positive reinforcement in a previous chapter), and toilet-training is rather sudden, although later there may be occasional accidents. Both the intense frustrations at one point and the intense gratifications later contribute to the adult character structures to be discussed later.

The Phallic Stage   Once the emotion concerning toilet activities passes, the child's attention is next drawn to the matter of his or her own sexuality. During this stage, parents frequently observe the child handling or manipulating his or her own sexual areas, and the child appears to find this pleasing and satisfying. This is called the *phallic* stage. Freud did not stop at this point, with simple description of the child's occupation in this activity. He went ahead to imply a type of instinct, whereby the dim awakening of genital sexuality is coupled with a vague awareness that opposite-sex individuals, in this case the opposite-sex parent, is somehow the fitting object for the sexual impulse. Freud then described the *Oedipus complex* in the little boy who develops a strong emotional attachment to the mother, with corresponding jealousy displayed toward the father, and the *Electra complex*, which is the corresponding situation involving the daughter and the father. Each of the two complexes is usually described under the broader term *Oedipus situation*.

The phallic stage progresses with the child continuing his interest in the genital areas and often exhibiting interest in the sexuality of children of the opposite sex. And, during this time, there is an increase both in the jealousy toward the same-sex parent and possessiveness toward the opposite-sex parent. At this age it is not unusual to see the child trying to wiggle in between the parents as they sit together on a sofa, or to verbalize as did a little girl once in my hearing: "When I grow up I'm going to marry my Daddy." Finally the friction is so great that the child begins to sense danger in the conflict that might develop. In the next chapter we shall discuss this process in more detail, but for now we shall simply sketch in a little description of *projection*. The child hates, and therefore sees himself hated in return, although this of course is usually baseless. He begins to see a possibility that the same-sex parent might harm him in order to "eliminate the opposition." In fact, and in line with the notion of the child's awakening instinct concerning genital sexuality, he begins to dimly perceive that the same-sex parent could harm his genitals. This resulted, said Freud, in the "castration complex," with the child beginning to feel fear, leading to a tactic of self-defense whereby the child relinquishes the opposite-sex parent as an object for possession, and from that time identifies with the same-sex parent. (If you can't fight them, join them.) From that point little boys become more masculine in attitudes and interests, and the little girls somewhat more feminine. With the resolution of the Oedipus situation the child moves out of the phallic stage.

The Latent Stage

The *latent* psychosexual stage of development comes after the Oedipus situation is resolved and the child begins to identify with the parent of the same sex. This period is said to begin somewhat earlier for boys than for girls, possibly at about age four to five for the male child and from five to seven for the female. During the latent stage the child does not focus his emotional energies on any particular situation. He has no great concerns or erotic influences that give him systematic patterns of anxiety or pleasure. Generally, interactions with peers are same-sex social patterns. This stage continues for several years until the individual approaches adolescence.

The Genital Stage

The final psychosexual stage is the *genital* stage, which accompanies heterosexual interests at about the beginning of adolescence. In the genital stage, the individual begins to focus an increasing amount of emotional concern toward affection patterns involving the opposite sex. Affection patterns at this stage become increasingly biological, involving sexual arousal, although during the earliest years of the genital stage the understanding and channeling of the biological aspects of heterosexual relationships may be vague.

C 12.10. *Psychoanalytic theory: The psychosexual stages of development.*

The five psychosexual stages of development, in the order of their development, are the _____

_____ , _____ , _____ , _____ , and

_____ stages.

The attachment of the child for the opposite-sex parent is called the _____

situation and develops in the _____ stage.

The _____ complex is one of the factors leading to the final resolution of the

Oedipus situation.

The Adult Character Structures

The psychosexual stages of development, described in the preceding section, can leave an emotional residual in the *adult character structure* of an individual. Psychoanalytic theory outlines nine adult character structures, in eight of which an individual will have fixated or regressed, which means that much of his present-day behavior is strongly influenced by significant emotional developments from earlier psychosexual stages. The fact that an individual may have fixated or regressed to, say, the oral stage does not mean that the individual may not be practicing appropriate heterosexual affection patterns that are said to reflect genital style interests; it simply means that the pattern of his behavior is strongly colored by his early experiences relating to orality.

The Oral Incorporative Structure

Corresponding to the oral stage, there are two possible resulting adult character structures. The first of these is the *oral incorporative* structure. Here the individual reenacts, emotionally, significant concerns and patterns that correspond to the first few months of life. As an infant he may have experienced intense emotional distress during hunger. As a result, he could be said to have experienced great emotional gratification when finally fed. The magnitude of this gratification might permanently influence his style of pleasure-seeking or his means of reducing emotional distress later in life. If you see that an individual pursues oral gratification quite extensively, resolving emotional upset through eating or drinking, it suggests the oral incorporative character structure. As an infant, the distressed child was given warm milk, and in drinking it his emotional distress melted away. Now, as an adult, when distressed he may eat, reawakening the infantile sense of gratitude and security. Or, in drinking alcohol, the warmth of the liquid and the ensuing drowsiness is similar in stimulus patterning to nursing and sleep as an infant. The oral incorporative character structure generally carries with it a pattern of affection-seeking and dependency, all of which corresponds to the primary emotions present during the very early stages of life.

The Oral Aggressive Structure

The next adult character structure, in the sense of the chronology of life, is the *oral aggressive* structure. This character is a residual of the emotional irritation experienced by the infant during the weaning process. Just as the oral incorporative character structure might have been triggered by repeatedly allowing the child to build up a too-high hunger level before feeding, so can the oral aggressive character structure have resulted from the child being weaned too abruptly, with punishment for any resistance displayed at that time. The essence of the oral aggressive character structure is that if the individual seeks pleasures but is frustrated, he tends immediately to flare up in anger. This causes an adult with this character structure to impress others as being rather immature and spoiled.

The Anal Aggressive Structure

Two adult character structures are associated with the anal psychosexual stage. Chronologically, the first is the *anal aggressive* structure. This goes back to the child's frustration and upset when the parents rejected him, punished him, and treated him as "unlovable" during the early stages of toilet-training. The child's natural activities were in a very real sense frustrated, but the emotional rejection had an even stronger influence. During this time of rejection the child literally seethed with anger, exhibiting frequent tantrums. Presumably, emotional fixation at this stage may result from an overly precise parent who insists upon perfect toilet behavior. The adult who demonstrates the anal aggressive character structure is an individual who resists the constraints of society, particularly when they concern personal habits and activities. Even decades ago, before popular interest in extreme fads of dress and hairstyle, psychoanalysts noted that many people resisted societal pressures to conform to what was "proper." They then, in a deliberate manner, were nonconformists, especially in resistance to dictates regarding neatness and cleanliness.

The Anal Retentive Structure

Next is the *anal retentive* structure. The general pattern leading to this character structure is first that the child, rejected by the parent during toilet training, becomes insecure. Then, at the time when he gains control over toilet habits and experiences the reacquired love, affection, and praise of the parent, the child feels unusually reassured. In a sense, "saving something" and having it available for the mother become synonymous with emotional security. Later in life the individual with the anal retentive structure becomes a "saver." As a youngster, when faced with various stresses of school and with separation from the parent during large parts of the day, it is not unusual for the child to develop interests in collecting things—rocks, matchbook covers, knives, or what-not. These cases, of course, are not full-blown character structures, but are partial and preliminary throwbacks to the emotional processes of the earlier stage.

The anal retentive adult character structure is sometimes seen in adults who, for various reasons relating to insecurity or lack of affection, save and stack up back issues of newspapers in their homes, sometimes running into the thousands. Often this is done by very elderly people who, as a result of the loss of a spouse, have lost the affection they were accustomed to. In these elderly persons, one sometimes sees the collection of bits of string, pieces of aluminum-foil or tin-foil, and not surprisingly, the hoarding of cash. Occasionally one reads an account of a very elderly person living in poverty, eating little, who dies leaving tens of thousands of dollars in bales of cash hoarded in a dresser drawer. We often wonder why the money was not spent for self-support by the individual who obviously needed many of life's necessities. The answer is simply that the individual derived emotional security, amounting to a nonrational feeling of being safe and loved, by having something accumulated. Some theorists have suggested that the modern-day materialism demonstrated by large segments of the population reflects a certain amount of this sort of fixation.

The Phallic Narcissistic Structure

Two resulting adult character structures correspond to the phallic stage. One is the *phallic narcissistic* structure. A narcissist is "in love" with himself, almost to the total exclusion of any real emotional involvement with others. In extreme cases one sees females who spend many hours before the mirror puttng every hair in place before they will appear in public, and who most of the time conduct themselves before others in ways that insure that they attract attention and are looked at appreciatively by large numbers of persons. The male narcissist could be the body builder who cultivates his physique through many hours of daily "mirror exercise." Some studies have suggested that such persons of both sexes have very little involvement in affectional interactions with others. They derive deep gratification from looking at themselves and savoring their own attractiveness. The phallic narcissist is an individual who is said to be re-experiencing the early interest that he once had when very young in his own body as a source of sexual pleasure. There is said to be an emotional correspondence between the child touching and rubbing the sexual areas and that person's later enjoyment of his or her own body as an object of almost-sexual admiration. Psychoanalysts do not appear to have firm ideas as to why an individual would become narcissistic, but they do feel confident of the relationship of the behavior of such adults to events during the early phallic stage.

The Psychopath

The next structure, also deriving from the phallic stage, is that of the *psychopath*. His emotional complex corresponds to that of the young child who wishes to possess the opposite-sex parent for himself and to destroy the same-sex parent, who is his competitor. In the young child the jealousy sometimes rises to massive proportions, and the whole process is a self-serving, selfish, and aggressive one. In the adult psychopath we have an individual who seemingly has no conscience. He is willing to gratify him-

BORN FREE?

Young Lennie Woodstock was brought to the psychologist when he was fifteen. He didn't study, didn't like to read books, and his mother reported that he spent most of his free time just hanging around with his friends. The friends were mostly like Lennie in being as nonacademic as he; it seemed that all they ever wanted to do was talk about automobiles, or kid around and play games like frisbee.

The parents were concerned over Lennie's expressing no interest in college.

"He even said that all he wanted to be was a truck driver, or work on construction projects," complained the mother. "His grades are almost all D's. We've threatened him and punished him, and I just don't know what else we can do."

Lennie's father was a college graduate, a hard-driving person who seemed to be all work and no play. He was a statistician with an insurance company, and felt that he owed all he was to his college education in mathematics. The mother was a tense, depressed individual who had been briefly institutionalized a few years previously for her depressions. She still visited a psychiatrist occasionally, and took a medication for the depressions. She was a very overweight woman as well.

When Lennie came to the psychologist's office he seemed open, friendly, and easygoing. Seemingly, he was well-adjusted. A battery of psychological tests was administered, and the test patterns suggested that he was an extremely mature and composed young man, relatively free from tension and anxiety, and without notable pathology. During the interview Lennie repeated his intent to become a construction worker, if possible. He liked automotive mechanics, he said, but if he were a mechanic he might not like it permanently since he liked to work in the outdoors.

A written report on the testing was prepared for the referring psychiatrist, and a copy was sent to the parents. The report stated, in essence, that the boy was normal and that no therapy seemed indicated. Upon reading the report the parents became irate. While the father went directly to the psychiatrist's office in an attempt to get him to agree to start Lennie in "therapy," the mother got on the phone to berate the psychologist directly. As she told the psychologist how wrong he was, she intermittently turned toward the dog or one of her younger children playing nearby to scream at them about the noise they were making.

The psychiatrist refused to treat Lennie, and the parents angrily refused to pay the billings of either the psychiatrist or the psychologist. One of the mother's final remarks was jotted down for further reflection: "It just breaks our hearts to see Lennie not growing up to be like us."

This true story reflects an all too true tendency for people to perceive those similar to themselves as being "good" or "right" and those dissimilar as being failures. Are you tolerant of those who may be marching to the beat of a "different drummer"?

self at other people's expense, and seems unaware of or unconcerned about the hurt he causes. The type of criminal activity whereby an elderly woman living on a small amount of savings may be cheated out of what little she has is an illustration of this. You can see the correspondence between selfish desires to take what one wants and eliminate the opposition during the phallic stage, and the later character structure of the psychopath.

The Homosexual

The next adult character structure is the *homosexual*. This is the first of two character structures associated with the latent psychosexual stage. The socially (not sexually) normal "homosexual" patterns during the latent years become a style of adult sexual interaction. Presumably, social activities with the same sex have been extremely gratifying, the exclusion of the opposite sex has been rather total, and coupled with this is typically a fear of the opposite sex transmitted through some interactions with the opposite-sex parent or other significant persons of the opposite sex. These factors, in combination, limit interactions to the homosexual area and finally the individual's warm social patterns mature, biologically, into warm sexual patterns. This explanation was essentially an early psychoanalytic one, and while modern psychologists tend to accept it as one explanation of some cases of homosexuality, they have identified what they think are several separate psychodynamic patterns in homosexuals of both sexes.

The Sexual Repressive

The next adult character structure is also associated with the latent psychosexual stage. This is the structure of the *sexual repressive*. These individuals have developed an aversion to interactions with the opposite sex, particularly of a sexual nature. However, they are cut off from affectionate interactions in that they have not entered into homosexual patterns or common sexual perversions. Sexual repressives are a cold, icy sort of people, and while they may marry, it is generally for social appearances rather than sexual satisfactions. Freud contended that the sexual repressive structure developed from feelings of fear of sexual activity instilled during the latent psychosexual stage. It should come as no great surprise that the majority of sexual repressives are females, because it is not unusual during the years immediately before adolescence for certain mothers to instill in their daughters a great fear of sexual activity. Stories are told, by such mothers, of pregnancies and venereal diseases, coupled with lurid descriptions of the "animal nature" of men, deliberately calculated to terrify the girl. These girls often grow up to be young women who are disgusted by the idea of sex, but who sometimes feel that "once they marry everything will be all right." Typically, after marriage, feelings of revulsion to sex persist and the sexual adjustment is quite poor.

We have described eight adult character structures which represent fixations or regressions to points preceding the genital psychosexual stage of development. Again, it should be stressed that while many people display *traces* of such behaviors both as older children and as adults, it is when such behaviors *dominate* the personality that we term it a regressive or fixated adult character structure.

The Adult Character Structure

The ninth character structure is simply called the *adult character structure,* and it is defined more by exclusion than inclusion. That is, the person does *not* demonstrate strong characteristics of any of the previous eight structures, and his concerns and pleasures typically are oriented in normal, heterosexual directions.

This is probably the ideal point to indicate how completely oriented toward sexuality Freud's theory was. Many persons who have graduated from the period of life when they were vitally concerned with who might be their Saturday night date, and whether or not they were sexually attractive to others have, in marriage, settled into a broad variety of interests and life-patterns, in which sexuality is an important but not a dominating part. Freud himself was not one of these individuals. Throughout his life he continued to be supremely concerned with sexuality, and he indicated, through his theory, that he considered others to have the same prevailing interests. Some persons have expressed the opinion that Freud's "sexuality" might be broadened to include the concerns that all individuals have that they be viewed fondly and affectionately by a variety of people, and that they not be rejected as loved ones or as friends. To that extent, Freud's theory seems more broadly applicable than would be the case where "sexuality" was viewed in a more narrow, strictly biological sense.

C 12.11. *Psychoanalytic theory: The adult character structures.*

Indicate which adult character structure is described in each of several short sentence-length cases which are presented here.

A person reduces his anxieties by getting drunk often.

_____

An individual is totally self-interested, admiring his own qualities to the total exclusion of almost anyone else.

_____

An individual is self-gratifying and seems to have little empathy or feeling for those whom he abuses in seeking his own aims.

_____

A highly-frustrated-appearing person is quick to anger and spends a great deal of time and energy talking about and criticizing other people.

_____

Living in messy surroundings, and presenting a disheveled appearance in both grooming and dress, characterize a rebellious attitude toward the generally recognized values of society.

_____

A middle-aged lady has very little use for men, suspecting that if given any opportunity they would probably initiate animalistic sexual overtures toward her.

_____

A young man who was reared by his mother has a characteristically feminine pattern of sensitivities and affections, and his primary affectional relationships are with men.

_____

Some persons, especially at difficult times in their lives when they are essentially without a close affectional relationship, collect, save, and stockpile incredible quantities of various things.

_____

Freud's theory has had an impact on those persons who are interested in the determinants of human behavior to an inestimable degree. So many social programs and other psychological explanatory frameworks are influenced by Freud's contributions that he may well have had the most impact on modern-day psychological thinking of any human being who ever lived. Many of his concepts are questioned, but there are many others that we tend to accept almost without hesitation.

Much of Freud's contribution lies in the ideas he had of how we struggle with anxiety-producing forces, and we shall return to such aspects of psychoanalytic theory in the next chapter.

PROGRESS CHECK   12.2

1. An ego-dominant personality functions according to _____ .

    a. the pleasure principle   b. the reality principle   c. the guilt principle

MATCH: _____ 2. Id   A. Consciousness

               _____ 3. Ego   B. Primary drives

               _____ 4. Superego   C. Conscience

                                       D. Develops through identification

                                       E. Develops through introjection

                                       F. Innate

5. The reservoir of energy or biological reserves, which could be expended on physical or mental activities, Freud called _____ .

    a. orgone   b. ego substance   c. life forces   d. libido

6. What model did Freud propose for the expenditure of energy? _____ .

    a. Lever model   b. Perpetual motion   c. Hydraulic model   d. Deterministic model

7. The son's attraction for the mother, which develops in the phallic stage, is _____ .

    a. perverted   b. a normal part of development

    c. the phallo-vaginal complex   d. the Oedipus complex

8. Freud's five psychosexual stages of development in correct order are _____ .

    a. oral, anal, phallic, latent, and genital

    b. oral, latent, anal, genital, and phallic

    c. oral, anal, latent, genital, and phallic

    d. anal, oral, latent, phallic, and genital

9. Freud would label an alcoholic as _____ .

    a. anal eliminative   b. oral incorporative   c. phallic narcissistic   d. repressed

10. Which person would be a phallic narcissist? _____ .

    a. A drug addict   b. A shoe fetishist

    c. A person hung up on redheads   d. A body builder

11. The oral aggressive character, says Freud, results from _____ .

    a. allowing the infant to get too hungry   b. abrupt weaning

    c. early toilet training   d. punitive toilet training

MATCH: _____ 12. Anal aggressive character   A. Collection of old magazines

            _____ 13. Anal retentive character   B. Non-conformist

14. Which adult character structure behaves as though conscienceless? _____ .

    a. Phallic narcissist   b. Homosexual   c. Psychopath   d. Sexual repressive

15. Which character structures are associated with the latent stage? _____ .

    a. Anal aggressive and psychopath   b. Psychopath and adult

    c. Psychopath and homosexual   d. Homosexual and sexual repressive

---

THE BEHAVIOR THEORY APPROACH TO PERSONALITY   A third look at approaches to personality will be that of the behaviorists, who base their conceptions on laboratory findings mainly in the research areas of learning and motivation. Actually, several approaches have been elaborated within behavior theory. B. F. Skinner's approach emphasizes operant processes and reinforcement almost exclusively. O. H. Mowrer, during the 1940-50 years, put together his "two factor" approach, emphasizing the dual processes of operant and respondent conditioning. Dollard and Miller, some years ago, conceptualized Freud's notions within a learning-approach framework. Much of what they did was in the nature of "translating'' Freud into learning terminology, and Freud's stress on critical environmental factors, such as feeding conflicts and toilet-training, remained. Albert Bandura has developed a systematic position that takes Skinner's emphases and additionally stresses both cognitive and social processes, especially the influence of social models.

These theorists all have a similarity of approach, at least in philosophy, and we shall not pursue the differences between them. We shall illustrate this overall approach to the understanding of personality by looking at a general notion put forward by Clark Hull, and later elaborated by Kenneth Spence. Our explanation of this point of view is somewhat amended and simplified, but is consistent with Spence's general ideas.

The approach can be embodied in a formula: $R = f (H \times D) - I$. This formula states that a response (behavior) is a function of habit times drive, minus inhibition. In order to properly understand how comprehensive this formula is, we shall examine the components of each of the factors.

Habit   *Habit strength* is a function of (a) magnitude of reinforcement, (b) number of reinforcements, and (c) delays of reinforcement. Each of these independent variables has been related in actual laboratory research to resulting response rates. The first factor, magnitude of reinforcement, has been further subdivided into two categories—quantity of reinforcement and quality of reinforcement. Often, but not always, reinforcers have a quality dimension. Dogs in laboratories condition more strongly to meat-reinforcers than to food that is partly meat but mostly cereal. In terms of quantity, they condition more strongly to large bits of the food than to smaller bits. As we saw in Chapter 9, the number of reinforcements that an organism has experienced for performing a certain behavior is perhaps one of the strongest and most straightforward of the functional relationships to response rate. The delay of reinforcement process also was discussed in Chapter 9. All of these components go together in a multiplicative way to create habit strength. The components are multiplicative in the sense that the product of their interaction is zero if any one of them is the equivalent of a zero value. Thus, if magnitude and number of reinforcers were adequate, too much delay of reinforcement still would have the effect of bringing about virtually no conditioning.

Drive   Drive strength is an outcome of five separate contributing variables. The first variable actually subdivides into one or another subcategory depending upon whether the drive concerned is appetitive or aversive. The five variables are (a_1) deprivation schedule / or/(a_2) drive stimulus intensity, (b) magnitude of the incentive, which subdivides into quality of incentive and quantity of incentive, (c) proximity to the incentive, (d) cues to the incentive, and (e) social facilitation.

Let us examine these components individually. First, if an *appetitive drive* is concerned, we know that the length of time the individual has been in a state of deprivation is a powerful variable. If the drive is an *aversive one,* then we know that the stimulus intensity is a primary factor.

The second concept, incentive, requires a little explanation. When we refer to reinforcement, we often call it reinforcement history, because we always use the term reinforcer in the past or current sense. The term *incentive* is used to refer to a *future* reinforcer that is perceived by the subject. In animal research it is necessary to place the incentive so that it can be sensed—visually, by smell, etc. Human subjects, on the other hand, can "visualize" an incentive that is promised verbally or that they "know" awaits the successful completion of a behavior.

Incentive effects have been studied by psychologists in ingenious ways. One researcher attached little harnesses to laboratory rats and measured the strength with which they pulled against a restraining leash toward an appetitive stimulus or away from an aversive stimulus. He was thereby able to investigate a variety of incentive effects. *Magnitude of incentive* is a powerful variable. An animal will pull more strongly against a restraining leash toward a large pile of food than toward a very small bit of food, if all other variables are kept constant. The quality effect is largely lost in animal data, but with human beings a strong quality as well as quantity effect is apparent. People will, for example, expend considerable time, effort, and money to have the opportunity of eating at a particular restaurant or drinking wine of a superior year.

If behavioral research has taught us one important thing, it is that incentive, although held in high esteem by many psychologists, is a very weak motivator when it is distant. An animal will pull against the restraining leash with twice the vigor when he is practically touching the incentive than he will when he is only a short distance from it. Human beings are no different. However, human beings are not limited to a conception of spatial distance to an incentive, as are research animals; human subjects are also able to experience distance to an incentive in terms of time, and therein lie many interesting phenomena. For example, consider the case of the student who has the aversive prospect (negative incentive) of an *F* for a term paper assignment if he does not get it completed. Our student procrastinates and waits until the last minute, for when the incentive is distant, it has very weak motivating properties. When such students later get into difficulties and take penalties, they tell themselves that they will never again put off studying or working on a project until it is too late to do it properly. The next time a similar situation arises, however, the strong functional relationship of *proximity to incentive* again prevails. Persons who contradict this principle seem to be motivated from their reinforcement histories, and not primarily by the incentive.

Cues to the incentive add to drive strength. Consider the times that you have walked by a restaurant and smelled the kitchen exhaust. It is no accident that in some of the big-city steakhouses the grills are placed just inside a front picture window so that passersby can see steaks cooking and can smell the aroma delivered by fans over the grills that exhaust directly onto the sidewalk area. There is no determining how many people have experienced a sharp increase in the hunger drive and may have entered because of these visual and olfactory (smell) cues to the incentive.

A recently developed research area is that of *social facilitation.* Zajonc, among others, has established that animals eat more when they are with other animals that are eating. The whole process of drive seems to be increased by others doing the same thing. A very similar process is involved at the respondent level, with emotions such as fear being increased sharply by another's high level of fear. The cry of "fire" in the crowded building and the resulting stampede of people toward an exit illustrates a respondent version of social facilitation, although this level of behavior is not exactly what Zajonc had in mind when he originated the term.

Inhibition   The final factor, *inhibition,* has five components. They are (a) fatigue, (b) extinction, (c) competing behaviors, (d) reactive inhibition, and (e) conditioned inhibition.

Fatigue is an obvious component. It is included because the authors of this explanation of behavior wished to establish a comprehensive theory— that is, one that explains *all* behavioral variation and change in organisms. Obviously, even if an organism is in a state of drive and is being reinforced, it may grow fatigued, and may then slow or stop responding. Fatigue, however, is a transient component. That is, the organism, after rest, will resume the behavior. The fatigue is said to dissipate with time.

Extinction already has been described in Chapter 9, and obviously it represents a *non*dissipatory component.

Competing behaviors are those that cannot be emitted simultaneously with the behavior in question. At a simple level, sitting down and standing up are competing behaviors. So is a child's disruptive behavior in a classroom and behaviors that could be called "productive" in the classroom. Competing behavior inhibits the target behavior to the extent that the competing behavior is emitted and thereby displaces the target behavior. The notion of *displacement* is simple—one behavior simply becomes so frequent that the time available for the other behavior is lessened. It should be recognized at this point that the competing behavior, also, has its own $R=f$ $(H \times D) - I$ formula, with the target behavior being a competing behavior within the I factor.

Reactive inhibition is the psychological counterpart of physical fatigue. It is a kind of mental fatigue, probably based on the need for stimulus variety. Reactive inhibition is a tendency, immediately after emitting a certain behavior, *not* to emit it again. If you were required to write your name over and over, indefinitely, you would begin to grow increasingly bored to the point of eventually wanting very badly to stop. The sameness and repetitive nature of the act would develop an aversive condition surrounding the behavior. Reactive inhibition is cumulative, growing stronger and stronger as the behavior is emitted repeatedly within a short space of time. And, like fatigue, it dissipates with time.

Psychologists formerly felt that reactive inhibition only partly dissipates, and that a residual amount was left. Later, the lasting effects were reconceptualized as *conditioned inhibition.* Conditioned inhibition is a conditioned—hence lasting—effect produced through negative reinforcement. Reactive inhibition creates an aversive drive condition. Cessation of the behavior that is creating reactive inhibition brings relief, and thereby negatively reinforces abstention from the behavior in situations where the behavior is emittable. According to the laws of reinforcement, the greater the prior level of reactive inhibition and corresponding aversiveness, the stronger is the reinforcement for deliberately *not* emitting the target behavior. Using the component of conditioned inhibition in the formula allows us to explain why people tend, almost permanently, to resist doing something they were once forced to do until they wished to stop very badly.

The Hull-Spence type of formulation has allowed the development of a number of novel approaches to the correction of some difficult behavior problems in clinics and counseling situations. These will be discussed in Chapter 14.

C 12.12. *Learning theory approaches to personality.*

State the Hull-Spence type of formula for behavior: $R = f$ _____ .

What are the components of the factor H?

   a. _____

   b. _____

   c. _____

What are the components of the factor D?

   a_1. _____

   a_2. _____

   b. _____

   c. _____

   d. _____

   e. _____

What are the components of the factor I?

   a. _____

   b. _____

   c. _____

   d. _____

   e. _____

Competing behaviors may reduce a target behavior by _____ it.

   a. suppressing   b. displacing   c. extinguishing

What form of inhibition dissipates with time? _____ .

   a. Reactive   b. Conditioned

Our presentation of a behavior theory approach to personality has been limited almost exclusively to the components of the Hull-Spence type of formula.

You might realize, however, that the Hull-Spence notions implicitly involve the classical conditioning processes as well as the operant. Also, you should bear in mind that by viewing reinforcers and incentives as both primary *and* conditioned, and as both positive *and* negative, one expands the scope of behavioral prediction immensely.

In the next two chapters you will see a continued and broadened use of a behavior-theory interpretation of behavior in various contexts.

ROGERS' SELF THEORY

As an example of modern *non*deterministic personality theory, we have chosen to describe the system developed by Carl Rogers. Rogers is a contemporary theorist of personality whose approach is generally termed "humanistic"; that is, the concepts he employs to explain why human beings are motivated to do the things they do are seen as totally different from those concepts which underlie animal motivation. Another label, sometimes placed upon Rogers and several other humanistic psychologists, is that of "phenomenological" theorist. This term refers to a heavy emphasis upon subjective experiences and upon individual interpretations of events. This stands in contrast to viewpoints which take stimuli and environmental events more or less at face value.

Most of the writings of Carl Rogers pertain to the delivery of psychotherapy to "clients," and the label *client-centered therapy* has sometimes been given to his therapeutic approach. One of the major factors which distinguishes Rogers' approach from that of most other theorists is an emphasis upon the client's ability to solve his problems himself, with the therapist acting in the role of a stimulator who provides an atmosphere which encourages the independence of the client and his reasoned examination of events.

C 12.13. *The nature of Rogers' approach to personality.*

Rogers' theory is essentially _____ .

    a. deterministic   b. nondeterministic

Rogers is said to be a _____ theorist.

    a. behavioral   b. dynamic   c. phenomenological

Rogers' approach to therapy has been termed _____ therapy.

    a. rational   b. supportive   c. client-centered

A phenomenological theorist is one who places heavy emphasis upon _____

_____

_____ .

Basic Assumptions in Rogers' Self Theory

Rogers states three basic assumptions in his approach (1959). The first of these is that the data of personality research should be viewed in terms of the client's subjective experiences. That is, the truth is not so important as is the client's perception of it. An example of this would be that, to a child, more important than the question of whether the parents love him is whether he *perceives* them as loving him. A dramatic and unusual point of view, for a psychologist, is the subsequent viewpoint expressed by Rogers that no one can truly understand the internal frame of reference of another person, even though, as Rogers has already stated, that kind of data are the only meaningful data in the study of personality.

A second major assumption in Rogers' self theory is that every individual has an actualizing tendency. Actualization refers to an inborn motive of the individual to develop his capacities in ways which appear, to him, to maintain and enhance his individual sense of being. This might be, for some, the optimum development of their intellectual capacities, while for others success and a positive self-viewpoint might be defined in totally different terms—power, wealth, and so forth.

The third major assumption in Rogers' self theory is that each individual pursues an experiential valuing process. All events, experiences, or behaviors are viewed as being either positive or negative in terms of their relationship to the actualizing tendency. Whatever sorts of experiences relate favorably to the individual's own actualizing tendency tend to be pursued, while negatively valued experiences tend to be avoided.

The Concept of Self

Early in the development of the personality the most important process to become evident is the emerging development of the self. Early in life

the child begins to think about his own characteristics and abilities. His self-concept is, then, made up of his characteristic ways of thinking about himself. It is small wonder that, as the child's intellectual capacities grow, he comes to reject those experiences and behaviors which are not in accord with his self-concept, while pursuing those behaviors which are consistent with and enhancing of his beliefs about himself.

One of the main determinants of individual differences has to do with the nature of the existing self-concept. There are those people whose ways of thinking about themselves are broad and flexible. These individuals will find that many different kinds of behaviors, attitudes and emotions are not seriously inconsistent with the self-concept. As a result of this broad self-image, this sort of individual will not neurotically attempt to ignore or avoid situations which might arouse such feelings. His life, therefore, tends to be one of relatively rich variety.

People whose self-concepts are narrow, on the other hand, are much less open to experience. Some individuals who consider themselves to be completely rational might therefore inhibit the expression of emotion and even the experiencing of it. The emotional leveling which results from such a self-image is an internal event, not readily evident to others, but the individual's behavior is affected as he attempts to avoid all situations which might threaten the existing self-concept. People who consider themselves as sexually "moral" would likely tend to avoid sexual stimuli, and similar explanations could be made which would describe a wide variety of similar inhibitions upon different people's behaviors and emotional experiences.

Rogers feels that every individual has the innate capacity to be aware of all events and emotions in his environment, and the individual's actual awareness of a wide spectrum of such events has to be reasonably complete and accurate if he is to be able to direct and control his life with any degree of satisfaction. In addition to literal avoidance of situations which might threaten the self-concept, individuals may deliberately misperceive cues in their environment in order to avoid or distort stimuli which would otherwise threaten. Rogers has introduced the term *subception* to explain how some people react to given situations with only partial awareness.

C 12.14.   *Self-concept and behavior.*

Rogers would feel that where people adopt a specific self-concept, such as "I am moral," "I am serious of purpose," and so forth, the self-concept is _____ .

   a. a broadening contributant to subsequent experiences

   b. a restrictive, narrowing influence upon subsequent experiences

Rogers feels that some individuals are motivated to remain partially unaware of events and experiences that otherwise would threaten their existing self-concepts. This tendency he calls _____ .

   a. perceived distortion   b. subception   c. threat defense

The Need for the Positive Regard by Others

One of Rogers' main points is that each person has a need for others to regard him positively. This is a "happy medium" sort of need, which may become unpleasantly exaggerated in certain individuals. Most children, from the beginning of life, receive various forms of positive expression— love, acceptance, human warmth, and eventually respect—from various individuals with whom they come into close contact. From the outset such negative reactions as hostility, emotional coldness, and lack of respect cause the child to be unhappy. With an overabundance of the latter sort of experience a child may develop in one of two directions.

One of these directions involves the child becoming more active in seeking positive emotional reactions from others. This type of individual may go to great lengths to impress, amaze, flatter, and so forth, in his efforts to bend others' reactions in ways that he seeks. On the one hand the child may be successful at doing this, and his or her subsequent need for positive regard will appear to be abnormally high and marked by vigorous deliberate attempts. On the other hand it is possible that the young individual will be unsuccessful in attempts to so influence others. It is possible that all that can occur, due to the crude and bungled social efforts of the individual, is an increased degree of social rejection. Individuals, thus rebuffed, may then cease to court the favor of others; their patterns of behavior may become those of rebellion, unorthodoxy, and contain both actions and statements which portray frustration and bitterness. Thus, from reasonably similar beginnings, one can see developed either a pathological emphasis on seeking others' positive regard or a pathological absence of the same factor.

The Need for Self-Regard

The need for self-regard grows out of the need for the positive regard of others. This need is said to develop as the child begins to perceive his own behaviors as being judged either bad or good by the significant people in his environment. The child comes to regard himself favorably when he acts in ways that lead to positive feedback from those who are important to him, and he eventually comes to feel badly about those behaviors which lead to negative feedback from others. (This is similar to Freud's notion of introjection of a value system, providing the basis for the superego.)

As you might anticipate, in the reasonably normal individual there is a high degree of coincidence between the perceptions involved in the need for self-regard and those involved in the need for positive regard for others. That is, the healthy person can generate behaviors that at one and the same time "feel right" to him and are positively regarded by others.

C 12.15. *The relation between self-regard and the regard of others.*

In the healthy personality, Rogers believes that _____ .

a. a person would behave in accord with his own beliefs, even if others disapprove

b. there would be consistency between behaviors that bring about self-regard and those that bring the positive regard of others

The Unhealthy Personality   Rogers conceives of pathological adjustment as being due to faulty experiences in life which interfere with the natural development of a healthy, self-actualizing personality. In one of the simpler models of maladjustment a person learns to think of a particular kind of behavior or experience as bad or unacceptable although it actually seems to be pleasurable and desirable; he or she will experience anxiety in situations which encourage this behavior. When this occurs, the individual's state of conflict generates one of two psychological defenses. In the first of these, denial to awareness, the person ignores what is really happening in the anxiety-arousing situation. In the other, distortion of awareness, the person thinks inaccurately about the situation and misinterprets events into patterns which are more acceptable to him. It is predictable that such defensive habits usually lead to further difficulties since they not only prevent the person from thinking creatively and constructively about the problem, but they may generate responses which are then negatively evaluated by others, leading to negative feedback. This, then, can intensify the tension that already exists.

Another form of maladjustment develops when distance increases between the individual's ideal self (what he or she would like to be in terms of self-actualizing tendencies) and the experienced self (the kind of person he or she is, according to the apparent evaluations by others). When this occurs the individual begins to behave in contradictory ways, sometimes acting in accordance with his or her own value processes, and at other times acting completely differently in accordance with what he or she believes others' wishes or expectations to be. The inconsistency, in itself, is further anxiety-arousing.

C 12.16.   *Rogers' view on sources of tension.*

Rogers conceives of unhealthy tension when on the one hand an experience seems pleasurable while on the other hand the person has "learned" that the experience _____ .

Tension occurs when there is a great distance between how others seem to view you and your _____ self.

Therapeutic Change   Rogers, as we have previously stated, adopts as a basic assumption the idea that the individual is capable of straightening out his own misperceptions and engaging in therapeutic change. The Rogerian therapist does not change the person in an active manner such as would be the goal in Freudian psychotherapy or in a learning-based therapy. Still, the therapist's role is vital.

The main reasons for the distortions in development that may already have occurred, and for their continuance, rest in the continuation of tension and anxiety generated by others' evaluations of one's self, and in turn one's own reactions to those evaluations. The need for positive regard, the need for self-regard and progress toward self-actualization are all intimately affected by the tensions that occur in the interpersonal processes.

In Rogerian client-centered therapy, Rogers stresses the necessity of the therapist joining the client in his own idiosyncratic perception of events. Rogers does not believe that interpreting to the patient the meaning of his behavior can lead to any ultimate good. Rather, this would tend to force the patient to begin looking at himself from the therapist's point of view, which would develop simply another categorical element within the client's own subjective experience. There would be no change in the self-image produced by the therapist's interpretations.

The key to client-centered therapy, and we might add that this has virtually become a social movement of sorts within the entire field of psychotherapy, is that the therapist must be accepting and nonevaluative in relation to the client. At first the client will be defensive, will feel vulnerable, and the effectiveness of the interpersonal relationship will be quite modest. Over time the client will come to trust the therapist, and increasingly will feel free to talk about even the most sensitive aspects of his own experiences. The client must feel liked and respected, despite whatever "unworthiness" he might reveal to the therapist.

Rogers gives little emphasis to the exploration and discussion of the distant past. His emphasis is on the currently perceived reality of the client's world. As the current situation is discussed in therapy, the client is expected to gradually integrate the conflicting elements of the self-image. Since no tensions are set up in therapy, and no conditions of human worth are implied, the client begins to admit all his experiences and feelings, and can unemotionally begin to fit the pieces together. The secret of change is that in the absence of defensiveness and emotional tension the client can begin to think very accurately about his or her perceptions and experiences, leading to a solution to those internal conflicts which have been interfering with self-actualization.

One of the interesting aspects of Rogerian client-centered therapy is the technique employed by the therapist during the interview. Where the Freudian therapist might probe directly through questioning, and use direct interpretive techniques to demonstrate the meaning of symptoms, the nondirective therapist listens closely to what the client has to say, then attempts to reflect the feelings. Thus, a sincerely expressed "Mmmm . . . hmmm" may be employed following meaningful statements by the client. At breaking points within a given topic, the therapist may summarize in a phrase or a sentence the client's essential communication. For example: after a lengthy complaint concerning the rigidity of a parent's expectations, the therapist might say, "You feel, then, that your mother simply cannot understand your thinking." Not only is this nonevaluative and accepting, but the patient is usually delighted to encounter another human being who seems to understand. There usually follows an increase in the patient's eagerness to continue and gain further insights into his or her thoughts and feelings.

C 12.17. *Techniques of client-centered therapy.*

Rogers _____ the interpretation of symptoms to a client.

    a. advocates   b. does not believe in

Rogers feels that a therapist should be _____ .

    a. an image and an example for the client to model after   b. accepting and nonevaluating

Rogers' attention in therapy is mainly to the _____ .

    a. client's childhood   b. future   c. present

> The objective of Rogerian client-centered therapy is to develop greater coincidence between reality as it exists and "reality" as it is interpreted by the client. As you can very well imagine, the data collected on the dependent variable in client-centered therapy is quite resistant to the usual processes of observation and measurement. Thus, it is no great surprise to find that Rogerian advocates feel misunderstood and even betrayed by "scientific" psychologists, while scientific psychologists express impatience over the type of research generated within the Rogerian therapeutic group.
>
> Regardless of any single individual's attitude toward Rogers' approach, there is no denying that this contemporary psychologist has had a tremendous impact upon theories of personality and of therapeutic change.

PROGRESS CHECK 12.3

1. The Hull-Spence formula for personality is _____ .

    a. $R=f(0)$ b. $R=f(H \times D)-I$ c. $P=(I+E) \div SE$ d. $P=(\frac{T}{n})r$

2. Habit strength in the Hull-Spence formula is a function of all but _____ .

    a. magnitude of reinforcement   b. number of reinforcements

    c. delays of reinforcement   d. expectation of reinforcement

MATCH: _____ 3. Drive   A. Incentivation

            _____ 4. Inhibition   B. Competing behaviors

5. Reactive inhibition _____ .

    a. has a lasting effect   b. dissipates with time

6. Which variable may displace a target behavior? _____ .

    a. Fatigue   b. Extinction   c. Competing behavior   d. Inhibition

7. Which is true of Rogers' approach to personality? _____ .

    a. It is deterministic   b. It is phenomenological

    c. It is directive   d. It places heavy emphasis on reinforcement

8. Rogers believes that people should adopt moral structures for better lives. _____ .

    a. True   b. False

9. A person misinterpreting a job loss to suit his self-concept is engaging in _____ .

    a. foolishness   b. lying   c. deception   d. subception

10. According to Rogers, healthy people do what? _____ .

    a. Stick to their beliefs under all circumstances

    b. Engage in an existential morality

    c. Try for consistency between self-regard and social compliance

    d. Always follow the dictates of society

11. Unhealthy tension, according to Rogers, arises from _____ .

    a. conflict over a desired yet forbidden event   b. suppressed libido

    c. learning unhealthy posture   d. experiences with masochism

12. Techniques of Rogerian client-centered therapy include _____ .

    a. acceptance   b. therapist interpretation of client symptoms

    c. orientation to a better future   d. all of these

CATEGORIES OF ASSESSMENT DEVICES

You have been introduced to one personality inventory, the 16 P–F. It is typical of one type of assessment instrument, but other methods of assessment also are in use. We shall describe five ways in which psychologists go about assessing the personality patterns of human beings.

The Interview Method

First is the *interview method*. This is a commonly used employment procedure. Typically an individual is interviewed by several people who then share their impressions, leading to a decision. The main problem with this method is that it has a poor level of reliability. You will remember from our earlier discussion (Chapter Six) that reliability is the consistency with which an instrument or technique performs a measurement function. The test-retest method has its counterpart here in the multiple interview. A job applicant (as an example) may be interviewed by one person who forms a very poor impression, while a second interviewer may be favorably impressed. It is in this sense that we say the interview method of assessment has low reliability. This is due to at least two things.

First, the two interviewers may ask different things. One interviewer may ask certain types of questions and get one impression, while a second interviewer may ask completely different questions and on that basis get a different impression. To control this variable, guided interview forms have been published which direct questions along certain lines and in a guided sequence. If more than one interviewer is involved, these forms allow the interviewers to know they have covered common ground. Research has shown, however, that even with guided interview forms, reliability of the judgments of different interviewers is quite low.

C 12.18. *The interview method of personality assessment.*

The main problem with the interview as an assessment technique is its poor _____ .

    a. face validity   b. reliability   c. construct validity

Referring to your answer just above, one means of remediating at least part of this problem came

in the development of _____ .

    a. the two-interviewer method   b. greater informality in the interview setting

    c. guided interview forms

Second, in the history of experiences of both the interviewer and the interviewee, a variety of events has led to conditioned emotional attitudes. Thus, one interviewer sees a behavior pattern as "smug and smart-aleck," while another interviewer is impressed by the person's "self-confidence and poise." Responsible for this is a certain amount of stimulus generalization on the parts of the interviewers. One interviewer will classify an individual's total personality in a certain configuration simply because he has known people with some of the same obvious traits. It seems natural to "fill in the gaps" by seeing the individual's personality as being similar in the rest of its aspects to people from one's past. Meanwhile, at another level, the interviewee tends to respond to the personality of the interviewer. With a warm, spontaneous interviewer, he, or she, relaxes and displays a sociable personality, while with the next interviewer, who is abrupt and critical-appearing, he may tense up and begin to appear nervous and flustered. The two interviewers then may get opposite impressions of the individual.

A great deal of the reaction of the interviewer to cues displayed by the interviewee can be easily anticipated. A job applicant may be a graduate of a famous university, known for its high standards; the interviewer is favorably impressed by this and judges the applicant as intelligent, with management potential, unless contradictory signs are very evident. Other interviewers, in a variety of contexts, have reactions to race, sex, physical attractiveness, age, and so forth, and their judgments are affected by these factors—sometimes deliberately, and at other times in a less conscious manner.

(Once, as a member of a management services organization, the author was called to a company in a large metropolitan area which had severe absenteeism and turnover problems in office staff. The problem, on examination, was obvious. The personnel supervisor was in the habit of hiring only young, single, attractive girls for the office. The supervisor was shown evidence that a broader mix was desirable and that he could expect lower turnover rates and lower absenteeism, on the average, in older women and married women. The recommended adjustment in hiring policy was made and the personnel problem began to be solved from that date forward. A few weeks later, in an unguarded moment, that personnel supervisor confided that early in his career with the organization he had hired an attractive and single young lady with whom he had subsequently developed a highly enjoyable and satisfying after-hours relationship. It appeared that from that point forward he was responding in accord with his history of reinforcement. Apparently he was not consciously aware of why he had decided that single attractive women would be more "efficient.")

The Rating Scale   A second method of personality assessment is the *rating scale*. Persons are given specific questions concerning an individual they are rating, and the answers are usually expressed in a ranked hierarchy.

For example, an executive in an organization may evaluate an employee on a rating scale. If that person is on a sales staff he, or she, might be evaluated on the extent to which he "projects a warm, genuine, friendly personality." The answer hierarchy may be as follows:

1. Make an outstanding impression on others in this regard.
2. Usually makes a good impression.
3. Is about average in the impression he makes on others.
4. Is subject to occasional shortcomings in the impression he makes on others.
5. Often gives a bad impression.

Rating scales are not known for their reliability, but they may (depending upon the circumstances) have fine validity. Let us explore this issue. Reliability may suffer from the failure of various observers to see the individual in the same situation. Thus, one observer may see an individual only over a cup of coffee while other observers may see him in different situations displaying entirely different patterns of behavior. In terms of validity, if the target behavior—the actual behavior of value which the individual is hired to do by the company—is observed and rated, the rating scale may have good validity. That is, it may reflect what it was actually designed to reflect. Notice that we said it *may* have good validity, because a second point of necessity emerges. The rating scale must ask for ratings of *actual observable behaviors* such as "seeks assistance readily when in difficulty," or "seldom is observed to be idle." It should not ask for ratings of unobservable processes such as "has a positive attitude toward superiors," or "is interested in his job."

C 12.19.   *The rating scale in personality or behavioral assessment.*

A rating scale's reliability depends upon the various raters having seen the individual _____ .

    a. performing the target behavior   b. in the same situation

A rating scale's validity depends upon the raters having seen the individual _____ .

    a. in the same situation   b. performing the target behavior

A rating scale's validity also depends upon the rating scale asking questions that pertain only to _____ .

    a. job-related attitudes and motives   b. actual observable behaviors

The Behavioral Assessment

A third method of personality assessment, and one that, peculiarly, is not often used, is the *behavioral assessment*. If an individual applies for a job as a salesman, it might be interesting to have that person try to do some selling under the observation of the individuals who are to make the assessment. If a person applies for a job as a professor, it would be useful to have that person come to the campus and teach an hour-long class on some general topic within the field. About the only area of endeavor that uses routine behavioral assessment for employment, in preference to interviews and possibly personality tests, is the entertainment business in which singers, actors, radio and TV performers actually "rehearse for a part." When a person shows his or her talent in an actual-role situation, the only question regarding reliability or validity comes from the possibility that the individual might later tense up in front of a large audience.

The Personality Inventory

A fourth method of personality assessment is the *personality inventory*, of which you have seen an example in the 16 P–F. Such an inventory simply asks a person to answer certain questions about his attitudes, behaviors, and so forth, and the results are put on a normative scale to assess highs and lows along the trait variables. The 16 P–F, described earlier, is a popular instrument used with persons outside of mental institutions. Another is the Edwards Personal Preference Schedule which assesses people along scales of psychological needs. The EPPS is not quite as behavioral as is the 16 P–F since persons typically admit to "needs" or "feelings" displayed in an EPPS score that may seldom be translated into actual behavior. The EPPS assesses needs for achievement, deference, orderliness, exhibition, autonomy, affiliation, interoception, succorance, dominance, abasement, nurturance, change, endurance, heterosexuality, and aggression.

Perhaps the best-known of the personality inventories is the MMPI (Minnesota Multiphasic Personality Inventory), which is generally used in mental health settings. This inventory was designed to diagnose severe disorders, and the labels for most of the scales are worded accordingly: hysteria, depression, hypochondria, psychopathic deviance, masculinity-femininity, paranoia, schizophrenia, and mania. The authors of this instrument proceeded in a somewhat unique way to develop their scales. About 30 years ago Hathaway and McKinley started with a large group of items—560 statements in all—which pertained to physical and psychological symptom reports, general habits, family matters, occupational and educational concerns, and attitudes toward a variety of religious, sexual, and social matters. Over several years, data on a group of 800 clinical cases, carefully studied and diagnosed, was accumulated. Each of the 800 persons was rated on the 560-item scale and, in addition, it was administered to a large number of persons who were considered not to have significant psychological disorders.

As an example of their procedure, let us take the category of depression. Examination of the entire set of 560 items produced the finding that 53 items significantly differentiated the group with depressive symptoms from other persons being tested. As you would expect, most (but not all) of the items pertained to reports of moods, pessimism, low energy level, feelings of self-worthlessness, and a lack of flexibility of action and thought. All of these are symptoms of depression. However, *all* items that differentiated depressives were placed into the depression scale, whether or not the items seemed to have a great deal of face validity pertaining to the relevant symptom. Later, more items were added and new research was conducted, but the scale remains largely as it was originally constructed and it has generated a great deal of research over the years. Interestingly it has "validity scales" not common to other tests. One scale indicates the individual's tendency to respond in socially desirable directions; it is called the "lie scale." Another shows patterns of deviation that suggest that the subject might not have understood some questions. And a third indicates tendencies to be defensive and deny certain symptoms. An examiner adjusts the other scale scores by a multiple derived from how much lying, defensiveness, and so forth appear in the validity scales.

C 12.20. *Behavioral assessments.*

In an employment setting, with applicants for a sales position being examined, a behavioral assessment would most likely take the form of _____ .

a. the interviewer conversing with the applicant about his attitudes and goals

b. the applicant being given a pencil and paper test of good sales procedure

c. the applicant being asked to learn a programmed sales training booklet

d. the applicant trying to "sell" something to the interviewer

C 12.21. *Personality inventories.*

Which of the personality inventories discussed is most appropriate for institutionalized mental patients?

_____ .

Often the instruments we have discussed under this heading (personality inventories) are called *objective* measures of personality. The word objective refers both to the straightforwardness of the questions and to the objectivity involved in the scoring, which involves a simple counting of answers within scales.

The Projective Measure In contrast to objective measures are the so-called *projective* measures of personality—the fifth method of personality assessment. A projective instrument is one into which the subject "projects" his personality. Generally these instruments present ambiguous stimulus situations, and the subject is asked to create a response. The nature of the response is then interpreted by the examiner. Probably the most familiar of the projective instruments is the Rorschach card series which consists of vague and cloudy appearing ink blots. The subject looks at the blots and tells what he can "see" there. It is true that there are a variety of common responses that are named by many people because of similarities in shapes, but beyond this a complex scoring technique has been derived which involves whether or not people tend to see human beings, and if they do whether they are "fairy tale" or monster types, etc. Also, some people tend to make something out of whole blots, some tend to concentrate on large details, and others on small details that go unnoticed by most. Some people tend to take the white areas within the dark ink blots and see such background as the actual object-form, a reversal of the figure-ground relationship. In addition there are literally hundreds of factors that can be taken into consideration in determining how the emotional and mental processes of the individual are operating. The extreme lack of structure in the Rorschach has led to the assumption that it touches upon very deep and unconscious forces in the personality.

Similar to the Rorschach, but with more structure, is the Thematic Apperception Test (TAT). This series of cards shows, in various environments, people with different facial expressions. Presumably the subject can "identify" with someone in the picture and, by telling a story of what is happening, what led up to it, and how it will end, he reveals the sorts of psychological concerns that are most meaningful to him. There are some general cards in a TAT deck, and there are certain others that portray themes most appropriate to either boys, girls, men, or women. Preparation usually is made ahead of time for a mix of cards, determined by the sex and age of the subject, and to some degree by what questions the examiner needs to answer about the subject's personality.

At another level of projective instruments are Incomplete Sentences Forms, of which there are several versions in professional use. A person is

"Because I'm happy, that's why."

asked to complete a number of partial sentences in writing. He is given sentence-beginnings such as "Sometimes I wonder if . . . ," and "I really got angry when . . . " Psychologists then analyze the pattern of answers and make judgments about the concerns and feelings of the subject.

There is a wide variety of other projective instruments. Lately the validity of projective instruments has been questioned by many psychologists, who stress the stronger validity coefficients of objective instruments. While projective instruments are certainly under attack, and the use of the Rorschach in particular is fading, it is likely that the wide use of projectives will persist for many years to come.

C 12.22. *Projective techniques in personality assessment.*

A general term that is used in contrast to "projective" and which indicates that a subject is simply

answering straightforward questions is _____ .

    a. subjective   b. objective

The famous ink blot test in which subjects try to perceive something is the _____ .

    a. Rorschach   b. MMPI   c. TAT   d. 16 P–F

The instrument which requires subjects to look at pictures of people and tell a story about what is

happening is called the _____ .

    a. Traumatic Awareness Test (TAT)   b. Thematic Apperception Test (TAT)

    c. (neither of these two answers is correct)

The section of text covering projective techniques mentioned which specific projective instruments?

    a. _____

    b. _____

    c. _____

PROGRESS CHECK   12.4

1. The interview method of personality assessment has good overall reliability. _____ .

     a. True   b. False

2. What method has been employed to improve interview methods? _____ .

     a. Use of more than one interviewer   b. Use of guided interview forms

     c. Both   d. Neither

3. Using a rating scale for on-task behavior analysis may produce _____ .

     a. a reliable measure   b. a valid measure

4. Actual role or on-the-job performance is what kind of assessment? _____ .

     a. Personality   b. Behavioral   c. Interview   d. Scaling

5. Which personality inventory is most appropriate for an institutionalized patient? _____ .

     a. MMPI   b. EPPS   c. CPI   d. All of these

6. Which of these is not a projective test of personality? _____ .

     a. TAT   b. Rorschach   c. EPPS

Now that you have completed this chapter on the topic of personality, you may find that your department of psychology offers an advanced undergraduate course on similar topics. Such courses are usually titled "Personality," or "Personality Theory," and there is also a related emphasis in courses titled "Psychology of Adjustment" or, at some universities, "Mental Hygiene."

Your further reading might go in a number of directions, since there are dozens of interesting books treating this overall topic. *Introduction to Personality*, by Walter Mischel (1971) and *The Psychology of Personality*, by Wiggins et al. (1971) are two of the best. An advanced presentation is given in a very well-known text, *Theories of Personality* (2nd Edition), by Hall and Lindzey (1970).

A specific treatment of Freudian theory that is excellently done is A. A. Brill's *Lectures on Psychoanalytic Psychiatry* (1959), and a specific treatment of a learning theory approach to personality is handled in Robert Lundin's *Personality: A Behavioral Analysis* (1969).

13

Frustration, Stress, and Conflict

STRESS

FRUSTRATION

Responses to Frustration: Persistence

Responses to Frustration: Aggression

Research with Humans into the Frustration-
Aggression Sequence

Responses to Prolonged Frustration

Apathy

Rationalization

Fantasy

The Choice of a Response to Frustration

Frustration Tolerance

CONFLICT

Approach-Approach Conflicts

Avoidance-Avoidance Conflicts

Approach-Avoidance Conflicts

Double Approach-Avoidance Conflicts

Conflict Gradients

Fixation in Conflict Situations

**HUMAN REACTIONS TO FRUSTRATION,
STRESS, AND CONFLICT**

Types of Anxiety

The Ego Defense Mechanisms

Identification

Introjection

Compensation

Conversion

Rationalization

Displacement of Aggression

Regression

Emotional Insulation

Isolation

Fantasy

Undoing

Projection

Sublimation

Denial

Escape Into Activity

Reaction Formation

Compulsive Control

Turning Against the Self

Displacement of Anxiety

Repression

Overview of the Ego Defense Mechanisms

We shall begin by showing the similarities and the differences among the three terms used in the title of this chapter. It is probably legitimate to use the overall term "stress" to encompass the chapter's problem area. Still, stress is usually induced in rather direct, uncomplicated ways in the laboratory, generally through physical-specific stimulation. Seldom is it experimentally administered through social agents. Also, the effects of stress are typically measured in terms of physiological changes. Still, we would hope that throughout the chapter you could conceptualize frustration and conflict as being specific forms of stress.

The term "frustration" refers to consequences to situations in which goal-directed behavior is blocked. Although stress is obviously associated with such events, we shall consider some special properties which are found in frustrating situations.

The third term, "conflict," refers to a special type of frustration in which goals may be available, but situational complexities associated with the goals introduce new problems. We shall make this clearer in later sections.

C 13.1. *The relationships among the terms "frustration," "stress," and "conflict." (See chapter introduction on previous page.)*

Of the three terms, which could be said to be the broadest, even to the point of encompassing the other two? _____ .

a. Frustration   b. Stress   c. Conflict

Stress is typically defined in research programs in terms of _____ _____ stimuli and resulting _____ changes.

STRESS   As we indicated, stress is usually defined, by laboratory psychologists, in terms of a physical-specific stimulus and a resulting physiological change. Perhaps the most important name associated with the experimental study of stress is that of Hans Selye of Canada. Beginning a number of years ago, Dr. Selye (1956) subjected laboratory animals to a wide variety of stressors. He was interested in seeing what sorts of physiological reactions these stressors produced. The very interesting finding was that, no matter what the type of stressor used, internal changes were similar. Selye used, at various times, intense cold, burns, intense noise, and electric shock, together with a variety of other less obvious stresses such as injections with foreign matter and immobilization for long periods of time. No major differences were noted among patterns of internal changes in animals subjected to different forms of stress.

Among the various internal changes were marked enlargement and dark discoloration of the adrenal glands, intense shrinkage of both the lymph nodes and the thymus, which produces white blood cells (Leukel, 1972), and production of numerous blood-covered stomach ulcers over a period of time. Some of the animals suffered "strokes," or ruptures of cerebral blood vessels, which can destroy the function of parts of the brain and cause wide-spread nervous system derangements. Interestingly, Selye's animals became extremely irritable and aggressive following such strokes, a change that is characteristic of senile mental derangements among some old people whose brains often show the same kind of deteriorative change. The animals in intense and prolonged stress also demonstrated a variety of sexual derangements. During stress the sex glands shrank and became less active in comparison with their normal condition. Disruptions of the typical appetitive eating cycles occurred in the animals, some losing weight and others eating to the point of obesity. (This variation was interpreted as probably due to hereditary predispositions.)

Other research programs have reported similar physiological changes in human beings subjected to stress. In human beings the prolonged experience of stress may lead to chronic changes in blood pressure, certain rheumatic disorders, respiratory disorders, and heart reactions. Great stress can even produce death.

Selye proposed the *general adaptation syndrome*, which includes three stages of reactions to stress. First is what he calls the *alarm reaction*. In this stage the autonomic nervous system becomes very active immediately upon the initial presentation of stress. The body's resources are brought to bear in defense, but little permanent damage is done to the individual unless these initial physiological reactions interact with existing physiological defects such as heart problems.

If the stress is prolonged, the individual enters the second stage, called the *stage of resistance*. In the stage of resistance, certain of the autonomic reactions partially subside, but remaining is an overall elevation of the autonomic actions to meet the continued stress. It is during the stage of resistance that the wide variety of physiological changes described earlier begin to develop.

Finally, after a considerable amount of time in the stage of resistance, the individual suffers from a virtual autonomic collapse. This is called the *stage of exhaustion,* and the organism is in great peril of life itself. In the stage of exhaustion, either the stress is removed or the organism dies. In an attempt to study this phenomenon further, some researchers removed the adrenal glands of animals, then subjected them to a stress situation. In every case, without the availability of the adrenal secretions, the animals quickly died. This entire area of research, stemming from Selye's initial work, has contributed a great deal to our understanding of many psychosomatic and other stress-related medical disorders of human beings.

C 13.2.   *Stress and the general adaptation syndrome (GAS).*

Selye found that, using different stressors, the resulting physiological changes in organisms were _____ .

    a. quite different   b. highly similar

Selye proposed _____ stages in his general adaptation syndrome.

    a. two   b. three   c. four

In Selye's GAS, the development of various psychophysiological ailments such as ulcers in the stomach occurs in the stage of _____ .

"Autonomic collapse" is described by Selye in the stage of _____ .

    a. alarm   b. resistance   c. exhaustion

Other researchers, following in Selye's footsteps, have investigated other forms of stress and have contributed other interesting findings. For example, in a large research program in St. Louis, rats were wrapped in gauze and tape until they were in virtual cocoons, with only their heads sticking out. These animals could shift position only slightly within their restraints, and it was found that within a very short period of time—perhaps as little as 48 hours—massive stomach ulceration was the frequent result. Following up this line of study, it was found that the hereditary factor was a major determinant in the development of stress-produced stomach ulcers.

The researchers first developed a large animal colony, within which many animals had given birth. The litters were clearly marked to indicate the parentage, and after weaning of the offspring the parents were used in the immobility stress experiment. Autopsy revealed, as expected, considerable variation in the condition of the stomach linings of various animals. Some suffered from massive ulceration (these were termed ulcer-prone individuals), some were intermediate or moderate in ulceration, and some showed little or no tendency towards ulceration (these were called the ulcer-resistant group).

In the second stage of the experiment second-generation animals, *both* of whose parents were ulcer-resistant, and those, *both* of whose parents were ulcer-prone, were reared, bred within the strain (that is, an animal with ulcer-resistant parents to another with ulcer-resistant parents, or the reverse), and their offspring (third-generation) were labeled for identification. Then the second-generation animals were given immobilization stress and a subsequent autopsy procedure. In this generation of animals it was found that most of them inherited the predominant characteristic of their parents—either ulcer-resistant or ulcer-prone tendencies.

In the third stage of the experiment only the offspring of *parents* and *grandparents* exhibiting a particular tendency were bred with offspring of *parents* and *grandparents* exhibiting the same tendency. In this manner, the two strains of ulcer-prone and ulcer-resistant animals were "purified." By the time this research had gone through seven generations of strain development, only 5 to 10 percent from the ulcer-resistant strain developed ulcers during 48 hours of immobilization stress, while well over 90 percent from the ulcer-prone strain did so.

Joseph Brady, a psychologist in the U.S. Army Medical Corps at Walter Reed Hospital, investigated another aspect of stomach ulcers, this time using monkeys as subjects (Brady et al., 1958). His important finding was an accidental product of an investigation of a separate problem, and the unexpected data generated a whole series of subsequent experiments. Brady used a pair of monkeys in a yoked-control experiment. (Yoked-control means that both animals were subjected to an identical pattern of stimulus presentation.) Brady called his two animals "the executive monkey" and "the dummy monkey." The two animals were confined in identical restraining chairs, with electrodes hooked onto their bodies. Control buttons were placed so that each monkey could press one. However, only the executive monkey's button was hooked up so that it could change the stimulus situation. The executive monkey could learn a technique of button-pressing that would immediately terminate an ongoing shock. The trick was to press the button quickly in order to escape and perhaps almost completely avoid the electric shock.

Early in the experiment both monkeys flailed about when shocked, sometimes hitting the button in front of them. Soon, through the process of negative reinforcement, the executive monkey's button-pressing decreased in latency and he began to cut off the electric shock (simultaneously for both animals) very quickly. The executive monkey became "aware" that there was something he could do about his situation, as indicated by the fact that he learned to sit during moments without shock with his hand on the button in a position where he could quickly press it. The dummy monkey, meanwhile, experienced all the shock relief that the executive monkey experienced, since he was a yoked control, but he was actually in a helpless position. He was a passive victim of whatever stimuli were presented, and nothing he did could terminate the shock.

At this point you might wonder which monkey would be subject to the greater stress—the animal that learns how to do something to escape stress or the animal that is a completely helpless victim of whatever events fate may deliver. Most people would suppose that the latter animal would suffer the greater stress, but if stomach ulcers are any indication, the reverse actually was true. In fact, the executive monkey in Brady's first experiment suddenly died of massive internal stomach hemorrhages, and only on autopsy was the cause of the monkey's death determined. At that point Brady's entire line of investigation switched to the study of stomach ulceration as a dependent variable. Using different pairs of monkeys, the "executive-monkey-ulcer" phenomenon was repeated again and again. The conclusion was that it is more stressful to experience stress stimulation and have to emit certain operant responses in order to save oneself than it is to experience stress without any opportunity to learn an operant behavior to gain relief.

C 13.3. *The development of psychophysiological disorders through stress.*

In the research in which rats were given immobilization stress, it was found that _____ plays an important role in the matter of whether or not the animal develops psychophysiological problems.

    a. heredity   b. whether the animal is alone   c. the reinforcement history

In Brady's executive monkey experiments, the conclusion was that it is the more stressful to _____ .

    a. be a helpless victim of circumstances

    b. be in a situation where you can learn to escape an aversive stimulus

All this research, as you can see, is linked to Dr. Selye's original work, published in 1956 in his book titled *The Stress of Life*. This is as far as we will go at this point in discussing stress research, and we will now turn to other aspects of the stress phenomenon, beginning with frustration.

PROGRESS CHECK 13.1

1. The most accurate analysis of the three concepts in this chapter is _____ .

    a. stress encompasses frustration and conflict

    b. frustration encompasses stress and conflict

    c. conflict encompasses frustration and stress

2. Which factor is defined in terms of a physical-specific stimulus resulting in physiological change?
   _____ .

   a. Frustration   b. Stress   c. Conflict

3. In Selye's GAS model of stress, when does the ANS first become active? _____ .

   a. Stage of exhaustion   b. Stage of resistance   c. Alarm reaction

4. According to Selye, the stage of resistance may produce _____ .

   a. loss of adrenal glands   b. psychophysiological ailments   c. death

5. When does the organism experience autonomic collapse or even death? _____ .

   a. Stage of exhaustion   b. Stage of resistance   c. Alarm reaction

6. Heredity was an important variable in the development of stress-induced psychophysiological problems in the _____ .

   a. rat immobilization experiments   b. executive monkey experiments

7. Which animal was more stressed? _____ .

   a. The passive monkey in Brady's experiments

   b. The executive monkey who controlled the escape button

FRUSTRATION

Frustration can be defined as an internal mental and emotional state directly resulting from blockage of goal-directed behavior, or from excessive delay in gaining an expected reward. As you can see, such a definition is not operational, and for an operational definition one must turn either to a statement about the degree of goal-blockage or to a measure of behavior in the goal-blocked situation. In our coverage of frustration, we shall tend to emphasize the latter type of definition, emphasizing actual behavioral effects.

Responses to Frustration: Persistence

A number of possible responses to frustration can be predicted with considerable accuracy if one knows the history of experiences of the organism. One of the most productive responses to frustration is *persistence*—a continuation of goal-directed effort. This seems a natural response to frustration, and one to be expected in the earliest stages of frustration in most experimentally naïve animals. In fact, in bar-press situations, a surge of responding at a very rapid rate usually occurs during the first few moments of the extinction trials. This surge has been said to illustrate the *frustration drive,* which is simply a way of saying that the overall drive state is elevated by the existence of frustration. It has even been suggested that the frustration drive might account for what we previously called scalloping—the sharp increase in responding shortly before the end of a fixed interval or a fixed ratio.

In addition, persistence in the face of an extinction schedule or some other difficulty in obtaining a goal is partly a function of the history of reinforcement for persistence in the past. That is, when an individual encounters difficulty, persists in his efforts, and finally achieves the goal, he is very likely to increase his tendency to persevere thereafter. On the other hand, if persistence leads only to continued failure, other responses to frustration typically begin to develop. Interacting in this situation, as you can see, would be variables such as intelligence. Highly intelligent people's attempts to persevere are more likely to lead to eventual success, which then reinforces persistence. Therefore, intelligent people tend to be the ones who do not give up as readily in the face of difficulty.

Another influence contributing to what at least appears to be persistence, and discussed in a previous chapter, is nearness to an incentive. When an individual has almost achieved a goal, and is blocked from reaching it when only a short distance away, he tends to demonstrate a considerably higher level of continued goal-directed effort than he does if blocked at a greater distance. This incentive effect can be translated into the terminology of frustration, so that we could say that there is a greater level of frustration when the organism is blocked close to the goal.

C 13.4. *Responses to frustration: Persistence.*

An early brief reaction to initial frustration in naïve organisms is persistence toward the goal, but in order to continue there must develop a history of _____ .

 a. eventual achievement of the goal through persistence

 b. escaping stress through the period of indecision

 c. encountering substitute goals after abandoning pursuit of the original one

An increase in response rate during the early stages of extinction is due to a so-called _____ .

 a. anger response   b. frustration drive   c. cognitive determination

Relative to the answer to the last question, this has been given as one explanation of the _____ effect sometimes seen in some partial (or intermittent) schedules of reinforcement.

 a. extinction   b. resistance to extinction   c. scalloping

The level of frustration resulting from goal-blockage, as indicated by the rate of frustration-induced behaviors, _____ if the goal-blockage occurs near to the goal.

 a. is relatively high   b. is relatively low

Responses to Frustration: Aggression

A second observed reaction to frustration is aggression. Aggression in frustrating circumstances is so common that it led to a statement, over three decades ago, of the *frustration-aggression sequence* (Miller et al., 1939). With little doubt, aggressive responses in a frustrated organism appear, to a certain degree at least, to be natural or innate. Some researchers believe that the aggressive response is, in fact, more natural to the naïve organism than is persistence toward the goal. At any rate, the experimental study of aggression by frustrated organisms has yielded a great deal of interesting information.

Generally, all factors that serve to increase the overall drive level have been shown to increase frustration-induced aggression as well. Thus, such factors as the deprivation level of the frustrated organism, the attractiveness of the goal, the degree to which the attractive values of the goal are obvious and visible, and the distance from the goal at the time further progress is blocked all relate to the probability and magnitude of the aggressive reaction to frustration. There also is considerable recent evidence that the harder one has worked toward a goal, the greater the aggressive response to frustration will be.

Additionally, habit strength has an effect on level of aggression, although the relationship is by no means as clear-cut as with the drive factor. The components of H (habit strength), translated, generally suggest that when individuals' past behaviors have easily gained the goal, subsequent interference makes the individual more prone to aggression. And, when the gained goal, in the past, has been very valuable or enjoyable (the quality of reinforcement variable), aggressive tendencies rise in response to frustration. In addition to these factors, evidence indicates that frustration can cumulate, so that many little frustrations may cause an eventual explosion of aggression in the frustrated individual.

Drawing by Frascino: © 1974 The New Yorker Magazine, Inc.

"Actually, he's afraid of us, but his inability to deal with his fear makes him angry. Anger is something he _can_ deal with."

Before we move on beyond the aggressive response, it should be pointed out that aggression is a very complex phenomenon. The emotional nucleus of aggression, generated from frustrations in the environment, can be operantly reinforced. Both positive and negative reinforcement of aggression can occur, and each can increase the aggressive tendency of the individual. In the area of positive reinforcement of animal aggression, aggressive responses can drive away competition for certain goal objects such as food, water, and sexual access. The animals that dominate, because of reinforcement, subsequently show increased tendencies to be aggressive. Similarly, when one is subjected to aversive stimuli, one way to stop the torment is to aggress and thereby drive away the individual who is causing the unpleasantness. If one succeeds, the aggressive pattern is negatively reinforced. Thus, aggression that originally began as a reaction to frustration can eventually develop, through reinforcement, into a behavior pattern that occurs quite generally in many situations.

C 13.5. *Responses to frustration: Aggression.*

A _____ correlation exists between the deprivation level of a frustrated organism and the magnitude of its aggressive reactions to frustration.

    a. positive   b. negative

A _____ correlation exists between the visibility and attractiveness of a goal object and the magnitude of aggressive reactions to frustration of efforts toward that goal.

    a. positive   b. negative

A _____ correlation exists between the distance from the goal when eventually blocked and the magnitude of aggressive reactions to that blockage.

    a. positive   b. negative

If an organism is accustomed to gaining a goal object easily, it will show _____ of frustration-induced aggression when blocked than would have been the case with a less consistent history of such positive reinforcement.

    a. a greater intensity   b. a lesser intensity

If, in the past, you have greatly enjoyed and appreciated the experience of a particular gained goal, there should be a relatively _____ tendency to become aggressive when that goal is thereafter blocked than would have been the case if the goal had been less satisfying.

    a. weaker   b. stronger

Aggression, starting in response to frustration, can be increased through _____ reinforcement.

    a. positive   b. negative   c. both positive and negative

As psychologists seek information on functional relationships concerning the frustration-aggression sequence, they have a number of concerns about the main body of existing research. One problem involves the level of frustration that can be imposed upon human subjects, which is usually quite limited. Much higher levels of frustration are customarily used in animal laboratories. A second major problem concerns the operational definition of the term "aggression" in human research. Such pencil-and-paper inventories as the Siegel Manifest Hostility Scale and the Buss Hostility Scale have been used, and the reader of published research involving these instruments is left on his own to interpret the relation between such assessments and any physical or verbal assaults on others that the subject may actually emit.

The situation is scarcely improved where behavioral measures are taken. The specification of behaviors to be called aggressive can be quite varied. Children may engage in a variety of pushing, pulling, holding, teasing, and verbal behaviors, and one is left to a variety of interpretations of what is actually happening—whether it is play or hostility. Even attempts in laboratory settings to operationalize aggression are not above criticism. Parton (1964) arranged a game in which seven-year-olds manipulated a doll that could knock down another doll controlled by the experimenter. Here we would wonder whether knocking down a doll is identical in motive and nature to more literal aggression against others. We might also wonder if children might vary in the degree to which they can express aggression in the presence of a strange adult. Cowan and Walters (1963) investigated aggression, measured by the number of hits on a big Bobo doll. The problem with this sort of measure is that the Bobo doll is never the actual stimulus to aggressive behavior, and considerable differences are found in the degrees to which various children tend to express their feelings on a safe target (displacement of aggression) rather than on the actual agent of frustration.

In summary, psychologists are understandably restricted in their ability to investigate the frustration-aggression sequence in human subjects by the limited degree to which they can ethically impose major frustration, and by the artificiality of the "aggression" that results. This latter factor stems largely from a reluctance to allow one human being to strike another in the name of research. This is yet another excellent justification of animal research in the establishment of the causes of basic behavior.

In 1966, Judith Elbert Favell set out to correct some of the limiting features of previous research with human subjects into the frustration-aggression sequence. Out of her careful efforts a remarkable experiment developed (Ulrich & Favell, 1971). She used four elementary school children as subjects. Each child was asked to place ten large rubber bottle stoppers, with the smaller ends down, into two stacks of five stoppers each. Whenever a child completed the two stacks without any falling over, he was rewarded with a dime from an automatic dispensing device. Any accident causing the stoppers to fall over during stacking ended that trial with no reward. A day's session consisted of twenty trials, so that a child could earn up to $2.00 if he had no accidents.

At the outset of the experiment each child was introduced to the apparatus in his booth. It was explained that the table he would use was attached to a vibrator motor that might shake the table surface from time to time. He was also told that there was another child (actually nonexistent) in a similar booth on the other side of the wall who was also stacking stoppers. The "other child" was said to control the button that would shake the subject child's table when pressed. The subject child was shown a button in his own booth, and he was told that pressing that button would shake the other child's table. Also, when pressed, the button activated a feedback light to "show it was operating."

The experiment began with each child being brought in for four initial sessions without any interfering vibrations. A baseline recording was taken of the number of previbration button-presses, showing an average of 36 button-presses per session. The button-presses that did occur during those sessions seemed to result from frustration when the stacks accidentally fell over, resulting in loss of the reward.

Following the initial previbration sessions, each subject proceeded to a series of ten sessions during which randomly spaced 4-second vibrations were delivered to his or her table during stacking. It was found that the rate of button-pressing under this condition went up to an average of 195—542 percent higher than the base rate—and most button-pressing was observed to occur immediately after vibration collapsed a partly completed stack. All four subjects showed an increase over the base-rate measure.

As an additional variable, the number of vibrations delivered was randomly assigned as either four, six, eight, ten, or twelve vibrations per session. A breakdown of data along that dimension showed that a higher number of vibrations per session experienced by the children resulted in a greater number of button-presses delivered by them. More than twice as many button-presses occurred, for example, under the twelve-vibrations-per-session condition than under the four-per-session condition. It again should be emphasized that retaliatory button-pressing was in no way effective in decreasing the disruptive vibrations. The only consequence of pressing the button was that the feedback light turned on, supposedly indicating to the child that the "other child's" table was being vibrated.

Favell observed considerable variation among individuals both in their base rates of button-pressing and in their percentage rate of increase, during table vibration, over the base rate, which suggests that either organismic variables influence the basic aggressive tendency or that aggression rate is affected by learned frustration tolerance or previous reinforcement history.

C 13.6. *The experimental study of aggression in human beings.*

A major limitation in frustration-aggression research with human subjects is that the response variable _____ .

   a. too often departs from being actual physical or verbal assault on another person

   b. is never operationally defined   c. cannot be observed directly

Favell's research with the vibrating table established that - - - was a predictive function of - - -. _____ .

    a. aggression/frustration   b. persistence/frustration   c. aggression/physical discomfort

Favell's subjects were _____ .

    a. children   b. laboratory rats   c. university students

Favell established that there is a _____ relation between the level of frustration and the amount of retaliatory responding.

    a. positive   b. negative

Favell found that, in her group of subjects, the basic level of aggressive response to a given degree of frustration _____ .

    a. was about the same from one subject to the next

    b. varied widely among the different subjects

Responses to Prolonged Frustration

In discussing persistence and aggression, we have been considering the sorts of responses to frustration that occur fairly immediately after frustration begins. There are other types of responses which seem to be reactions to prolonged frustration. It is assumed in these cases that strategies of persistence and aggression have failed, and the organism has drifted into alternative strategies. In such cases we attempt to determine what sorts of reinforcement might have occurred to stabilize such strategies.

Apathy

One of the reactions shown by organisms subjected to prolonged frustration is a state of *apathy*. The individual in such a state appears listless, shows little further interest in the goal, and in fact demonstrates little interaction with the environment in the frustrating situation. We do not know exactly how this state is reinforced, but is seems likely that previous attention to the environmental situation has resulted in continued disappointment. By diverting one's own attention away, perhaps almost not thinking about anything at all, the organism is negatively reinforced by a reduction of awareness of the frustration. A similar alternative explanation would hold that such detachment succeeds in lowering the drive state, thus reducing frustration, which would by definition be negatively reinforcing.

Rationalization

Another reaction to prolonged frustration (or failure) is that of *rationalization*. Although this reaction presumably is limited to human beings, the classic illustration comes from the Aesop Fable concerning the fox and the grapes. The fox in this story, who could not jump high enough to reach the delicious-appearing grapes hanging overhead, continued his journey down the road muttering about "sour" grapes. This is where our expression "sour grapes" comes from, and the fable shows the fox devaluing the object that he was frustrated from obtaining. Just as removal of attention (apathy) from the incentive value of the goal reduces the level of drive, so would devaluation of the blocked goal object succeed in reducing drive strength.

Bibler Feature Service

LITTLE MAN ON CAMPUS

"HE ASKED HIS ADVISOR HOW TO IMPROVE HIS GRADES."

Fantasy   A final form of response to prolonged frustration is that of *fantasy*. Researchers are not entirely clear on whether indulgence in fantasy revolving around goal attainment might actually reduce the relevant drive state. Some might point out that ideations concerning the goal object should heighten drive, but of course a peculiar character marks most frustration-produced fantasy. The individual does not simply imagine the pleasure to be obtained in achieving the goal, but actually works through a series of mental images involving the entire process of goal acquisition *and consumption*.

Cases of social fantasy are easily understandable. Socially and physically inadequate children often imagine themselves as conquering heroes. The popular story of Walter Mitty shows this type of response to prolonged feelings of ineffectiveness. It fits nicely into a reinforcement type of theory to suppose that Walter Mitty's "need" for success was at least partially met through daydreams, but as we indicated before this is not entirely clear. Therefore we are not certain how fantasy is reinforced to the point of becoming a high-rate, "typical" response to frustration, beyond the obvious provision of stimulus variety.

C 13.7. *Responses to prolonged frustration.*

When prolonged frustration occurs, one is likely to encounter in the frustrated subject patterns

of _____ .

a. apathy toward the goal object

b. rationalization concerning the value of the goal object

c. fantasy concerning attainment of the goal object

d. (two of the above three answers are true)

e. (all three of the first three answers are true)

Rationalization can be viewed as _____ the drive state.

a. increasing   b. decreasing

In line with your last answer, rationalization could be said most appropriately to be _____ reinforced.

a. negatively   b. positively

The Choice of a Response to Frustration It is likely that each individual develops what psychologists call a "habit-family hierarchy." This means that the individual has a history of varied success with the strategies he has used in the past when frustrated. Often these matters are dependent upon the sort of family situation and peer situation the individual is subjected to, which is one of the reasons that parents' behavior patterns, birth-order factors, and so forth are so often associated with different types of personality patterns. One child, for example, may have frequently tried again when frustrated and in many cases finally achieved the goal, while another child may have had a history of repeated failures. Moreover, one child's aggressive actions may have been punished and thereby suppressed in one family, while another child's aggression may not have been; in fact, varying degrees of reinforcement for aggression may occur in certain families. In some cases aggressive actions can perhaps only be directed against older, more powerful individuals by children who do not have easy access to many same-age peers; meanwhile, another child may have a frequent history of reinforcement for aggression due to his being the oldest or strongest among his siblings or in his peer group.

The concept of the habit-family hierarchy simply assumes a first, a second, a third level of habit development, and so forth, with the individual usually behaving in a predictable sequence. His strongest reaction, dictated by his particular history of reinforcement, is tried first. If it does not prove effective, the second behavioral level in the hierarchy is employed, and so forth. In this way we may explain the behaviors of some individuals who might typically show an initial redoubling of effort toward the goal, followed soon by a temper tantrum and aggression toward others.

C 13.8. *The habit-family hierarchy.*

A habit-family hierarchy is a notion of _____ .

a. a hierarchy of reflexes that exists in respondent behavior classes

b. rapid adaptability of an organism to the stimuli presented in a situation

c. an organism switching to a second, third, etc. strategy when thwarted, with the order dictated by the reinforcement history

d. groups of highly similar behaviors that are correlated from individual to individual

Frustration   A final note concerning reactions to frustration involves the notion of frus-
Tolerance   tration tolerance. This is a simple concept which holds that an individual
who has experienced little or no prior frustration tends to become angry
and aggressive very easily in frustrating circumstances, while an individual
who has experienced first mild, then moderate repeated frustrations, so long
as any subsequent aggression was not reinforced, is able to handle himself
much better. In his interesting paperback book *Walden Two*, B. F. Skinner
describes how one might go about developing frustration tolerance in
children in a very painless way. Skinner suggested, in this fictional account
of a psychological "Utopia," that at a very early age children should be
accustomed to minor frustrations and discomfort such as having to wait,
when hungry, for a few minutes before beginning to eat a meal placed
before them. If the reader is interested in a unique account of how children
might be reared, consistent with many notions advocated by behaviorists,
the novel *Walden Two* is certainly a painless, and in fact enjoyable, way
to explore some of these ideas.

C 13.9. *Frustration tolerance.*

Frustration tolerance is said to be developed in situations where _____ .

    a. the organism is exposed to major frustration almost from the time of birth

    b. the organism is "tested" repeatedly with intense frustration until tolerance develops

    c. frustration is gradually introduced a little at a time and builds in intensity

    d. there is adequate attention to incentives in the situation, making the temporary delay of goal
       attainment bearable

PROGRESS CHECK   13.2

MATCH: _____ 1. Reaction of naïve organ-   A. Increased response rate during initial extinction
                       isms to initial frustration
                                            B. Persistence
    _____ 2. Frustration drive

3. Frustration becomes lower with nearness to the blocked goal. _____ .

    a. True   b. False

4. A positive correlation exists between magnitude of aggression and _____ .

    a. amount of frustration   b. degree of deprivation of the frustrated organism

    c. nearness of a blocked goal   d. all of these

5. Which animal would probably show greater frustration-induced aggression? _____ .

    a. Rat 1 has a history of always achieving the goal box

    b. Rat 2 has experience with blocked goals

    c. Rat 3 is blocked from a neutral goal

6. Favell's research with the vibrating table _____ .

    a. used adult subjects

    b. established a positive relation between frustration and retaliation

    c. showed a consistent degree of aggression among subjects

7. With which group is it least restrictive to perform an experiment on aggression? _____ .

    a. Adults   b. Children   c. Animals

MATCH: _____ 8. Apathy   A. Devaluation of goal

            _____ 9. Rationalization   B. Imagining goal acquisition and consumption

            _____ 10. Fantasy   C. Listless and disinterested in goal

                                            D. Response to prolonged frustration

11. If rationalization decreases a frustrated drive state, then it is probably _____ .

    a. positively reinforcing   b. negatively reinforcing

12. A child would develop frustration tolerance _____ .

    a. if exposed to minor frustrations   b. if exposed to massive goal blocking

    c. both   d. neither

CONFLICT   An individual is placed in a state of conflict if he experiences mixed motives concerning a goal, or if he is required to choose between goals of more-or-less equal incentive value. Recognizing that some artificialities are the result of forced categorizing, psychologists still feel that it is useful to conceptualize four major models of conflict.

Approach-   The first major conflict model is known as the *approach-approach conflict.*
Approach   This exists where an individual must choose between two positive goals,
Conflicts   and cannot have both. If you wish to watch two television shows, but they are presented simultaneously on different channels, you have an example of an approach-approach conflict. These do not tend to be terribly problematic for human beings, although some situations, such as that of a young lady who cannot decide which of two men to marry, have significant implications. In one sense the approach-approach conflict is not a very tension-filled situation, and individuals tend to resolve this type of conflict fairly readily. A fable is told concerning a donkey who found himself midway between two piles of straw. He looked first at one and then the other, but could not make up his mind which pile of straw to eat. As the story goes, the donkey starved to death because he could not make up his mind. That story is totally misleading, because the approach-approach conflict involves what some

psychologists have called an *unstable equilibrium*. This means that the conflict tends not to be stable; it can be easily resolved by minor additional considerations. For example, if you go downtown to see a movie and find there are two movies of similar appeal, such an approach-approach conflict can be resolved by something so simple as which box office waiting line is the shorter. The problem of choice between two television shows scheduled for the same hour is often resolved simply by the knowledge of which channel receives the clearer signal. And when our friend the donkey found himself halfway between two piles of straw, the conflict would tend to be resolved by the animal being prone to go in the direction in which he was looking.

Avoidance-Avoidance Conflicts

The second type of conflict model, the *avoidance-avoidance conflict*, has a *stable equilibrium.* When an individual finds himself between two unpleasant alternatives, one of which he has to endure, he tends to put off a decision as long as possible. In a laboratory psychologists once tested an avoidance-avoidance conflict by having subjects decide which of two bad-tasting liquids they chose to drink—one was a mixture of salt with water, and the other was a mixture of vinegar with water. It is remarkable how long the subjects took to finally make up their minds. Serious cases of avoidance-avoidance conflict in a real-life environment are frequently found. An example would be the individual who must choose between continuing to

© 1971. Reprinted by permission of Saturday Review and Joseph Farris

"I think I'll stick it out here, but thanks, anyway."

endure nagging pain from an old injury or subjecting himself to a short period of more intense pain following an operation, but with the promise of permanent relief.

Approach-Avoidance Conflicts

A fairly stable equilibrium also exists in the third conflict model, the *approach-avoidance conflict*. Unlike the previous two models, both involving two goals with a decision to be made, the approach-avoidance conflict model involves only one goal. The difficulty comes in the decision as to whether it is worth putting up with certain negative aspects of the goal in order to enjoy certain positive aspects. If a young man wishes to enjoy the excitement of competitive football and the acclaim he may receive for his outstanding play, he must also endure long, uncomfortable practice sessions which have very little glamour. If a young man is deciding about marriage, he may weigh certain positive aspects of marriage against negative ones such as the surrender of social freedom and the assumption of increased financial responsibilities. The relatively *stable equilibrium* of the approach-avoidance conflict causes considerable delay in resolving this kind of conflict where the opposing motives are of comparable strength. We sometimes hear of individuals who become engaged to be married and then change their minds a half-dozen times, first setting the date, then withdrawing it, and later setting another date. Still, except for unusual cases, the equilibrium here is less stable than with the avoidance-avoidance conflict.

Double Approach-Avoidance Conflicts

The *double approach-avoidance conflict* is very much like the approach-avoidance conflict, except that rather than one goal with both positive and negative values attached to it, we have two goals, each with positive and negative characteristics. While this may seem to be an incredibly complex situation, it is likely that a majority of human conflicts fit this model. Consider the case of a young man who must make a decision about either going to college or staying in his hometown and working. Both goals have positive characteristics. If the young man goes to college, he will be preparing himself for an interesting vocation. He may be able to spend time with his girl friend who is going to go to that university. He may receive the approval and admiration of various members of his family, who are proud of his educational progress and are interested in his educational future. Staying at home also has its rewards. The young man may have a good job that pays him a fair amount of money. He has a circle of hometown friends. He may have the use of the family car, and he knows his way around the area, from long experience.

But both goals have negative aspects. If he goes to college it probably will be as a financially poor student, with the good hometown job left behind. He may be considerably threatened by academic competition, and he may be plagued with insecurity, doubt, and tension concerning whether or not he can make it at college. If he stays at home he will endure loneliness,

with his girl friend gone. Some of his other friends may be leaving to go to universities, and his family may become outspoken in their disappointment in him. So the young man must make a rather complex decision. He must move in one direction or the other, but he cannot embrace both goals simultaneously.

C 13.10. *The conflict models.*

Of the approach-approach and the avoidance-avoidance conflict models, which has the more stable

equilibrium? _____ .

    a. Approach-approach   b. Avoidance-avoidance

The conflict model with only one goal involved is the _____ model.

    a. approach-avoidance   b. avoidance-avoidance   c. approach-approach

Suppose you keep a dog in your apartment. You are vexed by the arrangements necessary to board

him during vacations and you hate to exercise him in winter. Still, you like your dog and he provides

good company. This is indicative of the _____ conflict model.

    a. approach-approach   b. avoidance-avoidance   c. approach-avoidance

Most human social situations where conflict is involved match the characteristics of the _____

conflict model.

    a. approach-avoidance   b. double approach-avoidance   c. avoidance-avoidance

Conflict Gradients

We can express the amount of motivation represented in an incentive situation in the form of a *gradient* on a chart. You will probably recall this procedure from our discussion which began in Chapter 7. Figure 13.1 indicates that as an individual draws nearer to a goal object, the level of motivation relative to that goal increases. Motivation toward an appetitive goal or situation is called approach motivation, and motivation away from an aversive situation is called avoidance motivation.

Several important experiments in research literature study the relation of the approach and avoidance gradients. As we briefly mentioned in Chapter 7, pulling strength against a restraining leash is a typical measure of motivation in an animal research situation. When animals are routinely fed in a special chamber and are then restrained as they run down an alleyway toward the chamber, the resulting gradient is similar to that labeled "approach" in Figure 13.1. When other animals are shocked in the chamber and their flight down the alleyway is restrained, the resulting gradient is similar to that labeled "avoidance."

It is also possible to combine the experiences. Animals may be fed numerous times in an experimental chamber and later shocked a given number of times there. When they are allowed into the alleyway leading to the chamber, they typically approach while they are at some distance from it, then slow and finally stop as they arrive at the physical location represented by the point where the gradients of approach and avoidance motives cross. At this point the individual typically "vacillates," swaying back and forth, too hungry to leave and too afraid to go forward. One researcher was fond of astounding visitors to his laboratory with the accuracy of his predictions of the exact spot where an animal would stop. The researcher would have a number of known values to calculate—the number of food presentations, the amounts of food given and under what deprivation level, the number, intensity, and durations of the shocks experienced, and the current deprivation level. By carefully relying upon known data from past research,

Figure 13.1

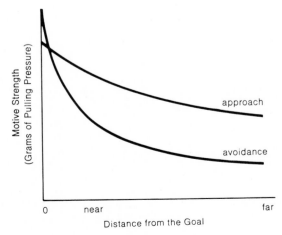

he predicted amazingly constant motivational gradients from individual to individual.

Let us summarize the findings on goal-gradient research:

(a) The closer to a positive goal or situation, the stronger the tendency to approach.

(b) The nearer to a negative situation (an aversive stimulus) the stronger the tendency to avoid it.

(c) The avoidance motive increases as a function of decreasing distance to the goal more rapidly than does the approach motive.

(d) When incompatible response tendencies are in conflict, the stronger will prevail.

An interesting elaboration on goal-gradient relationships pertains to the study of the effects of alcohol on conflict behavior. When animals are both stressed and rewarded in a given situation, it has been found that alcohol is very powerful in lowering the avoidance gradient. Human beings are subjected to a variety of situations, particularly in earning their livings, in which their fear of performing certain acts may be as strong as or stronger than their desire to perform those acts. A salesman afraid of initiating certain contacts, or an executive who fears having to deal with certain men higher in the organization, may find a few drinks help overcome hesitation. The dynamics of this phenomenon can be investigated with animals, since alcohol appears to have a similar direct effect of lowering the avoidance gradient.

Human behavior in conflict exhibits only a few more complexities than that of animals, one of the most important being man's capability of dealing with a goal in terms of his relation to it in time, and not just in distance. Man's behavior in terms of the variable of closeness in time is exactly analogous to behavior relative to closeness to a goal in space.

C 13.11. *Motivation gradients in conflict.*

Motive strength _____ as you draw nearer to an incentive object.

    a. increases   b. decreases

Motivation increases _____ sharply as one draws nearer to the incentive.

    a. less   b. more

When the approach and the avoidance gradients cross, the organism will _____ at that point relative to the incentive.

    a. vacillate   b. go ahead   c. retreat

Unlike lower organisms, man's tendencies to perceive conflicts and respond accordingly include _____ relative to distance to incentives.

    a. only perceptions of space   b. only perceptions of time

    c. both perceptions of space and of time

Fixation in Conflict Situations

In 1940 Maier first described an interesting behavior demonstrated by rats in a situation that prevented the animal from making a consistently correct response to escape an aversive stimulus. The problem situation was essentially this: the animal was placed on a jumping-stand, where he would gaze across an interval of space and see the outlines of two doorways confronting him, one round and one square. Since the animal would not jump without cause, a squirt of compressed air from behind would cause him to immediately leap to the other side. One of two things would happen. If the rat hit the "correct" doorway, the door would fall inward and the animal would pass through the opening, landing on a platform behind, with food available there as a special reward. However, if he hit the "wrong" doorway it would not yield, and in addition to banging his head, he would drop end-over-end several feet down into a suspended net, a circumstance apparently quite unpleasant. Early in the experiment one shape of doorway was always the correct one, and the animals very quickly learned the concept of squareness and circularity, and became capable of 100 percent correct performance whether they were to jump left or right.

After mastery of the described performance, the animals were placed in an impossible task situation. No longer would any strategy allow them to be consistently correct. The animals would leap toward their previously established "correct" doorway, only to meet with a random 50-50 chance of being correct. The animals would persist for a time in jumping toward the proper shape, whether it was placed on the left or the right. Finally, however, the rats "fixated"—that is, they began to jump repeatedly to the left or to the right side, regardless of which shape of doorway the choice entailed. Also, their fixation persisted regardless of the consequences of their act. In one series of experiments, at the time when an animal adopted such a position fixation, circumstances were then arranged so that that animal was always wrong when he persisted. If the animal fixated toward the right opening, the researcher would permanently lock the right doorway, and even go so far as to leave the left entrance open with the platform behind in plain view. Even under these circumstances, the animals persisted in fixated responses through hundreds of successive trials.

It is possible to hypothesize an explanation of such fixated behavior based on reinforcement theory. We would propose that an animal would find it more aversive to have to make a choice and be punished 50 percent of the time than to give up any form of choice and mindlessly persist at a fixated response which was punished 100 percent of the time. If this is true, future research should investigate such circumstances with human subjects. We have frequently noted that some children, and even some college students, who are called upon for an answer in the classroom, do not show a very high rate of correct answering. One form of fixated behavior, analogous to the animal's self-defeating behavior, is simply to give up responding in the classroom. The child who consistently mumbles, "I don't know," to even the simplest question is demonstrating fixation which may be negatively reinforced by no longer having to make decisions.

C 13.12. *Experimentally-induced fixation.*

Fixated behavior can be interpreted as being _____ reinforced.

    a. non-   b. positively   c. negatively

The "reinforcer" in fixation would likely be _____ .

    a. social reinforcement

    b. escape from having to make decisions in a stress situation

    c. primary reinforcement

PROGRESS CHECK   13.3

1. According to the conflict models, which has the most stable equilibrium? _____ .

    a. Approach-approach   b. Approach-avoidance

    c. Avoidance-avoidance   d. b and c

2. Which statement is often true of marriage? _____ .

    a. It can be an approach-avoidance conflict   b. A single goal is involved

    c. Both   d. Neither

3. The double approach-avoidance model typifies most human social conflict. _____ .

    a. True   b. False

4. Conflict gradients show what effects on motivation? _____ .

    a. Proximity does not affect the motive's strength

    b. Crossing gradients produces vacillation

    c. a and b   d. None of the above

5. Humans' behavior in conflict is more complex than animals' because _____ .

    a. humans have more cerebral cortex

    b. humans can philosophize

    c. human conflict situations follow more complex models

    d. humans have both space and time perception

6. Fixated behavior under conflict is probably negatively reinforced because _____ .

    a. it eventually pays off   b. it permits escape from decision making   c. both

HUMAN REACTIONS TO FRUSTRATION, STRESS, AND CONFLICT

We will now discuss the human subject under stress conditions from two different aspects. First we will consider the efficiency of the stressed individual, and second we will turn again to psychoanalytic viewpoints and consider how Freud saw man resolving his stresses.

First, let us look at the efficiency of the individual who is motivated by aversive stimuli. Essentially, the essence of this matter was presented in Chapter 7. In that chapter we spoke of the Yerkes-Dodson Principle which stated that for every task there is an optimum intermediate level of motivation. Research has shown that motivation levels can be too high, resulting in the disorganization and fragmenting of behavior patterns, and causing inefficiency. Many of the research findings that went into the formulation of the Yerkes-Dodson Principle were handled in laboratory settings in which human subjects were offered rewards on one hand and punishers on the other to motivate them through various tasks. In general, when the aversive threat was a serious one such as would be the case with threatened electric shock, it was found that human subjects performed much better on complex tasks under the lower, appetitive types of motivation. Threats of physical and other forms of punishment succeeded in overmotivating and disrupting performance. At the University of Iowa researchers related scores on the Taylor Manifest Anxiety Scale to subsequent grade point averages and, consistent with the Yerkes-Dodson Principle, it was found that low-anxiety and high-anxiety students were alike in making lower grade point averages than did students with intermediate levels of anxiety.

Types of Anxiety

Turning now to clinical types of stress reduction and conflict resolution, we shall examine Freud's thoughts on the matter. Remember that Freud stated that the ego was the conscious, experiencing part of the personality structure. The ego experiences pressure and resulting distress from three sources.

First, and easiest to understand, is pressure from the environment. When an individual perceives a real or imagined threat, such as possibly failing an important examination, he experiences anxiety. This form of environmentally produced anxiety is called *objective anxiety*.

The second source of anxiety is the superego. When the ego experiences the superego's pressures in the form of guilt, *moral anxiety* is the result.

Finally, and perhaps most difficult to understand, is the ego's experience of pressures from the id. Freud had the idea that when an individual represses or bottles up his impulses toward sexual and aggressive expression, the ego begins to suffer from pressures with resulting tensions that the individual finds very difficult to localize. The individual may feel impulses toward behaviors that are almost unspeakably horrible, and he may be upset by this sort of thing, or the pent-up id pressures may express themselves in dreams concerning violent, aggressive actions against certain people. However the impulses may be manifest, the build-up of unexpressed id impulses can make the individual very unhappy and anxious, according to Freud, and in this case the individual seldom is able to understand why he feels the way he does. This form of anxiety is called *neurotic anxiety*, but there is no significance to the selection of that term; it is not the type of anxiety that "makes a neurotic."

C 13.13. *Types of anxiety: Freud's theory.*

Anxiety arising from pressures of the superego is called _____ anxiety.

Neurotic anxiety originates from pressures from the _____ .

If you hesitate to walk through a field of tall grass in which you have heard there are quite a few snakes, this would be an example of _____ anxiety.

    a. neurotic   b. moral   c. objective

The Ego Defense Mechanisms

As we have said, the ego experiences discomfort because of pressures from one or more of three sources. When experiencing these discomforts, the ego naturally attempts to deflect the impulses and reduce the level of distress. A number of mental mechanisms may develop and, through what we would call reinforcement, may become part of the characteristic mental processes of the individual. The methods of anxiety control are called *ego defense mechanisms*—tactics used by the ego to defend against id impulses, super-ego pressures, and threats from the environment. We shall discuss each of these individually, with examples and short definitions.

1. Identification

1. *Identification* is a defense against objective (environment-produced) anxiety. Identification is defined as *building the ego by symbolically becoming another person,* all of which involves incorporating another's ego structure. You may have noticed how small children, helpless in many ways, seem to enjoy playing games that call for them to assume the identity of some power-ful—often gun-wielding—individual. Playing "police," "cowboy," or "sol-dier" is a way in which the child defends, at least momentarily in fantasy, against an otherwise ever present awareness of his own powerlessness.

Similarly, you may have read of occasional cases of people who experi-ence amnesia. In these accounts such persons invariably start to "seek" their identity, usually beginning with an approach to the police depart-ment. This act illustrates that being without an identity, and in a sense not knowing how one should act, is anxiety-producing.

The two preceding illustrations describe related psychological motives —the need for a release from helplessness and the need for a "personality." These needs most often combine, and the individual first begins by picking up personality patterns that he observes in others. The typical child main-tains a lasting and developing identification with the parents, later concen-trating on the same-sex parent. The parents become known to him intimately in terms of the finer points of their personalities and how they adjust to the various stresses of life. Most children also go through a series of transient identifications. They may see a movie featuring a certain hero, and they then act like, walk like, or talk like that person for a short period of time there-after. Or, they may make a transient identification with an admired peer and mimic many of his mannerisms. The problem with the transient iden-tification, if it is not supplemented by parent-identification, is that the child ordinarily does not get to know the patterned-after person well enough to know how to respond in a wide variety of stress situations.

Let us take for an example the young man who gets his first job, really enjoys it and tries hard, but gets fired for incompetence. This is a serious threat to one's emotional integrity. If as a child he, or she, has had the experience of living with his parents and seeing them go through a variety of emotional disappointments, he may then be able to show some kind of reasonably mature reaction to this development. If not, he may only have superficial ideas concerning the appropriate emotional handling of this stress. Perhaps he has seen a youngster in his peer group retaliate physically against a person who "insults" him. Or, some television character may provide a sort of model for expressions of what are actually immature or inappropriate reactions. The individual may resort to a primitive escape pattern—getting drunk—or he may hurt himself in some way, thus patterning after strategies that worked in recapturing affections when he was a very small child.

The concept of *ego-strength*, which we have said is not completely unlike the term *mental health*, depends upon two developments. First must come the opportunity to get to know someone intimately and learn how that person's emotional structure operates. This can happen in depth only if the child lives during practically his whole early developmental span in close daily association with a parent or parent image. Second, the model must have a strong, mature ego if the identifying child is to incorporate mature personality qualities. Lack of either of these two factors can engender a problem, and some psychoanalytic theorists think that what many psychologists consider to be genetic factors in neurotic and psychotic patterns actually may be the recycling, generation after generation, of immature and maladjustive emotional patterns transmitted through the identification process.

2. Introjection

2. *Introjection* is a defense against objective anxiety, but it may eventually contribute toward a paradoxical increase in subsequent moral anxiety. Introjection is defined as *incorporating another's values, thus building up the superego.* When young, a child is repeatedly punished for violating the rules. One way in which he can anticipate situations and thereby not do things that might bring about punishment is to adopt the rule-maker's set of values and concepts of what is right and wrong. In a manner very similar to the building of the ego by incorporating another's ego, one builds the superego by incorporating another's superego. Absence of an intimately known model results in a weak superego structure, as does introjection of a model's weak superego. Either situation may produce persons who seem to have low standards of ethical conduct and who eventually develop reputations of being untrustworthy. On the other hand, an overdeveloped superego can bring much grief, as such individuals may suffer constant feelings of guilt and may blame themselves for every failure or for everything that goes wrong. Introjecting another's overdeveloped superego typically results in an individual also developing an overdeveloped superego.

3. Compensation

3. *Compensation* is a defense against moral anxiety. Compensation is defined as *an unusual effort to make up for real or imagined worthlessness in*

some other area of endeavor. The belief that everyone *needs* some feeling of self-worth and accomplishment can be translated to an idea that everyone suffers from moral anxiety in the face of repeated failures. When an individual is a failure at certain important things, he tends to make up for it with an unusual effort toward success in something else. It is not unusual for a child who is a classroom failure in the elementary school to become the schoolyard bully, and thereby establish himself as someone with accomplishment and superiority. In the other direction, the male child who is not much of a success at sports may become very bookish, and be what teachers sometimes call an "overachiever" to make up for his feelings of physical worthlessness.

4. Conversion

4. *Conversion* seems mainly to be a defense against moral anxiety. Conversion is defined as *converting libidinal energy into physical channels in a symbolic fashion;* or, more loosely, *the draining of physical libido as in some psychosomatic problems.* In the original sense, as stated in the first phrase in the definition, one sometimes sees a dramatic physical development such as *hysterical blindness* or *paralysis* following some threatening or guilt-provoking incident. Such cases are much rarer now than they seem to have been in Freud's day—a fact that is sometimes laid to the reduction of sexual guilt in our modern-day society compared with Freud's Victorian times, and a fact that is sometimes offered as suggesting the validity of this part of Freudian theory.

The term "conversion," in contemporary use, more frequently refers to some psychosomatic type of problem produced by tension and anxiety. You can no doubt easily see the similarity of this type of conversion to the physiological problems developed in stressful situations, which were studied by Selye and discussed earlier in this chapter.

5. Rationalization

5. *Rationalization* is a defense against moral anxiety. Rationalization is defined as *maintaining feelings of self-worth by justifying shortcomings or personal indulgences.* To take a simple example, if you know you should be studying but you decide to accompany your friends who are going to a movie, you may "explain" to yourself that you are tense and the movie will relax you so that your subsequent study efforts will be more efficient. The psychoanalytic theorists emphasize that (1) your decision to go to the movie was made before you thought up the justification, and (2) although you may be talking to others in rationalizing your action, you are really trying to justify the act to yourself.

On a more serious level, you may have noticed in students doing poorly in a course a tendency to find fault with the teacher and his assignments or examinations. In an informal study done at one university, more than 80 percent of students in one auditorium section of a course rated the instructor as "above average or higher in teaching quality," but of those students who were maintaining a failing grade, more than 75 percent rated the same teacher as inferior. The assignment of blame to a source outside oneself—sometimes called "defensiveness"—can reduce feelings of guilt resulting from failure.

6. Displacement of Aggression

6. *Displacement of aggression* is a defense against objective anxiety. Displacement of aggression is the *act of discharging aggressive impulses on objects less dangerous than those which triggered the impulses.* If a boss chews out a subordinate, the subordinate may not dare fight back, so he fumes and is upset all day on the job. When he goes home he takes it out on his wife. If she is afraid to fight back, she probably will be exceptionally severe toward her son and punish him physically for small rule infractions. The child cannot hit back at the parent so he goes outside, crying, and kicks the dog. We might presume the chain would continue and, if the family cat came by, the otherwise-congenial dog might chase it up a tree, since animals, also, tend to displace aggression. Displacement of aggression seems amusing when illustrated in such a way, but it is the source of considerable brutality in human society.

7. Regression

7. *Regression* is primarily a defense against objective anxiety, and secondarily defends against both of the other forms of anxiety. *Regression refers to behavior appropriate to an earlier age.* For example, a child who is the center of attention until the new baby comes along may revert back to bed-wetting or infantile behaviors such as a pretense of helplessness. These were the behaviors that stimulated the parents' attention and interaction at a younger age. Sometimes adult mental patients grow quite childish and demonstrate patterns of giggling, word-rhyming, and so forth. In these cases the patients often are defending themselves against an awareness of their situation and concern about their future (objective anxiety) or against anxiety connected with the socially expected adult sexual role or the necessity for other forms of adult expressive behaviors (moral and neurotic anxieties). These patients simply maintain cognitive patterns that are happy, childlike, and devoid of the sort of content that threatens many adults.

8. Emotional Insulation

8. *Emotional insulation* is a defense against objective anxiety. It is defined as *emotional withdrawal that protects the individual from being hurt in close relationships.* Typically this pattern is found in persons whose parents were remote and punishing, and whose overtures to them resulted in aversive consequences. Such persons may go throughout their lives rejecting all attempts by others to gain emotional closeness. Sometimes a more superficial pattern of emotional insulation is adopted by an individual who, later in life, is treated badly within a close emotional relationship. Such persons decide they cannot trust others, so they withdraw emotionally into a shell and sometimes appear to be emotionally blunt and "tough."

9. Isolation

9. *Isolation* is also a defense against objective anxiety. It is the physical counterpart of emotional insulation, and is defined as *physical withdrawal to avoid the threat of interpersonal relationships.* Possibly some extreme cases of persons who are "hermits" living on a mountain might illustrate such patterns, but a more typical example would be the individual who stays alone in his room almost constantly, coming out only when it is necessary for meals or for the most important obligations. Such persons often present themselves as choosing isolation because they "want to think

about things," but the threat of interpersonal relationships is the real underlying basis. Isolation is a serious symptom, particularly when is seems to develop rapidly within a period of only a few weeks, and it is an indication that a mental health professional should be consulted.

10. Fantasy

10. *Fantasy* is a defense against objective anxiety. It is defined as *need gratification through either dreams or imagination.* The individual simply pushes aside thoughts concerning personal inadequacies or future threats by engaging in daydreaming. One study found a relationship of fantasy content to age, with elementary-age children concentrating on fantasies of power and physical superiority, and junior-high students continuing such fantasies but increasing the degree of their sophistication, including some fantasies with a romantic basis. High-school-age students move into sexual and romantic fantasy patterns, fantasies of athletic prowess, and begin to experience fantasies concerning expensive material possessions. College-age students continue the earlier occurring patterns to a considerable degree, and add patterns concentrating on high levels of brilliance or achievement. We can estimate a person's individual state of inadequacy feelings by looking at the content of his daydreams to see what is emphasized to a degree unusual for his own sex and age group. In certain extreme cases fantasy may totally dominate the cognitive patterning of the individual, and we then say the person has "lost touch with reality." In any case, extreme degrees of daydreaming suggest that the individual has massive feelings of inadequacy or unfulfillment concerning something important in his life.

11. Undoing

11. *Undoing* is a defense against moral anxiety. It is defined as a *repetitious activity symbolizing counteraction for guilt-producing ideas or impulses.* Like many other defenses, this one is practiced to some extent by most people, and religious rituals, apologies, and so forth fit the pattern. In extreme cases we may see people motivated to do something which is totally unnecessary and perhaps even highly inadvisable simply because they need to make up symbolically for some earlier behavior or impulse. One interesting pattern of undoing consists of a person's thinking over and over again, through the step-by-step details, of a guilt-provoking behavior from his past; presumably this is an effort, or represents a wish, to change what actually happened or to have the story "end" in a different fashion.

12. Projection

12. *Projection* is a defense against both objective and moral anxiety. Projection means *ascribing one's own unaccepted id impulses to others.* When possible environmental consequences prevent people from acting out sexual or aggressive impulses, and overdeveloped superegos prevent them from even thinking about their impulses, the libidinal energy is released (thus reducing neurotic anxiety) through preoccupation with the occurrence of that behavior in others. The "old maid" who constantly spies and complains about the teen-age girl across the street who remains parked for a while in her boy friend's car when he delivers her home after a date is thought to be releasing her own unaccepted sexual impulses through mental involvement

in others' sexual activities. In extreme cases projected impulses, particularly of an aggressive nature, assume frightening proportions and the person is said to have become "paranoid."

13. Sublimation

13. *Sublimation* is a defense against all three forms of anxiety. It is defined as the *channeling of libidinal energies into socially or morally acceptable patterns of behavior.* If you feel frustrated and want to hit someone, you can participate in certain kinds of sports and be praised for the aggressiveness of your play. You may work out your aggressions through maintaining absolute control over the activities of subordinates on the job or children in a classroom. Freud even proposed that the sexual dimensions of libidinal energy could be expressed in the creative arts. Great achievements in romantic classical music or in works of art emphasizing the human form were said to represent the only sexual outlet of certain great composers and artists. Freud went so far as to say that sublimation was the foundation of civilization. He felt that, out of fear of what society might do to punish you, or due to your own superego characteristics, energy that would otherwise have been expended in sexual behavior or aggression could be used to create something, with an unusual level of emotional involvement.

14. Denial

14. *Denial* is a defense against objective anxiety. Denial means *refusal to recognize the obvious.* It is not uncommon, when people are faced with catastrophic personal news, to sometimes hear them say, "No, it can't be true—I won't believe it." Then, when given time to rally other types of defenses, denial is relinquished and the individual accepts the truth. As another example, some persons just will not accept others' evaluations of their children as being destructive psychopaths, even though every acquaintance would agree on such a label. These are common, everyday patterns. Extreme cases of denial, however, are quite dramatic. Some mental patients refuse to recognize and admit where they are, or refuse to accept a report of their mate's or a parent's death. This sort of denial is crude and blunt, and usually indicates that the individual's ego is too nonfunctional to adopt a more sophisticated defense.

15. Escape Into Activity

15. *Escape into activity* is a defense against all three forms of anxiety. It is defined as the *continuous diversion of attention to some activity.* In a mild form it might be expressed by a depressed or disappointed person throwing herself into a job of total housecleaning to get her mind actively on other things. Often a depressed person is deliberately advised by his or her therapist to enter social volunteer activities so that escape into activity can develop. Often the activity is contributive to the individual's eventual welfare, so in this sense it is a good defense, but its value wanes somewhat if the individual continues to avoid an underlying problem.

16. Reaction Formation

16. *Reaction formation* is a defense against all forms of anxiety. Reaction formation is the *act of consciously adopting the exact opposite of the real, unconscious feelings or urges.* A person who harbors resentment against his children, because of personal sacrifices made for their benefit, might

George Dole

"You're not listening to a word I'm saying."

be totally unable to accept the existence of his feelings. To hate one's child is "horrible." So this same individual goes overboard to indulge the child and be a sugar-sweet, smothering type of parent, and consciously believes that this is the way he or she actually feels. Frequently we see reaction formation accompanied by certain sublimated acts against the target individual, as when a parent "loves" a child to the extent of making great sacrifices in order to provide the child with piano lessons requiring hours of necessary and possibly highly aversive practice.

17. Compulsive Control   17. *Compulsive control* is a defense against objective and neurotic anxiety. Compulsive control is defined as *rigid control of the environment in an effort to control one's own impulses.* On an everyday level we have all seen people who are neat to a completely unnecessary extent. The businessman may have ample opportunity to utilize compulsive control in his work and perhaps even be more effective professionally as a result, but a housewife, for example, may have little alternative but to be conspicuous as she almost continuously dusts, picks lint off rugs or fabrics, and empties and polishes ashtrays even while people are in the process of using them.

At the simplest explanatory level, we know that many persons grow up in environments that train them not to be spontaneous, but to plan everything carefully and refrain from making mistakes. A child learns that "spontaneity means risk" when he is punished for not being "careful." Extreme sorts of such backgrounds generally influence persons in the direction of compulsive control. With such persons, it is usually very easy to recognize the objective anxiety and the resulting use of this mechanism in relation to past punishment and reinforcement patterns.

Some of the very strong and dramatic cases of compulsive control seem to be defenses against neurotic anxiety. Persons who feel the need to count things compulsively or do things in a certain order are said, by psychoanalysts, to be attempting to hold in check the strong id impulses that the individual himself may describe as "bursting out." The ego feels the id pressure and, to counteract, increases the amount of constraint on any spontaneity in moment-to-moment behavior. Such people may even present a physically "stiff" appearance, showing wooden, tense movements and speaking in overly precise, exact phrases. The strain of constant compulsive control shows in many aspects of their behavior. There is a wide variety of compulsive control patterns, but this short summary may give you a feel for the basic dynamics.

18. Turning Against the Self

18. *Turning against the self* is a defense against moral anxiety. It is *an effort to ease guilt through self-punishment.* Basically, there seems to be a "need" to be punished in many persons who are experiencing guilt. In one study of children's behavior, it was found that children who were guilty of major rule violations, if obviously "caught" but not punished, had a greater-than-usual number of nightmare-type dreams. This was interpreted as indicating a need for punishment. In some cases people emit criminal behaviors with very little effort to conceal their identity, almost as if they were inviting punishment. In the psychoanalytic view, extreme turning against the self takes the form of suicide, presumably from a combination of overwhelming guilt and an ego that is too weak or disorganized to rally more effective defenses. Obviously these are extreme cases. In some studies it has been more commonly found that people do not "feel as guilty" after they have been punished in some way for whatever they feel they have done wrong.

A behavior theory type of explanation of this phenomenon might hold that if an individual is facing almost certain punishment, the additional burden of waiting for and anticipating that punishment is more aversive than just taking immediate punishment—a "let's get it over with" orientation. A similar alternative explanation is that for most children the experience of punishment for a behavior is paired with a fairly immediate change in the emotional climate. The child has "paid his debt" and some parents immediately comfort the upset child just after the punishment. So, in some families, you see a very aversive period of waiting to receive punishment, followed by quick punishment and almost immediate reinstatement of the love and affection that we know are positive reinforcers. In a conditioning paradigm, then, the undergoing of punishment is paired with receiving affection.

19. Displacement of Anxiety

19. *Displacement of anxiety* is a defense against objective anxiety. In using displacement of anxiety, *the individual switches his attention totally away from something that he is afraid of but can do nothing about to something he "becomes terrified of" but can avoid by certain methods.* In the next chapter we shall identify this mechanism rather clearly in cases of diversionary phobias. In such cases a person may begin to notice numbers, becoming terrified of sitting in the eighth seat, or in the eighth row, or being in some other situation involving the number 8, or may exhibit some other odd form of irrational-appearing fear. The level of fear is very great, but with a little care the individual can totally avoid the threatening stimulus. What is actually happening is that the individual has succeeded in diverting his attention completely away from the fact he is flunking out of college due to a low level of ability, or that he has recently begun to notice that he is aging or in worse general health. These are things that he cannot control. We might venture the conclusion that even an intense fear of an *avoidable* threat is less aversive than is moderate fear of an *unavoidable* threat. Thus, displacement of anxiety can be explained in terms of negative reinforcement, with reduction of the level of aversive stimulation being the vital variable.

20. Repression

20. *Repression* is the "master mechanism," and must be discussed either first or last in the series. It is defined as the *force with which the ego keeps anxiety-provoking thoughts or impulses from becoming conscious.* In the usual sense "repression" means the thoughts are never conscious, while the term "suppression" is sometimes used by Freudians to denote the process of pushing away previously conscious thoughts. This is a complex area of psychoanalytic theory, and for our purposes let us just describe how repression usually proceeds. In a typical case the individual simply does not become *aware* that he may deeply dislike his parent or his child. He may not become aware that he feels inferior to other people, and most important of all he is never fully aware of the true reasons behind his use of other ego defense mechanisms. It is for this latter reason that repression has been called the "master mechanism." Freud went so far as to say that all persons practice some degree of repression almost constantly. In therapy sessions a frequent fear is that a therapist may progress too fast, peeling away various defenses and exposing repressed thoughts that may overwhelm the patient before more sophisticated defenses or increased ego strength can handle them, and cause a relapse into a more serious condition.

Overview of the Ego Defense Mechanisms

The ego defense mechanisms are organized by writers in somewhat different ways. We have shown how the mechanisms can defend against anxiety from somewhat different sources. Other writers have pointed out that fairly strong and well integrated egos typically use the more sophisticated defenses such as rationalization, compensation, and so forth, while weak egos may tend to use "crude" mechanisms such as denial, regression, and isolation.

Freud felt that the ego defense mechanisms were largely unconscious strategies adopted by the ego. Subsequently, some psychologists, while agreeing upon the existence of the cognitive patterns, have preferred to interpret the development of such mechanisms in terms of reinforcement. The majority of the mechanisms, so such an interpretation goes, are negatively reinforced by the immediate reduction of the stress levels associated with guilt, unrelieved tension, and dread. As the practice of the mechanisms gains more and more reinforcement, the tendency to engage in those behaviors whenever in stressful situations increases.

C 13.14. *Ego defense mechanisms.*

We shall now present a variety of sample definitions relating to the ego defense mechanisms. Some mechanisms may be represented in more than one sample question. After identifying the ego defense mechanism described, note it in the space provided.

a. Which mechanism has been called the "master mechanism"? _____

b. Some people make excuses and thereby justify their behaviors. _____

c. If you get upset at your teacher you may later snap at your roommate over some minor incident. _____

d. An individual develops a phobia concerning some odd situation in the environment in order to shift his attention from unavoidable threats. _____

e. If we are threatened by the intensity of our hateful feelings toward someone, we may shift to an ultra-loving conscious attitude. _____

f. We may adopt the mannerisms and behavior patterns of older or superior people when we feel inadequate, especially during childhood. _____

g. Refusal to be vulnerable by resisting getting emotionally close to others.

_____

h. A weak or physically inept child may demonstrate extreme effort in the academic area, as well as later, toward the goal of financial success. _____

i. A person may reduce his feelings of guilt by self-inflicted injury, or ultimately in suicide.

_____

j. Sometimes lonely people become more childlike or infantile, which is a return to patterns that produced satisfactions at earlier ages. _____

k. When upset or depressed, some people get very involved in things and keep busy constantly.

_____

l. We can sometimes safeguard against the environment's punishments by adopting society's value system as our own. _____

m. Some persons symbolically safeguard against the threat of unexpected problems by taking great care to be prepared and be orderly and exact in everything they do.

_____

n. Some individuals who cannot face their own impulses and feelings tend to see their own repressed characteristics in others. _____

o. If persons cannot face the fact that they would like to hurt people and thereby express their aggressions, they sometimes do it in such "civilized" ways as close control and criticism in the development of subordinates on the job, etc. _____

p. You can often tell in what areas individuals feel inadequate simply by studying the patterns taken by their daydreams. _____

> We have now come to the end of our list of ego defense mechanisms. It is appropriate at this point to remark that often students become concerned because, in this material as well as in the subsequent chapter on psychopathology, they "see themselves." Clinical psychologists stress the following: (1) All people demonstrate patterns of ego defense mechanisms; (2) nobody is entirely free from anxiety and resulting symptoms; and (3) everyone goes through certain phases of life when pressures and resulting symptoms may become more prevalent. If you become convinced that you see your own patterns in the descriptions you have just read, you are very typical, and the important question to ask yourself is to what extent such patterns *actually control your total pattern* of daily activities. Answer this before you become concerned that you may be a candidate for a therapist.

PROGRESS CHECK 13.4

1. According to Freud, moral anxiety or guilt arises from _____ .

   a. superego pressures   b. environmental pressures   c. neurosis   d. learning

2. Which would be an example of objective anxiety? _____ .

   a. Fear of snakes in wooded areas   b. Guilt

   c. Fear of rejection because snake fears are silly

3. Close family ties with appropriate role models is the best situation for producing _____ .

   a. neurotic anxiety   b. psychotic anxiety   c. either   d. neither

MATCH: _____ 4. Displacement of aggression and emotional in-
sulation

A. Defense against objective anxiety

B. Defense against moral anxiety

_____ 5. Self-punishment

_____ 6. Denial

_____ 7. Rationalization

8. Symbolically becoming another person by role-playing is called _____ .

    a. conversion   b. introjection   c. identification   d. compensation

9. A child reaches for a forbidden cookie, stops, and says "No, no." This is an example of _____ .

    a. mental health   b. echolalia   c. isolation   d. introjection

10. Hysterical paralysis is attributed by Freud to _____ .

    a. conversion   b. compensation   c. regression   d. undoing

11. Offsetting worthlessness in one area by endeavor in another is to compensation as _____ .

    a. symbolic repetitious activity is to undoing   b. physical withdrawal is to isolation

    c. inappropriately blaming others is to projection   d. all of these

12. Oftentimes a first child will return to more infantile behaviors upon birth of a sibling. This is termed _____ .

    a. reaction formation   b. compulsive control

    c. regression   d. escape into activity

13. The "master mechanism" in Freud's theory is _____ .

    a. escape into activity   b. repression   c. reaction formation   d. regression

14. Which of these defends against all forms of anxiety? _____ .

    a. Escape into activity   b. Reaction formation

    c. Both   d. There is no such defense

15. An obsessively neat and orderly person exhibits compulsive control in Freud's model. _____ .

    a. True   b. False

      If you should have a continuing interest in the topics discussed in this chapter, you might possibly be interested in examining Reed Lawson's *Frustration: The Development of a Scientific Concept* (1965) or A. J. Yates' *Frustration and Conflict* (1962). Relating to the latter portion of this chapter is Anna Freud's *The Ego and the Mechanisms of Defense* (1946).

14

Psychopathology

DEFINITION OF PSYCHOPATHOLOGY

CHILDREN'S PSYCHOPATHOLOGIES
Problems with Operant Origins
Problems with Respondent Origins

ADULT PSYCHOPATHOLOGY

**THE MAJOR GROUPINGS OF
PSYCHOPATHOLOGIES**
Neurosis
Types of Neuroses
Anxiety State
Obsessive-Compulsive Neurosis
Phobias
Aesthenia
Hypochondria
Dissociative Reaction
Neurotic Depression
Other Neurotic Reactions
Psychosis
Schizophrenia
Simple Schizophrenia
Hebephrenic Schizophrenia
Catatonic Schizophrenia
Paranoid Schizophrenia
Manic-Depressive Psychosis

SOCIAL VARIABLES IN PSYCHOPATHOLOGY
Interpersonal Approaches to Psychosis
Societal Variables

**BIOLOGICAL FACTORS IN
PSYCHOPATHOLOGY**
Organic Psychosis
Genetic Basis of Functional Psychosis
Schizophrenia
Manic-depressive Psychosis
Diagnostic Considerations
Biochemical Theories of Psychosis
Role of Adrenalin
Role of Serotonin
Dietary Factors in Mental Disorder

PSYCHOPATHOLOGY AND THERAPY
Somatic Therapies
Psychological Treatment Approaches
to Psychopathology
Summary and Overview

Many of the concepts presented in earlier sections may be brought to bear upon the topic of psychopathology. The subject of disorganized behavior is complex and can be appreciated, perhaps, only by those who have had occasion to be in direct contact with mentally ill members of their families or those who have worked as mental health professionals. Deep frustration can be generated by daily contact with—and efforts to help—persons with severe pathologies. Those in the mental health professions have eagerly watched new developments in a variety of areas within psychology, and a number of minor breakthroughs have suggested that new answers to mental illness may not be completely out of reach. In this chapter we shall recognize contributions of several sorts which, combined, suggest multiple causation of psychopathology.

DEFINITION OF PSYCHOPATHOLOGY First, let us define our main term. "Psychopathology" refers to *patterns of behavior that show significant deviation from normal in socially undesirable directions.* Several words in the definition are worth following up. The words "significant" and "pattern" suggest that we are not concentrating upon behaviors that might be minor or inconsistent. The word "undesirable" is used because we do not wish to include behaviors that are different but are looked upon favorably, such as qualities of leadership, extreme talent, and so forth. The use of the words just mentioned allows us to exclude from pathological classification such things as the anxiety demonstrated by an unprepared student as he faces a difficult examination or the grief of a person who has just experienced the death of a close relative. Reactions to both situations are fairly extreme, but they do not form a continuing pattern that would represent a threat to society or incapacity for the individual himself.

C 14.1. *The definition of psychopathology.*

Psychopathology might be defined as _____ .

a. patterns of behaviors that show significant deviation of any sort

b. any behaviors that show significant deviation from normal in socially undesirable directions

c. patterns of behaviors that show recognizable deviation from normal in socially undesirable directions

d. patterns of behaviors that show significant deviation from normal in socially undesirable directions

Behavior patterns that would qualify as psychopathology under the above definition are numerous. Some people "define by description"—that is, they prefer to define psychopathology in terms of the existence of one of several patterns of behavior known to occur commonly, and generally labeled with such terms as "schizophrenic" or "compulsive." Since the definition of psychopathology given above is not very specific, we shall expand our understanding by noting and commenting on the main descriptive categories of psychopathology. In this chapter we shall use certain labels that reflect a number of ways to classify psychopathologies. Little real disagreement arises among clinical psychologists concerning the use of major groupings such as "neurosis" and "psychosis," but subdivision of each grouping has aroused many minor disagreements. Few psychopathology texts show the exact same listings of types of neuroses, schizophrenias, and so forth.

Perhaps the biggest objection to the "labeling" of people comes from behaviorists, who disapprove of diagnostic labels that sometimes seem almost an end in themselves. A label such as "schizophrenic" immediately brings a dozen behavior patterns to mind and, they feel, loses sight of the individual who may be unique among schizophrenics in the behavior he emits. Behaviorists would prefer to identify and measure the rates of actual behaviors and then attempt to modify objectionable behaviors by applying the principles of conditioning and extinction. We shall take a more moderate course and assume that, at the very least, communication among professionals is facilitated by the use of diagnostic labels; entire patterns of behavior can be fairly accurately anticipated once we know the diagnostic classification of an individual. This seems to have some advantage over the necessity to chart all the behaviors of each individual. Our presentation will adhere to a fairly simple system of classification, and the emphasis will not be merely upon the description of behavior patterns.

C 14.2. *The behavioristic approach to psychopathology.*

A psychologist who is a behaviorist would most likely be in the greatest disagreement with non-behavioristic psychologists over the matter of _____ .

a. whether psychopathology is of serious social significance

b. whether one should label pathological behaviors

c. just exactly "who" is normal

CHILDREN'S PSYCHO-PATHOLOGIES

Attempts to put standard labels such as "anxiety neurotic" on children have generally met with little success. Children's problems can be more appropriately placed into different sorts of "social categories," and in this presentation we shall show how the principles of conditioning that we have previously developed can relate to various kinds of children's (and some adults') problems.

Problems with Operant Origins

Operant problems generally can be divided into two groups—behavior deficits and behavior excesses. Meanings of the terms are fairly self-evident. A *behavior deficit* is an absence of a certain behavior pattern that would be appropriate, desirable, and expected of an individual of a given age. A *behavior excess,* on the other hand, is the presence of a behavior pattern to a degree undesirable in the individual.

Why do behavior deficits exist? It is of course possible that a problem might be organically based, as in cases of severely retarded children. If it can be traced to social origins, however, it can be attributed either to the lack of an appropriate behavior model or to a lack of reinforcement of the behavior when it occurred. Suppose, for example, that we are interested in a child's development of basic social skills. The matter of the behavior model is perhaps the most basic, so we shall take it up first. If a child witnesses the appropriate behavior being emitted by significant individuals in his environment, he tends to try out that behavior to a visible degree. On the other hand, if he associates almost exclusively with same-age and younger peers—which occurs in certain settings—without much chance to observe "mature" behavior, he will be severely handicapped in his ability to initiate appropriate patterns. But suppose he does have social models and the target behavior begins to appear in his behavioral repertoire. It may be taken for granted and ignored by the parents. Under such circumstances the behavior never achieves any regularity of occurrence, and the child continues to appear socially immature.

Table 14.1 presents common behavior deficits. It would be a good experience for you to try to visualize the type of family circumstance in which a child might either have no model for the appropriate behavior, or might gain little or no reinforcement despite existence of such a model.

Table 14.1

COMMON BEHAVIOR DEFICITS IN CHILDREN	
Shyness	Low dependency
Social isolation	Low attentiveness
Lack of social skills	Communications problems
Lack of confidence	Lack of self-control (or lack of
Low self-esteem	frustration tolerance)
Low self-assertion	Irresponsibility
Low cooperation	Motor inadequacies (walking, toilet
Lack of appropriate	habits, etc.)
masculinity or femininity	

The other type of problem—the behavior excess—results from the reinforcement of undesirable behavior patterns. Obviously undesirable social models for behaviors are frequently involved. Reinforcement of such behavior is often unintentional on the parts of parents or teachers. Frequently it comes in the form of attention. Earlier, in Chapter 9, we discussed how attention develops into an extremely powerful social reinforcer for the typical child. A child can gain attention by engaging in socially deviant behavior patterns, and it is typical of children who develop into problem cases that they seldom seem to be able to gain the attention of people in any other way. For example, if a child is never praised or noticed in the school for any sort of academic or other legitimate performance, he may respond very strongly to the peer and adult attention he gains by acting up in class, defying authority, and so forth. Usually the parents' and teachers' increasing awareness of the problem causes even more attention to be given to the child, and it is no wonder that the typical case grows increasingly worse as the years go by. About the only effective remedy for such problems is the deliberate removal of the attention the child receives by the behavior, coupled with deliberate delivery of attention for appropriate behaviors, however infrequently they may occur at first.

Some behavior excesses are developed through negative reinforcement. Usually in these cases the child is allowed to evade responsibilities through certain actions, or to remove himself from an aversive environment. Or he may, by certain actions such as shifting his attention to something else, reduce his anxiety concerning possible future punishment.

Table 14.2 presents some positively and negatively reinforced behavior excesses. It would be an excellent exercise for you to attempt to determine the manner in which the reinforcement is often delivered for each.

Table 14.2

COMMON BEHAVIOR EXCESSES	
Positively reinforced	*Negatively reinforced*
Nonconformity	Fearfulness
Attention-seeking	Fatigue
Aggression	Compulsiveness
Over-dependency	Daydreaming
Delinquency	Forgetfulness
Crying	Sickliness
Disruptions	Lying
Dominance	Truancy
Exploitation	
Depressed complaining	
Sickliness	
Lying	
Truancy	

C 14.3.   *Behavior deficits and behavior excesses.*

If little Billy is habitually truant from school, and in almost all cases it can be verified that he spent his days off engaged in vigorous, fun-filled play with other truant boys, then his behavior, at least to a considerable degree, is properly viewed as a _____ .

   a. behavior deficit   b. behavior excess

If Johnny seems almost unable to speak the truth, and gives evidence that he greatly fears that he will be blamed and punished for not being better than he is, so that his lies are of the nature of excuse-making and compensatory efforts, it is probable that the behavior is properly viewed as a _____ .

   a. behavior deficit   b. behavior excess

Behavior deficits seem largely developed due to _____ .

   a. the lack of a proper or appropriate social model

   b. failure of appropriate behavior to be reinforced when it occurred

   c. (both a and b are correct)   d. (neither a nor b is correct)

Where behavior excesses are positively reinforced, they seem very typically to be reinforced by _____ .

   a. escape from tension and anxiety   b. primary reinforcers

   c. attention   d. affection

Problems with Respondent Origins   You will recall from previous chapters that operants, which we have just discussed, are what organisms *do,* while respondents are *feelings.* A number of emotional problems of children are attributable to the processes of classical conditioning. You will recall the *UCS*s are of three general types—appetitive, aversive, and inescapable aversive—and they elicit at least three different sorts of emotional orientations. Those are, respectively, the approach, avoidance, and aggressive tendencies.

Let us look first at *approach* emotional orientations. These may not be generally thought of as problems, but when approach orientations are elicited by certain unusual stimuli, this may, in itself, define various sexual perversions or socially undesirable inclinations. In the area of sexual perversions, such things as fetishes, which are unusual sexually based object attachments, can be developed because of the pairing of sexual arousal (the intraphysical *UCS*) in the newly pubertal adolescent male with the *CS* of women's underclothing or other objects that bring to mind images of sexuality as it may be vaguely understood by an individual of that age. It is thought that some forms of homosexuality may be based on such backgrounds, as the child may have his first experiences of sexual arousal paired with same-sex peer experiences.

The qualities of masochism and sadism are other similarly founded approach orientations. In one laboratory a case of experimental masochism illustrated what is probably the basic human model. A hungry dog had a large sterilized needle passed through a fold of skin at the same moment that he was given a pan of food. He quickly grew to "appreciate" the pain in the sense that he begged to have the needle passed through his skin, even in the absence of food and when he was not hungry. Probably most cases of human sadism and masochism follow a similar model, but based on sexual *UCS*s rather than food stimuli.

A large number of *avoidance* orientations are generated by the pairing of various situational or object stimuli with aversive *UCS*s. We elaborated on this general development in Chapter 8, and these problems are so obvious that you should not need many additional examples in this chapter. Children's problems of this sort that most frequently come to view are cases of school phobia, social isolation (fear of peers), and fear of competing against others.

Aggressive emotional orientations are numerous, since many aversive situations are inescapable for small children. Children begin to respond to a variety of stimuli that have been repeatedly associated with inescapable punishment or frustration—such stimuli as authority figures, inanimate school property, and domineering personality characteristics in others. The forms taken by aggressive emotional orientations include direct aggression against the agent of punishment, displacement of aggression, attitudes of resentment, and in small children such things as breath-holding and tantrums.

Another possible emotional orientation recently has been developed in principle. This concerns depression. It is true that many depressive operant behaviors, such as complaining or threatening self-harm, can bring positive reinforcement from others. A basic respondent pattern of depression, however, appears to exist in many cases. The *UCS* of separation from the main agent of reinforcement (what clinicians would call the "love object") seems to trigger an unlearned emotional reaction that we generally label as depression. We can observe this clearly in animals—puppies separated from their mothers, or adult dogs separated from the human beings they are attached to. In humans it would appear that the separation may be literal, as when a young woman's husband goes overseas with a military unit, or it may be interactional, as where parents deliberately act cool and unloving as part of punishment given a child. In one such family I observed, the parents accented the freeze they put on the guilty child by having a special party for the other children, while the guilty one watched silently from another room. This sort of treatment, though not usual in such stark intensity, is fairly common, particularly in middle-class homes.

If some kind of guilt or failure brings about what the child perceives as withdrawal of the parents' love, cues which become associated with failure or guilt eventually can trigger depression. In this way a person may become irrationally depressed if fired from a job that he didn't like anyway, or if his "steady" unexpectedly announces she is breaking up with him, even though he was getting ready to leave her.

We should point out that what we have been calling the operant and respondent problems of children can and often do persist until they become adult problems. The patterns we have described are basic, however, and in adults they often are mixed and overlaid with certain additional patterns, leading to the use of diagnostic labels that typically classify adult cases.

C 14.4. *Classically conditioned psychopathologies.*

Certain sexual perversions involve people habitually seeking out a certain sort of activity or sex-object which is considered statistically unusual by a large percent of the general population. In terms of the preferred sex-object or activity, this sort of condition is best viewed as a classically conditioned emotional _____ orientation.

a. approach   b. avoidance   c. aggressive

Genuine phobias, developed on the basis of hurtful experiences, are best viewed as classically conditioned _____ orientations.

a. approach   b. avoidance   c. aggressive

There is indication that _____ can consistently be brought about as a *UCR* to the situational stimulus of separation from the main agent of reinforcement.

a. aggression   b. discouragement   c. depression   d. phobias

Conditioned depression can apparently be developed as a typical reaction in many social circumstances where parents repeatedly associate the child's awareness of his or her guilt or failure with _____ .

a. infliction of punishment   b. withdrawal of their own love and affection

c. discussions of other incidents of failure

PROGRESS CHECK   14.1

1. The study of patterns of behavior that deviate from the norm is termed _____ .

    a. anthropomorphism   b. normative pathology

    c. psychopathology   d. psychophysiology

2. Which of the following psychologists would most likely disagree with the labeling of individuals into psychological categories? _____ .

    a. Traditional clinical psychologists   b. Behaviorists

    c. Developmentalists   d. Humanists

MATCH the following operant terms with the descriptions:

    _____ 3. Behavior deficit   A. Aggression

    _____ 4. Behavior excess   B. Lack of appropriate behavior model

                                     C. Shyness

                                       D. Reinforcement of pattern

5. Problems arising from feelings or emotions that an individual may have are of _____ .

    a. an operant origin   b. a respondent origin   c. both   d. neither

6. Which two of the following problems would most likely be of an avoidance orientation? _____ .

    a. Depression caused by the death of a parent   b. School phobias

    c. Fear of competition   d. Tantrums

7. The respondent pattern of depression, in its development, usually involves _____ .

    a. aggressive emotional orientations   b. separation from the agent of reinforcement

    c. removal of an aversive stimuli   d. application of a positive reinforcer

---

ADULT PSYCHO-PATHOLOGY

We shall now turn to a variety of problems that are more or less the traditional topics of psychopathology, and we shall begin with a consideration of the question, "Who is abnormal?"

One approach to answering the question is to resort to statistical terms. An abnormal person is one who departs from being typical, in an undesirable direction. Even this simple kind of definition is not immune to criticism, and a very real question in the mental health professions concerns behavior which is strange or bizarre to the larger culture while being common and perhaps even regarded positively in the individual's particular subculture. I recall an interesting case of a "prophet." This man lived in the mountains of Kentucky, and presented a quite unusual appearance, with a long beard and flowing robe. He went from one small community to another in the mountain area, and was usually welcomed by many persons who invited him into the smaller churches to speak on his revelations. The man exhibited vivid hallucinations, during which he appeared to be hearing voices, and afterward he would tell the audiences about his direct communication with heaven. While he was perhaps not accepted by a majority of persons, he was admired within his own subculture by a significant number of people who certainly did not consider him to be psychologically abnormal. Nevertheless, his downfall came when he traveled by bus in order to enlarge his audiences. Alighting from the bus in downtown St. Louis, he proceeded to listen to the "voices" and talk to people on the sidewalks until he was finally removed by the police and taken to the State Hospital for observation. There he was diagnosed as schizophrenic. The question of whether such a man was abnormal *inside* his own mountain subculture is difficult to answer.

A second way of viewing psychopathology, and the method that seems to be most typically employed in institutions today, is an implied definition stating that psychopathologies are symptom patterns that correspond to specific diagnostic labels which are recognized by mental health professionals. Such a definition seems shallow, as it takes the philosophic consideration of the meaning of mental illness away from all but the professionals who do the diagnosing. Still, this approach has functional utility, and a portion of this chapter will pursue this point of view.

A third way of defining psychopathology was proposed by Marie Jahoda, a psychologist who became concerned that most definitive adjectives were expressed along some kind of negative dimension (i.e., "anxious," "aggressive," and so forth). She proposed measures of positive factors, asking if an individual is happy, friendly, trusting of others, unworried, and if that individual has a feeling of achievement. "Yes" answers imply mental health, and "no" answers imply pathology. Jahoda's point of view may be inappropriate for the institutional setting, but it has practical value for the individual in the general population who is considering the possibility of seeking the help of a mental health professional.

A final approach, mentioned earlier in this chapter in discussing problems of children, is not yet well established but is gaining ground. This is a definition of psychopathology in behavioral terms. We ask whether an individual manifests behavior deficits or behavior excesses to a degree that suggests remediation. Implicit in this approach is a consideration of the individual's reinforcement history and current environmental situation, which then sets the stage for a program of behavior therapy.

C 14.5. *Criteria of psychopathology.*

Which of the following have been noted by experts as legitimate criteria of psychopathology? _____ .

   a. An absence of positive attitudinal factors

   b. Correspondence of behavior to known diagnostic category symptom patterns

   c. Departure from statistical norms of behavior in undesirable fashion

   d. Use of actual behavioral criteria, noting excesses and deficits

   e. (*All* of the above are legitimate criteria)

THE MAJOR GROUPINGS OF PSYCHO-PATHOLOGIES

It is traditional to group psychopathologies into three "families": neuroses, psychoses, and finally what are termed character disorders.

In general, a *neurosis* is a maladaptive pattern, usually triggered by an intense experience of anxiety. Some of these may go almost unrecognized by friends and neighbors, while others may take on a very severe appearance. Seldom, however, do persons with even severe neuroses have to be institutionalized. The vast majority of them maintain their jobs and family relations, and continue their day-to-day style of living.

The second major category, *psychosis,* is roughly what we mean when we use the expression "mental illness." Within the framework of psychosis, it is customary to refer to two main subdivisions. The *functional psychoses* historically have been considered as being brought on by various stresses and experiences in the environment, while the *organic psychoses* are traceable to actual neurological dysfunctions.

Finally, *character disorders,* in the traditional sense, are continuing behaviors that seem to involve a moral lapse, such as alcoholism, drug addiction, pathological dishonesty, and similar disorders to which we attach moral blame. As you can see, we do not normally use such words as "wrong" or "immoral" to describe neurosis and psychosis, but we imply that a person is somehow ethically lacking if he manifests a character disorder. For reasons that we shall not go into at this point, the integration and manner of comparison of these three major groups of psychopathologies varies from one text to another. Within the framework of a behavior-theory interpretation, there are a number of justifications for treating most character disorders as types of neuroses, so that we shall not deal with the subject of character disorders as a separate group.

C 14.6. *Neurosis and the two main divisions of psychosis.*

Neuroses are maladaptive behavior patterns that seem to be triggered by an intense experience

of _____ .

    a. anxiety   b. amnesia   c. "aloneness"

"Mental illness" is more or less the same thing as the more technical term, _____ .

Of the psychoses, those which seem to be brought on primarily by the problems related to environmental

factors are called _____ psychoses.

    a. stress   b. organic   c. functional   d. guilt

Neurosis

It is difficult to define neurosis in such a way as to clearly differentiate it from psychosis. Generally the neurotic is an anxious, troubled individual found engaged in everyday-life activities outside the mental institution. (Psychotics are usually in institutions.) One problem in defining neurosis is the diversity of behavior found within each different type. Behavior theory, however, has done an acceptable job of systematizing the events going on in neurosis in a way that emphasizes the similarities. The term deserves one further comment. When used as a noun, the word neurosis (or neurotic) denotes an individual with significant problems. Often, however, the expression "neurotic" is used as an adjective. We may refer to a *neurotic way* of facing up to a problem, and so forth. Frequently this use of the term is encountered in reference to fairly normal individuals, and it may refer to ducking and dodging responsibilities in temporary situations, or to coping with new stresses in ways that do not really solve the problems. In this sense one can honestly say that almost everyone behaves neurotically to some degree at certain moments during his lifetime. For this reason, when a person "sees himself" in certain case-history descriptions it is not necessarily a cause for alarm. In fact there was a book on the market in which the author stated, in his title, "Be glad you're neurotic," and continued to point out certain kinds of neurotic patterns that might facilitate performance in some occupations, such as the case of the compulsive bookkeeper.

First and foremost, we will state that *anxiety* is the underlying cause of neurotic symptoms. Anxiety could be conceived of as an intervening variable, coming between S (stress) and R (expressions of unhappiness or tension). Therefore the *stress* might be considered the cause, but here we run into the difficulty that different persons manifest different degrees of anxiety to a given level of stress. Therefore anxiety, which can be operationally defined in terms of measurable autonomic reactions, is a somewhat more objective variable that can be studied as a "cause" of neurotic psychopathologies. Anxiety is most properly conceived of as a conditioned response (CR) to certain conditioned stimuli (CSs) that have, in the past, been associated with aversive UCSs. This interpretation, based on a behavior-theory structure, is perhaps the best model available to explain factors such as the reasons why certain situations are anxiety-provoking to some individuals but not to others.

If anxiety is the cause of neurosis, then the observable symptoms of the neurotic can be viewed as *operant behaviors* that are negatively reinforced by the momentary reduction of anxiety (bear in mind that anxiety has drive properties). In more subjective terms, we might interpret the neurotic's feelings in the following manner: 1) *Anxiety exists,* as a result of which the individual suffers serious discomfort and a deterioration in general efficiency, particularly in complex, patterned activities (we have already referred to this process in Chapter 7 in a discussion of the Yerkes-Dodson Principle); 2) symptoms such as compulsions, phobias, and so forth, begin to *reduce the anxiety.* These are then problems to the individual of a quite different sort—he is perceived by others as being strange, and some social consequences often ensue. Some years ago certain clinicians posed the *neurotic paradox* which was intended as a challenge to those who would explain neurosis in terms of learned responses. It was considered to be a paradox, unexplainable in reinforcement terms, that behavior could be *"self-defeating, yet self-perpetuating."* How could a punished behavior stay strong in the individual's behavioral repertoire? A knowledge of reinforcement principles, however, easily explained the paradox. Enactment of neurotic symptoms *immediately* reduces anxiety, and those symptoms are therefore negatively reinforced. Punishment, such as social rejection by others, is *delayed,* and therefore the punishment is ineffective in suppressing the neurotic behavior.

C 14.7. *The cause of neurosis.*

The basic cause of neurosis apparently is a high anxiety level which in turn is triggered by certain cues in the environment which have previously been linked with aversive events. These aversive events themselves have functioned as _____ in the conditioning model.

    a. *CS*s   b. *UCS*s   c. *CR*s   d. *UCR*s

C 14.8. *The neurotic paradox.*

The neurotic paradox was that neurotic behavior is _____ .

    a. fulfilling, yet ultimately dissatisfying   b. enjoyable, yet superficial

    c. self-defeating, yet self-perpetuating   d. an unhappy and ineffectual style of living

The neurotic paradox was explained by an understanding of the _____ .

    a. immediacy of the reinforcement and the delay of the punishment

    b. gratification at relief and the awareness of the defeat

    c. superficial nature of the neurotic's value system

C 14.9. *The reinforcement interpretation of neurotic symptoms.*

Neurotic symptoms seem mainly to be _____ reinforced.

    a. positively   b. negatively

The reinforcer for neurotic symptoms appears to be _____ .

    a. elevation in temporary gratification   b. social reinforcement

    c. reduction in momentary anxiety

    d. an intellectual appreciation of the domination being achieved over others

Types of Neuroses   Two points of orientation are in order before we list the types of recognized neuroses. Neurotic tendencies in an individual may appear to fit a typology but fail to qualify as a full-fledged neurosis for the reasons described earlier. As already noted, neurosis is not a black or white condition. Numerous tendencies, such as the simple escape behaviors of oversocialization and excessive television viewing, or too much sleeping, all of which are frequent in college student populations exposed to competition and other stresses, are simply inclinations toward neurosis. These escapes are sometimes generated by a fear of competition or failure, and at other times by loneliness and social rejection, or the moderately aversive demands of keeping up with one's assigned familial or social role. The anxieties generated usually are not great and not unduly prolonged, so neurotic tendencies are modest and transient. It is when anxieties derive from more formidable sources, or when responses are prolonged and exaggerated, that we place an individual into a formal "typology."

Second, our descriptions of neurotic reactions which follow will show a fault that is common in psychology books. At least we can point it out to you. Specifically it is this—the purity of the types is largely a fiction. The typical neurotic will show a number of mixed neurotic patterns, although he may show a predominance of a certain one.

Anxiety State   *Anxiety state* is the term used to describe one type of neurosis which is significant for a number of reasons. 1) In this neurosis, the only clearly observable consistent pattern is the anxiety itself, inferred from its autonomic components (sweating, trembling, heart palpitations, chills, etc.), without further visible symptoms. 2) It is an initial neurosis in many cases, followed by the later development of one of the other types of neuroses as the individual begins behaving in ways that gain negative reinforcement through reducing his anxiety. 3) In most cases it is not realistically resolved as it should be (by behavior therapy through extinction or counterconditioning), but is treated medically with tranquilizers, resulting in perpetual suppression of symptoms while basic causes remain.

Anxiety state is sometimes described as the breaking down of fairly minimal ego defense mechanisms due to a sudden upsurge in the degree of stress. Thus, it is seen that anxiety state frequently comes about as graduation nears, as one's employment status is undergoing revision, as marriage approaches, as one gets promoted to a new sort of responsibility, or as some other major change in life pattern comes about. At such a time a person can be overwhelmed by feelings of being caught up in an irreversible, doomed process. Often the stress is lifted and the problems are resolved. But if such stress continues, then it is typical that escape from the stress occasionally occurs when the individual casually engages in some cognitive process or performs some physical act that reduces the anxiety momentarily. This constitutes negative reinforcement, and symptoms beyond just the basic anxiety then begin to emerge.

Usually during this stage the individual is alarmed about his state of mental health and casts about for some identification of the reasons for his condition. The need to "know the reason" is strong, and typically leads the person to a conclusion which is inaccurate. Reasons such as "responsibilities of the job" do not take into account the fact that the conditioned emotional patterns that cause such job-reactions were established, in many cases, through events that took place years earlier.

Obsessive-Compulsive Neurosis   *Obsessive-compulsive neurosis* is a common pattern that, like the other types of neuroses, elaborates minor manifestations found in most people. The obsession is an involuntary *cognitive* response, while the compulsion is an involuntary *motor* response. It should be obvious that every compulsion

"I understand she's a terrific housekeeper."

involves an obsessive substratum, so that the former is simply a more elaborate manifestation of the latter. At the everyday level, the tune that one cannot keep from thinking about, or the cracks in the sidewalk that one may try to avoid stepping on, represent inclinations in the direction of obsessive-compulsive neurosis. The reinforcing function in this kind of disorder comes from the diversion afforded by the symptoms. One cannot pay a great deal of attention to several things at once, and—particularly when obsessions are complex—the individual may completely succeed in pushing out of awareness the anxiety-provoking CSs.

A number of subtypes of compulsions and obsessions have been described, and are extensively differentiated in some texts. For example, in "control" compulsions the individual demonstrates a need for equalizing and balancing factors in his environment, which indicates that the anxiety is provoked by a lack of ability to anticipate events and be free from error. The individual feels relief from having complete control over tangible environmental situations. The professor who spends hours every week adjusting and correcting little details in his bookshelf arrangement, and preparing a matching card-file system to indicate where everything can be located, is an example. The housewife who empties and polishes ashtrays while guests are in the middle of their cigarettes is another. It is consistent with behavior theory to propose an earlier environment in which the consequences of casualness and lack of preparation were not minor. In such a situation, very powerful response tendencies toward compulsion would develop.

The serial compulsion is a type of behavior in which the individual proceeds in a highly rigid manner in bathing, dressing, and so forth, and each movement must come in a particular order. Cases have been described of individuals who take two hours or more in dressing, due to their peculiar rigidities.

A number of other sorts of obsessions and compulsions could be described, but these examples will suffice to indicate the general sort of process involved.

Phobias

The *phobia* is an unreasonable fear of some source-object. There appear to be two types of phobia, with completely different origins. Similar to the obsessive-compulsive neurosis is the *diversionary phobia*. The CS-provoked anxiety is highly aversive, but by transferring attention and fear to some new specific fear-object—one that can be avoided—an unpleasant but nonetheless negatively reinforced condition comes into existence. The diversionary phobia is identifiable largely in terms of the fear-object. Odd fears, such as fear of the number 13 or of germs, are likely to be of this nature; they could not reasonably be expected to have been classically conditioned. By concerning oneself endlessly with thoughts of the fear-object, one escapes from conscious awareness of the otherwise unavoidable more realistic fear and the CSs which produce it.

On the other hand, persons who experience fear in the presence of bodies of water, dogs or other animals, opposite sex persons, or small enclosed spaces are likely to have undergone a different developmental process. Persons who fear water, though they may have been of such a young age as not to consciously remember, have usually had associated traumatic experiences. The toddler who experienced the physical trauma and shock (UCS) of falling into a pond may show the generalized response later in life to lakes, rivers, and other bodies of water. We call this sort of development a *conditioned phobia*. Treatments of the two types of phobias, obviously, would involve different procedures.

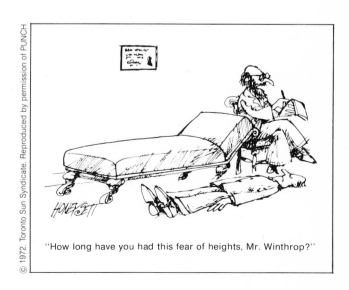

© 1972 Toronto Sun Syndicate. Reproduced by permission of PUNCH

"How long have you had this fear of heights, Mr. Winthrop?"

Aesthenia   *Aesthenia*, in the past, was called neuraesthenia, which literally meant "tired nerves." That interpretation is now recognized as absurd, but it was rather descriptive. This type of neurotic shows a fatigue reaction despite rest or lack of effort. It is common for fatigue reactions to be unusually severe just before participation in an unwelcomed activity. This, incidentally, can yield information regarding the source of the anxiety. The aesthenic gains a useful end-result from the symptoms, as his, or her, lack of endurance for uninteresting work may excuse him from that work. Some such people demonstrate the most pronounced fatigue on those days when they have done virtually nothing and are either bored or have nothing to distract thoughts concerning their troubles. Often this condition precedes a "nap" or extra-long sleep, which is an escape from conscious involvement with cognitive *CS*s. Statistical data indicates family copying patterns, so that social imitation and subsequent reinforcement appear frequently to be involved. However, traditionally oriented clinical psychologists still lean toward a libidinal explanation based on Freud's concepts. According to this view, anxiety drains off available energy.

Hypochondria   *Hypochondria* is a pattern with elements of both obsession and aesthenia. Imagined physiological ailments show family copying as well as a sudden appearance shortly after recovery from illness or injury, suggesting the reinforcement model. It is also possible that hypochondria might actually serve as an obsession with one's health, diverting conscious attention from more unavoidable *CS*s. Probably high on the list of reasons for the establishment and maintenance of both aesthenia and hypochrondria is the attention this behavior gains from others, and release from social or professional obligations. Persons widowed, or at emotionally vulnerable ages when they consider themselves unwanted, demonstrate this neurosis much more often than other people. When ignored, the hypochondriac may make his symptoms more colorful to the point of predicting imminent death. This strategy is usually good for at least a few days of temporary recovery of lost attention. Since hypochondria is typically *positively* reinforced, most cases may not be what we have indicated are "true" neuroses.

Dissociative Reaction *Dissociative reaction* is as familiar at "normal" levels as it is unusual at extreme levels. The term refers to a separation or dissociation of memory from conscious awareness. Simple lack of recall for those things which we do not particularly like to remember is common, and not of a degree to be called neurotic. Amnesia produced by the shock and horror of what one has done, on the other hand, involving feelings of massive guilt, is a severe neurotic reaction and fortunately is rare. Rarer still is the multiple personality portrayed in "The Three Faces of Eve." Only a handful of such cases have come to the attention of professionals. The phenomenon represents a crude but effective avoidance of cognitive *CS*s that provoke anxiety.

An everyday phenomenon that demonstrates dissociation in virtually everyone is the poor memory most people have for facts that oppose their own cherished beliefs or attitudes. To recognize reasons why your own opinions may be wrong produces the type of tension we earlier called *cognitive dissonance*. Dissociation from such memories reduces this anxiety. The often observed refusal of most persons to seek out newspaper or magazine editorials which may refute some of their own cherished beliefs is an example of such a preventive device to avoid cognitive dissonance.

Neurotic Depression *Neurotic depression,* like the other neuroses, is an elaborated development of a process found to some degree in practically everyone. What differentiates a normal depression from one of a neurotic nature are the degree and the duration of the depression, and the extent to which the degree is a realistic reaction to circumstances. Depression, to a greater extent than most other pathologies, appears to be related to middle-class child-rearing practices. Some theorists have stressed the cultural emphasis upon achievement in the middle-class home, with withdrawal of love as punishment for failure. The child who experiences this as a frequent situation soon becomes quite sensitive to any signs or indications of failure. These signs are the CSs that produce depression. Some theorists have tried to show that practically all situations which typically generate depression can, in some way, be seen as a type of failure. The individual who loses the beloved parent through death has suffered an irrationally perceived sort of rejection, resulting in emotional feelings of failure to be worthy of the parent's continued love in that the parent abandoned him. The person who reacts frequently in this manner has been conditioned too well to respond to cues suggesting failure.

So far, we have discussed a respondent form of depression. There is operant depression as well. Such patterns are characterized by the individual seeking out others for a "shoulder to cry on." These people do not seem to readily gain affection and other social reinforcers in more usual ways, but can often command the attention and sympathy of other people by their display of depression and despair. This form of depression is sometimes accompanied by various threats or actions that are self-injurious, all of which are established, maintained, and intensified (through shaping, see Chapter 9A) by sympathy and concern from others. Suicidal gestures are an extreme form of this pattern. Communication of suicidal intent is almost sure to bring about the increased concern and involvement of a person's friends, all of which reinforces this pattern of behavior at times when the individual is probably somewhat socially deprived. It may be relevant to mention that a number of publications claim that a different type of personality test profile may be identified in those persons who commit suicide, as compared with the more numerous group who have "attempted" suicide unsuccessfully.

Other Neurotic Reactions Other reactions to anxiety which may be exhibited by an individual are worth considering. In most cases these are given some other formal label than neurosis by experts. *Alcoholism* is a direct escape operant, triggered by anxiety and reinforced by reduction of the anxiety. The individual, through alcoholic indulgence, dulls perception of the stimuli which trigger anxiety. The duration and quantity of past drinking does not, itself, determine the "habit" of drinking. On the same drinking schedule one person may become alcoholic while another does not. The *presence of anxiety* is the determining factor. Similarly, though alcoholism shows a considerable degree of family patterning—that is, it shows some tendency to run in families—studies give little reason to conclude that it is genetic in the sense of being biologically inherited. Rather, the family pattern seems fairly well explained by the parent serving as a social model responding to stress.

Cats have been conditioned to prefer alcoholic liquid over nonalcoholic liquid when forced to endure electric shock in order to eat. These feline drunks become almost instantly cured when the shock grids are unplugged. Unfortunately it is not so easy to unplug the "emotional grid," represented by critical *CS*s, in the human being's perceptual field.

Sexual perversions in some cases (not all) are based, in the early stages, on the avoidance, due to fear, of certain types of experiences rather than upon approach motives. Sometimes the individual, as a youngster, has had traumatic interactions—perhaps sexual—with the opposite-sex parent or with some other opposite-sex adult, and the emotion thus generated can generalize to other opposite-sex individuals. Then, the sex drive being operative, a sexual outlet may be found with children, who would generate less generalized anxiety, with animals, with objects of clothing, etc. In the cases of homosexuality, a same-sex individual would generate less anxiety than would an opposite-sex individual.

As with other patterns, evidence indicates that in some cases a different situation—social imitation—brings about the condition. Here the individual patterns after the *emotional structure* of the opposite-sex parent, typically when a same-sex model is unavailable. Usually in such cases many overt mannerisms that are sexually inappropriate are simultaneously developed.

Again, we characterize reactions as neurotic in type where they appear to have been established as escape and avoidance patterns pertaining to deep-seated tensions and anxieties. Those reactions that do not involve a significant degree of anxiety reduction, hence negative reinforcement, are not properly categorized as neurotic in nature.

This completes a description of the major forms of neuroses. Underlying all of them is a hypothetical symptom cluster called the "neurotic nucleus." Some or all of the following usually exist in the neurotic: feelings of inferiority and inadequacy, low stress tolerance that expresses itself in dread of competition or being at the center of attention, hypersensitivity, egocentricity (in which most of your thoughts involve yourself), defensiveness, rigidity, tension, and irritability. It is easy to see how most of these patterns would be either the cause, or the result, of high levels of anxiety.

C 14.10.   *Identification of neurotic types.*

A true neurosis is one that is negatively reinforced. In cases of _____ we often suspect that older

persons have the behaviors reinforced through positive reinforcement, so that these cases then

would not represent true cases of neurosis.

   a. phobia   b. dissociative reaction   c. hypochondria   d. anxiety state

© 1971 by NEA, Inc.

"I don't know what's the matter with me, doctor—I've been feeling good!"

This reaction can be brought about by the various cues associated with failure. _____ .

   a. Phobia   b. Hypochondria   c. Depression   d. Aesthenia

The rare cases of multiple personality form one subgrouping of this neurosis. _____ .

   a. Anxiety state   b. Aesthenia   c. Dissociative reaction   d. Hypochondria

One form of this neurosis is a conditioned operant behavior of a strictly cognitive nature; the other form involves elements of the first, plus certain skeletal accompaniments that cannot easily be resisted. _____ .

   a. Phobia   b. Obsessive-compulsive neurosis   c. Depression

This reaction is statistically related to being reared in the middle-class home, and is caused presumably by the middle-class punishment pattern. _____ .

   a. Obsessive-compulsive neurosis   b. Depression   c. Aesthenia   d. Anxiety state

This is a typical first form of neurosis, which often later changes into a different type altogether. _____ .

   a. Dissociative reaction   b. Aesthenia   c. Anxiety state

There are two main groupings of this neurosis, the one being called the conditioned type and the other being called the diversionary type. _____ .

   a. Depression   b. Phobia   c. Dissociative reaction   d. Aesthenia

_____ is a neurosis characterized by fatigue and exhaustion that is unreasonable in terms of circumstances.

Functional (meaning not due to any physical injury) amnesia is an extreme form of the neurosis called

_____ _____ .

PROGRESS CHECK 14.2

1. Which of the criteria given below are used by experts to note psychopathology? _____ .

    a. Absence of positive attitude

    b. Behavior corresponds to category of symptom patterns

    c. Departure from statistical behavioral norms

    d. Behavioral criteria, such as deficits and excesses

    e. All of the above

MATCH: _____ 2. Neuroses   A. Maladaptive behavior triggered by anxiety

        _____ 3. Psychoses   B. Behaviors involving a moral lapse

        _____ 4. Character disorders   C. Usually called "mental illness"

5. An aversive UCS can be paired with certain CSs to produce _____ .

    a. pleasure   b. anxiety   c. job satisfaction   d. none of the above

6. The neurotic paradox expressed by some clinicians is that neurosis is _____ .

    a. self-defeating yet self-perpetuating   b. a state of mind

    c. an effective means of coping with some problems

7. Neurotic symptoms can be viewed as created and maintained by _____ .

    a. positive reinforcement   b. negative reinforcement   c. punishment

MATCH: _____ 8. Obsession   A. Involuntary cognitive responses

        _____ 9. Compulsion   B. Involuntary motor actions

10. Which condition is thought to be primarily caused by failure? _____ .

    a. Hypochondria   b. Phobia   c. Dissociation   d. Depression

11. Multiple personality is usually considered a subset of what reaction? _____ .

12. Usually anxiety is considered the underlying factor bringing about neuroses. _____ .

    a. True   b. False

13. Unreasonable fatigue and exhaustion is a neurosis termed _____ .

    a. amnesia   b. exhaustia   c. traumatic tiredness   d. aesthenia

14. A traumatic shock, such as getting caught in a rip tide, may produce _____ .

      a. diversionary phobia   b. conditioned phobia

15. What causes functional amnesia? _____ .

      a. Blows to the head   b. Drug overdose   c. Anxiety

Psychosis   When the expression "mental illness" is used, *psychosis* is the pattern being referred to. Psychotic behavior is at such deviance from social and physical reality as to present a considerable problem. Psychotics, due to the danger they sometimes pose to themselves or others, to their role as a frequent nuisance to society, or to their potential for becoming non-self-supporting burdens, are usually found in institutional settings. There, most of them receive only custodial care (which simply means they are fed, housed, and cannot leave) and possibly tranquilizing medications. This comment is intended as a recognition of the limited allocated tax money, rather than as a criticism of institutions which are trying to stretch their funds and personnel as far as they will go.

One of the key, and often unmentioned, factors in what we call *normal* behavior is its *predictability*. Most of us would usually expect certain behaviors from those persons whom we treat with courtesy, or from subordinates who are constructively criticized, or from persons politely informed by businesses of oversights in the paying of bills. We would be quite surprised if any of the above acted with extreme aggression, perhaps even assaulting the person making contact. Unpredictability is distressing to society. It works a hardship upon the individual who, as a result, quickly becomes friendless, loses sources of livelihood, and may become unemployable and unable to maintain himself. Unpredictable aggressiveness, as well as other types of deviance and unpredictability, are frequently indications of psychosis and suggest the advisability of institutionalization for the good of both society and the individual himself. The aggressiveness mentioned above is *overreactivity*. Forms of *underreactivity* also can violate the criterion of predictability, which is one of society's key measures of adjustment. The psychotic is the most unpredictable of those with behavior pathologies.

The traditional division of psychosis is into two groups—the organic and the functional. *Organic* psychoses are those assumed to be brought about by definite biological pathologies. These patients make up about half of most institutionalized populations. Among them are persons with brain damage resulting from accidents, birth defects, diseases of the central nervous system, toxic effects of leaded paints and certain types of alcohol, and age-related disorders such as extreme types of senility, cerebral arteriosclerosis, etc. The number of persons with age-associated mental disorders seems to be increasing in hospital populations due to increasing lengths of life. Organic psychosis is primarily a medical problem. It is obvious that damage to the central nervous system would have a profound effect upon behavior, making it much less predictable. Organic forms of psychosis are irreversible to a major extent, at least in terms of current knowledge.

Of more interest to the psychologist is the group of problems called *functional* psychoses. These, it has been traditionally assumed, are psychogenic problems—that is, they have their causes in the environment and in the individual's experiences. We will have more to say on the subject of cause after consideration of some major forms of functional psychosis.

Schizophrenia One of the two major forms of functional psychosis is *schizophrenia,* which is the diagnosis for 20 to 30 percent of the admissions to typical state hospitals. We can refer to (1) a basic schizophrenic substratum, and (2) overlaid symptoms which further indicate a subdivision of types. The basic schizophrenic substratum is one of strange and even bizarre verbal and motor behavior. Magical primitive thinking may be encountered, and in severe cases a break with reality may occur to the extent that the observer cannot communicate with or understand the attempted communications of the schizophrenic.

The following list of symptom clusters (adapted from Vetter, 1972) may be said to be typical of schizophrenic patients and to illustrate the schizophrenic substrate. Naturally, one would not expect to find every one of the listed symptoms in any single given case.

1. Withdrawal, seclusiveness, increased indifference to one's surroundings and social obligations.
2. "Flat" emotional state, or inappropriate emotional responses.
3. Bizarre posturing, peculiar gestures, aggressive behaviors, blatant sexual overtures.
4. Hallucinations, sensory disturbances, distortions of body perception, misinterpretations of physical experiences.
5. Delusional formations, beliefs of persecution or grandeur, ideas of reference (personal applications interpreted from nonpersonal events), unjustified sexual beliefs, religious fervor.
6. Increased autistic thinking (preoccupation with private fantasies), at the expense of continuing ties with reality.
7. Disturbances of thought, language, and communication with others. Stilted language tending toward disorganization, or mute. Inability to pursue an abstract line of reasoning, intrusive ideas.

Some or all of these patterns of behavior typically call attention to the individual well in advance of an actual "breakdown." The final crisis is heralded by panic, agitation, and an obvious need for immediate institutional aid.

Simple Schizophrenia

Simple schizophrenia is characterized mainly by withdrawal from any involvement with the environment. We shall present some details of one developing case:

The subject, a male about 20 years old, lived at home with his parents. His father was a self-made businessman who rose from poverty to the ownership of a medium-sized business. The subject, after graduation from high school, got a job selling small items of mechanical equipment across a counter. His behavior was not considered adequate by his employer and he was discharged after about three months. After this episode he was reluctant to follow-up advertised job openings. After going through a few motions of job-seeking, he developed a pattern of spending most of his days and evenings at home in his room. Over a period of about two years his behavior became more extreme. He refused to see or go out with his old high school friends who occasionally stopped at his home on their way to the neighborhood drug store which was a sort of hangout. The family was naturally concerned, but the gradualness of the withdrawal pattern and the nonthreatening nature of the disorder minimized their apprehensions, to the extent that professional help was not sought during this entire two-year span.

Reflection on this case will suggest that the simple schizophrenic perceives society as threatening, or at least as being somewhat aversive. A simple and direct disengagement from employment and social ties is the most obvious escape route. The simple schizophrenic, if provided financial support and a degree of "looking after," often is not committed to an institution; his otherwise quiet, withdrawn life seldom bothers anyone. Often prostitutes and vagabonds, whose circumstances have eventually brought them to the attention of legal or medical authorities, have been diagnosed as simple schizophrenics.

Hebephrenic Schizophrenia

Hebephrenic schizophrenia is characterized by childish, silly behavior that appears extremely regressive. Long series of "sense and nonsense" rhyming words are not uncommon, nor is giggling at any sort of remark— even those that would normally stimulate anger or grief. The hebephrenic schizophrenic maintains a continuous nonsexual, nonaggressive, noneconomic, and relatively nonsocial cognitive life, similar to that of a very small child. Continuous occupation of the cognitive processes with self-produced nonthreatening mental stimuli successfully diverts thought away from anxiety-arousing stimuli.

Catatonic Schizophrenia

Catatonic schizophrenia involves motor manifestations. The gestures, body positions, and movements in this form of pathology demonstrate, in a motoric manner, the general inappropriateness of the schizophrenic's behavior. Sometimes the motor manifestations are religiously oriented as the individual invokes physical rituals to avoid problems pressing in upon him. Sometimes verbal formulae are used to ward off threats or sinful impulses. The avoidance of threat involves, in severe cases, a detachment from reality through fantasy. Hallucinatory states place the individual in a less threatening fantasy environment, or at least remove him from his real environment. The severe catatonic schizophrenic, in a stuporlike condition, is often oblivious to reality, as the following case shows:

An undergraduate female student at a state university was found by a night patrol lying on the lawn in front of her dormitory. She was clad only in her nightgown, lying on her back with arms rigidly outstretched. Though not in communication with those who cared for her in a hospital during several subsequent hours, it became apparent from her occasional rambling, fragmented verbalizations that she was hallucinating, and that the arms-out-stretched position, which she continued to maintain, represented a cross—a common religious symbolization. While in this position her religious hallucinatory processes apparently rendered her "safe" from the anxieties which beset her during the times when she was more aware of her surroundings.

Paranoid Schizophrenia

Paranoid schizophrenia is the least likely of the schizophrenias to involve extremely fragmented behavior. In fact, groups of paranoid schizophrenics achieve higher mean IQ scores than do groups of other types of schizophrenics, and indications are that their preschizophrenic IQs were similarly superior. Such a person is frequently successful in getting other people involved in his pathology-produced beliefs, due to his intact intelligence and believability, though at later stages his behavior may be more obviously disturbed. The schizophrenic (of any type) is usually beset with a multitude of problems during the time immediately preceding breakdown. These problems derive from his increasing inability to maintain his former level of work quality and to manage his affairs and social relationships. As more and more problems beset him, he casts about for an answer. It is perhaps because of reasonably high intelligence that some paranoid schizophrenics finally find logical reasons for their misfortunes. A tightly logical "paranoid clarification" occurs, and the individual discovers "who" is behind all his misfortune. It is usually some authority figure in the community or in government. Occasionally the assignment of blame is upon some fantastic source, such as people from other planets. An important factor in paranoid

"I only growled at you because you looked as if you were going to growl at me. I'm sorry. I didnt' realize I'd become so paranoid."

Drawing by Frascino; © 1973 The New Yorker Magazine, Inc.

schizophrenia is the occasional occurrence of aggression against the supposed persecutor, which makes the paranoid schizophrenic, in some cases, dangerous. Paranoid processes are reinforced by escape from the self-blame and guilt resulting from failure, all of which is achieved by relinquishing responsibility and putting the blame upon someone else.

Schizophrenia, of one type or another, affects a large number of persons. Its incidence at any single moment in the general population at large is 0.85 percent, or 85/100 of 1 percent. Major implications are discernible from its age-selection of victims and the prognostic factors. Schizophrenia is sometimes referred to as a young person's disorder because most first-onset cases are initially diagnosed between the ages of 18 and 35. This, coupled with the fact that the prognosis is relatively poor for total and sustained recovery, means that society, through institutionalization, maintains the total welfare of a huge population for a considerable length of time. Fortunately the outlook for general recovery has undergone a sizable trend upward from the 15 percent figure of about a decade ago, the credit going largely to new developments in biochemical treatment.

C 14.11. *Identification of schizophrenic types.*

The _____ schizophrenic, among schizophrenics, is the least likely to be institutionalized.

A childlike cognitive pattern (regression) is characteristic of the _____ schizophrenic.

Strange motor (physical) mannerisms, sometimes ritualistic, are characteristic of the _____ _____ schizophrenic.

The _____ schizophrenic is the type most likely to arrive at the point of blaming specific other people for his troubles.

The _____ schizophrenic, among schizophrenics, is likely to be the most coherent and have a higher IQ.

The incidence of schizophrenia in the general population is _____ .

    a. less than one-half of one percent   b. a little less than one percent

    c. around five percent   d. around nine and a half percent

The _____ schizophrenic engages in a tightly logical search for the causes for all his troubles.

Incoherent, silly behaviors characterize much of the pattern of _____ schizophrenia.

The first onset of schizophrenia is typically between the ages of _____ and _____ .

**Manic-Depressive
Psychosis**

Manic-depressive psychosis involves extremes of mood, as opposed to schizophrenia which involves mainly disorders of thought processes. A first grouping under this heading are those patients of the *manic type*—persons whose moods show elation, a sort of "grim" excitement, expansive ambitions with blindness to barriers, and extreme social excesses involving sex, alcohol, and profanity. These persons typically exist on little sleep and frequently go at a rapid pace until they reach the point of total physical collapse. *Depressives*, at the psychotic opposite extreme, are melancholy to the point of stupor, their behaviors typically involving physical immobility and "frozen" thought patterns that preclude decision making or recognition of important factors in necessary day-to-day planning.

Cyclic types are found within the manic-depressive group—persons whose behaviors swing from one extreme to the other, typically with a period of several weeks or even a few months during which each mood runs its course. The three types of manic-depressive psychosis—manic type, depressive type, and cyclic type—are represented about equally in terms of rate within institutional populations.

The dynamics of *depression* are quite complex. It has been suggested that the depressed individual is usually reacting to some kind of loss or failure, and is turning inward his feelings of guilt. Others interpret depression as a frustration-aggression sequence brought about by lack of ability of the individual to control others to the degree he would like. Thus suicide attempts are interpreted, by the latter explanation, as attempts to force the important other person back into an emotional position where his or her feelings can again be controlled. (It is noted that unsuccessful suicide attempts far outnumber successful suicides.) The suicide who, after many unsuccessful attempts, finally achieves death is actually expressing his aggression in the final and most dramatic way left to him. Again, remember that these interpretations are quite theoretical.

The dynamics of *mania* are more obvious. It seems reasonable that mania is negatively reinforced by escape from depression, the aversive aspects of which can become overwhelming. Particularly in cases involving guilt, an escape into the overinvolved life of mania leaves little cognitive room for the aversive guilt patterns. This is little different from a less emphatic pattern by which a person relieves sadness or a guilty conscience by getting involved in activities that keep him busy. The manic shows an extreme degree of this "escape into activity."

Depressive mental illness is at one and the same time both a less severe social problem than schizophrenia and a still-devastating source of family and societal concern. The incidence of manic-depressive psychosis in the general population is estimated by one authority at .5 percent (one-half of one percent). Other authorities use figures somewhat lower but still in the same general range. Making the disability somewhat less devastating than schizophrenia are two additional facts. First, the median age at first hospital admission is approximately 40 years of age; second, the duration of hospitalization tends to be much shorter than is the case with schizophrenia. Even some years ago, prior to most modern psychopharmacological developments, hospitalizations for manic episodes tended to last only 60 to 90 days at the most, and for depressed psychotic episodes only 6 to 9 months at most. Thus, when comparing the ratio of hospitalized manic-depressives to hospitalized schizophrenics, one can see that manic-depressive psychosis represents a considerably less severe economic social problem.

On the other hand, it should be emphasized that there are many, many cases of severe depression that technically are not diagnosed as psychosis, but which nevertheless bring about significant psychological distress both for the patient and for the relatives of that patient, and which last in some cases for a considerable period of time. These depressive reactions are difficult to differentiate from depressive psychosis, and their incidence is undoubtedly much greater than that of formally diagnosed and institutionalized psychotic cases.

C 14.12. *Mania and depression.*

Which of the following is not a recognized subgrouping of manic-depressive psychosis? _____ .

    a. Manic type   b. Depressive type   c. Undifferentiated type   d. Cyclic type

The incidence of diagnosed manic-depressive psychosis in the population is estimated to be _____ .

    a. a little less than the incidence of schizophrenia

    b. a little more than the incidence of schizophrenia

    c. less than a fourth that of schizophrenia

    d. more than four times that of schizophrenia

One interpretation of manic behavior is that it is reinforced by _____ .

    a. attention   b. escape from depression

    c. a positive feeling of awareness of changing physiological balances

With reference to the last question, this would imply that manic behavior is _____ reinforced.

    a. positively   b. negatively

SOCIAL VARIABLES IN PSYCHOPATHOLOGY

The search for causes of psychopathology is made doubly difficult by the fact that it is not feasible to use experimental methods in the investigation. Ethical considerations allow us only to observe various correlates of mental illness, and the cause-and-effect relationship remains largely inferred. Perhaps we could summarize the situation involving social variables by saying that a large number of factors have been related to the occurrence of mental illness, but most of these factors are also correlationally related to one another. For example, a much higher rate of schizophrenia occurs in the lower socio-economic class than at other class levels. Other studies show higher rates of schizophrenia (in comparison with the general population) among black residents of the United States, in families with lower levels of education, and in families that live in high-transiency and more densely crowded neighborhoods. Some clinicians make a rational case for some of the correlates. For example, an individual of low education, instead of understanding the complexities of life, must endure frequent frustration from mistakes made in encounters with the institutions of a complex society. Living in a high-transiency neighborhood means that a child never feels the security of a real home. Being black brings a variety of social conflicts and derogatory experiences that have both the effects of arousing anger and tearing down one's feelings of self-worth.

What do we make of all this? If income level relates to mental illness and education level relates to mental illness, but income relates to education level, then we are in a position to seriously question whether both of the predictor variables are exercising a causative influence on rate of mental illness. Also, with the limitations of the survey method, it is quite possible that *neither* variable is an actual cause of mental illness.

In addition to the wide variety of social variables that we have listed, we encounter literally dozens of other established statistical relationships, including interpersonal interaction patterns in the home, personality patterns of mothers of schizophrenics, and so forth.

Interpersonal Approaches to Psychosis

One school of thought concerning causes of mental illness addresses itself to the various personal relationships formed by an individual, especially at the early stages of life, and possibly within the family environment. This line of thinking derives mainly from observations that the schizophrenic's patterns of social withdrawal and his various insecurities tend to reflect a general lack of confidence in or of satisfactions from relationships with others.

One of the basic approaches concerns the question of identity. As we mentioned in Chapter 3, in connection with Erikson's theory of developmental stages, each child needs to establish a firm sense of his or her own identity. Feelings of self-worth and independence as an individual seem to flow mainly out of the parents' attitudes toward the child. Whatever deficiencies occur in the child's abilities, and whatever stresses may develop in daily living, the basic pattern of parental affection and confidence in the child, together with a mutual understanding of their availability should assistance be necessary, seems vital in maintaining stability and self-confidence. Without these conditions, there is an effect upon the child's ability to persevere in the face of defeat, to recover from stresses, and to generally face a world that is at times hostile or rejecting. Even a sense of trust in other people derives from the basic interpersonal relationship with parents.

Buss (1966) states that two variables determine the individual's developing sense of adequacy. First is the matter of the talent possessed by the individual. That is, there is a basic level of ability that is perhaps necessary for an emerging sense of positive identity and mental health. It is quite likely that individuals deficient in talent, interacting consistently with others of greater abilities and sometimes with disparaging attitudes, cannot develop adequately. A second important variable pertains to positive models of effective behavior. This is particularly important for the development of sexual identification. Many psychologists feel that boys need an adult male model in order to assimilate the "normal" attitudes and behaviors of the male sex role in our society, and similarly girls need an adult female model in order to develop the typical "womanly" attitudes.

While there are many who might challenge the need for such conformism, this point of view mainly reflects a value system associated with the sexual role in our society and its ultimate effects upon individual human beings. Although an absence of predictable sex-appropriate role behavior might be considered desirable by some activists in contemporary society, others feel that the child should acquire the roles appropriate to his or her age, sex, and status if he or she is to move through life unchallenged by major prejudices and/or failures.

Another factor in the development of mental health appears to be the parental child-rearing practices. There are many dimensions along which child rearing may vary, some of them being the degrees of attention and care, discipline, freedom and independence, and basic respect given to the child. Any of these, as you can well imagine, can have an effect upon the developing psychological structure.

One of the patterns identified by researchers in child-rearing practices that seems related to the development of schizophrenia is the opposed message from a parent as a source of cognitive and emotional confusion. This has sometimes been referred to as the "double bind." At the simplest level the child may be told one message, yet that message may be contradicted by the facial and bodily response of the parent; or the verbal content of the message may be contradicted by the tone of voice with which it is delivered; or one part of the message may be contradicted by another part. Within this model the child may learn that the parent asks for demonstrations of affection, yet rejects or makes fun of affection-initiating behaviors. Or the child may be bullied into subservience, and simultaneously criticized for a lack of initiative and individuality. These contradictory stimuli produce the double bind, and result in a wary, uncertain child who continuously but vainly seeks some consistency in the incoming stimuli provided by the major individuals in his life. His expectations are that things will not usually be what they seem to be, and such children seem somewhat susceptible to becoming schizophrenic in late adolescence or early adulthood.

Various studies of the maternal interaction with the child have been performed. A variety of research methodologies have been employed, some with and some without control groups, and employing different variables in their designs. For this reason research publications do not offer easy comparison and analysis of research findings, but a few patterns seem to emerge. The one consistent finding from these investigations is that schizophrenics' mothers tend to be much more controlling of the developing child than are mothers of normals. Traditionally this finding is interpreted as meaning that overrestrictiveness makes it difficult for a child to mature emotionally, to initiate activities on his own, and to socialize on his own initiative. That is, the child has learned through the interaction with the mother to be passive and let others arrange his affairs and his thinking for him. It could also be interpreted from such research that the child in such a condition might be prone to "magical thinking," since his affairs so often are dominated by factors apart from anything he himself might initiate. Such magical thinking is often found to be an aspect of a schizophrenic cognitive style.

We should not cease our interpretation of the effect of the mother's restrictive control without an alternative interpretation. The data allow the possibility that the mother's overcontrol is a response to the child's already abnormal tendencies. Research lends credence to such an interpretation. First, the research of Klebanoff (1959) compared the child-rearing practices of mothers of schizophrenics, normals, and retarded children. It was found that the mothers of both of the nonnormal groups were more possessive and controlling than were the mothers of normal children. Klebanoff's interpretation was that mothers, confronted with aspects of deviant behavior in their children, develop strong, controlling attitudes and patterns of behavior toward those children.

An intersecting area of research was published some time ago by Hoskins (1946), who studied the early life records of persons later institutionalized as schizophrenics. Hoskins found in preschizophrenic childhood histories various lags in achievement skills, academic and social skills coupled with slow physiological maturation and poorly developing motor skills. Hoskins' point of view was that schizophrenia is a general biological immaturity that hits all levels of function and is manifest in very early signs, far predating the actual schizophrenic breakdown.

Thus, as you can see, there is some evidence that children who will later become schizophenic are different as children, and that mothers tend to overcontrol "different" children. Therefore, it is possible that the correlational data relating maternal child-rearing patterns and schizophrenia do not reflect a genuine cause-and-effect relationship.

The father's role in developing schizophrenia is not so clear. Various studies of fathers of schizophrenics can be summarized, however, to indicate two typical behavior patterns. In one of these the father is hostile toward the children, competing with them for the mother's involvement. He also remains aloof and isolated from the family in general, and is seldom found within the mainstream of family activities. The second pattern is that of the father who is a failure and a nonentity in the home, is passive and totally dominated by his wife. Too weak to assert parental authority, he retreats into a pattern of withdrawal with occasional aggression and resentfulness.

A variety of studies have been performed which relate high rates of schizophrenia to growing up in certain types of homes. There is an association between parental loss and later psychosis. For example, maternal deaths before the child reaches eight years of age have occurred more often in schizophrenic cases than in normals (Barry, 1949). Another comparison (Berg & Cohen, 1959) showed that separation from the mother before the age of six was an event in the lives of 35 percent of schizophrenic women versus 5 percent of a control group of neurotic women. In the same vein, Lidz and Lidz (1949) reported that 40 percent of a schizophrenic sample lost a parent before the age of nineteen, and Wahl (1956) reported an approximate 40 percent of a schizophrenic group losing a parent before the age of fifteen. Wahl gave the figure of 12 percent, in contrast, for the general population.

The data from research such as we have been discussing in this section are open to a variety of challenges. For example, even allowing that within a family the children may be treated somewhat differently, what does one make of the fact that many siblings of schizophrenics, emerging from deviant homes, are not themselves seriously deviant? Moreover, what can we make of the many cases of schizophrenia or other varieties of mental illness where no such home structure can be found that would match the extremes of predictor variables discussed in this section? It is obvious that the pattern and quality of parental interaction can exercise a great effect on the personality; however, at this point in time it would not be fair to conclude that the hypothesis of family dynamics causing mental illness has been clearly demonstrated.

C 14.13.   *Interpersonal variables in psychopathology.*

From Erikson's theory we derive the general idea that the parents' attitudes expressed toward the child contribute to his own developing _____ , a contributant to mental health.

  a. identity   b. ego strength   c. sense of sociability

Buss has expressed a point of view that psychopathology can be generated simply by the lack of a sense of adequacy, coming from the individual being _____ .

  a. an only child   b. left alone too often

  c. given too much assistance and help   d. of low ability or talent

Situations in which a parent gives off opposing messages to the perceiving child generate what is termed the _____ .

  a. approach-avoidance conflict model   b. double bind   c. aloof parent syndrome

It has generally been found that during the child-rearing years the mothers of children who later become schizophrenic are typically _____ .

  a. passive and depressed   b. themselves schizophrenic

  c. overcontrolling   d. hostile and aggressive

It was Hoskins' finding that children who later develop schizophrenia _____ .

  a. show many early signs of retarded development

  b. are very high in intelligence

  c. are highly dependent upon a few close friends

Related to high rates of later schizophrenia is the child's _____ .

  a. separation from the mother during childhood

  b. father being aloof, passive, and isolated

  c. being slow in both social and academic achievement

  d. (all three of the above are true)

Societal Variables   There are researchers who feel that, more than the family interaction pattern, the general environment in which one lives can be a predisposing factor toward mental illness. A basic assumption is that social disorganization leads to personal disorganization. When the individual lives in an environment which is unstable and chaotic, he can no longer rely on enduring structures to lend stability to his efforts to adjust and cope with his problems.

What are the specific factors relating to an unstable and disorganized society? Leighton (1959) has suggested the following indicators of societal disintegration:

Poverty—instability of income, as well as low income

Cultural confusion—"old country" versus new traditions

Absence of inspirational values

Frequency of broken homes

Few and weak associations with a group

Few and weak leaders

Little recreational opportunity for use with leisure time

High frequency of aggressive acts in the community

Weak and fragmented communications

Jaco (1954) found that the more disorganized communities contribute higher rates of schizophrenia, which suggests broad social causes.

One variation on such an interpretation of societal causes of schizophrenia relates community deterioration to the notions of maternal rearing practices such as were previously discussed. Faris (1944) suggested that societal disorganization itself does not lead to schizophrenia, rather, it is the pressure that such a community puts upon the child. He notes that in the more integrated communities, the relations that exist between adults and their children as well as between adults and others' children are such that they soften the impact of society on the deviant child. In slum areas, however, there is a certain isolation that exists within small groups, which creates barriers in social relationships. The deviant child cannot successfully cope with the lack of interpersonal cooperation and with the tradition of "toughness" that is a constant threat. This form of social isolation hypothesis was the outcome of research by Faris and Dunham (1939) who compared the rates of psychopathology in various areas of the city of Chicago. The city was divided into concentric rings. It had previously been established that the center of a city, as a residential area, provides the worst social conditions, and that residential neighborhoods improve along many dimensions with increasing distance from the center. Accordingly, it was found that the central area of the city had the highest generated rate of schizophrenia, the rate diminishing from ring to ring as they extended out into the suburbs.

In 1958, Hollingshead and Redlich published the results of a mental health census of an entire community—New Haven, Connecticut. Armed with credentials showing support by various professional agencies such as the American Psychiatric Association, the researchers examined the files of every public and private mental health treatment facility in the state, plus the files of all mental health professionals with private practices. They recorded the names and addresses of all New Haven patients. Having the names of patients allowed recognition of duplications, which might occur if an individual was treated by more than one private practitioner or facility. Next, a sociological census of New Haven was carried out, with each family being rated on a number of factors—the part of town lived in, the income level of the family, the job status of the head of the household, educational levels of family members, and so forth. Each family was placed into one of five classes. Class I was made up of those highest-status citizens with inherited wealth—the "established" rich. Class II was made up of reasonably wealthy families, most of whom had earned the wealth in their own lifetimes either through development of self-owned businesses or by working in top positions in industry. Class III was the upper-middle and middle class type of family, with the head of the household usually owning a small business or being in a top level blue collar occupation or a white collar position of intermediate responsibility. Class IV was made up of most of the so-called blue collar occupations, plus the lower-paid white collar occupations. Class V was comprised of the low-skill occupational group, many of whom are unemployed at any given time.

The rate of mental illness is indicated in Figure 14.1 for each of the groups just mentioned. Classes I and II were combined for purposes of rate calculation, because there were relatively few individuals in each.

In considering the data from the Hollingshead and Redlich survey, you should recognize that most individuals with an actual psychosis have little real chance of escaping detection by society and receiving some kind of medical treatment. For this reason, and because of the thoroughness of the data-gathering procedures, the Hollingshead and Redlich study stands as probably the most significant of its kind in existing literature.

When one observes the fantastic differences in rates from class to class, the conclusion of cause-and-effect at first seems warranted, but remember

Figure 14.1

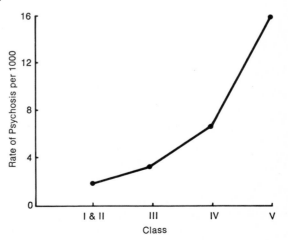

the many correlated variables that we stated were also related to mental illness and you will see the dangers in such inferences made from survey method research.

C 14.14. *Societal variables in psychopathology.*

Faris and Dunham showed that the rate of schizophrenia decreased _____ .

    a. as age increased   b. as educational level increased

    c. as distance of residence from the center of the city increased

    d. as number of children in the family decreased

Hollingshead and Redlich showed that the highest rate of psychosis occurs in the _____ socio-economic class of society.

    a. highest   b. middle   c. lowest

A major problem in drawing cause-and-effect inferences between social factor variables and mental illness is that almost all of the data in such research is _____ .

    a. contaminated with the researcher's sociopolitical bias

    b. collected by way of the survey method

    c. conducted on very small groups of subjects

    d. limited to urban area generalization

PROGRESS CHECK 14.3

MATCH: _____ 1. Simple schizophrenia   A. Bizarre physical posturing

           _____ 2. Hebephrenic schizophrenia   B. Withdrawn but often not institutionalized

           C. Regressive silly behavior

           _____ 3. Catatonic schizophrenia   D. Suspicious

           _____ 4. Paranoid schizophrenia

5. Which is a correct statement about schizophrenia? _____ .

    a. It does not affect a large number of persons

    b. Its onset usually occurs late in life

    c. Both   d. Neither

6. The persons who alternate between the manic and depressive aspects of manic-depressive psychosis are termed _____ .

    a. depressives   b. cyclic   c. maniacs

7. Which aspect of manic-depression represents negative reinforcement? _____ .

   a. Mania   b. Depression

8. Which psychologist emphasizes parental influences on the child's sense of identity? _____ .

   a. Erikson   b. Buss

9. The double bind in family situations contributing to psychopathology is caused by _____ .

   a. rejection of and forbidding demonstrations of affection

   b. opposed messages   c. directions issued in a stern voice

10. Mothers of potentially schizophrenic children typically employ what type of child-rearing practice? _____ .

    a. Overcontrol   b. Passivity   c. Nonverbal control

11. According to Hoskins, schizophrenics typically show academic, social, and maturational lags. _____ .

    a. True   b. False

12. Aloof fathers or absent mothers seem to correlate with schizophrenia how? _____ .

    a. Rarely   b. Negatively   c. Positively

13. According to Faris and Dunham, which children are more likely to exhibit deviant behavior? _____ .

    a. Suburban   b. Rural   c. Inner City

14. Some of the most conclusive data about cause and effect of psychological variables has arisen from studies of mental illness and society. _____ .

    a. True   b. False

BIOLOGICAL FACTORS IN PSYCHOPATHOLOGY

Of immense importance in recent research are the numerous findings which in various ways suggest a biological foundation beneath both organic and functional forms of psychosis.

Organic Psychosis

It is of course commonly recognized that a wide variety of known physical effects can bring about behavioral states in which the individual can no longer be responsible for himself or those around him. Brain damage resulting from physical trauma has this capability, as does toxic damage from the consumption of, or the body's absorption of, certain kinds of chemical substances. Very high prolonged fevers, loss of access to oxygen for an extended period, and congenital deformations of the structure of the brain tissue comprise still other known causes of organic psychosis. Finally, some individuals during their period of old age suffer a type and degree of degenerative physical change in brain tissue that produces a resulting psychotic state. This latter group, the so-called age-associated psychoses, make up a very large percent of the residential population of most mental institutions in this nation.

Genetic Basis of Functional Psychosis

While opinions differ, many experts feel that the weight of experimental evidence increasingly suggests that the so-called "functional" psychoses have organic bases. The first field of research which generally supports this notion is that of behavioral genetics. We shall first look at data pertaining to the genetics of schizophrenia.

Schizophrenia

Pertinent data were developed by Kallman (1953), mainly in the State of New York through the facilities of the New York State Department of Mental Hygiene. Kallman surveyed tens of thousands of hospitalized patients' family records and developed tables of concordance for persons with various degrees of genetic relationship to persons diagnosed as schizophrenic. One of Kallman's several concordance tables on schizophrenics shows the percentages of individuals with known genetic relationships to schizophrenics who are concordant in that they, too, have such a diagnosis. See Table 14.3.

Table 14.3

Relationship to Schizophrenic	Concordance Rate
Step-sibling	1.8%
Husband-wife	2.1
Half-sibling	7.0
Sibling (opposite-sex)	11.5
Sibling (same-sex)	14.3
Fraternal twin (opposite-sex)	11.5
Fraternal twin (same-sex)	17.7
Identical twin (reared apart)	77.8
Identical twin	91.5

In case you have any difficulty interpreting the data, the Kallman figures would show, for example, that 91.5 percent of the identical twins of patients institutionalized with schizophrenia are also institutionalized with schizophrenia.

A number of points of interest emerge from Kallman's figures. First, step-siblings and the husband-wife relationship are not genetic relationships. These figures, still, are higher than the 0.85 percent *general population incidence* figure for schizophrenia. Second, the degree of genetic relationship is identical among same- and opposite-sex siblings and same- and opposite-sex fraternal twins, so that any higher concordance figures for some groups probably reflect a greater commonality in environments and experiences. That is, parents have one way of handling their boys, and another way of handling their girls. Sets of expectations, discipline patterns, and so forth are quite likely to be influenced by the child's sex. It is also of interest that concordance rates of identical twins reared apart since infancy are so high (77.8 percent). Over many years Kallman was able to find a total of 18 such sets of identical twins in order to derive the figure. This figure is a powerful indication of a genetic basis for schizophrenia.

Finally, we shall comment upon the figure of 91.5 percent for identical twins, and by implication, upon the other figures as well. Kallman followed up family records and gathered data on whether or not relatives were in mental hospitals at a *single* point in time. This fact makes the various concordance rates conservative. If schizophrenia, for example, is totally biologically derived and genetically transmitted, the concordance rate should be 100 percent for identical twins. The fact that the rate approaches 100 percent is suggestive that if the 8.5 percent *non*concordant identical twins were followed up for the rest of their lives, eventually almost all would fall into the schizophrenic category. This should be recognized, however, as conjecture.

In Chapter 2 we devoted space to an examination of the basic principles of simple genetic transmission of structural characteristics. In that section we presented the notion of dominant- and recessive-gene effects, single-gene versus polygenic effects, and the notions of penetrance and expressivity. These various factors all come into play in one way or another in genetic psychopathology research.

We shall begin our discussion of schizophrenia with the point of view, usually associated with the work of Kallman (1953), that this disorder results from a recessive gene action, involving at least indirectly the actions of multiple minor genes. Kallman believes that the recessive gene causing the tendency toward schizophrenia produces an enzyme which has an effect on the metabolic balance, which in turn then has a major effect upon the general psychological state. In essence he feels that the affected individual is biologically predisposed to an inability to handle common life stresses. Under circumstances of stress, even moderate, the individual tends to develop schizophrenia with the particular pattern of symptoms being determined by specific life events.

The effect of multiple minor genes, mentioned a moment ago, may have to do with the individual's constitution. It was previously mentioned, in Chapter 12, that Sheldon found unusually high rates of schizophrenia in individuals with the ectomorphic body build. While the body build may be only a correlate of certain vital internal biochemical conditions determined by the same genes, it is Kallman's hypothesis that, in the ectomorph, the tendency toward schizophrenia would meet little resistance and the development of the schizophrenic state would be at a rate closely approximating theoretical predictions. In individuals with other body builds, the observed rates would be lower than the predicted rates due to the resistance of the multiple minor genes that interact with, and lower, the biological expression of schizophrenia.

Some investigators lean toward the hypothesis of a dominant gene effect in schizophrenia (Book, 1953). Here lowered penetrance is assumed to account for the fact that actual rates of genetic expression (concordance) are somewhat lower than predicted rates.

One interesting area of support for the single-gene theory comes from a study performed by McConaghy (1959), who selected various schizophrenics in a hospital who showed evidence of thought disorder on an object-sorting task (it might be pointed out that most diagnosed schizophrenics show such thought disorder). He then tested both parents of the schizophrenic patients on the same sorting task, and compared their performances with those of a control group of normal individuals, the latter being hospital employees. The first interesting fact was that, as a group, the parents of schizophrenics showed a much higher rate of thought disorder on the object sorting task than did the hospital employees. The second, and even more interesting, point was that every schizophrenic had at least one parent who demonstrated thought disorder on the sorting task, although only occasionally did both parents show the thought disorder. As you consider this data, you should bear in mind that the parents of the hospitalized schizophrenics were, as far as was known, "normal" insofar as any current medical diagnosis was concerned. The implications of this research are that there may be a single-gene trans-mission underlying the basic thought disorder found in most cases of schizophrenia.

There are various alternative points of view concerning the inheritance of a schizophrenic tendency. One of these (Weinberg & Lobstein, 1943) assumes that different mechanisms of heredity account for the different types of schizophrenia. Thus, catatonic schizophrenics would possibly have a somewhat different inheritance pattern than paranoid schizo-phrenics. This interesting point of view has received support from Rosenthal (1959), who has found that in identical twins there tends to be an extremely high concordance for a diagnosis of catatonic schizophrenia, but a lower con-cordance for paranoid schizophrenia. Rosenthal is of the opinion that paranoid schizophrenia is a different disturbance, reflecting milder thought disorder and less psychological deficit. He then groups the nonparanoid types of schizophrenia together, linking them with more severe thought disorder and a stronger genetic disposition. Parenthetically it might be pointed out that in certain biochemical research, in which body serums of schizophrenics have been injected or ingested into the bodies of animals or insects, there is evidence of a greater behavioral effect where the body serums of catatonic schizophrenics are involved than with serums of other schizophrenic types.

Meehl (1962) has proposed three distinct concepts—schizotaxia, schizotypy, and schizophrenia. He suggests that certain people inherit a neurological defect, the nature of which is largely unspecified in his theory, which he calls *schizotaxia*. The individual's developmental history interacts with this physical defect to produce a personality organization called *schizotypy*. All schizotaxic individuals become schizotypes, regard-less of what experiences they have during the developmental period. The schizotype consists of four tendencies which Meehl believes are present in all schizophrenic personalities—cognitive deficiency, a tendency to avoid others, an inability to experience pleasure in the normal sense, and ambivalent feelings toward a variety of significant environmental figures. Most schizotypes do not become schizophrenic. Factors in the environment as well as various constitutional factors such as physical rigor and a tolerance for stress combine so that some individuals may remain "peculiar" and somewhat idiosyncratic in their cognitive processes and social relationships, but they do not become psychotic. On the other hand a certain percentage of schizotypes become schizophrenic. Meehl's point of view thus combines genetic predisposition with both constitutional factors and the social environment.

C 14.15. *The genetic basis of schizophrenia.*

An indication of the predictability of certain illnesses as a function of the genetic degree of relationship to persons with the illness appears in tables of _____ .

There appears to be a likelihood that approximately _____ percent of the identical twins of individuals diagnosed schizophrenic will, themselves, be schizophrenic at any given point in time.

The concordance table data informs us that an individual whose identical twin is schizophrenic is about _____ times more likely to be schizophrenic than an individual whose same-sex fraternal twin is schizophrenic.

    a. two   b. five   c. fifteen   d. one hundred

An individual who has an opposite-sex sibling who is schizophrenic is about _____ times more likely to be schizophrenic than the general population incidence.

    a. 1½   b. 7½   c. 13½   d. 50

Manic-Depressive Psychosis The question of possible inheritance of manic-depressive psychosis has not undergone the same degree of research activity as has the inheritance of schizophrenia, but nevertheless there have been a number of sophisticated research programs carried out. Possibly for the reason that the diagnosis of this particular disorder is somewhat unreliable, there is a wide range of reported genetic concordances in the research that has been published. Buss has presented a summarization of a number of studies and reviews, and Table 14.4 indicates derived median concordance rates for a variety of degrees of relationship. Despite some deviation among

Table 14.4

Relationship to Manic-Depressive	Concordance Rate
Parent	13
Child	26
Sibling	17
Fraternal twin	20
Identical twin	81

Source: Adapted from Buss, 1966.

individual studies, the trend is clear. There is an obvious progression of the concordance rate as the genetic relationship tightens. Overshadowing all other concordance rates is the extremely high rate for monozygotic twins, suggesting a strong heredity factor in this particular disorder.

The most favored hypothesis among researchers is that manic-depressive psychosis is the work of a single recessive gene. This is partly a derivation from the finding that where the families of manic-depressive patients have been examined there appears to be a bimodal distribution of depression versus normal emotion. Some members of such families tend to be quite prone to depression while the other family members seem essentially normal in all aspects of their emotional reactions (Shields & Slater, 1961).

According to genetic theory, if a normal individual were to marry an individual with the manic-depressive phenotype, on the average 50 percent of their offspring should be manic-depressive, with the other 50 percent being normal. In actual practice, concordance rates are lower than such hypothetical predictions, but one study concerned cases of depression with the criterion broadened to include all individuals with pronounced mood swings, whether or not they were technically psychotic. The resulting parent-child and sibling-to-sibling concordances then were remarkably close to theoretical predictions (Fuller & Thompson, 1960).

C 14.16. *The genetic basis of manic-depressive psychosis.*

There appears to be a likelihood that approximately _____ percent of the identical twins of

individuals diagnosed as manic-depressive will, themselves, be manic-depressive at any given

time.

The data obtained from concordance research appears to fit the single recessive gene hypothesis for

manic-depressive psychosis fairly well if _____ .

a. one allows for missed diagnoses

b. one broadens "concordance" to mean all persons with pronounced mood swings

c. one considers only sibling concordances and not those of parents or children

Diagnostic Considerations   In the cases of both psychotic depressives and schizophrenics, we should note that research is made difficult by the fact that diagnosis is not as reliable ("reliable" means that multiple diagnosticians agree on the diagnosis of individual cases) as you might imagine. In cases of depression, a severe depression may be labeled manic-depressive psychosis by one diagnostician and severe neurotic depression, or even reactive depression, by another. Similarly, there is a "degree" of schizophrenia short of which the diagnostic label of schizophrenia is usually withheld. We generally term this state "schizoid."

We have not used the term schizoid before, so we shall take a moment for explanation. Kallman has suggested that schizoid individuals are fundamentally the same as schizophrenics, but with a milder form of symptoms. Heston (1970) reported a study of 5,000 relatives of diagnosed schizophrenics. The researchers found that many of the diagnostically "normal" relatives were judged by other relatives to be somewhat "odd." Descriptive terms that recurred fell into certain clusters—*paranoid eccentricities* such as sullen, resentful, suspicious; *other eccentricities* such as narrow-minded, humorless, rigid; *lack of feeling* characteristics such as cruel, unsympathetic; *social reserve* characteristics such as unsociable, seeks solitude; and *characteristics relating to one's social independence* such as dependent, subserviant, unreliable. Heston's conclusion was that while schizoids do not show the marked thought disorders characteristic of most schizophrenics, some of their occasional behavioral lapses are bizarre enough to suggest that these are "micro-psychotic episodes." It is generally the case that two or three times as many close relatives of schizophrenic patients can be diagnosed as schizoid as can be diagnosed schizophrenic (Heston, 1970).

C 14.17.   *Schizoid patterns of behavior.*

Expert opinion (that of Kallman, Heston) commonly holds that "schizoid" individuals _____ .

a. have a mild form of genuine schizophrenia

b. develop their symptoms from being in the continued presence of schizophrenics

c. are little different from "normals"

d. may more properly be lumped with depressives than with schizophrenics

Biochemical Theories of Psychosis

What is inherited, if indeed heredity underlies psychosis? Most tentative answers to this question involve the body's biochemistry. A number of studies have compared the various biochemical processes of schizophrenics and depressives with those of normal or neurotic groups, and most of these have indicated rather distinct differences. Various body fluids—perspiration, blood, urine—show chemical differences for psychotics. Scientists have injected some of these extracts into the bodies of animals and have observed resulting psychotic-like behaviors. The potential psychotic perhaps is not an intact organism at birth. His metabolic processes, his autonomic reactivity, and the like, may deviate significantly from the normal and make him more vulnerable to stress. There is even some evidence that the life expectancy of the psychotic is significantly lower than that of the nonpsychotic individual.

A very tentative notion—and note that it involves quite a few broad interpretations—holds that social factors such as those identified by Hollingshead and Redlich can be tied in with biochemical factors. A limited amount of research tends to suggest that perhaps a significant percentage of individuals from the lower-class population may be stress-avoidant for biological reasons, and for that very reason they stay in their social stratum, not engaging in a positive fashion in higher education or other "stresses."

They may then pass along through the genetic process whatever physiological factors cause low stress tolerance. This whole notion may relate to the fact that many individuals view fairly stressful experiences as challenges, while other individuals react to the same circumstances with aversion and anxiety.

As you have seen, most genetic theory is compatible with a biochemical notion of psychosis. That is, genetic theory does not stipulate exactly what the specific vehicle for expression of the schizophrenia in the individual might be. Buss (1966) has stated that there are two major families of biochemical theories of psychosis. One of these emphasizes adrenalin and its various products, and the other focuses on serotonin.

Role of Adrenalin
When an individual is made anxious, or is stressed, there is an excessive flow of adrenalin in the biological system. In the normal person the adrenalin is converted to various oxidized substances that have a variety of both psychological and physiological effects, but do not interfere with the basic metabolism in the cerebral area. In schizophrenics (Hoffer & Osmond, 1959), a separate enzyme which is the result of the schizophrenic gene is assumed to convert adrenalin to adrenochrome. Researchers apparently feel that this specific enzyme may be taraxein, a substance reported by Heath and his associates (1957) to be present only in schizophrenic blood. The adrenochrome is capable of moving through the blood-brain barrier (which prevents most diffused substances in the blood plasma moving to the brain where the biochemical environment might be upset) and subsequently expresses itself upon the brain metabolism, producing disturbed behavior. A variety of related research has been performed; one interesting result is the speculation that LSD may work in such a way as to interfere with the proper destruction of adrenochrome (through metabolic processes) and its conversion into harmless substances.

Role of Serotonin
The serotonin theory originates with Woolley and Shaw (1962). This theory was originally suggested by the fact that there is a close chemical relationship between LSD, which produces psychotic-like symptoms, and brain serotonin. Serotonin is a substance believed to be involved in the transmission of neurological impulses throughout brain tissue. Serotonin is found throughout the brain, together with an opposing natural agent, monamine oxydase, an enzyme which breaks down and destroys serotonin.

The theory assumes that normal metabolism of serotonin in the brain is required for normal psychological processes. Woolley (1962) states that schizophrenia is considered to begin with a failure to form enough brain serotonin, leading to the social withdrawal and mild depression which usually are early signs of the disease. When emotional strain is encountered, there is a process by which the controlling mechanisms governing the levels of brain serotonin begin to break down. The production levels may fluctuate, with the production of brain serotonin sharply increasing, accounting for the agitated conditions frequently seen in individuals in the process of a schizophrenic breakdown; or the production of brain serotonin may sharply decrease, which leads to the severe withdrawal patterns commonly observed in hospitalized chronic schizophrenics. Thus, either an excess or a deficiency in brain serotonin can cause psychological abnormalities.

There is a variety of research pointing to interpretations of schizophrenia based on biochemical processes related to, but not identical to, those just discussed. Moreover, this is a very active area of current research, and modifications and elaborations of theory frequently emerge in the literature.

There are certain problems associated with biochemical interpretations. First, it should not be overlooked that hospitalized patients are a unique group in several respects. First, the hospital diet is usually inexpensive and tending toward heavy starch and limited protein components. Moreover, even if the hospital diet were better balanced, there is no assurance that the psychotic patient would voluntarily eat a variety of dietary substances so as to provide a reasonably balanced diet. Additionally, the hospital routine is notable for its lack of physical demands on patients, leading to an extreme of general inactivity. There are effects upon the basic body chemistry from such prolonged inactivity. Finally, there is a pronounced lack of general stimulus variety in most public mental institutions. Patients sit by the hour with little to do, with their inactivity punctuated occasionally by a mealtime. It is known that, with species such as the monkey, a prolonged lack of stimulus variety can itself bring about changes in the brain chemistry. Therefore some of the biochemical differences that have been established between hospitalized psychiatric patients and normal control groups may be artifacts brought about within the hospitalization environment itself.

C 14.18.   *Biochemical theories of psychosis.*

Biochemical theories of the cause of psychosis are _____ genetic theories.

   a. contradictory to most   b. completely compatible with

   c. much more widely accepted than are

Interpretation of findings of biochemical differences in the body substances of psychotics is made

   difficult by knowledge of _____ .

   a. low-protein institutional diets

   b. the low activity level of hospitalized patients

   c. (both of the above answers are true)

Dietary Factors in Mental Disorder   A fascinating approach to the question of the cause of psychopathology has been proposed by Linus Pauling, the Nobel Prize winning chemistry professor at the University of California, San Diego. Pauling (1968) advanced the view that psychiatric disturbances may be the result of variations in concentrations of substances normally present in the human body, and that the factor of diet is a primary contributant to such deviations. Pauling conducted research on the nutritive basis of mental illness for 12 years prior to publication of his approach, termed *orthomolecular psychiatry.*

Pauling suggests that there is considerable variation in the minimum daily essential levels of the various vitamins and minerals in different people's diets. Some individuals, he believes, have a far higher need for a given vitamin than is true with the average individual. This may be due to individual differences in the efficiency with which the vitamin is metabolized into substances appropriate for the body's use. It is Pauling's contention that mental symptoms of vitamin insufficiency are typically observed long before physical symptoms appear. He states that the brain tissue itself is more sensitive to changes in the concentrations of vital substances than are other organs and tissues. He has related, for example, inadequacies of Vitamin C to symptoms of depression. Amino acids have been related to changes in personality as well as changes in apparent intelligence, as measured by IQ tests.

A variety of vehicles for the effect of vitamin inadequacy have been suggested by Pauling. One of these is a possibility that some persons may have a physiological abnormality such as a decreased permeability of the blood-brain barrier for vital substances that the brain may need for cerebral efficiency. Pauling has found that for some persons the cerebral-spinal fluid concentration of a given substance may be grossly low at the same time that the concentration in the blood is essentially normal. Another possibility suggested by Pauling relates to the work on concordance done by geneticists. Pauling accepts the notion that genes are involved and contribute to mental illness. But he suggests that these genes may well be those that regulate the metabolism of vital substances, many of them nutritional. He reports success in treating many cases of schizophrenia and other mental illnesses by the use of massive doses of vitamins.

C 14.19. *Dietary factors in mental disorder.*

Orthomolecular psychiatry is a term associated with the name of _____ .

    a. Freud   b. Hoskins   c. Pauling   d. Bugge

One of the hypotheses of orthomolecular psychiatry is that the minimum daily essential levels of vitamins and minerals _____ .

    a. vary widely from one individual to another

    b. are practically constant among different individuals

    c. are almost exactly predictable as a function of age

PSYCHOPATHOLOGY AND THERAPY

Just as there are several theories of what causes psychopathology, so are there numerous approaches to therapy with these disorders. Generally the theory predicts the treatment. In a brief space we shall attempt to outline some of the major forms of therapy in common practice today.

Somatic Therapies   Those individuals who feel that psychopathology is essentially a biological imbalance have proposed various somatic (relating to the biological aspects of the organism) therapies.

Depression is a condition which is frequently treated directly via some form of drug administration. A variety of tranquilizers are utilized for manic conditions, while energizers such as Tofranil are used for depressed states. These are short-term drugs which exercise their effects soon after administration and must be frequently used in order to be continuously effective. The usefulness of this sort of treatment is considered to be situational—that is, a depressed person who is overwhelmed by a variety of disappointments or defeats can be hospitalized for a few days during which medication is started and adjustments in dosages are made, then released with perhaps a supply of the medication for temporary outpatient use. The point is that the depression is "broken" temporarily while the individual has a chance to get away from direct involvement with the source of the difficulty. During this time the individual may find the energies and the inclinations to try again and finally gain control over the problems that exist.

Within the last few years a new treatment for depression has emerged within the field of psychiatry. The mineral lithium carbonate (usually referred to simply as lithium) has been used presumably to "rebalance" the body chemistry and prevent depressive relapses. Lithium is not a symptomatic treatment designed to improve the momentary mood of the patient. Rather, once the depressive episode is ended, it is felt that sustaining the patient on an appropriate dosage of lithium gradually brings about a physical condition less conducive to depressive recurrences. A number of studies have been reviewed by Prien, Caffey, and Klett (1973), all of which conclude that relapse rate is significantly lower after lithium treatment than in a control condition.

Still used by medical professionals is ECT (electroconvulsive therapy). The basic principles of this treatment were first described in a report in 1938 by two Italian clinicians. In modern practice the patient is allowed no breakfast, he is positioned comfortably in bed on his back and given an injection of a muscle relaxant drug. An electrode is placed on each temple and a current of around 80 volts is passed through the brain for a brief fraction of a second. A short time later the patient emerges from the post-convulsive sleep, usually with a sense of confusion and amnesia. A sense of his identity and situation soon return spontaneously, with the distant past reappearing most clearly, but it appears that much of the memory for the weeks just prior to the treatment is irretrievable.

ECT was originally developed as a treatment for schizophrenia, but it soon became apparent that results were far better with cases of depression, and it can now be said that the use of ECT with schizophrenic patients is seldom the treatment of choice.

The problem of a permanent memory loss in ECT patients is not insignificant, and is receiving an increased amount of attention from interested professionals. A fascinating first-person account of the experience of ECT and the resulting incapacitation from loss of memory can be found in the *New Yorker* in the September 9, 1974 issue.

Following its introduction in the mid-1950s, the drug chlorpromazine became the somatic treatment of choice in cases of schizophrenia. A dosage level of 2,000 mg/day of chlorpromazine is usually administered within the hospital setting for a period of several weeks or months. In one major study (Prien & Cole, 1970) involving over 800 chronic schizophrenics it was found that a 24-week treatment program with male patients hospitalized for less than ten years resulted in 38 percent of patients reported improved, 43 percent showing no appreciable change, and 19 percent reported as worsened. Concurrently a comparable placebo group, given a chemically inert substance rather than chlorpromazine, showed 11 percent improved, 26 percent showing no change, and 63 percent worsened. Problems associated with the administration of chlorpromazine at such levels include common side-effects of dizziness, drowsiness, and significant but reversible deterioration in vision.

C 14.20. *Somatic treatment for psychopathology.*

Lithium carbonate is a relatively new somatic therapy used in the treatment of patients with a diagnosis

of _____ .

Specifically, lithium is considered to be useful in _____ .

    a. symptom remediation present at the time

    b. lessening the probability of future relapse

    c. inducing a gradual loss of memory for unpleasant events

ECT is considered to be most effective with patients diagnosed as _____ .

A frequent side-effect of ECT which is causing growing concern among professionals is

    reported _____ .

    a. damage to the central nervous system   b. temporary memory loss

    c. irretrievable memory loss

An effective drug therapy for schizophrenia involves the use of the drug _____ .

Psychological Treatment Approaches to Psychopathology

A variety of approaches to the psychological treatment of psychopathology exist, most of them being subsumed under the general heading *psychotherapy*. In this section we shall limit ourselves to the task of pointing out the main dimensions along which some of the recognized approaches differ.

The first major division is between the so-called "talking therapies" and those which are based on behavioristic strategies. Behaviorists have generated two generally recognized areas of remediation. The first is usually termed *behavior therapy* and is based essentially on the concepts and principles of respondent behavior and classical conditioning. Chapter 8 included material pertaining to various conditioned emotions including anxiety, and the behavior therapist's approach to such problems is quite straightforward. He may choose to use the principles of extinction in handling the fears common to most neuroses. Once the situational stimulus that generates the emotional state is identified, the therapist gradually exposes the relaxed patient to situations of the same general type or to cognitively generated images of being in the situations. The rationale is that the CS is being presented without the simultaneous aversive UCS. Typically the patient has avoided all stimuli of the general nature of the CS for years, and thus the CR has never had the opportunity to extinguish. Extinction-based behavior therapy is generally quite effective, and it is usually referred to in the literature as *systematic desensitization*.

An elaboration of extinction is to simultaneously associate pleasant stimuli with the experience of the CS. This approach is called *counter-conditioning* and has the general effect of speeding up, somewhat, the elimination of the fear response to the CS.

As behaviorists have developed a therapy to remediate emotional states, they have developed *behavior modification* principles to remediate operant behavior deficits and excesses. In the first few pages of the present chapter we expanded upon such principles applied specifically to children's problems. As a simple example of the use of behavior modification principles with an adult patient, we shall discuss the treatment of a depressed woman by a behavioristically-oriented therapist. The patient had few friends and seemed to alienate others readily through interaction. In the first session it became clear why this was so. The woman griped, complained, criticized, and extensively discussed how unhappy she was and how life seemed not to be worth the effort of living it. The therapist reasoned that social reinforcement, through attention, was maintaining the depressive verbal behavior and, following the rationale of Premack (see Chapter 9A), the high-rate behavior of being allowed depressive talk was used as a reinforcer.

The patient was told that she would be timed and after each ten minutes of "normal" talk, she would be allowed two minutes to complain and talk about how unhappy she was. This had the immediate effect of making the patient quite angry, but she soon resumed treatment as the lesser of the available evils. During the ten minutes of normal talk the therapist paid a great deal of close attention to what she said and interacted pleasantly. When the signal began for depressed talk the therapist simply stared down at the table in front of him during the patient's talking period. Very soon the natural contingencies of attention to pleasant speech took control and the patient began not to have much to say during her depressed speech period, and she concurrently reported that, as her patterns of saying depressive things subsided, her overall mental condition improved. Within a short time the patient was self-judged and judged by the psychologist to be essentially recovered.

The basic philosophy of the behavior modification proponent is to downgrade the importance of both "insight" into one's problems and the pursuit of the history of how the patient "got that way." Rather, the problem behavior is attacked directly, with the behavior said to be controlled by its consequences. Even in cases of extreme pathologies such as are encountered in mental institutions, those who view behavior modification programs closely from the inside cannot doubt that they achieve a great deal of value. When "sick talk," various indices of irresponsibility and antisocial actions, and irritating personal characteristics are sharply reduced, and the rates of self-sustaining and desirable behavior patterns are increased, many patients are judged as being well enough to be discharged. Then, following discharge, their newly established social-behavioral habit patterns result in their getting jobs, relating again to family members and friends in socially appropriate ways, etc.

Other psychotherapists belong to schools of thought which Ullmann and Krasner term *evocative psychotherapy*. Their approach is to alter the person's behavior indirectly by first altering intrapsychic organization (Ullmann & Krasner, 1975). To most psychologists, Freud is the most outstandingly known representative of this form of therapy. The patient is guided, in Freudian psychotherapy, in reliving important emotional moments from childhood, experiencing "therapeutic" insights in working through unresolved conflicts with the therapist serving as parent-image, and the overall emotional structure established in childhood is broken up and to an extent recast in a more insightful and emotionally mature pattern. Often the goals of this form of therapy are not so much changed behavior as changed feelings regarding behavior—guilt, resentfulness, etc.

Many other therapeutic schools seem close to Freud's in their basic approach, though one of them may stress the image of the therapist being a "proper" model for emulation, while another may place stress upon the patient's view of a developing "relationship" with another person who can be trusted and whose reactions are always nonjudgmental. Carl Rogers' nondirective model of therapy is illustrative of the latter approach. It should be clear to you at this time that the structure of a therapeutic approach is derived from a theory of how the problem developed to begin with, and on the topic of any given form of psychopathology there are several theoretical approaches.

A final approach to therapy that we shall discuss has not previously been alluded to. This is the approach of Albert Ellis, who has developed *rational-emotive psychotherapy* (Ellis, 1962).

Ellis feels that pathological processes are caused by irrational or illogical thinking. He assumes that thought and emotion are essentially the same process, since emotion accompanies thought and can easily become highly personalized and irrational. Ellis is not clear on the origins of irrational thinking, placing this secondary in his therapeutic system. He speculates that irrational thinking may originate early in individuals biologically disposed in that direction. This assumption of a biological basis is modified, however, by Ellis' statement that the individual goes more deeply and specifically into irrational thinking through interaction with his parents and his culture.

An interesting key to pathology, according to Ellis, exists in the use of language. He emphasizes that thinking occurs strictly through the use of symbols and language, and the disturbed individual's illogical behavior can be defined in terms of his or her internal language of irrational thoughts and ideas. These internal statements the disordered individual keeps repeating to himself represent a process of continuing self-stimulation and are the reason that pathology persists.

Ellis feels that the nature of the culture indoctrinates the individual in regard to what the individual thinks others expect from him. He has, for example, demonstrated that our Western society has generated a number of irrational ideas which are quite common. Adherence to these ideas can become a source of great psychological distress.

Typical among these irrationalities is the idea that one must be *approved of* by virtually everyone, and that one should make significant sacrifices if necessary in order to bring this about. Another irrational idea is that there is a correct or "right" solution to every problem, and one should work unceasingly toward finding it if the end result is not to be catastrophic. You might consider that persons with such ideas continue to dwell upon past misfortunes and present frustrations, where a more judicious individual would become involved in more positive affairs.

Yet another idea of Ellis' is that one should become involved in others' troubles and be upset by others' misfortunes. Ellis continues to list almost a dozen such irrational ideas. An examination of these notions reveals that there is little of relevance to psychotic or depressive reactions, but the irrational ideas do seem to be realistically descriptive of the neurotic individual who becomes overinvolved in nonproductive and agitating events, and whose private thoughts are uncomfortable to say the least.

In therapy, Ellis attempts to change the individual's negative self-appraisals, and to reorganize perceptions and thinking so that thinking becomes logical and rational. The patient must be shown that his irrational self-verbalizations are the source of most of his problems, and the therapist shows the patient how to become more logical and efficient in generating new thought processes.

C 14.21.   *Psychologically based therapies.*

The term behavior therapy is usually employed to describe therapies based on the principles of _____ .

   a. classical conditioning and extinction

   b. operant conditioning and extinction

   c. alteration of intrapsychic organization

The term behavior modification is usually employed to describe therapies based on the principles of _____ .

   a. classical conditioning and extinction

   b. operant conditioning and extinction

   c. alteration of intrapsychic organization

The therapy that involves a patient interacting with the therapist with the same sort of emotional involvement that once accompanied his emotional interactions with a parent at critical early years is basically _____ .

a. Freudian   b. Ellis' system   c. a behavior modification approach   d. Rogers' system

The therapy in which an individual develops a relationship with another person which is always non-judgmental and within which the individual can express his own thoughts and "grow" without fear is basically _____ .

a. Freudian   b. Ellis' system   c. a behavior modification approach   d. Rogers' system

Replacement of irrational thoughts by a different set of self-verbalizations which are practiced until they are believed is basically _____ .

a. Freudian   b. Ellis' system   c. a behavior modification approach   d. Rogers' system

---

PROGRESS CHECK   14.4

1. Concordance tables would indicate the probabilities of a given diagnosis _____ .

    a. in persons with a certain genetic relationship to patients

    b. occurring in anyone within certain geographic areas

    c. as a function of weather and climate

    d. none of the above

2. Suppose you located 50 hospitalized male schizophrenics with living brothers and 50 hospitalized female schizophrenics with living brothers. The concordance table would predict that the numbers of these relatives who would at a single moment themselves be hospitalized with such a diagnosis would be closest to _____ .

    a. 7 and 14, respectively   b. 9 and 6, respectively

    c. 14 and 12, respectively   d. 6 and 7, respectively

3. In general, the concordance rates of manic-depressive psychosis, by categories of relatives, appear to be _____ .

    a. about half as high as those for schizophrenia

    b. roughly comparable to those for schizophrenia

    c. about twice as high as those for schizophrenia

4. Mild forms of schizophrenia-like disorders are termed _____ .

    a. schizophrenic residual   b. eccentric convolutions

    c. partial concordance   d. schizoid patterns

5. In investigating the biochemical causes of schizophrenia, which two of the following would offer problems to the researcher? _____ .

    a. Schizophrenics do not understand the impressions they make on others

    b. Hospitalized patients have little to do all day

    c. Little money is available to provide the most expensive element of a well-balanced diet in most public mental institutions

6. Orthomolecular psychiatry advocates the treatment of mental illnesses through _____ .

    a. transcendental meditation

    b. administration of critical minerals and vitamins

    c. innoculations with serums drawn from other patients

7. Lithium treatments seem almost immediately to reduce depressive symptoms. _____ .

    a. True   b. False

MATCH: _____ 8. Lithium   A. Depression

            _____ 9. ECT   B. Schizophrenia

            _____ 10. Chlorpromazine

MATCH: _____ 11. Behavior therapy   A. Therapist as a parent-image

            _____ 12. Behavior modification   B. Think more positive thoughts

            _____ 13. Freud   C. Classical conditioning

            _____ 14. Rogers   D. Operant conditioning

            _____ 15. Ellis   E. Therapist is nonjudgmental

Summary and Overview   In the preceding sections we have attempted to communicate the message that there have recently been a number of significant developments along several diverse lines of therapy. Psychopharmacology, as an independent field, has made giant strides forward, as have a number of behavioristically founded approaches to behavior change. The evocative psychotherapies, too, have seen a number of innovations and even totally new approaches, although the evaluation of these contributions does not result in so clear-cut a picture of improved technique.

Many professionals are proponents of a single position—somatic therapy, psychotherapy, or behavior therapy. Such individuals will argue the merits of one approach, and cast doubt upon the value of contributions of the other approaches. Typical criticisms are that somatic approaches result in "drugged" individuals who are not actually solving their problems and are subject to recurrences of the problems whenever tensions again arise. Psychotherapies (evocative therapies) are said not to result in any meaningful gain—this criticism is voiced mainly by behaviorists. Behavior therapies are said to be superficial in that while individuals are in a sense bribed to act in different ways, the "real, underlying" causes of the behavior are unchanged.

The advancement of a single approach is more typical in academic settings where individuals are committed to a single line of research than in applied settings such as mental hospitals and clinics. In such applied settings the professionals who work there have frequent opportunities to actually observe the gains being made in different kinds of settings, and it is then common to see eclectic theorists who employ one technique with one sort of patient, and other techniques with other types. For example, it would not be uncommon to find a practicing professional who advocated pharmacological approaches to depression, psychotherapy with obsessive and compulsive types of individuals, and behavior therapy with phobics and others demonstrating specific fears and anxieties.

At the present stage of development, few would propose that the cause (or causes) of psychopathology have finally been established. One major problem is that relationships among variables are often not as strong as we might assume. Theory would predict that certain individuals, such as those from certain types of families and social class backgrounds, should develop pathologies, yet they do not. Others who should not have developed the pathologies do develop them. Perhaps the biggest problem lies in the fact that ethical prohibitions prevent broad scale experimentation in the field of mental health. In many areas of psychopathology most of the available research evidence consists of data generated via the survey method. The result is that one must constantly wonder what correlated variables might have been inadequately controlled, rendering the research meaningless. However, with improvements in research technologies, and with tighter controls in research designs, it would appear that we are gradually unraveling the massive challenge of psychopathology.

If you should have a continuing interest in the questions raised in this chapter, you might find David Rosenthal's *Genetics of Psychopathology* (1971) and Arnold Buss's *Psychopathology* (1966) of interest. Most psychology departments also explore this area in greater detail in their course offerings in Psychology of Adjustment and Abnormal Psychology (or Psychopathology).

EXTENSION CHAPTERS

Research Methods

LEVELS OF MEASUREMENT

SAMPLING
  Sampling Procedures

ERROR
  Random Error
  Systematic Error
    Controlling Systematic Error
    Stratifying the Correlated Variable
  Experimentation and Systematic Error

INFERENTIAL STATISTICS
  Probability
  The Components of Inferential Statistics
  Inferential Formulas
  Interaction Effects

SUMMARY OF SCIENTIFIC INFERENCE

THE PURPOSES OF SCIENCE: AN OVERVIEW

In Chapter 5 you were introduced to the various methods of science, and you were shown some of the ways in which scientists represent data derived from their research. This chapter will extend the topics of Chapter 5 into the more complex developments connected with the collection and analysis of data. We shall begin with a section describing different levels of measurement that are taken on various behavioral events, discuss some of the problems introduced as error into our data, and explore ways of handling these problems. We will then discuss some of the different sampling techniques and conclude with a section on inferential statistical analysis. The latter topic refers to how scientists use statistical probabilities to make decisions concerning the hypotheses which they are investigating.

LEVELS OF MEASUREMENT

Differing precision levels of measurement occur with various kinds of data. In an ascending order of precision they are: (1) nominal measures, (2) ordinal measures, (3) interval measures, and (4) ratio measures. The researcher wishes to measure his independent and dependent variables in as precise a manner as possible, but he is often limited by the nature of the variable itself.

Nominal measures are actually designations which simply give names to the various levels of a variable, without implying any kind of rank or value. Variables such as sex or race would be examples. Nominal designations typically use labels (male, female) rather than numbers, although numbers such as those on racing cars are only nominal. An example of nominal independent and dependent variables would be in an investigation of attitudes toward the death penalty for capital crimes (in terms of being either for or against such punishment) as a function of the sex of the interviewee.

Ordinal measures give an order or rank to the levels of a variable, but the intervals between the ranks are not specified. We might consider the finishing position in a horse race as a typical ordinal measure; the statement "3rd" or "4th" does not tell us how far ahead of the fourth horse the third horse finished. It simply gives the order of finishing. An ordinal independent variable exists in a study of scores on exams as a function of the order of completion of the exam. In such a study the author once established that there was no difference among the mean scores of the first, third, and fifth exam completion quintiles (subgroups of 20 percent each of a larger group) of a class. That is, early finishers and late finishers were no different from intermediate finishers in terms of average test scores.

Interval measures employ scales with equal units. Temperature is an example. We can assume that if temperature A is 30 degrees and temperature B is 45 degrees, the difference between the two is the exact same amount of difference as exists between temperature C of 60 degrees and temperature D of 75 degrees—specifically, 15 degrees difference.

Ratio measures are very much like interval measures in that the scale employed is represented in equal units; additionally, ratio scales must have a true or absolute zero point. An example of a ratio scale is that of length. There is a hypothetical point beyond which there can be no smaller unit of length. Similarly, weight, stimulus intensity, and counts of the number of occurrences of behaviors all have true zero points. In differentiating ratio from interval measures, it is necessary to ask if the measure *does* have an absolute zero value beneath which lower values do not exist. If so, and this is the case at least 95 percent of the time, the measure is ratio.

C 5A.1. *Designation of precision levels of measurement.*

If we are going to study the frequency of hungry rats' bar-pressing for food during a given time period as a function of each animal's sex, the dependent variable is a _____ type of measure, while the independent variable is a _____ measure.

Suppose that in a monkey colony we study the "dominance hierarchy," which means that there is a boss monkey, a number two, and so forth. We are interested in seeing if any changes come about in the hierarchy if we occasionally deliver an electric shock through battery-powered collars to certain animals. The intensity of the shock is the dimension along which we vary our major independent variable. The dependent variable in this experiment is a(n) _____ type of measure, while the independent variable is a(n) _____ measure.

Suppose that a researcher injected nicotine directly into the brain tissue of young chickens and found that in this manner he could induce sleep lasting for periods of several minutes. In a subsequent experiment he studies the length of the period of sleep as a function of the amount of nicotine employed. The independent variable is a _____ type, while the dependent measure is a _____ type. If, on the other hand, the independent variable varied along the dimension of the specific area of the brain injected, with amount of nicotine held constant, the measure would be a _____ type.

Often we have no choice in the kind of measure we can employ. Sometimes we do, however, and whenever this happens we always want to use the most precise possible measure. Let us demonstrate a low-precision correlation formula for the coefficient, *rho*. *Rho* is used for assessing correlation when the measures employed are ordinal rather than interval or ratio. Suppose that we measure 11 different students on two measures (*x* and *y*), and then rank the standings on each measure for each student:

Student Number	Rank on *x*	Rank on *y*
1	11	10
2	10	11
3	9	8
4	8	9
5	7	6
6	6	7
7	5	1
8	4	5
9	3	4
10	2	2
11	1	3

As you can see, high-ranked persons on the *x* measure are generally high on the *y* measure as well. The formula for *rho* is:

$$rho = 1 - \frac{6 \, \Sigma(d^2)}{n(n^2 - 1)},$$

where *n* = number of persons and *d* = the difference in rank on the two measures for a single subject. For example, if an individual were third on one measure and first on another, $3-1=2$, which is the value of d for that one person. If you wish to calculate *rho*, using the data supplied above, you should come up with a value for *rho* of around .86 or .87, showing that there is a high degree of relationship between the x and y measures.

The problem with the use of low-precision measurement (and hence a low-precision computation such as *rho*) is that while linearity might be established *just between the rank scores,* the raw scores upon which the ranks are based might be quite nonlinear, in such a way as to render a much lower value of r. When one uses low-precision measurement where high-precision measurement is possible, one is throwing away information, and this is to be avoided. There are certain circumstances, of course, where low-precision measurement is dictated by the type of data available; and this is the reason for the development of the low-precision measurement rationale with its various formulas. You will learn more about this if you take courses in statistics or measurement at a later time.

SAMPLING Remarks should now be made about basic sampling procedures in conducting research. We always start with a group of people who have been selected to be subjects in our research. But how are they selected? Sometimes horrible blunders have been made by researchers because they failed to follow proper sampling procedures.

Let us start by defining a few terms, some of which we have already been using. First, what is a population? By "population" we do not typically mean the population of the United States. Actually, a *population* is the group from which a sample is selected. If you decide to conduct research on your own campus, you are drawing from the population of students at that specific university. You may be even more limited in your selection. If you take students who attend a particular course, you may get all freshmen, or mainly majors in a single academic area. As you can see, your actual population is sharply limited. This leads to an old saying in research—you can generalize research findings only to the type of population from which the sample was drawn. It is an error to sample political opinion in a freshman auditorium class and then generalize widely, saying that "people" or "students" have certain characteristics. What you actually mean is that freshmen at a particular university, probably disproportionately representing a certain academic major area, have those characteristics. Usually, unless there is good reason to believe otherwise, researchers will generalize from properly sampled university research to the entire population of American university students. Exceptions might be where the sample was drawn from a church-affiliated school or from a largely single-purpose (teacher education, for example) college or university. You should also be cautious about generalizing from a group of one sex to all persons regardless of sex, from college students to the general population, from young people to the general population, and so forth.

C 5A.2. *Populations and samples.*

A population is defined as the group from which the researcher _____

_____ .

One can generalize research findings only as far as the _____

_____ .

Sampling Procedures By far the most useful sampling technique is the random sample. In a *random sample* every individual in the population has an equal chance of being selected as a subject. A student directory might be used in selecting a sample. If you need 100 students and the student directory lists 3,000, you might start by drawing a number from a box of small papers numbered from 1 to 30. If you draw the number 7, you could start with the 7th person in the directory and take every 30th student thereafter, thereby using students numbered 7, 37, 67, 97, and so forth as their names occur in the alphabetical list.

Violation of randomness in selecting a sample may seriously bias the results of research. I recall two questionnaire projects which yielded peculiar-looking patterns. Upon inquiry I found that one of the student-researchers had gone into a socially popular area of the Student Union Building to ask opinions about issues (these students were by no means a typical cross-section of the university), and the other student-researcher had polled only his own friends and acquaintances who, predictably, had opinions very like his own.

Even experts can unthinkingly violate principles of random subject selection. In 1936 there was a classic case of this, where a polling organization predicted a landslide victory for the Republican candidate, Alf Landon. Following the overwhelming victory of Franklin D. Roosevelt, researchers took a closer look at the original polling procedure. It was found that the telephone was used to poll the sample group, but in 1936, in the middle of the Depression, the "average" person did not have a phone. Telephones were possessed mainly by the fairly well-to-do, who traditionally tended to be oriented toward the Republican Party. The population, in this case, was made up of persons whose names were listed in the telephone directory, which was not a random sample in the hard times of 1936.

The major alternatives to random sampling are *stratified sampling,* in which attempts are made to insure that certain important variables in the population (race, sex, age, etc.) are represented in the sample in the same exact proportions with which they occur in the population, and *cluster sampling,* in which the researcher, for reasons of convenience, uses persons grouped together for their own extraneous purposes. The most common type of cluster sampling is the brief use of one or more classrooms of students as research subjects. Cluster sampling has obvious risks of departure from randomness. For example, an auditorium class of psychology students might be disproportionately heavy in its proportions of freshmen and sophomores, and heavy in its proportion of majors in the various social sciences. The other technique, stratification, is a complex procedure, and will be discussed in more detail within the next few pages.

C 5A.3. *Types of samples: Random, stratified, cluster.*

Suppose that you wish to sample attitudes of municipal (city) workers toward the existing pay-scale structure. If your procedure is such that every single municipal worker has an equal probability of being included in the sample, the sample is called a _____ sample.

    a. random   b. stratified   c. cluster

In the above example, suppose you simply decided to use the workers in the office at the waterworks, and generalize from their responses to the entire population of municipal workers. That would be a _____ sample.

    a. random   b. stratified   c. cluster

In the above example, if you exercised care to insure 48 percent male, 52 percent female individuals in the sample, 37 percent clerical workers, 63 percent nonclerical, etc. because those are the *population* proportions, this would be a _____ sample.

    a. random   b. stratified   c. cluster

Suppose in the survey of municipal employees we find that there are approximately 900 employees, and we would like to sample the opinions of about 100 of them. We obtain an alphabetized list of all municipal workers and go down that list, selecting every 9th name for inclusion in the sample. The sample would be a _____ sample.

    a. random   b. stratified   c. cluster

By properly selecting for your sample individuals who actually represent the population from which they are drawn, you should be able to come up with data which can then be presented to others and can be statistically analyzed for significance. The statistical aspect of research will be the subject in a later section of this chapter.

PROGRESS CHECK 5A.1

MATCH the level of measurement with its definition.

    _____ 1. Nominal   A. Equal units having a true zero point

    _____ 2. Ordinal   B. Naming of levels without assigning rank or value

    _____ 3. Interval   C. Measures using equal units

    _____ 4. Ratio   D. Ordering or ranking without specifying intervals

5. Which of the following is a potential research population for studying the use of drugs in relation to academic achievement? _____ .

    a. All individuals over 50 years of age

    b. Students taking an Introductory Psychology course

    c. Individuals in drug rehabilitation programs

    d. None of the above

6. If you take a sample of every 1,000th person who is registered to vote in the U.S., you would be using _____ .

    a. random sampling   b. stratified sampling   c. cluster sampling

---

ERROR   Whenever we conduct research, we are greatly concerned about the possibility of error entering into our data. *Error* is simply the intrusion of data that is not truly representative of the population being sampled. There are two main types of error.

Random Error   *Random error* refers to the effects of sheer chance, any momentary irregularity of the environment or internal condition of a subject, that might throw off, in some way, the accuracy of the data. The subject might be distracted by the ringing of a phone or by someone walking through the laboratory unexpectedly, or a subject might feel sleepy or ill on the day of his participation. These things may occur randomly from time to time, but there is usually no reason to suspect that there is a loading of random error into just one level of the independent variable. In addition to taking reasonable care in arranging his research conditions, the researcher should bear several vital factors in mind in order to reduce random error.

First, he should *discard* an individual's data *if* he knows of a specific reason (unrelated to the independent variable under consideration) for that individual's exceptional performance. Second, he should *scatter* his use of subjects through the various time-of-day and time-of-week conditions so as to spread out individuals from the different levels of the independent variable in a reasonably similar manner. Third, he should *protect* his research against the statistical effects of random error by using no fewer than 30 subjects, if possible, at each level of the independent variable. In this manner, if one individual contributes random error to the data, his contribution is diluted to the point that it does not distort the average significantly.

Systematic Error   *Systematic error* is a dangerous threat to research. If it cannot be controlled, the research is virtually worthless. Systematic error arises from lack of control over correlated variables. A *correlated variable* is simply an extraneous variable that is correlated with the independent variable, and which might conceivably influence the dependent variable.

Suppose, for example, that we wished to test the hypothesis that student estimates of a course's value are a function of the teaching strategy employed. We might compare the lecture method with a group-discussion method (the independent variable). The method in which a course is taught is generally decided by the person who is teaching it. Therefore, although research may show that students like the discussion method best, the teacher in the discussion class might be a more experienced and better overall teacher than the teacher in the lecture section, so that the teacher is "correlated" with the method and is a major influence on student evaluations, completely apart from the teaching method itself.

Other correlated variables in the same program of research would be the textbook used, the time of day of the classes, the rooms where the classes are held, the size of the classes, the types and difficulty of the exams, the grading scales used, and so forth. Such correlated variables *must be controlled* if systematic error, in turn, is to be controlled.

Controlling Systematic Error

There are three main ways to control systematic error. The first two we shall discuss are typical within survey method research and the third occurs in experimentation.

Holding Correlated Variables Constant at One Level

First, correlated variables may be *held constant at one level*. In the case of the lecture-versus-discussion research, we might have the same teacher teach both class sections. We would then want to have the classes at virtually the same time of day—say ten and eleven o'clock—in the same room, using the same text, with the same exams and grading scale, and so forth. This method, where it can work smoothly, is very easy to employ.

Stratifying Correlated Variables

A second method of controlling correlated variables is to *stratify* them within the sample. This procedure is important in cases where a single level of the correlated variable would limit the scope of the research in terms of its generalizability to broad groups. The example we have been using is somewhat inappropriate, so let us look at another research problem.

Suppose that we are comparing males' versus females' attitudes on an issue such as women's "sexual liberation." Our hypothesis might be that women will be more liberal than men [*attitude =f (sex)*] on this issue. We might find that in the community being studied about 60 percent of the women, but only 42 percent of the men, are Catholic. We may be concerned that different religious groups may vary in attitude, so we could arrange to have both the men's and women's groups equal in the Protestant, Catholic, Jewish, other-religion, and non-religious group percentages. If the *overall* percentage of Catholics is 54 percent in the community, then we systematically pick and choose from our subject pool until we arrive at 54 percent of the men used in the study being Catholic, and 54 percent of the women, and we do the same then for Protestants, Jews, and other groups. Stratifying the correlated variable, as you can see, gives us a broader view of the relation of sex to attitude than would have been the case if we had held the correlated variable constant at one level—say Protestant.

C 5A.4.   *Controlling random and systematic error.*

If we are measuring physical strength as a function of height, the sex of a subject would be a _____ variable.

   a. correlated   b. dependent

We should make sure that each individual research subject is not distracted during his participation in order to prevent _____ error.

   a. random   b. systematic

No level of the independent variable should contain fewer than 30 subjects if the researcher wishes to prevent _____ error.

   a. random   b. systematic

Suppose you are investigating political attitude as a predictive function of the level of education. You might be concerned that the age of the subjects might influence the political attitude. Whenever you are faced with a problem of this sort, you can control the age variable by either

   a. _____ , or

   b. _____ .

Sometimes we might not get a true representation of a population in our sample if we control a correlated variable by _____ .

   a. holding the variable constant at one level   b. stratification

Advantages of a technique are usually matched by certain disadvantages, and stratification is no exception. You can readily see that it is more difficult to juggle people around so as to get a specific percentage representation of a correlated variable at each level of the independent variable than it is just to hold the variable constant at one level. Now, if we have several correlated variables to worry about, we are really in a bind.

Suppose there is considerable variation in ages in our subject group, and we wish to control for this factor, as well as race, educational level, and socioeconomic level. There are two ways to stratify several correlated variables. First, and the more complex, is to represent in the sample group's *combinations* of values of the correlated variables percentages corresponding to the population percentages. This is called *cross-stratification*. If 3 percent of the people in a community are white, Catholic, twenty-two- to twenty-four-year-old women from lower-middle class homes where the father is a college graduate (six variables), then exactly 3 percent of the sample at each level of the independent variable should have such combined characteristics, and we should have a similarly exact representation of every other combination of the six variables at each level of the independent variable. Think for a moment how difficult that would be to arrange. Due to the difficulty, this method is usually not used where there are more than two or three correlated variables.

A less exact method, but one that is considerably easier to arrange, is simply to make certain that each correlated variable, *by itself*, is properly represented at each level of the independent variable. Thus, to represent the 10 percent black people and the 32 percent Catholic people in a population, both these proportions should be reflected in the sample at each level of the independent variable. But even though 1 percent of the population may be black Catholics, *no* black Catholics necessarily would occur in the stratified groups, since combinations of factors were not taken into account. This latter method is termed *multiple stratification,* and is to be preferred where there are more correlated variables to stratify than is feasible with cross-stratification.

Now, as an exercise, try to design a study, employing reasonable control over systematic error. Suppose that you are interested in whether intelligence has something to do with choosing a political position. You would see whether students who have ultra-conservative political opinions are more or less intelligent than political moderates or ultra-liberal students. You could group the students into below average, average, and above average IQ.

(a) What is the independent variable? _____ .

(b) What is the dependent variable? _____ .

(c) State the labels for the obvious levels of the dependent variable:

  1. _____ ,

  2. _____ ,

  3. _____ .

(d) How many students (minimum) would you try to have *in total,* divided equally among the levels of the independent variable? _____

(e) State two correlated variables that you might try to control:

  1. _____ ,

  2. _____ .

(f) What methods might you choose to control the correlated variables?

  1. _____ ,

  2. _____ .

(g) What do you think you would probably end up using for your operational definition of the independent variable? _____

  _____ .

For the dependent variable?_____
_____ .

Now, check your answers below.

   To return to item (*f*) (above), it may not have occurred to you that we can control correlated variables in different ways in a single experiment. If we choose to control sex and age, we can represent each sex at its actual population proportion in the three political groups, but hold age constant within a narrow range of, say, nineteen to twenty-three years of age. Obviously, on the age factor, we are still getting a fairly true reflection of the "average student," but with sex, stratification is needed to represent realistically the student body.

   As we have stated, it is mainly in survey method research that we find control of correlated variables by holding them constant at one level or by representing the various levels proportionately through stratification. The two major shortcomings are (1) the difficulty of controlling a large number of known correlated variables, and (2) the problem that obviously exists when you do not know of certain important correlated variables. This latter point may not reflect a personal shortcoming in a scientist—it may be that future research will establish functional relationships between certain variables that, as yet, psychologists haven't even hypothesized. For this reason, *if the possibility of random assignment to levels of the independent variable exists,* it is vastly preferable to switch to *experimentation* and thereby employ the third method of controlling correlated variables. This shall be our next topic.

C 5A.5. *Types of stratified sampling.*

If I were to employ a research design wherein I was concerned about the effects of five different

   correlated variables, I could probably realistically employ the _____ method without too

   much difficulty.

   a. cross-stratification   b. multiple stratification

Which of the following is the more complex to set up? _____ .

   a. Multiple stratification   b. Cross-stratification

In a research design I am able to arrange 5 percent of the sample to be Jewish, in order to match

   population characteristics; I also arrange 11 percent of the sample to be of an education level

   less than high-school graduation. Yet, while the population is approximately one-sixth of 1 percent

----

The answer to (a) is intelligence; (b) is political opinion; (c) is ultraconservative, moderate, and ultraliberal; (d) is 90 or more; (e) there are a number of possibilities—race, age, sex, and year in school are four of the more obvious ones; (f) holding a variable constant at one level or stratifying it (it is possible to do one procedure with one correlated variable and the other procedure with the other correlated variable in a single study); (g) an IQ score and a score on a political opinion questionnaire or, perhaps, self-categorization.

Jewish high-school dropouts, I have no such individuals in my sample. I am using _____ .

a. multiple stratification   b. cross-stratification

Which procedure gives the more exact representation of a match between sample and population characteristics? _____ .

a. Cross-stratification   b. Multiple stratification

C 5A.6. *Identification of independent, dependent, and correlated variables.*

You should be able to identify the independent, dependent, and correlated variables that exist in statements of research designs. For example, if one studied groups of young-adult, middle-aged, and elderly monkeys in monkey colonies, calculating the numbers of aggressive incidents occurring in each age grouping, the ages of the monkeys would be the _____ .

a. independent variable   b. dependent variable   c. correlated variable

In the above research, species of the monkeys would be _____ .

a. the independent variable   b. a correlated variable

In the above research, rate of aggression (number of aggressive incidents per hour) would be _____ .

a. the independent variable   b. the dependent variable

In the above research, the size of the social colonies of monkeys would be _____ .

a. the dependent variable   b. a correlated variable

One research design was set up to investigate the relation that might exist between intelligence of children and the development of characteristics of leadership in the social groups being observed. Age of the children would be _____ .

a. the independent variable   b. a correlated variable

In the above research, the physical sizes of the different children would be _____ .

a. the dependent variable   b. a correlated variable

In the above research, IQ score would be _____ .

a. the independent variable   b. the dependent variable   c. a correlated variable

Experimentation and Systematic Error   Suppose that we are interested in the advantages of a new, innovative method of teaching at the first-grade level. But with survey research we might find that the school where the new method is being used is in an upper-middle-class neighborhood, while the comparison school where the traditional method is to be used is predominantly lower-middle class. Even if we intend to compare classes within a single school, we may see some mothers more eager than others to have their children enrolled in a certain teacher's "enriched" classroom. Such attitudes correlate with both parental intelligence and a child's abilities. We need to eliminate the problems that would be created by such systematic error. Therefore, we should try to use the experimental method wherever possible.

By taking all students from the first grades of both schools and randomly assigning them to the two levels of the independent variable (an alternating 1–2–1–2 procedure through an alphabetically arranged list of students would be acceptable), the correlated variables of parental intelligence and income level will *randomize out*. This means that about as many children from high income families will end up in one treatment condition as in the other, and the same holds true for the other income levels as well. The major necessary condition is that there again be at least 30 subjects per level of the independent variable.

Now, a powerful point—one that overshadows the mere greater ease of random assignment of subjects compared to the more difficult procedures of complex stratification. Random assignment of subjects to conditions of the independent variable allows correlated variables to randomize out, *even if we do not know of their existence!* If, through some freakish twist of genetics, we later find that learning ability correlates with blond hair and social introversion, and that those two factors should have been controlled, they will have been controlled through the procedure of random assignment.

C 5A.7. *Experimentation and systematic error.*

The problem of not knowing about important correlated variables can be dealt with *if* you are able

to use the _____ method in research.

(Refer to the last question.) Using this method, the effect of the correlated variable is said to

_____ _____ across the levels of the independent variable.

(Refer to the last question.) The critical factor in this procedure—the factor that brings it all about—

is that you must be able to do *what* with your initial group of subjects? _____

assign them to_____ .

PROGRESS CHECK   5A.2

MATCH: _____ 1. Random error

_____ 2. Systematic error

A. Noise outside of the experimental room

B. One subject has the flu

C. First subject group used in morning, other in late afternoon

D. 30 percent of one subject group female, 50 percent of other group

3. Which of the following is an example of holding correlated variables constant at one level when comparing two classes' test scores as a function of readability of their textbooks? _____ .

   a. Compare test scores using different texts   b. Compare test scores using same texts

   c. Compare test scores using same teacher   d. None of the above

4. You are conducting a study to find out if there is a correlation between the form of birth control used and religious preference. How might you control for systematic error? _____ .

   a. Stratification of correlated variables such as income level

   b. Use of an experimental room to reduce distraction

   c. Both   d. Neither

MATCH: _____ 5. Cross-stratification   A. Each correlated variable is represented proportionately at each level of the independent variable

       _____ 6. Multiple stratification

                                  B. Exact representation of the population's combinations of values of the correlated variables

7. One way you control for error is to use _____ .

   a. random assignment of subjects to the treatment levels

   b. the experimental approach with at least 30 subjects per condition

   c. both   d. neither

8. You want to study the effectiveness of bonus points to control the rate that students proceed through an individualized psychology course. Students' academic ability is _____ .

   a. the independent variable   b. the dependent variable   c. a correlated variable

---

INFERENTIAL STATISTICS

In all research we are (at least eventually) interested in the comparison of the data from two or more groups. Let us examine the various possibilities. In a typical research design we have two, three, four or more levels of the independent variable, and we are interested in comparing the dependent measures of the groups. We might think here of animals, induced by a food reward, learning a maze under four different levels of food deprivation.

In another type of research we refer to a *control group* and one or more *experimental groups*. We do something in terms of the independent variable to the experimental groups, but not to the control group. For example, in research into the effectiveness of psychotherapy one group might have one kind of therapy, a second group another kind, and a control group might spend time without therapy. We would call the no-therapy group a control group and the other two groups would be experimental groups.

C 5A.8. *Experimental and control groups.*

In all research we are eventually interested in the _____ .

    a. data of our target group   b. comparison of the data from two or more groups

If we were to administer a treatment condition to one group but not to another, then take the dependent

    variable measure on each group, we would refer to the first group as the _____

    group and the latter group as the _____ group.

> In some experiments, due to an unusual expense or time involved in the use of each subject, we cannot realistically use enough subjects to provide assurance that error has randomized out across conditions. Error can then be controlled by having the *subject be his own control,* passing each subject through all levels of the independent variable. In these cases we do not speak of a control group and an experimental group, since separate subject groups do not exist. We speak of the *control condition* and the *experimental conditions.*
>
> One more research model remains to be examined here. Often normative data exist on a population so that we are able to take a measure of a dependent variable on a group and compare it to known normative criteria. For example, if we wanted to determine the IQs of children from a community where all children attended a highly idiosyncratic school system, we could simply measure those children's IQs and compare the mean and standard deviation with the known mean and standard deviation in the general population, as determined by huge normative sampling done in the past during test standardization. Still, as you should be able to see, we are comparing two (or more) groups, even though in this latter case we did not test the larger normative group ourselves.

C 5A.9. *Control procedures in single or small sample research.*

Suppose it costs a small fortune to administer a complex experimental condition to even a half-dozen

    subjects. We wish to find the effect of three or four levels of the treatment variable, but are con-

    cerned about systematic error in so small a group. It would probably be advisable, then, to employ

    which control procedure? _____ .

> Now that we have established our interest in comparing two or more groups, what sorts of conclusions might we draw? Let us say that we measure two groups and get differences in the dependent measure. We need to know if the difference reflects a *true population difference* or whether it might be just the manifestation of random error. That is, we wish to know whether the obtained difference between groups might have occurred by chance. Toward this end we use *inferential statistics*—techniques for arriving at decisions based upon probabilities of the occurrence of given data. For example, suppose someone told you that a one-pound bag of gum-drops

contains one-half pound or more of green gum-drops. You sample ten from the bag without looking inside. None of the ten are green. Assuming the bag is mixed well, you can determine that if 50 percent of the gum-drops are green there would then be less than one chance in a thousand that you could have drawn ten without getting a green one. This allows you to decide, if you care to, that the statement that the bag contains at least 50 percent green candy is a false statement. The decision is based on probability.

C 5A.10. *Purpose of inferential statistics.*

Inferential statistics are techniques for arriving at _____

   based on _____ .

A scientist who is planning to do research generally expects to find a functional relationship between the variables he is investigating. This is understandable, as it is hard to whip up much enthusiasm about the expectation that nothing will occur. He then states his *experimental hypothesis,* abbreviated H_1 (H sub-one). H_1 is that $d = f(i)$, with d and i being the dependent and independent variables in the research. Two notes are appropriate here. First, the term "experimental hypothesis" is applied whether or not the experimental method is being employed. Second, in the few cases in which the scientist *does not predict* that $d = f(i)$, H_1 is still the statement that there *is* a functional relationship. Following the statement of H_1 the scientist states the *null hypothesis,* abbreviated H_0 (H sub-zero). This is the statement that $d \neq f(i)$, or "d is *not* a function of i." The null hypothesis at this stage is assumed to be true; subsequently the scientist determines the likelihood that it actually *is* true, based on its statistical probability.

C 5A.11. *The use of null and experimental hypotheses.*

H_0 is the _____ .

   a. null hypothesis   b. experimental hypothesis

If a scientist does *not* expect $d = f(i)$, then his statement of the experimental hypothesis would

   be _____ .

   a. $d = f(i)$ b. $d \neq f(i)$

Finally, after collection of the data, inferential statistical formulas either allow us to reject the null hypothesis in favor of H_1, or retain the null hypothesis on the basis that random error might have caused the observed differences between the groups. Let us examine the concept of probability in hypothesis testing.

Probability   Events have probabilities. Suppose we wonder if a coin has been "fixed" so that it will come up heads all the time. Our experimental hypothesis is that the "heads" score is a function of *which coin*—that is, the coin in question versus the known population of normal coins—is being tossed. The null hypothesis, then, is that there is *no* difference in the heads scores. We can begin tossing the questionable coin and calculating the probabilities of getting a run of heads. With normal coins, the probability of one head is .50; two heads in a row, .25; three heads, .125; four heads, .0625; five heads, .03125; six heads, .015625; seven heads, .0078125; eight heads, .00390625; nine heads, .001953125; and ten heads, .0009765625. How would we arrive at a decision to reject the null hypothesis of no difference between the coin in question and normal coins in general?

We would first establish an area of rejection of the null hypothesis. In practice this would refer to rejection whenever the obtained probability value fell below a certain *critical value*. Typically this area is defined as where the probability of getting the observed pattern of data, were the null hypothesis really true, is either less than 5 percent ($p < .05$) or less than 1 percent ($p < .01$). Once in a while the critical value necessary for rejection is set very low at $p < .001$. Using the probabilities we have worked out for coin tosses, we can say that when we get the fifth head in a row we could then reject the null hypothesis with $p < .05$. This means that we would have less than a 5 percent chance of being wrong if we rejected the null hypothesis. If we are holding out for $p < .01$, we must await the seventh head in a row, and it takes 10 heads in a row for $p < .001$. The procedure is that we either fail to reject the null hypothesis if the data does not have a low enough associated probability *or* we reject the null hypothesis and accept the experimental hypothesis as being demonstrated beyond a reasonable doubt. To put it another way, when the probability drops below our specified critical value, we conclude that the data are reasonably improbable unless there really is a relationship between the variables, and we accept the experimental hypothesis as having been demonstrated. This "probabilistic" model in science has led to an increasingly infrequent use of the word "proof" in the published literature.

In *interpreting* research, certain risks usually are involved, and it is because of the risk factor that we decide where to set our area of rejection. Suppose that we reject the null hypothesis when, in fact, the null hypothesis is true (this is called a Type I error). If we are studying the relationship of the sex of individuals to rate of religious conversion after adulthood, it is quite unlikely that funds will be spent, lives affected, or costly programs modified if we publish results containing a Type I error. On the other hand, if we cause existing medical therapy programs to be discarded in favor of new ones which eventually do not prove to be as effective as the original ones, there is actual risk of life and health. Therefore, while we might accept $p < .05$ for rejection of the null hypothesis in the religion study, we would demand a very low probability such as $p < .001$ in the medical research.

In a few cases we can associate serious risks with making Type II errors. This type of error involves failure to reject the null hypothesis when it is in fact false. In such cases, if Type II error has serious consequences, we use a relatively high (that is, $p < .05$) probability value for rejecting H_0.

C 5A.12.   *Errors in hypothesis testing: Types I and II.*

Type I error is an error made in interpreting research when one _____ the null hypothesis.

   a. accepts   b. rejects

Suppose that the means of scores in two groups are 34 and 39, $p < .05$. I reject the null hypothesis as being too unlikely. Subsequent research repeatedly shows that under comparable circumstances there really in no appreciable difference between comparable groups. It appears that I have made a _____ .

   a. Type I error   b. Type II error

Type I error is most reduced in likelihood by setting, as the critical value for rejection of H_0, _____ .

   a. $p < .05$ b. $p < .001$

With the critical value for rejection of the null hypothesis being $p < .001$, there is more likelihood of a - - - than a - - - error. _____ .

   a. Type I/Type II   b. Type II/Type I

The Components of Inferential Statistics

Three factors affect probability levels, and each is built into the formulas with which we calculate the values of the various inferential statistics.

First is the *size of the differences between the means* of the groups. Obviously the larger this difference, the more unlikely that the difference could have occurred by chance, and we can more readily reject the null hypothesis.

Second is the *size of the ns in the groups*. Obviously the confidence we have in the obtained sample differences being representative of actual population differences increases as the ns increase. All other things being equal, larger ns make it more unlikely that obtained differences could have occurred by chance, and we can more readily reject the null hypothesis. (*Note:* This statement is especially true when n is less than 30. When n is 30 or greater, there are only modest further effects on probability values associated with increasing n.)

Third is the amount of variability within the groups, expressed by the *sizes of the groups' standard deviations*. To use an extreme example, two groups with different means might have distributions that do not overlap at all and we would feel that the independent variable must certainly have had something to do with the obtained differences. On the other hand, with the same means, the distribution could be such that there would be considerable overlap and we would wonder if there was a "real" difference between the groups.

Examine these illustrations, first with relatively small amounts of variability around the means of 40 and 60:

Group I—32, 34, 36, 38, 40, 40, 40, 42, 44, 46, 48
Group II—55, 56, 57, 58, 59, 60, 61, 62, 63, 64, 65

Now, examine scores with the same means but with large amounts of variability:

Group I—0, 0, 0, 0, 10, 40, 70, 80, 80, 80, 80
Group II—0, 0, 40, 80, 80, 80, 80, 80, 80, 80

In the first example even the lowest score in Group II is higher than the highest in Group I, indicating a small probability that the two sample groups just "happened" by chance to show the difference between means. The scores in the second example, in contrast, would be much more likely to have occurred by chance. (*Note:* With some forms of data, particularly where nominal or ordinal measurement is used, inferential statistical formulas do not utilize amount of variability. For example, if measurement yielded a certain number of students who "passed" and a certain number who "failed," there would be no standard deviation on the measure.)

In summary, low probabilities and an increased likelihood of rejecting the null hypothesis are associated with (1) large differences between the means of the groups, (2) large ns in each group, and (3) small standard deviations in each group.

C 5A.13.   *Components of inferential statistics.*

In which of the following cases would you expect that a calculated probability

would be lower (a or b)? _____ .

a) $n_1 = 30$, $\bar{x}_1 = 14.6$, $s_1 = 2.7$

$n_2 = 30$, $\bar{x}_2 = 12.9$, $s_2 = 2.7$

b) $n_1 = 30$, $\bar{x}_1 = 15.9$, $s_1 = 2.7$

$n_2 = 30$, $\bar{x}_2 = 10.4$, $s_2 = 2.7$

As above: _____ .

a) $n_1 = 50$, $\bar{x}_1 = 28.7$, $s_1 = 5.6$

$n_2 = 40$, $\bar{x}_2 = 21.2$, $s_2 = 5.6$

b) $n_1 = 21$, $\bar{x}_1 = 28.7$, $s_1 = 5.6$

$n_2 = 13$, $\bar{x}_2 = 21.2$, $s_2 = 5.6$

As above: _____ .

a) $n_1 = 30$, $\bar{x}_1 = 41.2$, $s_1 = 12.7$

$n_2 = 30$, $\bar{x}_2 = 36.4$, $s_2 = 13.4$

b) $n_1 = 30$, $\bar{x}_1 = 41.2$, $s_1 = 3.4$

$n_2 = 30$, $\bar{x}_2 = 36.4$, $s_2 = 6.1$

If $n_1 = 20$, $n_2 = 20$, $\bar{x}_1 = 30$, $\bar{x}_2 = 33$, $s_1 = 4.0$, and $s_2 = 6.3$, and $p = .06$, is it conceivable that continued data collection causing an increase in n_1 and n_2, but not changing the mean or standard deviation values, would allow rejection of H_0? _____ .

a. Yes   b. No

PROGRESS CHECK   5A.3

1. To test an hypothesis by means of probabilities, you would use _____ .

    a. inferential statistics   b. descriptive statistics   c. both   d. neither

MATCH: _____ 2. Experimental group   A. Receives some manipulated value of the independent variable

          _____ 3. Control group   B. Does not receive manipulation of the indepen-
dent variable

4. The null hypothesis (H_0) states that _____ .

    a. d is a function of i b. d is not a function of i

    c. i is not a function of d d. i is a function of d

MATCH: _____ 5. Type I   A. Reject H_0 when H_0 is true

          _____ 6. Type II   B. Accept H_0 when H_0 is false

                                      C. Reject H_0 when H_0 is false

                                      D. Accept H_0 when H_0 is true

True or false. The likelihood of rejecting the null hypothesis is increased when:

        _____ 7. the differences between the means of the groups are small.

        _____ 8. the number of subjects in each group is large.

        _____ 9. the standard deviations in each group are small.

10. You would set the critical level for H_0 at $p < .001$ to _____ .

    a. increase the likelihood of a Type I error

    b. decrease the likelihood of a Type I error

    c. increase the likelihood of a Type II error

    d. decrease the likelihood of a Type II error

Inferential Formulas   Different inferential statistics are appropriate for different types of data. In one experiment we may compare differences between means; in another, differences in proportions. In one experiment we may have interval or ratio data and in another nominal or ordinal data. For each we need a specific formula.

One common formula is the t-test, which is used to assess the significance of the difference between two means. Suppose that I teach two classes by two different methods, then give them both the same examination. The mean of one class is 34.1 points and the mean of the other is 38.7 points. How likely is it that we could have obtained such a difference by chance alone, unrelated to teaching method?

$$t = \frac{\bar{x}_1 - \bar{x}_2}{\sqrt{s_1^2 + s_2^2}}$$

The formula for t, at the left, calls for the various components of inferential statistics described earlier, with the exception of n, which is built into the table of probabilities for t.

Tables of t-value probabilities are readily available, but to give you a feel for the operation of the formula for t, if one had ten subjects in each of two groups being compared, rejection of the null hypothesis with $p < .05$ would call for a t-score of 2.1 or higher; rejection with $p < .01$ would call for $t > 2.88$. If one had 15 subjects in each group, the respective t-values for $p < .05$ and $p < .01$ would be $t > 2.05$ and $t > 2.76$.

C 5A.14.   *The t-test.*

A t-test allows us to test the probabilities associated with getting particular differences between two

_____ .

    a. medians   b. standard deviations   c. means   d. ns

Suppose $n_1 = 15$, $n_2 = 15$, $\bar{x}_1 = 107.9$, $\bar{x}_2 = 99.9$; $s_1 = 2.95$, $s_2 = 2.63$. The associated value of t would

be _____ .

    a. 1.577   b. 2.025   c. 2.305   d. 2.950

Using the data just given, and your calculation of t, one would properly _____ .

    a. retain the null hypothesis as not being reasonably discounted

    b. reject the null hypothesis with $p < .05$

    c. reject the null hypothesis with $p < .01$

(*Note:* unless your instructor specifically instructs you otherwise, you can depend upon not being given any t-values to calculate on an exam without the simultaneous availability of the formula for t; this is the philosophy of most psychology instructors.)

Perhaps, instead of analyzing the difference between means, you are interested in the probability associated with a given correlation coefficient. Even with high correlation coefficients it is possible that an apparent correlation is due to random error, perhaps due to a too-small sample.

$$\frac{r}{\sqrt{1-r^2}} \cdot \sqrt{n-2}$$

You use the formula at the left. You then enter a probability table to find whether the value you have calculated has a low enough probability for rejection of the null hypothesis. (*Note:* In this case H_0 states that there is no real correlation.) If H_0 is rejected, your conclusion would be that a relationship actually exists between the two variables that the correlation coefficient was based upon. As you can see from the formula, the size of the coefficient (the difference between it and .00) and n are both critically involved.

Still other situations call for their own types of inferential statistics. For example, up to this point we have generally discussed variables that are measured with interval or ratio measures and which fall into a wide distribution range, such as score points on examinations or IQ scores. Suppose, however, nominal or ordinal measurement produces a very limited number of categories for each variable. Let us consider an example. We could plot a 2-by-2 table showing the numbers of persons falling into the categories of high grades and low grades, and high number of absences and low number of absences from classes, as follows:

Figure 5A.1

	High Grade	Low Grade
Low Absence	140	100
High Absence	30	50

As you can see in Figure 5A.1, in the simplest terms we might say that of the 320 students, only about 37 percent of the "high-absence" group made high grades, while around 58 percent of "low-absence" people made high grades. Superficially such figures may seem convincing, but one *might* find that such values could have happened by chance. It is by no means obvious in this example that there is a clear-cut relation between grades and attendance, so we would use a formula called *chi-square* for the analysis of such data. Using a box system with *A, B, C,* and *D* symbolizing upper left, upper right, lower left and lower right respectively, the formula is:

$$x^2 = \frac{N(AD - BC)^2}{(A+B)\,(C+D)\,(A+C)\,(B+D)}$$

We then enter a table of probability for x^2 and see if our obtained x^2 value has a probability of $< .05$, $< .01$, or $< .001$. If so, we could then reject the null hypothesis which assumes no relation between the absence rate and exam performance. If you were to calculate this particular value of x^2, you would arrive at a coefficient of 10.46, which has a probability lower than .01.

The data just provided gives an excellent example of a situation where a naïve investigator might not have held ability level constant. He should, instead of using everyone in a class, match high- and low-absence groups on the ability variable, then compare grades. When one does this, "differences" often begin to melt away. Taken from another direction, if one went into background data, one would very probably find that the high-absence group had a *previously earned* lower GPA than the other group.

Interaction Effects   In some cases we attempt to deal with a *group* of means and their associated distributions instead of just two as with the t-test. Here we have a more complex formula than t—it is called the analysis of variance. Analysis of variance and some of the formulas derived from it (called factorial designs) also are capable of measuring more than just one independent variable's influence on the dependent variable.

Suppose, for example, that we took the numbers of class absences (the independent variable) and grade-point, and introduced the additional variable of IQ. We could then, using an analysis of variance design, assess not only the contributions of each of the two independent variables to the dependent variable, but study any interaction between them. *Interaction* is a term that refers to the combined effect of certain values of two or more independent variables that is not exactly predictable from knowledge of the functional relationship of only one of the independent variables with the dependent variable.

For example, with our study of absences, we might find that both independent variables—IQ and absences—are significantly related to the dependent variable, but that absence rate's effect on the grade is almost entirely manifest at the low-IQ level. That is (and this is just imaginary data), low-ability people who are frequently absent may be *much* lower on exams than regularly attending low-ability students, but at the higher ability levels there might be hardly any difference between the scores of high- and low-absence groups.

Now, to really add complexity, there are analyses of variance and factorial design formulas which allow three, four, five, and more independent variables to be studied for their main effects and their interactions. This, however, is subject-matter content usually reserved for advanced statistics students.

C 5A.15. *Interaction effects.*

If I found that amount of dating affects grade point averages of university students, but that the effect is strong with women and weak with men, I have then established an _____ between subjects' sex and dating behavior in the study.

Research might show that sexual activity, in terms of degree and frequency of sexual experience, is a function of the sex of the individual, with males being the more sexually active, and of frequency of church attendance, with non-attenders being the more sexually active. However, it might be found that groups of males with different levels of church attendance show no differences in sexual activity. An interaction has been established between sex of subject and _____ .

a. sexual activity   b. church attendance

(*Note:* Interactions, if they exist, are always between independent or predictor variables in a situation, and never between an independent and a dependent variable.)

PROGRESS CHECK   5A.4

1. In an introductory psychology course, if we wished to find out the difference between exam means of one group studying together in pairs and other students who study independently, we would use a(n) _____ .

   a. chi square   b. test for significance of a correlation coefficient

   c. *t*-test   d. interaction correlation

2. If you wanted to measure the effects of more than one independent variable, you would use a(n) _____ .

   a. chi square   b. *t*-test

   c. analysis of variance   d. correlation coefficient

MATCH the research methods with what they are testing:

_____ 3. *t*-test	A. Difference between groups of means
_____ 4. Chi square	B. Difference between two means using an interval or ratio scale
_____ 5. Analysis of variance	C. Difference between using a nominal or ordinal scale

---

SUMMARY OF SCIENTIFIC INFERENCE

Let us again go through the procedure in scientific inference. In almost all cases we are considering how two or more groups differ from one another and this, then, tells us something about the relation of the independent variable to the dependent variable. We define the variables in operational terms, make sure we control correlated variables, and then compare the two groups on the dependent measure. We arrange the data in terms of frequency distributions, make calculations of standard deviations, means, and so forth, then state our hypothesis (H_1) that the dependent variable is a function of the independent variable. We then state the null hypothesis (H_0), put our data into an inferential formula and calculate the probability of getting data such as ours by sheer chance. If the probability value associated with the data is too small to be reasonable, we say that we have significant results, we reject the null hypothesis, and consider the experimental hypothesis to have been demonstrated beyond the .05, .01, or .001 level of probability, depending upon the probability value we have obtained. This figure, then, is the actual probability of our having made a Type I error.

You are now in a position to perhaps undertake an encounter with further information on scientific method and statistical inference. Three books on the topic of research methods that you might search out are (in an ascending order of difficulty) Arthur Bachrach's *Psychological Research: An Introduction* (1972), Robert Plutchik's *Foundations of Experimental Research* (1968), and Malcolm Arnoult's *Fundamentals of Scientific Method in Psychology* (1972). Such materials are appropriate to the content of a course in Research Methods or Introduction to Experimental Psychology, which you might later choose to take.

An interesting little statistics book that is not too difficult is *Elementary Statistics* (1968) by Janet T. Spence and her colleagues. Perhaps you may also take a beginning statistics course in the near future.

THE PURPOSES OF SCIENCE: AN OVERVIEW

Scientists conduct research for a number of reasons. These may be summarized as follows: First, they wish to investigate relationships between (and among) variables. Second, they may wish to establish more clearly the cause-and-effect processes that may hold between the variables. Third, they may wish to extend the range of values of variables that have already been used in research. And fourth, through replication, they may wish to increase the reliability of findings already reported by themselves or other scientists.

Functional relationships are established initially in individual research projects in which one can only make statements concerning the values of the variables actually employed, the species and ages of subjects actually used in the research, etc. These functional relationships, when added to others, often form a consistent pattern. Once a consistent pattern is established, we have a *system*. Let us illustrate this point: Suppose we find that monkeys will press a bar faster for food when they are very hungry than when they are only moderately hungry, rats will run down a runway faster for water when they are very thirsty than when they are only moderately thirsty, and so forth. Let us say that we find this sort of thing very consistently in the investigation of different primary drives and using different species of subjects. We might then state the rule, or system, that level of performance is a function of the level of the motivating drive state. Finally, we have what is known as a *theory*. The theory is an explanatory statement that is based upon related systems, but that extends beyond directly observable variables. In that sense a theory can never really be disproven, but when enough of the systems upon which a theory is based come to be seriously questioned by contradictory research data, the believability of a theory is threatened. The purposes of systems and theories are typically stated as (1) to integrate and organize existing data, and (2) to predict new data.

C 5A.16. *The purposes of systems and theories in science.*

What are the purposes of systems and theories?

a. _____ ,

b. _____ .

In Chapters 5 and 5A we have laid stress upon establishing cause-and-effect relationships after the initial establishment of functional relationships. We hope you appreciate the seriousness of this purpose, particularly in the behavioral sciences. If we find that persons who have had driver-education training in high school have fewer accidents than persons who have not, the typical survey-method research does not actually show us that such training results in lower accidents. It may simply mean that those persons who are careful, mature, thoughtful individuals and who are not prone to have accidents are the sort who typically choose to take driver education. Similarly, if we show that high-absence college students make lower grades than low-absence students, it may be that attending lectures improves exam performance, or it may just be that those persons who are not interested in the subject enough to study for exams are also not interested enough to attend class. A proper respect for the experimental method with its attendant power to establish cause-and-effect relationships is vital in modern psychology.

The goal of science is to discover rules which permit the association and foretelling of facts. It also seeks to reduce the connections discovered to the smallest possible number of mutually independent conceptual elements. It is in this striving for the rational unification of the manifold that it encounters its greatest success [Albert Einstein, *Ideas and Opinions by Albert Einstein*, p. 49].

Operant Conditioning: Advanced Principles

RESEARCH STYLES AND TERMINOLOGY
  Single Subject Research
      Use of the Subject as His Own Control
  Baselines and Cumulative Records
  Contingencies
  Exponential Graphs
  Operant Versus Instrumental Behaviors

ELABORATED OPERANT PROCEDURES
  Shaping
  Discriminative Conditioning
  Chaining
  Modeling and Vicarious Reinforcement
  The Premack Principle
  Noncontingent Reinforcement
  Token Economies
    Advantages of Tokens
    Types of Token Redemptions

PUNISHMENT

CONDITIONABILITY

THEORIES OF REINFORCEMENT
  Need Reduction Interpretation
  Hedonistic Interpretation
  Activation Level Interpretation
  Empirical Interpretation

SUMMARY

In Chapter 9 we introduced the concept of operant reinforcement. We discussed different types of reinforcers—positive versus negative and primary versus conditioned. We discussed some of the factors that influence the degree of operant conditioning—number of reinforcements, delay of reinforcement, and magnitude of reinforcement. We showed that reinforcers could be presented either continuously or within several formal intermittent schedules. Finally, we introduced the topic of punishment.

In the present chapter it is our intent to expand upon the basic topics studied in Chapter 9 and to introduce a number of other significant aspects of operant conditioning, as well as to provide exposure to the operant researcher's vocabulary.

**RESEARCH
STYLES AND
TERMINOLOGY**

**Single Subject
Research**

The operant psychologist has developed a number of concepts and approaches to the collection of data that are almost exclusively limited to his own research. One frequent characteristic of operant literature is the selection of a single subject for intensive study in preference to a more abbreviated treatment typically used with large subject groups. Let us compare the two approaches. Suppose that a researcher was interested in the comparison of two techniques for inducing an academic form of learning. The traditional method would be group oriented. One group would be exposed to one technique and the other group to a second technique, and the subsequent test scores of the two groups would be compared. Of prime interest to the researcher would be the control of ability level. The traditional researcher would hope, using random assignment of subjects to groups, that the correlated variable of academic ability would randomize out.

The operant technologist, on the other hand, takes a different approach to the control of this variable. By concentrating attention on a single subject, or perhaps on a half dozen or so individuals, the operant researcher prefers to control ability simply by keeping the *same subject* in all conditions of the independent variable. Let us assume that techniques *A* and *B* are being compared. Individual *X* is a subject. We teach individual *X* certain concepts using technique *A*, then other concepts using technique *B*. We then compare the ease or efficiency with which the concepts were acquired under the two conditions. We know that the learning ability variable was controlled, because individual *X* was the subject in both conditions and he could not reasonably be "more intelligent" at one time than at another. This is said to be the *use of the subject as his own control.*

Use of the Subject as His Own Control

Naïvely, we might assume that the reason the operant researcher prefers only one or two subjects instead of fifty or a hundred is simply to reduce his own investment of time. Actually, the strategy employed in a single subject or small sample design is for control purposes. Let us present another example.

If we were interested in learning whether social reinforcement is maintaining classroom misbehavior, a very important correlated variable would be each child's history of reinforcement for misbehavior. You can see how control could be attempted by "matching" children who show about the same rates of misbehavior, but the procedure might actually result in some very odd matches. Many interacting factors—a child's physiological system, situations of stress in the home—could contribute to classroom misbehavior. Widely varying factors affecting major individual differences cannot be totally matched among individuals simply by matching them on behavior rate. They *would be* controlled, however, if the *same child* were observed under a series of experimental conditions with the objective of calculating effects of the different conditions on his behavior.

Even more clearly you can see the futility of trying to control complex variables such as "intelligence" or "past experience" by matching groups. If we find an individual with an IQ of 100 and match him with another individual with an IQ of 100, we might find that the two are nevertheless of very *unequal* abilities. One individual might be particularly strong in verbal ability, while the second might be weak verbally but strong in math ability. Each of the abilities contributes to the IQ score. If we were to expose the first subject to an innovative math program and the second to a traditional math program we would probably conclude that the innovative program had no merit. Actually, *math ability*, not being adequately controlled, might have been the deciding influence rather than the independent variable. The difficulty in exactly assessing and matching ability factors, motivational variables and the like, and subsequently controlling them through a matched-groups procedure leads us to this general statement: *Where possible*, the use of a subject as his own control is the superior method of controlling correlated variables. The major limitation, of course, is that in some cases the process of exposing a subject to one condition, then another and another, may bring about a sequential or residual effect from experience. The learning of critical continuing skills at an earlier treatment level or the establishment of certain lingering emotional states in certain kinds of research may make single subject research impractical.

A second advantage lies in the objective pursued by operant psychologists that a researcher should not lose sight of the individual through averaged data. Suppose you present an insight problem to college-student subjects. One well-known problem is to have two strings hanging from a high ceiling down to about 7 feet above the floor, 10 feet apart. The task is to tie the ends of the strings together within 10 seconds without breaking anything. The strings are usually tied to some piece of hardware that is screwed into the ceiling, and the subject is provided with a stepladder, screwdriver, and a few other small tools. If he does not succeed in completing the task on the first trial, everything is put back as it was, and he is immediately started on his second trial. The problem is the difficulty in getting hold of the ends of both strings simultaneously. The strings are not heavy enough to swing, of course, and they are placed so far apart that when the subject holds the end of one and walks as far as possible toward the other, it is still a little out of his reach. "Insight" comes when the subject realizes that, rather than unscrew screws, which cannot be done within the few seconds allowed, the task requires tying the screwdriver onto the end of one string and swinging it, then walking to the other string and grabbing the swinging one.

Consider now how the data might appear. A graph would show an individual subject achieving at a zero-success level for several trials, then achieving 100 percent success thereafter. Some subjects would achieve insight sooner than others. Averaging the data would lead to a *curve*, suggesting gradual acquisition, which is unlike the performance of any subject in the research. Such an extreme distortion of the pattern of individual data resulting from data-averaging may not be common, but the point remains that some distortion usually does occur and can be avoided by conducting more intense investigations of functional relationships in single subject research designs.

C 9A.1. *Control procedures and purposes of single subject research designs.*

Research in which only one or two subjects are passed through successive conditions of the
independent variable is _____ typical of operant than of traditional psychologists.

a. more   b. less

Single subject research allows control of correlated variables through the technique of _____ .

a. matching groups   b. stratifying   c. using the subject as his own control

Operant psychologists prefer data plots on individual subjects largely because they feel that distortions may occur when data on multiple subjects is _____ .

a. collected   b. averaged   c. deliberately discarded when deviant

Baselines and
Cumulative Records

An important research procedure often followed by the operant psychologist
who uses subjects as their own controls is the comparison of (1) behavior
under some condition of the independent variable with (2) behavior in the
absence of that condition. The absence of the specially imposed condition
of the independent variable is termed the *baseline* condition. Baseline
conditions are the typical pretreatment conditions. In some cases the
experimental or treatment procedure would then call for *imposing* an event
during the second stage of the research, and in other cases the experimental
procedure might call for *withdrawing* an event in the second stage.

As an example of the latter, consider for a moment that a teacher might
be interested in trying to apply the concept of extinction in a classroom of
children in an effort to reduce the rate of classroom misbehavior. Here, as
you can imagine, typical teacher attention to misbehaviors is the normal
environmental phenomenon in the classroom—hence it is the baseline
condition. In an effort to explore the effects of deliberately withholding
teacher attention (extinction), the teacher first measures the baseline rate
(or base rate) of classroom misbehaviors under normal conditions. The
initial base rate of misbehavior is charted, and the teacher moves to the
second phase, which is the imposing of the special condition which he or
she has selected to investigate.

In our example the teacher would withhold attention whenever misbehavior occurs, and would thereby be able to derive a rate of misbehavior
under the *treatment condition*. Typically, in operant research, the baseline
period is called condition *A* and the treatment condition is called condition
B. The research model *ABA* is followed, wherein the researcher establishes
the base rate of the target behavior, establishes the rate under the treatment
condition, then re-establishes baseline procedures for a final measure. The
reversal of the behavioral effect in the return to baseline procedures is
considered by operant psychologists to be a vital part of demonstrating
that the treatment condition was the actual cause of the changes in behavior
that were observed.

C 9A.2. *Baseline data.*

An initial measure of typical behavior under normal conditions prior to the initiation of any treatment

condition is called a _____ measure.

In *ABA* research designs, the *A* condition produces the _____ measure, while the

B condition is the measure under the _____ condition.

ABA designs are important because the subsequent reversal of conditions from *B* back to *A* should

result in a return of the rate of the target behavior back toward the original base rate; and, if this

happens, it is considered to be a clear demonstration that the observed changes in the rate of the

target behavior are _____ .

a. actually being caused by the independent variable

b. due to correlated variables

c. capable of random fluctuation

In charting behaviors, psychologists have traditionally used a *rate curve*. This means that as a behavior increases in frequency, the line on the graph depicting the behavior goes up, and as the behavior decreases in frequency the line drops. Figure 9A.1 is a rate curve from an informal study reflecting the change in negative self-evaluatory remarks by clients during the progress of therapy. It is typical of rate curves in the research literature.

Operant behaviorists, on the other hand, frequently employ what is called a *cumulative record* to chart their results. The key to understanding a cumulative record is simply to recognize that instead of having the *rate* of a particular behavior plotted on the vertical axis, the graph portrays

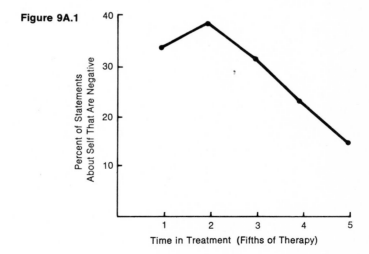

Figure 9A.1

Figure 9A.2

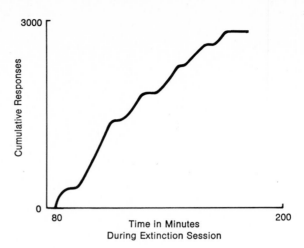

the *total number* of accumulated responses to that point in time. For example, if during the first time period a subject emits 50 responses, the line rises from 0 to 50 within that time period. If the subject then stops responding and emits no responses in the next recorded time period, the data plot for the second time period is again 50. It does not return to 0, because the cumulative record shows how many *total* responses have been emitted by the individual subject since measurement began. An understanding of the nature of the cumulative record is essential for any student who wishes to read and understand the published research of operant psychologists. Figure 9A.2 depicts a typical cumulative record. A pigeon had been extensively reinforced on a VR100 schedule. The pigeon's extinction session, during the interval of 80 to 200 minutes since the end of all reinforcement for disc-pecking, is portrayed in Figure 9A.2. The increasingly horizontal nature of the line indicates slowing of the response rate, with the final flat section indicating a complete ceasing of the behavior.

C 9A.3. *Rate curves versus cumulative records.*

A charting of behaviors that shows, at any given point, how many total behaviors have so far occurred

is called a _____ .

In a cumulative record, can the line depicting behavior rise from the horizontal and drop from the

horizontal as the behavior rate changes? _____ .

  a. Yes   b. No

A charting of behaviors that shows, for a given trial or time period on the horizontal axis, the frequency

or rate of behaviors occurring within that specific time period alone, is called a _____

_____ .

In a rate curve, can the line depicting behavior rise from the horizontal and drop from the horizontal as the behavior rate changes? _____ .

    a. Yes   b. No

Contingencies   An important term that we have not yet defined is *contingency*. We might say, in describing a contingency, that reinforcement is *contingent* upon a certain behavior. The expression means that if the subject behaves a certain way, he will be reinforced, but if he does not emit the behavior, he will not gain reinforcement. Therefore, to say that an event is contingent upon another simply means that it depends, for its occurrence, upon the occurrence of the other. Often operant psychologists refer to procedures where reinforcers are deliberately and broadly employed as *contingency management*.

C 9A.4. *Contingencies.*

In operant terminology it would be common to state that a - - - is contingent upon a - - -. _____ .

    a. reinforcer/behavior   b. behavior/reinforcer

A contingency relationship states that a certain event _____ .

    a. depends for its occurrence upon some other event

    b. is associated with, but not necessarily caused by, some other event

    c. will occur at set time intervals

Exponential Graphs   A device frequently employed by operant psychologists is the exponential graph, sometimes called a log (logarithmic) chart. The exponential graph is plotted upon specially designed graph paper that gives a constant size representation to a fixed percentage change. As shown in Figure 9A.3, the increase from *1* to *2* (100 percent) is the same physical distance on the vertical dimension of the graph as from *5* to *10* (100 percent) and from *100* to *200* (100 percent). Exponential graphs are helpful in illuminating changes in behavior that may escape notice unless represented in this way. For example, suppose that a teacher, by employing extinction procedures in a classroom, is able to reduce the total number of undesirable incidents from 100 per day to 50 per day. If such results are charted on a typical graph they will be quite impressive. Suppose, then, that in working intensively with one child she reduces a behavior rate from 4 incidents per day to 2. If this behavior change is plotted to the same spatial proportion, as was the reduction from 100 to 50, it is doubtful that one would take notice of the graphed difference between values of 4 and 2. Moreover, the teacher might not experience any personal awareness of behavioral change in the drop from four to two incidents per day for a given individual. Consider,

Figure 9A.3

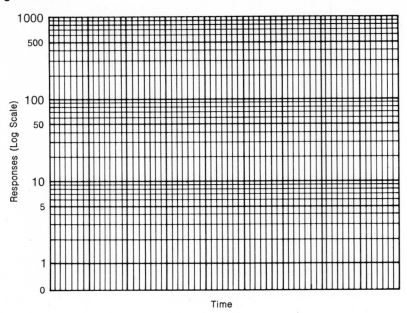

however, that the teacher has actually *cut in half* the number of emissions of the undesirable behavior by the child through her modification of the child's environment. A reduction of 50 percent is impressive, and the data for a single child, with behavior incidence reduced from four incidents per day to two, can be as vividly portrayed on an exponential graph as is the whole class's 50 percent reduction from 100 to 50 daily incidents.

C 9A.5. *Exponential graphs (log charts).*

A major purpose of the exponential graph is to _____ .

    a. save paper space where rates of different individuals differ widely

    b. bring graph lines together for easier comparison

    c. give emphasis to changes in low-rate behaviors

Operant Versus Instrumental Behaviors

Up to this point we have used the term "operant" to indicate all behaviors emitted voluntarily by the organism, in contrast to those reflexively elicited by stimuli. In research literature, at a more technical level, we find that there are two separate terms in use that are sometimes loosely combined under the single term "operant." First there is what is technically called "free operant" behavior, and second there is "instrumental" behavior.

    Let us consider the free operant. A technical definition would state that *free operant* is behavior that may be reinforced and the emission of which leaves the individual in a position immediately to make further responses of the same class for further reinforcement. If a monkey grasps a lever, and by pulling it can deliver a raisin to himself as a reinforcer, he is *free* to depress the lever again immediately if he chooses. In the same way, if a child is able to gain attention in the classroom by being out of his seat, talking to his neighbors, or throwing objects at another child, he may emit these behaviors again immediately and as often as he wants, unless he is literally pinned to his seat by the teacher. So, if a subject is free to emit a certain type of operant behavior at any time he chooses, it is appropriate to refer to the behavior as free operant.

While spontaneous response characterizes a free operant situation, a situation in which a response is to be emitted only once within an experimental trial or session is referred to as *instrumental*. Or, more broadly, the term "instrumental" is applied to a situation where a single emission of the response is appropriate at a given time, but multiple responses at that moment are inappropriate, and either time or some other factor determines when the behavior again becomes appropriate. With such a technical definition, examples are usually crucial.

Suppose we place a rat in a *T*-maze. After it goes up the center runway, it can then go left or right. It is not "free" to emit a right turn 20, 40, or 60 times per hour, but can only emit the behavior *one time per trial*. Thus, if we use a rat four times in the *T*-maze, it can make the choice to go right a maximum of only four times, and is not free to respond this way more often. Similarly, you emit the response of going to class, going to work, returning home, and so forth when the situation for emitting them is appropriate and, once emitted, they are inappropriate until situational factors such as general location or time of day again make their emission appropriate. All these examples, therefore, are instrumental behaviors.

C 9A.6. *Distinguishing instrumental from free operant behavior.*

Is using your umbrella to keep dry an instrumental or operant behavior? _____ .

Let us say that you have been reinforced with excellent grades for writing term papers. You are a "good"

paper writer. Is writing term papers an instrumental or operant behavior? _____ .

By going to work you are reinforced with paychecks. Is going to your job an operant or instrumental

behavior? _____ .

Conversation is reinforced by others' attention, and some people are so influenced by this form of

reinforcement that they are "compulsive talkers" in social groups, even when they are aware that

other people are turned off by their interruptions and too-frequent entries into the conversation.

During a social get-together, does such behavior have the characteristics of instrumental or

operant behavior? _____ .

PROGRESS CHECK   9A.1

1. Single subject research _____ .

    a. is typical of operant psychologists   b. uses the subject as his own control

    c. reduces the distortion of averaging data

    d. all of the preceding   e. none of the preceding

2. A return to the - - - rate of behavior after a treatment condition ceases indicates the effect of the - - -

    variable. _____ .

    a. baseline/independent   b. aversive/correlated

3. A cumulative record _____ .

    a. may go up or down indicating the rate of behavior

    b. shows total behavior occurrences at a given point

4. Response rate measures the frequency of - - - within a - - - time period. _____ .

    a. trials/lengthy   b. behaviors/specific   c. reinforcers/variable

5. A contingency relationship is one in which _____ .

    a. the occurrence of a behavior depends upon a reinforcer

    b. a reinforcer occurs indeterminately

    c. the delivery of a reinforcer depends upon a behavior

    d. the occurrence of a reinforcer precedes a behavior

6. Exponential graphs can plot both low-rate and high-rate behaviors. _____.

    a. True   b. False

MATCH: _____ 7. Operant   A. Behaviors that can be emitted many times within a short time period

           _____ 8. Instrumental

                                          B. Behaviors that are controlled as to rate

ELABORATED OPERANT PROCEDURES:

Shaping

Now that we have developed a broader operant vocabulary, let us turn again to laboratory procedures through which the behaviors of organisms can be modified and controlled. Often, when we analyze an operant behavior, we are interested in a behavior that is well-defined at an extremely simple level. One notes that the behavior either *is* or *is not* emitted, and there are few if any references to response quality. We thus think in terms of bar-presses in an operant chamber or pecks at a plastic button by a pigeon, or even acts such as pushing or shoving others on the part of a child. Many behaviors, however, are much more complex and do not readily occur in a polished form in very young individuals. We might wait years for an opportunity to reinforce a child for certain "mature" behaviors. Laboratory psychologists have approached the more rapid development of such behaviors through the strategy of shaping. *Shaping* is defined as the reinforcement of successive approximations to some final form of a behavior.

The words in the definition just given are not difficult to understand. We might envision a final or finished form of the behavior that we wish an individual eventually to attain. The individual is able to emit only a crude form or approximation of that final hoped-for behavior, but we may nevertheless reinforce the "better" instances whenever they occur, until we finally see the individual performing fairly consistently at the "better" level.

When we begin to train a very young child in proper table manners, such a crude initial approximation might be represented by the child holding a fork and trying to use it to spear the larger pieces of food and guide them to his mouth. Once the individual can fairly consistently operate without errors at that level, it is then time to raise the standard to the next successive approximation. We withhold reinforcement until the child demonstrates a little more sophisticated level of the behavior. This might simply be eating a certain number of bites without spilling, which we might follow with praise and perhaps give him a hug or promise of something he might like to do. Eventually we see that the behavior of eating without spilling begins to occur consistently. At that point one stops reinforcing merely eating without spilling, and the new criterion for reinforcement continues in the direction of the final form of table manners that we hope the child will eventually demonstrate. At the next level we might emphasize the proper holding and handling of the fork, or we might require proper ways of cutting solid foods with the table knife before reinforcement is given.

Shaping is often involved in the development of undesirable as well as desirable patterns. I recall the development of one such case over a period of about a year. A mother was in the habit of ignoring her four-year-old son when he came to her with questions while she was conversing with other adults. The initial stage of shaping consisted of her ignoring the questions or remarks of the child except for those few cases where the child spoke loudly or used a particularly high-pitched voice. Soon, whenever the child approached his mother while she was conversing with others, he would immediately launch into the louder, higher-pitched manner of speech. She then began to ignore most of the child's utterances even of this nature, and the child developed, over a period of months, a variety of more extreme attention-getting devices. He began putting his mouth closer and closer to his mother's ear, increasing both the volume and high-pitched quality of his voice, and he began to jerk on her sleeve during the time that he was asking for an answer or for a favor. After about a year of such reinforcement of successive approximations, the final form of the child's behavior was most unpleasant, yet entirely attributable to the mother's actions.

At this point it is well for you to clearly understand that in shaping we are interested in the development of behaviors that are *qualitatively* different from the behaviors observed at earlier stages. This is in contrast to changes in the quantitative (or rate) dimension of behavior through the procedure of reinforcement that we already have discussed extensively. Moreover, the type of behavior that is shaped tends to be a *unitary* form of behavior. In an encompassing fashion we might denote the "quality" of handwriting, the "level" of speech skills in a young child, the "degree" of social maturity in interpersonal interactions, the "quality" of table manners, the "level" of math skills, etc. While not necessarily simple in nature, such unitary behaviors still can be distinguished from actions that are *sequential*, such as tying a shoelace or necktie, reciting the months of the year in order, etc., all of which are processes that are developed by another means, to be discussed shortly.

When shaping behavior, psychologists generally prefer to use conditioned reinforcers. This is not hard to understand. In animal training, when one wishes an animal to learn a complex task swiftly, if the animal turns from the task to consume a primary reinforcer the resulting distraction produces an inhibiting effect. Most animal trainers are skilled in the use of little clickers that have previously been connected with food rewards. They deliver such clicks when the animal is responding at the criterion level for reinforcement at that stage of shaping.

C 9A.7. *Shaping.*

Shaping is defined as the reinforcement of _____

_____ .

Shaping involves behaviors that are _____ .

  a. complex and sequential, like tying a shoelace

  b. unitary, such as writing a "neat" letter *R* in script

Shaping progresses more swiftly if reinforced with _____ reinforcers.

  a. primary   b. conditioned

An interesting behavioral phenomenon that we should mention at this point involves shaping. The phenomenon is called *response generalization*. Very simply, this means that while a given behavior by a subject usually is of a fairly consistent style, the exact manner in which that behavior is emitted will show *some* variability. Further reinforcement generally produces an increasing stereotypy of the behavior so that each response of a given class begins to look very much like the others. In shaping, when we raise the criterion for reinforcement at a given stage, the overall response patterns do not generally get reinforced, and decreasing stereotypy occurs. That is, increasing variation occurs in the way the behavior is emitted. Some of these variations may meet the higher standard set for reinforcement, are then reinforced, and the behavior very quickly begins to correspond to the new performance standard. As those behaviors are reinforced, increased stereotypy again develops until the next level of successive approximation is initiated, and so on.

C 9A.8. *Response generalization.*

Response generalization refers to the fact that, as a behavior develops, certain _____ .

   a. variations in its enactment occur

   b. reinforcements of it occur

   c. acts fail to gain reinforcement

C 9A.9. *Response stereotypy (versus variability) as a function of conditioning.*

Variability in responding _____ during extinction.

   a. increases   b. decreases

Stereotyped responding _____ during conditioning.

   a. increases   b. decreases

Discriminative Conditioning

Once we have established a behavior in the repertoire of an organism, it is usually important to bring this behavior under some sort of stimulus control. You can see that we typically behave in one way toward persons who occupy certain social roles and behave in other ways, perhaps even directly contrasting with our former behaviors, toward other persons occupying different roles. There are certain different role-appropriate behaviors for a single individual in dealing with his parents, his employer, his mate, and his children. This, in a general sense, is why discrimination is important in the lives of individuals.

We shall begin with a very basic demonstration of discrimination. One useful way of viewing it is as the opposite of stimulus generalization. Stimulus generalization, when it occurs, suggests that the individual confuses a particular stimulus with other stimuli that are in some ways similar. In this manner, a dog that has been mistreated by someone may react negatively to all human beings, which could be interpreted as a form of confusion. Discrimination, on the other hand, means that the individual has learned what is to be reacted to in a certain manner and what is not.

Let us turn to the operant experimental chamber for an example of how discriminative conditioning proceeds. Suppose we have a pigeon that, as a result of being food-deprived, is now quite hungry. His behavior will be reinforced by food delivery. Since pigeons are sensitive to different colors of light, we can use discrimination between a green light and a blue light as the training task. Let us say that our chamber equipment includes a plastic disc built into the wall, with a food delivery cup located just beneath, and two colored lights built into the wall just above the disc. While the blue light is turned on, the "rules" are that pecking the disc will result in *no* consequence. When the green light is turned on, however, pecking the disc delivers grain into the food delivery cup.

As our experiment begins, we observe a low random base rate of disc-pecking on the part of the pigeon, since pigeons seem attracted by the novelty of lighted discs. We soon see that the behavior is beginning to come under stimulus control. At first the pigeon pecks about as many times under the blue condition as under the green, but gradually when the blue light comes on and the green goes off the rate of pecking decreases, increasing again when the green light switches on. We will observe that after a short while in the experimental situation, the pigeon pecks very rapidly and consistently under the green light condition, stopping abruptly and even walking away when the blue light comes on. The bird will rush back to the disc and resume pecking when it again sees the green light.

We refer to the stimulus lights as S^D and S^Δ. And S^D, or *discriminative stimulus,* is defined as a stimulus in the presence of which a given operant behavior *will* be reinforced. An S^Δ (pronounced S-delta), on the other hand, is defined as a stimulus in the presence of which a given operant *will not* be reinforced. The green light is S^D and the blue light is S^Δ in the case just described.

Sometimes we refer to the *presence* of a given stimulus as S^D and the *absence* of that stimulus as S^Δ. In this way, we might observe that when a light is turned on over the plastic disc the bird learns to peck, and when the light goes off the animal learns that it is not worthwhile to peck.

Before continuing, it is appropriate to note that one large group of learning researchers use the expression S^+ in place of what we have termed S^D, and S^- in place of what we termed S^Δ (Logan, 1970). The terms should be considered interchangable in the event you should encounter them elsewhere.

In a natural life setting organisms frequently come to demonstrate discriminatively controlled behavior. Imagine that your friends own a large dog. Let us say that they decide the dog should not be allowed to lie on their sofa. We might define an S^Δ condition of "owners being present," because it is under this condition that the response of lying on the couch will *not* be reinforced by favorable consequences. Under the stimulus condition of "owners absent" (S^D), the behavior of lying on the sofa will be reinforced by the comfort provided. Under certain conditions the animal will learn to make the discrimination perfectly, and the owners may be very disturbed to find that their well behaved dog who never visibly occupies the sofa nevertheless leaves traces of his presence (hair) all over the sofa, which they discover each time they return home after having gone out. The dog has been involved in an elementary discriminative conditioning procedure; he can discriminate readily whether lying upon the sofa will be reinforced. It is not necessary to hypothesize that the dog "understands" the contingencies involved.

At the human level it is very common to observe a small child act in very immature, dependent ways with his grandmother (S^D), who reinforces that sort of behavior, but emit much more responsible behavior in the presence of his mother who demands a higher level of maturity from him.

Discrimination can be carried out to a very high degree of precision if psychologists are careful in their methods. Some years ago a psychologist demonstrated how pigeons could be turned into quality control inspectors (Verhave, 1966). The psychologist undertook to have pigeons examine pharmaceutical capsules as they traveled along a conveyor system to the packaging point. The pigeons were to peck a disc, causing rejection of the capsule, whenever a capsule that had a visually evident flaw passed in front of them. The flawed capsules were called "skags." Capsules that had no flaws were to be allowed to pass on along the conveyor belt. The discrimination-training procedure was aided by the fact that birds tend to have extremely good eyesight. Each bird went through a training situation where, initially, a high percentage of skags were deliberately passed along at intervals. These capsules were electrochemically treated during training so that, as they passed the pigeon, they momentarily activated the food delivery mechanism. Any pecks during that brief moment resulted in food reinforcement. Skags thus functioned as S^D and good capsules as S^Δ, since the latter did not activate the food-delivery mechanism.

During training the birds encountered a progressively smaller percentage of skags on the conveyor system, while the total number of capsules within a given interval of time was increased eventually to a very high level. Toward the end of training, only about one in a thousand capsules would be a deliberately placed S^D. When switched from training to actual assembly line production, the trained pigeons were able to exercise excellent critical judgment as they visually inspected capsules.

Once the bird was trained, the food-delivery mechanism was permanently activated, so that every peck, regardless of circumstances, would deliver grain. But the bird fixed its attention on the assembly line, and only pecked at the appropriate times when a skag appeared. The only adjustment that had to be made in the regular assembly line procedure was to include a certain number of deliberately flawed capsules—perhaps one for every hundred in the production sequence—to maintain the bird's attention. Those skags that were deliberately introduced were easily treated electrochemically so that they could be located with sensors and removed if for any reason they passed the visual inspection of the pigeon.

It was found that a trained pigeon was easily able to outperform human quality control inspectors—the human inspector allowed almost 50 times as many skags to go undetected. Even this high rate of performance was further improved by the introduction of a second trained pigeon down the line at another inspection window. As was done for the first bird, deliberately flawed capsules were introduced, this time at an intermediate point, in order to maintain the second bird's attention. The introduction of the second bird multiplicatively reduced the number of skags passed, so that the eventual calculated rate of pigeon error was less than one three-thousandth that of a human inspector.

C 9A.10.   *Discriminative conditioning.*

An S^D is a stimulus in the _____ of which a behavior will _____ .

An S^Δ is a stimulus in the _____ of which a behavior will _____ .

The experimental literature sometimes equates the term S^+ with _____ .

    a. S^D b. S^Δ c. S^-

In the research where pigeons served as "quality control inspectors," "good" capsules were _____ .

    a. S^D b. S^Δ

In the training of the pigeons as quality control inspectors, the reason for the deliberate introduction

of flawed capsules after training was to maintain the _____ of the inspectors.

    a. attention   b. responding   c. lack of response

Numerous additional aspects of discriminative conditioning exist, only a few of which will be described here. It has been found that the type of *drive state* of an organism can function effectively as a discriminative stimulus for behavior. Animals have been trained to go up a *T*-maze and turn right under one primary drive state and turn left under another. They learn, for example, that the hunger drive is the discriminative stimulus for a turn in one direction and the thirst drive is S^D for the opposite behavior.

In the field of educational psychology, discrimination technology has been put to work by Terrace (1966) in what is called *errorless discrimination learning.* To a limited degree such a procedure is involved in the underlying philosophy of the program that you are studying in this psychology course. Essentially what Terrace attempts is progressive discrimination training in which errors are not allowed to occur. Cues to the answer to a given problem are given in formal errorless discrimination learning. For example, we might ask, "Who was the sixteenth president of the United States?" and the answer blanks might contain the initials "A. L." (*prompting*), which virtually eliminates the possibility of error as the association forms between "sixteenth president" and the man's name. As trials progress, less and less of the cue is given (called *fading*), until finally the student is able to supply answers for a long list of questions and he has never practiced error association. Terrace found that large bodies of material can be effectively learned using prompting and fading, without the necessity for "unlearning" the error associations that otherwise develop early in practice. The result is much swifter acquisition of concepts. The future of errorless discrimination learning seems quite promising, although relatively little development in actual educational practice has yet occurred.

C 9A.11.   *Errorless discrimination learning.*

Errorless discrimination learning involves _____ .

    a. a heavy emphasis on feedback relative to accuracy

b. preventing the individual from practicing errors

c. reward of success but avoids punishment of errors

In errorless discrimination learning, supplying cues to the correct answer is called _____ .

Withdrawal of cues as learning becomes firmer is called _____ .

Chaining   As we begin the topic of chaining, let us recall our previous discussion on the topic of shaping. You were asked then to note that shaping concerns behaviors that are unitary in the sense of *not* being made up of sequences of individual behaviors to be emitted in a given order. Now we come to behaviors that actually do consist of behavioral sequences or chains. Examples of behavior chains would be tying a shoelace, and reciting the alphabet or months of the year.

Perhaps you have experienced interesting phenomena in connection with these examples. If you were to take over the tying of a shoelace left partially completed by another person, it is likely that you would prefer to completely undo what had been done and start at the beginning. Or, if someone asks you what month of the year comes after September, it might be that you would have to begin earlier—perhaps with January—in order to get a sequence of months emitted to the point that you could give the answer. It is not uncommon if you ask a small child what letter comes after F that he must begin "A, B, C," and so forth until he is at last able to say "E, F, G." The reason is that chaining involves aspects of discriminative conditioning, which we have just discussed. To understand the degree of stimulus control over behavior that is typically involved, you must recognize that early behaviors in a chain serve as discriminative stimuli for later behaviors. Thus, in order to say "G" appropriately, one must start the sequence "A, B, C," and so forth. The sequence "E, F" is the vital discriminative stimulus for the correct production of the response "G." It should come as no surprise to you that *behaviors* can have *stimulus* properties. These are often called *response-produced cues.* In the example of the alphabet, the behavior of generating "E, F" becomes the S^D for the response "G."

Let us restate the necessary conditions for chaining. A behavior pattern exists that actually consists of smaller units of behavior, each of which must be emitted in its proper sequence. In developing the ability to enact these behaviors properly, organisms begin to rely upon the enactments of prior elements in the chain as their cues as to which next element should be enacted. Thus the prior response has stimulus properties and is, in fact, the critical S^D.

One of the more interesting research findings is that the usual forward-chaining procedure so normal for us as we instruct others through sequential steps is not as effective nor as swift as is backward chaining, by which the final element is taught first, then the last two elements in sequence, etc. Such a procedure has been tried with great success in math workbooks, in teaching multiplication and division. The reason for the superiority of backward chaining may be because the final behavioral element is instantly reinforced by success; and by association, the *situation* (or opportunity) in which that final element can be emitted becomes a *conditioned reinforcer*. Then the next-to-last behavioral element, by bringing the individual into the reinforcing situation in which the final element can be emitted, is reinforced, and so forth back through the chain.

C 9A.12. *Chaining.*

The S^D in chaining can be viewed as a _____ .

    a. response-produced cue   b. fading element   c. reinforced trial

Chaining refers to a process used to develop _____ behaviors.

    a. unitary   b. sequential

The proper interpretation of chaining is that the - - - in the chain serves as the - - - for the target response in the series. _____ .

    a. next response/S^D b. previous response/S^D c. starting point/stimulus

In an 8-element chain of behavior, a procedure whereby I teach the last or final element, reinforce it, then teach the 7th and 8th in sequence, followed by reinforcement, etc., is called _____ chaining.

Forward chaining appears to be _____ to backward chaining.

    a. superior   b. inferior

Modeling and Vicarious Reinforcement

Several forms of reinforcement have been discussed, including primary, conditioned, social, positive and negative. In a separate category is *vicarious reinforcement*. This term refers to the subsequent increase in the probability or rate of a behavior of an individual who views the behavior being emitted by a model. There is much in operant theory that reminds one of a sort of "grandma's law" in the sense that old admonitions and adages seem sometimes borne out when we closely observe the conditions surrounding behavior. Old sayings warn against the danger of association with "evil companions." Laboratory experiments with vicarious reinforcement verify that children who associate with other children who are emitting undesirable behaviors begin to emit many of the same behaviors themselves. Most parents are familiar with that special form of distress which comes from seeing their previously normal child turn into an ill-behaved brat when in the company of ill-behaved brats.

However, imitation of *all* behaviors that one observes on the part of others clearly does not happen. There are a number of functional relationships involved in imitation. First and perhaps foremost, one of the most powerful factors determining whether observed behavior is imitated is the consequence to the model. A young child was once observed pressing handles on a candy bar machine that was marked "out of order." The machine was paying off with a candy bar for each press of a handle, even though no coins had been inserted. A group of other children passing by noticed the bar-pressing behavior of the child, witnessed the consequences, and immediately rushed to the machine. They were all trying to press the bars and snatch up the candy as it was delivered.

Such an example as we have just given is fairly basic, carrying with it aspects of excitement and group action. More subtle examples abound, however. If a child in a classroom perceives that another child's misbehavior gains him the attention and admiration of peers, then the misbehavior tends to be imitated. If certain styles of clothing gain favorable comment from others, individuals who witness the process adopt those styles, etc. The general rule governing these processes simply is that if the observed behavior leads to the model's being visibly reinforced, we witness an increase in the likelihood that the observer will begin to emit the same behavior. Conversely, if the observed behavior is punished, there tends to be a vicarious suppression effect.

Another functional relationship involves the sex of the observer and the sex of the model. Same-sex modeling is far more prevalent than patterning after an opposite-sex model, and this is particularly pronounced when the observing individual is male.

Yet another powerful determinant of modeling behavior is the status of the model. In a peer group the tendency is to model after the leader's behavior. In a typical gang of boys, for example, the leader is often copied in his style of dress, speech, or actions. Seldom is individualized behavior of a low-status individual copied by anyone else in his peer group. It should come as no great surprise that even adults have varying degrees of status in the eyes of observing children. Some school teachers, for example, are regarded with disdain by students in their classes, while others are looked up to. Often boys of junior-high-school or high-school age are particularly impressed by athletic coaches, while they may be relatively unimpressed by "old fashioned" teachers whom they perceive as having never "done anything" nor acquired really useful knowledge. A warning concerning the possible harmful effects of smoking would be much more impressive to a junior-high-school-age male if it came from an idolized coach rather than from a very prim and proper "old maid" school teacher. The status of the model, in the eyes of the observer, is the important variable in this case.

These functional relationships should be suggestive to anyone who hopes to change the behaviors of children in ways that involve the peer group. Without a doubt, one of the most important considerations that can be given to a deliberate peer group make-up would be the characteristics of the group leader. If a young boy or young girl has some sort of behavioral or social adjustment problem, the problem often resolves itself quickly when the child begins to "look up to" a peer group leader who demonstrates desirable social characteristics.

C 9A.13. *Modeling and vicarious reinforcement.*

Vicarious reinforcement refers to an increase in _____ .

    a. a model's rate of a certain class of a behavior

    b. an observer's rate of a certain behavior seen reinforced for a model

c. an observer's rate of a behavior witnessed in a model, regardless of the consequences for the model

The phenomenon of vicarious reinforcement is a function of

1. _____ .

2. _____ .

3. _____ .

If an observed behavior leads to punishment delivered to the model, the rate of the behavior in the observer should _____ .

The phenomenon just described would be called _____ .

a. suppression   b. vicarious suppression   c. generalization

---

PROGRESS CHECK   9A.2

1. At intermediate points in a shaping procedure reinforcement is withheld except for _____.

   a. the few final trials in the practice session

   b. more vigorous attempts to express the behavior

   c. improved approximations of a final form of the behavior

   d. modeled behaviors

2. Which is an example of shaping? _____ .

   a. Reinforcing spoon eating, then skillful utensil use

   b. Reinforcing cake baking, then cookie making

   c. Sewing a dress, then buying a coat

3. Variability in a behavior is also called _____ .

   a. stereotypy   b. response shaping   c. response generalization

MATCH: _____ 4. S^+ A. A stimulus during which a behavior is reinforced

   _____ 5. Fading   B. A stimulus during which a behavior is not reinforced

   _____ 6. Errorless discrimination

   _____ 7. S^D C. The avoidance of practicing errors

   _____ 8. S^Δ D. The withdrawal of cues

   _____ 9. S^- E. The supplying of cues

   _____ 10. Prompting

11. Chaining involves _____ .

    a. shaping behaviors   b. unitary behaviors

    c. sequential behaviors   d. none of the preceding

12. Backward chaining is a procedure in which the - - - step is taught and reinforced, followed by the - - - step, etc. _____ .

    a. first/last   b. second/next-to-the-last   c. last/next-to-the-last

13. In most situations, forward chaining, as a method of teaching, is inferior to backward chaining.

    _____ .

    a. True   b. False

14. _____ describes an increase in the probability or rate of a behavior of an individual who views the behavior being emitted by a model and subsequently reinforced.

    a. Vicarious reinforcement   b. Modeling   c. Imitation

15. Vicarious suppression occurs when _____ .

    a. the rate of behavior in the observer increases

    b. the model's behavior is reinforced

    c. punishment is delivered to the model

    d. punishment is delivered to the observer

The Premack Principle

David Premack, a few years ago, offered an interesting idea concerning reinforcement of human beings. His idea, as are most, is not unique in a literal sense, but what is unique is a complete systematizing of what is a very simple notion in single instances. Premack stated that any low-rate behavior can be reinforced if the opportunity to engage in a higher-rate behavior is made contingent upon emission of the low-rate behavior. The logic behind the Premack Principle is that there are obvious reinforcing properties involved in many forms of behavior, which is why they are high-rate behaviors. A boy may ride his bicycle almost constantly, thus defining bicycle-riding as a high-rate behavior. If practicing the piano is a low-rate behavior, piano-practicing can be increased by requiring practice before bicycle-riding is allowed.

Parents probably have been using such "behavioral contracts" for centuries, but Premack's suggestions involve the complete cataloging of a child's activities, so that one is able to touch upon exactly which behaviors may be used to reinforce other behaviors. If such a complete hierarchy of behavior rates were produced for a single child, some rather amazing modifications of relative behavior rates could be planned easily.

C 9A.14. *The Premack Principle.*

The Premack Principle states that a behavior rate can be increased if _____ is made contingent

upon the target behavior.

a. escape from an aversive condition   b. imitation

c. an increase in the structure or organization of a situation

d. an opportunity to engage in a higher-rate behavior

Noncontingent Reinforcement   "Superstition" is said to result from *noncontingent reinforcement*. That is, if in the midst of emitting a certain behavior something unusually good happens, the rate of behavior is increased even if the emission of the behavior had nothing whatever to do with the associated event.

    Skinner has noted that superstition resulting from noncontingent reinforcement is very easily established in an organism. He has shown that, with a given pigeon in a chamber, the simple noncontingent delivery of food every five minutes typically will result in the development of odd habits. Perhaps a laboratory bird is stretching and arching its neck at the moment grain is delivered into a food cup. The reinforcement increases the rate of neck-arching so that neck-arching is more likely to be occurring at the moment of the next delivery of a noncontingent reinforcer. If two or three such reinforcements occur, unusual habit patterns develop. Perhaps the baseball player with a variety of largely unnecessary behaviors—tapping his spikes, tugging his cap, shifting his shoulders, and doing a variety of things with his bat—is one of the most extreme examples of how certain behaviors increase in frequency after being noncontingently reinforced by successful turns at bat.

C 9A.15. *Noncontingent reinforcement.*

In noncontingent reinforcement, the target behavior _____ .

a. is not followed by reinforcement

b. is followed by reinforcement

c. is suppressed by the contingent delivery of an aversive stimulus

In noncontingent reinforcement, the target behavior _____ .

a. is increased in rate   b. is unaffected in rate   c. is decreased in rate

It can be stated that, in noncontingent reinforcement, the target behavior _____ .

a. did not actually produce the reinforcer

b. produced the reinforcer

c. eliminated the reinforcer

An increase in the rate of the target behavior through noncontingent reinforcement _____ increase the number of reinforcers gained over subsequent periods.

    a. will   b. will not

Token Economies

As we have previously shown, when we wish to reinforce a behavior we may do so by delivering a primary reinforcer, some form of social reinforcer, or perhaps a token reinforcer. The latter, as you will recall, is some kind of tangible object that has no value except that it may be redeemed for "back-up" reinforcers which may themselves be primary reinforcers, money, or some other meaningful reinforcer. We generally differentiate between a *token system*, in which a relatively few target behaviors are selected for token reinforcement and a relatively small number of back-up reinforcers are available, and a *token economy*. A token economy operates much as a real economy does in society; that is, practically everything that is necessary or desirable can be gained only through token exchange, and a wide variety of desirable behavior patterns are reinforced with tokens. In general, token economies are found on some mental hospital wards, in some residential institutions for the retarded, and in some classrooms for disturbed children, although few have been established in public-school classrooms and similar settings.

The token economy is a very powerful tool by which psychologists can bring under control severely deviant behaviors—both behavior excesses and behavior deficits. A child may wish to resist the rules of the "system" and may do so with a fair degree of success in most classrooms and in many other settings. In the token economy, however, he rapidly learns that he is merely defeating himself if he does not conform to teacher expectations in his disciplinary patterns and work output.

Token reinforcement in the classroom is a somewhat controversial topic, and it is easy to imagine that unethical controllers might be in a position to use tokens to influence others unfairly. You may even question the general idea of developing conformity in children's behaviors. Let us explore this issue for a moment. First, in the types of institutions where token economies are usually put to use, there is generally a watchful public eye looking over both the operations and the objectives. If an institution's director seems to be pursuing questionable goals with those under his control, it is likely that he will be quickly removed from his position.

Second, on the general matter of conformity there is certainly a good side, as well as a bad, to conforming. The good aspects of conformity pertain to those behaviors directed toward achievement and gaining the approval of others. By definition, the opposite sorts of behaviors are self-defeating. It is probably a cruel jest to encourage or even allow youngsters to develop self-defeating patterns of nonconforming behaviors when we are aware of techniques that can easily remediate those patterns.

Advantages of Tokens Tokens have a number of advantages over other systems of reinforcement.

(1) If one gives a plain plastic poker chip or almost any other popular form of token item, there is *no distraction* effect, as the students do not stop to read them as they might comic books, or eat them as they might candy.

(2) Tokens *do not satiate* the organism, as might primary reinforcers.

(3) Tokens *do not extinguish* so long as back-up reinforcers are available, as might be the result with social reinforcers given alone.

(4) *Rate of administration* of tokens is *adjustable,* as the program director is usually able to adjust pay-off rates as he gains information about task difficulty.

(5) Tokens may be *redeemed flexibly,* as the program director adjusts prices to reflect supply and demand.

(6) Tokens *may be given immediately* upon the behavior's occurrence, to avoid the delay of reinforcement effect.

(7) Tokens can usually *reach* a number of children who are *unresponsive to social reinforcers.*

(8) Finally, an advantage that is related to the last-mentioned one is that use of tokens, if done properly, can *develop a sensitivity* to the existence of *behavior-reinforcement contingenices.*

The seventh advantage cited above should be elaborated further. A number of children, particularly the severely maladjusted and retarded, are relatively unreachable through the use of approval and other positive forms of attention delivered by adults. This can usually be traced to their developmental history, since some children have had almost consistently negative experiences with adults whenever those adults began to notice them. Also, in many families, approval of the children has almost never occurred, so that approval could not have developed as a conditioned social reinforcer for those children. As a program director dispenses tokens, which have a redeemable value for the child, he should attempt to dramatically pair the delivery of the token with praise for what the child has done. In this manner, over a period of time, a child usually begins to be responsive to adults' attention and approval, even when they are used without further rewards. That is, the program director has *conditioned* approval, within the classical conditioning model, into becoming a social reinforcer.

C 9A.16. *Token systems.*

In a setting where relatively few behaviors are reinforced with tokens and the tokens can be exchanged

for relatively few things, we call the procedure a _____ .

    a. token system   b. token economy

In a token program, the objects or privileges than can be redeemed with tokens are called _____ .

    a. back-up reinforcers   b. redemption processes   c. token objects

You should be able to recognize, from a list presented, some of the actual versus some false advantages

of token programs. Be prepared to do so.

Types of
Token Redemptions
Token economies depend largely upon the ingenuity of the program director. There are a number of very complex formats of token economies in existence, and only a few of the various strategies can be mentioned here. In one residential treatment center for delinquent children, tokens are given for a variety of behaviors, beginning with making beds in the mornings, sweeping the area, putting away clothing, dressing appropriately, keeping neat and clean, going to classes punctually, and rendering the proper classwork. In that particular setting the tokens can be redeemed for a wide variety of privileges.

Some of the older children are highly motivated by being given purchase access to cigarettes, and only tokens can buy them. Desserts after meals may also require tokens, as do visits to town, access to an individual TV set, and individual rooms which are rented by the week as an alternative to barracks-style living arrangements. In one particular setting, students "graduate" through four separate levels, with each level allowing a wider variety of back-up reinforcers. Any individual who runs away from the institutional setting has to go back to the beginning level upon his return, which is an effective technique to discourage potential run-aways.

Even the U.S. Army has experimented with a type of token economy and has found it extremely workable. A basic training program in California reversed the traditional demerit system, where privileges are taken away, in favor of a more positive approach. Inspections of barracks areas resulted in tokens being given to those individuals who had performed at or above standard. Success on the rifle range, proficiency during other aspects of training, and even promptness to formations all resulted in a trainee receiving tokens. The trainees were allowed a variety of privileges contingent upon having the tokens to purchase them. A relatively small number of tokens allowed a trainee to leave the area to go to the post exchange, and larger costs were associated with obtaining weekend passes and other major advantages. In this system a trainee could even buy his way out of certain assigned duties which might be personally aversive. At the end of one full year of experimentation with token rewards for positive behaviors, the Fort Commandant concluded that the method had been demonstrated to be superior to the traditional demerit system in terms of performance on training activities, morale as reflected on questionnaires and by rates of AWOL, etc.

PUNISHMENT
A considerable body of literature exists on the subject of punishment. While punishment is not the modification procedure of choice in most behavior modification settings, there are still a sizable number of known factors associated with its effectiveness and occasional lack of effectiveness.

Punishment is usually defined as the delivery of an aversive stimulus contingent upon the emission of some operant behavior. The resulting drop in response rate is called *suppression*. This term should be clearly understood in contrast to extinction, since both pertain to behavioral decreases.

The most obvious functional relationships in punishment, as we stated in Chapter 9, are between the degree of suppression and the factors of intensity and immediacy of punishment. A wide variety of punishers have been used in research which shows that intense punishment results in a greater degree of behavioral suppression than does moderate punishment, and moderate punishment in turn suppresses behavior more than does mild punishment. Also punishment should come *immediately* after the emission of the behavior. The longer it is delayed, the less suppressive effect it has, and only a few seconds delay causes the punishment to be virtually useless as a suppressor. In fact, the delay of punishment gradient looks remarkably like the delay of reinforcement gradient. To illustrate this, consider how one goes about training a puppy in what is generally termed "housebreaking." Most people keep a watchful eye on a new puppy, following it around with a rolled-up newspaper, and delivering a swat whenever the puppy makes a puddle where it is not supposed to. This, coupled with immediately taking the pup to the papers he is supposed to use, usually results in very rapid housebreaking.

I know of one family, however, that had a much more casual approach to housebreaking. They acquired a small female beagle dog as a puppy, but were quite inconsistent in their attempts to housebreak it. Both the husband and wife worked during the days, and the dog therefore was left alone indoors for considerable periods of time; nor did the owners appear to give the animal much watchful attention when they were at home. As a result the dog became adult without becoming housebroken, and as you might expect, she had managed to soil or ruin a number of carpets and other furnishings. One day when the dog was more than a year old, she made her puddle squarely in view of the husband of the family, whereupon she was seized by the nape of the neck and hurled directly through the open window and through the screening out into the yard. The dog never again made a puddle in the house. It is likely that the husband's act was the first occasion when immediate and intense punishment had followed the act of wetting on the floor.

Yet another functional relationship exists between the sudden (versus gradual) delivery of the ultimate level of aversive stimulation and the degree of suppression. It has been found that subjects, human and animal alike, can tolerate fairly high levels of aversive stimulation without a dramatic suppression effect if the stimuli slowly escalate to their ultimate level. The parent who disciplines a small child with mild scolding, then moderate scolding, then harsh scolding along with mild physical punishment, then moderate physical punishment, then more intense physical punishment may wonder why the punishment seems to have little permanent effect. If the first punishment of the behavior, after an initial "caution," were to have been fairly intense, however, the behavior would more likely have been suppressed.

Let us briefly examine some of the possible disadvantages of the use of punishment in educational, institutional, and other settings. There is currently a considerable degree of research interest, among operant psychologists, in the disadvantages of punishment, resulting in the fact that certain values of punishment are often neglected.

First, punishment tends only to suppress an undesirable behavior.

Suppression, in contrast to extinction, is often a transient affair. That is, suppression lasts only until a relatively high state of drive brings the behavior out into the open again—the reflex reserve phenomenon discussed earlier. Extinguished behaviors do not show this tendency to come back. In qualification, it should be pointed out that the tendency for suppressed behavior to re-emerge under high drive conditions is clearly apparent only where the previous punishment was mild or moderate. As punishment intensities increase, it appears that suppression may be more permanent.

As an example of the re-emergence of suppressed behavior, let us choose an everyday example of children playing in a group. You are probably familiar with the fact that many undesirable and previously punished behaviors of children continue to be suppressed during times when the child is engaged in isolated play, or even in play with one other child. When the child is involved in large-group play, however, his level of excitement increases, and he may then ignore the painfully learned lessons from earlier times. This is simply the emergence of suppressed behavior as the drive level (with social origins in this case) increases.

A second disadvantage of punishment is that, in itself, it gives no information about correct behavior. Put another way, punishing a behavior tells the child that what he has done is *not* right, but it does not tell the child what *is* right. A pathetic example of this phenomenon is the child of less-than-average intelligence who, after working very hard on a theme, receives a grade of F. This is punishment, and the child may readily understand that the theme was not good, but he does not understand what he should have done instead. If punishment is to be effective, the environment should be arranged with information that guides the individual into alternative behavior patterns that will then lead to success and reinforcement. This very important principle is frequently overlooked, with the result that training attempts that stress punishment sometimes fail.

A third disadvantage to punishment is that one often sees an effect called *generalized suppression*. This simply means that, for a period of time following punishment, the organism stops doing anything. In a laboratory rat on a shock grid this takes the form of "freezing" in position between shocks, making no leaping attempts to escape. In a school child, severely punished for some action, the child may stop doing assigned work, stop volunteering answers to questions, or even stop interacting spontaneously with other children. Generalized suppression has not been extensively investigated, but it would appear to be mainly a result of sudden and extremely aversive punishment with escape not easily achieved.

Other disadvantages to the use of punishment were discussed in Chapter 9, and you should bear in mind the problems that can develop after a child associates a number of stimuli in a certain setting with the frequent punishments received there. Fears of people, of situations, and even the broad attitudes individuals hold toward various social institutions can be molded within such conditions.

One of the interesting aspects of punishment concerns an apparent paradox between the typically suppressive effects of punishment and the seemingly masochistic characteristics of some individuals who appear to enjoy pain, or at least who frequently seem to get themselves into situations where pain is a result (and we could be speaking of "emotional" suffering as well as physical). Examination of cases reveals that a large number of such individuals, after "accidentally" getting hurt or even inflicting seemingly deliberate pain upon themselves, receive positive reinforcement in the form of the attention, sympathy, and concern of others.

Of contemporary interest are the writings of Eric Berne, who comments on the "games people play." The type of person we have been discussing is playing the game of "see what you made me do!" Not infrequently we encounter individuals whose reinforcement histories have shaped them into extreme cases of self-inflictive harm. In addition to the obvious concern of others that can reinforce the suicidal gesture, three individual cases come to mind as examples of this pattern.

One intelligent young woman was involved in a series of automobile accidents, all of which occurred shortly after quarrels with her fiancé. The consequence of each such event was that the young man rushed to the young woman as soon as he heard the news, and a newly established relationship of concern and affection was the inevitable result.

In another case, an estranged husband was in the habit of calling his wife from highway taverns in the after-midnight hours, and in a slightly intoxicated condition would imply that he would drive to a distant town as fast as his car would travel (and probably would be involved in a wreck) if he were not re-accepted by his wife. Usually the wife then re-accepted him for a day or two, which served as a reinforcer and caused the continuation of such behaviors.

In the third case, a male university student was in the habit, after serious quarrels or break-ups with his girl friend, of "failing" examinations and skipping all classes because he "could not concentrate." This behavior typically caused the girl to feel guilt and anguish, and she usually contacted her boy friend to smooth things over and thereby keep him from academic disaster.

You should recognize, in all these cases, that positive reinforcement was given to behavior patterns that were first established in early childhood. At such ages children often receive sympathy and affection from parents when they hurt themselves. You should recognize that (1) the individuals behaving in such ways may *feel* sincere in their emotional involvement, in that they may not "deliberately" use the behaviors in a cool and calculating manner to manipulate others, and (2) such patterns can persist for a significant amount of time within an inter-relationship between two people even if one *does not* reinforce the other. In such cases, the *entire reinforcement history* — not just current success in manipulating people — maintains the pattern and makes extinction prolonged.

The management of self-threat or self-inflicted harm is an interesting topic within the field of behavior modification. Some judgments must of course be made, in cases of "upset fiancés" and the like, of the actual likelihood of serious self-harm. While it is usually the best policy to refrain from reinforcing manipulatory behaviors, mental health professionals should be consulted in cases of likely suicide.

One type of self-inflicted pain is the sort sometimes encountered in institutionalized children. Often severe self-injury occurs in populations of retarded or psychotic individuals, and usually one can observe the concern of the staff members who rush to aid and calm the child, and thereby reinforce the behavior. Still, the fact of institutionalization sometimes allows suppression of the behavior in highly effective ways which utilize electric shock or other aversive stimuli.

In behavior therapy programs with schizophrenic children—a group that typically is difficult to remediate—some dramatic results were found in using punishment to suppress self-inflicted pain. The researcher in one case attached shock electrodes to the children, and whenever they harmed themselves he would deliver contingent shock.

Let us examine the plight of such children. One typical individual in the group so treated was in the habit of striking himself in the face repeatedly with his fists, so that he was constantly black and blue from the blows. These blows were extremely severe, and unless the child was restrained they tended to recur at a high rate throughout the day. Over the years this child had developed severe enlargement of the ear cartilage, and there were numerous disfiguring scars on the face. The child was beginning to lose vision in both eyes as a result of eye-tissue damage.

Now we might ask, "Why does not the pain from the blows suppress their reoccurrence?" The answer to this question has been very difficult to unravel. Clinicians have preferred to continue to use the suppressive advantage of contingent electric shock without exactly understanding why the shock works.

In one explanatory experiment, a number of college students were asked to be volunteers in an experiment involving electric shock. Using the subjects as their own controls, they were passed through two conditions. In one condition, the students pressed a button and thereby delivered shock to themselves. In the other condition they signaled to the experimenter that they were "ready" for the next shock. In both conditions a control device started the shocks at a very low intensity and shock intensity was gradually built up to the point at which the subjects decided that they could not continue. It was found that in the self-delivered shock condition subjects could endure a significantly higher ultimate level of shock than in the other-delivered shock condition—4.6 milliamperes versus 3.6 milliamperes—(Vernon, 1969).

The conclusion was that *self-inflicted* pain, for undetermined reasons, is considerably *less aversive* than the same apparent intensity of pain inflicted by another. This finding explains why contingent electric shock of moderate intensity can suppress self-inflicted pain that would at first appear to have equal or stronger aversive properties.

C 9A.17. *Punishment theory.*

State three functional relationships that hold between punishment and the degree of behavioral suppression:

1. _____ .

2. _____ .

3. _____ .

A disadvantage of the use of punishment (at least where the intensity is mild or moderate) is that under

conditions of _____ suppressed behavior tends to re-emerge.

    a. extinction   b. generalization   c. high drive

A disadvantage of the use of punishment is that punishment as it typically is used gives no _____ .

    a. concurrent reinforcement   b. opportunity to escape

    c. information about what is the correct behavior

An almost-total withholding of behavior of all sorts in situations in which intense punishment has previ-

ously been used is called _____ _____ .

Individuals sometimes make themselves vulnerable to harm because of their history of - - - reinforcement

when hurt, with other people's - - - serving as the reinforcer. _____ .

    a. positive/sympathy   b. negative/punishment

It appears that which of the following is the more aversive, stimulus levels being equal? _____ .

    a. self-inflicted pain   b. pain inflicted by another person

CONDITIONABILITY

In our examination of the variables that affect the degree of conditioning, we must not disregard the factor of individual conditionability. Conditionability seems to be due to characteristics of the central nervous system, hence is considered to be an O-variable, but there is not nearly as great a correlation between conditionability and what we term "intelligence"—phylogenetic or within species—as we might at first assume.

One research project into conditionability began in Canada, where Mahut (1958) tested reactivity to stimuli in 202 dogs of ten breeds. Certain breeds, especially poodles, collies, and German shepherds, were much more reactive to stimuli, and therefore potentially conditionable, than were other breeds, particularly the terriers. In related research it has been fairly well established that alert, excitable dogs condition more quickly than do those we usually visualize as being slow and easy-going, such as several types of hounds.

Human beings also exhibit wide differences in conditionability. In extreme cases, low conditionability might be the result of brain damage which limits the individual's ability to process information and thus make the associations necessary for conditioning. But beyond that, there seems to be a great deal of individual variation that appears to have a hereditary basis.

Speculation exists that adult behavior patterns, even to the extent of one's central personality characteristics, in some cases may relate to conditionability. One such pattern is that of a certain type of criminal personality that does not seem to "profit" from experiences of punishment. Research in penitentiary settings indicates that certain such individuals, strangely, do not seem to be very conditionable. Theoretically, we might hypothesize that, as children, these people were not conditioned, and hence sensitized to punishment contingencies, even though perhaps exposed to "normal" parental discipline and typical punishment for wrongdoings. We comment on further research into this topic, briefly, in Chapter 14.

Some individuals seem extremely sensitive to primary positive reinforcers, and as a consequence show high rates of behaviors that represent various "indulgences." Thus, in one study, persons who indicated a greater-than-average degree of personal pleasure from eating (and a large number of these individuals were overweight) also, on the average, indicated a greater-than-average amount of pleasure in sexual relations and various other appetitive indulgences. It would appear that some persons are simply more inclined to experience pleasure from the satisfaction of primary drives; perhaps this phenomenon is determined by differences in the neurological structure within and around the brain's hypothalamic regions.

There is some question as to whether conditionability might be further subdivided. In addition to ordinary conditionability, there is data to suggest that there may be certain individuals who, relatively, are extremely susceptible to the influence of negative reinforcement, and this has been proposed as a possible determinant of alcoholism. At any rate, this and similar interpretations are more fully discussed in Chapter 14. At this point we might merely say that individuals with high levels of anxiety seem particularly responsive to any reduction in the level of experienced tension. Thus, when they ingest alcohol and thereby temporarily relieve their anxieties, they are much more highly reinforced for drinking than is the average individual.

On another dimension, Eysenck, a British pyschologist, has associated the factor of conditionability to the human personality characteristic we term *introversion*. Like the breeds of dogs that are extremely sensitive to stimuli, it would appear that introverts are highly conditionable, while extroverts, perhaps because they are less aware of stimuli, do not as easily develop conditioned associations.

C 9A.18. *Conditionability.*

After fairly comparable conditioning histories, we may see that a given individual is more strongly conditioned than another. This is presumably due to _____ variable.

    a. an organismic   b. a stimulus   c. a response

The variable just mentioned is _____ .

    a. responsiveness   b. sensitivity   c. conditionability

A typical pattern seems to be that people who are highly responsive to "appetitive" pleasures are _____ responsive to other appetitive indulgences than are most other persons.

    a. more   b. less

Eysenck has linked conditionability to the personality characteristic of _____ .

    a. psychoticism   b. introversion   c. extraversion

**THEORIES OF
REINFORCEMENT**

Many years ago a famous educational psychologist named Thorndike stated the original law of effect. If a behavior leads to "pleasant" results, the behavioral habit is "stamped in," and if it leads to "unpleasant" results it is "stamped out" of an organism. According to such language, it would seem that *pleasure* underlies the phenomenon of reinforcement. Since that time several major positions have emerged to "explain" reinforcement.

**Need Reduction
Interpretation**

One of the most popular positions, at least up to a few years ago, is called the *need reduction law of effect.* This interpretation holds that a primary reinforcer is reinforcing because it reduces a need.

Interestingly, about 98 percent of research into learning is consistent with the need reduction interpretation in the sense that the reinforcers used *do* seem relevant to a need. When animals are thirsty, and a certain behavior leads to water and a consequent reduction in thirst, the water functions as a reinforcer and the relevant behavior is strengthened. With aversive drives, such as the sort produced by the delivery of electric shock, any behavior that eliminates or reduces the intensity of the ongoing shock is reinforced—also consistent with an interpretation involving biological needs. Certain contradictions begin to appear, however. For example, when an animal takes a turn in the *T*-maze and encounters a sexually receptive animal of the opposite sex, but is immediately removed, the typical result is that the animal thereafter tends to turn in that direction. The need reduction interpretation would have predicted that only a reduction of need could increase the frequency of the turn. Also, there is abundant evidence that human beings sometimes deliberately seek out stimulation which is need and drive *in*ducing rather than reducing. If we elect to go on a roller coaster ride or watch a horror movie on television, this tends to increase drive, yet the activities seem reinforcing.

Another problem is derived from the fact that need reduction could not *literally* take place within a second or two (in terms of blood sugar elevations, etc.), and so the need reduction interpretation is inconsistent with the delay of reinforcement effect. In order to investigate this, dogs have been prepared for laboratory research by having a tube divert all consumed water from the mouth out an opening in the throat to the outside of the body. These animals also can have their stomachs directly loaded with food or water by the experimenter, bypassing the mouth entirely. The results from this type of research are not absolutely clear. First, it appears that the animals are reinforced, to a degree, by consuming water, even though it does not enter the stomach. At least the water serves as a reward, as evidenced by the fact that the behavior that produced the water is strengthened. On the other hand, the direct loading of the stomach with the food or water also appears to have a certain degree of reinforcement value. That is, even though the animal has not "drunk" his reward, he will again emit the behavior that previously led to the direct stomach loading. This latter fact appears to give some support to the need reduction interpretation, while the former fact seems to refute it. Few psychologists at the present time emphasize need reduction in their own interpretations of the basis for reinforcement.

Hedonistic Interpretation

A second major form of the law of effect is the *hedonistic interpretation*. The hedonistic form of the law of effect is a statement that certain events are reinforcing because they give an organism pleasure. The hedonistic approach assumes that organisms are motivated by pleasure and by the avoidance of discomfort. This is a reasonably sound approach which contains far fewer contradictions in actual data than does the drive reduction point of view. We can imagine how the satisfaction of primary drives gives pleasure to the organism. Food and water are pleasant to consume and sexual arousal without drive reduction would, by this criterion, be called pleasurable.

As we have indicated, there is little inconsistency of the hedonistic interpretation with the various research data that we said largely discount the need reduction interpretation. Even the delay of reinforcement effect is consistent, since pleasure and displeasure would occur immediately upon experiencing or consuming the goal object. Objection to the hedonistic interpretation comes, rather, from a different source. At a largely philosophic level, many observers have considered the reinforcement effects in organisms that are, neurologically, extremely primitive. When a tiny worm that swims in water can be reinforced by dimming a bright light, and the direction of his swimming thus influenced, it may be questionable whether the organism is sophisticated to the point that it can *experience* mentalistic pleasure. The experience of such a cognitive quality simply could not take place (the critics say) in an organism with only a few memory cells and no "brain" as we usually understand the term. Psychologists who informally use language suggesting a hedonistic interpretation are quite numerous, but as a formal position espoused by recognized theorists, the interpretation is unpopular.

Activation Level Interpretation

A third formal position is the *activation level interpretation*. This interpretation holds that the level of activation of the neurological system mediates the reinforcement function. The activation level law of effect is rather complicated, so we will present it only in a very simple form. Briefly, it holds that every organism has some optimum level of neurological activation. Activation, as we stated in Chapter 7, is a variable conceptualized in terms of electrochemical activity in the central nervous system. Optimum activation levels for individuals differ, due to variations in their inherited biological structures, damage to the central nervous system, or for some other reason. Then, so the theory goes, something like this occurs: Let us assume that an individual has been in a very dull environment for several hours. Very little has taken place that is stimulating or interesting. The individual's brain circuitry is relatively inactive. He is bored, may get drowsy, and we would say that he is at a *low* level of activation. Suppose a second individual has had a hectic day. He has been hurrying, his pulse rate and blood pressure have been high all day, and he is feeling emotionally drained. His activation level is quite high. In essence, the activation level interpretation holds that any time the consequence of a behavior is a change in the activation level *in the direction of the optimum level,* that activity is reinforced. So, if the bored individual goes to a certain place and has a good time, he subsequently is more likely to return to that place. And, when the individual comes home after a hectic day, whatever behaviors are successful in relaxing him, and may thereby return the activation level to a near-optimum point, are reinforced and become habits.

One small qualification to the previous statement must be added. Staying at a *single level* of activation, even if that level is the usual "optimum" level, eventually becomes aversive. Under those circumstances any movement away from the point at which the organism has been fixed for so long is reinforcing, and then after a period of time, movement back toward the optimum point is again reinforcing. This qualification was added to explain the behaviors of the people who "have everything," in terms of comforts and amusements, and yet enjoy occasional short periods of excitement, hardship, or stress.

One of the interesting phenomena that supports an activation level interpretation of reinforcement, and in some ways a hedonistic interpretation as well, began with the research of James Olds and Peter Milner (1954). Rats were prepared with microelectrodes implanted in the septal area (adjacent to the hypothalamus) of their brains, through which tiny electrical currents of a half-second duration could be delivered. The animals could deliver their own stimulation by pressing a bar. The vast majority of the animals showed a dramatic development. Once they had pressed the bar and received the stimulus, they continued to press at a rapid rate until exhausted. When recovered they resumed stimulating themselves. Central stimulation (called that because the stimulation is directly to the CNS) took precedence even over the primary needs, so that hungry and thirsty animals spent more time stimulating themselves than eating or drinking. An interpretation of the effect was that psychologists finally had discovered the spot at which activation of the neurological structure *was* reinforcement. A hedonistic interpretation held that "pleasure" and accompanying activation eventuates in activation of that particular area, and that central stimulation simply bypasses the pleasure stage. Such "pleasure centers" have been located in similar structural locations in several other species, including man (Bishop et al., 1963).

Empirical Interpretation

One of the popular positions these days concerning the law of effect is sometimes referred to as the *empirical law of effect*. The empirical interpretation simply recognizes as fact that certain stimuli such as food and shock can influence behavior rates, and it attempts to discover appropriate functional relationships, but it does not attempt to explain why. The statement by Thorndike of the original law of effect was largely of this sort. Thorndike's statement was simply that acts are fixed or eliminated as functions of their effects. He also said that acts followed by a state of affairs which the individual does not avoid, and which he often tries to preserve or attain, are fixed, while acts followed by states of affairs which the individual avoids or attempts to change are eliminated. As you can see, there is no explanation of why the law of effect should hold, although in some of his minor publications Thorndike used such expressions as "pleasant" and "unpleasant." The psychologists who are the most active in operant laboratory research at this time generally subscribe to an empirical interpretation of the law of effect.

Many operant psychologists are less concerned with the theory of reinforcement than they are with the technologies of behavioral change that can be developed in applied settings. Still, a little reflection will show that a better knowledge of why reinforcers are reinforcing might open up radically new approaches that could have far-reaching effects.

C 9A.19. *Theories of reinforcement.*

A modern version of the law of effect emphasizes that most primary reinforcers seem to be relevant to needs. This is the _____ _____ interpretation.

A modern version of the law of effect emphasizing consummatory responding and using words like "pleasure" is the _____ interpretation.

A modern version of the law of effect emphasizing neurological arousal is the _____ _____ interpretation.

A modern version of the law of effect that simply catalogs the reinforcing effects of various stimuli, with no attempt to explain *why* reinforcers have a reinforcing effect, is the _____ interpretation.

Would the discussed experiments using sex-drive relevant stimuli seem to support or discredit the need reduction interpretation? _____ .

a. Support   b. Discredit

Would our knowledge of the delay of reinforcement effect seem to be consistent or inconsistent with the need reduction interpretation? _____ .

a. Consistent   b. Inconsistent

Would our knowledge of the delay of reinforcement effect seem to be consistent or inconsistent with the hedonistic interpretation? _____ .

a. Consistent   b. Inconsistent

Would our observations that many individuals deliberately seek out stress and "fear" stimulating situations seem to support or discredit the activation level interpretation? _____ .

a. Support   b. Discredit

PROGRESS CHECK   9A.3

1. The Premack Principle states that - - - behavior can be reinforced if the opportunity to engage in

   - - - behavior is contingent upon the emission of - - - behavior. _____ .

   a. high-rate/pleasurable/approved

   b. low-rate/high-rate/low-rate

   c. correct/pleasurable/low-rate

2. In noncontingent reinforcement _____ .

   a. the target behavior rate is increased

   b. the target behavior does not produce the reinforcer

   c. unusual habits can develop

   d. all of the above

MATCH: _____ 3. Back-up reinforcer

            _____ 4. Token economy

            _____ 5. Token system

A. Everything is gained only through token exchange

B. A few special favors can be redeemed with tokens

C. An object or privilege that is redeemable with tokens

6. Which is *not* a disadvantage of punishment? _____ .

   a. No information is given about correct behavior

   b. Under high-drive conditions suppressed behavior is likely to re-emerge

   c. Harsh punishment must often be used to achieve lasting suppression

   d. All of the above are disadvantages of punishment

   e. None of the above are disadvantages of punishment

7. Generalized suppression is _____ .

   a. caused by self-inflicted pain

   b. an almost total withholding of behavior

   c. the total withholding of reinforcers

8. Conditionability is _____ .

   a. an organismic variable   b. characteristic of extraversion   c. both of the preceding

MATCH: ———— 9. Need reduction interpretation

———— 10. Hedonistic interpretation

———— 11. Empirical interpretation

———— 12. Activation interpretation

A. Emphasizes neurological arousal

B. Emphasizes pleasure and avoidance of discomfort

C. Emphasizes relevance of reinforcers to primary drives

D. Catalogs reinforcing effects

SUMMARY We have devoted three full chapters to the basic manifestations of the phenomenon known as conditioning. This is largely because these chapters reflect perhaps the most rapidly developing and influential approach in the field of psychology in this decade. Also, you will see how these concepts will be applied in the topic areas of social processes, personality, and psychopathology in later chapters.

We have taken a great deal of space to indicate a variety of factors that can influence behavior patterns. We can inventory what we have discussed in the following listing of behavioral paradigms. Please bear in mind that in practically all cases of behavior, with the possible exception of certain intellectually motivated or "anticipatory" human patterns, the paradigm to explain behavioral occurrence and change should be represented below.

I. Respondent Behavior
   A. *UCS—R* (unconditioned respondent patterns)
     1. appetitive (approach) emotional orientation
     2. aversive (away from) emotional orientation
     3. aversive (attack) emotional orientation
   B. Adaptation to *UCS*
   CS—R (classical conditioning)
     1. appetitive (approach) emotional orientation
     2. aversive (away from) emotional orientation
     3. aversive (attack) emotional orientation
   D. Extinction
   E. Counterconditioning
   F. Stimulus generalization *(CS'—CR')*
   G. Higher order conditioning
   H. Generalization of extinction
II. Operant Behavior
   A. *R*
     1. Random *R*
     2. Imitative *R*

B. Operant conditioning (R—*S*)
    1. Random *R—S*
        a. positive reinforcement
            i. primary reinforcement
            ii. conditioned reinforcement
        b. negative reinforcement
            i. primary reinforcement
            ii. conditioned reinforcement
C. Extinction of operant behavior
D. Suppression
E. Discriminative conditioning
F. Chaining
G. Shaping

As you can see, items E, F, and G under Operant Behavior in the listing may overlap with categories under item B.

If you would be proficient at analysis of behavior in reinforcement terminology, we recommend that you attempt to explain to yourself what factors have established and may be maintaining the various behaviors with which you come in contact during each day. It is one thing to work at grasping certain definitions and a few examples, and quite another to be at ease and immediately familiar with concepts. Behaviors of organisms, normal or abnormal, can be observed and speculated upon almost by the minute if you seek them out. Only in this way can you achieve spontaneity in the terminology of behavior theory.

If you have further interest in the sorts of topics developed within Chapters 8 and 9, bear in mind that many psychology departments have developed specific operant emphases in different class sections of experimental psychology, and it is possible that your school may offer a section with a conditioning orientation. Also, courses with titles such as "Experimental Analysis of Behavior" and "Behavior Modification" develop out of what you have been studying.

For further reading we recommend *A Primer of Operant Conditioning*, by Reynolds (1968), *Motivating Children: Behavior Modification in the Classroom*, by Vernon (1972), *Behavior Therapy in Clinical Psychiatry*, by Meyer and Chesser (1970) and, for edited readings, *Control of Human Behavior: Volumes* I, II, and III (1966, 1970, and 1974) by Ulrich, Stachnik, and Mabry, and *Behavior Modification in Clinical Psychology*, by Neuringer and Michael (1970).

Social Processes: Ethological and Social Learning Viewpoints

THE STUDY OF ANIMAL SOCIETIES
"Natural" Social Tendencies
Simple Dyadic Tendencies
Unfamiliarity
Behavioral Dissimilarity
Proximity in Space
Higher Physical Positions
The Status Hierarchy
The Effects of Familiarity Within the Hierarchy

SOCIALIZATION VERSUS ISOLATION

AN EXPERIMENTAL ANALYSIS OF AGGRESSION
Types of Aggression
Natural Elicitors of Aggression
Frustration
Sexual Privileges
Territorial Intrusion
Aggressive Display
The Posture Variable
Pain
Learned Patterns of Aggression
Positive Reinforcement of Aggression
Negative Reinforcement of Aggression
Imitative Aggression
Punishment of Aggression
Classically Conditioned Aggression

THE EXPERIMENTAL ANALYSIS OF OTHER SOCIAL PATTERNS

HUMAN INTERPERSONAL RESPONSE PATTERNS
Roles and Cultures

CONCLUSION

For most of you reading this chapter, you will have just completed Chapter 10 which examines the nature of social processes in uniquely human situations. As noted in that chapter, the approach used there is most characteristic of social psychologists. A whole separate approach to the topic of basic social behavior exists, however.

Many researchers, most of them associated with areas of biology, study the processes involved in animal social behavior. It is their assumption that animal social processes provide the very foundation of any consideration of why human beings behave in the ways they do. This basic approach is often termed *ethology*. "Ethology" in turn is defined by Scott (1967) as "evolutionary psychology." What this actually means is that the investigators view patterns of animal behavior in terms of adaptability and the survival function, and attention is given to processes analogous to known human social processes. Understandably, such an approach is easily meshed with research which stresses modification of behavior through experience (classical and operant conditioning), and it is not unusual to see overlapping interests in a given animal behavior researcher.

Some teachers, especially those who share an operant emphasis, may have you read the present chapter before you start Chapter 10. Whatever the sequence, however, you should emerge with an increased awareness that the individual, regardless of his inner urgencies and self-direction, is influenced in the majority of his behaviors by the presence and the actions of those around him.

THE STUDY OF ANIMAL SOCIETIES   Our first interest shall be in an examination of social patterns in animal communities. Sometimes the reason for reliance on lower organisms as sources of data is not well understood by the student. We are asked, "Why not just study human beings?" We have already, to some degree, presented answers to this question.

We see in animals the basic unembellished fabric of organismic variables in interaction with obvious, visible environmental factors. We like to interpret the outcomes as reflecting *basic tendencies* of organisms, and we are vitally interested in the possible *continuity* of these tendencies between and among species. If continuity is found, particularly among phylogenetic levels near the level of man (for example, the primates), we then interpret the behaviors as being *basic patterns* that may generalize to man and allow us to understand him better. J. P. Scott, a leading expert in the study of animal behavior, says: "If it is found that a statement is true of a very large proportion of all species studied, it is correct to assume that the same statement is very likely true of human beings and that it concerns an important and basic element in human behavior [Scott, 1972, p. 4]." The prevailing interpretation of such generalization treats the discovered principles as representing a broad motivational under-structure in man, which itself may be modified by social learning characteristics and cultural processes. Man's inclinations to follow his basic behavioral tendencies still exist, it is argued, and this has led, recently, to great interest, even outside the academic community, in the writings of such men as Lorenz (*On Aggression,* 1966), Desmond Morris (*The Naked Ape,* 1967) and Ardrey (*The Territorial Imperative,* 1966). These books, slanted to the layman, are suggested for those wishing to pursue the subject at the popular reading level.

Another reason for research with infrahuman organisms is that the human being has a relatively long life-span. Many variables relating to the molding of social processes conceptually would require application of conditions to the young of a species, who would then be examined, during adulthood, for indications that their adult behavior might have been affected by the early experiences. It would be impractical to test many notions using human children because of the length of life factor. Many favored research species have much shorter relative developmental and total life spans.

The last stated reason, of course, suggests another that we have already treated in previous discussions. It is that many independent variables that we would have an interest in are, potentially, harmful to human beings. We would be quite reluctant to deliberately inflict harmful conditions on human subjects.

C 10A.1. *The use of animals in the study of social processes.*

One prime reason for the use of animals in psychological research is that patterns are considered

generalizable to man if and when _____ .

a. they are found in a large proportion of species studied

b. they clearly serve the evolutionary function

c. they are found in the most basic, lowest (phylogenetically) species

d. they do not fall within the "instinct" grouping

Animals are favored in developmental studies where the effects of experiences when young are studied in relation to later adult-behavior patterns. In this area the preference for animal subjects relates to _____ .

a. their more complex social environment

b. the natural mothering patterns in lower species

c. animals' typical shorter developmental spans and life spans

Animals are definitely preferred subjects where the _____ .

a. dependent variable is difficult to predict

b. independent variable is potentially harmful

c. correlated variables are unknown

"Natural" Social Tendencies   A large number of behavioral tendencies of human beings, matched by parallel tendencies in many lower species, are easily explainable in terms of evolutionary development. The tendency of man to live in groups, for example, has its counterpart in many animal societies. Examination of the life patterns of all such species demonstrates that unity brings safety to an animal colony (much research on the baboon is available); divides vital roles among members (the worker society of ants and the sentry duty of prairie dogs are indicative); and at the most basic level animals may even find a sufficient reward for socialization simply in huddling together for warmth in cold weather. You should recognize, of course, that much of our interpretation is speculative. We would like to assume that the most basic causes of action, in addition to relating to the biologically determined capacity to act, would be evolutionary factors that evolved along with modification in biological characteristics. We simply do not have the research capabilities to test these ideas, and only the behavioral residuals exist as food for speculation as to how they might have come about. We can examine several such "basic" tendencies.

Simple Dyadic Tendencies   In dyadic interactions (involving two individuals) it is known that *similarities in type* appear to promote increased amounts of socialization. It is reasonable to assume that one of the earliest capacities of organisms was that of recognizing species that might be expected to aggress, and differentiating these both from one's own species and from species that might safely be aggressed against (the latter might represent a food source).

Unfamiliarity   *Unfamiliarity* with an individual, in terms of identity, leads to physical spacing. This exists as a tendency not only in animal communities, but with human beings as well. Think for a moment how strangers have a tendency to draw apart when they accidentally touch their bare arms in a crowded elevator or bus.

There is some data to support a statement that organisms tend to limit their close involvement with individuals who are *physically different* in unfamiliar ways. Deformed offspring are sometimes driven away from a group and left to die. So, too, are injured adults in some species groups.

Behavioral Dissimilarity   Just as animals respond negatively to physical dissimilarity, so also do they respond negatively to *behavioral dissimilarity*. If an animal begins to vocalize loudly, stagger, or perhaps starts to rush about aimlessly, others in the group tend to become restless and move away to a considerable distance, or even take flight in alarm.

In human beings we see counterparts to lower animals' negative reactions to physical and behavioral unfamiliarity. We see an extreme amount of hesitation on the parts of many persons to prospects of interacting with patients in mental hospitals. We see aversion in many toward prolonged interactions with severe stutterers, with the deaf, with the blind, or with those with motor impairments. Many such persons are left almost totally alone by their peers, to a degree unsuspected by most of us.

Proximity in Space   Another interesting dimension of dyadic relationships is that *proximity in space* leads to *positive* socialization. In many animal groups the individual in the center of the group is the one with greatest power and dominance. Weak or old individuals are typically driven to the periphery of the area, where they are ignored, and where the supply of available food is usually limited and their chances of survival are reduced. Odd though it may appear, a related phenomenon is demonstrated in human groups. Those in the "middle" seem to be treated as having higher attraction and status, and are more sought out. Those on the periphery are ignored. A study made at a large midwestern university shortly after World War II found that in a veterans' housing unit, those students and their families who happened to have the most centrally located living units were sought out and interacted with a great deal more than were those persons positioned outside of the central area. Obviously there were certain exceptions—social popularity was no more guaranteed by being centrally positioned than unpopularity was by being positioned on the periphery. But on the average a clear and unmistakable tendency was present whereby, in terms of developing popularity, being centrally positioned favored social attractiveness.

C 10A.2.   *Basic dyadic tendencies: Effects of unfamiliarity, dissimilarity, and location.*

A dyad is an interaction involving _____ individuals.

A general tendency is that increased socialization occurs between individuals that are _____ .

    a. similar in type   b. dissimilar in type   c. not known to each other

There would be relatively less socialization between two individuals if _____ .

    a. they were of similar type   b. they were not known to each other

    c. they demonstrated quite similar behavior patterns

All other things being equal, which of the following is most positively interacted with? _____ .

   a. individuals spaced on the periphery of a group

   b. individuals located near the center of a group, close to many others

   c. an individual manifesting strange, unfamiliar behavior

If an unfamiliar individual drew close to you, the most basic social tendency would be to _____ .

   a. withdraw and increase the distance separating you

   b. retaliate or become aggressive

   c. feel a closer attraction and initiate further socialization

Higher Physical Positions   Elevation is a variable that may owe its importance to some sort of evolutionary development. There appears to be a tendency, in human groups, to literally seek *higher physical positions,* particularly in settings where some sort of status resolution is involved or in competitive settings. Think for a moment of where the executive suites are positioned in organizations that totally occupy a multistoried building. Observe also how many teachers stand for their lectures (the authority role), while the students sit (the subordinate role). One informal study (Jurgen & Vernon, 1967) was performed in a role-playing situation. A "boss" scolded a "subordinate" along certain prearranged lines, ostensibly to study the infectiousness of emotion. In the experimental condition the subordinate stood while the boss sat behind a desk, while in the control condition they both sat. Several different "bosses" were used, and several different "subordinates." In the experimental condition (subordinate standing), the bosses expressed more angry emotion, and the bosses also reported their feeling that the subordinate was putting forth greater resistance and counter-argument. A careful study of tape recordings of the sessions confirmed both of these impressions. Both the bosses and the subordinates presumably were responding to the elevation factor which created a greater impression of equality of status, and hence (1) increased the sense of threat for the superior, and (2) lowered the restraints of caution for the subordinate. In order to get a feeling for what we have discussed, consider for a moment the "naturalness" of a scene in which a standing individual talks very aggressively to another person who is seated, with the result that the seated individual gets quickly and angrily to his feet, thus equalizing the height "advantage."

     It is possible that the status-resulting-from-height phenomenon evolved mainly from an informational advantage that would exist in a natural setting for any species with reasonably good vision. Additionally, mountain sheep are only one of several species that seek a height advantage during actual fighting, from which they will propel themselves downward with added force toward the opponent.

C 10A.3. *The effects of higher physical positions upon dyadic socialization.*

It would appear that _____ status and social power accompany being physically lower than another.

   a. increased   b. decreased

Suppose that you were a "boss" wishing to interact with a somewhat angry subordinate. You wish to

correct him, but also to minimize the chances of his having an outburst of some sort that would call

for his termination. You would best arrange to have him _____ during your conversation.

a. standing   b. seated

The Status Hierarchy   In primates as well as human societies most existing social groups show a definite status hierarchy. Such a hierarchy may not be rigid, in the sense of there being a clear number one individual, a number two, etc., but levels typically exist that are perceived by all in the group.

The position of an individual on a status hierarchy seems basically to be determined by past interactions within the group, which can be translated into victory and defeat histories. In any conflicts the experience of victory by one of the participants tends *not only* to determine the subsequent relationship between the individuals involved, but *also* tends to make the victorious individual more dominant and aggressive and the defeated individual more submissive in terms of vocalization patterns, physical posturing and, in human groups, all sorts of dominant personality characteristics. Then, when an animal that is high statused within one group is introduced into a newly organized group, many of his dominant threat patterns are interpretable by his new companions. A high statused individual is quite likely to be afforded high status in the new organization, often without even a necessity for actual combat. In some species conflicts during mating season are formed almost entirely of ritualized threats, with "victories" and "defeats" resulting from no more than the effects of bluster and threat.

C 10A.4. *The effects of victory and defeat histories on socialization tendencies.*

Victory and defeat histories determine an individual's vertical position on _____ .

a. a status hierarchy   b. friendship preferences in groups

c. hierarchical lists of "enemies" prepared by human subjects

One's personality characteristics _____ affected by victory and defeat histories.

a. seem to be   b. are apparently not

In a newly formed group of *socially experienced* individuals, _____ occur for a new status hierarchy

to become firmly established.

a. aggression and physical combat must   b. it is not necessary for fighting to actually

The Effects of Familiarity Within the Hierarchy   In human and primate groups, most casual social interaction between individuals of different status levels tends to depress the status of the higher individual and elevate the status of the lower individual, with the exception of formal situations which will be discussed in a moment. The lower statused individual typically pursues status elevation through a variety of means, and one tactic may be familiarity toward superiors. This leads to his being called a "boot polisher," or any of a number of more colorful terms, as a result of his attempts to mingle with and ingratiate himself with his superiors. Conversely, the superior tends, through such informal social contact, to experience lowered status, which may account for the directive in military ranks for those of higher status to refrain from fraternizing with subordinates, and to slogans such as "familiarity breeds contempt." It might be added that perception by the higher-statused individual of his lowered status through such contacts may be affected by his own felt motives for power and superiority. Some individuals seem to have strong power motives and hold themselves socially aloof.

In attempting to initiate social contacts between status levels, making the overture is not without risk for the lower-statused individual. Specifically, any rebuff toward the lower-statused individual further reduces his status. Most individuals are quite sensitive to this factor, and gauge carefully whether a higher-statused individual is likely to rebuff them before they will risk anything more than the most superficial and casual overture. In business and industry, any individual of lower status who seems to lack sensitivity and caution in initiating social overtures toward those of higher status usually is looked upon as being lacking in a vital form of social intelligence.

Earlier we stated that, in general, many formal situations are exceptions to the general principle of status change from contacts between persons of different status levels. Such a formal situation is one in which the superior invites the subordinate into his office to discuss the subordinate's job satisfaction, rate of professional development, etc. Another formal setting may at first seem otherwise—this would be the formal social event such as a one-time-a-year Christmas drop-in at the employer's home. None of these situations provide for relative elevation of the subordinate's status simply through the interaction itself.

C 10A.5.   *The effects of social interaction on status in a social hierarchy.*

Normally, casual social interaction between individuals of different status levels _____ the status level of the lower-statused individual.

    a. increases   b. decreases   c. leaves unchanged

The lower-statused individual's status is lowered if, in his attempt to initiate social overtures toward another, he is _____ .

    a. rebuffed   b. given full opportunity to express himself   c. successful

Interactions between individuals of mixed-status level usually do not change the status of the lower-statused individual if the interaction takes place within _____ .

    a. an informal or casual situation   b. a formal situation

Studies of status level and the resulting effects upon accompanying social behavior have never been comprehensively undertaken. It is accepted, by many, that highly status-conscious individuals, who subscribe to the "rules" reflecting status rise and status maintenance, are those whose backgrounds suggest a significant degree of felt inferiority. Such an assumption, however, fails to account for the fact that by far the majority of individuals seem motivated, in many aspects of social interaction, to increase their status relative to other persons. This is not well understood, and is difficult to research since activities within human groups are typically outgrowths of a considerable number of separate but interacting motives. For example, how would we interpret ambitious striving on the part of a young corporation executive? Imitation of significant others, reinforcement for past achievements, professional dedication and interest, and financial motives are only a few of the factors that may have appearances of being attempts solely toward status elevation.

SOCIALIZATION VERSUS ISOLATION

One of the earliest socialization tendencies lies in the apparent need of the individual for social interactions. It is unclear whether deprivation of social contacts is simply deprivation of stimulus variety, but it is a fact that complete isolation of an individual from others has a debilitating psychological effect. Total and prolonged social isolation has been shown, in infant dogs and in monkeys, to later render physically mature individuals with severe intellectual or emotional retardations that inhibit adaptive responses to the environment, as well as inhibit such otherwise simple interactions as mating and caring for offspring (Harlow, 1958).

Normally the process of socialization is studied as a within-species phenomenon. Of considerable interest, however, is research which shows that the process of socialization can, and often does, cross species lines. Monkeys reared with humans apparently prefer the company of humans to monkeys (Sackett et al., 1965), and the same phenomenon applies to dogs, sheep, and other species. Birds, reared alone in cages, are found to attach themselves to humans and reject the social overtures of other birds. Cairns and Werboff (1967) even introduced isolated young puppies to a rabbit. It was reported that, following a socialization period as short as only two hours, separation from their new friend produced prolonged and agitated vocalization. You will note that the relationship was *not* based on feeding. Scott (1972) theorizes that the customary pack-orientation of adult dogs and wolves relates to the tendencies of parents of the species to leave the litters by themselves a great deal of the time after four to five weeks of age, so that the strongest developed relationship is to the group rather than to the mother.

Scott (1972) has identified a critical period for socialization, which occurs at varying times depending upon the species involved. It is known that birds of various sorts, including geese, ducks, and chickens, will "adopt," as their mother, whatever large moving object may be present in their visual fields during a critical and very short period that comes several hours after birth. Lorenz, a well-known animal biologist, is recognizable from the numerous published photographs that show him leading the way across a meadow with a long line of young geese following faithfully behind—he is their "mother." This phenomenon, conceptually limited to birds, is called *imprinting*.

Scott's own work, mostly with dogs, suggests that the phenomenon of the *critical period for socialization* is broader than just the imprinting effect in birds. He has suggested that from three to twelve weeks is a period within which the puppy is sensitive and receptive to whatever sorts of individuals with whom he has interaction, so that separation of the puppy around the seventh or eighth week of life, when puppies are typically weaned, usually results in appropriate socialization as an adult dog to both humans and other dogs. In those cases in which the dogs are separated earlier than three weeks of age (and usually are then hand-reared), they typically later experience great difficulty in social-sexual relations with other dogs; and in cases where puppies past the age of twelve weeks are still unfamiliar with human beings, the later life pattern almost never involves a close, dependent relationship with a human being (Scott, 1972).

C 10A.6.   *The basic socialization process in the young.*

The process of socialization takes place quite early in most species, and attachments to others apparently _____ .

   a. are contained within species   b. cross species lines

Birds will adopt, as parent, any large moving presence they see at a specific moment a few hours after hatching. This is a phenomenon known as _____ .

   a. mothering   b. movement reaction   c. nestling response   d. imprinting

Scott has termed the time during which an organism formulates its early social attachments as its _____ .

   a. critical period for socialization   b. incubation period

Scott, in his thorough research with puppies, found that the critical period for their socialization came between the _____ .

   a. third and sixth month   b. third and twelfth week   c. second and sixth week

---

PROGRESS CHECK   10A.1

1. Two of three reasons given for the preference for animals to humans in psychological research are _____ and _____ .

   a. continuity between species is obvious   b. generalization is easily suppressed

   c. some independent variables can be harmful   d. organismal basics are easily obtained

   e. life and development spans are shorter

2. Animal "instinct" is a prime justification for the use of animals in social research generalizable to humans. _____ .

    a. True   b. False

3. Greater physical height results in a presumably "higher" social status. _____ .

    a. True   b. False

4. Victory and defeat histories seem to have an effect on personality characteristics and status hierarchy. _____ .

    a. True   b. False

5. The status level of an individual usually is _____ while he/she is informally conversing with someone of higher social status.

    a. increased   b. decreased

6. Does the previous answer hold true during most formal social situations? _____ .

    a. Yes   b. No

7. The "critical period for socialization" refers to a time during which _____ .

    a. adolescence occurs   b. early social attachments are formed

    c. the offspring leave their mother   d. attachments are "locked" within one species

8. Fowl adopting as a parent the first large moving object that crosses their visual field soon after hatching is known as _____ .

    a. surrogating   b. socialization   c. imprinting

AN EXPERIMENTAL ANALYSIS OF AGGRESSION

As an example of what *can* be done in the experimental analysis of behavior, we have chosen to present a fairly comprehensive experimental analysis of aggression. In so doing we should point out that other areas—cooperation, dominance, patterns of sexual expression, etc.—can be handled in a similar manner. The treatment of aggression is alone subjected to a reasonably thorough analysis, partly due to space considerations and partly because this area represents such a commanding social problem in human society.

Types of Aggression

For convenience, let us categorize two major types of aggressive behavior which are both, in their separate ways, dependent upon environmental factors. First there is *respondent* aggression—patterns elicited in a reflexive manner as UCRs by certain classes of stimuli (UCSs). We shall consider both stimuli of pain and frustration as UCSs capable of triggering aggression. Second there is *operant* aggression. Aggressive patterns that occur, be they initially random or accidental in nature, imitative, or elicited, can become strengthened because of the immediate consequences of the aggressive act.

C 10A.7. *Types of aggression.*

It can be stated that two types of aggression can be differentiated, both due to environmental factors. These types are _____ .

a. random and elicited   b. imitative and random

c. operant and respondent   d. cognitive and accidental

Natural Elicitors of Aggression

There are numerous conditions that serve to bring about aggression, even in the absence of any previous experiences of an organism with the conditions in question. These unlearned patterns are termed *respondent behaviors* by psychologists. They are, of course, hereditarily determined, and so may vary in *style* from species to species, and may vary considerably in *degree* within a species as a function of individual organismic differences.

Frustration

The familiar frustration-aggression respondent behavior sequence has been extensively investigated with both human and animal subjects. Quite a few years ago it was demonstrated that such factors as the deprivation level of a frustrated animal, closeness to the goal when restrained, and the magnitude of a visible incentive from which the animal is restrained, all relate to both the probability and the intensity of a demonstrated rage response. More recently research has centered upon the schedule of reinforcement which precedes the extinction procedure which creates the frustration. Azrin, Hake and Hutchinson (1966) conditioned pigeons to peck at a key, reinforcing each peck immediately with food. After an appreciable time in this situation, the food supply was stopped. The subject pigeon would emit a burst of responses, breaking off this activity to rush at another bird in the chamber and begin attacking it about the head. The pigeons used in this experiment all showed a similar pattern of frustration-induced aggression following the termination of a 100 percent schedule of reinforcement; this behavior is probably related to that we call "spoiled" in human beings.

There is perhaps a lesson in the observation that pigeons that experienced fairly lean intermittent schedules of reinforcement, where considerably less than 100 percent of responses gained reinforcement, failed to demonstrate much if any aggression when their supply of food was cut off. Along the same general line of research, Knutson (1970) recently showed a high level of aggression by pigeons where food rewards were delivered on very lean schedules, such as one reinforcer per 100 to 120 responses. It is of interest that Knutson described aggression *during the conditioning sequence,* rather than during extinction. Apparently, positive reinforcement schedules should be carefully constructed from the standpoints of both Azrin's and Knutson's findings.

Little experimental research has been done relating aggression to frustrated drives other than hunger, although some might hold that fighting over mating privileges could be due to a frustrated sex drive. Along this line we could no double hypothesize frustration-aggression relationships to a number of naturally occurring deprivations.

On the basis of laboratory-derived knowledge, it seems safe to conclude that an aggressive response to the general situation we term "frustration" can occur when animals have not previously experienced frustration and have failed to develop a tolerance for it. Also, aggression occurs when schedules of reinforcement are such that a very large number of responses are necessary to produce only a few reinforcers. In line with the last remark, it appears that we might consider more frequent positive payoffs in the various human situations where frustration and aggression seem to be problems.

C 10A.8.   *The effects of schedules of reinforcement on aggression.*

Aggression sometimes occurs during extinction following a favorable schedule of reinforcement. This is less pronounced, however, if the prior schedule of reinforcement was _____ .

a. FI   b. crf   c. lean   d. VR

Aggression would be more likely to occur occasionally during conditioning trials if the schedule of reinforcement was _____ .

a. crf   b. VR5   c. VR20   d. VR400

Sexual Privileges   Fighting over females occurs frequently in many species. The males of some species have their season. This is called "rutting"—a periodically recurring sexual excitement. Species such as deer, moose, and mountain sheep engage in battles over the possession of harems of females. In species such as dogs, the occurrence of aggression related to sexual privileges seems more dependent upon there being a female animal in estrous in the presence of more than one male. The extent of fighting over possession of females is suggested by Zuckerman's (1932) study of baboons on a monkey island in the London Zoo. Zuckerman's observation was that fighting over sexual privileges was the principal cause of injury in that zoo population.

Territorial Intrusion   While fights concerning mating privileges seem to be seasonal, or at least situational, territorial defense is a reasonably continuous phenomenon, producing threats and actual combat whenever animals intrude upon the territories of same-species animals. Animals of different species mark their territories in various ways. Common is the spray of urine on landmarks which warns off others. It would similarly appear that birds' songs have an ominous quality about them, serving as threats which space out the species.

Presumably the function of the spacing provided by territorial behavior is that there are eventually, in an area, only the number of animals which can be adequately supported by the food and water supplies and, in the cases of smaller animals, the number which can be adequately shielded by the territory's hiding places.

C 10A.9. *Territorial behavior.*

"Territorial behavior" is a term that has to do with actions which _____ .

    a. lead to fighting   b. space out a species over an area

    c. relate to migrations of animal colonies

It is thought that territorial behavior serves the primary function of achieving a balance between the size of a local population and _____ .

    a. the available natural resources

    b. the degree of intraspecies fighting typical of the species

Such animal behaviors as sprays of urine by males serve as _____ .

    a. sexual invitations   b. warnings of territorial occupancy

A bit of recent research on the variable of population density, or crowding, suggests that crowding, itself, does *not* increase the level of aggression —at least not the typical forms of aggression with which we have been concerned.

There have been reports that cannibalism of newborn occurs in various species (Breder & Coates, 1932; Willis, 1966; Wynne-Edwards, 1962) when crowding reaches a certain level. This occurs even with food supplies in abundance. But most recent research shows other pathological patterns in dense crowds. Christian (1959, 1963) showed histological changes of the adrenal gland in a deer population on an island, presumably resulting from the stress of overcrowding. This produced the deaths of many otherwise healthy individuals. Endocrine changes in mice (Frank, 1953) have been reported, as well as stoppage of sexual activity, stoppage of the milk supply in mothers (von Holst, 1969), and even a breakdown in the general pattern of care for the young in crowded rat populations (Calhoun, 1962)—all being responses to overpopulation.

Aggressive Display Yet another important area of concern is with the effect of threats and aggressive displays on the incidence of aggression. It is taken to be practically a truism in most texts that aggressive display has the effect of intimidating opponents and presumably *decreasing* the likelihood of actual battle. There seems to be a variety of evidence, mostly impressionistic, that this is so, and it is common to hear that the piloerection (hair erection) response in a cat (as an example), by making the animal appear larger, *intimidates* and drives away the opponent; or that a vocal threat, delivered loudly, has the effect of momentarily *startling* the opponent and allowing the first individual to escape. Despite such common positions, one occasionally reads that in a species vocalization brings about counter-vocalization, leading to fighting; or that in male birds aggressive display attracts retaliatory display which frequently leads to damaging aggressive contact. Evidence is somewhat hard to come by in this area. There are many naturalistic observations of threats—even direct stares—which seem to be preliminaries to fighting, but there are as many anecdotal descriptions of the successful threat that drives away, or spaces, the participants.

It is possible that the latter group of findings is influenced by a systematic contributing factor. In no reported cases have the researchers made certain that the animals involved had not already accumulated victory and defeat experiences, or established social hierarchies. These factors would serve as artifacts in the situation and the effect of the aggressive display itself could not be properly assessed. A great proportion of the studies reported have used species that are prone to establish dominance hierarchies and, in many cases, have had the opportunity to do so. In such groups, the majority of the members of the colony are repeatedly subjected to punishments delivered by a single dominant individual. Dominance seems to be established through the infliction of punishment, and can even be reversed by this means.

Robinson (1969) has shown that when subordinate male monkeys are induced to attack dominant males through hypothalamic stimulation, several trials are completely sufficient to reverse the dominant-subordinate relationship. It was also shown that dominant monkeys frequently make certain kinds of vocalizations, while subordinate monkeys seldom do. The pairing of another animal's threat with frequent punishment delivered by that animal would obviously, through classical conditioning, sensitize an individual to aggressive vocal and physical displays and make more probable his retreat from them. But we need more research with species that do not so readily form dominance hierarchies. Further, we should insure that the animals' social histories do not make unexpected contributions to research findings.

The Posture Variable

Within a pain-elicited fighting experiment, which is in a series of experiments that we shall describe at a later point, we investigated the effects of a *threatening posture* with socially naïve male rats. A shock, delivered to paired animals, will produce fighting, and during an interval between shocks of, say, 20 seconds often one or both animals will remain erect in a fighting posture until the moment of the next shock. This posture presumably carries with it an aspect of threat. By careful analysis of the behaviors *preceding* the shocks, we were able to discover the effects, on rate of fighting, of there being both animals, one animal, or neither animal in a threatening fighting posture at the moment of shock onset. Thousands of fighting responses were analyzed, and the rate of fighting when both animals were in the fighting posture was seen to be approximately 85 percent; the rate when only one animal was erect was approximately 58 percent; and the rate when neither animal was erect was approximately 23 percent. Furthermore, visual observation indicated that at those moments when only one animal was erect, it was most typically the *other animal* that initiated the attack (Vernon, 1969). Thus threat seems to stimulate aggression.

As a final note on aggressive display, it appears perhaps to have certain innate effects on observer animals. Sackett (1969) showed that at approximately two-and-a-half months laboratory-reared rhesus monkeys begin to show fear responses to slide pictures of threatening adult monkeys. Before that age the animals simply show curiosity, and even learn to press a bar in order to view such a slide. None of the animals in Sackett's experiment had even had an actual live social encounter with a threatening monkey, nor had they seen their own mirror images, but at two and one-half months of age, bar-pressing ceased, and visible emotion was observed in response to the slide pictures when presented noncontingently.

C 10A.10. *The effect of threat on the probability of aggression.*

In a controlled laboratory experiment it appeared that the effect of threat, expressed through the posture of an animal, was to _____ the likelihood of an aggressive incident.

   a. increase   b. decrease

Without there having been any prior experience with other individuals, fear reactions to pictures of threatening individuals seem to have _____ in monkeys.

   a. a learned basis   b. an innate basis

Pain   The last *unlearned* stimulus to fighting that we shall discuss is pain. When pain is employed in a laboratory, it is customary for stimulation to be delivered to a lone animal. In the published literature concerning aversive stimulation, it was not until 1939 that an article appeared describing the behavior of pairs of animals in a shock chamber. In that article O'Kelly and Steckle (1939) noted that, when shocked, the animals leaped at one another and began fighting. They remained in a defensive fighting posture for periods of time during the intervals between shocks. The topography of rats fighting suggests little difference between the pattern of shock-elicited fighting and the fighting that occurs in natural environments. In fact, much fighting in the natural setting may well have a cause-and-effect aspect quite similar to shock-elicited fighting.

For example, Scott (1958) observed the mutual grooming that occurs between adult male mice; he noted that a rough period of grooming is often enough to trigger a fighting response on the part of the groomed mouse. Then the pain being delivered by the animal reacting to discomfort is sufficient to trigger fighting on the part of the animal originally doing the grooming. In most species, young littermates engage in a considerable amount of active play, typically involving wrestling and playful biting. When pain is experienced by one animal, a retaliatory attack is common, which turns the play into serious combat.

The aggressive response to pain is an extremely powerful reflex. It has been compared in strength to behavioral escape tendencies. Ulrich and Craine (1964) trained lone rats to press a bar to turn off grid shock. Then two trained rats were placed together in the chamber. In the situation with another animal present, both animals abandoned the bar-press behavior which could terminate the shock, and attacked one another. Later Ulrich and his colleagues trained rats side-by-side with a plexiglas transparent partition separating them. They became fully accustomed to the visual presence of the other animal. After bar-pressing was well established, negatively reinforced by shock termination, the simple removal of the partition brought about abandonment of bar-pressing and consistent fighting in the presence of shock.

Logan (1969) showed that if rats were shocked individually they could learn a wheel-turning response which would terminate the shock. When rats so trained were then brought together in pairs and shocked, they fought. However, Logan then found that a very simple escape response— namely running away to a safe area—persisted when the rats were given such an opportunity to escape.

In contrasting these findings we could conclude that the most basic reflexive orientation to aversive stimulation is escape, and fighting occurs when escape is impossible. Yet Ulrich's research also shows that when the escape behaviors contain complex components, or have been newly learned, the basic reflex hierarchy shifts in favor of the aggressive response. Logan's running-away escape pattern, offered to his animal subjects, was one that was much more basic than bar-pressing and probably had been practiced many times during each animal's lifetime—simple physical withdrawal away from a source of aversive stimulation.

C 10A.11.   *Pain-elicited aggression.*

Aggressive responses to frustration, aggressive display, and pain all seem to be essentially _____ .

    a. learned   b. innate

The fighting response to pain will displace escape responses if those responses are _____

_____ .

An animal is offered a "choice" when pain is inflicted upon it. It can attack another animal present, it

    can run out of the area (and has done so before), or it can run to a lever and press it down to

    terminate the pain stimulus (and has done so before). Under these circumstances it is likely that the

    animal would _____ .

PROGRESS CHECK   10A.2

1. Name the two types of aggression that are due to environmental factors.

    _____   _____

2. The level of aggression when extinction has followed a period of lean reinforcement rather than a period of rich reinforcement is _____ .

    a. higher   b. lower

3. Give an example of a "territorial" warning.

    _____ .

4. Territorial behavior serves the primary function of achieving a balance between population and available natural resources. _____ .

    a. True   b. False

5. A threatening appearance _____ the likelihood of aggression.

    a. increases   b. decreases

6. A fear reaction, without previous experience, to a threatening picture appears to be _____ .

    a. innate   b. learned

MATCH: _____ 7. An aggressive response to pain   A. Probably learned

              _____ 8. An aggressive response to frustration   B. Basically innate

9. When two animals are present and pain is inflicted on one, the inflicted animal is likely to _____ .

    a. attack the other animal   b. escape   c. learn to terminate the pain

---

Learned Patterns of Aggression

A great deal of aggression has been clearly shown to relate to environmental consequences. We will first consider the two patterns of operant reinforcement—positive reinforcement of aggression, where the consequences of fighting are the gaining of various rewards or privileges, and negative reinforcement, where the consequences are the reduction or elimination of an aversive situation.

Positive Reinforcement of Aggression

Fighting can be developed between paired animals or within groups by presenting food or water to deprived animals as the immediate consequence to any conflict which may involve them. Ulrich, Johnston, Richardson and Wolff (1963) were able to demonstrate this phenomenon in water-deprived rats by first pairing access to a water magazine with the onset of a buzzer, and then making both the buzzer and water contingent upon movements toward the head of the other animal. After such approach responses were developed, the stimuli were made contingent upon actual striking movements and, finally, prolonged aggressive contact. In this manner very vigorous fights were developed, the animals rearing, striking, pushing and often knocking one another to the floor. Often the animals would not even respond to the buzzer, but would continue to fight. The positively reinforced aggression apparently was being combined with the tendencies to fight that are elicited by the aversive aspects of the fight itself.

One of the less predictable findings in the recent literature is that when pain-elicited aggression is stimulated, the *availability of an attackable object* will, itself, serve as a positive reinforcer. Azrin (1964) shocked monkeys and observed a flurry of physical activity. One of the possible actions in the situation was to pull a chain. The only function served by the chain-pull was to produce a tennis ball, which could then be bitten by the monkey. The chain-pull had no relation to terminating the shock—it only produced the ball—but monkeys were observed to make thousands of chain-pull responses which allowed an attack on the tennis ball. More recently Dreyer and Church (1970) gave rats a series of shocks in a *T*-maze. While the shock was inescapable, the rats preferred to enter an arm of the *T*-maze that contained another rat which could be attacked. This lends further support to the notion that an attackable object, in certain circumstances, can function as a positive reinforcer.

C 10A.12. *Positive reinforcement of aggression.*

Which of the following are found to be effective in *positively* reinforcing aggressive behavior in animal research? _____ .

a. food and water   b. termination of shock

c. availability of an attackable object   d. (two of the first three choices are correct)

One might generalize from animal research to say that when an individual is experiencing intense physical discomfort, the presence of another individual _____ .

a. is so aversive as to enrage the first individual, and he aggresses

b. is "rewarding" in a sense, giving the first individual an opportunity to aggress as his behavior of choice

There are probably quite a few cases in the natural environment where aggressive responses produce positive reinforcers for both animals and human beings. No doubt extortion in the peer group and control of parents by tantrum aggression are clear-cut examples. Even more clearly, however, we can see the relation of aggression to negative reinforcement.

Negative Reinforcement of Aggression   In a natural setting the unpleasant stimuli necessary for negative reinforcement are typically delivered by another animal. Running away is one way of eliminating the aversive condition. Successful counterattack is another way of doing so. The choice of which of these strategies to use seems to be directly related to an animal's victory and defeat history. Animals with predominant win-records typically attack those animals that intrude or threaten, while those animals with predominant loss-records typically retreat from threat.

There has been little actual experimental demonstration of the negative reinforcement of aggression since Miller performed such an experiment in 1948. Miller shocked paired rats, causing them to fight. As soon as they had both assumed a fighting posture and begun to strike, the shock was turned off for one minute. Then the current was turned on again. This experiment actually combined shock-elicited fighting with the negative reinforcement procedure, and we now know that a fighting pattern would have occurred even if shock termination had not been made contingent upon fighting. Nevertheless, in a procedure such as Miller's, it would seem that negative reinforcement would probably increase the already substantial rate of fighting which initially was pain-elicited.

C 10A.13. *Negative reinforcement of aggression.*

Which of the following would probably represent *negative* reinforcement of aggression in the human social world? _____ .

a. Control of parents by a child's tantrums

b. Aggressive "bullying" through which the bully gains privileges

c. Driving away an irritating individual by finally blowing your top at him

d. Winning a prize as the most obnoxious loudmouth in your school

Imitative Aggression

The subject of social imitation is only recently capturing the widespread interest of psychologists. For some years we have known that many predatory patterns are dependent upon the parent instructing the young through example. Kuo in 1930 showed that cats are not ordinarily mouse-killers unless they have observed other cats performing this behavior. Recently, popular literature has related cases of hand-reared lions which were later released into a free wild state where they had considerable difficulty learning to kill their prey. When we think of the topic of aggression, we usually think of intraspecies fighting, however, and in this context a limited amount of material has accumulated on the imitative influence. Without detailing the research, it appears that aggression in most species is simultaneously *not dependent* upon an imitative model but *can be influenced* through imitative modeling (if this is clear to the reader).

Regarding the first part of the statement, King and Gurney (1954) found that mice reared in isolation attack others of their species that are introduced into their cages, and exhibit all of the species-typical patterns of threatening and fighting. Also, the frequency of aggression of isolation-reared mice was much higher than that of mice reared in social groups. Concerning the second part of the statement, a cross-litter experiment was performed by Lagersperz and Worinen (1965) in which litters of mice from an aggressive line were given to a docile mother to rear, and vice-versa. While the mice from the aggressive line continued to show more aggression than the docile-line mice, the level of their aggression fell off somewhat. Similarly there was a modest increase in the level of aggression of docile-line mice reared by aggressive mothers.

C 10A.14. *Imitative aggression.*

If predatory aggression is to properly develop in wild species, it appears critical that the young have

the opportunity to _____ .

Higher levels of aggression in groups occur in those animals that were reared _____ .

    a. in groups   b. in isolation

Punishment of Aggression

One of the contributions which the recent aggression literature has made toward socially relevant knowledge pertains to the modification of aggression through its punishment. It is relevant that man tends most typically to punish expressions of aggression in his children. We have already reviewed data which suggest that the infliction of pain, by itself, is often sufficient to induce aggressive behavior. This brings into the question the entire strategy of trying to reduce aggression through punishment. In human populations we can already see evidence that adolescent aggression is substantially higher where the adolescents have punitive home environments featuring harsh punishment. Parental punishment, of course, offers an aggressive imitative model, in addition to stimulating a reflexive form of aggression.

Ulrich and Craine (1964) subjected paired rats to continuous shock in an experimental chamber. When a nonfighting response occurred, as it occasionally did, the shock was immediately interrupted for a short time. All fighting responses received continuous punishment, however. It was found that in this situation the amount of fighting actually increased as the experiment progressed. Azrin (1964), however, provided evidence that punishment *can* reduce pain-elicited fighting between rats if the punishing stimulus is more intense than the stimulus which originally elicited the fighting. This is consistent with the observation by Ginsburg and Allee (1942) that, following severe defeats in mice, their participation in fights decreased considerably.

C 10A.15. *The control of aggression through punishment.*

Punishment (i.e., pain) generally tends to _____ the level of aggression.

    a. increase   b. decrease   c. leave unchanged

Pain-elicited aggression was suppressed in one experiment by contingent punishment, but this method

was effective only where the intensity of the contingent punishment _____

_____ the intensity of the pain stimulus which originally elicited the aggressive behavior.

Classically Conditioned Aggression

One other form of learned aggression remains to be described. Within the framework of classical conditioning, stimuli which are closely associated with those stimuli that elicit fighting can themselves begin to elicit the same response. The stimulus most investigated thus far in eliciting respondent aggression, as we have noted, is pain. Vernon and Ulrich (1966) combined the presentation of a pain stimulus—electric shock—with a *CS*-complex consisting of the simultaneous presentation of a buzzer and the increased illumination level of the chamber lights. The animals fought in this stimulus combination. Gradually we began to drop out the shock from some trials and saw the animals still leaping across the chamber and struggling as soon as the buzzer sounded and the lights brightened.

It is quite apparent that, in the natural setting, this model for the development of aggression is readily available in the social experiences of most animals. In this way we might anticipate an animal responding aggressively to the sight of an individual with whom he had had unpleasant experiences in the past. The same might be said for human beings who, to a much greater extent than animals, are often held unwillingly in inescapable aversive circumstances.

C 10A.16. *Classical conditioning of aggressive behavior.*

Classical conditioning of aggression in rats has been successfully developed, using _____ as the unconditioned stimulus (UCS).

    a. pain   b. a buzzer   c. food and water

At this particular point you may well feel like the little boy assigned a book report on the topic of dinosaurs. He simply summarized, "I learned a lot more about dinosaurs than I actually wanted to know." We have pursued the topic of aggression at such length because, as we explained, this is indicative of the ways in which those interested in the experimental analysis of behavior go about determining the causes of a given behavior, drawing substantially from animal literature, especially where appropriate experimental research with human subjects is unavailable.

THE EXPERIMENTAL ANALYSIS OF OTHER SOCIAL PATTERNS

We will not dwell upon the application of behavioral technologies to the study of other social processes. If you recognize that most such processes are quite complex, and the motives for similar behaviors may not be similar at all, then it should be easy for you to interpret such behaviors in terms of their being positively and negatively reinforced, and perhaps with other factors coming into play as well.

The determination of criminal behavior has been very thoroughly dealt with by Eysenck (1964). It is also possible to view creativity, social dominance, altruism (as we have done in Chapter 10), prejudice, patterns of mothering, the choosing of social associates, and a wide variety of related topics in the same general manner. Sections of the Ulrich and Mountjoy text, *The Experimental Analysis of Social Behavior* (1972) are given over to comprehensive experimentation on such topics as cooperation, competition, leadership, affection, sexual behavior, and communications patterns. The student who is interested in exploring this general approach to social behavior patterns should encounter little difficulty in finding material.

PROGRESS CHECK   10A.3

MATCH: _____ 1. Providing nourishment to an   A. Negative reinforcement of aggression

animal that bites the cage bars

_____ 2. Rewarding a tantrum with candy   B. Positive reinforcement of aggression

_____ 3. A parent stopping the scolding

of a teen-age boy when the boy

acts threateningly

4. "Observation" by the young plays an important part in predatory aggression. _____ .

a. True   b. False

5. Animals raised in an isolated environment would have _____ .

a. higher levels of aggression   b. lower levels of aggression

6. Punishment _____ .

a. disguises aggression   b. maintains the level of aggression

c. increases the level of aggression   d. decreases the level of aggression

7. Classical conditioning of aggression in rats has been successfully developed, using primary rein-

forcers as the UCS. _____ .

a. True   b. False

HUMAN INTERPERSONAL RESPONSE PATTERNS:

Roles and Cultures

An individual's present behavior, as we have shown, is largely a function of his history of reinforcement. The culture is the determiner of which behaviors will be reinforced and thus persist, and which will either go unreinforced and therefore extinguish or will be punished and thereby suppressed. The socialization of the child is largely an extended period of selective reinforcement and shaping, balanced by selective extinction and suppression.

The persistence of many types of deviant behavior in our culture can be interpreted by observing that these behaviors, while not reinforced by the dominant culture, are often reinforced by a *counterculture* whose reinforcement is perhaps stronger and more contingent to the individual than is reinforcement by the mainstream of society. The cultural reinforcement pattern that determines an individual's behavior is, then, a function of an individual's position in the society.

The *position* an individual is born into in society—that is, his socioeconomic level—will be a powerful determinant of the pattern of reinforcement contingencies he will be subjected to. It is not that an individual of a given socioeconomic class will be subjected to different kinds of rein-forcers, since there is no evidence that any single level has a monopoly on love and affection, attention, money rewards, candy, and other favors. Rather, it appears that different kinds of behaviors are valued differently by different socioeconomic class subcultures, and behaviors that are rein-forced by one subculture may be disapproved of and suppressed by another. A vast sociological literature exists which shows that there are considerable socioeconomic class differences in value systems, in attitudes regarding many social practices, in child-rearing patterns, religious patterns, and even in the psychological mechanisms one uses to defend against anxiety and maintain emotional equilibrium (Miller & Swanson, 1959).

Roles are response sets that are initially developed through imitation and reinforcement, and are appropriate to ascribed and acquired positions. One learns role-appropriate behavior largely through the processes of social imitation and vicarious reinforcement. We learn what parents and spouses are supposed to do in their roles when we, as children, observe our own parents. It is not irrelevant that many children despise certain behavioral patterns of their parents, yet use these same patterns when they become parents.

While we are interested in the ways in which appropriate role interactions develop, we tend to be even more interested in the ways in which problems can develop, as these produce the incidents that give us concern as neighbors, friends, relatives, or mental health professionals. The assumption of a role, and successful operation within it, depends largely upon one's having repeatedly witnessed competent role playing over a substantial period of time.

Sometimes orphaned children, those from broken homes, or those who for other reasons are reared in institutional settings, have little opportunity to witness and learn how to be an effective parent or spouse. Then, statistics indicate, individuals with such upbringings frequently have severe difficulties trying to adjust to the necessary roles expected of them. A child who has never known a family's love is often unable to effectively render love to others. The child who grows up in a home torn by marital strife more often than not experiences serious adjustment problems of his own, not knowing how to cooperate successfully within a marriage. Even in preparing for employment it is important that a developing child be exposed to social models of promptness, responsibility, and efficiency. Otherwise the child, when grown, will probably fail to reflect the minimal qualities expected of him and necessary for his retention as an employee in any significant occupation.

Roles, as sets of responses, are reinforced when practiced, usually in the presence of discriminative stimuli (S^Ds). To take a simple example, one learns over time that while the proper behavior of a sports fan in a stadium may be boisterous, proper behavior in a classroom is of a totally different quality. Individuals typically occupy numerous roles at one time or another, and are then conditioned to a number of different response sets, each tied to relevant S^Ds. A whole area of problems is shown by those individuals who have had a very limited set of S^Ds within their past experiences. If a young man has operated almost totally within the context of a lower-class subculture, he may very well experience considerable difficulty adapting to a radically different culture—one which projects unfamiliar S^Ds and expects precise patterns of behavior of a sort perhaps not significantly reinforced in his own subculture. Habits of punctuality, following instructions carefully when they are delivered by an authority figure, sensing the status levels of those being interacted with and adjusting one's remarks and expressed attitudes accordingly, are all patterns for which the S^Ds and the appropriate reinforcers may not have been linked or emphasized in some families and peer groups. In being projected into a new social world and sometimes experiencing rebuff and failure as a result of not emitting the appropriate behaviors others expect, many individuals grow frustrated and predictable aggressive actions develop. The nonliterate then make derogatory remarks about the unrealistic expectations of the literate; some blacks speak of the alien superficiality of the white, middle-class subculture, and so forth. It might be added that exactly the same difficulties would be presented to the middle-class individual attempting to fit himself into an unfamiliar ghetto subculture, so there is no justification for any feelings of "superiority" simply through a familiarity with a role assumption within any given social class of society.

A pattern of behavior may be given a different value in one subculture than in another, and thus may gain *differential reinforcement* in different subcultures. For the individual, this would mean that the behavior pattern he develops most strongly is a function of the subculture he is being reared in. The middle-class subculture emphasizes and reinforces intangible symbols of success to a much greater degree than does the lower-class subculture, as just one example.

For the middle-class child, failure tends to be paired with aversive stimuli, and eventually cues to failure produce anxiety and increased avoidance behaviors to a far greater extent than is the case with the lower class. When teachers of introductory-level courses in college witness that, even in the face of failing work, certain students still cut classes, fail to come to optional help sessions, and fail to obtain available extra credits, almost invariably investigation will reveal that a disproportionately large number of these students are from lower socioeconomic class backgrounds.

Hostility, completely apart from its respondent qualities that may be generated from frustration, has many role-associated characteristics. The lower socioeconomic class places a much higher degree of value, especially for the male, on having power, and not being weak. While a middle-class mother may spend much time telling others about the various high grades or achievement awards her child has received, the lower-class parent often is more impressed by her son's handling of physical threats from other children, or "standing up for his rights." The tendency, in the lower class, to value and reinforce physical expression and success in interpersonal conflict is perhaps a main factor underlying the higher rates of incidents of physical aggression among both children and adults in the lower socioeconomic class.

C 10A.17. *The conditioning of role-appropriate behavior.*

Many types of deviant behavior are maintained, against society's resistances, through _____ .

    a. the reinforcement delivered within a counterculture

    b. nonreinforced rebelliousness that ultimately serves no purpose

    c. an understanding of a lack of relevance for the individual

The individual's socioeconomic class membership in large part determines _____ .

    a. the types of reinforcers he will receive

    b. which of his behaviors will be reinforced

Role-appropriate behavior first originates in _____ .

    a. reinforcement of random responses

    b. imitation of social models

    c. logical awareness of what needs to be done

Problems in enacting proper roles appropriate to alien subcultures may originate in a lack of experience with many _____ .

    a. people of the sort being interacted with

    b. emphases such as time delays before acting

    c. critical discriminative stimuli

The qualities admired, relatively, by middle- and lower-class adults were reflected in a study done some years ago in which it was shown that individuals from the middle class tend to assign relatively higher ratings on a status hierarchy to occupations reflecting social responsibility, such as minister or social worker. Lower socioeconomic class persons tend to place occupations with social responsibility subordinate to occupations reflecting power and control over other adults, such as the job of foreman (which in turn is not highly rated by the middle class).

Perhaps this is an appropriate place to mention that the social psychological literature places considerable stress upon socioeconomic class level as an independent variable in research. Occasionally students are surprised by a discussion of the "lower class." Actually, while such a term may not sound particularly democratic, most individuals are quite clear on what is meant by the class labels. Once, in a survey, several hundred persons from all walks of life were asked to place themselves in their proper category on a three-level scale. The conclusion was that slightly more than 98 percent assigned themselves to the same category—upper class, middle class, or working class—as did the sociologists examining their personal data.

When social psychologists go about placing individuals into class categories, they take a number of factors into account. Of nearly equal importance, in most systems, are income level of the head of the family, educational level of both husband and wife, and the type of occupation pursued by the head of the family. Various secondary factors are sometimes included, even to the extent of what part of a town or city the family lives in and, if wealthy, whether their wealth was inherited.

Obviously there is a reality in the concept of class level. It is clearly seen as a variable in relation to other data both by the social scientists who study it and by those individuals who are classified within its various dimensions. As such it has proven to be a very valuable concept, since such a great number of dependent factors have been related to class level.

C 10A.18. *Relations between socioeconomic class and behavior.*

It appears clear that the lower socioeconomic class displays a higher level of _____ in both adult and child groups studied than does the middle class.

    a. ambition   b. anxiety   c. aggression

Relative to the lower socioeconomic class, the middle-class individual would assign higher status to a job reflecting _____ .

    a. direct supervisory responsibility over other adults

    b. a position of social responsibility and trust

When surveyed, approximately _____ of adults will place themselves into the same socioeconomic category (working, middle, upper class) as would trained social psychologists.

    a. 50%   b. 70%   c. 90%   d. 98%

PROGRESS CHECK   10A.4

1. Different behaviors are reinforced in different _____ .

    a. subcultures   b. environments   c. socioeconomic classes   d. all of the preceding

2. Role-appropriate behavior most strongly involves _____ .

    a. imitation   b. logic

3. The lack of exposure to a behavior in an alien subculture would have _____ .

    a. little effect on appropriate role behavior

    b. a great effect on appropriate role behavior

4. People are usually aware of their own socioeconomic category _____ .

    a. True   b. False

5. Aggressive tendencies are more prevalent (and admired) in _____ .

    a. lower socioeconomic groups   b. higher socioeconomic groups

6. Respect for roles of social responsibility is highest in the _____ class.

    a. lower socioeconomic class   b. middle to upper socioeconomic class

---

CONCLUSION   This brings us to the end of our brief consideration of social processes—how they develop, and how they in turn influence our further behaviors. From the topics developed in this chapter, and in Chapter 10, you can see that the field is extremely broad in scope.

    Early in the chapter we mentioned some of the books written from an ethological point of view that you might find interesting. Now that you have examined an actual review of research topics in the experimental analysis of aggression, you may be interested in further reading in this direction too. *The Experimental Analysis of Social Behavior*, a book of readings edited by Ulrich and Mountjoy (1972), would provide an excellent foundation in topics extending beyond just aggression, for this book covers such topics as cooperation and leadership, altruism, affection, verbal behavior, disordered social behavior, etc. A very comprehensive treatment of most approaches and topics in the entire field is found in Sahakian's *Systematic Social Psychology* (1974). You will see, if you continue to examine literature in this area, that social processes comprise one of the most vital and exciting areas of psychological research today.

Verbal Learning
in Context

THE IMPORTANCE OF CONTEXTUAL LEARNING

AREAS OF CONTEXTUAL LEARNING RESEARCH
Learning = f (Nature of the Verbal Materials)
   Meaningfulness of the Material
   Concreteness of the Material
   Organization of the Material
Learning = f (Conditions Under Which Verbal Materials Are Presented)
   Amount of Practice
   Whole vs. Part Learning
   Highlighting Effects
   Type of Examination Expected

OVERVIEW

In Chapter 9 you studied simple associative learning of the type called operant conditioning. In that chapter you found that the concept of reinforcement is the primary factor influencing this form of learning. In Chapter 11 you considered human learning, largely of a verbal type, and found that a number of additional factors are influential—among them meaningfulness, serial position, chunking. But research on the learning of simple word lists or nonsense syllables —what is called learning out-of-context material —is somewhat unlike the type of learning where you study a textbook in preparation for a classroom examination. You may have wondered if the relationships between variables pertaining to learning out of context would apply to contextual learning. If this question did occur to you, then you were anticipating the purpose of the present chapter, which is to present factors that affect how well you learn textbook material, and factors that will make it possible for you to present to others material in a more learnable fashion.

THE IMPORTANCE OF CONTEXTUAL LEARNING

You might ask if any argument could exist concerning whether contextual learning is vital to individual and societal well-being, and whether contextual learning might have any personal relevance to the educational drop-out who may spend his lifetime in a single fixed trade or at semiskilled labor. The only answer can be that for such an individual the issue would reduce down to feelings of personal fulfillment that accompany knowing and understanding what is going on in the world versus not having such awareness.

Also you might cite the point that has been made by some educators that much of our past learning may soon become deadweight as computer memory takes on more and more of the load now handled by our own rote memories. For the psychological researcher, for example, some day no longer will he have to remember that John Smith, Sam Brown, and Kenneth Jones are the three leading researchers in a given area. At the touch of a button he will have a printout of references to major published work in any specific research area. Rather than struggle with human memory and its numerous failings, a much better job can be achieved through the use of computer memory, according to this argument.

This interesting viewpoint is partly right, but partly wrong. Let us examine it in an historical framework. Yates (1966) has described how the ancients went about memorizing oratorical presentations. In the absence of the printing press, or of video and audio tapes, verbatim memory—with information passed from one person to another through the spoken word—was the major vehicle for the transmission of accumulated knowledge from one generation to another. Today, it is obviously unnecessary for an individual to memorize all the details of, for example, a war. With mass production, printed copies of books are available at little cost. Students can become minor experts after a few hours of study, and books serve as a ready reference should memories falter.

Still, the out-of-hand rejection of human memory and its replacement by computer memory suffers from two major shortcomings. First, many modern-day miracles in education, predicted only a short while ago as soon to be commonplace, are proving to be so expensive as to be available for use to only a tiny percentage of the population. While the portable hand calculator has virtually removed the need to learn to do pencil-and-paper calculations of square roots, the same does not apply to the big computers servicing other disciplines. Thus, economics comes into the picture as a realistic limiting factor for the foreseeable future.

A second factor relates to the schema behind information storage. At a basic level, you must learn how to retrieve information by knowing what retrieval codes to use. Here we see that the context within a section of an academic discipline usually provides the systems of categories and subcategories which serve as retrieval labels. Moreover, we now know that lengthy concept presentations in context are more easily learned than the same concepts presented in no fixed order of sequence nor with transitional sections. Therefore it is doubtful if retrieved information of an abstract or interdependent nature could be as effectively interpreted and utilized if retrieved by computer for a user who had no background of contextual knowledge. This is a major reason why we find most computer progress to be in areas of *non*-contextual information retrieval. For example, the fact that a record filed under an alphabetical system can be quickly looked up, and a computer printout can then display information on a person's medical history or about side effects of the use of a certain medicinal drug, can greatly facilitate the practice of medicine. But this is not to say that such computer-generated facts could actually substitute for a contextual medical education.

It is thus the position taken here that the continuing necessity for contextual learning can easily be demonstrated. We are therefore vitally concerned with the variables that can make efforts at contextual learning either more or less effective.

AREAS OF CONTEXTUAL LEARNING RESEARCH

Several factors affect the initial learning of verbal materials. These variables can be categorized under two broad headings. First there are those factors that have to do with the nature of the verbal materials; then there are those factors having to do with conditions under which the verbal materials are presented to the subject for learning.

Learning = f(Nature of the Verbal Materials)

Verbal materials may vary in several ways. We shall start with a brief discussion of (1) the meaningfulness of the verbal material, followed by (2) the concreteness of the verbal material, and (3) the organizational qualities of the verbal material. We must, of course, recognize that these categories are not mutually exclusive, and some overlapping of classifications will occur.

Meaningfulness of the Material

Would you prefer to learn concepts from a textbook that presented the material in common, everyday language and brought in many familiar illustrations, or would you prefer a text that presented illustrations from obscure areas, using words very uncommonly employed? As an example, "The tails of Manx cats tend to be either missing altogether (we call these 'rumpies') or tend to be quite short (these are called 'stumpies')" versus "The caudal appendages of Manx felines tend, partially or totally, to be truncated." Most of us would prefer the style of the first presentation, but more important we can learn concepts more readily in the simpler language format. In general, then, we find that not only do learners prefer to have verbal material presented to them in a simple, recognizable style (the variables of *familiarity* and *meaningfulness*), but they also learn more swiftly and with fewer errors under such conditions. This leads to two commonly recognized generalizations. First, the purpose of language is to communicate; and if you use unfamiliar words or examples to the degree that a high percentage of persons do not know what you are talking about, you have failed to communicate or to teach. Second, most teachers recognize the value of the introduction of "relevance" into their teaching through the development of familiar examples and applications. These teachers can show students how a concept applies to their daily lives and thereby increase meaningfulness and, through meaningfulness, learning.

C 11A.1.   *Effects of meaningfulness of material on contextual learning.*

In contextual-learning situations, it can be shown that concepts presented in familiar language and phraseology are _____ easily learned than if presented through the use of less commonly employed vocabulary.

    a. more   b. less

In reference to the above question, we are familiar with the fact that some students who read a great deal seem later to be better students and understand things more easily than is the case with students who seldom read. The functional relationship demonstrated within the last question and answer would be _____ with the notion of existing individual differences in learning ability independent of biological intelligence.

    a. consistent   b. inconsistent

Concreteness of the Material   A second variable that pertains to the nature of verbal materials is the concreteness of material to be learned. There is evidence that, in lengthy word lists, such elements as "dirt," "elephant," "red," and so forth are learned more rapidly than are elements such as "virtue," "reversal," "pledge." Why should this be, when presumably for educated adults the latter type of word is commonly known? The critical factor in this case appears to be that the former type of element is concrete, and the latter abstract. Consider this example: If stimulus *X* becomes a reinforcer due to repeated association with situation *C*, *C* being a primary reinforcer, then behavior (*B*) which leads to *X* comes to be reinforced in the same way as would be the case if *B* led to *C*. Contrast such a highly abstract presentation of the topic of conditioned reinforcement against this presentation: If coins begin to be traded repeatedly for candy by a very small child, soon one will find that coins can be used as rewards for the child just as effectively as the primary reinforcer of candy itself.

    The extent to which increases in abstraction cause a lowering in the degree of learning is a complex question at this time. It has been found that older-aged university students are comparatively more disadvantaged by an increased level of abstraction in printed materials, and that a continuous and linear relation exists between age of adults and difficulty with abstraction. Yet the older students can be subdivided into those for whom continuing formal or self-education has been relatively uninterrupted, who show little loss of ability to handle abstract material, and those who have not studied seriously for years, and who are typically greatly disadvantaged.

    One research project established a relation between such disadvantage and the type of intervening employment. In that study infrequently enrolled public-school teachers, on a college campus for summer courses, were studied using their ages and the grade level taught as the predictor variables. After initial matching for learning ability, using concrete tasks such as remembering lists of numbers and basic words on a word list, it was found that kindergarten and first-grade teachers had the most trouble with abstract material, followed by middle-year elementary, upper-year elementary, and finally junior/senior high-school teachers. An interaction with age was established, with the older teachers in each teaching-level group having the greater disadvantage with abstractions. As one older kindergarten teacher explained following the project, "I think I know what's wrong. For thirty years I've gone through each day thinking in concrete terms, just like all the children in my classes." For young as well as old, but especially for older individuals, abstractness of materials sharply decreases the efficiency of learning.

C 11A.2. *Effects of concreteness of material on contextual learning.*

Learning scores are _____ correlated with the degree of abstractness of the material to be learned.

   a. positively   b. negatively

Learning scores, where highly abstract material is concerned, are _____ correlated with age in adult subject groups.

   a. positively   b. negatively

In general, with young adults, performance on a learning task is _____ correlated with the concreteness of the material presented.

   a. not   b. positively   c. negatively

It is likely that _____ adult would be the most disadvantaged by an increase in the abstract level of material to be learned, other factors being held constant.

   a. a young   b. a middle-aged   c. an elderly

Organization of the Material   A third variable affecting contextual learning has to do with the basic organization and sequencing of the material. This requires a preliminary statement. First, it should be apparent to you that it would be a great deal harder to "memorize" nine hundred facts taken at random from a science textbook, all of which are unfamiliar to you, than it would be to systematically read the whole book and see how the facts are developed within a context. Having an understanding that separate principles may derive from the same theory, and recognizing generalizations, exceptions, and so forth—as opposed to simple rote memorization—lead consistently to better examination scores. Therefore, if we agree that the presentation of material in context increases its learnability, then it should follow that some contextual styles of development proceed more smoothly and with better internal organization than others. This is a fairly difficult variable to assess, but it is a vital one, especially in some academic areas.

As one example, the sequencing of topics in a math textbook is critical. The effective math teacher or textbook author is knowledgeable as to which topics should come first since some topics lead sequentially to other topics.

Textbook authors in areas such as psychology often wonder whether one should proceed from specific examples and points to general principles (the inductive process) or develop general principles and then show how those principles explain specific cases (the deductive process). Should one go from easy to difficult in one continuous escalation, or run up, down, and up the difficulty scale repeatedly? Note that our questions here are not directed at what style would best entertain or stimulate the student, but rather which style results in the most effective learning. These are vital questions; research is in progress, but few answers are yet available.

A first principle we might consider is that where verbal material can be incorporated within some meaningful or logical framework, it is more rapidly learned. From word list research we already know that where an individual can bring a general concept into use so that words in a word list fall into categories (e.g., names of trees), the list is learned more efficiently.

Generally this sort of interpretation by researchers comes to a sudden halt after consideration of the nature of the material—that is, one word list can be categorized, another partially so, and another not at all, with a strong functional relationship being demonstrated between "categorizability" of the list and subsequent rate of learning. Mandler (1967) decided to carry the notion on to the question of differences in individuals' abilities to categorize. He presented subjects with individual word cards prior to attempted learning. Subjects were asked to sort the cards into two to seven separate categories, and the categories could be designated on any basis other than words starting with the same letter. The finding was that the more categories a subject used, the better was his subsequent learning of the word list. Thus our ability to categorize materials into organizational arrangements seems strongly related to how easily and efficiently we can learn the materials.

Moving into more contextually styled material, Miller and Selfridge (1950) investigated subjects' memories for practiced material which either did or did not fall into a proper "structure" of content organization. They found that subjects could more easily learn lists of statements such as "The boy drove the car" than statements such as "Car boy the a drove."

A final illustration comes from an experiment in which recall of lists of sentences was assessed (DeVilliers, 1974). Subjects who wove these sentences into some kind of theme or story showed much higher recall at a later time for the sentences than did subjects whose memorization was more in the form of disconnected sentences. Our conclusion from this and related programs of research is that learning is facilitated considerably both by existing organizational structure in verbal material and by abilities of individual learners to recognize or introduce patterns of meaning.

We have now progressed from conceptual organization that extends from one word to another in a word list, through that which exists within sentence-length statements, and finally to organization of a group of sentences into a story.

So far we have considered situations in which we can assume that most of the organization was due to the presence or absence of certain content in the materials. Another dimension exists, however. The factor of *semantic generalization*—conceptualization introduced by similarities in word meaning—has also been investigated. In a recent experiment (Light & Carter-Sobell, 1970), subjects were presented sentences with adjective-noun pairings embedded within them. For example, "The boy saw a *Northern Seal.*" *Northern* and *Seal* comprised the pairing in this case. Later subjects were given a test for recognition of the noun from the various sentences they had studied. In some cases the modifying adjective was the same as it had been in the sentence—*Northern*—but in other cases changes were made along either the physical or both the physical and semantic dimensions. An example of the former would be *Alaskan Seal,* where the meaning of the modifier is somewhat the same and only the physical structure of the word is grossly changed. An example of the latter, where both the physical structure and the semantic dimension were changed, would be *Wax Seal.* Remember that the subject sees the initial sentence, then later an expression such as *Alaskan Seal,* and is asked only whether the noun, *Seal,* was presented earlier.

The finding in this research was very clear—by changing just the modifier, a reduction in the average recognition score was brought about: the scores were moderately reduced where the physical structure but not the semantic dimension was modified. That is, recognition of *Seal* from the *Alaskan Seal* presentation was worse than from the *Northern Seal* presentation. But by far the worst of all the performance categories was where both the physical structure and the semantic dimension were modified, as with *Wax Seal.*

In applying the results of this experiment to a general learning situation, the major inference is that any change in wording from the text definitions and statements to those on a later examination will lower the performance score. We think immediately of a textbook presentation of a definition of a term, followed by an example; later an exam might present one question using the example given in the textbook, but another question asking for the same term using a new, unfamiliar example. We would expect the better performance on the question utilizing the example given in the book. This pattern of research clearly suggests that better learning, with increased flexibility and ability to transfer learning to new situations, would result from (1) multiple examples in textbooks or lectures rather than single ones, and (2) a multiplicity of examples self-stimulated by the learner himself. In performing the latter task, the student should strive first to understand examples given in the lecture and text, then try to develop additional examples from his own history of experiences.

C 11A.3. *Effects of organization of materials on contextual learning.*

A conclusion from the Miller and Selfridge research on learning lists of statements might be that if a subject perceives _____ in what he studies, his memory for the material will be better.

    a. a dimension of meaning   b. rhyming similarities   c. personal relevance

The DeVilliers research extends the concept of organization from individual sentence statements to the combination of such elements to form a _____ .

    a. group reference   b. logical conclusion   c. story

Where elements are changed within the context from the material practiced to its presentation on a recognition test, we generally expect a _____ score than would have been the case with no element changes.

    a. higher   b. lower

Where elements are changed within the context from the material practiced to its presentation on a recognition test, the highest retention score would be achieved in a situation where only the _____ dimension were changed.

    a. physical   b. semantic

We should not let the opportunity pass without a word concerning what verbal learning research suggests about the concept of "intelligence" as it applies to learning in an academic setting. We might draw a parallel between students in a classroom who face an array of contextual verbal material and individuals presented with a list of disconnected words to learn. On the word list task we find individuals searching for some element of structural meaning, in this case usually some commonality of categories, within the words given. Let us assume that one student finds such a category, at least for a portion of the words in the list, due (hypothetically) to his past experiences with office equipment. That student, then, seems to be more "intelligent" in terms of the later test for learning. Just as was the case with the word list example, we see that contextual material presented to a classroom of students first of all has certain patterned characteristics that permit it to be conceptually organized. But, related to this, we find that students' past histories of experiences allow them to seize upon various ways of organizing and conceptualizing the material.

It is then our contention that such past histories, including the degrees to which the students have read extensively, largely dictate the degree of difficulty in learning. With a little imagination you can see how a background in Greek and Roman mythology or cultural knowledge, derived through casual reading or from classics courses or indirectly from foreign language classes, might cause a student to gain a great deal more insight and more easily organize historical material. Parallels could be drawn through a vast array of different kinds of experiential backgrounds. Put in everyday terms, one teacher said that a certain student had trouble learning concepts in a course because that student "had nothing to relate new knowledge to." This, in essence, translates to an inability to form conceptual categories due to a limited set of experiences.

**Learning =
f(Conditions Under
Which Verbal
Materials Are
Presented)**

We shall begin this section by making the following claim—more than any other factor, the number of times verbal material is practiced by a subject determines the extent of learning. When we seek to arrange learning experiences for ourselves or others, amount of practice is our strongest single tool.

Amount of Practice   As was the case with some of the other functional relationships already discussed, amount of practice has clearly been shown to be a strong determining variable in learning research using nonsense syllables and word lists. In such out-of-context learning situations the power of this variable is quite clear. In context learning, the effect is not as powerful, but it still dominates other factors.

In out-of-context learning research, the variable of amount of practice is varied along two dimensions. The first simply involves repeating the elements (the words in a list, etc.) once, twice, three times, or more, and it is found under these conditions that with more exposures a greater percentage of the material is retained. The second dimension consists of the amount of time each element is presented to a subject. In one research procedure, elements from a word list were presented one at a time to two groups of subjects. One group experienced a one-second exposure of each element, while subjects in the other group were allowed to view each element for a two-second time period. Following a single exposure to each element in the 20-word list, the first group was able to recall an average of 6.9 words while the second group (the two-second exposure) recalled an average of 8.5 words, representing an approximately 24 percent difference in average scores (Murdock, 1962).

Turning to contextual-learning research concerning the variable of amount of practice, we see that it is conducted along quite similar lines. However, as you can readily see, exact control over "time spent per element" is lacking since there are no contextual elements in a clearly defined sense. On the one hand the experimenter can have subjects read through prose material once, twice, or three times, comparing the acquisition scores at each level; however, there naturally exists a possibility of certain subjects re-reading a line or sentence that they find difficult at first presentation. Or, a researcher could do as King (1974) did, and simply present a page of contextual material, allowing different groups of subjects different time periods to study. Under either of these circumstances, it is consistently found that the variable of amount of practice is strongly related to the recall score.

C 11A.4.   *Effects of amount of practice.*

The variable of amount of practice has been proposed as _____ in determining level of recall in contextual learning.

   a. perhaps the most powerful of all relevant variables

   b. being probably of only second-order importance

Strategies employed in investigating the effects of amount of practice include _____ .

   a. allowing subjects varying numbers of times to read the material

   b. allowing subjects varying amounts of time to view segments of the material

   c. both of the above are true   d. neither of the first two answers is true

Whole vs. Part Learning   A number of other important variables, all falling under the broad category of conditions under which verbal material are presented, influence learning. One of these is whole versus part learning. You will recall from a point earlier in Chapter 11 that, in research concerning out-of-context learning, word lists were more efficiently learned if long lists were first broken into shorter lists which could then be learned one at a time. In learning lines of a play, or poetry, you may have noticed that your best approach is to tackle a short section, learn it, then proceed to the next section. Perhaps this is the place where we should apply the knowledge of one learning phenomenon to the explanation of another. Most learning theorists would agree that the serial position effect is largely influenced by an accumulation of proactive and retroactive interference as learning proceeds. Using word lists, the first few words are scarcely affected by proactive interference (take a moment and think about this), and the last few words in the list are scarcely affected by retroactive interference. Now, suppose that both forms of interference are a function of the amount of interfering material, and that the functional relationship between amount of interfering material and degree of interference, when drawn, has the appearance of an ogival curve.

Figure 11A.1 presents two hypothetical curves, one for proactive interference and one for retroactive interference, which taken together could explain the serial position effect. Suppose, for example, that we calculate the amount of interference delivered to the 20th element in a 20-element list. All the interference would be proactive, and Figure 11A.1 suggests ten "units" (units are hypothetical levels) of interference in such a case. The first element, on the other hand, would receive only retroactive interference, and 20 interfering elements in this case would yield around 5 units of interference. The 11th or 12th element in a 20-element list would receive around 10 units of proactive interference and around 3 or 4 units

Figure 11A.1

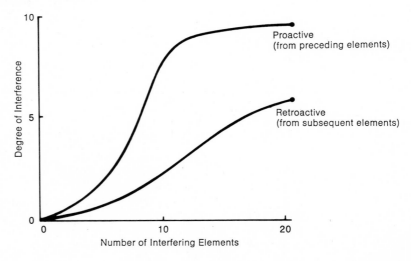

of retroactive interference, and would thus be most affected by serial position. This sort of analysis oversimplifies the dynamics of the serial position effect, but is useful in showing that an analysis of the effect is possible, given data derived from experimentation.

When we section a 20-element list into four 5-element lists and require the subject to learn each to criterion one at a time, we find that a relatively shorter total time period is required for complete acquisition. This could also relate to the "chunking" phenomenon described earlier. The greater efficiency of learning chunked material can be explained on the basis of the lessened serial position effect upon the midrange of shorter masses of material. It is quite possible for an individual to chunk contextual material on the basis of the content of a page or the content between major headings in a textbook, or it is possible for contextual material to be so organized as to be presentable in conceptual chunks. That is, the material can be written so that the learner is vividly aware of his progression from topic to topic, with accompanying awareness of the overall format outline of the material being studied. Both would appear to be effective strategies for learning lengthy masses of material.

Does the serial position effect appear in contextual learning? The research that has been done on this topic is limited, but one illustrative project was that of Sehulster, McLaughlin, and Crouse (1974), who presented four stories sequentially to subjects. It was found that recall of details from the first story was better than that for later stories. The serial position curve as we typically know it from word list or nonsense syllable learning research was not reproduced in the Sehulster research, however, since recall for the details of the final story in the sequence was not better than that for intermediate material. One very tentative conclusion might be that while the effects of proactive interference remain quite strong in shaping a serial position curve in contextual learning, contextual retroactive interference is relatively much weaker. Further research will clarify this topic.

Our illustration has ranged into distant theoretical matters, but let us bring the discussion back to the initial question of whether the whole or the part method of learning is best in contextual learning situations. It would seem that with contextual materials, as with word lists and lists of nonsense syllables, the part method yields the better results. The reason for this phenomenon appears to rest on the fact that division into small parts prevents the serial position effect from being as pronounced, since the middle of any ordering of elements is not very far from either end.

C 11A.5. *Serial position effects in contextual learning.*

In contextual learning situations, it was hypothesized that _____ interference is relatively stronger.

    a. proactive   b. retroactive

There _____ appear to be a "classical" serial position effect in contextual learning.

    a. does   b. does not

C 11A.6. *Whole versus part learning in contextual learning research.*

From contextual learning research data, it would appear that the _____ method is the best strategy

for acquisition.

a. whole   b. part

Highlighting Effects   It has long been known that setting key terms or phrases in italic type in a textbook is one way to call attention to their significance, and the terms or phrases seem to be retained better at a later examination. This line of research first began with a finding by Von Restorff (1933) that perceptually isolated materials are better retained than are materials which are not perceptually isolated. At a basic level it has been found that subjects rehearse an item more when it is set in italic type, underlined, or otherwise perceptually isolated (Rundus, 1971), but this still does not get at the heart of *why* extra rehearsal occurs.

There are two main ideas explaining this effect and each one is represented by a question, as follows. Do most subjects simply spend a longer period of time looking at highlighted material and thus learn it better? Or, is some cognitive message communicated through the high-lighting that tells the learner that the term is important and likely to appear on an examination? The effect probably is a mix of both factors, with the weighting of each depending upon characteristics of the materials to be learned.

To consider the first of those two possibilities, Cashen and Leicht (1970) compared two conditions in the study of contextual material. In the control condition students were presented nonhighlighted passages of material to be learned; in the experimental condition the important prin-ciples were underlined in red. On a later test covering important principles, learning of the highlighted passages was 18 percent better for the students in the experimental condition. The researchers' interpretation was simply that the students perceived the underlined material as "isolated," therefore more perceptually vivid, and that these sections were then given more attention.

While we would not go so far as to disagree with the observation that a contribution to learning is made simply by the attention-drawing qualities of highlighting, it is possible that relatively more of a contribution comes from the learner realizing that highlighted material deliberately is being given a higher-quality value. In the Cashen and Leicht research, the researchers could not claim as a fact that subjects did not reason that underlining meant a statement was relatively important.

It should not be lost upon you that another form of highlighting is employed in the makeup of learning materials, as in this book. In addition to italics of single words or phrases, this method sets apart sample questions which tie in to whole concepts. The logic behind this form of presentation is that (1) highlighted materials are better learned, and therefore (2) we should highlight a large proportion of the important content; then (3) the important content will be better learned than is the case with traditional materials.

One question that has come up since the introduction of this type of heavy highlighting (in contrast to the limited highlighting through italic type in traditional texts) is whether nonstressed sections in a heavily highlighted book are adequately learned. It is not uncommon to encounter a reasoning that in such learning students pay no attention to anything other than the specific answers to the sample questions. One research project, within a contextual learning setting, investigated this question. Compared with scores on the same material in a control group where heavy highlighting was not used, subjects with highlighted material had much *higher* scores on the stressed elements (95 percent versus 71 percent), but somewhat *lower* scores on the nonstressed elements tested (61 percent versus 73 percent). However, one important uncontrolled factor seems to have had an effect. In that project the students with the highlighted material were led to believe that the elements stressed, being the total of performance objectives, would be the only ones selected for the examination. Their strategy, then, was to concentrate mainly upon material which, they assumed, was important and would be on their test. Still, significant learning of the nonstressed learning elements was shown in this group (Aiken, 1973).

C 11A.7. *Effects of highlighting material on contextual learning,*

The theory of the operation of the highlighting effect is that the learner _____ .

    a. perceives highlighted material more vividly

    b. understands that the highlighted material is more vital

    c. (both of the above explanations have been invoked to explain the effect)

Research shows that nonstressed elements in material using highlighting are _____ .

    a. learned extremely well   b. learned to a 60 percent level   c. not learned at all

Type of Exam Expected   Yet another of the various conditions under which verbal learning material is presented to the subject has to do with the expectations of the learner concerning the type of examination to follow. This variable is initially dependent upon the instructions given by the researcher or teacher.

People appear to learn material (1) to different levels, and (2) in different ways, depending upon the type of examination they expect. Let us consider why this should be so. Suppose that you are told to expect an *essay* exam over a chapter of material. You would probably study the chapter in such a way as to recognize the main points, see relationships between sections, and understand the thematic currents that flow through the material. As an extreme case in point, qualifications stated on the last page of the chapter are typically learned not in isolation but, rather, in relation to general principles developed in earlier sections of the material.

On the other hand, when you expect a multiple-choice test you typically learn along a different dimension. What then becomes important is to recognize associative pairings or groupings in terms or facts. For example, "Who developed psychoanalytic theory?" becomes two associative elements—the name *Freud* and the label *psychoanalytic theory*. Or, "What is an operational definition?" associates two elements: the term *operational definition* and a short definitive meaning of the term. Other associative formats might involve five elements in "The four reasons why," or the four elements in "The three types of," and so forth.

Evidence suggests that when a student studies for a multiple-choice exam and then unexpectedly receives an essay exam, he does more poorly than would have been the case had he expected an essay test during his preparation. Conversely, though to a much lesser extent, the student preparing for an essay test, then unexpectedly presented with a multiple-choice exam, is also handicapped. In this case there is a mix of evidence, with the best conclusion being that the degree to which a student may or may not be slightly hurt by studying for an essay test and then being given a multiple-choice test is largely determined by the type of material being studied. If many associative elements are presented in a minimally integrated chapter, the handicap can be pronounced; if the chapter is highly abstract but interconnected, there would be little if any resulting handicap.

Why is there a relatively stronger handicapping effect to the student preparing with the expectation of a multiple-choice test, then surprised with an essay test, than is the case where events are the other way around? It appears that the student usually learns to a higher level, all other things being equal, when the material is to be tested by means of an essay examination. This factor is an important element of the overall rationale of the classroom examination, so we shall consider it in detail.

As we stated earlier, various levels of learning have been identified and related to certain methods of measurement. We identified the *level of recognition* as the lowest commonly conceived level of retention. This is what is directly tested by a multiple-choice exam. The person may be able to recognize the correct answer from a list of names where the question is "Who was the founder of psychoanalytic theory?" The names Jung, Freud, Reik, and Adler might be presented, and the student would only need to recognize the correct answer from those presented. A fill-in-the-blank test asking the same question would call for knowledge to the *level of recall*. It is found that if a class is randomly divided, half its members being given a multiple-choice test and half a fill-in-the-blank test with identical question stems, the percent correct will be quite a bit higher for the multiple-choice group, indicating that recall is at a higher (more difficult) level. At the still higher level, the *level of reconstruction*, the learner has, presumably, to pick his way through sequences of reasoning, understanding, and concluding, and his own analytical processes may have to match the processes demonstrated in the material studied. It is quite difficult to directly compare elements of a recall test format with matching elements present in a reconstruction or essay style of examination, but to the extent that this has been attempted, it seems that the "percent correct" type of scoring of contained elements would give the lower score to the group taking the essay examination. It appears that a learner must be able to recognize analogous circumstances, reason while using the principles learned, retrace arguments, and make comparisons on the basis of the knowledge acquired if he or she is to do well on a typical essay examination. Thus, learning to the level of reconstruction is a higher level of academic learning.

We earlier made the case that if a student expects a multiple-choice exam he will study in ways that best prepare him for that particular kind of exam, and we have now made the case that he then learns to a relatively lower level. It follows, therefore, that student preparation for an essay examination will result in superior learning. If this is so, then why do teachers persist in using the multiple-choice exam? The reasons are several.

First, with the advent of large classes, many teachers have had little alternative. Even in a "small" class of about 40 students, a teacher must spend ten to fifteen hours to carefully read and evaluate a class's essay examination. Second, many teachers are disturbed by having to confer with certain students after each essay examination. The objective scoring system used with the multiple-choice exam, coupled with careful exam preparation, means that fewer questions generate discussion over what is the correct answer. Finally, disregarding the fact that exam expectancy influences learning level, it can be shown that the results of different types of exams show high positive correlations. It is found that the people falling into the top 10 or 20 percent on a multiple-choice test are the same ones who tend to score in the same level on an essay test over the same material. There are occasional exceptions, but with most people the relationship is quite strong. Therefore the multiple-choice exam—designed as a measure of learning to the level of recognition—can be taken as an estimate of learning to the level of reconstruction.

C 11A.8. *Effect of type of exam expected on contextual learning.*

Evidence suggests that modifying the type of exam a student expects will change _____ .

    a. the type of learning strategy the student uses

    b. the actual level of learning that subsequently occurs

    c. both of the above are correct   d. neither of the first two answers is correct

The student who expected an essay test and had studied for it, then received a multiple-choice exam unexpectedly, would probably do _____ on the exam than would a student expecting a multiple-choice exam who then received an essay exam unexpectedly.

    a. better   b. more poorly

A fill-in-the-blank type of exam tests the student to the level of _____ .

    a. recall   b. reconstruction   c. recognition

The processes of logical reasoning, analogous thinking, and the making of comparisons based upon initial knowledge call for learning to the level of _____ .

    a. recall   b. reconstruction   c. recognition

A test of learning to the level of recognition is reflected in the _____ .

    a. essay exam   b. fill-in-the-blank test   c. multiple-choice exam

It is known that when a multiple-choice exam and an essay exam over the same material are given to a group of individuals, the resulting two distributions of scores show a _____ correlation.

    a. strong positive   b. weak positive   c. strong negative   d. weak negative

---

PROGRESS CHECK   11A.1

1. Contextual learning is easier, when _____ .

    a. familiar language is used

    b. obscure language is used

    c. either circumstance is equally difficult

2. The fact that practice improves performance indicates _____ .

    a. biological intelligence   b. learned intelligence

    c. general intelligence   d. native intelligence

3. Which statement is untrue of the correlation between learning scores and abstractness of the material? _____

    a. Learning scores are negatively correlated with degree of abstraction

    b. As one ages, learning abstract material gets easier

    c. Almost anyone will learn concrete material better than abstract material

MATCH: _____ 4. Miller and Selfridge's research   A. Lists in story form were more easily learned

    _____ 5. DeVillier's research   B. Proper sentence structure facilitated learning

    _____ 6. Changing the context   C. Lower performance scores

7. Which strategies have not been emphasized in typical research on practice and contextual learning? _____ .

    a. Repetition   b. Amount of time   c. Reinforcements

8. Acquisition improves with whole (versus part) learning. _____ .

    a. True   b. False

9. Which is an accurate statement on highlighting? _____ .

    a. Cashen and Leicht believed highlighted material was made more perceptually vivid

    b. Highlighting may signal value of content

    c. Highlighting material improves its acquisition

    d. All of these

10. Although study for a multiple-choice test hurts later performance on an essay test, studying for an essay test may not hurt later multiple-choice test performance. _____ .

     a. True   b. False

MATCH: _____ 11. Fill-in-the-blank test   A. Recognition

              _____ 12. Logical reasoning   B. Recall
                        and comparison   C. Reconstruction

              _____ 13. Multiple-choice

OVERVIEW   At no point in this section have we gone into such matters as rewards and punishments in contextual learning. Nor have we made mention of a wide array of additional functional relationships that perhaps have less immediate application to how we might arrange our own study—such factors as whether material presented through the visual or through the auditory sensory modalities is the more easily learned, or whether multimodal presentations are effective.

At this point we shall simply indicate that research into learning in context is exceedingly difficult. Nowhere, however, is there as great a likelihood of valuable and socially relevant payoff as in the relatively young field of the experimental study of learning in context.

References

References

Adams, J. S. Injustice in social exchange. In L. Berkowitz (Ed.), *Advances in experimental social psychology.* New York: Academic Press, Vol. II, 1965.

Aiken, S. Variables in mastery instruction. Unpublished research paper, Illinois State Univer., 1973

Allen, K. E., Hart, B. M., Buell, J. S., Harris, F. R., and Wolf, M. M. Effects of social reinforcement on isolate behavior of a nursery school child. *Child Devel.,* 1964, **35,** 511–18.

Ardrey, R. *The territorial imperative.* New York: Atheneum, 1966.

Arnoult, M. D. *Fundamentals of scientific method in psychology.* Dubuque, Iowa: W. C. Brown, 1972.

Aronfreed, J. The socialization of altruistic and sympathetic behavior: Some theoretical and experimental analyses. In J. Macauley and L. Berkowitz (Eds.), *Altruism and helping behavior: Social psychological studies of some antecedents and consequences.* New York: Academic Press, 1970.

Aronson, E. Gain and loss of esteem as determinants of interpersonal attractiveness. *J. exp. soc. Psychol.,* 1965, **1,** 156–72.

Aronson, E. *The social animal.* San Francisco: W. H. Freeman & Co., 1972.

Aronson, E., and Carlsmith, J. M. Experimentation in social psychology. In G. Lindzey and E. Aronson (Eds.), *Handbook of social psychology.* Reading, Mass.: Addison-Wesley, 1969.

Aronson, E., and Mills, J. The effect of severity of initiation on liking for a group. *J. ab. soc. Psychol.,* 1959, **59,** 177–91.

Asch, S. E. Effects of group pressure upon the modification and distortion of judgments. In H. Guetzkow (Ed.), *Groups, leadership, and men.* Pittsburgh: Carnegie Press, 1951.

Ashley, W. R., Harper, R. S., and Runyon, D. L. The perceived size of coins in normal and hynotically induced economic status. *Amer. J. Psychol.,* 1951, **64,** 564–72.

Ayllon, T. Intensive treatment of psychotic behaviour by stimulus satiation and food reinforcement. *Beh. Res. Ther.,* 1963, **1,** 53–61.

Ayllon, T., and Michael, J. The psychiatric nurse as a behavioral engineer. *J. exp. anal. Behav.,* 1959, **2,** 323–34.

Azrin, N. H. Aggression. *Amer. Psychol.,* 1964, **19,** 501.

Azrin, N. H., Hake, D. F., and Hutchinson, R. R. Elicitation of aggression by a physical blow. *J. exp. anal. Behav.,* 1965, **8,** 55–57.

Azrin, H. H., Hake, D. F., and Hutchinson, R. R. Extinction-induced aggression. *J. exp. anal. Behav.,* 1966, **9,** 191–204.

Asimov, I. *Asimov's guide to science.* New York: Basic Books, 1972.

Auerbach, C. *The science of genetics.* New York: Harper & Row, 1961.

Bachrach, A. *Psychological research: An introduction.* (3rd ed.) New York: Random House, 1972.

Bales, R. F. *Interaction process analysis: A method for the study of small groups.* Cambridge, Mass.: Addison-Wesley, 1950.

Bales, R. F. *Personality and interpersonal behavior.* New York: Holt, Rinehart & Winston, 1970.

Bandura, A. Vicarious and self-reinforcement. In R. Glaser (Ed.), *The nature of reinforcement.* New York: Academic Press, 1971.

Banks, E. M. A time and motion study of prefighting behaviors in mice. *J. gen. Psychol.,* 1962, **101,** 165–83.

Barry, H., Jr. Significance of maternal bereavement before age eight in psychiatric patients. *Arch. Neur. Psychiat.*, 1949, **62,** 630–37.

Bartley, S. H. *Principles of perception.* (2nd ed.) New York: Harper & Row, 1969.

Bartley, S.H. *Perception in everyday life.* New York: Harper & Row, 1972.

Beadle, G., and Beadle, M. *The language of life.* Garden City, N.Y.: Doubleday & Co., 1966.

Bennett, E. L., Krech, D., and Rosenzweig, M. R. Reliability and regional specificity of cerebral effects of environmental complexity and training. *J. comp. physiol. Psychol.,* 1964, **57,** 440–41.

Berg, M., and Cohen, B. B. Early separation from the mother in schizophrenia. *J. nerv. ment. Dis.,* 1959, **128,** 365–69.

Berlyne, D. E., and Boudewijns, W. J. Hedonic effects of uniformity in variety. *Canad. J. Psychol.,* 1971, **25,** 195–206.

Berne, E. *Games people play: The psychology of human relationships.* New York: Grove Press, 1972.

Berscheid, E., and Walster, E. Physical attractiveness. In L. Berkowitz (Ed.), *Advances in experimental social psychology.* New York: Academic Press, Vol. VII, 1974.

Bishop, M. P., Elder, S. T., and Heath, R. Intracranial self-stimulation in man. *Science,* 1963, **140,** 394–96.

Bogardus, E. S. A social distance scale. *Soc. soc. Res.,* 1933, **17,** 265–71.

Bond, E. A. Tenth grade abilities and achievements. Teachers College, Columbia University Contribution to Education, 1940, p. 813.

Böök, J. A. Schizophrenia as a gene mutation. *Acta Genetica,* 1953, **4,** 133–39.

Borgatta, E. F., Bales, R. F., and Couch, A. S. Some findings relevant to the great man theory of leadership. *Amer. soc. Rev.,* 1954, **19,** 755–59.

Botwinick, J. *Aging and behavior.* New York: Springer, 1973.

Bowlby, J. *Attachment and loss.* London: Hogarth, 1969.

Brady, J. V., Porter, R. W., Conrad, D. G., and Mason, J. W. Avoidance behavior and the development of gastroduodenal ulcers. *J. exp. anal. Behav.,* 1958, **1,** 69–72.

Breder, C. M., Jr., and Coates, C. W. A preliminary study of population stability and sex ratio of *Lebistes. Copeia,* 1932, **38,** 147–55.

Bridges, K. M. B. Emotional development in early infancy. *Child Dev.,* 1932, **3,** 324–41.

Brill, A. A. *Lectures on psychoanalytic psychiatry.* New York: Vintage Books, 1959.

Brislin, R. W., and Lewis, S. A. Dating and physical attractiveness: Replication. *Psychol. Rep.,* 1968, **22,** 976.

Brown, J. S. Gradients of approach and avoidance responses and their relation to level of motivation. *J. comp. physiol. Psychol.,* 1948, **41,** 450–65.

Brown, J. S. *The motivation of behavior.* New York: McGraw-Hill, 1961.

Brownfield, C. A. *Isolation. Clinical and experimental approaches.* New York: Random House, 1965.

Bruce, C. L., and Livingston, F. B. On creeping Jensenism. In C. L. Bruce et al. (Eds.), *Race and intelligence.* Washington, D.C.: American Anthropological Association, 1971.

Brunswick, E. *Perception and the representative design of psychological experiments.* Berkeley: Univer. of Calif. Press, 1953.

Bryan, J. H., and Test, M. Models and helping: Naturalistic studies in aiding behavior. *J. Personal. soc. Psychol.,* 1967, **6,** 400–407.

Burke, H. R. Raven's progressive matrices: A review and critical evaluation. *J. genet. Psychol.,* 1958, **193,** 199–228.

Burt, C., and Howard, M. The multifactorial theory of inheritance and its application to intelligence. *Brit. J. statist. Psychol.,* 1956, **9,** 95–131.

Buss, A. *Psychopathology.* New York: Wiley, 1966.

Cairns, R. B., and Werboff, J. Behavior development in the dog: An interspecific analysis. *Science,* 1967, **158,** 1070–1072.

Calhoun, J. B. Population density and social pathology. *Sci. Amer.,* 1962, **206,** 139–48.

Cannon, W. B. Hunger and thirst. In C. Murchinson (Ed.), *A handbook of general experimental psychology.* Worcester, Mass.: Clark Univer. Press, 1934. Pp. 247–63.

Cashen, V., and Leicht, K. Role of the isolation effect in a formal educational setting. *J. ed. Psychol.*, 1970, **61,** 484–86.

Casler, L. Perceptual deprivation in institutional settings. In G. Newton and S. Levine (Eds.), *Early experience and behavior.* Springfield, Ill.: Charles C Thomas, 1968.

Cattell, R. B. Theory of fluid and crystallized intelligence: A critical experiment. *J. ed. Psychol.*, 1963, **54,** 1–22.

Cattell, R. B., and Eber, H. W. *Handbook for the sixteen personality factor questionnaire (16 P-F).* Champaign, Ill.: Inst. for Personality and Ability Testing, 1970.

Christian, J. J. The roles of endocrine and behavioral factors in the growth of mammalian populations. In A. Gorbman (Ed.), *Comparative endocrinology.* New York: Wiley, 1959. Pp. 71–97.

Christian, J. J. Endocrine adaptive mechanisms and the physiologic regulation of population growth. In M. V. Meyer and R. Van Gelder (Eds.), *Physiological mammalogy.* New York: Academic Press, 1963. Pp. 189–353.

Cialdini, R. B., Braver, S. L., and Lewis, S. K. Attributional bias and the easily persuaded other. *J. Personal. soc. Psychol.*, 1974, **30,** 631–37.

Coats, W. D., and Smidchens, U. Audience recall as a function of speaker dynamism. *J. educ. Psychol.*, 1966, **57,** 189–91.

Cowan, P., and Walters, R. Studies of reinforcement of aggression: I. Effects of scheduling. *Child Devel.*, 1963, **34**(3), 543–51.

Crutchfield, R. S. Conformity and character, *American Psychologist,* 1955, **10,** 191–98.

Darwin, C. *On the origin of species.* London: J. John Murray Publishers, 1859.

Davis, C. M. Self-selection of diet by newly weaned infants. *Amer. J. Dis. Child.*, 1928, **36,** 651–79.

Deese, J., and Hulse, S. *The psychology of learning.* (3rd ed.) New York: McGraw-Hill, 1967.

Deese, J., and Kaufman, R. A. Serial effects in recall of unorganized and sequentially organized verbal material. *J. exp. Psychol.*, 1957, **54,** 180–87.

DeValois, R. L. Analysis and coding of color vision in the primate system. In *Cold Spring Harbor Symposium in quantitative biology,* 1965, 30.

DeVilliers, P. A. Imagery and theme in recall of connected discourse. *J. exp. Psychol.*, 1974, **103,** 263–68.

DiMatteo, M. R. The effects of perceived deviancy on interpersonal evaluation. *Psychonomic Science,* 1972, **29,** 97–99.

Dion, K. K., and Berscheid, E. Physical attractiveness and social perception of peers in preschool children. Unpublished manuscript, University of Minnesota, 1972.

Doland, D. J. and Adelberg, K. The learning of sharing behavior. *Child Devel.*, 1967, **38,** 695–700.

Dollard, J., and Miller, N. E. *Personality and psychotherapy: An analysis in terms of learning, thinking and culture.* New York: McGraw-Hill, 1950.

Dollard, J., Miller, N. E., Doob, L. W., Mowrer, O. H., and Sears, R. R. *Frustration and aggression.* New Haven, Conn.: Yale Univer. Press, 1939.

Dreyer, P. I., and Church, R. M. Reinforcement of shock-induced fighting. *Psychonom. Sci.*, 1970, **18,** 147–48.

Ebbinghaus, H. *Das Gedachtnes: Untersuchungen zur experimentellen Psychologie.* Leipzig. Duncker and Humblot, 1885. (Trans. *Memory: A contribution to experimental psychology,* translated by Ruger, H. A., and Bussenuis, C. E. New York: Teachers College, Columbia Univer., 1913).

Edwards, A. J. *Individual mental testing.* Vol. 1—*History and theories;* Vol. 2—*Measurement.* Scranton, Pa.: Intext, 1972.

Efran, M. G. The effect of physical appearance on the judgment of guilt, interpersonal attraction, and severity of recommended punishment in a simulated jury task. *J. Res. Personal.*, 1974, **8,** 45–54.

Einstein, A. *Ideas and opinions.* New York: Crown Publishing, Inc., 1954.

Ellis, A. *Reason and emotion in psychotherapy.* New York: Lyle Stuart, 1962.

Erikson, E. H. *Insight and responsibility.* New York: Norton, 1964.

Eysenck, H. J. *Experiments in personality.* London: Routledge & Kegan Paul, 1960.

Eysenck, H. J. *Crime and personality*. Boston: Houghton Mifflin, 1964.

Fantz, R. L. Pattern vision in newborn infants. *Science,* 1963, **140,** 296–97.

Faris, R. E. L. Ecological factors in human behavior. In J. McV. Hunt (Ed.), *Personality and the behavior disorders*. New York: Ronald Press, 1944.

Faris, R. E. L., and Dunham, H. W. *Mental disorders in urban areas*. Chicago: Univer. of Chicago Press, 1939.

Feather, N. T., and Simon, J. G. Reactions to male and female success and failure in sex-linked occupations: Impressions of personality, causal attributions, and perceived likelihood of different consequences. *J. Personal. soc. Psychol.,* 1975, **31,** 20–31.

Fejer, D., and Smart, R. G. Drug use, anxiety and psychological problems among adolescents. *Ontario psychologist,* 1972, **4,** 10–21.

Festinger, L. *A theory of cognitive dissonance*. Stanford, Calif.: Stanford Univer. Press, 1957.

Fischer, W. F. Sharing in preschool children as a function of amount and type of reinforcement. *Genet. Psychol. Monogr.,* 1963, **68,** 215–45.

Frank, F. Uber den Zusammenbruch von Feldmausplagen. *Zool. Jahrb. Abt. System,* 1953, **82,** 1–156.

Freedman, D. G. Smiling in blind infants and the issue of innate vs. acquired. *J. child Psychol. Psychiat.,* 1964, **5,** 171–84.

French, J. D., Porter, R. W., Cavanaugh, E. B., and Longmire, R. L. Experimental observations on "psychosomatic" mechanisms. I. Gastrointestinal disturbances. *A.M.A. Arch. Neurol. Psychiat.,* 1954, **72,** 267–81.

Freud, A. *The ego and the mechanisms of defence*. New York: International Univer. Press, 1946.

Fuller, J. L., and Thompson, W. R. *Behavior genetics*. New York: Wiley, 1960.

Fuster, J. M. Effect of stimulation of brain stem on tachistoscopic perception. *Science,* 1958, **127,** 150.

Galambos, R., and Davis, H. Action potentials from single auditory nerve fibers? *Science,* 1948, **108,** 513.

Galton, F. *Hereditary genius*. London: Clay & Sons, 1869.

Galton, F. *Memories of my life*. London: Methuen, 1908.

Gergen, K. *The psychology of behavior exchange*. Reading, Mass.: Addison-Wesley, 1969.

Gibson, E. J. *Principles of perceptual learning and development*. New York: Appleton-Century-Crofts, 1969.

Gibson, J. J. *The senses considered as perceptual systems*. New York: Houghton Mifflin, 1966.

Gibson, J. J. What gives rise to the perception of motion? *Psychol. Rev.,* 1968, **75,** 335–46.

Ginsburg, B., and Allee, W. C. Some effects of conditioning on social dominance and subordination in inbred strains of mice. *Physiol. Zool.,* 1942, **15,** 485–506.

Goldschmidt, R. *Theoretical genetics*. Berkeley: Univer. of Calif. Press, 1955.

Gouldner, A. W. The norm of reciprocity: A preliminary statement. *Amer. soc. Rev.,* 1960, **25,** 161–79.

Gregory, R. L. *The intelligent eye*. New York: McGraw-Hill, 1970.

Grice, G. R. The relation of secondary reinforcement to delayed reward in visual discrimination. *J. exp. Psychol.,* 1948, **38,** 1–16.

Grusec, J. Demand characteristics of the modeling experiment: Altruism as a function of age and aggression. *J. Personal. soc. Psychol.,* 1972, **22,** 139–48.

Guilford, J. P. Theories of intelligence. In B. B. Wolman (Ed.), *Handbook of general psychology*. Englewood Cliffs, N. J.: Prentice-Hall, 1973.

Hall, C., and Lindzey, G. *Theories of personality*. (2nd ed.) New York: Wiley, 1970.

Handlon, B. J., and Gross, P. The development of sharing behavior. *J. ab. soc. Psychol.,* 1959, **59,** 425–28.

Harlow, H. F. The nature of love. *Amer. Psychologist,* 1958, **13,** 673–85.

Harrell, R. F., Woodyard, E., and Gates, A. I. *The effects of mothers' diets on the intelligence of the offspring*. New York: Teachers College, Columbia Univer., 1955.

Harvard Educational Review. *Science, heritability, and IQ*. Cambridge, Mass.: Harvard Educational Review, 1969.

Hathaway, S. R., and McKinley, J. C. *The Minnesota multiphasic personality inventory*. (Rev. ed.) Minneapolis: Univer. of Minn. Press, 1943.

Hays, W. L. *Statistics for psychologists*. New York: Holt, Rinehart & Winston, 1963.

Heath, R. B., Martens, S., Leach, B. E., and Angel, C. Effect on behavior of humans with the administration of taraxein. *Amer. J. Psychiat.*, 1957, **114**, 14–24.

Hebb, D. O. *Textbook of psychology* (3rd ed.) Philadelphia: W. B. Saunders, 1972.

Heidbreder, E. *Seven psychologies*. New York: Century, 1933.

Heider, F. *The psychology of interpersonal relations*. New York: Wiley, 1958.

Held, R., and Hein, A. Movement-produced stimulation in the development of visually-guided behavior. *J. comp. physiol. Psychol.*, 1963, **56**, 872–76.

Heron, W. The pathology of boredom. *Scientific Amer.*, 1957, **199**, 52–56.

Herrnstein, R. J. *I. Q. in the meritocracy*. Boston: Little, Brown, 1973.

Hess, R. D., and Shipman, V. C. Cognitive elements in maternal behavior. In J. P. Hill (Ed.), *Minnesota symposia on child psychology*. Minneapolis: Univer. of Minn. Press, 1967.

Heston, L. The genetics of schizophrenia and schizoid disease. *Science*, 1970, **167**, 249–56.

Hoffer, A., and Osmond, H. The adrenochrome model and schizophrenics. *J. nerv. ment. Dis.*, 1959, **128**, 18–35.

Hollingshead, A. B., and Redlich, F. *Social class and mental illness*. New York: Wiley, 1958.

Homans, G. C. *The human group*. New York: Harcourt, Brace, 1950.

Homans, G. C. Social behavior as exchange. *Amer. J. Soc.*, 1958, **63**, 597–606.

Honzik, M. P. Developmental studies of parent-child resemblance in intelligence. *Child Development*, 1957, **28**, 215–28.

Horney, K. *The neurotic personality of our time*. New York: Norton, 1937.

Horrocks, J. E. *The psychology of adolescence*. (3rd ed.) Boston: Houghton Mifflin, 1969.

Hoskins, R. G. *The biology of schizophrenia*. New York: Norton, 1946.

Hovland, C. I., and Janis, I. L. (Eds.), *Personality and persuasibility*. New Haven, Conn.: Yale Univer. Press, 1959.

Hubel, D. H., and Wiesel, T. N. Receptive fields, binocular interaction and functional architecture in the cat's retina. *J. Physiol.*, 1962, **160**, 106–54.

Hull, C. L. *A behavior system*. New Haven: Yale Univer. Press, 1952.

Hunt, J. McV. (Ed.) *Human intelligence*. New Brunswick, N.J.: Transaction Books, 1972.

Hunter, W. S. *General psychology*. Chicago: Univer. of Chicago Press, 1919.

Iwawaki, S., and Lerner, R. M. Cross-cultural analyses of body-behavior relations: I. A comparison of body build stereotypes of Japanese and American males and females. *Psychologia: An International Journal of Psychology in the Orient*, 1974, **17**, 75–81.

Jaco, E. G. The social isolation hypothesis in schizophrenia. *Amer. soc. Rev.*, 1954, **19**, 567–77.

Jencks, B., and Porter, P. B. Need reduction and primary reinforcement: Varied goal situations as reinforcement in maze learning of rats. *J. Psychol.*, 1960, **49**, 139–43.

Jensen, A. R. How much can we boost IQ and scholastic achievement? *Harvard Educational Review*, 1969, **39**, 1–123.

Jensen, A. R. Input: Arthur Jensen replies. *Psychol. Today*, 1969, **3**, 8.

Jensen, A. R. *Genetics and education*. New York: Harper & Row, 1972.

Johnson, R. C., and Medinnus, G. R. *Child psychology*. (3rd ed.) New York: Wiley, 1974.

Johnston, J. M., and Pennypacker, H. S. A behavioral approach to college teaching. *Amer. Psychol.*, 1971, **26**, 219–44.

Jones, E. E., Rock, L., Shaver, K. G., Goethals, G. R., and Ward, L. M. Patterns of performance and ability attribution. *J. Personal. soc. Psychol.*, 1968, **10**, 317–40.

Jones, E. E., and Sigall, H. The bogus pipeline: A new paradigm for measuring affect and attitude. *Psychol. Bull.*, 1971, **76**, 349–64.

Jones, M. B. Genetics review section. *Claremont M. H. Abstr. Quart.*, 1956, **2,** 42.

Jurgen, K., and Vernon, W. M. Physical height and social height. Unpublished paper, Illinois State Univer., 1967.

Kallman, F. J. *Heredity in health and mental disorder.* New York: Norton, 1953.

Kendler, H. H. *Basic psychology.* New York: Appleton-Century-Crofts, 1963.

Kimble, G. A., and Bilodeau, E. A. Work and rest as variables in cyclical motor learning. *J. exp. Psychol.*, 1949, **39,** 150–57.

King, D. J. Total presentation time and total learning time in connected discourse learning. *J. exp. Psychol.*, 1974, **103,** 586–89.

King, J. A., and Gurney, N. L. Effect of early social experiences on adult aggresive behavior in C57BL/10 mice. *J. comp. physiol. Psychol.*, 1954, **47,** 326–36.

Klebanoff, L. B. Parental attitudes of mothers of schizophrenic, brain-injured and retarded, and normal children. *Amer. J. Orthopsychiat.*, 1959, **24,** 445–54.

Knutson, J. F. Aggression during the fixed-ratio and extinction components of a multiple schedule of reinforcement. *J. exp. anal. Behav.*, 1970, **13,** 221–31.

Kuffler, S. W. Discharge patterns and functional organization of mammalian retina. *J. Neurophysiology*, 1953, **16,** 37–68.

Kuo, Z. Y. The genesis of the cat's responses to the rat. *J. comp. Psychol.*, 1930, **11,** 1–35.

Lagerspetz, K., and Worinen, K. A cross-fostering experiment with mice selectively bred for aggressiveness and non-aggressiveness. *Rept. psychol. Inst. Univ. Turku,* 1965, *No. 17,* 1–6.

Latane, B., and Hothersall, D. Social attraction in animals. In P. C. Dodwell (Ed.), *New horizons in psychology 2.* Baltimore: Penguin Books, 1972. Pp. 259–75.

Lawson R. *Frustration: The development of a scientific concept.* New York: Macmillan, 1965.

Lee, E. S. Negro intelligence and selective migration: A Philadelphia test of the Klineberg hypothesis. *Amer. Sociol. Rev.*, 1951, **16,** 227–33.

Leighton, A. *My name is legion.* New York: Basic Books, 1959.

Lenneberg, E. H. *Biological foundations of language.* New York: Wiley, 1967.

Leukel, F. *Introduction to physiological psychology* (2nd ed.) St. Louis: C. V. Mosby, 1972.

Lidz, R., and Lidz, T. The family environment of schizophrenic patients. *Amer. J. Psychiat.*, 1949, **106,** 332–45.

Light, L. L., and Carter-Sobell, L. Effects of changed semantic context on recognition memory. *J. verb. Learn. verb. Behav.*, 1970, **9,** 1–11.

Logan, F. A., and Boice, R. Aggressive behaviors of paired rodents in an avoidance context. *Behaviour,* 1969, **34,** 161–83.

Lorenz, K. Z. Die angeborenen Formen moglicher Erfahrung. *Z. Tierpsychologie,* 1943, **5,** 235–409.

Lorenz, K. *On aggression.* New York: Harcourt, Brace & World, 1966.

Lorge, I. The influence of regularly interpolated time intervals upon subsequent learning. *Teach. Coll. Contr. Educ.*, 1930, **No. 438.**

Luginbuhl, J. E., Crowe, D. H., and Kahan, J. P. Causal attributions for success and failure. *J. Personal. soc. Psychol.*, 1975, **31,** 86–93.

Lugo, J. O., and Hershey, G. L. *Human development.* New York: Macmillan, 1974.

Lundin, R. *Personality: A behavioral analysis.* New York: Macmillan, 1969.

McCleary, R. A. (Ed.) *Genetic and experimental factors in perception.* Glenview, Ill.: Scott, Foresman, 1970.

McGaugh, J. L. (Ed.) *Psychology: Behavior from a biological perspective.* New York: Academic Press, 1971.

McGhie, A. *Pathology of attention.* Baltimore: Penguin, 1969.

Mahut, H. Breed differences in dogs' emotional behaviour. *Canad. J. Psychol.*, 1958, **12,** 35–44.

Maier, N.R.F., Glaser, N. M., and Klee, J. B. Studies of abnormal behavior in the rat: III. The development of behavioral fixations through frustration. *J. exp. Psychol.*, 1940, **26,** 521–46.

Mandler, G. Organization and memory. In K. W. Spence and J. T. Spence (Eds.), *The psychology of learning and motivation.* New York: Academic Press, 1967.

Marks, W. B., Dobelle, W. H., and MacNichol, E. F., Jr. Visual pigments of single primate cones. *Science,* 1964, **143,** 1181–83.

Maslow, A. H. *Motivation and personality.* New York: Harper & Row, 1954.

Maslow, A. H. *Toward a psychology of being.* (2nd ed.) Princeton, N.J.: Van Nostrand, 1968.

Mathews, S. R., Jr., and Finger, F. W. Direct observation of the rat's activity during food deprivation. *Physiol. and Behav.,* 1966, **1,** 85–88.

McClelland, D. C. *The achieving society.* Princeton, N. J.: Van Nostrand, 1961.

McClelland, D. C., Atkinson, J. W., Clark, R. A., and Lowell, E. L. *The achievement motive.* New York: Appleton, 1953.

McConaghy, N. The use of an object sorting test in elucidating the hereditary factor in schizophrenia. *J. Neurol. Neurosurg. Psychiat.,* 1959, **22,** 243–46.

Meehl, P. E. Schizotaxia, schizotypy, schizophrenia. *Amer. Psych.,* 1962, **17,** 827–38.

Meyer, V., and Chesser, E. *Behavior therapy in clinical psychiatry.* Baltimore: Penguin, 1970.

Mikula, G., & Egger, J. The acquisition of positive and negative attitudes while facing previously neutral persons. *Zeitschrift für Experimentelle und Angewandte Psychologie,* 1974, **21,** 132–45.

Milgram, S. Some conditions of obedience and disobedience to authority. *Human Relations,* 1965, **18,** 57–75.

Miller, G. A., and Selfridge, O. G. Verbal context and the recall of meaningful material. *Amer. J. Psychol.,* 1950, **63,** 176–85.

Miller, N. E. Studies of fear as an acquirable drive: I. Fear as motivation and fear reduction as reinforcement in the learning of new responses. *J. exp. Psychol.,* 1948, **38,** 89–101.

Miller, N. E., Dollard, J., Doob, L. W., Mowrer, A. H., and Sears, R. R. *Frustration and aggression.* New Haven, Conn.: Yale University Press, 1939.

Miller D. R., and Swanson, G. E. *Inner conflict and defense.* New York: Holt, 1960.

Mischel, W. *Introduction to personality.* New York: Holt, Rinehart & Winston, 1971.

Moment, B. G. *General zoology.* Boston: Houghton Mifflin, 1958.

Morris, D. *The naked ape.* New York: McGraw-Hill, 1967.

Mowrer, O. H. *Learning theory and personality dynamics.* New York: Ronald Press, 1950.

Munsinger, H., and Weir, M. W. Infants' and young children's preference for complexity. *J. exp. child Psychol.,* 1967, **5,** 69–73.

Munson, P., and Kiesler, C. A. The role of attribution by others in the acceptance of persuasive communications. *J. Personality,* 1974, **42,** 453–66.

Murdock, B. B., Jr. The serial position effect of free recall. *J. exp. Psychol.,* 1962, **64,** 482–88.

Murray, H. A. *Explorations in personality.* New York: Oxford Univer. Press, 1938.

Neuringer, C., and Michael, J. *Behavior modification in clinical psychology.* New York: Appleton-Century-Crofts, 1970.

O'Kelly, L. W., and Steckle, L. C. A note on long-enduring emotional responses in the rat. *J. Psychol.,* 1939, **8,** 125–31.

Olds, J., and Milner, P. M. Positive reinforcement produced by electrical stimulation of septal area and other regions of rat brains. *J. comp. physiol. Psychol.,* 1954, **47,** 419–27.

Osgood, C. E. The similarity paradox in human learning: A resolution. *Psychol. Rev.,* 1949, **56,** 132–43.

Parton, D. A. The study of aggression in boys with an operant device. *J. exp. Child Psychol.,* 1964, **1,** 79–88.

Pauling, L. Orthomolecular psychiatry. *Science,* 1968, **160,** 265–71.

Piaget, J. *The language and thought of the child.* New York: Harcourt, Brace, 1923.

Piaget, J. *The child's conception of physical causality.* London: Kegan Paul, 1930.

Piaget, J. *The origins of intelligence in children.* New York: International Universities Press, 1952.

Piaget, J. *The child and reality.* New York: Grossman Publishers, 1973.

Plutchik, R. *Foundations of experimental research.* New York: Harper & Row, 1968.

Porteus, S. D. *The Porteus maze test and intelligence.* Palo Alto, Calif.: Pacific Books, 1950.

Porteus, S. D. *Porteus maze tests: Fifty years' application.* Palo Alto, Calif.: Pacific Books, 1965.

Prien, R. F., Caffey, E. M., and Klett, C. J. Prophylactic efficacy of lithium carbonate in manic-depressive illness. *Arch. gen. Psychiat.,* 1973, **28,** 337–41.

Prien, R. F., and Cole, J. O. High dose chlorpromozine therapy in chronic schizophrenia. In T. Rothman (Ed.), *Changing patterns in psychiatric care.* New York: Crown Publishers, 1970.

Premack, D. Reinforcement theory. In D. Levine (Ed.) *Nebraska symposium on motivation.* Lincoln, Nebr.: Univer. of Nebraska Press, 1965, 123–88.

Pritchard, R. M. Stabilized images on the retina. *Scientific Amer.,* 1961, **204**(6), 72–78.

Regan, D. T. Straus, E., and Fazio, R. Liking and the attribution process. *J. exp. soc. Psychol.,* 1974, **10,** 385–97.

Regan, D., Williams, M., and Sparling, S. Voluntary expiation of guilt: A field experiment. *J. Personal. soc. Psychol.,* 1972, **24,** 42–45.

Reynolds, G. S. *A primer of operant conditioning.* Glenview, Ill.: Scott, Foresman, 1968.

Robinson, B. W., Alexander, M., and Bowne, G. Dominance reversal resulting from aggressive responses evoked by brain telestimulation. *Physiol. and Behavior,* 1969, **4,** 749–52.

Rogers, C. R. A theory of therapy, personality, and interpersonal relationships, as developed in a clinet-centered framework. In S. Koch (Ed.), *Psychology: A study of a science.* Vol. 3. New York: McGraw-Hill, 1959. Pp. 184–256.

Rosenthal, D. Some factors associated with concordance and discordance with respect to schizophrenia in monozygotic twins. *J. nerv. ment. Dis.,* 1959, **129,** 1–10.

Rosenthal, D. *Genetics of psychopathology.* New York: McGraw Hill, 1971.

Rosenthal, R., and Jacobson, L. *Pygmalion in the classroom.* New York: Holt, Rinehart & Winston, 1968.

Rundus, D. An analysis of rehearsal processes in free recall. *J. exp. Psychol.,* 1971, **89,** 63–77.

Rushton, W. A. H. *Visual pigments in man.* Liverpool: Liverpool University Press, 1962.

Sackett, G. P. Monkeys reared in isolation with pictures as visual input: Evidence for an innate releasing mechanism. *Science,* 1969, **154,** 1468–73.

Sackett, G. P., Porter, M., and Holmes, H. Response of rhesus monkeys to social stimulation presented by means of colored slides. *J. percep. motor Skills,* 1965, **20** (3, pt. 2), 1027–28.

Saegert, S., Swap, W., and Zajonc, R. B. Exposure, context, and interpersonal attraction. *J. Personal. soc. Psychol.,* 1973, **15,** 234–42.

Sahakian W. S. *Systematic social psychology.* New York: Chandler, 1974.

Savage, R. D. *Psychometric assessment of the individual child.* Baltimore: Penguin Books, 1968.

Schachter, S. Duration, rejection, and communication. *J. ab. soc. Psychol.,* 1951, **46,** 190–207.

Schachter, S. *The psychology of affiliation.* Stanford, Calif.: Stanford Univer. Press, 1959.

Scheidt, F. J. Deviance, power, and the occult: A field study. *J. Psychol.,* 1974, **87,** 21–28.

Scott, J. P. *Aggression.* Chicago: Univer. of Chicago Press, 1958.

Scott, J. P. Comparative psychology and ethology. In P. R. Farnsworth, et al, (Eds.), *Annual review of psychology.* Palo Alto, Calif.: Annual Reviews, Inc., Vol. XVIII, 1967.

Scott, J. P. *Early experience and the organization of behavior.* Belmont, Calif.: Brooks-Cole, 1968.

Scott, J. P. *Animal behavior.* (2nd ed.) Chicago: Univer. of Chicago Press, 1972.

Scott, W. A. attitude change through reward of verbal behavior. *J. ab. soc. Psychol.,* 1958, **55,** 72–75.

Sehulster, J. R., McLaughlin, J. P., and Crouse, J. H. Separation of storage and retrieval processes in recall of prose. *J. exp. Psychol.*, 1974, **103,** 583–86.

Seligman, C., Paschall, N., and Takata, G. Effects of physical attractiveness on attribution of responsibility. *Canad. J. behav. Sci.*, 1974, **6,** 290–96.

Selye, H. *The stress of life.* New York: McGraw-Hill, 1956.

Senden, M. V. *Space and sight* (trans. by P. Heath), New York: Free Press, 1960.

Sheldon, W. H. *The varieties of temperament.* New York: Harper & Row, 1942.

Sheldon, W. H., Stevens, S. S., and Tucker, W. B. *The varieties of human physique.* New York: Harper & Row, 1940.

Shepherd, C. *Small groups: Some sociological perspectives.* San Francisco: Chandler, 1964.

Sheppard, W. C., and Willoughby, R. H. *Child behavior.* Chicago: Rand McNally, 1975.

Shields, J., and Slater, E. Heredity and psychological abnormality. In H. J. Eysenck (Ed.), *Handbook of abnormal psychology.* New York: Basic Books, 1961.

Skeels, H. M. Adult status of children with contrasting early life experiences. *Monogr. Soc. Res. Child Devel.*, 1966, **297,** 312–13.

Skinner, B. F. *The behavior of organisms: An experimental analysis.* New York: Appleton-Century-Crofts, 1938.

Skinner, B. F. *Walden two.* New York: Macmillan, 1948.

Skinner, B. F. Some contributions of an experimental analysis of behavior to psychology as a whole. *Amer. Psychologist*, 1953, **8,** 69–78.

Skinner, B. F. "Superstition" in the pigeon. *J. exp. Psych.*, 1948, **38,** 168–72.

Skodak, M., and Skeels, H. M. A final follow-up study of 100 adopted children. *J. genet. Psychol.*, 1949, **75,** 85–125.

Sosis, R. H. Internal-external control and the perception of responsibility of another for an accident. *J. Personal. soc. Psychol.*, 1974, **30,** 393–99.

Spearman, C. E. "General intelligence" objectively determined and measured. *Amer. J. Psychol.*, 1904, **15,** 72–101.

Spence, K. W. *Behavior theory and conditioning.* New Haven: Yale Univer. Press, 1956.

Spence, J. T., Underwood, B. J., Duncan, C. P., and Cotton, J. W. *Elementary statistics.* (2nd ed.) New York: Appleton-Century-Crofts, 1968.

Spitz, R. A. Hospitalism: An inquiry into the genesis of psychiatric conditions in early childhood. *Psychoanal. Stu. Child*, 1945, **1,** 53–74.

Spitz, R. A. Hospitalism: A follow-up report. *Psychoanal. Stu. Child*, 1946, **2,** 113.

Spuhler, J. N. and Lindzey, G. Racial differences in behavior. In J. Hirsch (Ed.), *Behavior-genetic analysis.* New York: McGraw-Hill, 1957. Pp. 366–414.

Stanley-Jones, D. The biological origin of love and hate. In M. B. Arnold (Ed.), *Feelings and emotions: The Loyola symposium.* New York: Academic Press, 1970. Pp. 25–38.

Stein, Z. S., Susser, M., Saenger, G., and Marolla, F. Nutrition and mental performance. *Science*, 1972, **178,** 708–13.

Taylor, D. M., and Jaggi, V. Ethnocentrism and causal attribution in a south Indian context. *J. cross-cultural Psychol.*, 1974, **5,** 162–71.

Teevan, R. C., and Birney, R. C. (Eds.), *Color vision.* New York: Van Nostrand, 1961.

Templeton, R. D., and Quigley, J. P. The action of insulin on motility of the gastrointestinal tract. *Amer. J. Physiol.*, 1930, **91,** 467–74.

Terman, L. M. *Genetic studies of genius.* Stanford, Calif.: Stanford Univer. Press, 1925.

Terrace, H. S. Discrimination learning with and without "errors." *J. exp. anal. Behav.*, 1966, **6,** 1–27.

Thompson, C. W., and Thompson, M. A. Mental deficiency review section, *Claremont M. H. Abstr. Quart.*, 1966, **11,** 29.

Thurstone, L. L. *The measurement of social attitudes.* Chicago: Univer. of Chicago Press, 1931.

Thurstone, L. L. Primary mental abilities of children. *Educ. psychol. Measmt.*, 1941, **1,** 105–16.

Toch, H., and Smith, H. C. (Eds.) *Social perception.* New York: Van Nostrand, 1968.

Tompkins, S. S. Affect as the primary motivational system. In M. B. Arnold (Ed.), *Feelings and emotions.* New York: Academic Press, Inc., 1970.

Tryon, R.C. Genetic differences in maze-learning ability in rats. *Yb. nat. soc. stud. Educ.*, 1940, **39** (1), 111–19.

Ullmann, L. P., and Krasner, L. *A psychological approach to abnormal behavior.* (2nd ed.) Englewood Cliffs, N. J.: Prentice-Hall, 1975.

Ulrich. R. E., and Azrin, N. N. Reflexive fighting in response to aversive stimulation. *J. exp. anal. Behav.*, 1962, **5**, 511–20.

Ulrich, R. E., Johnston, M., Richardson, J., and Wolff, P. C. The operant conditioning of fighting behavior in rats. *Psychol. Rec.*, 1963, **13**, 465–70.

Ulrich, R. E., and Craine, W. H. Behavior: Persistance of shock-induced aggression. *Science*, 1964, **143**, 971–73.

Ulrich, R. E., and Mountjoy, P. T. *The experimental analysis of social behavior.* New York: Appleton-Century-Crofts, 1972.

Ulrich, R. E., Stachnik, T. J., and Mabry, J. (Eds.) *Control of human behavior.* Glenview, Ill.: Scott, Foresman, Vol. I, 1966; Vol. II, 1970; Vol. III, 1974.

Ulrich, R. E., and Favell, J. E. Human aggression. In C. Neuringer, and J. Michael (Eds.), *Behavior modification in clinical psychology.* New York: Appleton-Century-Crofts, 1971.

Verhave, T. The pigeon as a quality-control inspector. *Amer. Psychologist*, 1966, **21**, 109–15.

Vernon, W. M. A sequence of reactions to a directional pain stimulus. Unpublished paper, Univer. of S. C., 1959.

Vernon, W. M. A longitudinal study of the IQs of university students. Unpublished paper, Washington Univer. (St. Louis), 1962.

Vernon, W. M. The relation of intelligence and education level to promotability in management. Unpublished paper, The Quaker Oats Co., Chicago, 1963.

Vernon, W. M., and Ulrich, R. E. Classically conditioned aggression. *Science*, 1966, **152,** 668–69.

Vernon, W. M. Comparative aversiveness of self-delivered vs. other-delivered shock. *Proceedings of the 77th annual convention of the Amer. Psychological Association*, 1969, 813–14.

Vernon, W. M. Relation of postural threat to the incidence of pain-elicited fighting. *Proceedings of the 77th annual convention of the Amer. Psychological Association*, 1969, 95–96.

Vernon, W. M. Rate of shock-elicited fighting in rats through trials. Unpublished paper, Illinois State Univer., 1969.

Vernon, W. M. *Motivating children: Behavior modification in the classroom.* New York: Holt, Rinehart & Winston, 1972.

Vetter, H. J. *Psychology of abnormal behavior.* New York: Ronald Press, 1972.

Von Holst, E. *Zur Verhaltenphysiologie bei Tieren und Menschen.* Munich: Piper, 1969.

Von Restorff, H. Uber die Virkung von Bereichsbildungen im Spurenfled. *Psychologie Forschung*, 1933, **18**, 299–342.

Wahl, C. W. Some antecedent factors in the family histories of 568 male schizophrenics of the U. S. Navy. *Amer. J. Psychiat.*, 1956, **113,** 201–10.

Walker, R. N. Body build and behavior in young children: I. Body build and nursery school teachers' ratings. In F. Rebelsky and L. Dorman (Eds.), *Child development and behavior.* (2nd ed.) New York: Knopf, 1973.

Watson, J. B. A schematic outline of emotions. *Psychol. Rev.*, 1919, **26**, 165–96.

Watson, J. S. The development and generalization of "contingency awareness" in early infancy: Some hypotheses. *Merrill-Palmer Quart.*, 1964, **12**, 123–35.

Weinberg, I., and Lobstein, J. Inheritance in schizophrenia. *Acta Psychiatrica Neurologica*, 1943, **18**, 93–140.

Werner, M. The relationship of dominant and submissive personality characteristics to parental dominance patterns. Unpublished paper, Illinois State Univer., 1970.

Werner, M. "Forgiving" behavior in relation to religiosity of judges. Unpublished research paper, Illinois State Univer., 1975.

Wever, E. G. *Theory of hearing.* New York: Wiley, 1949.

Wever, E. G., and Bray, C. W. Action currents in the auditory nerve in response to acoustical stimulation. *Proc. Nat. Acad. Sci.,* 1930, **16,** 344–50.

Wever, E. G., and Lawrence, M. The acoustic pathways to the cochlea. *J. acous. Soc. Amer.*, 1950, **22,** 460–67.

Wever, E. G., and Smith, C. H. The problem of stimulation deafness. I. Cochlear impairment as a function of tonal frequency. *J. exp. Psychol.*, 1944, **34,** 239–45.

White, R. W. Motivation reconsidered: The concept of competence. *Psychol. Rev.*, 1959, **66,** 297–333.

Whiteman, M., Brook, J. S., and Gordon, A. S. Children's motivational perception as related to the instrumentality and effect of action. *Devel. Psychol.*, 1974, **10,** 929–35.

Whitten, P. and Kagan, J. Stimulus/response: "Jensen's dangerous half-truths." *Psychol. Today*, 1969, **3,** 8.

Wiggins, J., Renner, K. E., Clore, G. L., and Rose, R. *The psychology of personality.* Reading, Mass.: Addison-Wesley, 1971.

Williams, C. D. The elimination of tantrum behavior by extinction procedures. *J. ab. soc. Psychol.*, 1959, **59,** 269.

Williams, R. L. Psychological testing of blacks. Paper presented to convention of Assoc. of Black Psychologists, 1973.

Willis, F. N., Jr. Fighting in pigeons relative to available space. Psychonom. Sci., 1966, **4,** 315–16.

Winterbottom, M. R. The relation of need for achievement to learning experiences in independence in mastery. In J. W. Atkinson (Ed.), *Motives in fantasy, action, and society.* Princeton, N. J.: D. Van Nostrand, 1958.

Wooley, D. W. *The biochemical bases of psychoses.* New York: Wiley, 1962.

Wooley, D. W., and Shaw, E. A biochemical and pharmacological suggestion about certain mental disorders. *Proc. Nat. Acad. Sci.*, 1954, **40,** 228–31.

Wynne-Edwards, V. C. *Animal Dispersion in Relation to Social Behaviour.* New York: Hafner, 1962.

Yates, A. J. *Frustration and conflict.* New York: Wiley, 1962.

Yates, F. A. *The art of memory.* Chicago: Univer. of Chicago Press, 1966.

Zamenhof, S., Marthens, E. V., and Margolis, F. L. DNA (cell number) and protein in neonatal brain: Alteration by maternal dietary protein restriction. *Science*, 1968, **160,** 322–23.

Zuckerman, S. *The social life of monkeys and apes.* New York: Harcourt, Brace, & World, 1932.

Index

Index

Abnormal behavior, *see* Psychopathology
Abscissa, 174
Absolute refractory phase, 44
Abstract thought, 102
Achievement tests, 232
Activation level, 236–37, 627
Activity, general, 238
Adams, J., 261
Adaptation, 14
Additive color mixture, 124
Adolescent stage, 85–87
Adrenal gland, 47, 51
Adrenaline, 554
Aesthenia, 528
Affect, *see* Emotions
Affection as reinforcer, 316
Afferent pathways, 45
Afterimages, 125
Aggression, 168, 371, 644–55
Alcoholism, 529
All-or-none principle, 43
Altruistic behaviors, 87, 369–71
Analysis of variance, 589
Animal research, reasons for, 195–96, 636
Anxiety, types of, 498
Anxiety state, 525
Apathy, 486
Appetitive deprivation effect, 250
Approval as reinforcer, 316
Aptitude tests, 231
Aristotle, 9
Aronfreed, J., 369
Aronson, E., 355, 363, 387
Asch, S., 346, 377
Asimov, I., 62
Asymptote, 180
Attention, 146, 315
Attitudes, 352ff.
Attraction, 361–62
Attractiveness, 364, 379
Attribution theory, 373–81
Auerbach, C., 62
Autonomic nervous system, 46
Avoidance conditioning, 311
Ayllon, T., 337–38
Azrin, N., 645, 654

Backward conditioning, 294–95
Balance theory, 388
Bales, R., 390
Barry, H., 542
Baseline procedures, 598
Base rates, 598
Behavior deficits, 515–17
Behavior excesses, 515–17
Behavior paradigms, 323, 631
Behaviorism, 20, 22, 454–58, 558–60
Beadle, G. and M., 62
Bennett, E., 75
Berg, M., 542
Berlyne, D., 249
Berscheid, E., 365
Binet, A., 204
Binet-Simon test, 204
Biochemistry, 553
Body type, 380, 436
Bogardus Social Distance Scale, 353
Bogus pipeline procedure, 355
Bond, E., 216
Borgatta, E., 391
Bowlby, J., 78
Brain, *see* Cerebral cortex
Bridges, K., 270
Brislin, R., 364
Brown, J., 255
Bruce, C., 222
Brunswick, E., 150
Bryan, J., 370
Burt, C., 193
Buss, A., 540, 551

Cannon, W., 244
Casler, L., 80
Cattell, J., 203
Cattell, R., 225, 433
Cause-and-effect inference, 5, 159
Central tendency, measures of, 176–79
Cerebellum, 38
Cerebral cortex, 38, 40ff., 75
Chaining, 661
Character disorders, 522
Character structures, 447–52
Chi-square, 588
Chlorpromozine, 558

Chromosomes, 52–53
Chunking, 410
Cialdini, R., 375
Classical conditioning, 285–95, 334
Client-centered therapy, 459–65
Coats, W., 248
Cognitive dissonance, 384–87
Cognitive psychology, 22, 93, 398
Color blindness, 57, 125–27
Color vision, 116, 120–27
Competence, 365
Conditionability, 34, 624
Conditioned discrimination, 303
Conditioning, definition of, 284
Cones, 113–16
Conflict gradients, 494–95
Conflict models, 490–93
Conformity, 364, 617
Contact comfort, 246
Context learning, 407, 663ff.
Contrast effect, 146
Control group, 580
Correlation, 183–87, 569
Cowan, P., 484
Crutchfield, R., 346
Culture-fair tests, 229
Cumulative records, 599

Darwin, C., 14, 28ff., 195, 203
Deafness, 145
Death, 88
Dennis, W., 148
Depression, 80, 518, 529, 538, 557
Deprivation, 238
Depth perception, 134–37
Descriptive statistics, 176–87
Determinism, 435
DeValois, R., 121
DiMatteo, M., 381
Dion, K., 364
Discriminative conditioning, 607
Discriminative stimuli, 608
Displacement of anxiety, 507
Displacement of behavior, 457
Dissociative reaction, 528
Distribution of practice, 421
DNA, 53
Doland, D., 370
Dominance, 317
Dominant gene action, 55
Donders, F., 11
Double bind, 541
Dove, A., 217
Drives:
    appetitive, 243
    aversive, 243
    effects on activity level, 238–39
    primary, 241–52
    strengths of, 252
Dutch famine study, 73
Dyads, 637

Ebbinghaus, H., 9, 402
Edwards, A., 233
Edwards Personal Preference Schedule, 263
EEG, 236
Effectors, 45
Efferent pathways, 45
Efficiency, 256
Efran, M., 379
Ego-defense mechanisms, 499–508
Ego strength, 500
Ellis, A., 560
Ellis-van Crevald syndrome, 34
Emotions, 50, 267–72
Emotional orientations, 279ff.
Empiricism, 149
Epinephrine, 47
Erikson's developmental theory, 84–88
Error:
    random, 573
    systematic, 573–75
    type I & II, 583
Escape conditioning, 311
Experimental group, 580
Experimental hypothesis, 582
Experimental method, 171, 578–79
Exponential graphs, 601
Expressivity, 58
Extinction:
    in classical conditioning, 298–99
    in operant conditioning, 321
Eye color, 54
Eye structure, 112ff.
Eysenck, H., 625, 655

Factor analysis, 433
Fantasy, 487, 503
Fantz, R., 148
Faris, R., 544
Favell, J., 484
Fear, 366
Feather, N., 379
Fechner, G., 10
Feedback, 422
Fejer, D., 159
Festinger, L., 384
Figure-ground perception, 131
Fischer, W., 370
Fixation, 496

Forgetting, theories of, 415–19
Freedman, D., 79
French, J., 236
Frequency distributions, 173
Frequency theory of hearing, 143
Freud, S., *see* Psychoanalytic theory
Frontal lobes, 42
Frustration:
    and aggression, 481, 645
    and persistence, 480
    drive, 480
    tolerance, 489
Functional psychosis, 534
Functional relationships, 158–59
Functionalism, 14, 22
Fuster, J., 237

Galambos, R., 143
Galton, F., 35, 195, 202
General adaptation syndrome, 476
Generalization of extinction, 302–03
Genes, 52–58
Genetic drift, 34
Genius, *see* Gifted children
Genotype, 53–58
Genovese, K., 369
Gestalt psychologists, 17, 22, 132, 150
Gibson, E. and J., 151
Gifted children, 228–29
Glaze, J., 403
Goal gradients, 255
Goldschmidt, R., 195
Gouldner, A., 370
Graphing, 174–75
Grice, G., 320
Grusec, J., 370
Guilford, J., 224
Guilt, 506

Habit family hierarchy, 488
Habituation, 237
Handlon, B., 370
Harlow, H., 81, 245–46
Harrell, R., 73
Hearing, 140–45
Heath, R., 554
Hebb, D., 150
Hedonism, 627
Heider, F., 373, 388
Height and weight, 70
Held, R., 148
Heredity, 52, 193
Hering theory of color vision, 121
Heron, W., 250
Herrnstein, R., 194

Hess, R., 78
Heston, L., 553
Higher-order conditioning, 305
Highlighting, 674
Hollingshead, A., 544–45
Homeostasis, 242
Honzik, M., 194
Horney, K., 271
Hoskins, R., 542
Hovland, C., 347
Hull, C., 236, 455
Humanistic psychology, 261
Hunt, J., 233
Hunter, W., 258
Hypochondria, 528
Hypothalamus, 39, 50

Identification, 441, 499
Identity, sense of, 86
Imitation, *see* Social imitation
Incentives and incentivation, 254–56, 456
Incomplete sentences forms, 471
Inferential statistics, 580–89
Inhibition, 457
Instincts, 258–60
Instrumental behaviors, 602
Intelligence (*see also* IQ):
    and heredity, 60, 193–97, 220–23
    and nutrition, 68, 72–75
    and sensory discrimination, 203
    components of, 223–25
    concept of, 92
    definition of, 192
    effects of environment, 75, 195, 197–201
    in animals, 196
    measuring, 202–33
    Piaget's theory of, 90–103
    tests, *see* Intelligence tests
Intelligence tests:
    culture-fair, 229–30
    fairness, 217–18
    group, 210, 216
    history of, 202–06
    individual, 210, 215
    infant, 230
Interaction effects, 589
Interaction Process Analysis (IPA), 390–92
Interval frequency distributions, 173–74
Interview method, 466
Introversion, 625
IQ:
    and kindergarten, 199
    calculation of, 206

constancy, 198
deviation, 209
Item analysis, 213

Jaco, E., 544
Jencks, B., 248
Jensen, A., 220–23
Johnson, R., 71
Jones, E., 349, 355
Jones, M., 33

Kagan, J., 222
Kallman, F., 548
Kendler, H., 258
Kimble, G., 421
Kinesthesis, 42
Klebanoff, L., 542
Knowledge, sources of, 156
Krech, D., 75
Kuffler, S., 117

Latane, B., 269
Latency of response, 292
Learning, levels of, 405, 676
Learning to learn effect, 412
Lee, E., 201
Leighton, A., 544
Lenneberg, E., 69
Leukel, F., 476
Libido, 443
Lidz, R., 542
Light-dark adaptation, 115–16
Lithium, 557
Locus of control, 376
Logan, F., 650
Lorenz, K., 78
Lorge, I., 421
Love, 87
Luginbuhl, J., 379

Maier, N., 496
Malnutrition, see Nutrition
Manic-depressive psychosis, 538, 551, 557
Marks, W., 121
Maslow, A., 262, 264–67
Maternal age, 68
Maternal diseases, 68
Maternal emotions, 68
Mathews, S., 239
McClelland, D., 261–62
McGaugh, J., 29
Meaningfulness in learning, 401, 665

Means, 176
Measurement, levels of, 568
Measurement, psychological, 191ff.
Medians, 176
Medulla, 38
Meehl, P., 550
Mental age, 205
Mental retardation, 193, 226–28
Metabolism, 39
Michael, J., 337
Midbrain, 39
Mikula, G., 376
Milgram, S., 371
Miller, N., 653
MMPI, 469
Mnemonics, 412
Modes, 177
Modeling, see Social imitation
Moment, B., 30
Mothering, 79–83, 245–46
Motion perception, 138
Motives, see Drives, Incentives and incentivation
Motor development, 69–71
Motor learning, 419–20
Mowrer, O., 454
Munsinger, H., 249
Munson, P., 377
Murray, H., 263
Mutation, 30

Nativism, 149
Natural selection, 28ff., 48, 51, 241, 269, 277–79
Needs, 241ff.
Nervous system:
    autonomic, 47ff.
    central, 37, 45
    peripheral, 37, 45
Neural code, 109
Neurology, 36ff.
Neuron, operation of, 37ff., 43
Neurosis, 522ff.
Neurotic depression, 518, 529
Noncontingent reinforcement, 616
Nonsense syllables, 402
Norepinephrine, 47
Normal curve, 178
Norms, 343
Null hypothesis, 582
Nutrition:
    effects on intelligence, 68, 72–75
    effects on mental health, 555–56

Obsessive-compulsive neurosis, 525
Occipital lobes, 42

Ogive, 180
Operant behavior, 282–83, 515
Operant conditioning, 310–24
Operation Headstart, 195, 201
Operational definitions, 167–69
Ordinate, 174
Organic psychosis, 533, 547
Orphans, 75, 80
Orthomolecular psychiatry, 556

Pain-elicited aggression, 649–50
Paired associate method, 407
Pancreas, 50
Paradigms of behavior, 323, 631
Paranoid behavior, 536
Parietal lobes, 42
Partial reinforcement effect, 332–33
Parton, D., 484
Pauling, L., 555–56
Pavlov, I., 20, 291
Penetrance, 58
Perception, 128–53:
    and motivation, 146
    definition of, 128
    of motion, 138
    organizational principles, 130–38
Personality:
    and body type, 436
    definition of, 432, 436
    inventories, 469
    tests as behaviors, 469
Personalized systems of instruction
    (PSI), 6
Phenotype, 53–58
Phobias, 527
Photic energy, 110
Piaget's developmental theory, 90–103
Piloerection response, 49
Pituitary gland, 47
Place theory of hearing, 143
Pleasure center, 39
Polygenic effects, 59
Pons, 38
Porteus maze test, 229
Predictive functions, 159
Prejudice, *see* Attitudes
Premack Principle, 615
Pride, 84
Primacy effect, 348
Proactive effects, 425
Probabilistic functionalism, 150
Probabilities, 585
Projective techniques, 470–72
Psychoanalytic theory, 16, 22, 440–52,
    560
Psychology, areas of, 4
Psychology, definition of, 155

Psychopathology:
    definition of, 514
    of childhood, 515
    major classifications, 522ff.
Psychosis, 533ff.
Punishment, 335–39, 619–23
Purkinje shift, 116

Range, 180–81
Rating scales, 468
Rationalization, 486, 501
Raven's Progressive Matrices, 230
Receptors, 45, 108
Recency effect, 350
Recessive gene action, 55
Reciprocity, 366
Reflexes, 278
Refractory phases, 44
Regan, D., 370, 380
Reinforcement:
    conditioned, 313
    delay of, 320
    negative, 310, 334
    positive, 310, 334
    primary, 313
    social, 315
    theories of, 626
Reliability of tests:
    internal, 213
    overall, 213
Reminiscence effect, 410
Research, types of, 171
Respondent behavior, 278ff., 517
Response generalization, 606
Reticular system, 38, 50, 236–37
Retroactive effects, 425
RNA, 53
Rods, 113–16
Rogers, C., 459–65
Roles, 86, 343, 389–90, 657
Rorschach technique, 471
Rosenthal, D., 62
Rosenzweig, M., 75
Rushton, W., 121

Sagert, S., 362
Sampling, 570–72
Scalloping, 327, 329
Schachter, S., 347, 366
Schedules of reinforcement, 327–32
Scheidt, F., 377
Schools of psychology, 12ff.
Science, 591–92
Scientific method, 157
Schizophrenia, 534–37, 548
Scoring distributions, 173

Scott, J., 83
Seguin Form Board, 229
Sehulster, J., 673
Self-actualization, 265
Self-confidence, 85
Seligman, C., 379
Selye, H., 51, 476
Semantic differential, 354–55
Senden, M., 147
Sensory deprivation, 249–50
Serial anticipation method, 407
Serial position effect, 408
Serotonin, 554
Sex-linked genetic effects, 57
Sexual deviations, 288, 530
Sexual drive, 250–51
Shaping, 604–7
Sheldon, W., 436, 549
Similarity, effects of, 363
Sixteen P-F Test, 433–35
Skeels, H., 75, 194
Skewed curves, 179
Skinner, B. F., 21, 336, 454, 489, 616
Skodak, M., 194
Smiling behavior, 78
Social class, 544–46, 659
Social imitation, 283, 357, 612, 657
Social isolation, 643
Sosis, R., 376
Spearman, C., 223
Spence, K., 294, 455
Spitz, R., 78–79
Spontaneous recovery, 298
Spuhler, J., 28
Standard deviation, 181, 207
Stanford-Binet IQ Test, 205
Stanley-Jones, D., 270
Startle reflex, 48
Statistical methods, 172–87
Status levels, 640
Stein, Z., 73
Stereotypes, 352
Stimulus deprivation, 83
Stimulus generalization, 301
Stimulus, types of, 161–62
Stimulus variety, 75, 247, 487
Stratification, 574–77
Stress reactions, 83, 476
Structuralism, 12, 22
Subject, use of as own control, 581, 596
Submission of others, 317
Sugar storage, 51
Suppression, 335, 621
Survey method, 171
Synapse, 43, 45

TAT, 471

Taylor, D., 380
Temperament, 436
Temporal lobes, 42
Terman, L., 205, 229
Territoriality, 646
Thalamus, 40
Thinking, 90–103
Thyroid glands, 47
Threat, 647–49
Thresholds, 43, 48
Thurstone, L., 224
Thurstone scale, 354
Token reinforcers, 318
Token systems and economies, 617–19
Tomkins, S., 268
Traits, 433
Transducers, 108
Transfer of training, 423–27
Trigrams, 403
Trust, 84
Tryon, R., 196

Ulcers, 479
Ulrich, R., 484, 650, 651, 654, 655

Validity:
    concurrent, 212
    construct, 212
    face, 212
    of IQ tests, 215
    of tests, 211
    predictive, 212
Variability, measures of, 180–87
Variables:
    definition of, 158
    dependent, 159–60
    independent, 159–60
    organismic, 163–65
    response, 163–65
    stimulus, 161–62, 164–65
Variation, 30
Verbal learning, 401ff.
Vernon, W., 216, 272, 280, 649, 655
Vetter, H., 534
Vicarious reinforcement, 612
Vision, 108–38
Visual acuity, 113
Volley theory of hearing, 143
Von Helmholtz, H., 149

Wahl, C., 542
Walden Two, 489
Walker, R., 439
Walking, *see* Motor development

Warm-up effect, 411
Watson, J. B., 20, 271
Watson, J. S., 78
Weber-Fechner ratio, 10
Wechsler Intelligence Scales, 209–10
Wever, E., 144
White, R., 261
Whiteman, M., 377
Whitten, P., 222
Whole *vs.* part learning, 404, 672
Williams, R., 217–19

Wooley, D., 544
Wundt, W., 12

Yerkes-Dodson Principle, 257, 498
Young-Helmholtz theory of color vision, 121

Zajonc, R., 362
Z-scores, 207–8

Answers to
Progress Checks

Answers to Progress Checks

Chapter 1

PROGRESS CHECKS

1.1

Answer		Text Page
1.	b	9
2.	a	10
3.	c	10
4.	c	10
5.	b	11
6.	d	12

1.2

1.	a	14
2.	a	16
3.	c	21

Chapter 2

PROGRESS CHECKS

2.1

1.	c	28
2.	A	28
3.	C	30
4.	B	30
5.	b	29
6.	a	34
7.	c	35

2.2

1.	b	37

Answer		Text Page
2.	b	37
3.	b	37
4.	d	38
5.	c	38
6.	B	42
7.	C	42
8.	D	42
9.	A	42
10.	a	43
11.	B	44
12.	A	44
13.	d	48
14.	b	49

2.3

1.	d	53
2.	d	61
3.	a	52
4.	b	53
5.	c	55
6.	a	55
7.	c	56
8.	c	57
9.	b	57
10.	C	58
11.	A	58
12.	B	59

Chapter 3

PROGRESS CHECKS

Answer		Text Page

3.1

1.	a	66
2.	b	66
3.	b	70
4.	c	69
5.	d	72
6.	d	72
7.	b	73
8.	a	75

3.2

1.	b	79
2.	c	80
3.	b	82
4.	a	83
5.	d	84
6.	a	85
7.	A	85
8.	B	86
9.	C	85
10.	D	87
11.	b	88
12.	c	78
13.	b	78
14.	c	79

3.3

1.	c	94
2.	a	96
3.	a	98

Answer	Text Page		Answer	Text Page		Answer	Text Page
4. a	101		2. b	116		8. b	132
5. d	101		3. a	116		9. E	136
6. b	92		4. a	116		10. A	135
7. A	93		5. b	117		11. B	135
8. B	93		6. c	117		12. D	136
9. a	97					13. c	136
10. d	99					14. a	138
				4.4		15. b	138
			1. c	120			
Chapter 4			2. b	121			
PROGRESS CHECKS			3. a	123			**4.6**
			4. B	123		1. a	146
			5. A	123		2. b	147
	4.1		6. C	123		3. c	148
			7. b	123		4. a	148
1. b	108		8. c	124		5. d	150
2. c	108		9. a	124		6. b	149
3. A	108		10. blue, green, red	124		7. a	149
4. C	108		11. blue, yellow, red	124		8. a	150
5. B	108		12. d	125		9. a	150
6. B	108		13. b	125		10. a	150
7. a	109		14. A	126		11. C	151
			15. C	126		12. A	151
			16. B	126		13. B	151
	4.2		17. c	126		14. b	151
1. a	110						
2. B	110					**Chapter 5**	
3. A	110			**4.5**		**PROGRESS CHECKS**	
4. 600	110		1. A	130			
5. violet	110		2. B	130			
6. 380–760 *nm*	110		3. b	130			**5.1**
7. c	112		4. b	131		1. b	157
8. a	112		5. b	132		2. b	157
9. b	113		6. a	132		3. B	157
10. b	113		7. proximity, similarity, closure, good continuation, common fate	133		4. A	157
11. a	114					5. C	157
						6. c	158
	4.3						
1. b	115						

Answer	Text Page
7. B	158
8. A	158
9. cause and effect, predictive function	159
10. B	161
11. A	163
12. C	163
13. d	162
14. b	163
15. a	162

5.2

Answer	Text Page
1. a	167
2. A	171
3. B	171
4. c	167
5. d	168

5.3

Answer	Text Page
1. Scores f 99 3 98 1 97 1	173
2. b	174
3. A-4; B-3; C-1; D-2	175
4.	174

Answer	Text Page
5. b	176
6. a. 15; b. 10; c. 15	176–77
7. c	176
8. A. mean; B. median; C. mode	179
9. b	179

Answer	Text Page
10. A	180
11. B	180
12. 6	180
13. $s = \sqrt{1.414}$ or $\sqrt{2}$	181

5.4

Answer	Text Page
1. a	183
2. d	184
3. a	184
4. b	187

Chapter 6

PROGRESS CHECKS

6.1

Answer	Text Page
1. c	194
2. b	196
3. b	196
4. a	197
5. b	198
6. B	199
7. A	199
8. c	199, 200

6.2

Answer	Text Page
1. b	205
2. d	206
3. c	207
4. a	209
5. d	209
6. b	209
7. d	209

6.3

Answer	Text Page
1. c	210

Answer	Text Page
2. a	211
3. d	213
4. d	213
5. b	213
6. A	215
7. B	216

6.4

Answer	Text Page
1. b	217
2. a	222
3. d	223
4. C	223
5. B	224
6. A	225
7. D	224

6.5

Answer	Text Page
1. a	226
2. a	227
3. d	227
4. b	229
5. c	229
6. d	229
7. c	230
8. B	231
9. A	232

Chapter 7

PROGRESS CHECKS

7.1

Answer	Text Page
1. d	236
2. c	237
3. b	236

Answer	Text Page	Answer	Text Page	Answer	Text Page
4. d	237	14. b	269		**9.1**
5. c	237	15. A	271	1. c	309
6. a	237	16. B	271	2. B	310
7. a	238			3. A	310
			Chapter 8	4. b	311
			PROGRESS CHECKS	5. c	311
	7.2			6. b	313
1. B, C, D	242		**8.1**	7. d	318
2. A, E	242	1. c	279		
3. a	243	2. a	279		**9.2**
4. d	243	3. b	279	1. c	320
5. c	242	4. d	280	2. b	321
6. b	244	5. d	282	3. b	322
7. b	245	6. b, c	283	4. a	328
8. d	246			5. d	329
9. c	247			6. a	323
10. c	250		**8.2**	7. c	325
11. a	250	1. c	284		
12. A, B	252	2. c	287		
13. A, C	252	3. c	288		**9.3**
14. a	252	4. d	288	1. d	330
		5. b	289	2. c	331
		6. a	292	3. b	332
	7.3	7. a	293	4. b	334
1. b	256	8. c	295	5. a	335
2. d	256	9. b	298	6. d	336
3. c	257	10. d	298	7. A	337
4. a	257			8. B	338
5. b	258		**8.3**		
6. d	258	1. a	301		**Chapter 10**
7. b	259	2. b	302		**PROGRESS CHECKS**
8. b	260	3. c	303		
9. a	261	4. d	305		**10.1**
10. c	261			1. c	343
11. d	263		**Chapter 9**	2. a, d	345
12. c	266		**PROGRESS CHECKS**	3. b, c	344
13. c	268				

Answer	Text Page	Answer	Text Page	Answer	Text Page
4. c	346	2. a	373		**11.1**
5. c	346	3. b	374	1. c	398
6. a	346–47	4. a, d; b, c	373	2. b	401
7. a, b, e; c, d, f	350	5. b	375	3. c	402
		6. c	375	4. b	401
	10.2	7. a	376	5. d	403
1. a	353	8. a, d; b, c	373–77	6. a	404
2. d	353	9. c	377	7. a	404
3. C	354	10. b	377	8. b	405
4. A	355	11. B	379	9. d	405
5. B	355	12. C	379		
6. c	356	13. A	379		**11.2**
7. c	358	14. D	379	1. a	407
8. a	359	15. b	380	2. b	407
9. b	359	16. b	379	3. d	408
		17. c	381	4. B	409
	10.3	18. b	379	5. A	409
1. b	362	19. a	380	6. d	410
2. b	362			7. c	410
3. b	363		**10.6**	8. d	412
4. b	364	1. a	384	9. a	407
5. a	365	2. c	385	10. a	411
6. a	365	3. c	386		
7. b	365	4. c	386		**11.3**
8. a	365	5. a	387	1. A	415
9. c	366	6. b	388	2. B	415
10. b	366	7. b	388	3. d	415
		8. a	388	4. a	415
	10.4	9. a	388	5. c	416
1. c	366	10. c	390	6. d	416
2. a	366	11. a	391	7. c, d	418
3. c	367	12. c	391	8. b	420
4. c	368			9. d	419
			Chapter 11	10. a	419
	10.5		**PROGRESS CHECKS**	11. b	421
1. a	373				

Answer	Text Page		Answer	Text Page		Answer	Text Page
12. c	422			**12.3**		2. A	480
13. b	423		1. b	455		3. b	482
14. b	427		2. d	455		4. d	482
			3. A	455		5. a	482
			4. B	457		6. b	484
Chapter 12			5. b	457		7. c	484
PROGRESS CHECKS			6. c	457		8. C, D	486
			7. b	459		9. A, D	486
			8. b	460		10. B, D	487
	12.1		9. d	461		11. b	486
1. b	432		10. c	462		12. a	489
2. c	432		11. a	463			
3. d	433		12. a	464			**13.3**
4. a	433					1. c	490
5. d	435					2. c	492
6. B	436			**12.4**		3. a	492
7. A	436		1. b	466		4. b	494
8. d	437		2. c	466		5. d	495
9. c	437		3. b	468		6. b	496
			4. b	469			
			5. a	469			**13.4**
	12.2		6. c	469		1. a	498
1. b	442					2. a	498
2. B, F	440					3. d	498
3. A, D	441		**Chapter 13**			4. A	502
4. C, E	441		**PROGRESS CHECKS**			5. B	506
5. d	443					6. A	504
6. c	444					7. B	501
7. b, d	446			**13.1**		8. c	499
8. a	444		1. a	475		9. d	500
9. b	447		2. b	476		10. a	501
10. d	449		3. c	476		11. d	500
11. b	448		4. b	477		12. c	502
12. B	448		5. a	477		13. b	507
13. A	448		6. a	477		14. c	504
14. c	449		7. b	479		15. a	505
15. d	451			**13.2**			
			1. B	480			

Answer	Text Page	Answer	Text Page	Answer	Text Page
		6. b	538	5. b	570
Chapter 14		7. a	538	6. a	570
PROGRESS CHECKS		8. a	540		
		9. b	541		
	14.1	10. a	541	**5A.2**	
1. c	514	11. a	542	1. A, B	573
2. b	514	12. c	542	2. C, D	573
3. B, C	515	13. c	544	3. c	574
4. A, D	516	14. b	545	4. a	574
5. b	517			5. B	575
6. b, c	518			6. A	576
7. b	518		**14.4**	7. c	579
		1. a	548	8. c	574
	14.2	2. b	548		
1. e	520	3. b	551		
2. A	522	4. d	552	**5A.3**	
3. C	522	5. b, c	555	1. a	581
4. B	522	6. b	555–56	2. A	580
5. b	523	7. b	557	3. B	580
6. a	523	8. A	557	4. b	582
7. b	523	9. B	557	5. A	583
8. A	525	10. B	558	6. B	584
9. B	525	11. C	558	7. False	584
10. d	529	12. D	559	8. True	584
11. dissociative	528	13. A	560	9. True	584
12. a	523	14. E	560	10. b	583
13. d	528	15. B	561		
14. b	527			**5A.4**	
15. c	528	**Chapter 5A**		1. c	587
		PROGRESS CHECKS		2. c	587
	14.3			3. B	587
1. B	534		**5A.1**	4. C	588
2. C	535	1. B	568	5. A	589
3. A	535	2. D	568		
4. D	536	3. C	568	**Chapter 9A**	
5. d	537	4. A	568	**PROGRESS CHECKS**	

Answer	Text Page	Answer	Text Page	Answer	Text Page
	9A.1	8. a	625	4. a	653
1. d	596	9. C	626	5. a	653
2. a	598	10. B	626	6. c	654
3. b	599	11. D	628	7. b	655
4. b	599	12. A	627		
5. c	601				**10A.4**
6. a	601		**Chapter 10A**	1. d	656
7. A	603		**PROGRESS CHECKS**	2. a	657
8. B	603			3. b	657
			10A.1	4. a	659
	9A.2	1. c, e	636	5. a	658
1. c	605	2. b	636	6. b	659
2. a	605	3. a	639		
3. c	606	4. a	640		
4. A	608	5. a	641		**Chapter 11A**
5. D	610	6. b	641		**PROGRESS CHECKS**
6. C	610	7. b	643		
7. A	608	8. c	643		**11A.1**
8. B	608			1. a	665
9. B	608		**10A.2**	2. b	670
10. E	610	1. operant, respondent	644	3. b	666
11. c	611			4. B	668
12. c	611	2. b	645	5. A	668
13. a	611	3. urine sprays, birds' sprays	646	6. C	669
14. a	612	4. a	647	7. c	671
15. c	613	5. a	649	8. b	673
		6. a	649	9. d	674
	9A.3	7. B	645	10. a	676
1. b	615	8. B	649	11. B	676
2. d	616	9. a	649	12. C	676
3. C	617			13. A	676
4. A	617		**10A.3**		
5. B	617	1. B	651		
6. d	620	2. B	651		
7. b	621	3. A	652	*Printed in U.S.A.*	